Language Arts

Patterns of Practice

Language Arts

Patterns of Practice

EIGHTH EDITION

Gail E. Tompkins

California State University, Fresno, Emerita

PEARSON

Boston | Columbus | Indianapolis | New York | San Francisco | Upper Saddle River

Amsterdam | Cape Town | Dubai | London | Madrid | Milan | Munich | Paris | Montreal | Toronto

Delhi | Mexico City | Sao Paulo | Sydney | Hong Kong | Seoul | Singapore | Taipei | Tokyo

Vice President and Editor-in-Chief:	Aurora Martínez Ramos
Development Editor:	Hope Madden
Editorial Assistant:	Michelle Hochberg
Executive Marketing Manager:	Krista Clark
Production Editor:	Janet Domingo
Editorial Production Service:	Nesbitt Graphics, Inc./Cenveo Publisher Services
Manufacturing Buyer:	Megan Cochran
Electronic Composition:	Nesbitt Graphics, Inc./Cenveo Publisher Services
Interior Design:	Carol Somberg
Cover Designers:	Diane Lorenzo and Candace Rowley
Cover Illustrator:	Story Book Arts Inc./Karelyn Siegler
Quilt art:	Carol Taylor

10 9 8 7 6 5 4 3 2 1

PEARSON

www.pearsonhighered.com

ISBN 10:   0-13-268575-2
ISBN 13: 978-0-13-268575-7

To Ava and Ivan and their mother, Kimberly Clark.

May these children always be joyful language arts learners, engaged by teachers like those described in this text.

A Note From the Author

Orange is my favorite color, and I'm excited that it's being used as the second color in this edition of *Language Arts*. I think that orange, a combination of yellow and red, is an exciting, energetic color. You can see from my picture that my new car—a convertible—is orange!

I'm a teacher, first and foremost. I began my career as a first grade teacher in Northern Virginia in the 1970s. I remember one first grader who cried as the first day of school was ending. When I tried to comfort him, he sobbed accusingly, "I came to first grade to learn to read and write, and you forgot to teach me." I've never forgotten that child's comment and what it taught me: Teachers must understand their students and meet their expectations.

My first few years of teaching left me with more questions than answers, and I wanted to become a more effective teacher, so I started taking graduate courses. In time I earned a master's degree and then a doctorate in reading/language arts, both from Virginia Tech. Through my graduate studies, I learned a lot of answers, but more importantly, I learned to keep asking questions.

Then I began teaching at the university level. First I taught at Miami University in Ohio, then at the University of Oklahoma, and finally at California State University, Fresno. I've taught preservice teachers and practicing teachers working on master's degrees, and I've directed doctoral dissertations. I've received awards for my teaching, including the Provost's Award for Excellence in Teaching at California State University, Fresno, and I was inducted into the California Reading Association's Reading Hall of Fame. Through the years, my students have taught me as much as I've taught them, and I'm grateful to all of them for what I've learned.

I've been writing college textbooks for more than 25 years, and I think of the book I write as teaching, too. I'll be teaching you as you read this text. Some of my other textbooks are *Literacy for the 21st Century: A Balanced Approach,* 5e, *Teaching Writing: Balancing Process and Product,* 7e, and *50 Literacy Strategies: Step-by-Step,* 4e.

Now I spend half the year in Fresno, California, and the other half on Cape Cod in Massachusetts. When I'm not writing, I like to make quilts. Piecing together a quilt is a lot like planning effective language arts instruction, but instead of cloth, teachers use the patterns of practice and other instructional procedures to design instruction for the diverse students in 21st-century classrooms. That's why I like to use a quilt on the cover of *Language Arts*.

Gail E. Tompkins

Contents

CHAPTER 3

Emergent Literacy **58**

CHAPTER 4

Personal Writing **86**

CHAPTER 7

Visual Language: Viewing and Visually Representing   176

CHAPTER 10

Investigating Nonfiction   276

Special Features

Differentiated Instruction

Digital Classroom

Preface

Your goal is to teach children and adolescents to communicate effectively using oral, written, and visual language. Helping all children in our culturally diverse, technologically changing society meet this goal is daunting—even for experienced teachers. I've carefully revised this eighth edition of *Language Arts: Patterns of Practice* with this ambitious goal in mind. I've written a brand-new chapter on visual language, and I've added new components on integrating technology and Engaging English Learners to most chapters, plus a new feature connecting content in each chapter with the Common Core State Standards for the English Language Arts. In this text, you'll learn how to teach students to comprehend and communicate using all six language arts—listening, talking, reading, writing, viewing, and visually representing—and to incorporate technology to support and demonstrate their learning. Plus, the text retains its time-tested focus on modeling the most effective and practical methods for teaching language arts so you'll be prepared to teach language arts in preK–8 classrooms.

New to This Edition

I've added a new chapter and new features to this edition to reflect the changes in language arts and to highlight innovative instructional practices. The new chapter on visual language provides essential information about viewing and visually representing and identifies ways to integrate the language arts, and new features and chapter sections address the Common Core State Standards, differentiation, and technology.

- **Chapter 7: Visual Language: Viewing and Visually Representing** explores what teachers need to know and what students need to know how to do to truly learn these two essential, but underrepresented, language arts.
- **Integrating Technology** chapter sections lay the groundwork for the meaningful integration of cutting-edge technologies, including blogs, podcasts, and digital storytelling, to teach language arts.
- **Digital Classroom** features provide in-depth information about technology tools and how to use them in preK–8 classrooms.
- **Common Core State Standards for English Language Arts** features highlight the standards related to each chapter's topic and make connections between the chapter content and learning expectations.
- **Differentiated Instruction** features suggest ways to modify instruction using oral, written, and visual language activities to ensure that all students can be successful.
- **Engaging English Learners** chapter sections describe English learners' specific instructional needs and provide in-depth guidance about how to meet them.
- **Assessment** chapter sections explain how to plan for assessment, monitor students' progress, and evaluate achievement.
- **Spotlight** features throughout the text share classroom research related to a chapter's topic and zero in on how teachers can apply the results in prekindergarten and middle school classrooms.
- **Booklist** features provide new and time-tested favorite titles that teachers use as mentor texts.

PATTERNS OF PRACTICE

The text begins with the background information you need to understand your students and to develop a community of learners, and the research and theories that provide the foundation for contemporary language arts instruction. I go on to clarify the specific instructional approaches best suited to an integrated study of language arts, modeling instruction and pinpointing the concepts and strategies you'll be expected to teach. You'll be guided in ways to get to know your students, and learn what they need to succeed.

I'll lead you through the materials, foundational information, research findings, and methods you must understand to skillfully prepare to teach these students. Finally, you'll learn the tools that you can take directly into your first classroom to make a difference in your students' learning. The text illustrates the way language arts and instructional methodologies, known as patterns of practice, fit together, like the carefully constructed pieces of a quilt, crafted and organized to form one complete picture.

Modeling Effective Instruction

Chapter-opening Vignette:s begin every chapter with a snapshot of authentic instruction. These features describe how individual teachers use the different instructional approaches to develop language arts competencies. They set the tone for each chapter, clearly illustrating chapter concepts as they're played out in successful language arts classrooms.

Authentic samples of student work pepper every chapter, modeling the kinds of interaction and response you can expect in your own classroom.

 New! **Differentiated Instruction** features describe ways to adapt instruction to meet the needs of all students.

New! **Spotlight** features throughout the text zero in on how chapter topics are artfully taught in prekindergarten and middle school classrooms, helping you pinpoint instruction for appropriate grade ranges.

New! **Engaging English Learners** sections lay out the specific instructional needs of English learners and provide in-depth guidance about how to meet them. These features arm you with concrete advice for planning instruction to address the needs of culturally and linguistically diverse students.

Preparing You to Teach

New! **Common Core State Standards for English Language Arts** features in every chapter pinpoint instructional goals for K–8 language arts classrooms. You'll notice the close connection between chapter content and the Standards.

PreK Spotlight

Do young children really need explicit vocabulary instruction?

You might be surprised that vocabulary instruction is an essential component of the preschool language arts program. Word knowledge is necessary for reading comprehension, and children's level of word knowledge predicts their later literacy achievement (Cunningham & Stanovich, 1997). PreK teachers typically teach vocabulary as they read aloud picture books. In *One Duck Stuck* (Root, 2003), teachers can target *stuck*, *deep*, and *slither*, and in *Lunch* (Fleming, 1996), they can focus on *crisp*, *tend*, and *tart*, for instance. Read-aloud sessions are often recommended as the best way to teach vocabulary because the expressive language and rich illustrations in picture books facilitate word learning. Recently, Silverman and Crandell (2010) examined vocabulary instruction during both read-aloud and non-read-aloud times and concluded that a focus on words should be infused throughout the school day. They recommended these instructional techniques:

Acting Out and Illustrating Words. Teachers dramatize and show pictures of targeted words as they're reading aloud or during other language arts activities. This technique is effective for children with low levels of vocabulary development but not for those with higher levels.

Defining Words Explicitly in Rich Context. Teachers explicitly define targeted words as they're reading aloud or during a discussion so children understand what the word means and how to use it. This technique is effective for everyone, but more useful for children with higher levels of word knowledge. The researchers speculated that children with less vocabulary development need more scaffolding than conversations provide.

Viewing Words. Teachers write targeted words on a whiteboard and draw children's attention to some of the sounds and letters in them. This technique is effective for all children during both read-aloud and non-read-aloud sessions.

Applying Words in New Contexts. Teachers encourage children to use targeted words and to make personal connections to them. This technique is effective for all children, but especially for those with higher levels of vocabulary knowledge.

The researchers' most far-reaching conclusion is that children's level of vocabulary knowledge influences the effectiveness of instructional techniques. In particular, children with less vocabulary knowledge need more scaffolding than those with higher levels of development.

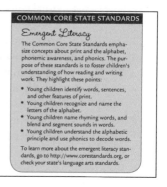

COMMON CORE STATE STANDARDS

Emergent Literacy

The Common Core State Standards emphasize concepts about print and the alphabet, phonemic awareness, and phonics. The purpose of these standards is to foster children's understanding of how reading and writing work. They highlight these points:

- Young children identify words, sentences, and other features of print.
- Young children recognize and name the letters of the alphabet.
- Young children name rhyming words, and blend and segment sounds in words.
- Young children understand the alphabetic principle and use phonics to decode words.

To learn more about the emergent literacy standards, go to http://www.corestandards.org, or check your state's language arts standards.

New! **Integrating Technology** sections equip you to enlist technology to motivate and engage tech-savvy 21st-century students.

New! **Chapter Assessment** sections have been revised to address the integral elements of assessment: planning, monitoring, and evaluating. The new organization and material provide a more detailed picture of meaningful language arts assessment that both guides instruction and assesses learning.

Colorful inserts in Chapter 2 identify the patterns of practice and clarify processes and procedures for using each instructional approach—the four instructional approaches most appropriate for integrating the six language arts. These pages provide detailed classroom examples of teachers in action, illustrating how motivating and engaging each approach can be for students learning language arts.

Patterns of Practice features illustrate how chapter concepts—the reading and writing processes, vocabulary, visual language, reading, and so on—fit into the patterns of practice: literature focus units, literature circles, reading and writing workshop, and thematic units.

Providing the Tools

New! **Booklist** features present mentor texts to use in teaching. Language arts teachers use these books to shape students' learning, and the Booklists provide new and time-tested favorites on a variety of topics for prekindergarten through eighth grade.

Booklist

VOCABULARY	
PreK–Grade 2	DeGross, M. (1998). *Donovan's word jar*. New York: HarperCollins. Mammano, J. (2001). *Rhinos who play soccer*. San Francisco: Chronicle Books. (Check other books in the series.) Moss, L. (2005). *Zin! Zin! Zin! A violin*. New York: Aladdin Books. O'Connor, J. (2008). *Fancy Nancy's favorite fancy words: From accessories to zany*. New York: HarperCollins.
Grades 3–5	Barretta, G. (2007). *Dear deer: A book of homophones*. New York: Henry Holt. Cleary, B. P. (2007). *How much can a bare bear bear? What are homonyms and homophones?* New York: First Avenue Editions. Clements, A. (1998). *Frindle*. New York: Atheneum. Falwell, C. (2006). *Word wizard*. New York: Sandpiper. Frasier, D. (2000). *Miss Alaineus: A vocabulary disaster*. San Diego: Harcourt Brace. Heller, R. (1998). *A cache of jewels and other collective nouns*. New York: Putnam. Melmed, L. K. (2009). *Heart of Texas: A lone star ABC*. New York: HarperCollins. Napier, M. (2002). *Z is for Zamboni: A hockey alphabet*. Farmington Hills, MI: Sleeping Bear Press. Pallotta, J. (2006). *The construction alphabet book*. Watertown, MA: Charlesbridge. (See other alphabet books by this author.)
Grades 6–8	Agee, J. (2009). *Palindromania!* New York: Farrar, Straus & Giroux. (See other books by this author.) Bauer, P. (2009). *B is for battle cry: A Civil War alphabet*. Farmington Hills, MI: Sleeping Bear Press. Evans, D. (2004). *MVP**. Blodgett, OR: Hand Print Press. Fine, E. H. (2004). *Cryptomania! Teleporting into Greek and Latin with the Cryptokids*. Berkeley, CA: Tricycle Press. Lederer, R., & Morice, D. (1998). *Word circus: A letter-perfect book*. Springfield, MA: Merriam Webster. Terban, M. (2006). *Building your vocabulary and making it great!* New York: Scholastic. Terban, M. (2006). *The Scholastic dictionary of idioms*. New York: Scholastic.

Step-by-Step features present detailed directions for preparing and carrying out specific instructional strategies and procedures, providing a clear and precise map to use in the classroom.

Minilessons throughout the text provide detailed examples that model effective instructional practice, giving you tools to take into the classroom.

FOR PROFESSORS AND STUDENTS

MyEducationLab™

Proven to **engage students**, provide **trusted content**, and **improve results**, Pearson MyLabs have helped more than 8 million registered students reach true understanding in their courses. **MyEducationLab** engages students with real-life teaching situations through dynamic videos, case studies, and student artifacts. Student progress is assessed, and a personalized study plan is created based on the student's unique results. Automatic grading and reporting keep educators informed to quickly address gaps and improve student performance. All of the activities and exercises in MyEducationLab are built around essential learning outcomes for teachers and are mapped to professional teaching standards.

In *Preparing Teachers for a Changing World,* Linda Darling-Hammond and her colleagues point out that grounding teacher education in real classrooms—among real teachers and students and among actual examples of students' and teachers' work—is an important, and perhaps even an essential, part of training teachers for the complexities of teaching in today's classrooms.

In the MyEducationLab for this course, you will find the following features and resources.

STUDY PLAN SPECIFIC TO YOUR TEXT

MyEducationLab gives students the opportunity to test themselves on key concepts and skills, track their own progress through the course, and access personalized Study Plan activities.

The customized Study Plan—with enriching activities—is generated based on students' results on a pretest. Study Plans tag incorrect questions from the pretest to the appropriate textbook learning outcome, helping students focus on the topics they need help with. Personalized Study Plan activities may include eBook reading assignments, and review, practice and enrichment activities.

After students complete the enrichment activities, they take a posttest to see the concepts they've mastered or the areas where they may need extra help.

MyEducationLab then reports the Study Plan results to the instructor. Based on these reports, the instructor can adapt course material to suit the needs of individual students or the entire class.

CONNECTION TO NATIONAL STANDARDS

Now it is easier than ever to see how coursework is connected to national standards. Each topic, activity, and exercise on MyEducationLab lists intended learning outcomes connected to the either the Common Core State Standards for Language Arts or the IRA Standards for Reading Professionals.

ASSIGNMENTS AND ACTIVITIES

Designed to enhance your understanding of concepts covered in class, these assignable exercises show concepts in action (through videos, cases, and/or student and teacher artifacts). They help you deepen content knowledge and synthesize and apply concepts and strategies you read about in the book. (Correct answers for these assignments are available to the instructor only.)

BUILDING TEACHING SKILLS AND DISPOSITIONS

These unique learning units help users practice and strengthen skills that are essential to effective teaching. After presenting the steps involved in a core teaching process, you are given an opportunity to practice applying this skill via videos, student and teacher artifacts, and/or case studies of authentic classrooms. Providing multiple opportunities to practice a single teaching concept, each activity encourages a deeper understanding and application of concepts, as well as the use of critical thinking skills. After practice, students take a quiz that is reported to the instructor gradebook.

LESSON PLAN BUILDER

The **Lesson Plan Builder** is an effective and easy-to-use tool that you can use to create, update, and share quality lesson plans. The software also makes it easy to integrate state content standards into any lesson plan.

IRIS CENTER RESOURCES

The IRIS Center at Vanderbilt University (http://iris.peabody.vanderbilt.edu), funded by the U.S. Department of Education's Office of Special Education Programs (OSEP), develops training enhancement materials for preservice and practicing teachers. The Center works with experts from across the country to create challenge-based interactive modules, case study units, and podcasts that provide research-validated information about working with students in inclusive settings. In your MyEducationLab course, we have integrated this content where appropriate.

LITERACY PORTRAITS

Yearlong case studies of second graders—complete with student artifacts matching each video clip, teacher commentary, and student and teacher interviews—track the month-by-month literacy growth of five second graders. You'll meet English learner Rakie, struggling readers Rhiannon and Curt-Lynn, bilingual learner Michael, and grade-level reader Jimmy, and travel with them through a year of assessments, word-study instruction, reading groups, writing activities, buddy reading, and more.

A+RISE ACTIVITIES

A+RISE activities provide practice in targeting instruction. A+RISE®, developed by three-time Teacher of the Year and administrator Evelyn Arroyo, provides quick, research-based strategies that get to the "how" of targeting instruction and making content accessible for all students, including English language learners.

A+RISE® Standards2Strategy™ is an innovative and interactive online resource that offers new K–12 teachers research-based instructional strategies that:

- Meet the linguistic needs of ELLs as they learn content
- Differentiate instruction for all grades and abilities
- Offer reading and writing techniques, cooperative learning, use of linguistic and nonlinguistic representations, scaffolding, teacher modeling, higher order thinking, and alternative classroom ELL assessment
- Provide support to help teachers be effective through the integration of listening, speaking, reading, and writing along with the content curriculum
- Improve student achievement
- Are aligned to Common Core Elementary Language Arts standards (for the literacy strategies) and to English language proficiency standards in WIDA, Texas, California, and Florida

COURSE RESOURCES

The Course Resources section of MyEducationLab is designed to help you put together an effective lesson plan, prepare for and begin your career, navigate your first year of teaching, and understand key educational standards, policies, and laws.

It includes the following:

The Grammar Tutorial provides content extracted in part from *The Praxis Series™ Online Tutorial for the Pre-Professional Skills Test: Writing*. Online quizzes built around specific elements of grammar help users strengthen their understanding and proper usage of the English language in writing. Definitions and examples of grammatical concepts are followed by practice exercises to provide the background information and usage examples needed to refresh understandings of grammar, and then apply that knowledge to make it more permanent.

The Database of Children's Literature offers information on thousands of quality literature titles, and the activities provide experience in choosing appropriate literature and integrating the best titles into language arts instruction.

The Certification and Licensure section is designed to help you pass your licensure exam by giving you access to state test requirements, overviews of what tests cover, and sample test items.

The Certification and Licensure section includes the following:

- **State Certification Test Requirements:** Here, you can click on a state and will then be taken to a list of state certification tests.

- You can click on the **Licensure Exams** you need to take to find:
  - Basic information about each test
  - Descriptions of what is covered on each test
  - Sample test questions with explanations of correct answers

- **National Evaluation Series™** by Pearson: Here, you can see the tests in the NES, learn what is covered on each exam, and access sample test items with descriptions and rationales of correct answers. You can also purchase interactive online tutorials developed by Pearson Evaluation Systems and the Pearson Teacher Education and Development group.

- **ETS Online Praxis Tutorials:** Here, you can purchase interactive online tutorials developed by ETS and by the Pearson Teacher Education and Development group. Tutorials are available for the Praxis I exams and for select Praxis II exams.

Visit http://www.myeducationlab.com for a demonstration of this exciting new online teaching resource.

Instructor's Resource Center

The Instructor's Resource Center at http://www.pearsonhighered.com has a variety of print and media resources available in downloadable, digital format—all in one location.

As a registered faculty member, you can access and download pass code–protected resource files, course-management content, and other premium online content directly to your computer.

Digital resources available for *Language Arts: Patterns of Practice*, 8e, include the following:

- A test bank of multiple choice and essay tests.
- PowerPoint presentations specifically designed for each chapter.
- Chapter-by-chapter materials, including objectives, suggested readings, discussion questions, and in-class activities, and guidance on how to use the Vignette:s meaningfully in your instruction.

To access these items online, go to http://www.pearsonhighered.com and click on the Instructor option. You'll find an Instructor's Resource Center option in the top navigation bar. There you will be able to log in or complete a one-time registration for a user name and password. If you have any questions regarding this process or the materials available online, please contact your local Pearson sales representative.

ACKNOWLEDGMENTS

I've been privileged to work with very talented teachers. I want to express my heartfelt thanks to the teachers highlighted in the chapter opener vignettes and the color inserts in Chapter 2. I also want to acknowledge the teachers who have influenced my teaching over the years, in particular: Eileen Boland, Kimberly Clark, Stephanie Collom, Pat Daniel, Whitney Donnelly, Laurie Goodman, Sandy Harris, Terry Kasner, Susan McCloskey, Kristi McNeal, Jennifer Miller-McColm, Carol Ochs, Judy Reeves, Jenny Reno, and Susan Zumwalt. Thanks for welcoming me into your classrooms. I've learned as I watched and worked side by side with you and your students. The students whose writing samples appear in the book deserve special recognition; you've breathed life into the pages of this book.

To my editors and the production team at Pearson Education, I offer my heartfelt thanks. A special thank-you to Hope Madden, my savvy taskmaster. You're an amazing woman, and after working together for a decade or more, it's so difficult to say good-bye as you move on to other projects. Thank you for trying to keep me on track to meet deadlines and for being a friend. A special note of thanks to Diane Lorenzo for designing a beautiful quilt cover—you're amazing! I want to express my appreciation to Aurora Martinez, my exceptional acquisitions editor, for her support. I extend my gratitude to Janet Domingo, who has again successfully moved this text through the maze of production details, and to Melissa Gruzs, who has again cleaned up my manuscript and proofread the typeset text; I'm grateful for your careful attention to detail.

Finally, I want to acknowledge my colleagues who served as reviewers for this edition: John Barnitz, University of New Orleans; Elaine Pierce Chakonas, Northeastern Illinois University; Kenneth M. Holmes, Webster University; Eileen Kaiser, Northeastern Illinois University; and Vernelle Tyler, University of South Carolina, Aiken. I appreciate your thoughtful analyses and insights. This text is more effective because of your efforts.

Language Arts

Patterns of Practice

Learning and the Language Arts

FIRST GRADERS APPLY THE SIX LANGUAGE ARTS   The first graders in Mrs. McNeal's classroom are rereading their collaborative retelling of Maurice Sendak's *Where the Wild Things Are* (2003). It's written on large charts, one for the beginning, one for the middle, and one for the end:

Beginning	*Max wore his wolf suit and made mischief. His mother called him, "Wild Thing!" He was sent to bed without any supper!*
Middle	*Max went to his room and a forest grew. Max got into his private boat and sailed to where the wild things are.*
End	*Max wanted to go home to where somebody loved him best of all. When he got home his supper was waiting for him and it was still hot!*

Mrs. McNeal used interactive writing for the retelling so that all of the words would be spelled correctly, and the children could easily reread it. The "middle" chart is shown on page 4; the boxes around some letters and words represent the correction tape that Mrs. McNeal used to correct spelling errors and poorly formed letters.

Japmeet holds the pointer and leads the class in rereading the "beginning" chart, moving the pointer from word to word as the children read aloud. Next, Henry leads the rereading of the "middle" chart, and Noelle does the "end" chart. As they finish reading, the children clap their hands because they're proud of their retelling of a favorite story.

Mrs. McNeal's students are learning about stories; they know that stories have beginnings, middles, and ends. They can pick out the three parts in stories that Mrs. McNeal reads aloud, and they try to include all three parts in the stories they write.

How do teachers incorporate the six language arts in their teaching?

Listening, talking, reading, writing, viewing, and visually representing are the six language arts; two of the language arts are oral, two are written, and two are visual. Effective teachers integrate instruction and incorporate opportunities for students to use all six every day in their language arts programs. As you read this vignette about first graders participating in writing workshop, notice that Mrs. McNeal provides opportunities for her students to use all six language arts.

The first graders participate in a 60-minute writing workshop each day, beginning with a 15-minute word work lesson that involves reading and writing high-frequency words. The first graders sit on the floor in front of the word wall, a bulletin-board display with 20 sheets of construction paper on which the letters are printed in alphabetical order and word cards with high-frequency words are posted according to beginning letter. Currently, 52 words are posted on the word wall, and several new words are added each week.

The lesson begins with a quick review of the words. First, Hanna holds the pointer and leads the children in reading the words. Next, Mrs. McNeal passes out small whiteboards, pens, and erasers, and they play a word game: The teacher gives phonological, semantic, and syntactic clues about a word on the word wall, and the first graders identify the word. Mrs. McNeal says, "I'm thinking of a word with three letters. It begins with /y/ and it fits in this sentence: _____ are my friend. What's the word?" The children identify *you* and write it on their whiteboards. They hold up their boards so Mrs. McNeal can check their work. Then they erase their boards, and the game continues.

Next, Mrs. McNeal teaches a 15-minute minilesson on a writing concept, such as adding details, writing titles, or using punctuation marks correctly. Today, she reviews beginning, middle, and end. She asks Sachit to read his draft aloud. He reads:

> *I love school. I have lots of friends. One is Yaman. He is a good friend to me. We play with Alex. We play basketball. We are good friends. I can't get a ball in the hoop.*

The children pick out the beginning and middle sections of the story but notice that Sachit's story needs an ending. After several children suggest possible endings, Sachit decides to use Yaman's suggestion and finishes his story this way: *But I still play basketball anyway.*

A 25-minute writing period follows. On most days, children write stories independently, but sometimes they work together to write collaborative compositions, as they did to retell *Where the Wild Things Are*. Today, some children are beginning new stories. They sit

Children's Retelling of the "Middle" of the Story

Max went to his room and a forest grew. Max got into his private boat and sailed to where the wild things are.

knee-to-knee with a classmate and plan their stories by telling them aloud. Some children work on stories they began the previous day, and others meet with Mrs. McNeal to share their writings. They read their stories to the teacher and talk about them, checking that they make sense and have a beginning, a middle, and an end. If the story is ready to be

Noelle's Story

The Birthday Party

Once it was my grandpa's birthday. We had a party.
We played lots of games. My dad played and my sister
played and my cousin played. All of us had fun.

published, Mrs. McNeal types it on the computer, leaving space at the top for an illustration and correcting spelling and other mechanical errors so that the children can read it.

For the last 5 minutes of the workshop, children share their newly published compositions. Noelle reads aloud her story, "The Birthday Party," which is shown on the previous page. The children tell her that they like her story because it reminds them of the time they spend with their grandparents. Mrs. McNeal ceremoniously hangs Noelle's story in a special section of the bulletin board for everyone to reread.

oday, teachers face new challenges and opportunities. The students who come to your classroom may speak a different language at school than they speak at home, and they're growing up in varied family structures: Many live in two-parent families, but others live with single parents or grandparents, in blended families, or with two moms or dads. Far too many children are growing up in poverty, some with parents in prison and siblings in gangs. Still others are homeless. Sadly, some have lost sight of the American dream, believing that a college education is out of reach. Clearly, the way you teach language arts must address not only your beliefs about how children learn but also the language and culture of the students you teach.

OW CHILDREN LEARN

Swiss psychologist Jean Piaget (1886–1980) radically changed our understanding of how children learn with his constructivist framework (Piaget & Inhelder, 2000). He described learning as the modification of children's cognitive structures as they interact with and adapt to their environment. He believed that children construct their own knowledge from their experiences. Related to Piaget's theory is the information-processing theory (Flavell, Miller, & Miller, 2001), which focuses on how learners use cognitive processes to think about what and how they're learning.

The Process of Learning

Children's knowledge is not just a collection of isolated bits of information; it's organized in the brain, and this organization becomes increasingly integrated as their knowledge grows (Tracey & Morrow, 2006). The organization of knowledge is the cognitive structure, and knowledge is arranged in category systems called *schemata*. (A single category is a *schema*.) Within the schemata are three components: categories of knowledge, features or rules for determining what constitutes a category and what's included in each category, and a network of interrelationships among the categories.

These schemata can be likened to a conceptual filing system in which people organize and store the information derived from their past experiences. Taking this analogy further, information is filed in the brain in "file folders." As children learn, they add new file folders to their filing system, and as they study a topic, its file folder becomes thicker.

Children enlarge existing schemata or construct new ones using two cognitive processes— *assimilation* and *accommodation* (Piaget & Inhelder, 2000). Assimilation takes place when information is integrated into existing schemata, and accommodation occurs when schemata are modified or new schemata are created. Through assimilation, children add new information to their picture of the world; through accommodation, they change that picture to reflect new information.

Learning occurs through the process of equilibration. When children encounter something they don't understand, disequilibrium, or cognitive conflict, results. This disequilibrium typically produces confusion and agitation, feelings that impel children to seek equilibrium, a comfortable balance with the environment. In other words, when confronted with new or discrepant information, children are intrinsically motivated to try to make sense of it. If their schemata can assimilate or accommodate the new information, then the disequilibrium caused by the new experience will motivate them to learn. Equilibrium is then regained at a higher developmental level. Here's the three-step process:

1. Equilibrium is disrupted by the introduction of new or discrepant information.
2. Disequilibrium occurs, and the dual processes of assimilation and accommodation function.
3. Equilibrium is attained at a higher developmental level.

The process of equilibration happens again and again during the course of a day. In fact, it's occurring right now as you're reading this chapter. Learning doesn't always occur when we're presented with new information, however: If the new information is too difficult and we can't relate it to what we already know, we don't learn. The new information must be puzzling, challenging, or, in Piaget's words, "moderately novel."

Learning Strategies

We all have skills that we use automatically plus self-regulated strategies for things that we do well—driving defensively, playing volleyball, training a new pet, or maintaining classroom discipline. We unconsciously apply skills we've learned and thoughtfully choose among strategies. The strategies are problem-solving mechanisms that involve complex thinking processes. When we're learning how to drive a car, for example, we learn both skills and strategies. Some of the first skills we learn are how to make left turns and parallel park. With practice, these skills become automatic. One of the first strategies we learn is how to pass another car. At first, we have only a small repertoire of strategies, and we don't always use them effectively; that's one reason why we get a learner's permit that requires a more experienced driver to ride along with us. With practice and guidance, we become more successful drivers, able to anticipate driving problems and take defensive actions.

Children develop a variety of learning strategies, including rehearsal—repeating information over and over—that they use to remember something. They also learn to use these strategies:

PREDICTING. Children anticipate what will happen next.

ORGANIZING. Children group information into categories.

ELABORATING. Children expand on the information presented.

MONITORING. Children regulate or keep track of their progress.

Information-processing theory suggests that as children grow older, their use of learning strategies improves (Flavell, Miller, & Miller, 2001). As they acquire more effective methods for learning and remembering information, children also become more aware of their own cognitive processes and better able to regulate them. They can reflect on their literacy processes and talk about themselves as readers and writers. For example, third grader Mario reports that "it's mostly after I read a book that I write" (Muhammad, 1993, p. 99), and fifth grader Hobbes reports that "the pictures in my head help me when I write stuff down 'cause then I can get ideas from my pictures" (L. Cleary, 1993, p. 142).

Children become more realistic about the limitations of their memories and more knowledgeable about which learning strategies are most effective in particular situations. They also become increasingly aware of what they know and don't know. The term *metacognition* refers to this knowledge that children acquire about their own learning processes and to their regulation of these cognitive processes to maximize learning (Tracey & Morrow, 2006).

Teachers play an important role in developing children's metacognitive abilities. During large-group activities, teachers introduce and model learning strategies. In small-group lessons, they provide guided practice, talk with children about learning strategies, and ask them to reflect on their own use of these cognitive processes. Teachers also guide children about when to use particular strategies and which strategies are more effective with various activities.

Social Contexts of Learning

Cognitive development is enhanced through social interaction. Russian psychologist Lev Vygotsky (1896–1934) asserted that children learn through socially meaningful interactions and that language is both social and an important facilitator of learning (Vygotsky, 1986, 2006). Experiences are organized and shaped by society, but rather than merely absorbing these experiences, children negotiate and transform them as a dynamic part of culture. They learn to talk through social interaction and to read and write through interaction with literate children and adults (Dyson, 1997, 2003). Community is important: Students talk with classmates about books they're reading, and they turn to classmates for feedback about their writing (Zebroski, 1994).

Through interactions with teachers and collaboration with classmates, students learn things they couldn't on their own (Tracey & Morrow, 2006). Teachers guide and support students as they move from their current level of knowledge toward a more advanced level. Vygotsky (2006) described these two levels as the *actual developmental level*, the point at which learners can perform a task independently, and the *level of proximal development*, the point at which learners can perform a task with assistance. Students can do more difficult things in collaboration than they can on their own, which is why teachers are important models and why students often work with partners and in small groups.

A child's "zone of proximal development" is the range of tasks that the child can perform with guidance from others but cannot yet perform independently. According to Vygotsky, children learn best when what they're attempting to learn is within this zone. He believed that children learn little by performing tasks they can already do independently—at their actual developmental level—or by attempting tasks that are too difficult, or beyond their zone of proximal development.

Vygotsky and Jerome Bruner (2004) used the term *scaffold* as a metaphor to describe adults' contributions to children's learning. Scaffolds are support mechanisms that teachers, parents, and others provide to help children successfully perform a task within their zone of proximal development. Teachers serve as scaffolds when they model or demonstrate a procedure, guide children through a task, ask questions, break complex tasks into smaller steps, and supply pieces of information. As students gain knowledge and experience about how to perform a task, teachers gradually withdraw their support so students make the transition from social interaction to internalized, independent functioning.

Implications for Learning Language Arts

How students learn has important implications for how they learn language arts. Contributions from the constructivist, information-processing, and sociolinguistic theories include these ideas:

- Students are active participants in learning.
- Students learn by relating the new information to prior knowledge.

- Students organize their knowledge in schemata.
- Students apply strategies consciously as they learn.
- Students learn through social interactions with classmates and the teacher.
- Teachers provide scaffolds for students.

Think about these implications and how they'll affect your teaching.

LANGUAGE LEARNING AND CULTURE

Language is a complex system for creating meaning through socially shared conventions (Halliday, 2006). Before children enter kindergarten, they learn the language of their community. They understand what community members say to them, and they share their ideas with others through that language. In an amazingly short period of three or four years, children master the exceedingly complex system of their native language, which allows them to understand sentences they've never heard before and to create sentences they've never said before. Young children aren't taught how to talk; this knowledge about language develops unconsciously.

The Four Language Systems

Language is organized using four systems, sometimes called *cueing systems*, which together make communication possible:

- The phonological, or sound, system of language
- The syntactic, or structural, system of language
- The semantic, or meaning, system of language
- The pragmatic, or social and cultural use, system of language

The four language systems and their terminology are summarized in Figure 1–1. Children have an implicit understanding of these systems, and they integrate information simultaneously from them in order to communicate. No one system is more important than any other, even though the phonological system (sometimes called the *visual system*) plays a prominent role when young children are learning to read and write.

The Phonological System. There are approximately 44 speech sounds in English. Children learn to pronounce these sounds as they learn to talk, and they associate the sounds with letters as they learn to read and write. Sounds are called *phonemes*, and they're represented in print with diagonal lines to differentiate them from *graphemes*, or letter combinations. For example, the first letter in *mother* is written *m,* and the phoneme is represented by /m/; the /ō/ phoneme in *soap* represented by the grapheme *oa*.

The phonological system is important in both oral and written language. Regional and cultural differences exist in the way people pronounce phonemes. For example, John F. Kennedy's speech was typical of New England. Similarly, the English spoken in Australia is different from American English. English learners must learn to pronounce English sounds, and sounds that are different from those in their native language are particularly difficult to learn. For example, Spanish doesn't have /th/, and children who have immigrated to the United States from Mexico and other Spanish-speaking countries have difficulty pronouncing this sound; they often substitute /d/ for /th/ because the sounds are articulated in similar ways (Nathenson-Mejia, 1989). Younger children usually learn to pronounce the difficult sounds more easily than older English learners do.

FIGURE 1–1   The Language Systems

System	Description	Terms
Phonological System	The sound system of English with approximately 44 sounds	• Phoneme (the smallest unit of sound) • Grapheme (the written representation of a phoneme using one or more letters) • Phonological awareness (knowledge about the sound structure of words, at the phoneme, onset-rime, and syllable levels) • Phonemic awareness (the ability to manipulate the sounds in words orally) • Phonics (knowledge about phoneme-grapheme correspondences and spelling rules)
Syntactic System	The structural system of English that governs how words are combined into sentences	• Syntax (the structure or grammar of a sentence) • Morpheme (the smallest meaningful unit of language) • Free morpheme (a morpheme that stands alone as word) • Bound morpheme (a morpheme that's attached to a free morpheme)
Semantic System	The meaning system of English that focuses on vocabulary	• Semantics (meaning) • Synonyms (words with similar meanings) • Antonyms (opposites) • Homophones (words that sound alike)
Pragmatic System	The system of English that varies according to social and cultural uses	• Function (the purpose for which a person uses language) • Standard English (the form of English used in textbooks and by television newscasters) • Nonstandard English (other forms of English)

Children use their knowledge of phonology as they learn to read and write. In a purely phonetic language, there's a one-to-one correspondence between letters and sounds, and teaching students to sound out words is an easy process. But English isn't a purely phonetic language, because there are 26 letters and 44 sounds and many ways to combine the letters—especially the vowels—to spell some of the sounds. Phonics, which describes the phoneme-grapheme correspondences and related spelling rules, is an important part of early literacy instruction, because students use phonics to decode words. They also use their understanding of the phonological system to spell words. Second graders, for example, might spell *school* as *skule,* based on their knowledge of phoneme-grapheme relationships and spelling patterns. As students learn more, their spellings become increasingly sophisticated and finally conventional.

The Syntactic System. The syntactic system is the structural organization of English. This system is the grammar that regulates how words are combined into sentences. Here the word *grammar* means the rules governing how words are organized into sentences, not the parts of speech or the conventional etiquette of language. Children use the syntactic system as they combine words to form sentences. Word order is important in English, and English speakers must arrange words into a sequence that makes sense. Young Spanish-speaking English learners, for example, learn to say, "This is my red sweater," not "This is my sweater red," the literal translation from Spanish.

Students use their knowledge of the syntactic system as they read. They anticipate that the words they're reading have been strung together into meaningful sentences. When they come to an unfamiliar word, they recognize its role in the sentence. For example, in the sentence "The horses galloped through the gate and out into the field," students may not be able to decode the word *through*, but they can easily substitute a reasonable word or phrase, such as *out of* or *past*. Many of the capitalization and punctuation rules that students learn reflect the syntactic system. Similarly, when they learn about simple, compound, and complex sentences, they're learning about the syntactic system.

Another component of syntax is word forms. Words such as *dog* and *play* are *morphemes*, the smallest meaningful units in language. Word parts that change the meaning of a word are also morphemes. When the plural marker *-s* is added to *dog* to make *dogs*, for instance, or the past-tense marker *-ed* is added to *play* to make *played*, these words now contain two morphemes because the inflectional endings change the meaning. The words *dog* and *play* are *free morphemes* because they stand alone; the endings *-s* and *-ed* are *bound morphemes* because they must be attached to a free morpheme to convey meaning. As they learn to talk, children quickly learn to combine words and word parts, such as adding *-s* to *cookie* to create a plural and adding *-er* to *high* to indicate a comparison. They also learn to combine two or more free morphemes to form compound words such as *birthday, sailboat,* and *grandfather*.

Children also learn to add affixes to words. Affixes added at the beginning of a word are *prefixes*, and those added at the end are *suffixes*. Both kinds of affixes are bound morphemes. For example, the prefix *un-* in *unhappy* is a bound morpheme, but *happy* is a free morpheme because it can stand alone.

The Semantic System. The third language system is the semantic, or meaning, system; it focuses on vocabulary. Researchers estimate that children have a vocabulary of 5,000 words by the time they enter school, and they continue to acquire 3,000 words each year (Stahl & Nagy, 2005). Children probably learn 7 to 10 words a day, many of which are learned informally through reading and through social studies, science, and other curricular areas.

At the same time students are learning new words, they're also learning that many words have multiple meanings. Meaning is usually based on the context—the surrounding words. The common word *run*, for instance, has more than 30 meanings! The meaning of *run* in these sentences is tied to the context in which it's used:

> Will the mayor run for reelection?
> The bus runs between Dallas and Houston.
> The advertisement will run for three days.
> Did you run in the 50-yard dash?
> The plane made a bombing run.
> Run to the store and get a loaf of bread for me.
> The dogs are out in the run.

Students often don't have the full range of meanings; rather, they learn meanings through a process of refinement.

Students learn other sophisticated concepts about words as well. They learn about shades of meaning—for example, the differences among these *sad* words: *unhappy, crushed, desolate, miserable, disappointed, cheerless, down,* and *griefstricken*. They also learn about synonyms and antonyms, wordplay, and figurative language.

The Pragmatic System. The fourth language system is *pragmatics*, which deals with the social and cultural aspects of language use. People use language for many purposes, and how they talk or write varies according to purpose and audience. Language use varies among social classes, cultural and ethnic groups, and geographic regions; these varieties are known as *dialects*. School is one cultural community, and the language of school is Standard English; this register, or style, is formal—the one used in textbooks, newspapers, and magazines and by television newscasters. Other forms, including those spoken in inner cities, in Appalachia, and by Mexican Americans in the Southwest, are generally classified as nonstandard English; these nonstandard forms are alternatives in which the phonology, syntax, and semantics differ from those of Standard English, but they aren't inferior or substandard. They reflect the communities of the speakers, and the speakers communicate as effectively as those who use Standard English in their communities. The goal is for students to add Standard English to their repertoire of language registers, not to replace their home dialect with Standard English. Interestingly, researchers have found regional differences in how people spell words on Twitter (Eisenstein, O'Connor, Smith, & Xing, 2011). For example, *cool* is spelled *coo* in southern California but *koo* in northern California, and in New York City *suttin* is shorthand for *something*.

Academic Language

The type of English used for instruction is called *academic language*. It's different than the social or conversational language we speak at home and with friends in two ways. First, academic language is more cognitively demanding and decontextualized than social language in which speakers carry on face-to-face conversations about everyday topics (Wong-Fillmore & Snow, 2002). Teachers use academic language when they teach language arts and other content areas and when they give directions for completing assignments. It's also the language used in content-area textbooks and standardized achievement tests.

Second, academic language has semantic, syntactic, and pragmatic features that distinguish it from social language. The ideas being expressed are more complex; the meaning is less obvious and takes more effort to understand. The vocabulary is more technical and precise; many words are unfamiliar or are used in new ways. The sentence structure is different: Academic language uses longer, more complex sentences that may be difficult to understand. Academic language has a different style, too: Speakers and writers present detailed, well-organized information about complex and abstract topics, usually without becoming personally involved in the topic. The contrasts between social and academic language are summarized in Figure 1–2.

Even when students are proficient users of social language, they're likely to have difficulty understanding and using academic language in the classroom without instruction (Wong-Fillmore & Snow, 2002). Through instruction and frequent opportunities to use academic language in meaningful ways, students develop the knowledge, vocabulary, and language patterns associated with academic English. Although learning academic language is essential for all students, the challenge is greater for English learners.

Culturally and Linguistically Diverse Students

The United States is a culturally pluralistic society, and our ethnic, racial, and socioeconomic diversity is reflected in classrooms. Today, more than a third of us classify ourselves as non-European Americans, and the percentage of culturally diverse students is even higher: In California, more than half of school-age children belong to ethnic minority groups, and in New York state, 40% do. Given current birthrates and immigration patterns, researchers estimate that within a few years, Hispanic American and Asian American populations will grow by more than 20%, and the African American population by 12%. These changing demographic realities are having a significant impact on schools, as more and more students come from linguistically and culturally diverse backgrounds.

Because the United States is a nation of immigrants, dealing with cultural diversity isn't a new responsibility for public schools; however, the magnitude of diversity is much greater now. In the past, the United States was viewed as a melting pot in which language and cultural differences

FIGURE 1–2	Contrasts Between Social and Academic Language	
	Social Language	**Academic Language**
Topics	Topics are familiar, everyday, and concrete; they're often examined superficially with few details being presented.	Topics are unfamiliar, complex, and abstract. More details are provided, and they are examined in more depth.
Vocabulary	Everyday, familiar words are used.	Technical terms, jargon, and many multisyllabic words are used.
Sentence Structure	Sentences are shorter and dependent on the context.	Sentence structure is longer and more complicated.
Viewpoints	One opinion or viewpoint is shared, and it's often subjective or biased.	Multiple viewpoints are considered and analyzed, usually objectively.

would be assimilated or combined to form a new, truly American culture. What actually happened, though, was that the European American culture remained dominant. That idea has been replaced with cultural pluralism, which respects people's right to retain their cultural identity within American society, recognizing that each culture contributes to and enriches the total society.

Children of diverse cultures come to school with a broad range of language and literacy experiences, although their experiences may be different than those of mainstream or European American children (Samway & McKeon, 1999). They've learned to communicate in at least one language, and, if they don't speak English, they want to learn English to make friends, learn, and communicate just like their classmates. Brock and Raphael (2005) emphasize that teachers must take students' diverse backgrounds into account as they plan instruction, making sure to provide a variety of opportunities for students to participate in classroom activities.

English Learners. Learning a second language is a constructive process, and students learn English in a predictable way through interactions with classmates and adults. Jim Cummins (1989) theorized that English learners must develop two types of English proficiency. First, children learn social or everyday language, which Cummins called Basic Interpersonal Conversational Skills (BICS). Social language is characterized as context embedded because context cues that make the language easier to understand are available to speakers and listeners. This type of language is easy to learn, according to Cummins, because it's cognitively undemanding and can usually be acquired in only two to three years.

Cummins's second type is Cognitive Academic Language Proficiency (CALP). CALP is academic language, the type of language that students need to understand and use for school success, and it's much harder to learn because it's context reduced and more cognitively demanding. Context-reduced language is more abstract and less familiar, and because technical terms, complex sentence structures, and less familiar topics are involved, it's less cognitively demanding. English learners require five to seven years or more to become proficient in this type of English, and too many English learners never reach proficiency.

How quickly English learners learn academic English depends on many factors, including their native language proficiency, school experiences, motivation, and personality. The family's literacy level, socioeconomic status, and cultural isolation are other considerations. In addition, when families flee from social unrest or war in their native countries, children often take longer to learn English because of the trauma they experienced. So that students grow in their knowledge and use of academic language, Courtney Cazden (2001) challenges teachers to incorporate more academic language in their instruction and classroom activities.

Critical Literacy

It's easy for teachers to focus on teaching language arts without considering how language works in society, but language is more than just a means of communication; it shapes our perceptions of society, justice, and acceptance. Standard English is the language of school, but today, many students speak a different language or nonstandard English at home. These language differences and the way that teachers and classmates respond to them affect how students think about themselves and their expectations for school success. Some students are more eager to share their ideas than others, and research suggests that teachers call on boys more often than girls. Also, classmates encourage some students to participate more than others. These language behaviors silence some students and marginalize others.

Language isn't neutral. Both children and adults use language for a variety of purposes—to entertain, inform, control, and persuade, for example. Language used for these purposes affects our beliefs, opinions, and behavior. Martin Luther King Jr.'s "I Have a Dream" speech, for example, had a great impact on American society, calling people to action during the civil rights movement. Essays, novels, and other written materials also affect us in powerful ways. Think about the impact of *Anne Frank: The Diary of a Young Girl* (Frank, 1995): The madness of the Holocaust appalled us.

Critical literacy focuses on the empowering role of language. This theory emphasizes the use of language to communicate, solve problems, and persuade others to a course of action. It emphasizes the interactions among students in the classroom, and the relationship between language and students in the context of the classroom, the neighborhood, and society.

Critical literacy grew out of the critical pedagogy theory that suggests that teachers and students should ask fundamental questions about knowledge, justice, and equity (Wink, 2010). Language becomes a means for social action. Teachers do more than just teach students to use language; both teachers and students become agents of social change. The increasing social and cultural diversity in our society adds urgency to resolving inequities and injustices.

Language arts instruction doesn't take place in a vacuum; the content that teachers teach and their instructional approaches occur in a social, cultural, political, and historical context (Freire & Macedo, 1987). Grammar instruction is a good example. Some people argue that grammar shouldn't be taught because it's too abstract and won't help students become better readers or writers; however, others believe that not teaching grammar is one way the majority culture denies access to nonstandard English speakers. Both proponents and detractors of grammar instruction want what's best for students, but their views are diametrically opposed. Think about these issues related to teaching and learning:

Does school perpetuate the dominant culture and exclude others?
Do all students have equal access to learning opportunities?
How are students who speak nonstandard English treated?
Is school more like family life in some cultures than in others?
Do teachers interact differently with boys and girls?
Are some students silenced in classrooms?
Do teachers have different expectations for minority students?
Are English learners marginalized?
Does the literature that students read reflect diverse voices?

Language arts isn't just a body of knowledge; instead, it's a way of organizing knowledge within a cultural and political context. Giroux (1997) challenges teachers not to accept the status quo, but to be professionals and to take control of their own teaching and consider the impact of what they do in the classroom.

Implications for Learning Language Arts

Language and culture have important implications for how students learn language arts in school:

- Students use the four language systems simultaneously as they communicate.
- Students need to understand and use academic language.
- Students from each cultural group bring their unique backgrounds of experience to the process of learning.
- Students' cultural and linguistic diversity provides an opportunity to enhance and enrich the learning of all students.
- Students use language arts to reflect on cultural, social, and political injustices and work to change the world.

Think about these implications and how they'll affect the way you teach language arts.

 ## OW STUDENTS LEARN LANGUAGE ARTS

Language arts instruction is changing to reflect the greater oral, written, and visual communication needs of the 21st century. The Steering Committee of the Elementary Section of the National Council of Teachers of English (NCTE, 1996) identified seven characteristics of competent language users, which are presented in Figure 1–3; students exemplify them as they perform these activities:

- Compare the video and book versions of the same story
- Interview community resource people who have special knowledge, interests, or talents in connection with literature focus units and thematic units
- Examine propaganda techniques used in print advertisements and television commercials
- Use the Internet to gather information as part of thematic units
- Assume the role of a character while reading a story, and write journal entries from that character's viewpoint
- Use the writing process to write stories, and share the stories with classmates
- Analyze an author's writing style during an author unit
- Create multimedia projects involving digital technology

These activities are *meaningful*, *functional*, and *genuine*; they represent the characteristics of all worthwhile language arts experiences. First, they use language in meaningful rather than contrived situations. Second, they're functional, or real-life, activities. And third, they're genuine rather than artificial activities, because they communicate ideas.

A Community of Learners

Language arts classrooms are social settings. Together, students and teachers create the classroom community, and the type of community they create strongly influences students' learning.

FIGURE 1–3   Characteristics of Competent Language Users

Personal Expression
Students use oral, written, and visual language to express themselves, to make connections between their experiences and their social world, and to create a personal voice.

Aesthetic Appreciation
Students use language aesthetically to read literature selections, view illustrations and artistic productions, talk with others, and enrich their lives.

Collaborative Exploration
Students use language as a learning tool and to work in collaboration with classmates.

Strategic Language Use
Students use strategies as they create and share meaning through oral, written, and visual language.

Creative Communication
Students use text forms, genres, and artistic style as they share ideas through oral, written, and visual language.

Reflective Interpretation
Students use language to organize and evaluate learning experiences, question personal and social values, and think critically.

Thoughtful Application
Students use oral, written, and visual language to solve problems, persuade others, and take action.

Effective teachers establish a classroom community in which students are motivated to learn and actively involved in language arts activities. Teachers and students work collaboratively and purposefully. Perhaps the most striking quality is the partnership that teachers and students create. Students are a "family" in which all the members respect one another and support each other's learning. They value culturally and linguistically diverse classmates and recognize that everyone makes important contributions to the classroom (Wells & Chang-Wells, 1992).

Students and teachers work together for the good of the community. Consider the differences between renting and owning a home. In a community of learners, students and teachers are joint owners of the classroom. Students assume responsibility for their own learning and behavior, work collaboratively with classmates, complete assignments, and care for their classroom home. In contrast, in traditional classrooms, the classroom belongs to the teacher, and students are renters. This doesn't mean that in a community of learners, teachers abdicate their responsibility. On the contrary, teachers retain their roles as organizer, facilitator, participant, instructor, model, manager, diagnostician, evaluator, coordinator, and communicator. These roles are often shared with students, but the ultimate responsibility remains with the teacher.

Researchers have identified the characteristics of effective classroom communities. These characteristics, which are described in Figure 1–4, show how the learning theories presented earlier in this chapter are translated into practice.

The process of establishing a community of learners begins when teachers make deliberate decisions about the kind of classroom culture they want to create (Whatley & Canalis, 2002). School is "real" life for students, and they learn best when they see a purpose for learning. The social contexts that teachers create are key. Teachers must think about their roles and what they believe about how students learn. They must decide to have a democratic classroom where students' abilities in reading and writing develop through meaningful literacy activities.

Teachers are more successful when they take the first 2 weeks of the school year to establish the classroom environment. They can't assume that students will be familiar with the procedures and routines used in communities of learners or that they'll instinctively be cooperative, responsible, and

FIGURE 1–4   Effective Classroom Communities

Responsibility
Students are responsible for their learning, their behavior, and the contributions they make. They're valued and contributing members of the classroom community.

Opportunities
Students participate in language arts activities that are meaningful, functional, and genuine. They read real books and write books for authentic audiences—their classmates, parents, and other community members.

Engagement
Students are motivated to learn and to be actively involved in language arts activities because the activities are interesting, and they often choose which books to read and which projects to create.

Risk Taking
Students explore topics, make guesses, and take risks. Rather than thinking of learning as the process of getting the right answers, teachers promote students' experimentation with language.

Instruction
Teachers are expert language users, and they provide instruction though minilessons and differentiate instruction to meet students' needs.

Demonstration
Teachers demonstrate procedures, concepts, and strategies—with modeling and scaffolding—as part of minilessons.

Response
Students respond to literature through writing in reading logs, participating in discussions called *grand conversations*, and taking part in dramatic activities.

Choice
Teachers offer choices because students are more motivated to work and value their learning experiences when activities are meaningful to them. Students often choose books to read, topics for writing, and multimedia projects to create within parameters set by the teacher.

Time
Teachers need 2 to 3 hours of uninterrupted time each day for language arts instruction, and it's important to minimize disruptions during this time, especially in the primary grades.

Assessment
Students take an active role in assessment. Teachers and students work together to establish guidelines for assessment, and students monitor their progress and self-evaluate their achievement.

Based on Cambourne & Turbill, 1987.

respectful of classmates. Teachers explicitly explain classroom routines, such as how to get supplies out and put them away and how to work with classmates in a collaborative group, and they set the expectation that students will adhere to the routines. Next, they demonstrate literacy procedures, including how to choose a book from the classroom library and how to provide feedback in a revising group. Third, teachers model ways of responding to literature, respecting classmates, and collaborating with classmates on multimedia projects.

Teachers are the classroom managers. They set expectations and clearly explain to students what's expected and what's valued in the classroom. The classroom rules are specific and consistent, and teachers set limits. For example, students might be allowed to talk quietly with classmates when they're working, but they aren't allowed to shout across the classroom or talk when the teacher's talking or when classmates are making presentations. Teachers also model classroom rules themselves as they interact with students. The process of socialization at the beginning of the school year is planned, deliberate, and crucial for establishing an environment that's conducive to learning.

Not everything can be accomplished quickly, however, so teachers continue to reinforce classroom routines and procedures. One way is to have student leaders model the desired routines and behaviors and encourage classmates to follow the lead. The classroom schedule is consistent because students feel comfortable, safe, and more willing to take risks in a predictable environment. This is especially true for students from varied cultures, English learners, and struggling students.

Self-Efficacy

Students who are engaged, or interested, in learning activities are intrinsically motivated, and they're more likely to succeed (Guthrie & Wigfield, 2000). They have *self-efficacy*, the belief in their capability to succeed and reach their goals (Bandura, 1997). They have high aspirations, and each achievement increases their self-efficacy. Students with high self-efficacy are resilient and persistent, despite obstacles and challenges that get in the way of success. Teachers play a crucial role in engaging students by planning instructional activities that are interesting, incorporating authentic materials, and often involving students in small collaborative groups. Pressley, Dolezal, Raphael, Mohan, Roehrig, and Bogner (2003) studied nine second grade teachers, examined the most engaging teachers' instructional practices, and identified these teacher behaviors that engage students:

- Establishing a community of learners
- Creating a positive classroom environment with books, charts, and posters used as teaching tools, colorful bulletin board displays, and a display of student work
- Setting clear expectations for learning and behavior so students know what's expected of them
- Encouraging cooperation rather than competition
- Providing positive feedback and giving compliments for good behavior and learning
- Encouraging students to take risks and be persistent
- Planning instruction thoroughly with little "downtime" between activities
- Using authentic, hands-on activities
- Scaffolding or supporting students' learning
- Teaching strategies through a combination of instruction and modeling
- Monitoring students' learning and behavior
- Stimulating creativity, curiosity, and critical thinking
- Emphasizing depth over breadth as they teach
- Making home–school connections
- Modeling interest and enthusiasm for learning

- Emphasizing the value of education
- Enjoying being with students and communicating that they care for them

Edmunds and Bauserman (2006) found similar results when they interviewed students in prekindergarten through fifth grade.

Often students' engagement diminishes as they reach the upper grades. Penny Oldfather (1995) conducted a 4-year study to examine the factors influencing students' engagement and found that when students had opportunities for authentic self-expression as part of activities, they were more highly motivated. The students she interviewed reported that they liked having ownership of the learning activities. Specific activities that they mentioned included choosing their own topics for writing and books for reading, expressing their own ideas and opinions and talking about books they're reading, sharing their writing with classmates, and pursuing authentic activities—not worksheets—using the language arts.

Students with low self-efficacy often adopt defensive tactics for avoiding failure rather than strategies for success (Paris, Wasik, & Turner, 1991). They give up or remain passive, uninvolved in activities. Some students feign interest or pretend to be involved even though they aren't or focus on other curricular areas—math or physical education, for instance. Others complain about feeling ill or that classmates are bothering them. They place the blame on anything other than themselves. The solution? The immediate solution is to engage students in authentic activities that interest them and provide enough support so they can be successful. At the same time, teachers should examine the climate in their classrooms and incorporate the suggestions for engaging learners described in this section.

The Six Language Arts

Traditionally, the language arts were defined as the study of the four modes of language—listening, talking, reading, and writing—but more than a decade ago, the National Council of Teachers of English and the International Reading Association (*Standards,* 1996) proposed two additional language arts—viewing and visually representing. These new language modes reflect the growing importance of visual language.

Listening. Beginning at birth, a child's contact with language is through listening. Too often listening instruction is neglected at school because teachers assume that students already know how to listen, and they believe that instructional time should be devoted to reading and writing. This text presents a contemporary view of listening instruction and focuses on these key concepts:

- Listening is a process of which hearing is only one part.
- Students listen differently according to their purpose.
- Students use listening strategies and monitor their understanding in order to listen more effectively.

Talking. As with listening, teachers often ignore talking because students already know how to talk, but research has emphasized the importance of talk in the learning process (Dwyer, 1991). For example, students use talk to respond to literature, provide feedback about classmates' writing in revising groups, and present oral reports as part of thematic units. You'll learn more about these concepts as you continue reading:

- Talk is an essential part of learning.
- Students participate in grand conversations as they respond to literature.
- Students create oral projects, including reports and PowerPoint presentations.

Reading. Reading is a process, and students use strategies to decode words and comprehend texts. Students vary how they read according to their purpose: They read for pleasure differently than they do to locate and remember information (Rosenblatt, 2005). I focus on these key concepts about reading in this text:

- Reading is a strategic process.
- The goal is comprehension, or meaning making.
- Students vary how they read according to their purpose.
- Students participate in different types of reading, including independent reading, shared reading, and guided reading.

Writing. Like reading, writing is a strategic process (Dean, 2006). Students use the writing process to write stories, reports, poems, and other genres (D. Graves, 1994). They also do informal writing, such as writing in reading logs and making graphic organizers. You'll learn about these concepts as you continue reading:

- Students use the writing process to develop and refine their writing.
- Students apply the writer's craft to make their compositions more effective.
- Students write compositions representing a variety of genres.
- Students use informal writing to develop writing fluency and as a learning tool.

Viewing. Visual media include film and DVDs, print advertisements and commercials, photographs and book illustrations, and the Internet. These media have become commonplace in 21st-century life, so students need to learn how to comprehend visual language and to integrate visual knowledge with other learning (T. Williams, 2007). You'll read more about these visual-language concepts in this text:

- Viewing has become an essential part of literacy in the 21st century.
- Students view visual media for a variety of purposes.
- Students use similar strategies in reading and viewing.
- Students learn about propaganda techniques to critically analyze commercials and advertisements.

Visually Representing. Students create meaning using multiple sign systems such as video presentations, digital photos, dramatizations, posters, and illustrations in books they're writing (Burmark, 2002; Moline, 1995). Projects involving visual texts are often completed as part of literature focus units and thematic units. I develop these concepts about visually representing:

- Students consider audience, purpose, and form as they create visual texts.
- Students create visual texts to share information learned during literature focus units and thematic units.
- Students use drama as a learning tool and a powerful way of communicating.
- Students combine real and virtual worlds to make successful presentations.

The six language arts can be characterized in several ways: Listening and talking are *oral*, reading and writing are *written*, and viewing and visually representing are *visual*. Also, three of the language modes—listening, reading, and viewing—are *receptive* because students receive or take in language. The other three modes—talking, writing, and visually representing—are *productive* because students compose or create language.

Relationships Among the Language Arts. Discussing the language arts one by one suggests a division among them, as though they could be used separately. In reality, they're used simultaneously and reciprocally, just as Mrs. McNeal's students in the vignette at the beginning of the chapter used all six language arts during writing workshop. In fact, almost any language arts activity involves more than one mode. In a seminal study, researcher Walter Loban (1976) documented the language growth and development of a group of 338 students from kindergarten through 12th grade. Two purposes of his longitudinal study were to examine differences between students who used language effectively and those who didn't, and to identify predictable stages of language development. Three of Loban's conclusions are especially noteworthy. First, he reported positive correlations among listening, talking, reading, and writing. Second, he found that students with less effective oral language abilities tended to have less effective written language abilities. And third, he found a strong relationship between students' oral language ability and their overall academic ability. Loban's study demonstrates clear relationships among the language arts and emphasizes the need to teach oral, written, and visual language.

Language Arts Strategies

Students learn strategies through language arts instruction. Strategies are problem-solving methods or behaviors, and students develop and use both general learning strategies and specific strategies related to language arts. Although there isn't a definitive list of language arts strategies, researchers have identified some strategies that capable students use (Fletcher & Portalupi, 2007). These 25 strategies are highlighted in this text:

ACTIVATE BACKGROUND KNOWLEDGE. Students think about their knowledge and prior experiences related to a topic and vocabulary related to it.

CONNECT. Students make connections between texts and their personal experiences, world events, literature, and media.

CONSIDER THE AUDIENCE. Students adapt their oral, written, and visual presentations to meet the needs of their audience.

DETECT BIAS. Students are alert to propaganda and other types of bias in oral, written, and visual language.

DETERMINE IMPORTANCE. Students use their knowledge of genres and text features or nonverbal cues to identify the big ideas, and they emphasize these important ideas in oral, written, and visual projects.

DRAW INFERENCES. Students use clues in the text and their background knowledge to deepen their understanding about oral, written, and visual texts.

ELABORATE. Students add details and examples to develop ideas more completely in projects they're creating.

EVALUATE. Students assess how well they're meeting the goals they set.

FORMAT. Students arrange the presentation of ideas to enhance their effectiveness.

GENERATE. Students brainstorm topics, ideas, or vocabulary for a project.

INTEGRATE MULTIMEDIA. Students combine oral, written, and visual language in projects.

MONITOR. Students ask themselves questions and evaluate their work to monitor their progress.

NARROW. Students limit the breadth of topics they're developing in oral, written, and visual projects.

NOTICE/APPLY NONVERBAL CUES. Students understand a speaker's use of gestures, facial expressions, and tone of voice to highlight big ideas and recognize artistic elements in visual presentations. They also highlight big ideas using gestures, expressions, and tone of voice when they're giving oral presentations and incorporate artistic elements in visual projects.

OBSERVE. Students examine visual presentations, identifying artistic elements to deepen their understanding.

ORGANIZE. Students create a structure for the ideas they're developing in oral, written, and visual projects.

PLAY WITH LANGUAGE. Students use language playfully by creating rhymes and riddles, inventing words, crafting metaphors, and adding alliteration or onomatopoeia.

PREDICT. Students make predictions while they're listening, reading, and viewing, based on the text, knowledge of genre characteristics, and prior experiences with literature.

PROOFREAD. Students use a special reading procedure to identify mechanical errors in their writing.

RECOGNIZE/INCORPORATE GENRE CHARACTERISTICS. Students notice characteristics to determine the genre of a text, and they apply their knowledge about a genre when they make projects.

REPAIR. Students use a variety of techniques to fix problems they encounter while using the language arts.

REVISE. Students make changes to clarify and extend meaning in their written and visual presentations.

SET GOALS. Students identify why they're involved in an activity and what they hope to accomplish.

TAKE NOTES. Students write big ideas and draw diagrams to highlight relationships among ideas to learn the information more easily.

VISUALIZE. Students form pictures in their minds to make texts more vivid and easier to understand.

These strategies are listed according to language mode in Figure 1–5. You'll notice that some strategies, such as activating background knowledge, evaluating, and monitoring, are applied in all six language arts, but others are more specialized. Also, compare the receptive and productive modes, and you'll see that students use many of the same strategies for listening, reading, and viewing and others for talking, writing, and visually representing.

Skills, in contrast, are techniques that students use automatically and unconsciously as they construct meaning. Many skills focus at the word level, but some require students to attend to larger chunks of text. For example, readers use skills such as decoding unfamiliar words, noting details, and sequencing events, and writers employ skills such as forming contractions, using punctuation marks, and capitalizing people's names. Researchers agree that skills and strategies aren't the same thing; however, controversy continues about what the terms mean. The interpretation used in this text is that the important difference between skills and strategies is how they're used: Skills are used unconsciously, and strategies are applied deliberately (Paris et al., 1991).

Teachers use minilessons to teach students about strategies. In these brief, 15- to 30-minute lessons, they explicitly explain a strategy, model its use, share examples, and provide opportunities for practice. Teachers also take advantage of teachable moments to reexplain a strategy to a student or clarify a misconception. Both types of instruction are necessary to ensure that all students are successful.

Teachers plan strategy instruction that grows out of language arts activities using a whole-part-whole sequence: The language arts activity is the first *whole*, the minilesson is the *part*, and having students apply what they're learning in new activities is the second *whole*. This instructional

FIGURE 1–5   Language Arts Strategies According to Mode

Mode	Strategies	
Listening	Activate background knowledge Connect Detect bias Determine importance Draw inferences Evaluate Monitor Notice nonverbal cues	Play with language Predict Recognize genre Repair Set goals Take notes Visualize
Talking	Activate background knowledge Consider the audience Elaborate Evaluate Generate Highlight big ideas Incorporate genre characteristics	Integrate multimedia Monitor Narrow Organize Set goals Use nonverbal cues
Reading	Activate background knowledge Connect Detect bias Determine importance Draw inferences Evaluate Monitor	Play with language Predict Recognize genre Repair Set goals Take notes Visualize
Writing	Activate background knowledge Consider the audience Elaborate Evaluate Format Generate Highlight big ideas Incorporate genre characteristics	Integrate multimedia Monitor Narrow Organize Proofread Revise Set goals
Viewing	Activate background knowledge Connect Detect bias Determine importance Draw inferences Evaluate Monitor Notice nonverbal cues	Observe Predict Recognize genre Repair Set goals Take notes Visualize
Visually Representing	Activate background knowledge Consider the audience Elaborate Evaluate Format Generate Highlight big ideas Incorporate genre characteristics	Integrate multimedia Monitor Narrow Organize Proofread Revise Set goals Visualize

sequence ensures that instruction is meaningful and that students learn to use the strategies independently (Mazzoni & Gambrell, 2003).

The goal is for students to be able to use strategies independently. Dorn and Soffos (2001) identified four behaviors that teachers use to develop self-regulated learners:

MODELING. Teachers demonstrate how to use strategies and skills.

COACHING. Teachers direct students' attention and encourage their active engagement in activities.

SCAFFOLDING. Teachers adjust the support they provide according to students' needs.

FADING. Teachers relinquish control as students become more capable of using a strategy or performing an activity.

It's not enough to simply explain the strategies or remind students to use them. Teachers must actively engage students, encourage and scaffold them while they're learning, and then gradually withdraw their support, if they want their students to be able to use the language arts strategies independently.

INTEGRATING TECHNOLOGY

The Internet is rapidly changing what it means to be literate. Students are increasingly becoming involved in online activities such as these:

- Reading electronic storybooks
- Crafting multimodal stories
- Writing blogs about books
- Creating video podcasts
- Emailing messages
- Researching nonfiction topics
- Exploring the websites of favorite authors
- Collaborating with students in other schools on projects

These students are excited about literacy because the World Wide Web fosters their engagement with language arts.

Some students learn to surf the web, locate and read information, and communicate using email and instant messaging outside of school; others, however, haven't had as many experiences with new technologies. Teaching students how to use the Internet has become a priority so they can become fully involved in today's digital world (Henry, 2006).

Internet texts are different than books (Castek, Bevans-Mangelson, & Goldstone, 2006). Print materials are linear and sequential, but online texts are a unique genre with these characteristics:

NONLINEARITY. Hypertext lacks the familiar linear organization of books; instead, it's dynamic and can be used in a variety of ways. Readers impose a structure that fits their needs and configure the organization when necessary.

MULTIPLE MODALITIES. Online texts are multimodal; they integrate words, images, and sound to create meaning. Students need to know how to interpret each type of text and appreciate how it contributes to the overall meaning.

INTERTEXTUALITY. Many related texts are available on the Internet, and they influence and shape each other. As students read these texts, they prioritize, evaluate, and synthesize the information being presented.

INTERACTIVITY. Webpages often include interactive features that engage readers and allow them to customize their searches, link to other websites, play games, listen to video clips, and send emails.

Because of these features, the Internet requires students to become proficient in new ways of accessing, understanding, and communicating information, which are referred to as *new literacies.*

Four Internet strategies are navigating, coauthoring, evaluating, and synthesizing. Students navigate the Internet to search for and locate information; coauthor online texts as they impose an organization on the information they're reading; evaluate the accuracy, relevance, and quality of information on webpages; and synthesize information from multiple texts (Leu, Kinzer, Coiro, & Cammack, 2004). Because the Internet presents new ways of using the language arts, it's essential that teachers prepare students to use the Internet and other information communication technologies successfully (Karchmer, Mallette, Kara-Soteriou, & Leu, 2005). ■

Communicative Competence

The goal of language arts instruction is for students to develop *communicative competence,* the ability to use language appropriately in both social and academic contexts (Hymes, 1972). Communicative competence is context specific: This means that students may participate effectively in classroom conversations but not know how to give a more formal oral presentation. Similarly, students may know how to read nonfiction books but not how to write a report to share information. At each grade level, teachers expand students' abilities to use the six language arts in new contexts. Through language arts instruction, students acquire the characteristics of competent language users. They become more strategic and more creative in their use of language, better able to use language as a tool for learning, and more reflective in their interpretations.

ENGAGING ENGLISH LEARNERS

When teachers work with English learners, they scaffold students' language development at the same time they're teaching language arts. Teachers adapt instruction and engage students in language arts activities in these ways:

- Create a stress-free environment in the classroom
- Show genuine interest in students, their language, and their culture
- Build students' background knowledge using artifacts, videos, photos, maps, and picture books
- Use oral language that is neither too hard nor too easy for students
- Embed language in context-rich activities
- Highlight important words on word walls and encourage students to use these words orally and in writing
- Have students dramatize vocabulary words they're learning, stories they've read, and other topics to enhance their learning
- Demonstrate how to do projects, and show samples so students understand what they're expected to do
- Read aloud to students every day
- Avoid forcing students to speak
- Expand the two- and three-word sentences that students produce

{
- Have students work together with partners and in collaborative groups
- Have students share ideas with a partner as a rehearsal before sharing with the whole class
- Provide many opportunities for students to use English in low-risk situations

Teachers don't lower their expectations for any group of students; instead, they create a nurturing classroom environment, differentiate their instruction, and engage English learners in meaningful, functional, and genuine oral, written, and visual language activities. ■

SUMMING UP

The goal of language arts instruction is to develop students' communicative competence in all six language arts—listening, talking, reading, writing, viewing, and visually representing—and the best way to achieve communicative competence is through instruction that's based on theories about how children learn combined with meaningful, functional, and genuine activities. Language and culture also influence achievement, especially when students aren't fluent English speakers or don't live in middle class communities. The language used at school is academic language; it's cognitively demanding and decontextualized.

MyEducationLab™

Go to the topic Reading in the MyEducationLab (http://www.myeducationlab.com) for *Language Arts: Patterns of Practice*, where you can:

- Find learning outcomes for Reading, along with the national standards that connect to these outcomes.
- Complete Assignments and Activities that can help you more deeply understand the chapter content.
- Apply and practice your understanding of the core teaching skills identified in the chapter with the Building Teaching Skills and Dispositions learning units.
- Examine challenging situations and cases presented in the IRIS Center Resources.
- Check your comprehension of the content covered in the chapter with the Study Plan. Here you will be able to take a chapter quiz, receive feedback on your answers, and then access Review, Practice, and Enrichment activities to enhance your understanding of chapter content.

On the **MyEducationLab** for this course, you'll also be able to:

- **A+RISE** Go to the topic A+RISE, an innovative and interactive database of strategies that differentiate instruction across the language arts and provide particular insight into research-based methods to meet the needs of English learners.
- Explore the topic Literacy Portraits—yearlong case studies of second graders, complete with student artifacts, teacher commentary, and student and teacher interviews, tracking the month-by-month language arts growth of five students.
- Gain practice with the Grammar Tutorial, online guided instruction to improve your own ability with grammar.

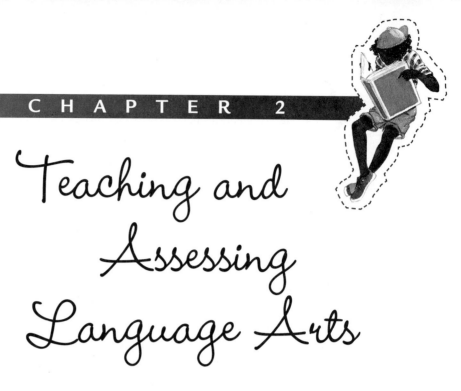

Teaching and Assessing Language Arts

A SIXTH GRADE LANGUAGE ARTS CLASS Mrs. Miller-McColm picks up Natalie Babbitt's *Tuck Everlasting* (2007), the highly acclaimed story of a family who drinks from a magical spring and becomes immortal. "Yesterday, we stopped halfway through Chapter 6," she says to her sixth graders. "Who remembers what was happening?" A sea of hands go up, and Mrs. Miller-McColm calls on Junior. "Winnie wanted to run away from home, but she got kidnapped by the Tucks. I don't know why, though," he says. Next, Isabel says, "I think she goes with the Tucks because she wants to. She wants an adventure so she'll stay with them forever."

The students briefly talk about the story, and then Mrs. Miller-McColm begins reading aloud. After she reads page 34, she asks, "Why does Mae Tuck say, 'We're not bad people, truly we're not. We had to bring you away—you'll see why in a minute—and we'll take you back just as soon as we can. Tomorrow. I promise'?" The students break into small groups to talk about whether the Tucks are "bad" people for kidnapping Winnie and to speculate about why they abducted her. After several minutes, Mrs. Miller-McColm brings the class together to continue the discussion. "We don't think the Tucks are bad people," Noemi offers, "because bad people aren't nice, and Mae Tuck is. They must have a good reason for what they did." Donavon says, "They may be nice people but we don't think Winnie will get free 'tomorrow.'" Iliana agrees, "Winnie won't get free until the book ends, and there are a lot of pages to read." After the students share their ideas, the teacher reads to the end of the chapter and continues reading the next one, where the Tucks explain to Winnie about their "changelessness" and why they abducted her. She finishes reading the last page of Chapter 7, puts the book down, and looks at the students. They look back, dazed; no one says a word.

How do teachers organize for instruction?

Teachers organize for instruction using four patterns of practice—literature focus units, literature circles, reading and writing workshop, and thematic units. Teachers vary the patterns they choose and sometimes add other programs, including basal readers. No matter which patterns teachers use, they combine direct instruction, small-group activities, and independent activities into their plans. As you read this vignette, notice how Mrs. Miller-McColm incorporates all four patterns of practice in her language arts program.

To help the sixth graders sort out their ideas, Mrs. Miller-McColm asks them to quickwrite in their reading logs. The students write for about 5 minutes, and then they're ready to talk. Some read their journal entries aloud, but others share their ideas. Mrs. Miller-McColm asks, "Do you believe the Tucks?" About half of the students think that the Tucks are truthful; others aren't so sure. Next, she asks them to write in their reading logs again, this time about whether they believe the Tucks' story.

Mrs. Miller-McColm uses the novels she reads aloud to teach about story structure. Her focus for this book is plot. She's talked about how authors develop stories, and the students understand that authors introduce the problem in the beginning, the problem gets worse in the middle, and it's resolved in the end. Yesterday, they learned the problem in this story—the Tucks abduct Winnie Foster. The teacher has also taught them about conflict situations, and at this point in the story, they think the conflict is between characters—between Winnie and the Tucks. Later, they'll see that the conflict is within Winnie as she decides whether to live with the Tucks forever.

Mrs. Miller-McColm spends the first hour of language arts teaching a literature focus unit using a book from her district's list of "core" literature selections. She reads the book aloud because nearly half of her sixth graders couldn't read it on their own. She's already read *Holes* (Sachar, 2008) and *A Wrinkle in Time* (L'Engle, 2007); by the end of the school year, she will have read 11 or 12 novels.

Mrs. Miller-McColm's daily schedule is shown in the box on page 28. Her students participate in a variety of activities using the four patterns of practice during the morning and connect language arts to social studies and science through thematic units in the afternoon.

Next, Mrs. Miller-McColm's students participate in book clubs, another name for literature circles. They read at fourth through eighth grade levels, and she divides them into seven book clubs according to reading level. The students choose novels to read after their teacher introduces several choices for each group. Currently, they're reading these books:

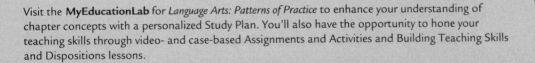

Mrs. Miller-McColm's Daily Schedule

8:30–8:45 Opening

8:45–9:45 Literature Focus Unit
Mrs. Miller-McColm reads aloud a featured book, involves students in response activities, and teaches story structure, vocabulary, and strategies and skills.

9:45–10:30 Book Clubs
Students divide into groups according to reading level and participate in literature circles. They choose books, read them independently, and meet together with Mrs. Miller-McColm to discuss them. They apply what they're learning about story structure during the literature focus unit to the books they're reading now and create graphic displays that they post on a special bulletin board.

10:30–10:45 Recess

10:45–11:15 Word Work
Mrs. Miller-McColm teaches minilessons on word-identification and spelling strategies and skills, including idioms, synonyms, syllabication, root words, and affixes. Students also study spelling words and take weekly spelling tests.

11:15–12:15 Writing Workshop
Students use the writing process to write stories and other genres. They meet in revising groups and editing conferences. They share their published writing from the author's chair.
Mrs. Miller-McColm also teaches minilessons on writing procedures, concepts, strategies, and skills.

12:15–1:00 Lunch and Recess

1:00–2:00 Math

2:00–3:15 Social Studies/Science
Mrs. Miller-McColm alternates teaching monthlong social studies and science thematic units. Students apply what they're learning in language arts as they participate in content-area study and develop projects to share their learning.

3:15–3:25 Clean-up and Dismissal

Stone Fox (Gardiner, 2003) (level 4)
Sarah, Plain and Tall (MacLachlan, 2005) (level 4)
Shiloh (Naylor, 2000) (level 5)
Ralph the Mouse (Cleary, 1993) (level 5)
Maniac Magee (Spinelli, 2002) (level 6)
The BFG (Dahl, 1998) (level 6)
Harry Potter and the Goblet of Fire (Rowling, 2002) (level 8)

The students read during this period and at home; then they meet with Mrs. Miller-McColm two or three times each week to talk about their books. Groups create displays about the books they're reading on a bulletin board on one side of the classroom, and for this round of book clubs, they focus on plot development: Each group makes a sign with the title and author of the book and then creates a graphic display emphasizing the conflict situations in their novel.

Mrs. Miller-McColm meets with the group reading *Shiloh*. They've just finished reading this novel about a boy who sticks his neck out to save an abused dog, and they're eager to talk about the book and make connections to personal experiences and to other dog stories they've read. Mrs. Miller-McColm rereads the last paragraph of the story aloud and asks what Marty means when he says, "nothing is as simple as you guess . . . " Omar begins, "At first Marty thought he was all good and Judd Travers was all bad, but then Marty did something dishonest to get Shiloh. He didn't like doing bad things but he did them for a good reason so I think that's ok." The students talk about being responsible for your own actions, both good and bad. After the discussion ends, the teacher checks the group's section of the bulletin board, and reminds them to finish it by Friday. Mrs. Miller-McColm also introduces them to *Shiloh Season* (Naylor, 1996) and *Saving Shiloh* (Naylor, 2006), the other books in the Shiloh trilogy. Then she moves on to another group.

After recess, Mrs. Miller-McColm teaches a minilesson on suffixes, beginning with the word *changelessness* from *Tuck Everlasting*. She points out the two suffixes, *-less*, meaning "without," and *-ness*, meaning "state of being." They talk about the word's meaning and how the suffixes affect the root word. Then she shares a list of other words ending in *-less*, including *weightless, effortless,* and *careless*. They talk about each word's meaning and how it changes when it takes on the suffix *-ness*, such as *weightlessness*. Then students take 10 minutes to practice their spelling words.

Writing workshop is next, and Mrs. Miller-McColm begins with a minilesson on narrative leads. She displays a chart of techniques that writers use to hook their audience and explains each one:

ACTION. The main character does something interesting.

DIALOGUE. The main character says something interesting.

A THOUGHT OR A QUESTION. The main character shares something that he or she's thinking or asks a question.

A SOUND. The author begins with an interesting sound related to the story.

She reads aloud the first sentences from *The Sign of the Beaver* (Speare, 2005), *The Breadwinner* (Ellis, 2000), and other familiar novels, and the students identify the hook used in each one. For the next couple of days, they'll practice writing leads.

After the minilesson, students write independently for 40 minutes. They've been writing on self-selected topics, but Mrs. Miller-McColm has announced that they should finish their projects by Friday because next week, they'll start preparing projects for their unit on ancient Egypt during writing workshop. Today, some students are working independently, and others are meeting in small groups to revise their writing, conferencing with the teacher, or working with partners to proofread their drafts. The four computers are all occupied, too, as students word process their compositions and print out final copies. They place their final copies in a box on the teacher's desk and she binds their compositions—handwritten or word processed—into books for them.

During the last 5 minutes of the workshop, students sit in the author's chair to read their compositions aloud. Students sit on the floor and listen attentively. Ricky, who wants to be a race car driver, reads his book about the Winston Cup Series; afterward, students ask questions. Junior asks, "What does NASCAR stand for?" and Ricky explains that it's an acronym for the National Association for Stock Car Automobile Racing. Omar asks for more clarification about how the races are run, and Briana asks how winners of each race gain points. The students get so interested that they don't want to end the discussion, even though it's lunchtime!

In the afternoon, Mrs. Miller-McColm is teaching a thematic unit on ancient Egypt. Today, she talks about the projects students will prepare. She begins by asking them to brainstorm a list of the Egyptians' achievements, and their list includes the pyramids, mummification, hieroglyphics, gods and goddesses, and women's make-up. Then she explains that students will choose one achievement that interests them, research it, and share what they learn in a project. The students are excited, quickly choosing topics. Mrs. Miller-McColm distributes the rubric that students will use to self-assess their projects and that she'll use to grade them. Then she shares several projects from last year, which the students examine and compare to the rubric to better understand their assignment.

eachers use the four patterns of practice to involve students in meaningful, functional, and genuine language-learning activities: literature focus units, literature circles, reading and writing workshop, and thematic units. Teachers incorporate a combination of these approaches in their instructional programs, just as Mrs. Miller-McColm did in the vignette. It's not enough to teach language arts using a basal reader or a literature textbook.

Assessment goes hand in hand with teaching. It should be authentic—based on students' using the six language arts in genuine and worthwhile ways. Teachers begin by determining students' background knowledge before instruction, and they continue as they monitor students' progress during instruction. Teachers and students collaborate to document students' learning; there are innovative ways to involve students in assessing their own learning and determining grades.

PATTERNS OF PRACTICE

There are many ways to organize language arts instruction. This text focuses on four patterns or instructional approaches for teaching language arts: literature focus units, literature circles, reading and writing workshop, and thematic units. All four patterns embody the characteristics of learning described in Chapter 1 and provide opportunities for students to use oral, written, and visual language in meaningful, functional, and genuine ways. Teachers organize their instructional programs in different ways, but students need opportunities to participate in all four approaches during each school year. Figure 2–1 provides an overview of the four patterns of practice.

Teachers usually organize their daily schedule to include two or more of the instructional approaches, as Mrs. Miller-McColm did in the vignette. When teachers don't have that much time available, they alternate teacher-led literature focus units with student-selected literature circles or reading and writing workshop. Both teacher-led and student-selected instructional patterns provide valuable language-learning opportunities, and no one approach provides all the opportunities that students need. The logical solution is to use a combination of patterns.

Literature Focus Units

Teachers organize literature focus units around a featured selection. Books chosen for literature focus units represent the finest in children's literature; they're books that every student should read. Several books for each grade level are suggested in the Booklist on page 34. The books must be appropriate for students' interest level, but sometimes they aren't written at their reading level. When they're too difficult for students to read themselves, teachers read them aloud.

Students read the featured selection as a class, and they develop their understanding of the story with the teacher's guidance. In the vignette, for example, Mrs. Miller-McColm was teaching a literature focus unit on *Tuck Everlasting* (Babbitt, 2007). Literature focus units include these components:

READING. Students read books together as a class or in small groups. They may read independently or together with a partner, or they may read along as the teacher reads the book aloud or guides their reading.

RESPONDING. Students record their initial impressions about the selection to develop their comprehension. They write in reading logs and participate in discussions called *grand conversations*.

TEACHING MINILESSONS. Teachers teach minilessons on language arts procedures, concepts, strategies, and skills and connect their instruction to the featured selection (Atwell, 1998). The steps in teaching a minilesson are shown in the Step-by-Step feature below.

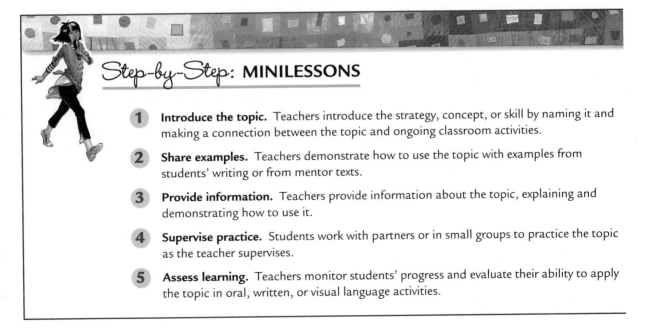

Step-by-Step: MINILESSONS

1. **Introduce the topic.** Teachers introduce the strategy, concept, or skill by naming it and making a connection between the topic and ongoing classroom activities.

2. **Share examples.** Teachers demonstrate how to use the topic with examples from students' writing or from mentor texts.

3. **Provide information.** Teachers provide information about the topic, explaining and demonstrating how to use it.

4. **Supervise practice.** Students work with partners or in small groups to practice the topic as the teacher supervises.

5. **Assess learning.** Teachers monitor students' progress and evaluate their ability to apply the topic in oral, written, or visual language activities.

FIGURE 2-1   The Patterns of Practice

Features	Literature Focus Units	Literature Circles
Description	Teachers and students read and respond to one text together as a class or in small groups. Teachers choose texts that are high-quality literature selections. After reading, students explore the text and apply their learning by creating oral, written, and visual projects.	Teachers choose five or six books and collect multiple copies of each one. Students choose the book they want to read and form groups or "book clubs" to read and respond to the book. They develop a reading and discussion schedule, and the teacher participates in some of the discussions.
Strengths	<ul><li>Teachers develop units using the stages of the reading process.</li><li>Teachers select high-quality picture books or novels for units.</li><li>Teachers scaffold reading instruction as they read with the whole class.</li><li>Teachers teach minilessons on reading strategies and skills.</li><li>Students explore vocabulary and literary language.</li><li>Students develop projects to apply their reading.</li></ul>	<ul><li>Books are available at a variety of reading levels.</li><li>Students are more strongly motivated because they choose the books they read.</li><li>Students have opportunities to work with their classmates.</li><li>Students participate in authentic literacy experiences.</li><li>Activities are student directed, and students work at their own pace.</li><li>Teachers may participate in discussions to help students clarify misunderstandings and think more deeply about the book.</li></ul>
Limitations	<ul><li>Students all read the same book whether or not they like it and whether or not it's at their reading level.</li><li>Many of the activities are teacher directed.</li></ul>	<ul><li>Teachers often feel a loss of control because students are reading different books.</li><li>Students must learn to be task oriented and to use time wisely in order to be successful.</li><li>Sometimes students choose books that are too difficult or too easy for them.</li></ul>

CREATING PROJECTS. Students create projects to apply their learning (Luongo-Orlando, 2001). Projects may involve any of the language arts, but students usually choose the projects they create based on their interests and the opportunities the selection presents to them. Oral language projects include puppet shows, PowerPoint presentations, and podcasts; written language projects include poems, wikis, and reports; and visual language projects include posters, video presentations, and collections of artifacts.

Literature Circles

Students meet in small-group literature circles to read and respond to self-selected books (Daniels, 2002; Day, Spiegel, McLellan, & Brown, 2002). What matters most is that students are reading and discussing something that interests them and is manageable in a supportive community of learners. As students participate in literature circles, they learn to view themselves as readers. They have opportunities to read high-quality books that they might not have chosen on

FIGURE 2-1   continued

Features	Reading and Writing Workshop	Thematic Units
Description	Students choose books and read and respond to them independently during reading workshop and write books on self-selected topics during writing workshop. Teachers monitor students' work through conferences. Students share the books they read and the books they write with classmates during a sharing period.	Students study social studies and science topics. They use the six language arts as they participate in activities and demonstrate learning. Although content-area textbooks may be used, they're only one resource. Students also identify topics they want to investigate, so thematic units are authentic learning opportunities.
Strengths	• Students read books appropriate for their reading levels. • Students are more strongly motivated because they choose the books they read. • Students work through the stages of the writing process during writing workshop. • Teachers teach minilessons on reading strategies and skills. • Activities are student directed, and students work at their own pace. • Teachers have opportunities to work individually with students during conferences.	• Students read text sets of stories, nonfiction, and poetry related to the unit. • Students write in learning logs. • Teachers and students make clusters and other charts to organize information. • Teachers scaffold instruction as students work independently, in small groups, and together as a class. • Students use talk to clarify meanings and give presentations. • Students use computers and technology tools to enhance learning. • Students create projects.
Limitations	• Teachers often feel a loss of control because students are reading different books and working at different stages of the writing process. • Students must learn to be task oriented and to use time wisely in order to be successful.	• Teachers must design thematic units and locate needed resources and other materials. • Thematic units are more time-consuming than textbook-driven social studies and science units.

their own, to learn responsibility for completing assignments, and to self-assess their learning and work habits. Literature circles involve these components:

READING. Teachers collect five or six copies of each of six books and give a book talk to introduce each book. Students sign up for the book they want to read and form literature circles to read the book. After working together as a group to create a reading and responding schedule, students read the first part of the book to be ready to participate in the discussion.

RESPONDING. Students meet to discuss the book and to reflect on their reading. To facilitate their responding, they often assume roles ranging from discussion director to illustrator and word wizard, and they prepare for their roles before they meet to talk about the book. A list of roles is presented in Figure 2–2.

SHARING. Students meet as a class, and each group shares its book. Sometimes students prepare a book talk to share the book; at other times, they create projects to tell about the book.

They provide enough information to create interest in the book, but they never tell the ending because they want to encourage classmates to read the book through the sharing activity.

In the vignette, Mrs. Miller-McColm's students participated in literature circles that they called book clubs. These sixth graders participated in activities representing all four components of literature circles.

Reading and Writing Workshop

Students participate in two types of workshops—reading workshop and writing workshop. Reading workshop fosters real reading of self-selected stories, poems, and nonfiction books, and writing workshop fosters real writing for genuine purposes and authentic audiences (Atwell, 2007; Cohle & Towle, 2001). Teachers often use the two workshops concurrently, but if their schedule doesn't allow them to do so, they may alternate them. Schedules for reading and writing workshop at the second, fifth, and eighth grade levels are presented in Figure 2–3.

Booklist

BOOKS FOR LITERATURE FOCUS UNITS	
PreK–Grade 2	Brett, J. (2009). *The mitten*. New York: Putnam. Bunting, E. (1999). *Smoky night*. San Diego: Harcourt Brace. Choi, Y. (2001). *The name jar*. New York: Knopf. Dorros, A. (1991). *Abuela*. New York: Dutton. Henkes, K. (1991). *Chrysanthemum*. New York: Greenwillow. Look, L. (2004). *Ruby Lu, brave and true*. New York: Atheneum. Meddaugh, S. (1995). *Hog-eye*. Boston: Houghton Mifflin. Rathmann, P. (1995). *Officer Buckle and Gloria*. New York: Putnam. Simont, M. (2001). *The stray dog*. New York: HarperCollins.
Grades 3–5	Cohen, B. (1999). *Molly's pilgrim*. New York: Scholastic. Curtis, C. P. (2000). *The Watsons go to Birmingham—1963*. New York: Delacorte. DiCamillo, K. (2003). *The tale of Despereaux*. New York: Candlewick Press. Gardiner, J. R. (2003). *Stone Fox*. New York: Harper Trophy. Lowry, L. (2011). *Number the stars*. New York: Sandpiper. MacLachlan, P. (2005). *Sarah, plain and tall*. New York: HarperCollins. Naylor, P. R. (2000). *Shiloh*. New York: Aladdin Books. Ryan, P. M. (2000). *Esperanza rising*. New York: Scholastic. White, E. B. (2006). *Charlotte's web*. New York: HarperCollins.
Grades 6–8	Avi. (2003). *Nothing but the truth: A documentary novel*. New York: Orchard Books. Babbitt, N. (2007). *Tuck everlasting*. New York: Square Fish Books. Cushman, K. (2005). *Catherine called Birdy*. New York: HarperCollins. Hale, S. (2007). *Princess academy*. New York: Bloomsbury. Hesse, K. (2005). *Witness*. New York: Scholastic. Lowry, L. (2006). *The giver*. New York: Delacorte. Paulsen, G. (2007). *Hatchet*. New York: Simon & Schuster. Sachar, L. (2008). *Holes*. New York: Farrar, Straus & Giroux. Whelan, G. (2000). *Homeless bird*. New York: Scholastic.

FIGURE 2-2   Literature Circle Roles

Discussion Director

The discussion director guides the group's discussion and keeps the group on task. To get the discussion started or to redirect the discussion, the discussion director may ask:

- What did the reading make you think of?
- What questions do you have about the reading?
- What do you predict will happen next?

Passage Master

The passage master focuses on the literary merits of the book. This student chooses several memorable passages to share with the group and tells why he or she chose each one.

Word Wizard

The word wizard is responsible for vocabulary. This student identifies four to six important, unfamiliar words from the reading and looks them up in the dictionary. The word wizard selects the most appropriate meaning and other interesting information about the word to share.

Connector

The connector makes meaningful personal, world, or literary connections. These connections might include events at school or in the community, current events or historical events, or something from the connector's own life. Or the connector can make comparisons with other books.

Summarizer

The summarizer prepares a brief summary of the reading to convey the main ideas to share with the group. This student often begins the discussion by reading the summary aloud to the group.

Illustrator

The illustrator draws a picture or diagram related to the reading; it might involve a character, an event, or a prediction. The student shares the illustration with the group, and the group talks about it before the illustrator explains it.

Investigator

The investigator locates some information about the book, the author, or a related topic to share with the group. This student may search the Internet, check an encyclopedia, or interview a person with special expertise.

Reading Workshop. Students read self-selected books independently during reading workshop and respond to books by writing in reading logs (Atwell, 1998). They focus on comprehension and practice applying the reading strategies they've learned. One way teachers differentiate instruction is by having students select books that interest them and that are written at an appropriate level of difficulty. They also individualize instruction as they conference with students about books they're reading and their use of reading strategies. There are three components of reading workshop:

READING AND RESPONDING. Students spend 30 to 60 minutes independently reading books and other reading materials. They also keep reading logs for writing responses to their reading and participate in conferences with the teacher to enrich their understanding of favorite books.

SHARING. For the last 15 minutes of reading workshop, the class gathers together to share books they've read and enjoyed.

TEACHING MINILESSONS. The teacher spends approximately 15 minutes teaching minilessons on reading workshop procedures, literary concepts, and reading strategies and skills.

There are many benefits to reading workshop: Students become more fluent readers and deepen their appreciation of books and reading, they develop lifelong reading habits, they're introduced to different genres, and they choose favorite authors. Most importantly, students come to think of themselves as readers (Daniels, 2002).

Writing Workshop. Writing workshop is a way of implementing the writing process (Atwell, 1998; Fletcher & Portalupi, 2001). Students usually write on topics they choose themselves, and they assume ownership of their learning. The classroom becomes a community of writers who write and share their writing, and students come to see themselves as writers (Samway, 2006). They practice writing skills and strategies and learn to choose words carefully to articulate their ideas. Perhaps most important, they see firsthand the power of writing to entertain, inform, and persuade.

Students' writing grows out of their personal experiences, books they've read or listened to read aloud, and content-area study (Gillet & Beverly, 2001; Heffernan, 2004). They write

---

FIGURE 2–3	Schedules for Reading and Writing Workshop

Second Grade Schedule	
15 minutes	Reading aloud to students
15 minutes	Teaching a minilesson (on a reading or writing topic)
30 minutes	Reading and responding
15 minutes	Sharing
	—Later—
30 minutes	Writing
15 minutes	Sharing

This 2-hour schedule is broken into two parts. The first 75 minutes, scheduled in the morning, focuses on reading, and the last 45 minutes, scheduled after lunch, is devoted to writing.

Fifth Grade Schedule	
40 minutes	Reading and responding
20 minutes	Teaching a minilesson (on a reading or writing topic)
40 minutes	Writing
20 minutes	Sharing

This schedule is also planned for 2 hours. The minilesson separates the two independent work sessions, and during the sharing session, students share books they've read, response projects they've created, and compositions they've published.

Eighth Grade Schedule	
40 minutes	Reading and responding or writing
15 minutes	Teaching a minilesson (on Mondays–Thursdays)
	Sharing (on Fridays)

The eighth grade schedule is for 55 minutes. Because of time limitations, students alternate reading and writing workshop, minilessons are scheduled for 4 days each week, and sharing is held on Fridays.

personal narratives about experiences and events in their lives, create sequels to favorite books, and retell stories from different viewpoints. Young children often use the pattern or refrain from a familiar book, such as *Brown Bear, Brown Bear, What Do You See?* (Martin, 2010) and *The Important Book* (Brown, 1990), to structure their writing. Students experiment with other genres, such as poetry and scripts, after reading examples of the genre and learning about them. They also use writing workshop to write letters, book reviews, reports, and other projects as part of thematic units. In the vignette at the beginning of the chapter, Mrs. Miller-McColm's sixth graders were writing reports and developing other projects about ancient Egypt during writing workshop.

Writing workshop is a 60- to 90-minute period scheduled each day. During this time, students are involved in these activities:

WRITING. Students spend 30 to 45 minutes working independently on writing projects. They move at their own pace through all five stages of the writing process—prewriting, drafting, revising, editing, and publishing. Many times, students compile their final copies to make books during writing workshop, but sometimes they attach their writing to artwork, make posters, write letters that are mailed, or perform scripts as skits or puppet shows.

SHARING. Students gather together to share their new publications and to make related announcements. For example, a student who has just finished writing a puppet-show script and making puppets may ask for volunteers to help perform the puppet show, which could be presented several days later during sharing time. Younger children often sit in a circle or gather together on a rug for sharing time. The student who is sharing sits in a special chair, labeled the "author's chair," to read his or her composition. After the reading, classmates clap and offer compliments. They may also make other comments and suggestions, but the focus is on celebrating completed writing projects, not on revising the composition to make it better.

TEACHING MINILESSONS. During this 15- to 30-minute period, teachers present minilessons on writing workshop procedures, literary concepts, and writing skills and strategies (Fletcher & Portalupi, 2007; Portalupi & Fletcher, 2001). They also talk about authors of children's trade books and the writing strategies and skills these authors use.

Teachers often add a fourth component in which they read stories aloud to share examples of good writing with students. This activity helps students to feel a part of the community of writers.

Thematic Units

Thematic units integrate language arts with social studies, science, and other curricular areas (Lindquist & Selwyn, 2000). Students use all the language arts as they investigate, solve problems, and learn during a unit (Rief, 1999). They also use language arts to demonstrate their new learning at the end of the unit. These language arts activities are integrated with content-area study during thematic units:

READING. Students read nonfiction books and magazines, stories, and poems related to the unit as well as content-area textbooks. They also research topics on the Internet.

KEEPING LEARNING LOGS. Students keep learning logs in which they write entries about new concepts they're learning, record new and interesting words, make charts and diagrams, and reflect on their learning.

MAKING GRAPHIC REPRESENTATIONS. Students create clusters, maps, time lines, Venn diagrams, data charts, and other diagrams and displays. They use these visual representations as tools to organize information and represent relationships about the topic they're studying (Moline, 1995).

CREATING PROJECTS. Students create projects to apply their learning and demonstrate their new knowledge. These projects range from alphabet books and oral reports to posters and dramatizations.

In the vignette, Mrs. Miller-McColm's students were involved in a thematic unit on ancient Egypt, and they used all six of the language arts during the unit.

THE TEACHER'S ROLE

Teachers direct the life of the classroom: They are instructors, coaches, facilitators, and managers. Figure 2–4 lists some of the roles teachers assume. They use the four patterns of practice and adapt activities to meet the needs of their students; their goal is to develop students' communicative competence so students can meet grade-level standards.

Scaffolding Learners

Teachers scaffold students' language arts development as they demonstrate, guide, and teach, and they vary the amount of support according to the instructional purpose and students' needs. For example, they demonstrate how to create a digital slide show, record students' dictation when they're developing a collaborative composition, or guide students as they respond to the film version of a book they've read. Teachers use five levels, moving from more support to less as students become more proficient (Fountas & Pinnell, 1996):

Modeled Level. Teachers provide the greatest amount of support when they model how experts use language. When teachers read aloud, they're modeling: They read fluently and with expression, and they talk about their thoughts and the strategies they're using. The same is true when they draw a Venn diagram or another graphic organizer or write an ode or another poetic form. Teachers use this level of support to demonstrate procedures or introduce new strategies, and they do think-alouds to share what they're thinking. The steps in a think-aloud are listed in the Step-by-Step feature on page 40.

Shared Level. Teachers "share" language tasks with students at this level. Probably the best known example of shared support is shared reading, which teachers use to read big books with young children. Teachers do most of the reading, but children join in to read familiar and predictable words and phrases. This level differs from modeled support in that students actually participate in the activity rather than simply observing the teacher.

Interactive Level. Students participate more actively at the interactive level. Teachers organize and lead activities, and students work collaboratively with classmates. Three examples are *interactive writing*, where students and the teacher create a text and write a message together; *choral reading*, where students read poems aloud with classmates; and *readers theatre*, where they read scripts expressively. Teachers use activities at this level to provide hands-on instruction and to allow students to participate in activities they can't do independently.

Guided Level. Teachers continue to support students, but at the guided level, students do the activities themselves. In guided reading, for example, small, homogeneous groups of students

FIGURE 2–4   Teachers' Roles

Role	Description
Organizer	Creates a language-rich environment Sets time schedules Uses the four patterns of practice Uses the language arts as tools for learning across the curriculum
Facilitator	Develops a community of learners Stimulates students' interest in language and literacy Allows students to choose books to read and topics for projects Provides opportunities for students to use language in meaningful, functional, and genuine ways Involves parents in classroom and out-of-classroom literacy activities
Participant	Reads and writes with students Learns along with students Asks questions and seeks answers to questions
Instructor	Provides information about books, authors, and illustrators Explains language arts procedures Teaches minilessons on concepts, skills, and strategies Activates and builds background knowledge before reading, writing, and viewing Groups students flexibly for instruction
Model	Demonstrates procedures, strategies, and skills Reads aloud to students every day
Manager	Sets expectations and responsibilities Monitors students' progress Keeps records Arranges the classroom to facilitate learning Provides technology hardware and software to support language arts activities
Diagnostician	Conferences with students Observes students participating in language arts activities Assesses students' strengths and weaknesses Plans instruction based on students' needs
Evaluator	Assesses students' progress in language arts Helps students self-assess their learning Assigns grades Examines the effectiveness of the language arts program
Coordinator	Works with librarians, aides, and parent volunteers Works with other teachers on grade-level projects, pen pal programs, and cross-age reading programs
Communicator	Expects students to do their best Encourages students to become lifelong readers and writers Communicates the language arts program to parents and administrators Shares language arts goals and activities with parents and the community

meet with the teacher to read books at their instructional level. The teacher introduces the book and guides students as they begin reading, then students continue reading on their own while the teacher supervises. Minilessons are another example; during these lessons, teachers provide practice activities and supervise as students apply what they're learning, usually in small groups or with a classmate. Teachers use activities at this level to provide instruction and assistance as students participate in language arts activities.

Independent Level. Students work independently on authentic activities, such as reading novels, writing poems, and creating visually representing projects at this level. During independent reading, for example, students usually choose their own books and work at their own pace as they read and respond to books. Teachers continue to monitor students at the independent level, but they provide much less guidance. They furnish authentic language arts experiences at this level so students can apply the knowledge and strategies they've learned.

Figure 2–5 summarizes these levels of scaffolding for language arts activities.

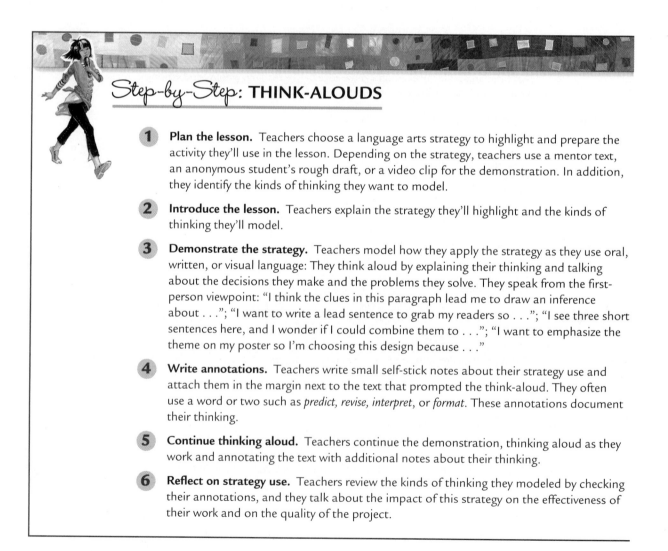

Step-by-Step: THINK-ALOUDS

1. **Plan the lesson.** Teachers choose a language arts strategy to highlight and prepare the activity they'll use in the lesson. Depending on the strategy, teachers use a mentor text, an anonymous student's rough draft, or a video clip for the demonstration. In addition, they identify the kinds of thinking they want to model.

2. **Introduce the lesson.** Teachers explain the strategy they'll highlight and the kinds of thinking they'll model.

3. **Demonstrate the strategy.** Teachers model how they apply the strategy as they use oral, written, or visual language: They think aloud by explaining their thinking and talking about the decisions they make and the problems they solve. They speak from the first-person viewpoint: "I think the clues in this paragraph lead me to draw an inference about . . ."; "I want to write a lead sentence to grab my readers so . . ."; "I see three short sentences here, and I wonder if I could combine them to . . ."; "I want to emphasize the theme on my poster so I'm choosing this design because . . ."

4. **Write annotations.** Teachers write small self-stick notes about their strategy use and attach them in the margin next to the text that prompted the think-aloud. They often use a word or two such as *predict, revise, interpret,* or *format*. These annotations document their thinking.

5. **Continue thinking aloud.** Teachers continue the demonstration, thinking aloud as they work and annotating the text with additional notes about their thinking.

6. **Reflect on strategy use.** Teachers review the kinds of thinking they modeled by checking their annotations, and they talk about the impact of this strategy on the effectiveness of their work and on the quality of the project.

FIGURE 2–5	Levels of Scaffolding	
Level	**Purpose**	**Examples**
Modeled	Teachers demonstrate how to use language in new ways and share their thinking with students during the demonstration. This level has the most scaffolding.	Book talks Reading aloud
Shared	Teachers engage students in a limited way in oral, written, or visual language activities that they lead.	Shared reading K-W-L charts
Interactive	Teachers and students share the work and responsibility in completing language activities.	Readers theatre Interactive writing
Guided	Teachers supervise as students practice new procedures and strategies and as they participate in collaborative language activities.	Guided reading Making words
Independent	Students apply what they've learned as they work independently or with partners on authentic language projects. This level has the least scaffolding.	Reading workshop Revising groups

Differentiating Instruction

Teachers know that students vary—in their interests and motivation, their background knowledge and prior experiences, and their culture and language proficiency as well as their intellectual capabilities—so it's important to adapt instruction to take these differences into account. According to Carol Ann Tomlinson (2001), differentiated instruction "means 'shaking up' what goes on in the classroom so that students have multiple options for taking in information, making sense of ideas, and expressing what they learn" (p. 1). Differentiating instruction is especially important for students who haven't been successful and for very capable students who aren't challenged by grade-level assignments.

Teachers use these techniques to differentiate instruction within the patterns of practice:

CHOICES. Teachers encourage students to make choices. For example, students select books to read in literature circles and in reading workshop, choose topics and genres for compositions during writing workshop, and decide on projects they create during literature focus units and thematic units.

SMALL GROUPS. Teachers group students flexibly for literature circles, guided reading, revising groups, and other instructional activities. Students also work in small groups to develop projects and to write reports and other compositions.

CENTERS. Teachers set up centers with instructional materials so students can practice concepts they're learning and explore topics that interest them.

THE SIX LANGUAGE ARTS. Teachers provide opportunities for students to use oral, written, and visual language because many students are better able to understand and express themselves through oral and visual language than through written language. Using all six language arts scaffolds students' learning.

PROJECTS. Teachers have students create individual, partner, or small-group projects to demonstrate their learning in authentic ways at the end of literature focus units and thematic units.

When teachers consider the needs of their students and incorporate these techniques to differentiate instruction, students are more successful.

ENGAGING ENGLISH LEARNERS

Teachers adapt instruction to meet the needs of students who are learning to speak English at the same time they're learning to read and write. They use these techniques to engage English learners and differentiate instruction:

CLASSROOM ENVIRONMENT. Creating a community of learners is especially important for ELs so that they feel valued and are comfortable taking risks and admitting when they're confused or need assistance.

GROUPING PATTERNS. Teachers vary grouping patterns so that ELs have regular opportunities to work in small groups, individually, and with the whole class. Working in small groups is especially important because when students work in small groups, they collaborate and learn English from their classmates.

MINILESSONS. Teachers teach minilessons regularly, and they preteach and reteach the lessons to ELs who need more background knowledge or additional practice.

VISUALS. Teachers integrate visuals, including realia, photographs, charts, maps, and diagrams, into the language arts program because visual language scaffolds ELs' oral and written language use.

BACKGROUND KNOWLEDGE. Teachers take time to build ELs' background knowledge, and introduce academic vocabulary words before teaching new concepts.

TALK. Teachers provide daily opportunities for ELs to chat with classmates and use talk to support their reading and writing.

CENTERS. Teachers incorporate centers in the language arts program so ELs have more opportunities to work collaboratively on activities and projects and learn from their classmates.

MONITOR STUDENTS. Teachers monitor ELs' progress closely and provide assistance when needed so they can be successful.

At the same time they're adapting the language arts program to scaffold English learners, teachers celebrate these students' special contributions. For example, ELs offer unique perspectives as they talk about their interpretations of books they're reading, and ELs create fresh images and metaphors in poems they write and the posters and other visual projects they create. English learners know that they're valued members of the classroom community when teachers acknowledge their perspectives, praise their talents and abilities, and recognize their effort. ■

Teaching Struggling Students

Struggling students have significant difficulty learning to read and write. Some students exhibit difficulties in first grade, but others develop difficulties in fourth or fifth grade or even later. Providing high-quality instruction and adding an intervention, if necessary, are the best ways to prevent difficulties in the first place (Cooper, Chard, & Kiger, 2006). But once students fall behind their classmates, there's no quick fix. Helping struggling students requires both high-quality classroom instruction and "a comprehensive and sustained intervention effort" (Allington, 2006, p. 141).

Teachers combine explicit instruction that is standards driven and that incorporates research-based procedures and activities with daily opportunities for students to apply what they're learning in authentic language activities (Allington, 2006). Teachers address these components to enhance the language development of all students:

Differentiating Instruction. Teachers adapt their instructional programs to match student needs using flexible grouping, tiered activities, and respectful tasks (Opitz & Ford, 2008). Results of ongoing assessment are used to vary instructional content, process, and assignments according to students' developmental levels, interests, and learning styles.

Choosing Appropriate Instructional Materials. Most of the time students read interesting books written at their reading levels in small groups or individually. Teachers usually have plenty of books available for on- and above-grade-level readers, but finding appropriate books for struggling readers can be difficult. Teachers choose award-winning books for literature focus units, but even though these "teaching texts" are important, Allington (2006) recommends using a single text with the whole class only 25% of the time because students need more opportunities to read books at their reading levels.

Expanding Teachers' Expertise. Teachers continue to grow professionally during their careers by joining the National Council of Teachers of English (NCTE), the International Reading Association (IRA), Teachers of English to Speakers of Other languages (TESOL), or other professional organizations. They read journals and books published by NCTE, IRA, TESOL, Heinemann, and Scholastic, among others. They participate in professional book clubs, attend workshops and conferences, and find answers to questions that puzzle them through teacher-inquiry projects. Teachers also attend local, state, and national conferences sponsored by NCTE, IRA, and TESOL to learn more about teaching language arts and participate in workshops and seminars sponsored by local sites affiliated with the National Writing Project. To locate the nearest site, check the organization's website (http://www.nwp.org).

Collaborating With Literacy Coaches. Literacy coaches are experienced teachers with special expertise in working with struggling students and their teachers (Casey, 2006). They work alongside teachers in their classrooms, demonstrating instructional procedures and evaluation techniques, and they collaborate with teachers to design instruction to address students' needs. Toll (2005) explains that "literacy coaching is not about telling others what to do, but rather bringing out the best in others" (p. 6). Through their efforts, teachers develop more expertise, and schools become better learning environments. The quality of classroom instruction has a tremendous impact on how well students learn (Block, Oakar, & Hurt, 2002).

Interventions. Schools use intervention programs to address low-achieving students' difficulties and accelerate their learning (Cooper, Chard, & Kiger, 2006). Some intervention programs are provided in addition to regular instruction, but others replace regular instruction. The classroom teacher or a specially trained teacher diagnoses students' areas of difficulty and focuses instruction on these areas; paraprofessionals shouldn't be used because they aren't as effective (Allington, 2006).

Response to Intervention (RTI) is a promising schoolwide initiative to identify struggling students quickly, promote effective classroom instruction, provide interventions, and increase students' success (Allington, 2009; Mellard & Johnson, 2008). It involves three tiers:

TIER 1: SCREENING AND PREVENTION. Teachers provide high-quality instruction, screen students to identify those at risk for failure, and monitor their progress. If students don't make adequate progress toward meeting grade-level standards, they move to Tier 2.

TIER 2: EARLY INTERVENTION. Teachers provide enhanced, individualized instruction targeting students' specific areas of difficulty. If the intervention is successful and students' problems are resolved, they return to Tier 1; if they make some progress but need additional instruction, they remain in Tier 2; and if they don't show improvement, they move to Tier 3, where the intensity of the intervention increases.

TIER 3: INTENSIVE INTERVENTION. Special education teachers provide more intensive intervention to individual students and small groups and more frequent progress monitoring. They focus on remedying students' problems and teaching compensatory strategies.

This schoolwide instruction and assessment program incorporates data-driven decision making, and special education teachers are optimistic that it's a more effective way to diagnose learning-disabled students (Bender & Shores, 2007).

Standards delineate specific grade-level expectations in language arts, but the developers recommend integrating them through genuine, functional, and meaningful activities and projects. Improving classroom instruction, diagnosing students' specific learning difficulties, and implementing intensive intervention programs to remedy students' learning problems are three important ways that teachers work more effectively with struggling students.

Language Arts Standards

In the 1990s, the states published standards documents that identify what students should know and be able to do at each grade level; these standards were developed to ensure that all students had access to a high-quality education that would prepare them for college and careers in the 21st century. The documents that are now in place across the United States articulate achievement benchmarks with K–12 end-of-year expectations in language arts, math, and other content areas. More recently, the National Governors Association spearheaded an initiative to create national standards in language arts and math that build on the individual state standards. Administrators and teachers worked to build consensus on what students should learn at each grade level to ensure that they're prepared for success in the increasingly competitive global economy. These new standards are known as the Common Core State Standards (2010).

The Common Core State Standards for Language Arts consist of these strands with integrated research and media requirements:

READING. Students will become fluent readers, read fiction and nonfiction texts, develop comprehension, and respond to literature.

WRITING. Students will apply the writing process, vary their writing according to genre, conduct research and report results, and employ technology to enhance and produce writing.

LISTENING AND SPEAKING. Students will use listening and talking as learning tools, communicate effectively using oral language, integrate media and visual displays into oral presentations, and collaborate with classmates.

LANGUAGE. Students will learn academic vocabulary, use Standard English grammar and conventions in speech and writing, use language purposefully in varied contexts, and make effective choices for meaning and style.

The Common Core State Standards box on the next page summarizes the four strands. These standards mesh with the content of this text, and in upcoming chapters, look for Common Core State Standards boxes that highlight oral, written, and visual language standards related to that chapter's content.

More than 80% of the states plus the District of Columbia have adopted the Common Core State Standards, and the remaining states are considering their adoption. Once a state adopts the standards, teachers design curriculum and locate instructional materials that align with the standards and develop assessment instruments. Within a few years, teachers will adjust their instructional programs and implement the standards. Teachers can also use the Common Core State Standards to determine when students aren't making expected progress so they can provide interventions, using RTI or another program.

COMMON CORE STATE STANDARDS

Language Arts Standards

The Common Core State Standards for Language Arts address all six language arts. The four traditional language arts are discussed individually, but the visual language arts—viewing and visually representing—are integrated into the other modes. The standards comprise these four strands:

- Reading
- Writing
- Listening and Speaking
- Language

To learn more about the language arts standards, go to http://www.corestandards.org, or check your state's educational standards website.

ASSESSING LEARNING

Assessing students' learning in language arts is a difficult task. Although it may seem fairly easy to develop and administer a criterion-referenced test, tests measure language skills rather than students' ability to use language in authentic ways. Nor do tests measure listening, talking, and viewing very well. A test on punctuation marks, for example, doesn't demonstrate students' ability to use punctuation marks correctly in their own writing. Instead, a test typically evaluates whether students can add punctuation marks to a set of sentences created by someone else or proofread to spot punctuation errors in someone else's writing. A better alternative approach is to examine how students use punctuation marks in their own writing.

Classroom assessment should be authentic; that is, students should be evaluated on how well they can use the six language arts in meaningful and genuine activities and projects (Valencia, Hiebert, & Afflerbach, 1994). Teachers examine both the processes that students use as they listen, talk, read, write, view, and visually represent and the artifacts or products they create, such as projects, reports, and reading logs.

Authentic assessment has five purposes:

- Identify students' strengths and needs before instruction
- Evaluate students' learning
- Determine grades
- Help teachers learn more about how students become strategic readers and writers
- Document milestones in students' oral, written, and visual language development

Assessment is an integral part of teaching and learning (Tierney, 2005). It begins when teachers plan for instruction and continues during instruction. Finally, it's used to evaluate learning. Teachers use these three components:

PLANNING FOR INSTRUCTION. Teachers determine students' background knowledge about a topic to know how to differentiate instruction to meet students' needs.

MONITORING PROGRESS. Teachers monitor students' progress to make sure they're making adequate progress, and when they're not, teachers modify instruction so all students can be successful.

EVALUATING LEARNING. Teachers evaluate students' achievement with checklists, rubrics, and other assessment tools and use the results to determine grades.

Through authentic assessment, teachers learn about their students, about themselves as teachers, and about the impact of their instructional program. Similarly, when students reflect on their learning, they learn about themselves as learners and also about their achievement.

Monitoring Progress

Teachers monitor students' progress during literature focus units, literature circles, reading and writing workshop, and thematic units, and they use the results of their monitoring to inform their teaching. Four ways to monitor students' progress are classroom observations, anecdotal notes, conferences, and checklists.

Classroom Observations. Language arts teachers engage in "kid watching," a term that Yetta Goodman coined, as they informally watch students participating in language arts activities (Owocki & Goodman, 2002). To be effective kid watchers, teachers must understand how children develop language and appreciate the role of errors in language learning. Teachers use kid watching spontaneously when they interact with students and are attentive to their behavior and comments. In addition, they plan observation times to focus on particular students and make anecdotal notes about their involvement in oral, written, and visual language activities. The focus is on what students do as they use language, not on whether they're behaving properly or working quietly. Of course, little learning can occur in disruptive situations, but during these observations, the focus is on language use, not behavior.

Anecdotal Notes. Teachers write brief notes as they observe students; the most useful notes describe specific events, report rather than evaluate, and relate the events to other information about the students (Rhodes & Nathenson-Mejia, 1992). Teachers make notes about students' performance in listening, talking, reading, writing, viewing, and visually representing activities; about the questions students ask; and about the strategies they're using or confusing. These records document students' growth and pinpoint instructional needs (Boyd-Batstone, 2004). A yearlong collection of records provides a comprehensive picture of a student's achievement. An excerpt from a fifth grade teacher's anecdotal notes about one student's progress during a unit on the American Revolution appears in Figure 2–6.

Several organizational schemes for anecdotal notes are possible, and teachers choose the format that's most comfortable for them. Some teachers make a card file with dividers for each student and write anecdotes on notecards. They feel comfortable jotting notes on these small cards or even carrying around a set of cards in a pocket. Other teachers divide a spiral-bound notebook into sections for each student and write anecdotes in the notebook, which they keep on their desk. A third technique is to write anecdotes on small sheets of paper and clip the notes in students' assessment folders.

Conferences. Teachers meet with students in conferences to monitor their progress in language arts activities as well as to set goals and help students solve problems (Gill, 2000). They hold conferences for these purposes:

ON-THE-SPOT CONFERENCES. The teacher visits with students at their desks to monitor their work or to check on their progress. These conferences are brief; the teacher often spends less than a minute with each student.

PATTERNS OF PRACTICE

Literature Focus Units

Reading

The fifth graders in Mrs. Kenney's class are reading Roald Dahl's delicious fantasy, *Charlie and the Chocolate Factory*. It's the story of Charlie Bucket, an honest and kind boy, who finds the fifth winning Golden Ticket, entitling him to a visit inside Willy Wonka's famous chocolate factory. Charlie and the four other children who also found winning tickets have a wild time visiting the factory, and, in the end, Mr. Wonka gives Charlie the best present of all—his factory!

Mrs. Kenney varies the ways students read each chapter. She reads the first chapter aloud, using whole-class shared reading, and students follow along in their copies of the book. For the other chapters, students alternate reading independently, reading with a buddy, reading in small groups, and reading together as a class.

Create your own Wonka goodie.

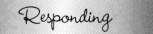

Responding

Mrs. Kenney's students respond to the story in two ways. They participate in small-group and whole-class discussions called *grand conversations*. In these lively discussions, they share their ideas about the story, ask questions to clarify misunderstandings, and make connections to their own lives. Mrs. Kenney participates in the whole-class grand conversations and often asks students to think about Charlie and compare him to the other four children.

The fifth graders also write in double entry reading logs. At the beginning of the literature focus unit, students staple together booklets of paper for their journals and divide each page into two columns. After reading each chapter, they choose a quote and write it in the left column and then write a response in the right column.

Quote	Response
Ch. 19 Pg. 94 "The place was like a witch's kitchen!"	I chose this quote because did you know — it's a simile!

QUOTE	MY THOUGHTS
Ch 11 Pg 50 "You've got a Golden Ticket! You found the last Golden Ticket! Hey, what do you know?"	I feel excited and happy because Charlie never had anything much in his life. Maybe now his life will take a turn for the better.

Teaching Minilessons

Mrs. Kenney and her students choose important words from each chapter as they read *Charlie and the Chocolate Factory*. The words are organized by parts of speech on the word wall because Mrs. Kenney is teaching a series of grammar minilessons. The noun list includes *hooligan*, *precipice*, and *verdict*; the verb list includes *beckoned*, *revolt*, *stammer*, and *criticize*. The adjective list includes *despicable*, *scraggy*, and *repulsive*; *ravenously*, *violently*, and *frantically* are on the adverb list.

Mrs. Kenney also uses the words from the word wall as she teaches minilessons on root words and affixes to small groups of students. Students take turns choosing a word from the word wall and breaking apart the word's prefix, root, and suffix as Mrs. Kenney writes the information on the whiteboard. Then students record the information on small, individual whiteboards.

In this literature focus unit, Mrs. Kenney is focusing on character. During a series of minilessons, students investigate how Roald Dahl developed Charlie's character and compare him with Willy Wonka and the other four children with winning Golden Tickets.

After studying about the characters, students create open-mind portraits of one of the characters. One student's open-mind portrait of Willy Wonka is shown here. The portrait goes on top and the page showing his thoughts goes underneath.

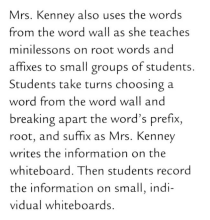

Creating Projects

Students create a variety of projects to extend the book and apply their learning. These two boys created a model of Willy Wonka's chocolate factory. Other students researched how chocolate is made and created a poster to display what they learned, wrote poems about each of the characters in *Charlie and the Chocolate Factory*, or read another of Roald Dahl's stories.

As the concluding activity, Mrs. Kenney and her students view *Willy Wonka and the Chocolate Factory*, the film version of the story starring Gene Wilder. Afterward, students work in small groups to create Venn diagrams comparing the book and the film versions. One student's Venn diagram is shown here. After discussing the differences, most students agree that they preferred the book.

PATTERNS OF PRACTICE

Literature Circles

Reading

Mrs. Goodman's eighth graders participate in literature circles. The teacher introduces six books written at varying levels of difficulty, and students sign up for the book they want to read. The students are currently reading these books:

- *The Outsiders*, by S. E. Hinton
- *The Face on the Milk Carton*, by Caroline Cooney
- *Holes*, by Louis Sachar
- *I Am the Cheese*, by Robert Cormier
- *To Kill a Mockingbird*, by Harper Lee
- *What Jamie Saw*, by Carolyn Coman

Students have set a reading schedule and they spend time reading during class and at home.

Students in each literature circle assume roles to deepen their understanding of the story and ensure the smooth functioning of their group. They rotate these roles each day so that everyone has the opportunity to experience all roles.

ROLES	
Discussion Leader	This student keeps classmates focused on the big ideas in the story.
Harmonizer	This student helps everyone stay on task and show respect to classmates.
Wordsmith	This student identifies important words in the story and checks the meaning of words in a dictionary.
Connector	This student connects events in the story with real-life experiences.
Illustrator	This student draws pictures to help classmates visualize events in the story.

Responding

Students frequently meet in their literature circles to discuss the story they're reading, and students fulfill their roles. They talk about what's happening in the story, ask questions to clarify confusions, make connections to their own lives, and predict what will happen next. As students talk, Mrs. Goodman circulates around the classroom, joining each group for a few minutes.

Students also write in reading logs. Sometimes they write summaries and make predictions, and at other times they write reflections and ask questions. After writing, students often divide into groups of two or three to read their entries to classmates.

Reading Log

I am liking <u>To Kill a Mockingbird</u> a lot. But it's very different from other books I've read. Instead of describing the scenery and how the people look, it tells the history of everything. The book tells you what has happened. That makes it harder to picture what is happening but easier to make up what you want. I don't think I've ever read a description of Scout anywhere in the book. I didn't quite understand the beginning of the book because it was introducing everything really fast. But now, I'm beginning to understand what is going on.

Reading Log

My questions are:

•   Why don't Scout and Jim call their father Dad but use his real name (Atticus)?

•   Why doesn't Scout play with other girls?

•   What does everyone look like?

•   Why doesn't anyone search for the truth about the Radleys?

Creating Projects

Students create projects after they finish reading and discussing a story. They write poems and sequels, research a topic on the Internet, develop PowerPoint presentations, create artifacts related to the story, and design story quilts.

After students identify a project they want to develop, they meet with Mrs. Goodman and she approves their choice and helps them get started.

"When Jamie saw Van Throw Nin"

This picture is a square from a story quilt about *What Jamie Saw*, a story about child abuse. Students in the literature circle draw pictures to represent events from the book and put them together to make the quilt, which presents a strong message about the effects of child abuse.

Sharing

Sharing is the concluding activity. Students in each literature circle share the book they've read and their project with Mrs. Goodman and the class. Sometimes students work together to give a group presentation to the class, and sometimes students develop individual presentations. The students demonstrate their understanding of the story through their presentation, and they hope to interest their classmates in choosing the book and reading the story.

Mrs. Goodman explains how students will be graded before the literature circle begins and posts the criteria in the classroom. For this literature circle, students are graded on four items; each item is worth 25 points. At the end of the literature circle, Mrs. Goodman prepares a grading sheet with the criteria, evaluates students' work, and assigns the grades.

GRADING SHEET

Name _Justin_

Book _The Face on the Milk Carton_

1. Reading Log — 20
2. Roles in the Literature Circle — 25
3. Working Together in a Group — 25
4. Project at the End — 22

(92)

PATTERNS OF PRACTICE

Reading and Writing Workshop

Reading & Responding

Mrs. McClenaghan's fifth and sixth graders participate in reading workshop for an hour each morning. The students read books they've selected from the classroom library, including *A Wrinkle in Time*, by Madeleine L'Engle; *The Sign of the Beaver*, by Elizabeth George Speare; *Harry Potter and the Sorcerer's Stone*, by J. K. Rowling; *Missing May*, by Cynthia Rylant; and *Tuck Everlasting*, by Natalie Babbitt.

Students also respond to the books they're reading, and their response activities vary according to what Mrs. McClenaghan is teaching. This week's focus is on a reading strategy—forming interpretations. The students identify a big idea in the chapter they're reading and provide evidence from the text to support the idea on T-charts they've made.

Conferencing

As her students read and respond, Mrs. McClenaghan moves around the classroom, stopping to conference with students. She asks students to read a short excerpt and tell about their reading experience and the reading strategies they're using. They talk about the story so Mrs. McClenaghan can monitor their comprehension and clarify any misunderstandings. She carries a clipboard with her and writes notes about each student, including what book the student is reading and the progress he or she is making.

PATTERNS OF PRACTICE *Reading and Writing Workshop*

Reading Aloud

Mrs. McClenaghan is reading aloud Theodore Taylor's *The Cay*, a survival story about an elderly African American man and a Caucasian boy who are shipwrecked in the Caribbean and become friends through the experience. She reads aloud a chapter or two each day and the students talk about the story in a grand conversation. She also uses the book in the minilessons she's teaching.

Teaching Minilessons

These fifth and sixth graders have been examining the strategies that good readers use, such as asking questions, making connections, and visualizing, in a series of minilessons. Today, Mrs. McClenaghan focuses on making inferences. She explains that good readers read between the lines to figure out the author's message. She rereads a passage from *The Cay* and asks the students to identify the big idea in the passage. Then she makes a T-chart on a whiteboard and records their answers. In the first column, she writes the big idea, and in the second, a quote from the text to support the big idea. Then she reads another passage several pages later in the text, and they rephrase the big idea to clarify it and finish the chart.

BIG Idea	Text Evidence
It's about friendship.	p. 76 I said to Timothy, "I want to be your friend." He said softly, "Young bahss, you 'ave always been my friend."
It doesn't matter what color you are, you can still be friends.	p. 79 "I don't like some white people my own self, but 'twould be outrageous if I didn't like any o' dem."

Writing

After spending 60 minutes in reading workshop, students begin writing workshop, which lasts for 45 minutes. Students usually write two- to four-page stories about events in their own lives—personal narratives—during writing workshop. They work at their own pace, moving through the stages of the writing process. Most students write three or four drafts as they develop and refine the content of their writing.

Really Hungry

One day, when it was close to dinner time, my big brother was so hungry he got there before any of us. He was waiting impatiently and when we were at the table with our food in front of us he already started devouring the vegetables and rice.

My mother looked at him, and he stopped stuffing himself. He waited very impatiently while she said grace. Mother's grace isn't short but it isn't very long either. He fidgeted and squirmed untill she finished. "You should make it shorter," he said.

He gobbled all of his rice, vegetables and chicken. We watched him in amazement. He asked for seconds and he started to swallow his food.

"Don't eat like that," snapped my mother. "Disgusting!" She bit her chicken wing and chewed.

Responding

Students meet with classmates and with Mrs. McClenaghan several times during the writing process to revise and edit their writing. The students provide useful feedback to classmates because they've learned about the qualities of a good piece of writing and they know how to identify problem spots.

Teaching Minilessons

In this writing minilesson, Mrs. McClenaghan shares an essay written by a student from another class. She asks the students to rate it using their district's 6-point writing rubric. They raise their hands and show with their fingers the score they'd give the paper. Most students rate it a 4, and Mrs. McClenaghan agrees. They talk about the strong points in the paper and the areas where improvement is needed.

Then Mrs. McClenaghan reviews the asking-questions and magnifying-a-sentence revision procedures and the symbols students use to represent them. Next, students reread the essay and attach small self-stick notes to the paper with the symbols written on them to indicate revision points. Students also underline the specific sentence each sticky note refers to.

Sharing

During the last 5 minutes of writing workshop, one student sits in the author's chair and shares a newly published composition. The classmates clap and offer compliments after the student finishes reading. They are an appreciative audience because Mrs. McClenaghan and her students have developed a supportive classroom community.

PATTERNS OF PRACTICE

Thematic Units

Reading

Ms. McCloskey works with 40 kindergarten through third grade students in their multiage classroom. The students are engaged in a thematic unit on insects, integrating all areas of the curriculum. They participate in a variety of reading activities. They listen to Ms. McCloskey read books aloud and read along with her as she shares big books. During centers time, they reread familiar books with buddies and read independently. They also read other books at their own reading levels during guided reading.

Learning Logs

Each day, children write entries for their learning logs at the writing center. They meet with Ms. Russell, a student teacher working in the classroom, to write about insects. Many of the children are English learners, so Ms. Russell helps them to expand their sentences and include science words in their entries. She also reviews spelling, capitalization, punctuation, and grammar skills with individual children. Then children file their papers in their learning log folders, which are kept at the writing center. At the end of the thematic unit, children compile their learning logs and decorate the covers.

This entry, titled "Wings," was written by a kindergartner who is still learning about capital letters and punctuation marks. He added the second part, "because it has wings," in response to Ms. Russell's question, "How can a ladybug fly?"

WFs

A LadeBug can fly, BeKCse it nS wfs.

Graphic Representations

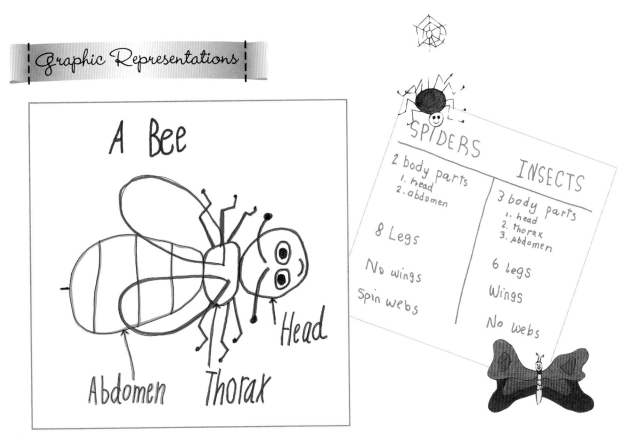

The children make diagrams, charts, and drawings to record information they're learning about insects. They learn to draw insects accurately with three body parts and six legs. They use diagrams to organize information they're learning as Ms. McCloskey reads a book or presents a demonstration. They also use attribute charts to record descriptive words as they observe insects in the "Look and Learn" science center.

Creating Projects

The children are creating a multigenre display on insects. Each child writes a story, poem, or report for the display, which will cover an entire wall of the classroom. The children use the writing process to develop their compositions, and all children, even the kindergartners, type their final copies on the computer with a teacher's assistance.

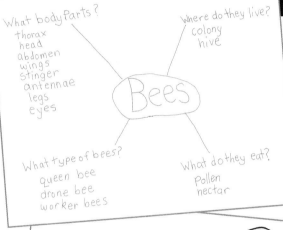

The Bees

Bees have three body parts: a thorax, an abdomen, and a head. On their body they have some little and big wings, a stinger, two antennae, six legs, and two large black eyes.

The bees live in a hive. Sometimes bees live in a group of bees, and it is called a colony. A lot of bees live in a colony and a lot of bees live in a hive.

There are three kinds of bees. There is a queen bee, a drone bee, and worker bees. The queen lays eggs on the hive and the worker bees take care of the baby bees. One of the worker bees gets pollen from the flowers. When the worker bees get pollen, they dance because they can't talk.

Bees eat pollen and nectar to make honey. When bees make honey they have to go get pollen and nectar. We need bees because bees could make honey for us. If bees is not in this state there will be no honey for us.

Dragonfly

Dragonfly fly, fly, fly.
Dragonfly fly around the pond.
Dragonfly fly by the flower.
Dragonfly fly by me.
Dragonfly fly, fly, fly.

PREREADING OR PREWRITING CONFERENCES. The teacher and students make plans for reading or writing. At prereading conferences, they talk about information related to the book, difficult concepts or vocabulary related to the reading, or which strategies to practice. At prewriting conferences, they discuss writing topics, how to narrow a broad topic, or where to locate information related to a topic.

REVISING CONFERENCES. A small group of students meets with the teacher to get specific suggestions about revising their compositions. These conferences offer student writers an audience to provide feedback on how well they've communicated.

BOOK DISCUSSION CONFERENCES. Students and the teacher meet to discuss the book they've read. They may share reading log entries, talk about the writer's craft, or compare the story to others they've read.

EDITING CONFERENCES. The teacher reviews students' proofread compositions and helps them correct spelling, punctuation, capitalization, and other mechanical errors.

PROJECT CONFERENCES. The teacher meets with individual students or small groups to plan projects related to literature focus units and thematic units.

FIGURE 2–6   Notes About Matthew

March 5	Matthew selected Ben Franklin as historical figure for American Revolution project.
March 11	Matthew fascinated with information he has found about B. F. Brought several sources from home. Is completing B. F.'s life line with many details.
March 18	Simulated journal. Four entries in four days! Interesting how he picked up language style of the period in his journal. Volunteers to share daily. I think he enjoys the oral sharing more than the writing.
March 25	Nine simulated journal entries, all illustrated. High level of enthusiasm.
March 28	Conferenced about cluster for B. F. biography. Well-developed with five rays, many details. Matthew will work on "contributions" ray. He recognized it as the least developed one.
April 2	Three chapters of biography drafted. Talked about "working titles" for chapters and choosing more interesting titles after writing that reflect the content of the chapters.
April 8	Drafting conference. Matthew has completed all five chapters. He and Dustin are competitive, both writing on B. F. They are reading each other's chapters and checking the accuracy of information.
April 11	Writing conference. Matthew confused Declaration of Independence with the Constitution. Chapters longer and more complete since drafting conference. Compared with autobiography project, writing is more sophisticated. Longer, too. Reading is influencing writing style—e.g., "Luckily for Ben." He is still somewhat defensive about accepting suggestions except from me. He will make 3 revisions—agreed in revising group.
April 15	Revisions: (1) eliminated "he" (substitute), (2) resequenced Chapter 3 (move), and (3) added sentences in Chapter 5 (add)
April 23	Editing conference—no major problems. Discussed use of commas within sentences, capitalizing proper nouns. Matthew and Dustin more task-oriented on this project: I see more motivation and commitment.
April 29	Final copy of biography completed and shared with class.

ASSESSMENT CONFERENCES. The teacher meets with students after they've completed a project to talk about their achievement. Students reflect on their work and set goals for the next project.

Often these conferences are brief and impromptu, held at students' desks as the teacher moves around the classroom; at other times, the conferences are planned, and students meet with the teacher at a designated conference table.

The teacher's role is to be listener and guide. Teachers can learn a great deal about students and their learning if they listen as students talk about their reading, writing, or other activities. When students explain a problem they're having, the teacher is often able to decide on a way to work through it. Graves (1994) suggests that teachers balance the amount of their talk with the student's talk during the conference and, at the end, reflect on what the student has taught them, what responsibilities the student can take, and whether the student understands what to do next.

Checklists. Teachers use checklists as they observe students; as they track students' progress during literature focus units, literature circles, reading and writing workshop, and thematic units; and as they document students' use of language arts strategies. For example, when students participate in revising groups in which they read their compositions to small groups of class-mates and ask for suggestions on ways to improve their writing, teachers note whether students participate fully in the group, share their writing with classmates, gracefully accept improvement suggestions, and make substantive changes in their writing based on some of their classmates' suggestions. Students can even help develop the checklists so that they understand what types of behavior are expected of them.

A "Weekly Reading-Writing Workshop Activity Sheet" appears in Figure 2–7. Third graders complete this checklist each week to monitor their work during reading and writing workshop. Notice that students are directed to write a letter to the teacher on the back of the sheet, reflecting on their progress that week.

Evaluating Learning

Assigning grades is one of the most difficult responsibilities placed on teachers. The authentic assessment procedures described in this chapter document how students are using language in authentic ways; the difficult part is reviewing and translating this documentation into grades. Assignment checklists and rubrics are useful tools that teachers use to assign grades.

Assignment Checklists. Students use assignment checklists to keep track of assignments during literature focus units and thematic units. Teachers create the checklist as they plan the unit, and students receive a copy of it at the beginning of the unit and keep it in their unit folder. As students complete assignments, they check them off, so it's easy for teachers to monitor students' progress. Then at the end of the unit, teachers collect the unit folders and grade the work. Figure 2–8 presents a checklist for a second grade thematic unit on hermit crabs. The assignments include both science and language arts activities. Students put a check in the boxes in the "Student's Check" column when they complete each assignment, and the teacher adds the grade in the right-hand column.

Rubrics. Both teachers and students develop and use scoring guides called *rubrics* to assess writing (Skillings & Ferrell, 2000). Rubrics make the analysis of writing easier and assessment more reliable and consistent. Rubrics may have 3, 4, 5, or 6 levels, with descriptors at each level related to ideas, organization, language, and mechanics. Teachers and students read the composition and highlight words or check statements in the rubric that best describe it. Rarely are all the highlighted words or checked statements at the same level; the score is determined by examining what's marked and

FIGURE 2–7   Weekly Reading-Writing Workshop Activity Sheet

Name _____   Week _____

Reading		Writing	
Read independently	M T W Th F	Made a cluster	M T W Th F
Wrote in a reading log	M T W Th F	Wrote a rough draft	M T W Th F
Listened to the teacher read aloud	M T W Th F	Went to a revising group	M T W Th F
Read with a classmate	M T W Th F	Made revisions	M T W Th F
Read at the listening center	M T W Th F	Proofread my own writing	M T W Th F
Had a reading conference	M T W Th F	Had a writing conference	M T W Th F
Shared the book with classmates	M T W Th F	Shared my writing with classmates	M T W Th F
Other		Other	
Interesting words read this week		Spelling words needed this week	
Titles of books read		Titles of writings	

Write a letter on the back, thinking about the week and your reading and writing.

determining which level best represents the overall quality of the composition. The steps in developing a rubric are described in the feature on page 51.

Some rubrics are designed for specific writing assignments, but others are general and appropriate for almost any writing project. A class of sixth graders developed the 4-level rubric shown in Figure 2–9 to assess reports they wrote during a unit on ancient Egypt. In contrast, Figure 2–10 shows a general, 5-level writing rubric that can be used to assess almost any type of formal writing assignment.

Implementing Portfolios

Portfolios are systematic and meaningful collections of artifacts documenting students' language arts development over a period of time (Porter & Cleland, 1995). These collections are dynamic, and they reflect students' day-to-day learning activities in language arts and across the curriculum.

Students' work samples provide windows on the strategies they employ as oral, written, and visual language users.

Portfolio programs complement language arts instruction in many ways. The most important benefit is that students become more involved in assessment and more reflective about the quality of their work. There are other benefits as well:

- Students feel ownership of their work.
- Students become more responsible about their work.
- Students set goals and are motivated to accomplish them.
- Students reflect on their accomplishments.
- Students make connections between learning and assessing.
- Students' self-esteem is enhanced.
- Students recognize the connection between process and product.

In addition, portfolios are useful for student and parent conferences, and they complement the information provided in report cards.

FIGURE 2–8   Checklist for a Thematic Unit on Hermit Crabs

Name _____   Begin _____
                                                          End _____

	Student's Check	Teacher's Grade
1. Keep an observation log on the hermit crab on your table for 10 days.	_____	_____
2. Make a diagram of a hermit crab and label the parts.	_____	_____
3. Make a map of the hermit crab's habitat.	_____	_____
4. Read three books about hermit crabs and do quickwrites about them.	_____	_____
_____ Hermit Crabs		
_____ A House for Hermit Crab		
_____ Is This a House for Hermit Crab?		
5. Do two science experiments and write lab reports.	_____	_____
_____ Wet-Dry Experiment		
_____ Light-Dark Experiment		
6. Write about hermit crabs. Do one.	_____	_____
_____ All About Hermit Crabs book		
_____ A poem about hermit crabs		
_____ A story about hermit crabs		
7. Do a project about hermit crabs. Share it.	_____	_____
8. Keep everything neatly in your hermit crab folder.	_____	_____

Step-by-Step: RUBRICS

1 **Choose a rubric.** Teachers pick a rubric that's appropriate to the project or create one that reflects the assignment.

2 **Introduce the rubric.** Teachers distribute copies to students and talk about the criteria listed at each level; they focus on the requirements at the proficiency level, which specifies grade-level expectations.

3 **Self-assess.** Students use one color pen to mark the rubric as they self-assess their work. They highlight phrases in the rubric or check off items that they believe best represent their work. Then they determine which level has the most highlighted phrases or checkmarks; that level is the overall score, and students circle it.

4 **Assess students' work.** Teachers use another color pen to assess students' work by highlighting phrases in the rubric or checking off items that best describe the work. Then they assign the overall score by determining which level has the most highlighted phrases or checkmarks and circling it.

5 **Conference with students.** Teachers talk with students about the assessment, identifying strengths and weaknesses. Afterward, students set goals for the next project.

Collecting Work in Portfolios. Portfolios are folders, large envelopes, or boxes that hold students' work. Teachers often have students label and decorate folders and then store them in plastic crates or cardboard boxes. Students date and label items as they place them in their portfolios, and they attach notes to the items to explain the context for the activity and why they selected a particular item for inclusion in the portfolio. Students' portfolios should be stored in a place where they're readily accessible to students. Students review their portfolios periodically and add new pieces to them.

Students usually choose the items to place in their portfolios within the guidelines the teacher provides. Some students submit the original piece of work; others keep the original, so they place a copy in the portfolio instead. In addition to the writing and art samples that can go directly into portfolios, students also record oral language and drama samples on audiotapes and flash drives to place in their portfolios. Large-size art and writing projects can be photographed, and the photographs placed in the portfolio. These types of student work might be placed in a portfolio:

autobiographies	podcasts
biographies	poems
books	posters
boxes of artifacts	PowerPoint presentations
choral readings	puppets and puppet shows
copies of letters, along with replies	reading logs
drawings, diagrams, and charts	reports
essays	simulated journals
learning logs	slide shows
lists of books read	stories
multigenre projects	websites and wikis

FIGURE 2–9	Rubric for Assessing Reports on Ancient Egypt

4   EXCELLENT REPORT

_____ Three or more chapters with titles

_____ Main idea clearly developed in each chapter

_____ Three or more illustrations

_____ Effective use of Egypt-related words in text and illustrations

_____ Very interesting to read

_____ Very few mechanical errors

_____ Table of contents

3   GOOD REPORT

_____ Three chapters with titles

_____ Main idea somewhat developed in each chapter

_____ Three illustrations

_____ Some Egypt-related words used

_____ Interesting to read

_____ A few mechanical errors

_____ Table of contents

2   AVERAGE REPORT

_____ Three chapters

_____ Main idea identified in each chapter

_____ One or two illustrations

_____ A few Egypt-related words used

_____ Some mechanical errors

_____ Sort of interesting to read

_____ Table of contents

1   POOR REPORT

_____ One or two chapters

_____ Information in each chapter rambles

_____ No illustrations

_____ Very few Egypt-related words used

_____ Many mechanical errors

_____ Hard to read and understand

_____ No table of contents

FIGURE 2–10   Writing Rubric

5   EXCEPTIONAL ACHIEVEMENT

- Creative and original
- Clear organization
- Precise word choice and figurative language
- Sophisticated sentences
- Essentially free of mechanical errors

4   EXCELLENT ACHIEVEMENT

- Some creativity, but more predictable than an exceptional paper
- Definite organization
- Good word choice, but little figurative language
- Varied sentences
- Only a few mechanical errors

3   ADEQUATE ACHIEVEMENT

- Predictable paper
- Some organization
- Adequate word choice
- Little variety of sentences and some run-on sentences
- Some mechanical errors

2   LIMITED ACHIEVEMENT

- Brief and superficial
- Little organization
- Imprecise language
- Incomplete and run-on sentences
- Many mechanical errors

1   MINIMAL ACHIEVEMENT

- No ideas communicated
- Lacks organization
- Inadequate word choice
- Sentence fragments
- Overwhelming mechanical errors

This variety of work samples represents all six language modes. Students place their written work directly into their portfolios, but for work involving the other language arts, they take photos, make videos, and save work on flash drives. They usually include samples of their work from workshops, literature focus units, literature circles, and thematic units in their portfolios.

Many teachers collect students' work in folders, and they assume that portfolios are basically the same as work folders; however, the two types of collections differ in several important ways. Perhaps the most striking difference is that portfolios are student oriented, but work folders are usually teachers' collections. Students choose which samples will be placed in portfolios, and teachers often place all completed assignments in work folders. Next, portfolios focus on students' strengths, not weaknesses. Because students choose items for portfolios, they choose samples that they believe best represent their development. Another difference is that portfolios involve reflection (D'Aoust, 1992): Through reflection, students become aware of their strengths as readers, writers, and language users. They also use their work samples to identify the language arts strategies they can apply effectively as well as the ones they don't know how to use.

Involving Students in Self-Assessment. Portfolios are a useful vehicle for engaging students in self-reflection and goal setting (Courtney & Abodeeb, 2005). Students can learn to reflect on and assess their own language arts activities and their development as oral, written, and visual language users. Teachers begin by asking students to think about their language arts abilities in terms of contrast. For example, in reading, students identify the books they've read that they liked most and least and ask themselves what these choices suggest about themselves as readers. They also identify what they do well in reading and what they need to improve about their reading. By making these comparisons, students begin to reflect on their language arts development.

Teachers use minilessons and conferences to talk with students about the characteristics of good listeners, good writers, good storytellers, and good viewers. In particular, they discuss these characteristics:

- What good listeners do as they listen
- How to view a film or videotape
- What fluent reading is
- How to prepare to give an oral report
- Which language arts strategies students use
- How students choose books for reading workshop
- How students demonstrate comprehension
- What makes a good project to extend reading
- How students decide what to write in journals
- How students adapt their writing to their audience
- How students visually represent important concepts
- How to use writing rubrics
- How to participate in a grand conversation

As students learn about what it means to be effective language users, they acquire both the tools they need to reflect on and evaluate their own language development and vocabulary to use in their reflections, such as *goal, strategy,* and *rubric.*

Students write notes on the items they choose to put into their portfolios. In these self-assessments, students explain the reasons for their selections and identify strengths and accomplishments in their work. In some classrooms, students write their reflections and comments on index cards; in others, students design special comment sheets that they attach to the items in their portfolios. A first grader wrote this reflection to explain why she chose to make a poster about author Eric Carle and his books and to include it in her portfolio: "I have a favorite author. Mr. Eric Carle. I read five of his books!" A fifth grader chose to put the reading log he wrote while reading *Shiloh* (Naylor, 2000) in his portfolio. He wrote this reflection: "I put my journal on the computer. It looks good! I used the SPELCHEK. I put in lots of details like I was him. I should of put some illustrations in the book."

Showcasing Students' Portfolios. At the end of the school year, many teachers organize "Portfolio Share Days" to celebrate students' accomplishments and to provide an opportunity for students to share their portfolios with classmates and the wider community (Porter & Cleland, 1995). Often family members, local businesspeople and politicians, school administrators, college students, and others are invited to attend. Students and community members form small groups, and the students share their portfolios, pointing out their accomplishments and strengths. This activity is especially useful in involving community members in the school and showing them the types of language arts activities students are doing as well as how students are becoming effective readers, writers, and language users.

These sharing days also help students accept responsibility for their own learning—especially those students who haven't been as motivated as their classmates. When less motivated students listen to their classmates talk about their work and how they've grown as readers, writers, and language users, they often decide to work harder the next year.

INTEGRATING TECHNOLOGY

Teachers are experimenting with a variety of online assessment tools, including these:

TEACHER BOOK WIZARD. Scholastic has a handy free tool, the Teacher Book Wizard (http://bookwizard.scholastic.com), that teachers use to find appropriate books for their students. They can locate books by grade level, reading level, genre, or subject. In addition to locating books, teachers can join the website's online community to connect with other teachers, exchange booklists, and create text sets for units. At the Scholastic website, teachers can also locate book and author information, book talks, discussion guides, and book-based lesson plans.

ONLINE WRITING ASSESSMENT TOOLS. Writing Roadmap, Criterion, and My Access are automated scoring programs that enable teachers in fourth through eighth grades to quickly evaluate students' word processed compositions and provide feedback writers can use to revise and edit their writing. One program claims to evaluate a composition in 20 seconds! These scoring tools provide feedback to students as well as holistic scores and generate class reports for teachers and administrators. The use of scoring programs is controversial, however, because they equate writing quality with word frequency, sentence structure, and grammatical correctness. The evaluation is generic; it can't be tailored to individual compositions.

DIGITAL PORTFOLIOS. Students create digital collections of projects and other work samples to share with classmates, teachers, and parents using HyperStudio or another multimedia software program or a web authoring program. They use hyperlinks to connect compositions to reflections, rubrics, and rough drafts, and viewers can interact with and respond to them. Students can also scan handwritten papers, use a digital camera to photograph visual projects, film oral presentations with a video camera, and store their portfolios on flash drives.

Technology is rapidly changing how teachers assess students' work. ■

High-Stakes Assessments

Authentic assessment tools and tests provide different kinds of information. Authentic assessment gives a more complete picture of what students know and the strategies they can apply, but tests judge students' performance against a grade-level standard (Wilson, Martens, & Arya, 2005). A student who scores 95% on a unit test is judged to have learned more than one who scores 70%, but it usually isn't clear exactly what the student knows or which strategies he or she has learned to use. In recent years, state and federal mandates have increasingly dictated instructional approaches and assessment procedures. The No Child Left Behind (NCLB) Act of 2001 was designed to close the achievement gap between affluent, white students and other students. Schools are now required to administer standardized tests each year to students in grades 3–8 to monitor their progress. Guidelines for preparing students for "high-stakes" testing are presented in Figure 2–11.

Because of the NCLB Act, state-designated lists of grade-level standards, and other mandated programs, teachers feel a loss of professional autonomy in determining what and how to teach. There's increased pressure from parents, administrators, and politicians for teachers to "teach to the test" rather than to develop students' communicative competence by engaging them in meaningful, functional, and genuine language arts activities. Some teachers have embraced the new instructional programs, and others have quietly resisted them and continued to use student-centered approaches as often as they could. Still others are actively resisting the imposition of these programs because they reject the conformity and loss of teacher control inherent in new state and federal mandates (Novinger & Compton-Lilly, 2005).

Teachers, administrators, and parents can point to both positive and negative outcomes of these mandates (Valencia & Villarreal, 2003). Some teachers feel more confident now because

FIGURE 2–11   How to Prepare Students for High-Stakes Testing

Test-Taking Strategies
Teach test-taking strategies by modeling how to read, think about, and answer test items.

Practice Tests
Design practice tests with the same types of items used on the tests that students will take.

Easy-to-Read Materials
Use easy-to-read reading materials for practice tests so students can focus on practicing test-taking strategies.

Variety of Passages
Include a combination of unrelated narrative and expository passages on practice tests.

Regular Schedule
Have students take practice tests on a regular schedule.

Untimed and Timed Tests
Begin with untimed tests and move to timed tests as students gain experience with test-taking strategies.

Testing Conditions
Simulate testing conditions in the classroom, or take students to where the test will be administered for the practice sessions.

Graphs of Test Results
Graph students' results on practice tests so they can see their progress.

they're told how to teach language arts, and in many schools, students' test scores are rising. At the same time, however, other teachers are frustrated because they aren't allowed to use the instructional approaches that have been effective for them. They're concerned about the amount of time diverted from instruction for testing. In some schools, testing consumes more than one month of the school year. In addition, some students have developed test anxiety and are preoccupied with the "high-stakes" tests they must pass each spring.

SUMMING UP

Teachers plan language arts instruction using four patterns of practice: literature focus units, literature circles, reading and writing workshop, and thematic units. Literature focus units are teacher directed; teachers and students read and respond to one book. In literature circles, students read and discuss self-selected books. Reading and writing workshop provide opportunities for students to read self-selected books independently and write compositions on topics they've chosen. Thematic units are interdisciplinary: They integrate language arts with social studies, science, and other curricular areas. In each of these instructional approaches, teachers differentiate instruction to meet the needs of all students, and they assess students' learning and use portfolios to document their achievement.

MyEducationLab™

Go to the topic Assessment in the MyEducationLab (http://www.myeducationlab.com) for *Language Arts: Patterns of Practice*, where you can:

- Find learning outcomes for Assessment, along with the national standards that connect to these outcomes.
- Complete Assignments and Activities that can help you more deeply understand the chapter content.
- Apply and practice your understanding of the core teaching skills identified in the chapter with the Building Teaching Skills and Dispositions learning units.
- Check your comprehension of the content covered in the chapter with the Study Plan. Here you will be able to take a chapter quiz, receive feedback on your answers, and then access Review, Practice, and Enrichment activities to enhance your understanding of chapter content.

On the **MyEducationLab** for this course, you'll also be able to:

- **A+RISE** Go to the topic A+RISE, an innovative and interactive database of strategies that differentiate instruction across the language arts and provide particular insight into research-based methods to meet the needs of English learners.
- Explore the topic Literacy Portraits—yearlong case studies of second graders, complete with student artifacts, teacher commentary, and student and teacher interviews, tracking the month-by-month language arts growth of five students.
- Gain practice with the Grammar Tutorial, online guided instruction to improve your own ability with grammar.

CHAPTER 3

Emergent Literacy

K–1 STUDENTS READ AND WRITE   In Mrs. Kirkpatrick's kindergarten–first grade multiage classroom, the children are involved in a weeklong literature focus unit featuring Laura Numeroff's *If You Give a Mouse a Cookie* (1985), a circular story about a mouse who, after receiving a cookie, wants a glass of milk, a straw, a napkin, other items, and finally another cookie. Mrs. Kirkpatrick has copies of both the regular-size and the big-book versions of the story as well as copies of other books by Numeroff that incorporate the same circular pattern: *If You Give a Moose a Muffin* (1991), *If You Give a Pig a Pancake* (1998), *If You Take a Mouse to the Movies* (2000), and *If You Take a Mouse to School* (2002).

Mrs. Kirkpatrick teaches language arts for 2½ hours each morning. Children sample cookies and talk about their favorite cookies on Monday before Mrs. Kirkpatrick reads the featured book using shared reading. Children read the big-book version of the story several times, and each time they're able to read more of the words themselves; the text's predictable pattern and picture clues make it easier for everyone to be successful. Later in the week, the children read the regular-size versions of the book with buddies and individually. Mrs. Kirkpatrick moves through the reading process as children respond to the story in a grand conversation, compare it to other Laura Numeroff books, and draw pictures and write in reading logs.

The children also participate in exploring-stage activities. Mrs. Kirkpatrick draws their attention to specific words in the story, and together they write vocabulary words on a word wall. She also teaches high-frequency words, which are posted on another word wall in the classroom. One of the high-frequency words this week is *you*; the children locate the

How do teachers support children's emergence into reading and writing?

In kindergarten and first grade, children acquire phonemic awareness and phonics knowledge, learn to recognize and print the letters of the alphabet, and develop concepts about print. Literature focus units facilitate children's emergence into literacy because the book provides the foundation for a combination of direct instruction and authentic reading and writing activities. As you read this vignette, notice how Mrs. Kirkpatrick provides instruction and opportunities to nurture her students' emergence into literacy.

word again and again in the story and reread all the high-frequency words that have been posted on the word wall in the classroom. Mrs. Kirkpatrick teaches minilessons on phonics concepts, using words from the featured book to emphasize that phonics knowledge is useful for reading and writing. She also teaches minilessons about irregular plurals after children ask whether *mouses* or *mice* is the correct plural form. They also practice reading skills at centers.

Children work on two culminating projects. They write pages for a class book following Laura Numeroff's pattern and using their own names. For example: *If you give Graciela a bag of popcorn, she will want a glass of juice.* They also make a cookie quilt to hang on the wall of the classroom. Each child makes a square for the paper quilt by designing a cookie in the center of the square and writing or dictating a sentence that's written underneath. The box on page 60 shows how Mrs. Kirkpatrick uses the reading process to teach *If You Give a Mouse a Cookie.*

Later in the morning, Mrs. Kirkpatrick meets with small groups for guided reading while their classmates work at these centers, most of which are related to the featured story:

COMPREHENSION CENTER. Children wear a mouse hand puppet as they sequence objects and retell the story. Copies of the book are available for children to review the order of events in the story.

LISTENING CENTER. Children listen to other books written by Laura Numeroff and write and draw pictures in their listening logs.

PHONICS CENTER. *M* is the featured letter. Some children sort a collection of objects, including a toy mouse, a valentine, a milk carton, a banana, macaroni, a car, and a mitten, into baskets labeled with letters, and others use magnetic letters to spell *man, mop, make, me,* and other words beginning with *m.*

Visit the **MyEducationLab** for *Language Arts: Patterns of Practice* to enhance your understanding of chapter concepts with a personalized Study Plan. You'll also have the opportunity to hone your teaching skills through video- and case-based Assignments and Activities, and Building Teaching Skills and Dispositions lessons.

QUILT CENTER. Children make cookie blocks for the class paper quilt. A variety of art materials are available for children to use.

READING CENTER. Children choose leveled books to read independently from plastic tubs at the center.

WORD CENTER. Children mark *you*, the high-frequency word of the week, on charts posted at the center using Wikki-Stix (pipe cleaners covered in wax) shaped into circles. Some children also spell the word with plastic linking letters.

WRITING CENTER. Children make books about cookies or write retellings of the story. A word wall with story-related words is posted nearby.

A Literature Focus Unit on *If You Give a Mouse a Cookie*

1. Prereading

- Children sample several types of cookies, talk about their favorite cookies, and create a graph to chart their favorite cookies.
- The teacher introduces the book using a big-book version of the story and shares a book box of objects or pictures of objects mentioned in the story (e.g., cookie, glass of milk, straw, napkin, mirror, scissors, broom). The children talk about how the items might be used in the story.
- Children and the teacher begin the word wall with the words *cookie* and *mouse*.

2. Reading

- The teacher uses shared reading to read the big-book version of *If You Give a Mouse a Cookie*.
- The teacher rereads the book, and children join in when they can repeat each sentence after the teacher reads it.

3. Responding

- The children and the teacher talk about the book in a grand conversation.
- Children dramatize the story using objects in the book box.
- Children draw pictures in reading logs and add words and sentences (using invented spelling) to record their reactions to the book.

4. Exploring

- Children and teacher add important words to the word wall.
- Children read regular-size versions of the book with partners and reread the book independently.
- The teacher teaches minilessons on phonemic awareness and phonics concepts.
- The teacher explains the concept of a circular story, and children sequence picture cards of the events in the story to make a circle diagram.
- The teacher presents a minilesson about the author, Laura Numeroff, and reads other books by the author.
- Children make word posters of words on the word wall.
- The teacher teaches a minilesson on irregular plurals (e.g., *mouse—mice, child—children*).
- The teacher sets up centers for children to sort objects related to the phonemic awareness/phonics lesson, listen to *If You Give a Moose a Muffin* (Numeroff, 1991), write books about cookies, and use cards to sequence story events.

5. Applying

- Children write their own versions of the story or original circle stories.
- Children create a cookie quilt.

Two sixth graders come to the classroom to help supervise centers so Mrs. Kirkpatrick can concentrate on the reading groups. Children work at their own pace and move freely from center to center, carrying their work folders with them. Stapled inside the folders is a weekly list of centers, and the sixth grade aides place a stamp beside the center's name when children complete work there.

s there a magic age when children become readers and writers? Researchers used to think that at age 6, most children were ready to learn to read and write, but now we know that children begin the process of becoming literate gradually during the preschool years. Very young children notice signs, logos, and other environmental print. Who hasn't observed children making scribbles on paper as they try to "write"? As parents and caregivers read to young children, they learn how to hold a book and turn pages, and they observe how the text is read. Most children come to prekindergarten and kindergarten with sophisticated knowledge about written language and a background of experiences with reading and writing.

Language arts instruction in prekindergarten through first grade is known as *emergent literacy*, a term that New Zealand educator Marie Clay coined in 1966 (Vukelich & Christie, 2009). Researchers look at literacy learning from the child's point of view, and the age range has been extended to include children as young as 12 months of age who listen to stories being read aloud, notice labels and signs in their environment, and experiment with pencils. The concept of literacy has broadened, too, to incorporate the cultural and social aspects of language learning, and children's experiences with and understanding of written language—both reading and writing—are part of emergent literacy.

Teale and Sulzby (1989) paint a portrait of young children as written language learners with these characteristics:

- Learning the functions of literacy through observing and participating in real-life settings in which reading and writing are used
- Developing reading and writing abilities concurrently and interrelatedly through experiences in reading and writing
- Constructing their understanding of reading and writing through active involvement with literacy materials

They describe young children as active learners who construct their own knowledge about reading and writing with the assistance of parents and other literate people. The Common Core State Standards emphasize the importance of teaching children how reading and writing work. The box on page 62 highlights the emergent literacy standards; they address written language concepts, the alphabet, phonemic awareness, and phonics.

The No Child Left Behind Act of 2001 has brought unprecedented attention to how young children learn to read and write. Teachers and administrators, parents,

COMMON CORE STATE STANDARDS

Emergent Literacy

The Common Core State Standards emphasize concepts about print and the alphabet, phonemic awareness, and phonics. The purpose of these standards is to foster children's understanding of how reading and writing work. They highlight these points:

- Young children identify words, sentences, and other features of print.
- Young children recognize and name the letters of the alphabet.
- Young children name rhyming words, and blend and segment sounds in words.
- Young children understand the alphabetic principle and use phonics to decode words.

To learn more about the emergent literacy standards, go to http://www.corestandards.org, or check your state's language arts standards.

researchers, and policy makers are all focused on ensuring that every child reads at grade level by the end of third grade. Although all of the interested groups have the same goal, they're divided on the most effective ways to teach language arts in the primary grades. Many state and national policy makers contend that "scientific" evidence specifies that a skills-based, direct instruction approach is the most effective way, but many other teachers and researchers prefer a balanced approach of blending direct instruction with authentic reading and writing activities (Barone & Morrow, 2003; Burns, Griffin, & Snow, 1999; Cowen, 2003; National Reading Panel, 2000a; Vukelich & Christie, 2009). The approach taken in this book is that children are more successful when teachers use research-based practices to provide direct instruction within the context of meaningful literacy activities.

OSTERING CHILDREN'S INTEREST IN WRITTEN LANGUAGE

Children's introduction to written language begins before they come to school. Parents and other caregivers read to young children, and the children observe adults reading. They learn to read signs and other environmental print in their community. Children experiment with writing and have parents write for them. They also observe adults writing. When young children come to school, their knowledge about written language expands quickly as they participate in meaningful experiences with reading and writing.

Children also grow in their ability to stand back and reflect on language. The ability to talk about concepts of language is called *metalinguistics* (Yaden & Templeton, 1986), and children's ability to think metalinguistically develops through experiences with reading and writing.

Written Language Concepts

Through experiences at home and at school, young children learn that print carries meaning and that reading and writing are used for varied purposes (Bennett-Armistead, Duke, & Moses, 2005). They read menus in restaurants to know what foods are being served, write and receive letters to communicate with friends and relatives, and read (and listen to) stories for enjoyment. Children also learn as they observe parents and teachers using written language for all of these purposes.

Children's understanding about the purposes of reading and writing reflects how written language is used in their community. Although reading and writing are part of daily life for almost every family, families use written language for varied purposes in different communities (Heath, 1983b). It's important to realize that children have a wide range of literacy experiences in both middle- and working-class families, even though those experiences might be different (Taylor & Dorsey-Gaines, 1987). In some communities, written language is used mainly as a tool for practical purposes, such as paying bills, and in some communities, reading and writing are also used for leisure-time activities. In other communities, written language serves even wider functions, such as debating social and political issues.

Teachers demonstrate the purposes of written language and provide opportunities for children to experiment with reading and writing in these ways:

- Posting signs in the classroom
- Making a list of classroom rules
- Using literacy materials in dramatic play centers
- Writing notes to children in the class
- Exchanging messages with classmates
- Reading and writing stories
- Making posters about favorite books
- Labeling classroom items
- Drawing and writing in journals
- Writing morning messages
- Recording questions and information on charts
- Writing notes to parents
- Reading and writing letters to pen pals
- Reading and writing charts and maps

Concept of a Word. Children's understanding of the concept of a "word" is an important part of becoming literate. Young children have only vague notions of language terms, such as *word, letter, sound,* and *sentence,* that teachers use in talking about reading and writing (Invernizzi, 2003). Preschoolers equate words with the objects the words represent. As they're introduced to reading and writing experiences, children begin to differentiate between objects and words, and finally they come to appreciate that words have meanings of their own.

Researchers have investigated children's understanding of a "word" as a unit of language. Papandropoulou and Sinclair (1974) identified four stages of word consciousness. At first, young children don't differentiate between words and things, but at the next level, children describe words as labels for things. They consider words that stand for objects as words, but don't classify articles and prepositions as words because words such as *the* and *with* can't be represented with objects. At the third level, children understand that words carry meaning and that stories are built using words. At the fourth level, more fluent readers and writers describe words as autonomous elements having meanings of their own with definite semantic and syntactic relationships. Children might say, "You make words with letters." Also, at this level, children understand that words have different appearances—they can be spoken, listened to, read, and written.

Environmental Print. Young children's "reading" experiences often begin with environmental print. Many children begin reading by recognizing logos on fast-food restaurants, department stores, grocery stores, and commonly used household items within familiar contexts (Harste, Woodward, & Burke, 1984). They recognize the golden arches of McDonald's and say "McDonald's," but when they are shown the word *McDonald's* written on a sheet of paper without the familiar sign and restaurant setting, they can't read the word. Researchers have found that young emergent readers depend on context to read familiar words and memorized texts (Sulzby, 1985). Slowly, children develop relationships linking form and meaning as they learn concepts about written language and gain more experience reading and writing.

When children begin writing, they use scribbles or single letters to represent complex ideas (Clay, 1991). As they learn about letter names and phoneme-grapheme correspondences, they use one, two, or three letters to stand for a word. At first they run their writing together, but they gradually learn to segment words and leave spaces between words. They sometimes add dots or lines as markers between words, or they draw circles around words. They also move from capitalizing words randomly to using a capital letter at the beginning of a sentence and to mark proper nouns. Similarly, children move from using periods at the end of each line of writing to marking the ends of sentences with periods. Then they learn about other end-of-sentence markers and, finally, about punctuation marks that are embedded in sentences.

Literacy Play Centers. Young children learn about the functions of reading and writing as they use written language in their play. As they construct block buildings, children write signs and tape them on the buildings; as they play doctor, they write prescriptions on slips of paper; and as they play teacher, they read stories aloud to friends who are pretending to be students or to doll and stuffed-animal "students." Young children use these activities to reenact familiar, everyday activities and to pretend to be someone or something else. Through these literacy-enriched play activities, children use reading and writing for a variety of functions.

Prekindergarten and kindergarten teachers adapt play centers by adding literacy materials to enhance their value for written language learning. Housekeeping centers are probably the most common play centers, but teachers can transform them into grocery stores, post offices, or medical centers by changing the props and adding written language materials (Bennett-Armistead, Duke, & Moses, 2005). Food packages, price stickers, and money are props in grocery store centers; letters, stamps, and mailboxes in post office centers; and appointment books, prescription pads, and folders for patient records in medical centers. Literacy play centers can be set up to coordinate with thematic units. Figure 3–1 lists ideas for literacy play centers; each center includes authentic materials that children experiment with to learn more about the functions of written language.

Alphabet Concepts

Young children also develop concepts about the alphabet and how letters are used to represent sounds. Children use this phonics knowledge to decode unfamiliar words during reading and to create spellings as they write. Too often phonics is assumed to be the most important component of the reading instruction, but phonics is only one of the four language systems. Emergent readers and writers use all four language systems—phonological, semantic, syntactic, and pragmatic—as well as their knowledge about written language concepts as they read and write.

The Alphabetic Principle. The one-to-one correspondence between the phonemes (or sounds) and graphemes (or letters), such that each letter consistently represents one sound, is known as the *alphabetic principle*. In phonetic languages, there's a one-to-one correspondence, but English isn't a purely phonetic language. The 26 letters represent approximately 44 phonemes, and three letters—*c, q,* and *x*—are superfluous because they don't represent unique phonemes. The letter *c*, for example, can represent either /k/ as in *cat* or /s/ as in *city*, and it can be joined with *h* for the digraph /ch/. To further complicate matters, more than 500 spellings represent the 44 phonemes. Consonants are more consistent and predictable than vowels; long *e*, for instance, is spelled more than 10 ways in common words.

Words are spelled phonetically approximately half the time (Hanna, Hanna, Hodges, & Rudorf, 1966). The nonphonetic spellings of many words reflect morphological information. The word *sign*, for instance, is a shortened form of *signature*, and the spelling shows this relationship. Spelling the word phonetically (i.e., *sine*) might seem simpler, but the phonetic spelling lacks semantic information.

FIGURE 3–1   Literacy Play Centers

Post Office Center

mailboxes	wrapping paper	package seals
envelopes	tape	address labels
stamps (stickers)	packages	cash register
pens	scale	play money

Hairdresser Center

hair rollers	towel	curling iron (cordless)
brush and comb	posters of hairstyles	ribbons, barrettes, clips
mirror	wig and wig stand	appointment book
empty shampoo bottle	hair dryer (cordless)	open/closed sign

Restaurant Center

tablecloth	napkins	aprons/vests for waitstaff
dishes	menus	hat and apron for chef
silverware	tray	order pad and pencil

Medical Center

appointment books	thermometer	prescription pad
white shirt/jacket	tweezers	patient record folders
medical bag	bandages	prescription bottles
stethoscope		

Grocery Store Center

grocery cart	price stickers	grocery bags
food packages	cash register	cents-off coupons
plastic fruit/vegetables	play money	advertisements

Letter Names. The most basic information children learn about the alphabet is to identify letter names and form the letters in handwriting. They notice letters in environmental print and learn to sing the ABC song. Four- and five-year-olds recognize some letters, especially those in their own names, in names of family members and pets, and in common words in their neighborhood. They also write some of these familiar letters.

Young children associate letters with meaningful contexts—names, store signs, and cereal boxes. Children don't learn alphabet letter names in any particular order or by isolating letters from meaningful written language; instead, as McGee and Richgels (2012) conclude, learning letters of the alphabet requires many, many experiences with meaningful written language. They recommend that teachers take these steps to encourage children's alphabet learning:

CAPITALIZE ON CHILDREN'S INTERESTS. Teachers provide letter activities that children enjoy and talk about letters when children are interested in talking about them. Teachers know what features to comment on because they observe children during reading and writing activities to find out which letters or letter features children are exploring. Children's questions also provide insights into what they're curious about.

TALK ABOUT THE ROLE OF LETTERS IN READING AND WRITING. Teachers talk about how letters represent sounds and how letters combine to spell words, and they point out capital and lowercase letters. Teachers often talk about the role of letters as they write with children.

TEACH ROUTINES AND PROVIDE OPPORTUNITIES FOR ALPHABET LEARNING. To teach the letters of the alphabet, teachers use children's names and environmental print in literacy activities, do interactive writing, encourage children to use invented spellings, share alphabet books, and play letter games.

Teachers begin teaching letters of the alphabet using two sources of words—children's own names and environmental print. They also teach children to sing the ABC song so that they'll have a strategy to use to identify a particular letter: Children sing the song and point to each letter on an alphabet chart until they reach the unfamiliar letter. This is an important strategy because it gives them the ability to identify unfamiliar letters. Teachers also provide routines, activities, and games for talking about and manipulating letters. During these familiar, predictable activities, teachers and children say letter names, manipulate magnetic letters, and write letters on whiteboards. At first the teacher guides the activities, but with experience, the children internalize the routine and do it independently, often at a literacy center. Figure 3-2 presents 10 routines to teach the letters of the alphabet.

It's crucial that explicit instruction to teach children to identify and print the letters of the alphabet be embedded in meaningful and authentic reading and writing experiences. Instruction is meaningful when children can tie what they're learning to their own world and authentic when they can apply what they're learning to reading and writing stories and other books. Children recognize and write the letters found in environmental print and in their classmates' names, find familiar letters and words on classroom signs and in books, write letters and words as they respond to literature, and make books.

Being able to name the letters of the alphabet is a good predictor of beginning reading achievement, even though knowing the names of the letters doesn't directly affect a child's ability to read (Adams, 1990). A more likely explanation for this relationship between letter knowledge and reading is that children who have been actively involved in reading and writing activities before entering first grade know the names of the letters, and they're more likely to begin reading quickly. Simply teaching children to name the letters without the accompanying reading and writing experiences doesn't have this effect.

Phonemic Awareness. *Phonemic awareness* refers to children's basic understanding that speech is composed of a series of individual sounds, and it provides the foundation for phonics (Yopp, 1992). When children can choose a duck as the animal that begins with /d/ from a collection of toy animals, identify *duck* and *luck* as rhyming words, or blend the sounds /d//ŭ//k/ to pronounce *duck*, they're phonemically aware. The emphasis is on the sounds of spoken words, not reading letters or pronouncing letter names. Developing phonemic awareness enables children to use sound-symbol correspondences to read and spell words. It isn't sounding out words for reading or using spelling patterns to write words; rather, it's the ability to manipulate sounds orally.

Understanding that words are composed of smaller units—phonemes—is a significant achievement for young children because phonemes are abstract language units. Phonemes carry no meaning, and children think of words according to their meanings, not their linguistic characteristics (Griffith & Olson, 1992). When children think about ducks, for example, they think of animals covered with feathers that swim in ponds and make noises we describe as "quacks"; they don't think of *duck* as a word with three phonemes or four graphemes or as a word beginning with /d/ and rhyming with *luck*. Phonemic awareness requires that children treat speech as an object. They shift their attention away from the meaning of words to the linguistic features of speech. This focus on phonemes is even more complicated because phonemes are not discrete units in speech. Often they are slurred together; think about the blended initial sound in *tree* and the ending sound in *eating*.

Children develop phonemic awareness in two ways. They learn playfully as they sing songs, chant rhymes, and listen to parents and teachers read wordplay books to them. Yopp (1995) recommends that teachers read books with wordplay aloud and encourage children to talk about the books' language. Teachers ask questions and make comments, such as "Did you notice how _____ and _____ rhyme?" and "This book is fun because of all the words beginning with the _____ sound." Once children are very familiar with the book, they can create new verses or make other variations. Books such as *Cock-a-Doodle-Moo!* (Most, 1996), *The Hungry Thing* (Slepian & Seidler, 2001), and *The Stuffed Animals Get Ready for Bed* (Inches, 2006) stimulate children to experiment with sounds, create nonsense words, and become enthusiastic about reading. When teachers read books with alliterative or assonant patterns, such as *Busy Buzzing Bumblebees and Other Tongue Twisters* (A. Schwartz, 1992), children attend to the smaller units of language.

FIGURE 3–2   Routines to Teach the ABCs

Environmental Print
Teachers collect food labels, toy traffic signs, and other examples of environmental print for children to use in identifying letters. Children sort labels and other materials to find examples of a letter being studied.

Alphabet Books
Teachers read aloud alphabet books to build vocabulary and teach the names of words that represent each letter. Then children reread the books and consult them to think of words when making books about a letter.

Magnetic Letters
Children pick all examples of one letter from a collection of magnetic letters or match upper- and lowercase letterforms. They also arrange the letters in alphabetical order and use the letters to spell their names and other familiar words.

Letter Stamps
Students use letter stamps and ink pads to stamp letters on paper or in booklets. They also paint letters using letter-shaped sponges and make cookies using letter-shaped cookie cutters.

Key Words
Teachers use alphabet charts with a picture of a familiar object for each letter. It's crucial that children be familiar with the objects or they won't remember the key words. Teachers recite the alphabet with children, pointing to each letter and saying, "A—apple, B—bear, C—cat," and so on.

Letter Containers
Teachers collect coffee cans or shoe boxes, one for each letter. They write upper- and lowercase letters on the outside of the containers and place several familiar objects or pictures of objects representing the letter in each one. Teachers use these containers to introduce the letters, and children use them at a center for sorting and matching activities.

Letter Frames
Teachers make circle-shaped letter frames from tagboard, collect large plastic bracelets, or shape pipe cleaners or Wikki-Stix (pipe cleaners covered in wax) into circles for students to use to highlight particular letters on charts or in big books.

Letter Books and Posters
Children make letter books with pictures of objects beginning with a particular letter on each page. They add letter stamps, stickers, or pictures cut from magazines. For posters, the teacher draws a large letterform on a chart and children add pictures, stickers, and letter stamps.

Letter Sorts
Teachers collect objects and pictures representing two or more letters. Then children sort the objects and place them in containers marked with the specific letters.

Whiteboards
Children practice writing upper- and lowercase forms of letters and familiar words on whiteboards.

Teachers also teach lessons to help children understand that their speech is composed of sounds (Ball & Blachman, 1991). The goal of phonemic awareness activities is to break down and manipulate spoken words. Children who have developed phonemic awareness can manipulate spoken language in these five ways:

- Match words by sounds
- Isolate a sound in a word
- Blend individual sounds to form a word
- Substitute sounds in a word
- Segment a word into its constituent sounds (Yopp, 1992)

Teachers teach minilessons focusing on each of these tasks using familiar songs with improvised lyrics, riddles and guessing games, and wordplay books. These activities should be playful and gamelike. Figure 3–3 describes different types of phonemic awareness routines.

Children experiment with oral language in these wordplay activities. Teachers have avoided asking children to read and write letters and words during these activities because the focus is on speech. More recently, however, teachers are finding that once children develop a rudimentary level of phonemic awareness, the activities are more effective when teachers begin with an oral language activity and then move into decoding and spelling words.

The relationship between phonemic awareness and learning to read is extremely important. Researchers have concluded that some phonemic awareness is a prerequisite for learning to read (Gillon, 2004). Interestingly, phonemic awareness seems to be both a prerequisite for and a consequence of learning to read (Perfitti, Beck, Bell, & Hughes, 1987). As they become phonemically aware, children recognize that speech can be segmented into smaller units, and this knowledge is very useful when children learn about sound-symbol correspondences and spelling patterns. Moreover, phonemic awareness is the most powerful predictor of later reading achievement. Klesius, Griffith, and Zielonka (1991) found that children who began first grade with strong phonemic awareness did well regardless of the kind of reading instruction they received.

Phonics. *Phonics* is the set of relationships between phonology (the sounds in speech) and orthography (the spelling patterns of written language). Sounds are spelled in different ways, for several reasons. One reason is that sounds, especially vowels, vary according to their location in a word (e.g., *go–got*). Adjacent letters often influence how letters are pronounced (e.g., *bed–bead*), as do vowel markers such as the final *e* (e.g., *bit–bite*) (Shefelbine, 1995).

Phonics has been a controversial topic for years. At first, some parents and politicians, as well as even a few teachers, believed that many of our educational ills could be solved if children were taught to read using a phonics-only program, but that view ignores what we know about the interrelatedness of the four language systems. Now the controversy centers on how to teach phonics. Marilyn Adams (1990), in her landmark review of the research on phonics instruction, recommends that phonics be taught within a balanced approach that integrates instruction in reading strategies and skills with meaningful opportunities for reading and writing. She emphasizes that phonics instruction should focus on teaching the most useful information for identifying words; it also should be systematic and intensive, and it should be completed by the third grade.

Teachers teach sound-symbol correspondences, how to blend sounds to decode words and segment sounds for spelling, and the most useful phonics generalizations, or "rules." Phonics concepts build on phonemic awareness. The most important concepts that children learn are consonants, vowels, rimes and rhymes, and phonics generalizations:

FIGURE 3–3   Phonemic Awareness Routines

Sound Matching
Teachers create matching games using familiar objects and pictures. From a collection, children choose two items that begin with the same sound. Or, children choose one of several items beginning with a particular sound. Children also identify rhyming words: They name a word that rhymes with a given word and identify rhyming words from familiar songs and books.

Sound Isolation
Children identify the sounds at the beginning, middle, or end of the word, or from a collection of objects children choose the one that doesn't begin with the sound. Yopp (1992) created new verses to sing to the tune of "Old MacDonald Had a Farm":

What's the sound that starts these words:
Chicken, chin, and cheek?
(wait for response)
/ch/ is the sound that starts these words:
Chicken, chin, and cheek.
With a /ch/, /ch/ here, and a /ch/, /ch/ there,
Here a /ch/, there a /ch/, everywhere a /ch/, /ch/.
/ch/ is the sound that starts these words:
Chicken, chin, and cheek. (p. 700)

Teachers change the question at the beginning of the verse to focus on medial and final sounds.

Sound Blending
Children play the "What am I thinking of?" guessing game. The teacher identifies several characteristics of an object and pronounces its name, articulating each of the sounds separately (Yopp, 1992). Then children blend the sounds together and identify the word using the phonological and semantic information that the teacher provided. For example:

I am thinking of an animal that lives in a pond when it's young, but that lives on land when it's an adult. It's a /f/ /r/ /ŏ/ /g/. What is it?

The children blend the sounds together to pronounce the word *frog*.

Sound Addition or Substitution
Children create nonsense words as they add or substitute sounds in words in song lyrics and in wordplay books that teachers read aloud. For example, in Hutchins's *Don't Forget the Bacon!* (2002), a boy leaves for the store with a mental list of four items to buy. As he walks, he repeats his list, substituting sounds and creating new words each time. "A cake for tea" becomes "a cape for me" and then "a rake for leaves." Children suggest other substitutions, such as "a pail for maple sugar trees." They also substitute sounds in song refrains (Yopp, 1992). For example, children change the "Ee-igh, ee-igh, oh!" refrain in "Old MacDonald Had a Farm" to "Bee-bigh, bee-bigh, boh!" to focus on the initial /b/ sound, or teachers choose one sound, such as /sh/, and children substitute this sound for the beginning sound in their names and in familiar words: *José* becomes *Shosé* and *clock* becomes *shock*.

Segmentation
Children slowly pronounce a word, identifying all its sounds. Yopp (1992) suggests singing a song to the tune of "Twinkle, Twinkle, Little Star" in which children segment entire words. Here's one example:

Listen, listen, to my word.
Then tell me all the sounds you heard: *coat*
/k/ is one sound, /o/ is two
/t/ is last in *coat*; it's true. (p. 702)

After several repetitions of the verse segmenting other words, the song ends this way:

Thanks for listening to my words
And telling all the sounds you heard! (p. 702)

CONSONANTS. Letters are classified as either consonants or vowels. The consonants are *b, c, d, f, g, h, j, k, l, m, n, p, q, r, s, t, v, w, x, y,* and *z.* Most consonants represent a single sound consistently, but there are exceptions. *C,* for example, doesn't represent a sound of its own: When it's followed by *a, o,* or *u,* it's pronounced /k/ (e.g., *castle, coffee, cut*), and when it's followed by *e, i,* or *y,* it's pronounced /s/ (e.g., *cell, city, cycle*). *G* represents two sounds, as the word *garbage* illustrates. It's usually pronounced /g/ (e.g., *glass, go, green, guppy*), but when *g* is followed by *e* or *i,* it's pronounced /j/, as in *giant. Gy* isn't a common English spelling, but when *g* is followed by *y* (e.g., *energy, gypsy, gymnasium*), it's usually pronounced /j/. *X* is also pronounced differently according to its location in a word. When *x* is at the beginning of a word, it's often pronounced /z/, as in *xylophone,* but sometimes the letter name is used, as in *x-ray.* At the end of a word, *x* is pronounced /ks/, as in *box.* The letters *w* and *y* are particularly interesting: At the beginning of a word or syllable, they're consonants (e.g., *wind, yard*), but in the middle or at the end of a word or syllable, they're vowels (e.g., *saw, flown, day, by*). Combination consonants are blends and digraphs. *Consonant blends* are two or three consonants that appear next to each other and the individual sounds are blended together, as in *grass, belt,* and *spring. Consonant digraphs* are letter combinations that represent single sounds. The four most common are *ch* as in *chair* and *each, sh* as in *shell* and *wish, th* as in *father* and *both,* and *wh* as in *whale.* Another consonant digraph is *ph,* as in *graph* and *photo.*

VOWELS. The five letters *a, e, i, o,* and *u* are vowels, and *w* and *y* are vowels when they're used in the middle and at the end of syllables and words. Vowels represent several sounds; the most common are short and long vowels. The short vowel sounds are pronounced as /ă/ as in *cat,* /ĕ/ as in *bed,* /ĭ/ as in *win,* /ŏ/ as in *hot,* and /ŭ/ as in *cup.* The long vowel sounds are pronounced like the letter names; they're illustrated in *make, feet, bike, coal,* and *suit.* Long vowels are usually spelled with two vowels, except when *e* or *y* is used at the end of a word or syllable (e.g., *belong, try*). When *y* is a single vowel, it's pronounced as long *e* or long *i,* depending on the word's length: In one-syllable words (e.g., *by* and *try*), *y* is pronounced as long *i,* but in most longer words (e.g., *baby* and *happy*), it's pronounced as long *e.* Many vowel combinations represent long vowels and other vowel sounds, such as *au* as in *laugh* and *caught, aw* as in *saw, ea* as in *peach* and *bread, oa* as in *soap, oi/oy* as in *oil* and *toy, oo* as in *cook* and *moon, ou* as in *house* and *through,* and *ow* as in *now* and *snow.* Most vowel combinations are vowel digraphs or diphthongs. When two vowels represent a single sound, the combination is a vowel digraph (e.g., *nail, snow*), and when two vowels represent a glide from one sound to another, the combination is a diphthong. Two vowel combinations that are consistently diphthongs are *oi* and *oy,* but other combinations, such as *ou* in *house* (but not in *through*) and *ow* in *now* (but not in *snow*) are diphthongs only when they represent a glided sound. In *through,* the *ou* represents the sound o̅o̅ as in *moon,* and in *snow,* the *ow* represents the ō sound. When *r* follows one or more vowels in a word, it influences the pronunciation of the vowel sound, as in *car, air, are, ear, bear, first, for, more, murder,* and *pure;* these sounds are called *r-controlled vowels.* Because they're difficult to sound out, students learn these words as sight words. In multisyllabic words, the vowels in the unaccented syllables are often softened and pronounced "uh," as in the first syllable of *about* and *machine* and the final syllable of *pencil, tunnel,* and *selection.* This vowel sound is called a *schwa* and is represented in dictionaries with ə, which looks like an inverted *e.*

RIMES AND RHYMES. One-syllable words and syllables in longer words can be divided into two parts, the onset and the rime. The onset is the consonant sound, if any, that precedes the vowel and the rime is the vowel and any consonant sounds that follow it. For example, in *show, sh* is the onset and *ow* is the rime, and in *ball, b* is the onset and *all* is the rime. For *at* and *up,* there is no onset; the entire word is the rime. Research has shown that children make more errors decoding and spelling final consonants than initial consonants and that

FIGURE 3–4   The 37 Rimes

Rime	Examples	Rime	Examples
-ack	black, pack, quack, stack	-ide	bride, hide, ride, side
-ail	mail, nail, sail, tail	-ight	bright, fight, light, might
-ain	brain, chain, plain, rain	-ill	fill, hill, kill, will
-ake	cake, shake, take, wake	-in	chin, grin, pin, win
-ale	male, sale, tale, whale	-ine	fine, line, mine, nine
-ame	came, flame, game, name	-ing	king, sing, thing, wing
-an	can, man, pan, than	-ink	pink, sink, think, wink
-ank	bank, drank, sank, thank	-ip	drip, hip, lip, ship
-ap	cap, clap, map, slap	-ir	fir, sir, stir
-ash	cash, dash, flash, trash	-ock	block, clock, knock, sock
-at	bat, cat, rat, that	-oke	choke, joke, poke, woke
-ate	gate, hate, late, plate	-op	chop, drop, hop, shop
-aw	claw, draw, jaw, saw	-or	for, or
-ay	day, play, say, way	-ore	chore, more, shore, store
-eat	beat, heat, meat, wheat	-uck	duck, luck, suck, truck
-ell	bell, sell, shell, well	-ug	bug, drug, hug, rug
-est	best, chest, nest, west	-ump	bump, dump, hump, lump
-ice	ice, mice, nice, rice	-unk	bunk, dunk, junk, sunk
-ick	brick, pick, sick, thick		

they make more errors on vowels than on consonants (Treiman, 1985). These problem areas correspond to rimes, and researchers now speculate that teaching onsets and rimes could provide a key to developing children's phonemic awareness.

Children can focus their attention on a rime, such as *ay*, and create rhyming words, including *bay, day, lay, may, play, say*, and *way*. These words can be read and spelled by analogy because the vowel sounds are consistent in rimes. Wylie and Durrell (1970) identified 37 rimes that can be used to produce nearly 500 words that children learn to read and write. Figure 3–4 lists these rimes and some common words using them.

PHONICS GENERALIZATIONS. Because English doesn't have a one-to-one correspondence between sounds and letters, generalizations or rules clarify English spelling patterns. One rule is that *q* is followed by *u* and pronounced /kw/ (e.g., *queen* and *earthquake*), and there are very few exceptions. Another generalization with few exceptions focuses on *r*-controlled vowels: *r* influences the preceding vowel so that its sound is neither long nor short (e.g., *car, market, birth*, and *four*). There are exceptions, however; for instance, *fire*.

Many generalizations aren't very useful because there are more exceptions to the rule than words that conform (Clymer, 1996). A good example is the "when two vowels go walking" rule: When two vowels are side by side, the long vowel sound of the first one is pronounced and the second is silent. Examples of words conforming to this rule are *meat, soap*, and *each*, but there are more exceptions, including *food, said, head, chief, bread, look, soup, does, too, again*, and *believe*.

Only a few phonics generalizations are useful. Students should learn those that work most of the time (Adams, 1990). Figure 3–5 lists eight high-utility generalizations. Even though these rules are fairly reliable, very few of them approach 100% utility. The *r*-controlled vowel rule is useful in 78% of words in which the letter *r* follows the vowel (Adams, 1990), but other commonly taught rules have even lower percentages of utility. The CVC pattern rule—which says that when a one-syllable word has only one vowel and the vowel comes between two consonants, it is usually short, as in *bat, land*, and *cup*—is estimated to work 62% of the time. Exceptions include *told, fall, fork*, and *comb*. The CVCe pattern rule—which says that when there are two vowels in a one-syllable word and one vowel is an *e* at the end of the word, the first vowel is long and the final *e* is silent—is estimated to work in 63% of CVCe words. Examples of conforming words are *came, hole*, and *pipe*, and two very common exceptions are *have* and *love*.

Children acquire some concepts about phonics as a natural part of reading and writing activities, but teachers teach phonics directly and systematically in the primary grades. They explain many phonics concepts as they engage children in authentic literacy activities using children's names and environmental print. During these teachable moments, teachers answer children's questions about words, model how to use phonics knowledge to decode and spell words, and have children share the strategies they use for reading and writing. For example, as part of a literature focus unit on *The Very Hungry Caterpillar* (Carle, 2001), teachers might point out that *very* begins with *v* but that not many words do. Children might mention other

FIGURE 3–5   Useful Phonics Generalizations

Pattern	Description	Examples	
Two sounds of *c*	The letter c can be pronounced as /k/ or /s/. When *c* is followed by *a, o*, or *u*, it's pronounced /k/—the hard *c* sound. When *c* is followed by *e, i*, or *y*, it's pronounced /s/—the soft *c* sound.	cat cough cut	cent city cycle
Two sounds of *g*	The letter g can be pronounced as /g/ or /j/. When *g* is followed by *a, o*, or *u*, it's pronounced /g/—the hard *g* sound. When *g* is followed by *e, i*, or *y*, it's usually pronounced /j/—the soft *g* sound. Exceptions include *get* and *give*.	gate go guess	gentle giant gypsy
CVC pattern	When a one-syllable word has only one vowel and the vowel comes between two consonants, it's usually short. One exception is *told*.	bat cup land	
CVCe pattern	When there are two vowels in a one-syllable word and one of them is an *e* at the end of the word, the first vowel is long and the final *e* is silent. Two exceptions are *have* and *done*.	home safe dune	
CV pattern	When a vowel follows a consonant in a one-syllable word, the vowel is long. Exceptions include *the, to*, and *do*.	go be	
r-controlled vowels	Vowels that are followed by the letter *r* are overpowered and are neither short nor long. One exception is *fire*.	car for birthday	
-igh	When *gh* follows *i*, the *i* is long and the *gh* is silent. Two exceptions are *neighbor* and *eight*.	high night	
kn- and *wr-*	In words beginning with *kn-* and *wr-*, the first letter isn't pronounced.	knee write	

Based on Clymer, 1996.

v words, such as *valentine*. Teachers also demonstrate how to apply phonics information as they read big books with the class and do interactive writing. As they read and spell words, teachers break words apart into sounds and apply phonics concepts and generalizations.

Teachers also teach minilessons on high-utility phonics concepts and generalizations as part of a systematic program. According to Shefelbine, the program should be "systematic and thorough enough to enable most students to become independent and fluent readers; yet still efficient and streamlined" (1995, p. 2). Phonics instruction is always tied to reading and writing because without meaningful reading and writing applications, children see little reason to learn phonics (Cunningham, 2009).

INTEGRATING TECHNOLOGY

Today, young children are immersed in electronic and interactive media. Three-, four-, and five-year-olds observe as adults use digital media for communication and entertainment, and they explore and learn from technology tools themselves. Children are digital natives (Prensky, 2006), approaching learning and literacy development in ways that weren't possible a decade ago. Computers, ebooks, smart toys, and other types of digital media are transforming early reading and writing development (Blanchard & Moore, 2010; Coiro, Knobel, Lankshear, & Leu, 2008):

TELEVISION. When you think about educational television programming for young children, you probably think of the venerable Sesame Street program featuring Big Bird, Elmo, Cookie Monster, Oscar the Grouch, and other Muppets and human characters. After 40 years, Sesame Street has received many awards and is recognized as having a significant educational impact on its viewers. Today, many other excellent TV programs are available, including Blue's Clues, Dora the Explorer, Word Girl, and The Electric Company, and these programs are linked to affiliate websites and podcasts. There are more opportunities for children to interact with these programs, too; they're asked to make choices, shout out encouragement, and sing along. In some programs, the emphasis is on written language; for instance, the characters in the PBS Kids series SuperWhy! have unique literacy super powers and teach letter recognition, spelling, and reading comprehension.

EBOOKS. Electronic books are digital versions of stories, and these picture books enhance children's reading experience using animation and interaction. The most popular collection of handheld electronic books for beginning readers is LeapFrog's Tag Reading Series. Children use a Tag pointer to read stories and play interactive games. More than 40 titles are available in the LeapFrog library. Other ebooks are available in online libraries; each word in these books is highlighted as it's read aloud. PBS's Between the Lions offers a free collection of high-quality online fiction and nonfiction books on topics ranging from feelings to food, but other websites charge fees. Sesame Street (http://ebooks.sesamestreet.org) offers a monthly subscription service to its collection of more than 125 books, and Tumble Books' library (http://www.tumblebooks.com) contains more than 200 ebooks, including *How I Became a Pirate* (Long, 2003) and *Diary of a Fly* (Cronin, 2007).

DIGITIZED TOYS. Children's play increasingly involves digitized toys, including talking animals, interactive board games, and Leap Frog and other toys equipped with learning software. These toys often feature characters from Disney and Pixar movies, including Ariel, Woody, Buzz Lightyear, and Lightning McQueen.

COMPUTERS. Young children are fascinated with computers, and they can easily learn to use a mouse to point and click and play software programs on home and school computers. In addition, some computers are specifically designed for 4- and 5-year-olds, including

PeeWee PC, Disney Netpal, and Intel Classmate. These kid-friendly computers are durable and inexpensive, and some have touch screens and offer USB ports and wireless capabilities.

WEBSITES. At age-appropriate websites, including PBS Kids, Scholastic, KerPoof, Webkinz Jr., National Geographic Little Kids, Nick Jr., Thomas and Friends, and Jump Start, young children play games, view videos, do craft projects, and participate in other interactive activities.

VIDEO GAMES. Young children play games using handheld electronic game boards with color LCD screens and sound effects, such as the Nintendo DS and LeapFrog's Leapster. These game boards use game cartridges offering multiple levels of game play. Children also play video games based on TV programs, movies, and book characters, such as Dora the Explorer, Blue's Clues, Clifford, the Big Red Dog, and Word Girl, that are available at Nick Jr, PBS Kids, and other websites.

SMART PHONES. Children borrow their parents' smart phones and play games using applications, such as Tickle Tap, SuperWhy!, and Toggle, that develop fine motor skills and support emergent readers' literacy development. They also can read "Itsy Bitsy Spider," "Wheels on the Bus," and other ebooks using storybook apps.

Involving young children in digital technology clearly affects their academic success (Wohlwend, 2010). In addition to enhanced literacy knowledge, they develop the fine motor skills needed for keyboarding and the problem-solving abilities necessary for navigating search engines. They also develop the ability to multitask, to moderate their attention according to the difficulty of the activity, and to attend to confusing content for longer periods. ■

YOUNG CHILDREN BECOME READERS

Children move through three stages as they learn to read: emergent reading, beginning reading, and fluent reading (Juel, 1991). In emergent reading, children gain an understanding of the communicative purpose of print. They notice environmental print, dictate stories for the teacher to record, and reread predictable books after they've memorized the pattern. With this foundation, children move into the beginning reading stage where they learn phoneme-grapheme correspondences and begin to decode words. In the third stage, fluent reading, children have learned to read most words automatically and decode unfamiliar words quickly; children should reach this stage by third grade. Once they're fluent readers, children can concentrate more of their cognitive energy on comprehension. This accomplishment is significant, because beginning in fourth grade, reading becomes a learning tool.

Primary grade teachers organize language arts instruction into the same four patterns of practice that teachers of older students use, but they make special adaptations to accommodate young children's developing written language abilities. Two instructional adaptations that preK–2 teachers use are shared reading and the Language Experience Approach.

Shared Reading

Teachers and children read books together in shared reading. Usually the teacher reads aloud as children follow along in regular-size or enlarged, big-book picture books. Teachers use this approach to share the enjoyment of high-quality literature when students can't read the books independently (Fisher & Medvic, 2000; Holdaway, 1979). As they read, teachers also demonstrate how print works, provide opportunities for children to use the prediction strategy, and increase children's confidence in their ability to read. Shared reading is often used with emergent readers; however, teachers also use shared reading with older students who can't read independently. The steps in shared reading are listed in the Step-by-Step feature on the next page.

Step-by-Step: SHARED READING

1 **Introduce the book.** Teachers introduce the book by activating children's prior knowledge about the topic or by presenting new information on a topic related to the book, and then by showing the cover of the book and reading the title and the author's name. Then children make predictions about what will happen in the book.

2 **Read the book.** The teacher reads the book aloud while children follow along in individual copies or on a big book positioned on a rack beside the teacher. The teacher models fluent reading and uses a dramatic style to keep the children's attention. Teachers encourage children to chime in on words they know and on refrains. Periodically, teachers ask children to make predictions to redirect their attention to the text.

3 **Respond to the book.** Children respond to the book by drawing and writing in reading logs and by sharing their responses in grand conversations.

4 **Reread the book.** Children take turns using the pointer to track the text and turning pages as they read the book. Teachers invite children to join in reading familiar and predictable words. Also, they take advantage of teachable moments to explain phonics concepts and reading strategies.

5 **Continue the process.** Teachers continue to reread the book with children one or two more times over a period of several days, again having them turn pages and take turns using the pointer to track the text while reading. They encourage children who can read the text to read along with them.

6 **Read independently.** After children become familiar with the text, teachers distribute individual copies of the book for children to read independently.

Predictable Books. The stories and other books teachers use for shared reading with young children often have repeated words and sentences, rhyme, or other patterns; books that use these patterns are known as *predictable books*. The repeated words and sentences, patterns, and sequence enable children to predict the next sentence or episode in the story or other book (Tompkins & Webeler, 1983). Predictable books have these characteristics:

REPETITION. Phrases and sentences are repeated to create a predictable pattern in many books for young children. Examples include *I Went Walking* (S. Williams, 1990), *Barnyard Banter* (Fleming, 1994), and *Polar Bear, Polar Bear, What Do You Hear?* (Martin, 1992). Sometimes each episode or section ends with the same words or a refrain, and in other books, the same statement or question is repeated. For example, in *The Little Red Hen* (Pinkney, 2006), the animals repeat "Not I" when the Little Red Hen asks them to help her plant the seeds, harvest the wheat, and bake the bread. After their refusals to help, the hen each time says, "Then I will."

CUMULATIVE SEQUENCE. Phrases or sentences are repeated and expanded in each episode in these books. In the traditional story *The Gingerbread Boy* (Galdone, 2008), for instance, Gingerbread Boy repeats and expands his boast as he meets each character on his run away from Little Old Man and Little Old Woman. Other examples include *Jack's Garden* (Cole, 1997) and *Jump, Frog, Jump!* (Kalan, 2002).

RHYME AND RHYTHM. Rhyme and rhythm are important devices in some books. Many of the popular Dr. Seuss books, such as *Hop on Pop* (2003), are good examples. The sentences have a strong beat, and rhyme is used at the end of each line or in another poetic scheme. Also, some books have an internal rhyme—within lines rather than at the ends of lines. Other books in this category include familiar songs, such as *Shoo Fly!* (Trapani, 2000), and book-long verses, such as *Pattern Fish* (Harris, 2000).

SEQUENTIAL PATTERNS. Some books use a familiar sequence—such as months of the year, days of the week, numbers 1 to 10, or letters of the alphabet—to structure the text. For example, *The Very Hungry Caterpillar* (Carle, 2001) combines number and day-of-the-week sequences as the caterpillar eats through an amazing array of foods, and *Shiver Me Letters: A Pirate ABC* (Sobel, 2006) incorporates an alphabet sequence.

The Booklist on the next page presents predictable books illustrating each of these patterns.

Big Books. Teachers use enlarged picture books called *big books* in shared reading, most commonly with preK–2 students (Ditzel, 2000). In this technique, developed in New Zealand, teachers place the enlarged picture book on an easel or chart rack where all children can see it, and the teacher reads the book aloud with small groups or with the whole class (Holdaway, 1979). Trachtenburg and Ferruggia (1989) used big books with their class of transitional first graders and found that making and reading big books dramatically improved children's reading scores on standardized achievement tests. The teachers reported that children's self-concepts as readers were improved as well.

Many popular picture books, including *Click, Clack, Moo: Cows That Type* (Cronin, 2011), *How Much Is a Million?* (D. Schwartz, 1994), *There Was an Old Lady Who Swallowed a Fly* (Taback, 1997), and *Eating the Alphabet: Fruits and Vegetables From A to Z* (Ehlert, 2006), are available in big-book editions from Scholastic. Teachers and children can also make big books themselves by printing the text of a book on large sheets of posterboard and adding illustrations.

Cross-Age Reading Buddies. Another way to use shared reading in kindergarten and first grade is with cross-age reading buddies. Upper grade students are paired with emergent readers, and the students become reading buddies. Older students read books with younger children, using shared reading techniques so that the younger children do more and more of the reading as they become familiar with the book. Research supports the effectiveness of cross-age tutoring, and teachers report that children's reading fluency increases and their attitudes toward school and learning become more positive (Caserta-Henry, 1996).

Teachers arranging a buddy reading program decide when the students will get together, how long each session will last, and what the reading schedule will be. Primary grade teachers explain the program to their students and talk about activities the buddies will do together. Upper grade teachers teach a series of minilessons about how to work with young children, how to read aloud and encourage children to make predictions, how to use shared reading, how to select books to appeal to younger children, and how to help them respond to books. Then older students choose books to read aloud and practice reading them until they can read the books fluently.

At the first meeting, students pair off, get acquainted, and read together. They also talk about the books they have read and perhaps write in special reading logs. Buddies also may want to go to the library and choose the books they'll read at the next session.

There are significant social benefits to cross-age tutoring programs. Children get acquainted with other children that they might otherwise not meet, and they learn how to work with older or younger children. As they talk about books they've read, they share personal experiences. They also talk about reading strategies, how to choose books, and their favorite authors or illustration styles. Sometimes reading buddies write notes back and forth, or they plan holiday celebrations together to strengthen the social connections between the children.

Traveling Bags of Books.   Another way to encourage shared reading is to involve parents by using traveling bags of books. Teachers collect text sets of three or four books on various topics for children to take home and read with their parents (Reutzel & Fawson, 1990). For example, teachers might collect copies of *The Gingerbread Boy* (Galdone, 2008), *Flossie and the Fox* (McKissack, 1992), *Fox and His Friends* (Marshall, 1994), and *Rosie's Walk* (Hutchins, 2005) for a traveling bag of fox stories. Then children and their parents read one or more of the books and draw or write a response to the books they've read in the reading log that accompanies the books in the traveling bag. Children keep the bag at home for several days and then return it to school so that another child can borrow it. Teachers can also add small toys, stuffed animals, audiotapes of one of the books, or other related objects to the bags.

Booklist

PREDICTABLE BOOKS	
Repetitive Sentences	Florian, D. (2000). *A pig is big*. New York: Greenwillow. Guarino, D. (2006). *Is your mama a llama?* New York: Scholastic. Hoberman, M. A. (2001). *"It's simple," said Simon*. New York: Knopf. Martin, B., Jr. (2010). *Brown bear, brown bear, what do you see?* New York: Holt. Westcott, N. B. (2003). *The lady with the alligator purse*. Boston: Little, Brown.
Cumulative Sentences	Brett, J. (2004). *The umbrella*. New York: Putnam. Egielski, R. (1997). *The gingerbread boy*. New York: HarperCollins. Pinkney, J. (2006). *The little red hen*. New York: Dial Books. Taback, S. (1997). *There was an old lady who swallowed a fly*. New York: Viking. West, C. (1996). *"I don't care!" said the bear*. Cambridge, MA: Candlewick Press.
Rhyme and Rhythm	Harris, P. (2006). *The night pirates*. New York: Scholastic. Lies, B. (2006). *Bats at the beach*. Boston: Houghton Mifflin. Martin, B., Jr., & Archambault, J. (2009). *Chicka chicka boom boom*. New York: Beach Lane Books. Raffi. (1999). *Down by the bay*. New York: Crown.
Sequential Patterns	Carle, E. (1984). *The very busy spider*. New York: Philomel. Kraus, R. (1995). *Come out and play, little mouse*. New York: HarperCollins. Numeroff, L. J. (2002). *If you take a mouse to school*. New York: HarperCollins. Wadsworth, O. A. (2002). *Over in the meadow*. New York: North-South Books. Wood, A. (2004). *The napping house*. San Diego: Harcourt Brace.

Teachers often introduce traveling bags at a special parents' meeting or an open house get-together and explain how parents use shared reading to read with their children. It's important for parents to understand that their children may not be familiar with the books and that they aren't expected to be able to read them independently. Teachers also talk about the responses that children and parents write in the reading log and show sample entries from the previous year.

Language Experience Approach

The Language Experience Approach (LEA) is based on children's language and experiences (Ashton-Warner, 1965; Stauffer, 1970). Children dictate words and sentences about their experiences, and the teacher takes down the dictation for them; the text they develop becomes the reading material. Because the language comes from the children themselves, and because the

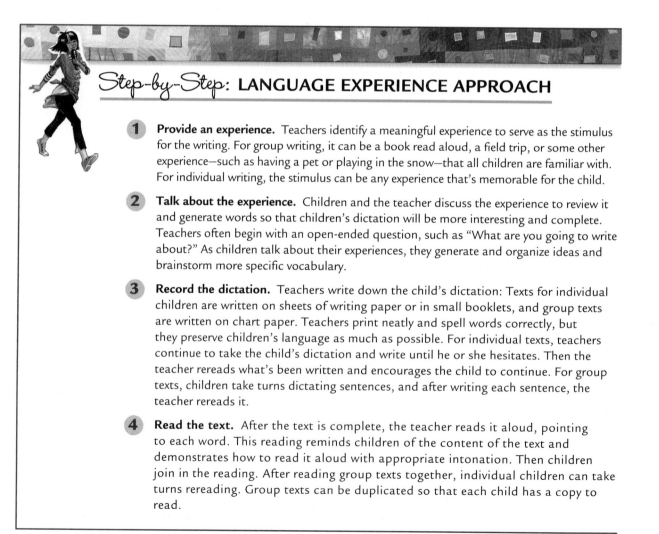

Step-by-Step: LANGUAGE EXPERIENCE APPROACH

1 **Provide an experience.** Teachers identify a meaningful experience to serve as the stimulus for the writing. For group writing, it can be a book read aloud, a field trip, or some other experience—such as having a pet or playing in the snow—that all children are familiar with. For individual writing, the stimulus can be any experience that's memorable for the child.

2 **Talk about the experience.** Children and the teacher discuss the experience to review it and generate words so that children's dictation will be more interesting and complete. Teachers often begin with an open-ended question, such as "What are you going to write about?" As children talk about their experiences, they generate and organize ideas and brainstorm more specific vocabulary.

3 **Record the dictation.** Teachers write down the child's dictation: Texts for individual children are written on sheets of writing paper or in small booklets, and group texts are written on chart paper. Teachers print neatly and spell words correctly, but they preserve children's language as much as possible. For individual texts, teachers continue to take the child's dictation and write until he or she hesitates. Then the teacher rereads what's been written and encourages the child to continue. For group texts, children take turns dictating sentences, and after writing each sentence, the teacher rereads it.

4 **Read the text.** After the text is complete, the teacher reads it aloud, pointing to each word. This reading reminds children of the content of the text and demonstrates how to read it aloud with appropriate intonation. Then children join in the reading. After reading group texts together, individual children can take turns rereading. Group texts can be duplicated so that each child has a copy to read.

content is based on their experiences, they're usually able to read the text easily. Reading and writing are connected because children are actively involved in reading what they've written. The steps are shown in the Step-by-Step feature on the previous page.

The Language Experience Approach is an effective way to help emergent readers. Even older children who haven't been successful with other reading activities can read what they've dictated. There's a drawback, however: Teachers provide a "perfect" model when they take children's dictation—they write neatly and spell all words correctly. After Language Experience activities, some young children aren't eager to do their own writing, because they prefer their teacher's "perfect" writing to their own childlike writing. To avoid this problem, teachers have young children do their own writing concurrently with the Language Experience activities so that they learn that sometimes they do their own writing, and at other times, the teacher takes their dictation.

 OUNG CHILDREN LEARN TO WRITE

Many young children become writers before they're 5 years old; others are introduced to writing during kindergarten (Schulze, 2006). Young children's writing development follows a pattern similar to their reading development: emergent writing, beginning writing, and fluent writing. In emergent writing, children make scribbles to represent writing. At first, the scribbles appear randomly on a page, but with experience, children line up the letters or scribbles from left to right and from top to bottom. Children also begin to "read," or tell what their writing says. The second stage is beginning writing, and it signals children's growing awareness of the alphabetic principle. Children use invented spelling to represent words, and as they learn more about phoneme-grapheme correspondences, their writing approximates conventional spelling. They move from writing single words to writing sentences and experiment with capital letters and punctuation marks. The third stage is fluent writing, when children write in paragraphs and vary their writing according to genre. They use mainly correct spelling and other conventions of written language, including capital letters and punctuation marks.

Opportunities for writing begin on the first day of school and continue daily throughout the primary grades, regardless of whether children have already learned to read or write letters and words. Children often begin using a combination of art and scribbles or letterlike forms to express themselves (Ditzel, 2000). Their writing moves toward conventional forms as they apply concepts that they're learning about written language.

Figure 3–6 presents four samples of young children's writing. The first is a kindergartner's letter to the Great Pumpkin; the writing is at the emergent stage. The child wrote using scribbles that look like cursive handwriting, and followed the left-to-right, top-to-bottom orientation. The Great Pumpkin's comment, "I love you all," can be deciphered. The second sample is characteristic of the beginning stage. A kindergartner wrote this list of favorite foods as part of a literature focus unit on *The Very Hungry Caterpillar* (Carle, 2001). The list reads, "orange, strawberry, apple, pizza, birthday cake." The third is an excerpt from a first grader's reading log; it's another example of beginning-stage writing. The child used invented spelling to list the animal characters that appear in *The Mitten* (Brett, 2009). The fifth animal from the top is a badger. The fourth sample is a page from a first grader's dinosaur book. The text reads, "No one ever saw a real dinosaur," and this child used a capital letter to begin the sentence and a period to mark the end. This sample shows the start of the transition from beginning to fluent writing.

FIGURE 3-6 Samples of Young Children's Writing

Introducing Young Children to Writing

Young children's writing grows out of talking and drawing (Schickedanz & Casbergue, 2004). As they begin to write, their writing is literally their talk written down, and children can usually express in writing the ideas they talk about. At the same time, children's letterlike marks develop from their drawing. With experience, children learn to differentiate between drawing and writing. Kindergarten teachers often say that children use crayons to draw and pencils to write. Teachers also differentiate where on a page children write and draw: The drawing often goes at the top of a page and the writing at the bottom, or children can use paper with space for drawing at the top and lines for writing at the bottom.

Teachers help children emerge into writing beginning on the first day of school when they give children pencils and encourage them to write. You might call young children's writing "kid writing" and contrast it with teachers' "adult writing." When young children understand that their writing is allowed to look different from adults', they're more willing to experiment with forming letters to represent ideas. Teachers show children how to hold a pencil and demonstrate how to do kid writing with scribbles, letterlike marks, or letters. Gradually children's writing more closely approximates adult writing because teachers are modeling writing, teaching minilessons about written language, and involving them in writing activities.

Kid writing takes many different forms. Their scribbles may resemble letterlike forms, or sometimes children imitate adults' cursive writing. At first, the letters they string together don't have phoneme-grapheme correspondences, but with more experience, children invent spellings that represent more sound features of words and apply some spelling rules. A child's progressive writings of "Abbie is my dog. I love her very much" over a period of 18 months are presented in Figure 3–7. This child moves from using scribbles, to using single letters to represent words (top two entries), to spelling phonetically and misapplying a few spelling rules in the third and fourth entries. Note that in the fourth example, the child is experimenting with using periods to mark spaces between words. In the fifth example, the child's writing is more conventional, and more than half of the words are spelled correctly. The message is written as two sentences, which are marked at the beginning with capital letters and at the end with periods.

Kid writing gives young children permission to experiment with written language. Too often, children assume that they should write and spell like adults do, but when they can't, they get frustrated and don't want to write, or they ask teachers to spell every word or copy text out of books or from charts. Kid writing empowers young children because it allows them to invent spellings that reflect their knowledge of written language. Glover (2009) emphasizes the importance of "honoring children's approximations" (p. 9) and "nudging rather than pushing" (p. 11) children toward adult standards.

Interactive Writing

Teachers use interactive writing to model conventional writing (McCarrier, Pinnell, & Fountas, 2000; Tompkins & Collom, 2004). Children and the teacher collaborate on constructing the text to be written and then write it together. Teachers reinforce concepts about written language as they focus children's attention on individual words and on sounds within words. This procedure grew out of the Language Experience Approach, and conventional writing is used so that everyone can read the completed text.

Topics for interactive writing can come from stories children have read, classroom news, and information learned during thematic units. Children take turns holding the marking pen and doing the writing themselves. They usually sit in a circle on the carpet and take turns writing the text they construct on chart paper that's displayed on an easel. While one child is writing at the easel, the others are writing on small whiteboards in their laps.

| FIGURE 3-7 | One Child's "Kid Writing" |

Scribble Writing

One-Letter Labeling

Invented Spelling Without Spacing

More Sophisticated Invented Spelling With Spacing

More Conventional Writing in Sentences

Teachers begin by collecting the necessary materials. For whole-class or small-group activities, they collect chart paper, colored marking pens, white correction tape, an alphabet chart, magnetic letters, and a pointer. They also collect small whiteboards, pens, and erasers for children to use. The steps in interactive writing are shown in the Step-by-Step feature on the next page.

When children begin interactive writing in kindergarten, they write letters to represent the beginning sounds in words and write familiar words such as *the, a,* and *is*. The first letters that children write are often the letters in their own names. As children learn more about sound-symbol correspondences and spelling patterns, they do more of the writing. Once children are writing words fluently, they can continue to do interactive writing as they work in small groups. Each child in the group uses a particular color pen, and children take turns writing letters, letter clusters, and words. They also learn to use the white correction tape to correct poorly formed letters and misspelled words.

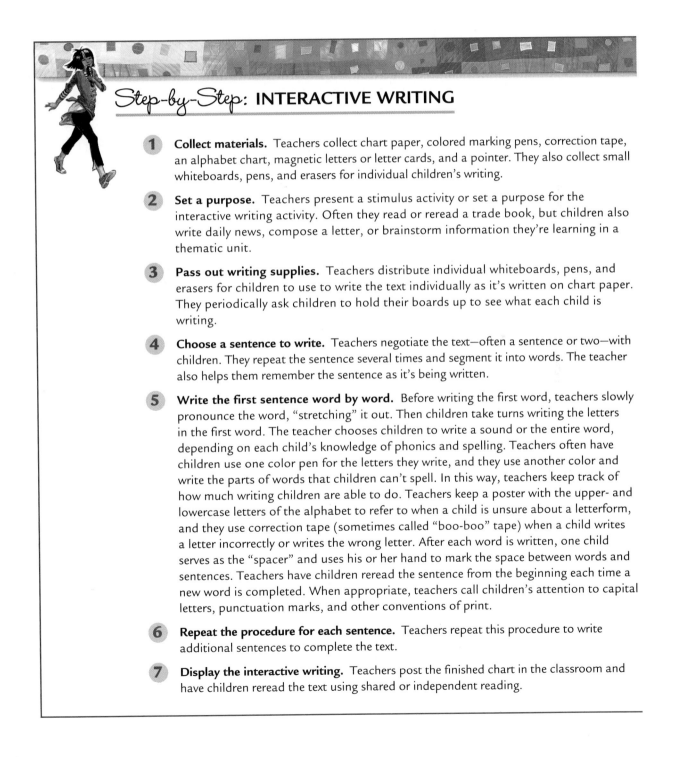

Step-by-Step: INTERACTIVE WRITING

1 **Collect materials.** Teachers collect chart paper, colored marking pens, correction tape, an alphabet chart, magnetic letters or letter cards, and a pointer. They also collect small whiteboards, pens, and erasers for individual children's writing.

2 **Set a purpose.** Teachers present a stimulus activity or set a purpose for the interactive writing activity. Often they read or reread a trade book, but children also write daily news, compose a letter, or brainstorm information they're learning in a thematic unit.

3 **Pass out writing supplies.** Teachers distribute individual whiteboards, pens, and erasers for children to use to write the text individually as it's written on chart paper. They periodically ask children to hold their boards up to see what each child is writing.

4 **Choose a sentence to write.** Teachers negotiate the text—often a sentence or two—with children. They repeat the sentence several times and segment it into words. The teacher also helps them remember the sentence as it's being written.

5 **Write the first sentence word by word.** Before writing the first word, teachers slowly pronounce the word, "stretching" it out. Then children take turns writing the letters in the first word. The teacher chooses children to write a sound or the entire word, depending on each child's knowledge of phonics and spelling. Teachers often have children use one color pen for the letters they write, and they use another color and write the parts of words that children can't spell. In this way, teachers keep track of how much writing children are able to do. Teachers keep a poster with the upper- and lowercase letters of the alphabet to refer to when a child is unsure about a letterform, and they use correction tape (sometimes called "boo-boo" tape) when a child writes a letter incorrectly or writes the wrong letter. After each word is written, one child serves as the "spacer" and uses his or her hand to mark the space between words and sentences. Teachers have children reread the sentence from the beginning each time a new word is completed. When appropriate, teachers call children's attention to capital letters, punctuation marks, and other conventions of print.

6 **Repeat the procedure for each sentence.** Teachers repeat this procedure to write additional sentences to complete the text.

7 **Display the interactive writing.** Teachers post the finished chart in the classroom and have children reread the text using shared or independent reading.

FIGURE 3–8   A Kindergarten Class's Interactive Writing Chart

Brushing Teeth
Brush your teeth after
you eat food.
Brush your teeth in the morning
and at night.
If You don't you will get
cavities.

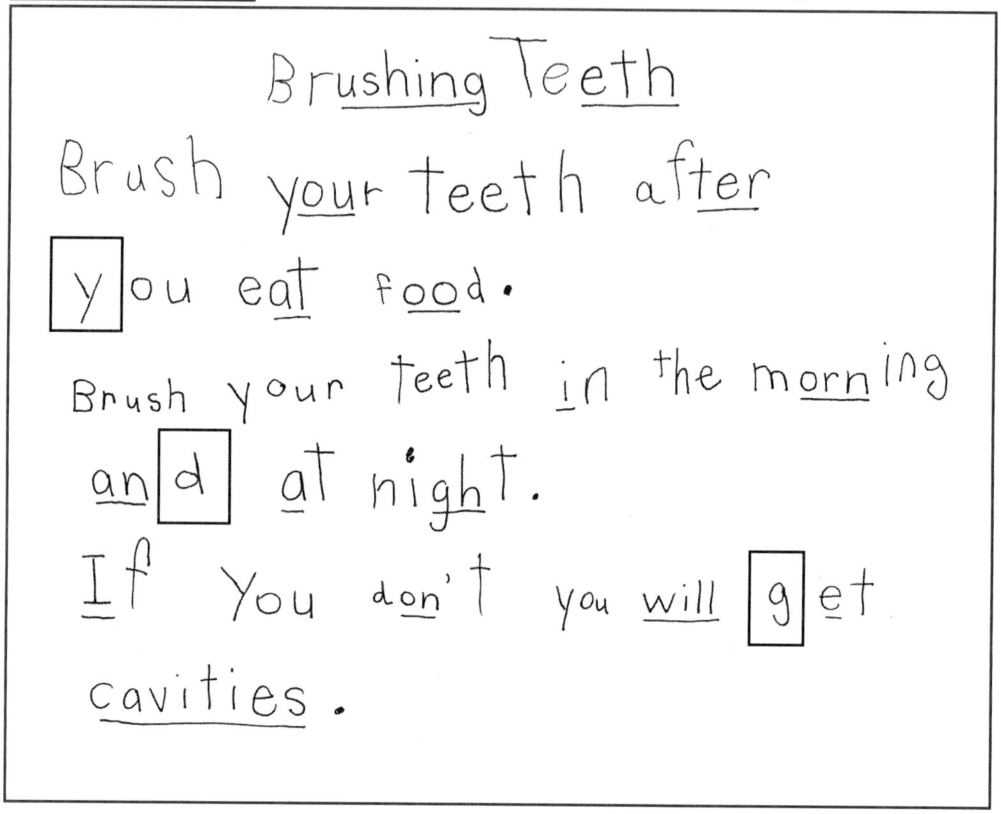

Figure 3–8 presents an interactive writing chart about brushing teeth, which was written over several days by a kindergarten class after a visit to a dentist. Notice that the children knew most beginning and ending sounds and the sight words *you* and *the*. Underlining has been added to show the letters the teacher wrote, and the boxes around letters indicate the use of correction tape.

Minilessons

Teachers teach minilessons about reading and writing topics to children in kindergarten and the primary grades. Children learn about how reading and writing are used to convey messages and how children behave as readers and writers. A minilesson showing how to teach children to make predictions is on the next page. These minilessons can be taught during literature focus units, reading and writing workshop, and thematic units.

Minilesson

Mr. Voss's Kindergartners Learn to Predict

1. Introduce the Topic

Mr. Voss explains to his kindergarten class that before he begins to read a book, he thinks about it. He looks at the illustration on the book cover, reads the title, and makes a prediction or guess about the story.

2. Share Examples

Mr. Voss shows the cover of *The Wolf's Chicken Stew* (Kasza, 1996) and thinks aloud about it. He says, "This book is about a wolf who is going to cook some delicious chicken stew. Yes, that makes sense because I know that wolves like to eat chickens. I think the wolf on the cover is looking for chickens to cook in the stew." Then Mr. Voss asks the kindergartners to agree or disagree. Most agree, but one child suggests that the wolf's looking for a supermarket to buy the chickens.

3. Provide Information

Mr. Voss reads the book aloud, stopping several times to confirm or revise predictions. Children confirm the prediction once the hen and her chicks are introduced, but by the end, no one's surprised when the wolf befriends the chickens. After reading, they talk about how their predictions changed as they read the story.

4. Supervise Practice

During story time for 5 days, the kindergartners make predictions before reading aloud. If the prediction seems far-fetched, Mr. Voss asks the child to relate it to the book or make a new prediction. Children confirm or revise predictions as they listen and discuss their predictions after reading.

5. Reflect on Learning

Mr. Voss's students make a chart about predicting. The kindergartners dictate these sentences for the chart:

You have to turn on your brain to think before you read. You can make a prediction. Then you want to find out if you are right.

SUMMING UP

Young children learn concepts about written language as they experiment with reading and writing. They move from recognizing environmental print to reading decontextualized words in books. Children use phonics as well as information from the other three language systems as they learn to read. Researchers have documented the emergent, beginning, and fluent stages in children's reading and writing development. Children learn about writing as they watch their teachers write and as they experiment with writing, and they use "kid writing" to experiment with written language concepts and invented spelling. Teachers use shared reading, interactive writing, and other instructional procedures to teach reading and writing.

CHAPTER 4

Personal Writing

SEVENTH GRADERS RESPOND TO LITERATURE   Ms. Meinke's seventh graders participate in literature circles. One group of six students is reading *The Great Gilly Hopkins* (Paterson, 1987), the story of an angry, mistrustful, disrespectful foster child who eventually finds love and acceptance. To begin their 3-week period of literature circles, the students sign up to read one of the six books that Ms. Meinke has introduced. The students divide into groups, and each group selects a leader and sets its schedule for reading and discussing the book. Students also construct reading logs by stapling paper into booklets and adding construction paper covers.

Ms. Meinke meets with *The Great Gilly Hopkins* group to talk about the book. She explains that the story is about a foster child named Gilly Hopkins. They talk about foster care and why children become foster children; several students mention that they know someone who's a foster child. She also passes out the list of topics for reading log entries shown on page 88, and students place the sheet in their reading logs. Ms. Meinke varies the types of entries that she asks students to write in reading logs because she's found that each chapter is different, and she believes that the content of the chapter should determine the type of response. Also, she's found that students tire of writing regular reading log entries because of their repetitiveness and predictability.

The students read in class and at home, and every 2 days, they meet to discuss their reading. Often Ms. Meinke sits in on at least part of their discussions where students ask questions and clarify misunderstandings, share their favorite excerpts, and make predictions about what will happen next. Sometimes, too, they share their reading log entries or talk about how they'll write their entries.

Timothy wrote this simulated-journal entry after reading Chapter 2:

Dear Diary,

I can't live here, it's a dump. I have to live with Miss Trotter and that colored (or black) man Mr. Randolph. I will have to get out of this dump and fast. Today was the first day Mr. Randolph came and I can't escort him every day to dinner. I don't belong here, even Mrs. Nevin's house was better than here.

I cannot believe Miss Ellis took me to this awful place. I got to find a way to call Courtney Hopkins. She'll take me outta this place. Everyone's trying to be nice to me but I'll show them who's the boss, and I bet there is something wrong with W. E.

After reading Chapter 6, about how mean Gilly is to her teacher, Miss Harris, Steven wrote this simulated letter to Gilly:

Hey Gilly,

That was the best note you have ever written. That was cool because you actually made Miss Harris curse. I bet you none of the kids at this school could ever make a teacher do that. I wish I could write cards like that and make teachers curse. You are also very brave because you wrote that to a teacher. No kid is crazy enough to do something like that. That is how crazy I think you are.

Your classmate,

Steven

Johanna wrote this response about whether it's ever right to lie and steal after reading Chapter 7:

I think she shouldn't be forgiven. I know she has had a horrible life, but it's never right. It is one thing to steal and it's another to steal from a blind man. That is just mean. I kind of feel bad for her because of everything she's been through. She lies, cheats, and steals. I am not sure which side to take because in one way she should be forgiven but on another side she shouldn't be because she's done too many bad things. Especially stealing from Mr. Randolph.

Reading Log Assignments for *The Great Gilly Hopkins*

Chapter 1 "Welcome to Thompson Park"
What is a foster child? How do foster children feel and behave? Why?

Chapter 2 "The Man Who Comes to Supper"
Write a diary entry from Gilly's viewpoint.

Chapter 3 "More Unpleasant Surprises"
Write a double entry with a quote from the chapter and your response.

Chapter 4 "Sarsaparilla to Sorcery"
Write a diary entry from Gilly's viewpoint.

Chapter 5 "William Ernest and Other Mean Flowers"
Do a character study on Maime Trotter. Identify and list three characteristics. Then locate and copy two quotes as evidence for each characteristic.

Chapter 6 "Harassing Miss Harris"
Write a letter to Gilly telling her what you think of what she did to Miss Harris.

Chapter 7 "Dust and Desperation"
Gilly does two things that are considered immoral: she lies and she steals. She has had a rough life, so maybe doing these things is excusable. Perhaps, however, lying and stealing are wrong under any circumstances. Take a position and support it with evidence from the book.

Chapter 8 "The One Way Ticket"
Draw a scene from the chapter and write a brief description of the scene.

Chapter 9 "Pow"
There is a definite change in Gilly's behavior and feelings in this chapter. Describe how she changes and then describe the causes of these changes using examples from the book.

Chapter 10 "The Visitor"
Draw a picture of Gilly and her family at Thanksgiving dinner. Then, in a paragraph, describe Gilly's foster family and how they make each other feel needed. Or, draw Nonnie, Gilly's grandmother. Then, in a paragraph, tell what she looks like, what kind of person she seems to be, how she behaves, and how she gets along with her daughter, Courtney.

Chapter 11 "Never and Other Canceled Promises"
So where should Gilly go? List three reasons why she should stay with Trotter and list three reasons why she should go with her grandmother Nonnie. Then write a short paragraph telling where you would like her to go and why.

Chapters 12 and 13 "The Going" and "Jackson, Virginia"
Select eight to ten images, details, interesting phrases, or parts of sentences from the book and arrange the "found" parts into a poem.

Chapters 14 and 15 "She'll Be Riding Six White Horses" and "Homecoming"
In this final response, write about your feelings. What did you like? dislike? Why?

Sarah wrote about how Gilly has changed after reading Chapter 9:

> *Gilly changes because she sees that Trotter really cares for her. Trotter got in an argument about what Gilly did. Miss Ellis wanted to take Gilly back but Trotter wouldn't let her. Gilly becomes more liking toward Trotter. Gilly even starts liking W. E. Gilly doesn't think he is dumb any more. Another example is "Look, W. E.," she bent over close to his ear and whispered hoarsely into it, "I'm going to teach you how to fight. No charge or anything. Then when some big punk comes up to you and tries to start something, you can just let them have it," said Gilly.*

After reading Chapters 12 and 13, Timothy composed this found poem:

> *He tore a piece of him and gave it to you.*
> *Don't make it harder for us, baby.*
> *This was supposed to be a party, not a funeral.*
> *Sometimes it's best not to go visiting.*
> *You make me proud.*
> *Why would anybody leave peace for war?*
> *Stop hovering over me.*
> *Inside her head, she was screaming.*

Steven reflects on the book in his last entry:

> *I thought that at the end Gilly was going to go with her mom. I also thought Gilly's mom was going to be nice and sweet. I thought this was very good because it had an unexpected ending. I didn't think that Gilly's mom would be so rude and mean. Now I wish that Gilly would go back with Trotter because Courtney is mean. Those are my reasons why she should be with Trotter.*

Ms. Meinke is especially interested in the students' responses in this last entry. She finds that many students, like Steven, want Gilly to stay with Trotter, but she's pleased when they realize that Nonnie, who never even knew of Gilly's existence, is family and is delighted to provide a home for her only granddaughter.

Ms. Meinke collects the students' reading logs twice—once halfway through the literature circle and again at the end—to grade them. She's found that students appreciate the opportunity to pace themselves as they read and write the entries. She awards points for each entry, and these points are part of students' grades for the literature circle.

All kinds of people do personal writing. People record the everyday events of their lives and the issues that concern them in journals and letters. The personal writing of some public figures has survived for hundreds of years and provides a fascinating glimpse of their authors and the times in which they lived. For example, the Renaissance genius Leonardo da Vinci recorded his daily activities and plans for his engineering projects in more than 40 notebooks, and American explorers Meriwether Lewis and William Clark kept a journal of their travels across the North American continent.

Dutch artist Vincent Van Gogh wrote more than 1,000 letters during his lifetime, many to his brother Theo; these letters document the artist's tragic life. Anne Frank, who wrote while in hiding from the Nazis during World War II, is the best known child diarist.

Students do personal writing for many of the same reasons—to record events in their lives and to share information with others. Increasingly, students are sharing their ideas on classroom blogs and commenting on their classmates' posts. And, there are other reasons for using personal writing: Students use it as a tool for learning; they write in learning logs, for instance, as part of thematic units, and young children develop writing fluency as they do personal writing. They practice handwriting skills, writing conventions, and spelling high-frequency words.

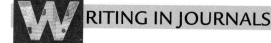

WRITING IN JOURNALS

Students use journals for a variety of purposes during language arts and across the curriculum:

- Recording experiences
- Stimulating interest in a topic
- Exploring thinking
- Personalizing learning
- Developing interpretations
- Wondering, predicting, and hypothesizing
- Engaging the imagination
- Asking questions
- Activating prior knowledge
- Assuming the role of another person
- Sharing experiences with trusted readers

Figure 4–1 describes different types of journals. In most types, the focus is on the writer; the writing is personal and private. Students' writing is spontaneous and loosely organized, often containing mechanical errors, because they're focusing on thinking, not on spelling, capitalization, and punctuation. James Britton and his colleagues (1975) compare journal writing to a written conversation with oneself or with trusted readers who are interested in the writer.

Personal writing gives students valuable writing practice. Young children use a combination of drawing and writing in their journal entries (McGee & Richgels, 2012). They write scribbles, random letters and numbers, simple captions, or extended texts using invented spelling. Their spellings often seem bizarre by adult standards, but they're reasonable in terms of children's knowledge of phoneme-grapheme correspondences and spelling patterns. In first and second grades, children gain fluency and confidence that they can write through journal writing. Older students experiment with writing conventions that are necessary in more public writing.

Personal Journals

Personal journals are usually the first type of journal writing that young children do. Kindergartners begin writing in journals early in the school year, and their writing becomes more conventional as they learn concepts about written language, letters of the alphabet, and phonics concepts. Hannon (1999) recommends beginning with personal or dialogue journals. Figure 4–2 shows two kindergartners' journal entries. In the left entry, a 5-year-old draws a detailed picture

FIGURE 4–1	Types of Journals

Personal Journals
Students write in personal journals about events in their own lives and about other topics of special interest. These journals are the most private type. Teachers respond as interested readers, often asking questions and offering comments about their own lives.

Dialogue Journals
Dialogue journals are similar to personal journals except they're written to be shared with the teacher or a classmate. Whoever receives the journal reads the entry and responds to it. The entries are like written conversations.

Reading Logs
Students respond in reading logs to stories, poems, and informational books they're reading. They write and draw entries after reading, record key vocabulary words, make charts and other diagrams, and record memorable quotes.

Double-Entry Journals
Students divide each page of their journals into two columns and write different types of information in each column. Sometimes they write quotes from a story in one column and add reactions to the quotes in the other, or they write predictions in one column and what actually happened in the story in the other.

Learning Logs
Students write in learning logs as part of thematic units. They write quickwrites, draw diagrams, take notes, and write vocabulary words.

Simulated Journals
Students assume the role of a book character or a historical personality and write journal entries from that person's viewpoint. They include details from the story or historical period in their entries.

of a football game (notice that the player in the middle-right position has the ball) and adds five letters for the text so that his entry will have some writing. In the entry on the right, another child writes, "I spent the night at my dad's house."

Students often keep personal journals in which they recount events in their lives and write about topics that interest them such as learning to ice skate, a new baby brother or sister, or a family camping trip. It's normal for students to misspell a few words in their entries because their emphasis is on what they say, not on writing conventionally. It's helpful to develop a list of journal-writing topics on a chart in the classroom or make copies for students to clip inside their journal notebooks because students choose their own topics for personal journals. Although they can write about almost anything, some students will complain that they don't know what to write about, so a list of topics gives them a crutch. Referring students to the list or asking them to brainstorm several topics encourages them to become more independent writers.

When students share personal information in their journals, sometimes teachers learn details about students' problems and family life that they don't know how to deal with. Entries about child abuse, suicide, or drug use may be a student's way of asking for help. Although teachers aren't counselors, they have a legal obligation to protect their students and to report possible abuse and neglect to appropriate school personnel. Occasionally a student invents a personal problem as an attention-getting tactic; however, asking about the journal entry or having a school counselor do so will help to ensure that the student's safety is fully considered.

FIGURE 4–2   Two Kindergartners' Journal Entries

Dialogue Journals

Students use dialogue journals to have a written conversation with the teacher or with a classmate; these journals provide opportunities for authentic communication. Students write informally about something of interest, a book they're reading, or what they're learning in a thematic unit. They choose their own topics and usually control the direction the writing takes. As teachers or classmates respond to students' entries, they answer as they would in an oral conversation: They react to the other person's comments, ask questions, and offer suggestions. Teachers acknowledge students' ideas and encourage them to continue to write, and they provide new information, so that students will want to read their responses. Teachers' responses don't need to be lengthy; a sentence or two is often enough, and they should avoid unspecific comments, such as "good idea" or "very interesting." Even so, it's time-consuming to respond to 25, 30, or more journal entries regularly. To address this problem, many teachers monitor students' journal entries on a rotating basis; they might respond to one group one week and another group the next week.

In this fifth grader's dialogue journal, Daniel shares the events in his life with his teacher, and she responds sympathetically. Daniel writes:

 Over spring break I went down to my grandma's house and played basketball in their backyard and while we were there we went to see some of my uncles who are all Indians. Out of my whole family down there they are all Indians except Grandpa Russell.

And Daniel's teacher responds:

What a fun spring break! That is so interesting to have Indians in your family. I think I might have some Indian ancestors too. Do you still plan to go to Padre Island for the summer?

The next day, Daniel writes:

My family and I plan to go to Padre Island in June and I imagine we will stay there for quite a while. I think the funnest part will probably be swimming or camping or something like that. When we get there my mom says we will probably stay in a nice motel.

Daniel's teacher responds:

That really sounds like a fun vacation. I think swimming is the most fun, too. Who will go with you?

Daniel continues to talk about his family, now focusing on the problems his family is facing:

Well, my mom and dad are divorced so that is why I am going to court to testify on Tuesday but my mom, me, and my sister and brother are all going and that kind of makes me sad because a couple of years ago when my mom and dad were together we used to go a lot of places like camping and hiking but now after what happened we hardly go anywhere.

His teacher responds:

I am so sorry your family is having problems. It sounds as if your mom and dad are having problems with each other, but they both love you and want to be with you. Be sure to keep talking to them about how you feel.

Daniel replies:

I wish my mom and dad did not have problems because I would have a lot more fun and get to go and do a lot more things together, but since my mom and dad are divorced I have to take turns spending time with both of them.

This journal isn't a series of teacher questions and student answers; instead, Daniel and his teacher are having a conversation that's built on mutual trust and respect.

Dialogue journals are especially effective in promoting English learners' writing development. Researchers have found that ELs are more successful writers when they choose their own topics and when their teachers request a reply (Reyes, 1991). Not surprisingly, when a student was particularly interested in a topic, it was less important what the teacher did, and when the teacher and the student were both interested in a topic, the topic seemed to take over as they built on each other's writing. Reyes also found that English learners were much more successful in writing dialogue journal entries than in writing in response to books they'd read.

Reading Logs

Students write in reading logs about stories they're reading or listening to the teacher read aloud during literature focus units, literature circles, and reading workshop. Rather than simply summarizing their reading, students delve into important ideas and relate their reading to their own lives or to other literature. They also list interesting words, jot down memorable quotes, and take notes about characters, plot, or other story elements; but the primary purpose is to think about the book and develop their interpretations, as Ms. Meinke's students did in the vignette at the beginning of the chapter.

Even 4- and 5-year-olds make reading logs using a combination of drawing and writing, as the two samples in Figure 4–3 show. A kindergartner wrote the entry on the left after listening to his teacher read *The Three Billy Goats Gruff* (Finch, 2001). He read the text this way: "You are a mean, bad troll." Another child wrote the entry on the right after listening to her teacher read *The Jolly Postman, or Other People's Letters* (Ahlberg & Ahlberg, 2006). This child drew a picture of the three bears receiving a letter from Goldilocks. She labeled the mom, dad, and baby bear in the picture and wrote, "I [am] sorry I ate your porridge."

Hancock (2007) examined students' responses and noticed patterns in their reading log entries; she identified nine categories, which are described in Figure 4–4. The first four are immersion responses in which students make inferences about characters, offer predictions, ask questions, or discuss confusions. The next three categories focus on students' involvement with the story. The last two are literary connections, in which students make connections and evaluate the book they're reading.

PreK *Spotlight*

How can teachers develop home–school partnerships?

Amy Kay uses home–school journals to build bridges and maintain a dialogue with her students' families (Kay, Neher, & Lush, 2010). Her 4- and 5-year-old students are culturally diverse, and many come from low SES families. She uses dialogue journals because she recognizes the importance of creating strong home–school partnerships, especially when teachers and students are from different cultures. Kay distributes notebooks at the back-to-school event held at the beginning of the school year and invites parents, grandparents, and other caregivers to write entries to tell her about their children. She responds to each entry, and in her responses, Kay offers encouragement, provides information, responds to issues parents raise, and celebrates children's accomplishments. Through these journals, she learns about her students' home life and their out-of-school reading and writing experiences:

Relationships With Families. Parents share information about their children's past experiences and family life. As Kay shows respect through her responses and parents develop trust, families share more personal information. For example, one father shared that his child hadn't completed an assignment because he was involved in wedding activities, and another parent explained her child's behavior changes because of a recent family tragedy. Kay speculates that the journal format allows families to share personal information that they might not in face-to-face interactions.

Home Literacy Experiences. Parents relate their children's experiences with reading and writing at home. For example, one grandparent shared her granddaughter's response to a read-aloud book, and a guardian explained her child's developing awareness of environmental print. Through their entries, Kay becomes more aware of parents' and other caregivers' involvement in her students' literacy development and the value that the families place on learning.

Home–school partnerships lead to better understanding, greater mutual respect, and an enhanced learning experience. Kay concluded that dialogue journals "allowed relationships to develop with families and students that would not have existed within the typical school-coordinated events" (p. 424), and that through home–school dialogue, "respect can grow, understanding can be deepened, and trust-based relationships can be formed" (p. 425).

FIGURE 4-3   Two Kindergartners' Reading Log Entries

These categories expand the possibilities for response by introducing teachers and students to a wide variety of response options. Teachers assess the kinds of responses students are currently making by categorizing their entries and tallying the results. Often students use only a few types of responses, not the wide range that's available, so teachers teach minilessons and model types of responses that students aren't using and ask questions when they read journal entries to prompt students to think in new ways.

Seventh graders' reading log entries about *The Giver* (Lowry, 2006b) are shown in Figure 4-5. In these entries, students react to the book, make predictions, deepen their understanding of the story, ask questions, assume the role of the main character, and value the story. Each entry is categorized according to Hancock's patterns of response.

Double-Entry Journals

Students divide each entry into two columns when they write double-entry journals (Berthoff, 1981). In the left column, they usually write quotes from the story or other book they're reading, and in the right column, they relate each quote to their own life, the world around them, or other literature. In this way, students become more engaged in what they're reading, notice sentences that have personal meaning, and become more sensitive to the author's language.

Students in a fifth grade class wrote double-entry journals as they read C. S. Lewis's classic *The Lion, the Witch and the Wardrobe* (2005). After reading each chapter, students reviewed it and selected one or two brief quotes. They wrote these excerpts in the left column, and in the right column they wrote reactions beside each quote. Excerpts from a fifth grader's journal are presented in Figure 4-6; this student's responses indicate that she's engaged in the story and connecting the story to her own life.

Double-entry journals can be used in other ways, too. Students can write "Reading Notes" about the events in a story in the left column and then add "Reactions" or personal, world, or

FIGURE 4–4   Response Patterns

Type	Patterns	Descriptions
Immersion Responses	Understanding	Students share their understanding of characters and plot. Their responses include personal interpretation as well as summaries.
	Character Introspection	Students share their insights into the feelings and motives of a character. They often begin their comments with "I think."
	Predicting	Students speculate about what will happen later in the story and confirm predictions they made previously.
	Questioning	Students ask "I wonder why" questions and write about confusions.
Involvement Responses	Character Identification	Students show personal identification with a character, sometimes writing "If I were _____, I would . . . " They express empathy, share related experiences from their own lives, and sometimes give advice to the character.
	Character Assessment	Students judge a character's actions and use evaluative terms such as *nice* or *dumb*.
	Story Involvement	Students reveal their involvement by expressing satisfaction with how the story is developing. They comment on their desire to continue reading or use terms such as *disgusting, weird,* or *awesome* to react to sensory aspects of the story.
Literary Connections	Connections	Students make text-to-self, text-to-world, text-to-text, and text-to-media (TV shows and movies) connections.
	Literary Evaluation	Students evaluate part or all of the book. They offer "I liked/I didn't like" opinions and praise or condemn an author's style.

Based on Hancock, 2007.

literary connections in the right column. Or, students can write "Reading Notes" in one column as they read or immediately after reading, and later, after discussing the chapter, they add "Discussion Notes" in the other column. As with other types of double-entry journals, it's in the second column that students make interpretive comments.

Young children use the double-entry format for a prediction journal (Macon, Bewell, & Vogt, 1991), labeling the left column "Predictions" and the right column "What Happened." In the left column, they write or draw a picture of what they predict will happen in the story before reading it, and afterward, they draw or write what actually happened in the right column.

Learning Logs

Students write entries in learning logs to record information and think about what they're learning in math, science, social studies, or other content areas. As they write in these journals, students reflect on their learning, discover gaps in their knowledge, and explore relationships between what they're learning and their past experiences. For example, in math journals students record explanations and examples of concepts and react to what they're learning and any problems they're encountering. Figure 4–7 presents an entry from a sixth grader's learning log in which she describes how to change improper fractions. Notice that after she describes the steps, she reviews them. In addition, upper grade teachers often use the last 5 minutes of the math lesson to summarize the day's lesson and have students respond in their learning logs.

FIGURE 4–5   Entries From Seventh Graders' Reading Logs

Student	Excerpt	Response Pattern
Tiffany	I think the book <u>The Giver</u> is very scary because when you do something wrong you get released from the community. I think it would be terrible to be pushed out of your community and leave your family. Your family would be ashamed and embarrassed. It is like you are dead.	Story involvement
Scott	I don't think I could handle being a friend of Jonas's. In other words NO I would not like to be a friend of his. There would be too much pain involved and most of the time I wouldn't see Jonas.	Character identification
Rob	The part that hooked me was when the book said Jonas took his pills and did not have feelings about Fiona.	Understanding
Jared	As I'm reading I'm wondering if they get married at twelve because they get jobs at twelve.	Questioning
Elizabeth	Something that surprised me so far in the story was when Lily said she wanted to be a birthmother. Lily's mom became mad and said three years, three births, and then you're a laborer. Being a birthmother is not a good job at least after the three years. I hope that doesn't happen to Lily but I don't know what other job she should have.	Character assessment
Graciela	So far I think that the story is really sad. The story is sad because everyone has sameness except Jonas and the Giver. Jonas and the Giver are the only ones who can see color because of the memories. The story is also sad because no one has feelings.	Story involvement
Rob	Why didn't Jonas use the fire in his favorite memory to stay warmer on his long journey through the rain and snow, and the terrible coldness? Also, why didn't the author explain more about the things that are between the lines so the reader could really grasp them?	Literary evaluation
Marcos	Well, I can't really make a prediction of what is going to happen because I already read the book. If I hadn't read ahead my prediction would be that Jonas would get drowned in the river because he couldn't handle the pain.	Understanding
Rob	I think Jonas will confront his father. He won't ever forget what he saw his father do and it is wrong. Just wrong, wrong, wrong. If my father ever did that to an innocent little baby I would never forgive him. It's like abortion. I would confront him and tell him that I know. I will always know and so will God.	Predicting
Elizabeth	I don't exactly understand what happens at the end. It sounds like they froze to death. I think they died but I wish they found freedom and happiness. It is very sad.	Questioning
Mark	The ending is cool. Jonas and Gabe come back to the community but now it is changed. There are colors and the people have feelings. They believe in God and it is Christmas.	Story involvement
Graciela	At first I thought it would be good to have a perfect community. There would be no gangs and no crime and no sickness. But there is a lesson in this story. Now I think you can't have a perfect community. Even though we have bad things in our community we have love and other emotions and we can make choices.	Connections

| FIGURE 4-6 | Excerpts From a Fifth Grader's Double-Entry Journal |

In the Text	My Response
Chapter 1 I tell you this is the sort of house where no one is going to mind what we do.	I remember the time that I went to Beaumont, Texas to stay with my aunt. My aunt's house was very large. She had a piano and she let us play it. She told us that we could do whatever we wanted to.
Chapter 5 "How do you know?" he asked, "that your sister's story is not true?"	It reminds me of when I was little and I had an imaginary place. I would go there in my mind. I made up all kinds of make-believe stories about myself in this imaginary place. One time I told my big brother about my imaginary place. He laughed at me and told me I was silly. But it didn't bother me because nobody can stop me from thinking what I want.
Chapter 15 Still they could see the shape of the great lion lying dead in his bonds. They're nibbling at the cords.	When Aslan died I thought about when my Uncle Carl died. This reminds me of the story where the lion lets the mouse go and the mouse helps the lion.

Students make daily entries in science logs to track the growth of plants or animals. For instance, a second grade class observed caterpillars as they changed to chrysalides and butterflies over a period of 4 to 6 weeks. They each kept a log with daily entries, in which they noted the changes they observed using words describing shape, color, size, and other properties. Figure 4–8 presents two pages from a second grader's log documenting the caterpillars' growth and change.

Simulated Journals

Some novels, such as *Catherine, Called Birdy* (Cushman, 2005), the story of a disenchanted English noblewoman of the 13th century, are written as journals; authors research the time period, assume the role of a character, and write from the character's point of view. These books might be considered simulated journals. They're rich with historical details and incorporate both the words and phrasing of the period. At the end of these books, authors often include information about how they researched the period and explanations about the liberties they took with the character, setting, or events that are recorded. Scholastic Books publishes three series of historical journals appropriate for fourth through eighth graders. The books include *I Walk in Dread: The Diary of Deliverance Trembley, Witness to the Salem Witch Trials* (Fraustino, 2004), which recounts events during the Salem witch hunts of 1692; *The Journal of Jesse Smoke: A Cherokee Boy* (Bruchac, 2001), which records the Cherokee removal on the Trail of Tears in 1838; and *Catherine: The Great Journey* (Gregory, 2005), which chronicles the 14th year in the life of the German princess who became empress of Russia. Each book provides a glimpse into history from a girl's or boy's perspective and is handsomely bound to look like an old journal. The paper is heavy and rough cut around the edges, and a ribbon page marker is bound into the book.

Students write simulated journals, too, assuming the role of another person and writing from that person's viewpoint. For example, they assume the role of a historical figure when they

FIGURE 4-7   A Sixth Grader's Entry in a Math Learning Log

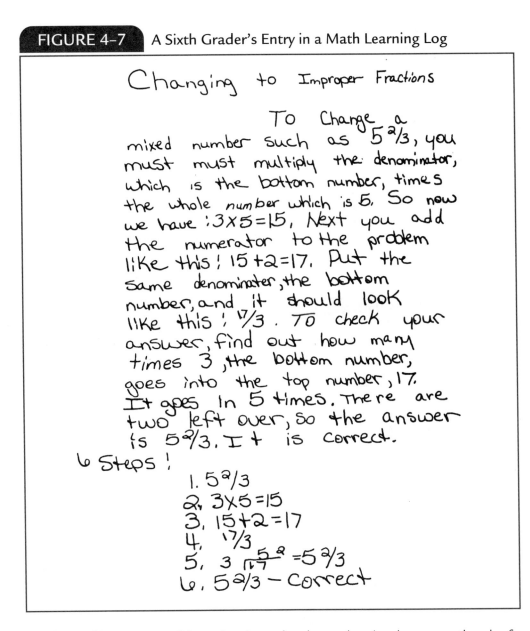

Changing to Improper Fractions

To Change a mixed number such as $5\frac{2}{3}$, you must must multiply the denominator, which is the bottom number, times the whole number which is 5. So now we have : 3×5=15. Next you add the numerator to the problem like this : 15+2=17. Put the same denominator, the bottom number, and it should look like this : $\frac{17}{3}$. To check your answer, find out how many times 3, the bottom number, goes into the top number, 17. It goes in 5 times. There are two left over, so the answer is $5\frac{2}{3}$. It is correct.

6 Steps !

1. $5\frac{2}{3}$
2. 3×5 =15
3. 15+2 =17
4. $\frac{17}{3}$
5. $3\overline{)17}$ $=5\frac{2}{3}$
6. $5\frac{2}{3}$ — correct

read biographies or as part of thematic units, and as they read stories, they assume the role of a character. In this way, students gain insight into other people's lives and into historical events. A look at a series of diary entries written by a fifth grader who has assumed the role of Betsy Ross shows how she carefully chose the dates for each entry and wove in factual information:

May 15, 1773

Dear Diary,

This morning at 5:00 I had to wake up my husband John to get up for work but he wouldn't wake up. I immediately called the doc. He came over as fast as he could. He asked me to leave the room so I did. An hour later he came out and told me he had passed away. I am so sad. I don't know what to do.

June 16, 1776

Dear Diary,

Today General Washington visited me about making a flag. I was so surprised. Me making a flag! I have made flags for the navy, but this is too much. But I said yes. He showed me a pattern of the flag he wanted. He also wanted six-pointed stars but I talked him into having five-pointed stars.

July 8, 1776

Dear Diary,

Today in front of Carpenter Hall the Declaration of Independence was read by Tom Jefferson. Well, I will tell you the whole story. I heard some yelling and shouting about liberty and everyone was gathering around Carpenter Hall. So I went to my next door neighbors to ask what was happening but Mistress Peters didn't know either so we both went down to Carpenter Hall. We saw

FIGURE 4–8   Two Entries From a Second Grader's Science Log

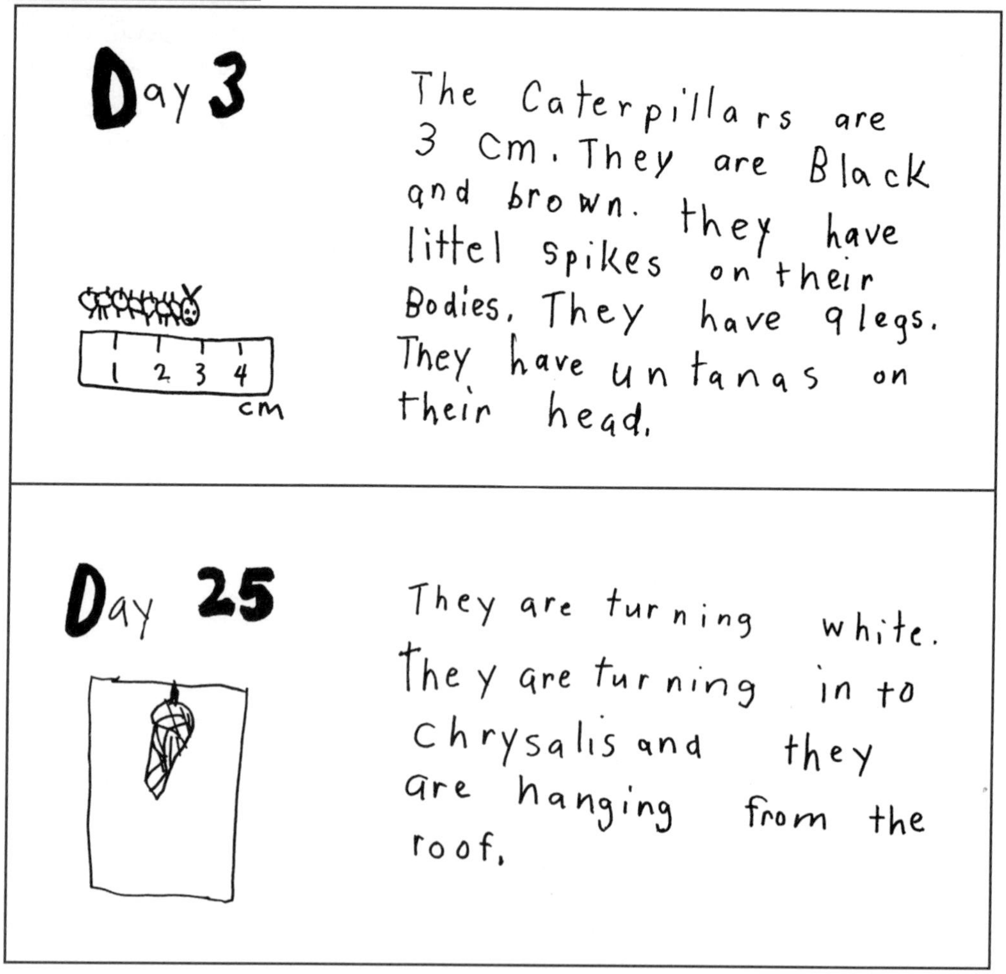

Day 3

The Caterpillars are 3 cm. They are Black and brown. they have littel spikes on their Bodies. They have 9 legs. They have untanas on their head.

Day 25

They are turning white. They are turning in to chrysalis and they are hanging from the roof.

firecrackers and heard a bell and the Declaration of Independence was being read aloud. When I heard this I knew a new country was born.

June 14, 1777

Dear Diary,

Today was a happy but scary day. Today the flag I made was adopted by Congress. I thought for sure that if England found out that a new flag was taking the old one's place something bad would happen. But I'm happy because I am the maker of the first American flag and I'm only 25 years old!

Students use simulated journals in two ways: as a tool for learning or as a project. When students use simulated journals as a learning tool, they write entries as they read a book to get to know the character better or during a thematic unit as they're learning about the historical period. In these entries, students are exploring concepts and making connections between what they're learning and what they already know. These journal entries are less polished than when students write a simulated journal as a project. Students often choose to write a simulated journal as a culminating project for a literature focus unit or a thematic unit. For these journals, students carefully plan out their journals, identify important dates or events, and use the writing process to draft, revise, edit, and publish their journals.

OCIAL NETWORKING

Today, students lead increasingly sophisticated digital lives, especially after fourth or fifth grade. They're more adept at playing interactive games, downloading music, and uploading pictures and videos than their parents and teachers are, and they exchange instant messages and email messages with friends and family members. Kist (2010) describes this online communication as *social networking*. Teens and adults use Facebook, Twitter, Ning, and other websites to place messages and connect with "friends" and other "followers." These social networks require participants to publish a profile that includes a photo and personal details, so users' anonymity isn't safeguarded. Children under age 13, however, can't have accounts on these social networks, but Class Blogmeister, 21 Classes, and other kid-friendly networking sites have been specifically designed for classroom use because privacy controls have been built into them.

Classroom Blogs

Teachers set up classroom weblogs or blogs to develop students' understanding of online communities and to allow them to safely engage in written friendly conversations with classmates (Parker, 2010). In addition, blogs are an online instructional tool where students respond to books they're reading, publish their writing, and work with classmates on projects, for instance. Teachers like to use blogs because students usually exert more effort in developing and expressing their thoughts because they know that their classmates will read and comment on their entries. Classmates' comments stimulate discussion, expand topics, and keep students thinking and writing. Teachers ensure that all students are respected and valued because they monitor students' comments before they're published. The Step-by-Step feature on page 102 describes the procedure for setting up and managing classroom blogs.

Teachers use blogs in a variety of ways to support their instructional programs (Prensky, 2010). They ensure that the applications are relevant to language arts instruction and thematic units; for example, students respond to books they're reading in literature focus units or

Step-by-Step: CLASSROOM BLOGS

1. **Review school and district Internet policies.** Teachers learn and follow all school and school district rules about students' use of social networking sites and request parents' permission for students to participate.

2. **Choose a blogging platform.** Teachers select a kid-friendly gated site designed for classroom use. These sites control who can post, comment, and view blogs; and they require teacher approval to publish posts and comments. These sites have an overarching classroom website with students' accounts protected underneath the umbrella to safeguard students from cyberbullying and online predators.

3. **Establish the classroom website.** Teachers establish the classroom website and make decisions about how they'll run the blog, who will have access to it, and which features to enable. In addition, they invite students to help choose a name, background, and graphics for the website.

4. **Set up student blogs.** Teachers either create accounts for each student ahead of time or guide students through the process of setting up their own blogs. Students also choose pseudonyms to use online to protect their privacy. These sites don't allow students to have online profiles with personal information or photos. Teachers play a few games so classmates learn each other's online names.

5. **Decide on ground rules.** Teachers explain ground rules, before the website and blogs become active. Rules usually focus on protecting students' pseudonyms, the format and length of blog entries, acceptable content for posts and comments, and directions for uploading multimedia. Other considerations are when students blog at school and whether they can access their blogs at home.

6. **Manage blogging activity.** Teachers read and approve students' entries before they're posted and monitor that students are writing their own posts and commenting on classmates' posts.

literature circles, publish their writing during writing workshop, and create online learning logs during thematic units. These applications provide opportunities for students to communicate with classmates, share ideas and information, and develop writing fluency:

CLASSROOM-TO-CLASSROOM BLOGS. Students become epals and write back and forth to students in another city, state, or country.

HOT TOPICS BLOGS. Teachers pose a topic or link to a website or podcast and invite students to share their opinions and comment on classmates' posts.

INDEPENDENT READING BLOGS. Students post entries about books they're reading independently and classmates add comments.

MESSAGE CENTER. Students communicate with classmates by posting messages.

PUBLICATION CENTER. Students post their compositions on their blogs after revising and editing them, and classmates read and comment on them.

SIMULATED JOURNALS. Students assume the role of a book character or historical personality and write a series of posts from that person's viewpoint.

TRADE BOOK BLOGS. Students respond to teacher-posted prompts about a book they're reading and make comments about classmates' posts.

THE WEEKLY REVIEW. Students work in small groups to summarize the week's events to post on the classroom website for parents to read and comment on.

THEMATIC UNIT BLOGS. At the beginning of a thematic unit, teachers pose a topic and students share their knowledge about the topic and questions they have about it. Later during the unit, teachers ask students to reflect on what they're learning.

VIRTUAL MUSEUMS. Students post images and video clips with accompanying information to create a virtual museum about a topic they're studying in a thematic unit.

Even young children can participate in social networking by sharing personal or classroom activities using a combination of photos, videos, and quotes.

Safety Concerns

Teachers are responsible for teaching students to conduct themselves safely and responsibly on the Internet, and for monitoring that they're respectful digital citizens. Online anonymity can lead to dangerous behaviors, including cyberbullying, inappropriate photo and video uploads, and meeting strangers offline, and it's often difficult for students to appreciate that the digital footprint they're creating will last a long time in cyberspace. Teachers are responsible for addressing these grade-appropriate safety concerns with their students:

PRIVACY. Students shouldn't reveal personal information about themselves—name, address, telephone number, or school name—online or post personal or family photos; instead, they should use screen names or choose avatars that highlight their personalities. They also need to protect the passwords to their online accounts. Teachers explain the importance of online anonymity and encourage students to take responsibility for their online behavior by being very selective about sharing personal information. Teachers design classroom social networks so that they're safe for students to use.

INAPPROPRIATE COMMENTS. Online anonymity allows some students to make hurtful comments that they'd never say in person, so it's important to teach them to behave respectfully on the Internet. Students need to know what's appropriate and what isn't. They also need to learn how react to inappropriate comments and respond politely to critical comments. Teachers monitor students' comments because they're the first line of defense in the classroom. If students make inappropriate comments online, teachers should treat them the same way they would if the words were spoken in class.

CYBERBULLYING. Cyberbullying occurs when a student is threatened, harassed, or embarrassed online by another kid. It's a real concern and should be treated seriously because children have killed each other or committed suicide afterward. Children act out fantasies online, and sometimes they're violent, leading them to issue death threats even though they usually don't intend to carry them out. Teachers help to prevent cyberbullying by explaining what it is and the consequences, teaching students to stop and think before they post messages, and taking a stand against bullying.

STRANGERS. Before age 13 or 14, many students have begun to use social networking sites to communicate with friends as well as to make new friends. They don't expect to meet anyone online who will try to hurt them, but some strangers are predators who use sophisticated manipulation techniques to gain children's trust and lure them to offline meetings. "Stranger-danger" warnings don't work very well; it's better to teach students how to assess the safety of online encounters.

Teachers are responsible for showing students how to prevent, detect, and respond to online concerns.

ETTER WRITING

Letters are a way of talking to people who live too far away to visit. Because they involve a genuine audience, students usually take more care to think through what they want to say, to write legibly, and to use spelling, capitalization, and punctuation conventions correctly. Students' letters are typically classified as friendly or business letters. Figure 4–9 presents the two formats. The choice of format depends on the writer's purpose. Friendly letters are informal, chatty messages to pen pals or thank-you notes to a television newscaster who has visited the classroom. When students write to the National Park Service requesting information about the Grand Canyon or send letters to the president expressing an opinion, they use the more formal, business-letter style.

Friendly Letters

After teachers have introduced the format for friendly letters, students need to choose a "real" someone to write to. Writing authentic letters that will be delivered is much more valuable than writing practice letters to be graded by the teacher. Students write friendly letters to classmates, friends who live out of town, relatives, and pen pals. They may want to keep a list of addresses of people to write friendly letters to on a special page in their journals or in address booklets. In these casual letters, they share news about events in their lives and ask questions to learn more about the person they're writing to and to encourage that person to write back. Receiving mail is the real reward of letter writing!

Robinson, Crawford, and Hall (1991) examined the effects of letter writing on young children's writing development. In the study, a group of 20 kindergartners wrote back and forth to the researchers over a 2-year period. In their early letters, the children told about themselves, promised to be friends with their correspondents, and asked questions. Over the 2-year period, they matured as letter writers and continued to be eager correspondents. Their letters became more sophisticated, and they took their readers into account. The researchers concluded that authentic, purposeful, and sustained letter-writing experiences are extremely valuable for children.

Pen Pal Letters. Teachers can arrange for their students to exchange letters with students in another class by contacting a teacher in a nearby school or local educational associations, or by answering advertisements online or in educational magazines. Another possible arrangement is to have your class become pen pals with college students in a language arts methods class. Over a semester, the children and the preservice teachers can write back and forth four, five, or six times, and perhaps even meet at the end of the semester. The children have the opportunity to be pen pals with college students, and the preservice teachers have the opportunity to get to know a student and examine his or her writing development.

FIGURE 4–9   Forms for Friendly and Business Letters

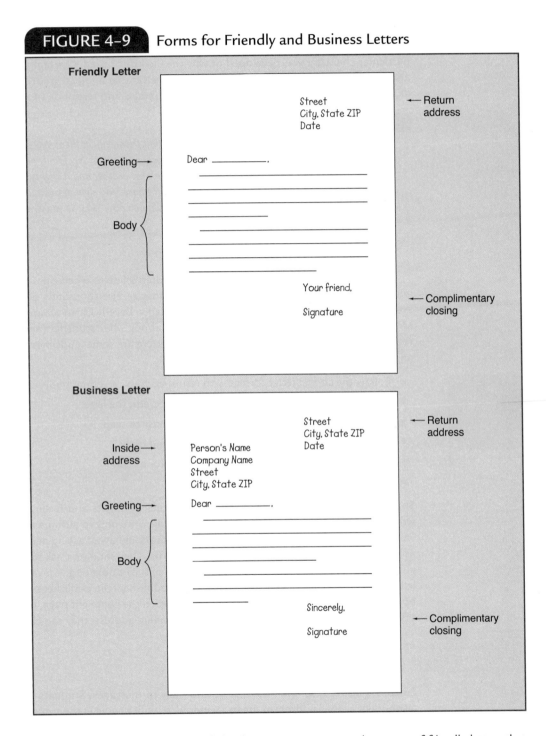

Courtesy Letters. Invitations and thank-you notes are two other types of friendly letters that students write. They may write to parents to invite them to an after-school program, to the class across the hall to invite them to visit a classroom exhibit, or to a person in the community to invite him or her to be interviewed as part of a thematic unit. Students also write letters to thank people who have been helpful.

Letters to Authors and Illustrators. Students write letters to favorite authors and illustrators to share their ideas and feelings about the books they've read. They ask questions about how a particular character was developed or why the illustrator used a certain art medium. Students also describe the books they've written. Here's a letter that a fourth grader wrote to Eve Bunting at the end of an author study, after the class had read and responded to eight of her books:

Dear Eve Bunting,

I have read some of your books. All of them had friendship in them. My favorite book is Smoky Night. I think the theme is get along and respect each other. My family needs to learn to respect each other and to get along because I fight with my brother and he fights with my sister.

How many picture books have you written? I have read eight of them. Have you ever met Chris Van Allsburg because we did an author study on him also. Why do you write your books?

Sincerely,

Jeffrey

Most authors and illustrators reply to children's letters when possible, and Eve Bunting answered this fourth grader's letters. However, they receive thousands of letters from children every year and cannot become pen pals with students. Beverly Cleary's award-winning book *Dear Mr. Henshaw* (2000) offers a worthwhile lesson about what students (and their teachers) can realistically expect from authors and illustrators. Here are some guidelines for writing to authors and illustrators:

- Follow the correct letter format with return address, greeting, body, closing, and signature.
- Use the process approach to write, revise, and edit the letter.
- Recopy the letter so that it will be neat and easy to read.
- Write the return address on both envelope and letter.
- Include a stamped, self-addressed envelope for a reply.
- Be polite in the letter.

Students should write genuine letters to share their thoughts and feelings about the author's writing or the illustrator's artwork, and they should write only to authors and illustrators whose work they're familiar with. In their letters, students should avoid asking personal questions, such as how much money the author or illustrator earns. They shouldn't ask for free books, because authors and illustrators usually don't have copies of their books to give away. Students send their letters to the author or illustrator in care of the publisher (the publisher's name appears on the book's title page, and the address usually appears on the copyright page, the page following the title page). If students can't find the complete mailing address, they can check online.

Email Messages

Email is a fast and simple way to send and reply to messages. Students learn to type the correspondent's email address in the top window, specify a topic in the subject window, and write their message in the large window. They begin by greeting their correspondent, and then they write their message. Students should keep their messages short—no longer than one or two screens—so that they can easily be read on the computer screen. They end with a closing, much like in letters. McKeon (1999) studied the email messages that a class of third graders wrote about the books they were reading and concluded that email is a constructive way to enhance students' learning as well as an effective strategy for teachers to interact with students.

Business Letters

Students write business letters to seek information, to complain and compliment, and to transact business. They use this more formal letter style and format shown in Figure 4–9 to communicate with businesses, local newspapers, and government agencies. Students may write to businesses to order products, to ask questions, and to complain about or compliment specific products; they write letters to the editors of local newspapers and magazines to comment on articles and to express their opinions. It is important that students support their comments and opinions with facts if they hope to have their letters published. Students can also write to local, state, and national government officials to express concerns, make suggestions, or seek information.

Simulated Letters

Students can write simulated letters, in which they assume the identity of a historical or literary figure (Roop, 1995). Simulated letters are similar to simulated journals except that they're formatted as letters. Students can write letters as though they were Davy Crockett or another of the men defending the Alamo, or Thomas Edison, describing his invention of the lightbulb. They can write from one book character to another; for example, after reading *Sarah, Plain and Tall* (MacLachlan, 2005), students can assume the persona of Sarah and write a letter to her brother William, as a third grader did in this letter:

Dear William,

I'm having fun here. There was a very big storm here. It was so big it looked like the sea. Sometimes I am very lonesome for home but sometimes it is very fun here in Ohio. We swam in the cow pond and I taught Caleb how to swim. They were afraid I would leave. Maggie and Matthew brought some chickens.

Love, Sarah

Even though these letters are never mailed, they're written to a specific audience. Classmates can assume the role of the person to whom the letter is addressed and respond to the letter from that point of view. Also, these letters show clearly how well students comprehend the story, and teachers can use them to monitor students' learning.

TEACHING PERSONAL WRITING

Personal writing is very versatile; it's easy to incorporate journals, blogs, and other informal writing activities into all four patterns of practice. The Patterns of Practice feature on page 108 points out some of the ways personal writing can be used in K–8 classrooms.

Teachers teach personal writing in a variety of ways. Different types of journals, email, and blogs are introduced as they're used, but teachers often teach letter writing separately. Teachers introduce students to journal-writing using minilessons in which they explain the purpose of the journal-writing activity and the procedures for gathering ideas, writing the entry, and sharing it with classmates. They model the procedure by writing a sample entry on chart paper as students observe; this sample demonstrates that the writing is informal, with ideas emphasized over correctness. Then students make their own first entries, and several read their entries aloud. Through this sharing, students who are confused or unsure have additional models on which to base their own writing. Minilessons are used to introduce each type of journal. Even though most types of journals are similar, the purpose of the journal, the information included in the entries, and the writer's viewpoint vary.

How Personal Writing Fits Into the Patterns of Practice

Literature Focus Units

Students usually write in reading logs, but sometimes they use double-entry journals and simulated journals or respond in blogs. They also write letters to authors.

Literature Circles

Students create reading logs for each book. They write entries as they're reading and take notes as classmates share information during small-group discussions.

Reading and Writing Workshop

In reading workshop, students write entries in reading logs and blogs, and during writing workshop, they sometimes write blogs to reflect on the pieces they're writing.

Thematic Units

Students record information in learning logs, write simulated journals, and share ideas in blogs. They also write business letters to request information related to the topic.

COMMON CORE STATE STANDARDS

Personal Writing

The Common Core State Standards don't directly address personal writing or mention journals, blogs, or letters by name, but when K–8 students are doing personal writing activities, they're addressing these points:

- Students develop writing fluency.
- Students spell high-frequency words correctly.
- Students respond to literature.
- Students analyze nonfiction texts.
- Students write texts for a variety of purposes and audiences.
- Students use technology, including the Internet, to produce writing.

To learn more about the language arts standards, go to http://www.corestandards.org, or check your state's language arts standards.

Teachers use personal writing to help students meet language arts standards related to responding to literature, identifying big ideas and details in nonfiction texts, and learning use a variety of writing genres. This Common Core State Standards box highlights the standards.

Minilessons

Teachers teach minilessons on procedures about writing in journals. It's especially important to teach a minilesson when students are learning a new type of journal or when they're having difficulty with a particular procedure or strategy, such as changing point of view for simulated journals or writing in two columns in double-entry journals. Teachers also present minilessons about letters, including how they're formatted and how to craft letters to encourage correspondents to respond. A minilesson on writing simulated letters appears on the next page. These lessons are sometimes conducted during language arts, but at other times, teachers teach minilessons on letter writing as part of a thematic unit because students often write letters as they're learning about social studies and science topics. For instance, students write business letters to request information or simulated letters from the viewpoint of historical figures as part of a thematic unit.

Mentor Texts

Teachers often share books that feature journals or letters during minilessons. Characters, such as Amelia in *Amelia's Notebook* (Moss, 2006), Harriet in *Harriet the Spy* (Fitzhugh, 2001), and and Birdy in *Catherine, Called Birdy* (Cushman, 2005), keep journals in which they demonstrate the process of journal writing and illustrate both the pleasures and the difficulties of keeping a journal. A list of books in which contemporary characters and historical personalities keep journals is presented in the Booklist on page 110. In addition, *Red, White and True Blue Mallory* (Friedman, 2009) is an unusual multigenre journal that combines text entries with photos and souvenirs. After teachers share this book, students may want to experiment with writing their own multigenre journals.

Teachers also use trade books that incorporate letters, postcards, and email. *With Love, Little Red Hen* (Ada, 2001), for instance, is a collection of letters that tells a story, and Ann Turner's *Nettie's Trip South* (1995) is a book-length letter about the inhumanity of slavery. Others are epistolary novels in which the story is told through a collection of letters, such as *Dear Whiskers* (Nagda, 2000), the story of a fourth grader who befriends her second grade pen pal, a Saudi

Minilesson

Mr. Rinaldi's Eighth Graders Write Simulated Letters

1. Introduce the Topic

Mr. Rinaldi's eighth graders are studying the American Civil War, and each student has assumed the persona of someone who lived in that period. Many students have become Union or Confederate soldiers and given themselves names and identities. Today, Mr. Rinaldi asks his students to think about the war as their persona would. He explains that they will write simulated letters to Abraham Lincoln or Jefferson Davis, arguing an issue as their persona might. He explains that a simulated letter is written as if the writer were someone else.

2. Share Examples

Mr. Rinaldi assumed the persona of a Confederate bugle boy when his students assumed personas, and he reads a letter he has written to Abraham Lincoln as that bugle boy, begging Lincoln to end the war. He gives three reasons why the war should end: the South has the right to choose its own destiny; the South is being destroyed by the war; and too many boys are dying. He ends his emotional letter this way: *I 'spect I'ma gonna die, too, Mr. President. What ya' gonna do when there be no more of us to shoot? No more Johnny Rebs to die. When the South has all died away, will you be a-smilin' then?* The students are stunned by the power of their teacher's simulated letter.

3. Provide Information

Mr. Rinaldi explains that he did three things in his simulated letter to make it powerful: He wrote in persona—the way a scared, uneducated boy might write—he included vocabulary words about the war, and he argued his point of view persuasively. Together they brainstorm a list of arguments or persuasive appeals—for better food and clothing for soldiers and to end the war or to continue the war. He passes out a prewriting form that students use to plan their simulated letters.

4. Supervise Practice

The students write their letters using the writing process. The planning sheet serves as prewriting, and students draft, revise, and edit their letters as Mr. Rinaldi conferences with them, encouraging them to develop the voice of their personas. Afterward, students share their letters with the class.

5. Reflect on Learning

After the lesson, Mr. Rinaldi talks with his students about their simulated letters. He asks them to reflect on what they've learned, and the students emphasize that what they learned was about the inhumanity of war, even though they thought they were learning about letters.

Booklist

JOURNALS	
Contemporary	Amato, M. (2008). *Please write in this book*. New York: Holiday House. M Cronin, D. (2005). *Diary of a spider*. New York: HarperCollins. P Green, J. (2007). *Diary of a would-be princess: The journal of Jillian James, 5B*. Watertown, MA: Charlesbridge. M Hays, A. J. (2008). *Smarty Sara*. New York: Random House. P Kinney, J. (2007). *Diary of a wimpy kid*. New York: Abrams. (and sequels) M Kline, L. W. (2008). *Write before your eyes*. New York: Delacorte. U Moss, M. (2006). *Amelia's fifth grade notebook*. New York: Simon & Schuster. M Perez, A. I. (2002). *My diary from here to there/Mi diario de aquí hasta allá*. San Francisco: Children's Book Press. P Portis, A. (2010). *Kindergarten diary*. New York: HarperCollins. P Wells, T. (2009). *Mackenzie Blue*. New York: HarperCollins. M–U
Historical	Augarde, S. (2009). *Leonardo da Vinci*. New York: Kingfisher. M–U Hesse, K. (2000). *Stowaway*. New York: McElderry. M–U Hite, S. (2003). *Journal of Rufus Rowe, witness to the battle of Fredericksburg*. New York: Scholastic. M–U Ma, Y. (2005). *The diary of Ma Yan: The struggles and hopes of a Chinese schoolgirl*. New York: HarperCollins. M–U McKissack, P. C. (2000). *Nzingha: Warrior queen of Matamba*. New York: Scholastic. M–U Moss, M. (2002). *Galen: My life in imperial Rome*. San Diego: Harcourt Brace. M–U Pettenati, J. K. (2006). *Galileo's journal, 1609–1610*. Watertown, MA: Charlesbridge. P–M Philbrick, R. (2001). *The journal of Douglas Allen Deeds: The Donner party expedition*. New York: Scholastic. M–U Platt, R. (2005). *Egyptian diary: The journal of Nakht*. New York: Candlewick Press. M Platt, R. (2009). *Roman diary: The journal of Iliona of Mytilini, who was captured and sold as a slave in Rome, AD 107*. Somerville, MA: Candlewick Press. U

P = primary grades (preK–2); M = middle grades (3–5); U = upper grades (6–8)

Arabian girl who has recently come to the United States. The Booklist on the next page presents mentor texts that teachers can use as they're teaching students how to write letters.

ENGAGING ENGLISH LEARNERS

Writing can be difficult for English learners, and journals are the best way to introduce writing. It's essential that English learners have daily opportunities to practice writing because they need to develop writing fluency, the ability to get words down on paper. Through sustained writing, their handwriting skills improve, and their ability to spell high-frequency English words increases. In addition, there's less pressure because when students write in journals, the emphasis is on ideas rather than on correctness and neatness.

Students usually write about events in their own lives before writing about books they're reading and the content they're learning in thematic units. Peregoy and Boyle (2009) recommend that English learners write in buddy journals, which are a lot like dialogue journals: Students write back and forth to other English learners, and in these entries that are like written conversations, they write about topics that interest them, sharing ideas and asking questions. And as they're developing writing fluency, students are also learning that the purpose of writing is communicating ideas.

Many English learners write brief entries, often using and reusing familiar words and sentence patterns, and their entries are typically sprinkled with grammatical errors and misspelled words. Too often, teachers conclude that their English learners just can't write, but they can help these students write better journal entries. The first step involves examining students' entries to determine whether the problems center on undeveloped ideas, limited vocabulary, nonstandard grammar, or spelling errors. Often teachers notice problems in these areas, but they prioritize the problem areas and then work to resolve them:

IDEAS AND VOCABULARY. Ideas and vocabulary usually go hand in hand. Teachers model how to brainstorm ideas and related words before beginning to write, and they also demonstrate how to write entries with interesting, well-developed ideas. Teachers can also help individual students talk out their ideas and brainstorm a bank of words before they begin writing.

GRAMMAR. To focus on correcting nonstandard grammar errors, teachers teach minilessons on particular grammar concepts and then have students locate examples of the concept in their journal entries and make any needed corrections.

SPELLING. Even though students usually misspell some words in their journal entries, they should be expected to spell most high-frequency words correctly. Teachers explain how useful high-frequency words are to writers, and they demonstrate how to locate high-frequency words on the classroom word wall or on individual word walls that students keep in their

Booklist

LETTERS

Email	Danziger, P., & Martin, A. M. (2000). *Snail mail no more.* New York: Scholastic. M
Epistolary Stories	Ada, A. F. (1998). *Yours truly, Goldilocks.* New York: Atheneum. P
	Ada, A. F. (2001). *With love, Little Red Hen.* New York: Atheneum. P
	Ahlberg, J., & Ahlberg, A. (2006). *The jolly postman, or other people's letters.* New York: LB Kids. P
	Danziger, P., & Martin, A. M. (1998). *P. S. Longer letter later.* New York: Scholastic. M
	Horse, H. (2008). *The last gold diggers.* Atlanta, GA: Peachtree. M
	Lyons, M. E. (1992). *Letters from a slave girl: The story of Harriet Jacobs.* New York: Scribner. U
	Lyons, M. E. (2009). *Letters from a slave boy: The story of Joseph Jacobs.* New York: Simon & Schuster. M
	Nolen, J. (2002). *Plantzilla.* San Diego: Harcourt Brace. P–M
	Olson, M. W. (2000). *Nice try, tooth fairy.* New York: Simon & Schuster. P
	Woodson, J. (2009). *Peace, Locomotion.* New York: Putnam. M–U
Multigenre Books	Avi. (2003). *Nothing but the truth.* New York: Orchard Books. U
	Klise, K. (1999). *Letters from camp.* New York: Avon. U
	Klise, K. (2006). *Regarding the bathrooms: A privy to the past.* San Diego: Harcourt. U
Pen Pals	Clements, A. (2009). *Extra credit.* New York: Atheneum. M–U
	Nagda, A. W. (2000). *Dear Whiskers.* New York: Holiday House. M
	Pak, S. (1999). *Dear Juno.* New York: Viking. P
Postcards	Cherry, L. (1994). *The armadillo from Amarillo.* San Diego: Harcourt Brace. M
	Crawford, L. (2008). *Postcards from Washington, D.C.: Traveling with Anna.* McHenry, IL: Raven Tree Press. M
	Gravett, E. (2007). *Meerkat mail.* New York: Simon & Schuster. P–M
	Leedy, L. (2006). *Postcards from Pluto.* New York: Holiday House. P–M

journals. English learners can also return to a previously written journal entry and check for misspelled words using the word wall as a resource. ■

Assessing Students' Personal Writing

Teachers assess students' personal writing differently than other types of writing. Most journal writing is informal because the emphasis is on developing writing fluency or using writing as a learning tool; however, when students create journals as projects to document their learning, teachers evaluate them, often using a checklist or rubric. Blogs are usually informal, too, so teachers expect students to complete a specific number of posts and comments, but they don't evaluate their quality. In contrast, teachers evaluate the letters that students write, but because they'll be mailed, teachers use a checklist or rubric for evaluating letters without marking on them.

PLANNING. As teachers plan for instruction, they decide how they'll incorporate personal writing to support students' learning, and they identify topics for minilessons and mentor texts they'll use.

MONITORING. Sometimes students write in journals independently with little or no monitoring, but they're usually more successful when they make daily entries that the teacher monitors or reads regularly. The sheer quantity of journal entries that students produce can be overwhelming, so teachers often monitor that students are writing every day but read and respond to their entries on a rotating basis.

EVALUATING. When students use journals as a learning tool, their writing is informal, so teachers don't evaluate the entries or grade them for mechanical correctness. Instead, teachers often give points for each entry made, especially in personal journals. However, some teachers grade the content in learning logs and simulated journals because they can determine whether the entries include particular pieces of information. For example, if students are writing simulated journals about the Crusades, they may be asked to include five pieces of historically accurate information in their entries. It's helpful to ask students to identify the pieces of information by underlining and numbering them. Teachers evaluate the friendly and business letters that students write more formally. A third grade teacher developed the checklist for evaluating letters in Figure 4–10; it identifies specific behaviors and measurable products. The

---

FIGURE 4–10   Pen Pal Letter Checklist

Name _____

		Yes	No
1.	Did you complete the cluster?	☐	☐
2.	Did you include questions in your letter?	☐	☐
3.	Did you put your letter in the friendly letter form?	☐	☐

_____ return address
_____ greeting
_____ 3 or more paragraphs
_____ closing
_____ salutation and name

		Yes	No
4.	Did you write a rough draft of your letter?	☐	☐
5.	Did you revise your letter with suggestions from people in your revising group?	☐	☐
6.	Did you proofread your letter and correct as many errors as possible?	☐	☐

teacher shares the checklist with students before they begin to write so that they know what's expected of them and how they'll be graded. At an evaluation conference before the letters are mailed, the teacher reviews the evaluation with each student. A grading scale can be developed from the checklist; for example, points can be awarded for each checkmark in the Yes column so that five checkmarks equal a grade of A, four checkmarks a B, and so on.

SUMMING UP

Students make entries in various types of journals, use social networking tools, and write friendly and business letters to develop writing fluency and use writing for authentic communication purposes. They use personal journals, dialogue journals, reading logs, double-entry journals, learning logs, and simulated journals. Young children draw and write in personal journals and reading logs, and English learners gain writing fluency by using dialogue journals. Students use blogs to communicate with classmates, respond to books, and reflect on what they're learning. Letters are the third type of personal writing. Students exchange emails and write friendly and business letters that they mail to authentic audiences and simulated letters that they write as part of literature focus units and thematic units.

MyEducationLab™

Go to the topic Writing in the MyEducationLab (http://www.myeducationlab.com) for *Language Arts: Patterns of Practice*, where you can:

- Find learning outcomes for Writing, along with the national standards that connect to these outcomes.
- Complete Assignments and Activities that can help you more deeply understand the chapter content.
- Apply and practice your understanding of the core teaching skills identified in the chapter with the Building Teaching Skills and Dispositions learning units.
- Examine challenging situations and cases presented in the IRIS Center Resources.
- Use the Lesson Plan Builder Activities to practice lesson planning and integrating national and state standards into your planning.
- Check your comprehension of the content covered in the chapter with the Study Plan. Here you will be able to take a chapter quiz, receive feedback on your answers, and then access Review, Practice, and Enrichment activities to enhance your understanding of chapter content.

On the **MyEducationLab** for this course, you'll also be able to:

- **A+RISE** Go to the topic A+RISE, an innovative and interactive database of strategies that differentiate instruction across the language arts and provide particular insight into research-based methods to meet the needs of English learners.
- Explore the topic Literacy Portraits—yearlong case studies of second graders, complete with student artifacts, teacher commentary, and student and teacher interviews, tracking the month-by-month language arts growth of five students.
- Gain practice with the Grammar Tutorial, online guided instruction to improve your own ability with grammar.

CHAPTER 5

Oral Language: Listening and Talking

SECOND GRADERS READ FOLKTALES The second graders in Mr. Hernandez's classroom are reading folktales, and this week, they're comparing versions of "The Little Red Hen." On Monday, Mr. Hernandez read aloud Galdone's *Little Red Hen* (2006a), and the next day, he read aloud Pinkney's *The Little Red Hen* (2006) and compared it to Galdone's version. On Wednesday and Thursday, the children read "The Little Red Hen" in their reading textbooks and compared it with the others.

Parent volunteers came into the classroom on Wednesday to make bread. The second graders learned how to read recipes and use measuring cups and other cooking tools. They baked the bread in the school kitchen and ate the freshly baked bread—still warm from the oven—dripping with butter and jam. The next day, Mr. Hernandez read aloud *Bread, Bread, Bread* (Morris, 1993), about the breads that people around the world eat, and parents brought in different kinds of bread for children to sample, including tortillas, corn bread, bagels, and Indian chapatty.

Today, Mr. Hernandez's reading aloud *Cook-a-Doodle-Doo!* (Stevens & Crummel, 2005), the story of the Little Red Hen's great-grandson, Big Brown Rooster, who bakes a strawberry shortcake with the help of three friends—Turtle, Iguana, and Pig. He sets out objects related to the story: a chef's hat, a flour sifter, an egg beater, an oven mitt, a plastic strawberry, a shortcake pan, a pastry blender, and measuring cups and spoons. The children identify the objects, and then Mr. Hernandez places them at a center so the class can investigate them further. Quickly, Mikey guesses, "I know what the story is about! Little Red Hen is going to cook something, but it isn't bread. Um . . . Maybe it's strawberry jam for the bread."

Should teachers encourage discussion during a read-aloud?

Some teachers ask students to listen quietly while they read aloud and then talk about the selection afterward. Other teachers, however, invite students to become actively involved as they're reading. These teachers stop reading periodically to pose questions to stimulate discussion, ask students to make predictions, and encourage them to offer spontaneous comments while they're listening. As you read this vignette, notice how Mr. Hernandez uses discussion to support his second graders' comprehension.

"That's a good prediction, Mikey, but let me share one more clue about this story," Mr. Hernandez says, as he reaches over to a nearby rack of puppets for a rooster puppet. He looks at the children expectantly, and Mallory asks, "Is that a hen?" "No, it isn't," Mr. Hernandez replies. Again he waits until Cristina offers, "I think it's a rooster." "You're right! A *rooster* is a male chicken, and a *hen* is a female chicken," he explains. Then Mikey revises his prediction, "Now I know! It's a story about a rooster who cooks something with strawberries."

Mr. Hernandez shows the cover and reads the title. At first the children laugh, but then several repeat the title. "What does the title make you think of?" Mr. Hernandez asks. Jesus jumps up and imitates a rooster as he calls, "Cock-a-doodle-doo! Cock-a-doodle-doo!" The children compare the sound a rooster makes to the book's title and conclude that the rooster is going to do some cooking. Next, Mr. Hernandez asks, "What's he going to cook?" Lacey and Connor both answer "strawberry pancakes," and everyone agrees. He asks if anyone has tasted strawberry shortcake, but no one has. He explains what it is and tells the class it's his favorite dessert.

Mr. Hernandez reads the first two pages that introduce the Little Red Hen's great-grandson, Big Brown Rooster. The children point out the similarity between Little Red Hen's and Big Brown Rooster's names: They're each three words long, each has a size word, a color word, and an animal name, and words are in the same order. Mr. Hernandez continues reading, and they learn that the Rooster does plan to make strawberry shortcake. "What's shortcake?" Larry asks. "Is it the opposite of long cake?" Everyone laughs, including Mr. Hernandez. He explains that shortcake is flatter than cake, more like a biscuit. Mikey asks, "Is it like a brownie? Brownies are flatter than chocolate cake." "That's a good comparison," Mr. Hernandez says. Sammy offers: "A tortilla is flatter than a piece of bread." "Good! That's another good comparison," the teacher responds. "All this talk about food is making me hungry."

The teacher continues reading. He turns the page and shows the illustration, a picture of Big Brown Rooster talking to a dog, a cat, and a goose, and the children, remembering the events from

"Little Red Hen," spontaneously call out to Rooster, "No, don't ask them. They won't help you!" Big Brown Rooster does ask the three animals to help him, and as the children predicted, they refuse. As Mr. Hernandez reads the "Not I" refrain, everyone joins in. Sondra comments on the similarities to the "Little Red Hen" story: "There's a dog, a cat, and a goose like in the other story, and they won't listen to the Big Brown Rooster either." The children predict that Big Brown Rooster, like Little Red Hen, will have to cook alone.

On the next several pages, they learn that three other animals—Turtle, who can read recipes, Iguana, who can get "stuff," and Pig, who is a tasting expert—offer to help. The children get excited. "I think this story is going to be different. It's better," Cristina comments. Mr. Hernandez wonders aloud if these three animals will be good helpers, and the children agree that they will be.

The rooster calls the four of them a "team" on the next page, and Mr. Hernandez asks, "What is a *team*?" The second graders mention basketball teams, so the teacher rephrases his question: "What do teams do?" Children respond that players work together to win a game. "So, what kind of team are the rooster, the turtle, the iguana, and the pig?" Connor explains, "They're a cooking team. I predict they'll cook strawberry shortcake together." The second graders make charts in their reading logs to help them remember important ideas, such as how the characters formed a team; the box below shows one child's chart.

Mr. Hernandez continues reading, as Turtle reads the recipe and Iguana collects the ingredients for strawberry shortcake, but Iguana doesn't know the difference between a *flower* and *flour*. Because the children seem confused, too, the teacher explains about homophones. Iguana doesn't know about cooking tools and procedures either; he wants

A Second Grader's Chart

Rooster	Iguana	Turtle	Pig
I need a Team.	I can get stuf!	I can read the recipe!	I am the taster! I like to eat.

to use a ruler instead of a measuring cup to measure flour, and he looks for teaspoons in a teapot, for example. Because the children recently used measuring cups and spoons when they baked bread, they're more knowledgeable than Iguana, and Sammy says, "That iguana isn't very smart." On the next page, Iguana misunderstands "stick of butter." He breaks a stick from a tree branch, and Lacey calls out, "No, Iguana, that's the wrong kind of stick."

Pig keeps offering to taste the batter, but Big Brown Rooster replies "not yet." Mr. Hernandez pauses after he reads this and reflects, "Pig is eager to taste the shortcake batter. I wonder how long he'll wait patiently for his turn to taste." "Maybe Big Brown Rooster should give him something else to do," Sondra offers. "I'd tell him to go in the living room and watch a video because that's what my mom tells my brother," says Connor. Mr. Hernandez continues reading, and in the story, Pig is getting more desperate to taste the batter. Jesus calls out, "Oh no! Now Pig really, really wants to taste it. Something bad is going to happen." Everyone agrees. The characters finish mixing the ingredients and put the batter in the oven to bake. "Wow! I'm surprised that Pig is being so good," Mallory offers. "I thought he would gobble up all the shortcake from the mixing bowl." The others agree. "So, now you think the shortcake is going to turn out right?" Mr. Hernandez asks. Most of the children think that it will, but Jesus and Mikey disagree.

The teacher continues reading: The characters cut the strawberries in half and make whipped cream while the shortcake bakes. As he reads, some of the children spontaneously pretend to cut strawberries or use the egg beater to whip the cream. The next several pages tell how Rooster takes the shortcake out of the oven, lets it cool, slices it in half, and assembles the layers of cake, whipped cream, and strawberries. Mikey notices that Pig really wants to taste the shortcake when it comes out of the oven. "I still think that Pig is bad news," he says.

Finally, the strawberry shortcake is ready to eat, and Rooster says, "If Great-Granny could see me now!" Mr. Hernandez asks what the sentence means. Connor answers, "Rooster wants her to know he's a good cook, too!" Lacey suggests, "Rooster is really proud of himself." Raymond says, "I think Rooster wants Little Red Hen to know that he has a team to help him cook."

Mr. Hernandez turns the page and the children gasp. The illustration shows the strawberry shortcake falling off the plate as Iguana carries it to the table. "Oh no, it's ruined!" Mallory says. "They can't eat it because it's on the floor." "Pig can! Yes, Pig can. Now it's really his turn," Mikey says gleefully. Jesus cheers. "Well, I guess pigs can eat food on the floor," Mallory allows.

"What about the other animals?" Mr. Hernandez asks. "Won't they get any strawberry shortcake?" At first the children guess that they won't, and then Jacob offers, "Well, they could make another strawberry shortcake." Most of the children agree that Jacob has a good idea, but Larry disagrees, "No way. 'Snip, snap, snout. This story's told out,' said Pig." Everyone laughs as Larry suggests an alternative ending using the final words from the "Gingerbread Man" story they read earlier.

Mr. Hernandez reads the last few pages in the book, and the children learn that the animals do make another strawberry shortcake for everyone to eat. They're satisfied with the ending. "I'm glad everyone got to eat strawberry shortcake," Cristina says. "It's a good story," Sammy reflects, "because it's funny and serious, too." "What's funny?" the teacher asks. The children say that Iguana is the funniest character, and the funniest part is when the shortcake falls on the floor and Pig gobbles it up. Then Mr. Hernandez asks, "What's serious?" The children recognize the authors' message—a job is easier to do when you work as a team. "I'm glad Rooster had a team," said Sondra. "What about us?" Mr. Hernandez asks, "Do we have a team?" Mikey says, "I think that our class is a team." Mr. Hernandez responds, "What do you think makes us a team?" "We help each other learn and do our work," Larry answers. The other children agree. Finally, Mr. Hernandez shows the last page with Little Red Hen's recipe for strawberry shortcake and surprises everyone by announcing that they'll make strawberry shortcake after lunch.

tudents use oral language to explore ideas and communicate with others. Listening and talking also play essential roles in learning (Vygotsky, 1986); as they listen to the teacher read books aloud, for example, students acquire new information and related vocabulary words, and as they participate in discussions, they explore their own thinking and deepen their understanding. Teachers facilitate meaningful talk in preK–8 classrooms in three ways (Gilles, 2010). First, they set ground rules and teach students how to work collaboratively and engage in effective conversations with classmates. Second, teachers monitor students as they participate in discussions, checking that they're respectful, keep their conversations focused, make eye contact with classmates, and handle disagreements successfully. Third, teachers integrate oral language across the curriculum so that students have opportunities to apply what they've learned about small-group and whole-class conversations during thematic units (Barnes, 2008).

LISTENING

Listening is something most people take for granted. It's an invisible process by which spoken messages are received and converted to meaning in the mind (Lundsteen, 1979; National Communication Association, 1998). Students are often admonished to listen, but few teachers teach them how to improve their ability to listen. Instead, teachers usually assume that students already know how to listen. Also, some teachers believe that it's more important to spend instructional time on reading and writing instruction. Despite these concerns, most teachers agree that students need to learn more about listening because it's essential for learning (Opitz & Zbaracki, 2004).

Types of Listening

When asked why they listen, students often say that they listen to learn or to avoid punishment, but according to Wolvin and Coakley (1996), people listen differently according to their purpose. They've identified these four types of listening:

- Discriminative listening
- Aesthetic listening
- Efferent listening
- Critical listening

FIGURE 5-1	The Four Types of Listening	
Type	**Description**	**Examples**
Discriminative	Students distinguish among sounds.	Participate in phonemic awareness activities Notice rhyming words in poems and songs Recognize alliteration and onomatopoeia Experiment with tongue twisters
Aesthetic	Students listen for pleasure or enjoyment.	Listen to stories and poems read aloud View video versions of stories Listen to stories at a listening center Watch students perform a play or readers theatre reading Participate in grand conversations Participate in tea party activities
Efferent	Students listen to understand messages.	Listen to nonfiction books read aloud or at a listening center Listen to oral reports Use clusters and graphic organizers View informational videos Participate in discussions Participate in revising groups Listen during minilessons Listen to classmates share projects
Critical	Students evaluate messages.	Listen to debates and political speeches View commercials and other advertisements Evaluate themes and arguments in books read aloud

Figure 5–1 reviews these types of listening.

Discriminative Listening. People use discriminative listening to distinguish sounds. Young children use discriminative listening as they develop phonemic awareness, the ability to blend and segment the sounds in spoken words. Students also "listen" to nonverbal messages. They learn the meanings of more sophisticated forms of body language and recognize how teachers emphasize main ideas, such as by writing them on the whiteboard, speaking more loudly, or repeating information.

Aesthetic Listening. People listen aesthetically when they're listening for enjoyment to stories read aloud, as Mr. Hernandez's students did in the vignette at the beginning of the chapter. The focus is on the lived-through experience of the literature and the connections students make to their own lives, the world around them, and other literature (Rosenblatt, 2005). Viewing film, DVD, and videotape versions of stories are other examples.

Three of the most important aesthetic listening strategies are predicting, visualizing, and connecting:

PREDICTING. As students listen, they're predicting what will happen next, and they revise their predictions as they continue listening. When they read aloud, teachers encourage students to predict by stopping and asking them what they think will happen next.

VISUALIZING. Students create an image or picture in their minds while listening to a story that has strong visual images. They practice by closing their eyes, thinking about the descriptive words and phrases they hear, and trying to draw mental pictures while they're listening.

CONNECTING. Students make three types of connections. First, they make text-to-self connections between the story and events in their own lives. Next, they make text-to-world connections between the story and familiar current events. Third, they make text-to-text connections between the story and other stories they've read or TV shows and movies they've watched. Teachers help students use this strategy by asking them to talk about connections they've made as they discuss the story.

The second graders in the vignette used these strategies as they listened to their teacher read aloud *Cook-a-Doodle-Doo!* (Stevens & Crummel, 2005). Mikey offered predictions spontaneously, and at key points in the story, Mr. Hernandez asked the children to make additional predictions. They made personal connections to their families' cooking experiences and literary connections to the "Little Red Hen" stories they had read. The children also made literary connections when they noticed the similarity between the names *Big Brown Rooster* and *Little Red Hen* and the "not I" refrain from "The Little Red Hen." The children used visualizing when they made character charts after listening to Mr. Hernandez read the story. Students don't always use every strategy as they listen to a story, but this story provided many opportunities, and Mr. Hernandez knew how to take advantage of them.

Efferent Listening. People listen efferently to understand a message and remember important information. The term *efferent,* first applied to language arts by Louise Rosenblatt (2005), means "carrying away." It's the most common type of listening that students do in school. They use efferent listening as they listen to teachers present information or read nonfiction books aloud. They determine the speaker's purpose, identify the big ideas, and organize the information to remember it.

Students use strategies as they listen efferently; some are the same ones they use for reading and viewing, but others are unique to efferent listening. The purpose of each strategy is to help listeners organize and remember the information. These four strategies are the most important:

ORGANIZING. Students often use graphic organizers to visualize the organization of informational presentations (Yopp & Yopp, 2006). When students are listening to a presentation or a nonfiction book that contains information on three or more categories, they make a cluster, a diagram that resembles a spider web. They write each category on a ray and then add descriptive information. For example, while listening to a presentation on simple machines, fifth graders made a cluster with five rays, one for each type of simple machine, and added words and drawings about each type. Figure 5–2 shows a fifth grader's cluster.

SUMMARIZING. Speakers present several main ideas and many details during oral presentations, so students need to learn to focus on the main ideas; otherwise, they quickly feel overwhelmed with information. Once students can identify the main ideas, they can chunk the details to the main idea. When teachers introduce the summarizing strategy, they ask students to listen for two or three main ideas. Then teachers give an oral presentation, having students raise their hands when they hear the first main idea stated. Students then raise their hands when they hear the second main idea, and again for the third main idea. After students gain practice in detecting already-stated main ideas, teachers give a very brief presentation with one main idea and ask students to identify it. Once students can identify the main idea, teachers give longer oral presentations and ask students to identify two or three main ideas. A teacher might make these points when giving an oral presentation on simple machines:

There are five kinds of simple machines.
Simple machines are combined in specialized machines.
Machines make work easier.
Almost everything we do involves machines.

FIGURE 5–2   Cluster About Simple Machines

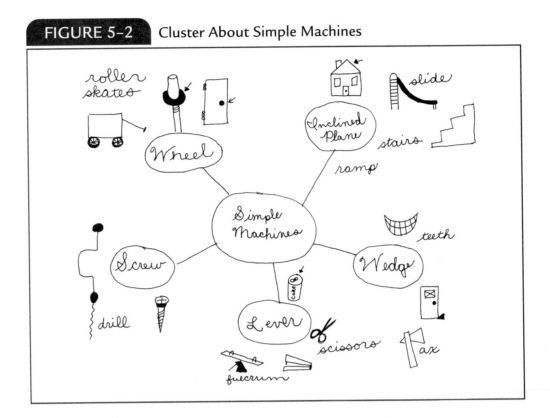

After students identify the main ideas, they chunk details to each one. This hierarchical organization is the most economical way to remember information, and students need to understand that they can remember more information when they use the summarizing strategy.

GETTING CLUES FROM THE SPEAKER. Speakers use both visual and verbal clues to convey their messages and direct their listeners' attention. Visual clues include gesturing, writing or underlining important information on the whiteboard, and changing facial expressions. Verbal clues include pausing, raising or lowering the voice, slowing down speech to stress key points, and repeating important information. Surprisingly, many students aren't aware of these attention-directing behaviors, so teachers must point them out. Once they're aware of these clues, students can use them to increase their understanding of a message.

MONITORING. Students monitor whether they're understanding while they're actively involved in listening. They ask themselves these questions as they begin to listen:

- Why am I listening to this message?
- Do I need to take notes?
- Does this information make sense?

They ask these questions as they continue listening:

- Is my strategy still working?
- Am I organizing the information effectively?
- Is the speaker giving me clues about the organization of the message?
- Is the speaker giving me nonverbal clues, such as gestures and facial expressions?

Monitoring is an important strategy because students need to know when they're not listening successfully or when a listening strategy isn't working so that they can correct the situation.

Critical Listening. People listen critically to evaluate a message. Critical listening is an extension of efferent listening. Students listen to understand a message, but they also filter the message to detect propaganda devices, persuasive language, and emotional appeals. It's used when people listen to debates, commercials, political speeches, and other arguments.

The most important strategy for critical listening is evaluating because students need to judge the message (Lundsteen, 1979). As they listen, students consider these questions simultaneously:

- What's the speaker's (or author's) purpose?
- Is there an intellectual appeal? a character appeal? an emotional appeal?
- Are propaganda devices being used?
- Are deceptive words or inflated language used?

As students listen to books read aloud, view commercials and advertisements, and listen to speakers, they ask themselves these questions to critically evaluate the message.

Reading Aloud

Reading aloud to children is a cherished classroom routine. In a study of sixth graders' reading preferences, an overwhelming 62% of students reported that they enjoy listening to the teacher read aloud (Ivey & Broaddus, 2001). Children's author Mem Fox (2001) and reading-aloud guru Jim Trelease (2006) both urge teachers to make time to read aloud every day because as students listen, they gain valuable experiences with books, enrich their background knowledge and vocabulary, and develop a love of literature. Reading aloud is an art; effective readers are familiar with the book they're reading, and they read fluently and with expression, changing the tone of their voices and using pauses to enhance students' listening experience.

It's easy to take reading aloud for granted, assuming that it's something teachers do for fun in between instructional activities. However, reading aloud is an important instructional activity with these benefits:

- Students' interest in reading is stimulated.
- Students' reading interests and their taste for quality literature are broadened.
- Students are introduced to the sounds of written language.
- Students' knowledge of vocabulary and sentence patterns is expanded.
- Students are introduced to books that are "too good to miss."
- Students see their teachers model what capable readers do.
- Students' background knowledge is expanded.
- Students are introduced to genres and elements of text structure.

And, most importantly, students who regularly listen to stories and informational books read aloud are more likely to become lifelong readers.

Interactive Read-Alouds. Reading aloud has been an informal activity in most classrooms: Teachers pick up a book, read the title aloud, and begin reading while students listen quietly. Often young children sit in a group on the floor around the teacher, and older students sit attentively at their desks. They're passive as they listen, but afterward, they're more engaged as they talk briefly about the book and perhaps participate in a follow-up activity. The focus has been on sharing literature, with little or no student involvement until afterward. Researchers have concluded, however, that students are better listeners when they're involved during reading, not afterward (Dickinson & Tabors, 2001). This conclusion has led to the development of the interactive read-aloud procedure (Barrentine, 1996).

In an interactive read-aloud, teachers introduce the book and activate students' background knowledge before they begin to read. They model listening strategies and fluent oral reading as they read aloud, and they engage students during reading. Then afterward, they provide opportunities for students to respond to the book. The most important component is student involvement during the read-aloud (Fisher, Flood, Lapp, & Frey, 2004). The Step-by-Step feature below describes the steps in an interactive read-aloud.

One way that teachers engage students is to stop reading periodically to discuss what they've just read. When they're reading stories, it's most effective to stop at points where students can make predictions and suggest connections, after reading episodes that students might find confusing, and just before it becomes clear how the story will end. For poems, teachers often read the entire poem once, and then stop as they read it a second time for students to play with words, notice poetic devices, and repeat favorite words and lines. When they're reading informational books aloud, teachers stop to talk about big ideas as they're presented, briefly explain technical terms, and emphasize connections among the big ideas. Figure 5–3 presents additional ways to actively involve students with read-aloud books. Deciding how often to stop for discussion and knowing when to end the discussion and continue reading develop through practice and vary from one group of students to another.

Books to Read Aloud. Guidelines for choosing books to read aloud are simple: Choose ones that you like and that you think will appeal to your students. Trelease (2006) makes these suggestions:

- Books should be fast-paced to hook students' interest as quickly as possible.
- Books should contain well-developed characters.

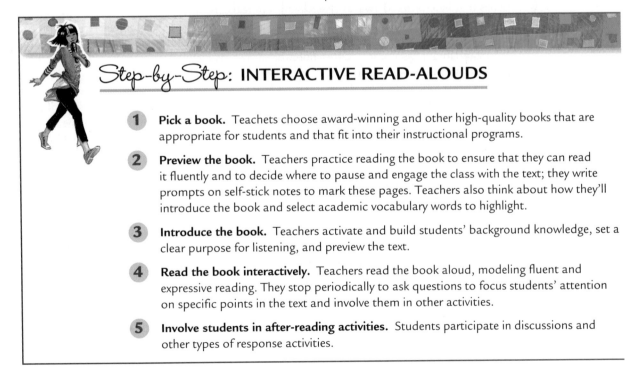

Step-by-Step: INTERACTIVE READ-ALOUDS

1. **Pick a book.** Teachers choose award-winning and other high-quality books that are appropriate for students and that fit into their instructional programs.

2. **Preview the book.** Teachers practice reading the book to ensure that they can read it fluently and to decide where to pause and engage the class with the text; they write prompts on self-stick notes to mark these pages. Teachers also think about how they'll introduce the book and select academic vocabulary words to highlight.

3. **Introduce the book.** Teachers activate and build students' background knowledge, set a clear purpose for listening, and preview the text.

4. **Read the book interactively.** Teachers read the book aloud, modeling fluent and expressive reading. They stop periodically to ask questions to focus students' attention on specific points in the text and involve them in other activities.

5. **Involve students in after-reading activities.** Students participate in discussions and other types of response activities.

FIGURE 5-3   Ways to Actively Involve Students With Books

Stories
Make and revise predictions at pivotal points in the story
Share personal, world, and literary connections
Talk about visualizations and other uses of listening strategies
Draw a picture of a character or an event
Assume the persona of a character and share what the character might be thinking
Reenact a scene from the story

Poems
Add sound effects
Mumble-read along with the teacher as the poem is read
Repeat lines after the teacher
Clap or snap fingers for rhyming words, alliterations, onomatopoeia, or other poetic devices

Nonfiction Books
Ask questions or share information
Raise their hands for specific information
Restate headings as questions
Take notes
Complete graphic organizers

- Books should include easy-to-read dialogue.
- Books should keep long descriptive passages to a minimum.

Books that have received awards or acclaim from teachers, librarians, and students make good choices. The two most prestigious awards are the Caldecott Medal, for outstanding picture books, and the Newbery Medal, for distinguished children's books, awarded annually by the American Library Association. Other noteworthy awards include the Pura Belpré Award, honoring Latino writers and illustrators whose books celebrate the Latino cultural experience; the Coretta Scott King Book Awards, recognizing African American authors and illustrators for outstanding contributions; and the Sibert Informational Book Medal, honoring the best nonfiction books. Many states give awards to outstanding books selected by students, such as the Buckeye Book Award in Ohio and the Sequoyah Book Award in Oklahoma. The International Reading Association also sponsors a Children's Choices competition, in which students read and select their favorite books, and a similar Teachers' Choices competition; lists of these books are published annually in *The Reading Teacher*. Teachers choose grade-appropriate books for read-alouds that are too difficult for students to read independently; the point is that even if students can't read the words, they can understand the ideas.

Sometimes students complain that a book's "boring," but what they generally mean is that they don't understand it. They may lack sufficient background knowledge on the topic or may be overwhelmed by unfamiliar vocabulary, but teachers can address these problems by building background knowledge by showing a video, reading a picture book, or sharing a box of objects related to the book and introducing essential academic vocabulary. Making sure that students understand often solves the problem, but sometimes teachers create interest by asking students to assume a role as a character and dramatize events from the story. Once in a while, however, a book really doesn't suit a group of students, so teachers try a different one.

Students—especially young children—often beg to have familiar books reread. Although it's important to share a wide variety of books, researchers have found that students benefit in specific ways from repeated readings (Yaden, 1988). In particular, they gain control over the parts of a story and are better able to synthesize those parts into a whole. The quality of students' responses changes, too, as they become more familiar with a story.

Persuasion

Students—even those in the primary grades—need to become critical listeners because they're exposed to persuasion and propaganda. Interpreting books and films requires critical thinking and listening. And social studies and science lessons on topics such as the Ku Klux Klan, illegal drugs, and climate change demand that students listen and think critically. Television commercials are another form of persuasion and source of propaganda, and because many commercials are directed at children, it's essential that they listen critically and learn to judge the advertising claims. For example, do the jogging shoes actually help you run faster? Will the breakfast cereal make you a better football player? Will a particular video game make you more popular?

People can be persuaded in three ways. The first is by using reason. We seek logical conclusions, whether from absolute facts or from strong possibilities; for example, we can be persuaded to practice more healthful living as the result of medical research. It's necessary, of course, to distinguish between reasonable arguments and illogical appeals. To suggest that diet pills will bring about extraordinary weight loss is illogical.

A second way is an appeal to character. We can be persuaded by what another person recommends if we trust that person. Trust comes from personal knowledge or the reputation of the person who is trying to persuade us. We believe what scientists say about the dangers of nuclear waste, but can we believe what a sports personality says about the taste of a particular brand of coffee?

The third way is by appealing to people's emotions. Emotional appeals can be as strong as intellectual appeals. We have strong feelings and concern for ourselves and other people and animals. Fear, a need for peer acceptance, and a desire for freedom of expression are all potent feelings that influence our opinions and beliefs.

Any of these types of appeals can be used to persuade someone. For example, when a child wishes to convince her parents that her bedtime should be delayed by 30 minutes, she might argue that neighbors allow their children to stay up later—an appeal to character. It's an appeal to reason when the argument focuses on the amount of sleep a 10-year-old needs. And when the child announces that she has the earliest bedtime of anyone in her class and it makes her feel like a baby, the appeal is to emotion. The same three appeals apply to in-school persuasion. To persuade classmates to read a particular book in a book report "commercial," a student might argue that they should read the book because it's written by a favorite author (reason); because it's hilarious (emotion); or because it's the most popular book in the seventh grade and everyone else is reading it (character).

It's essential that students become critical consumers of commercials and advertisements because they're bombarded with them (Brownell, 2006; Lutz, 1997). Advertisers use appeals to reason, character, and emotion just as other persuaders do to promote products, ideas, and services; however, advertisers may also use propaganda to influence our beliefs and actions. Propaganda suggests something shady or underhanded. Like persuasion, propaganda is designed to influence people's beliefs and actions, but propagandists may use certain techniques to distort, conceal, and exaggerate. Two of these techniques are deceptive language and propaganda devices.

People seeking to influence us often use words that evoke a variety of responses. They claim that something is "improved," "more natural," or "50% better"—loaded words and phrases that are deceptive because they're suggestive. When a product is advertised as 50% better, for example, consumers need to ask, "50% better than what?" Advertisements rarely answer that question.

Doublespeak is deceptive language that's evasive, euphemistic, confusing, and self-contradictory. It's language that only pretends to communicate (Lutz, 1997). Two kinds of doublespeak that children can understand are euphemisms and inflated language. *Euphemisms* are words or phrases (e.g., "passed away") that are used to avoid a harsh or distasteful reality, often out of concern for someone's feelings rather than to deceive. *Inflated language* includes words intended to make the ordinary seem extraordinary. Thus, car mechanics become "automotive internists," and used cars become "pre-owned" or even "experienced."

Students need to learn that people sometimes use words that only pretend to communicate; sometimes they use words to intentionally misrepresent, as when someone advertises a vinyl wallet as "genuine imitation leather" or a glass stone in a ring as a "faux diamond." When students can interpret deceptive language, they can avoid being deceived.

To sell products, advertisers use propaganda devices, such as testimonials, the bandwagon effect, and rewards. Figure 5–4 describes six devices that students can identify. They can listen to commercials to find examples of each propaganda device and discuss the effect the device has on them. They can also investigate how the same devices vary in commercials directed toward youngsters, teenagers, and adults. For instance, a commercial for a snack food with a sticker or toy in the package will appeal to a youngster, and an advertisement for an appliance offering a factory rebate will appeal to an adult. The same propaganda device—a reward—is used in both ads. Propaganda devices can be used to sell ideas as well as products; both public service announcements and political advertisements use these devices.

FIGURE 5–4 Propaganda Devices

Device	Description
Glittering Generality	Propagandists use generalities such as "environmentally safe" to enhance the quality of a product. Even though the generality is powerful, listeners need to think beyond it to assess the product.
Name Calling	Persuaders try to pin a bad label on someone or something they want listeners to dislike, such as calling a person "unpatriotic." Listeners then need to consider the effect of the label.
Bandwagon	Advertisers claim that everyone is using their product; for example, "four of five physicians recommend this medicine." Listeners must consider whether everyone recommends this product.
Testimonial	Advertisers associate a product with an athlete or movie star. Listeners must consider whether the person offering the endorsement has the expertise to judge the quality of the product.
Card Stacking	Propagandists often use only items that favor one side of an issue; unfavorable facts are ignored. To be objective, listeners need to seek information about other viewpoints.
Rewards	Propagandists offer rewards for buying their products—children are lured by toys and adults by discounts or rebates. Listeners need to ask whether the reward makes the product worth buying.

TALK

Noted researcher Shirley Brice Heath (1983a) explored the value of talk in classrooms and concluded that students' talk is an essential part of language arts and is necessary for academic success. Quiet classrooms were once considered the most conducive to learning, but researchers now emphasize that talk is a necessary ingredient for learning (Boyd & Galda, 2011). Talk is often thwarted in classrooms because of large class size and the mistaken assumption that silence facilitates learning; instead, teachers must make an extra effort to provide opportunities for students to use talk for both socialization and learning.

Talking in Small Groups

Students get together in small groups to respond to literature they're reading, talk about each other's writing, organize information they're learning, and work on projects. The most important benefit of talk is that it promotes higher level thinking. Teachers take students' ideas seriously, and students are validated as thinkers (Nystrand, Gamoran, & Heck, 1993). As they converse with classmates, students use talk for different purposes: to control classmates' behavior, maintain social relationships, convey information, and share personal experiences and opinions, for instance. Small-group conversations about literature can also support students' use of interpreting and other comprehension strategies (Berne & Clark, 2008). Students need to know how to use the strategies, and it's important for teachers to encourage them to apply the strategies while they're reading and to talk about how they used them during the discussions.

Students learn and refine their strategies for talking with classmates as they participate in small-group conversations (Kaufman, 2000). They learn how to begin conversations, take turns, keep the conversation moving forward, support comments, respond to questions that classmates ask, deal with conflicts, and bring the conversation to a close. And, they learn how powerful talk is in creating knowledge and deepening understanding. The characteristics of small-group conversations are described in Figure 5–5.

To begin the conversation, students gather in groups at tables or other areas in the classroom, bringing with them any necessary materials. One student in each group begins the conversation with a question or comment; classmates then take turns making comments and asking questions and support the other group members as they elaborate on and expand their comments. The tone is exploratory, and throughout the conversation, the group is progressing toward a common goal: deepening students' understanding of a book they've read, responding to a question the teacher has asked, or creating a project. From time to time, the conversation slows down and there may be a few minutes of silence. Then a group member asks a question or makes a comment that sends the conversation in a new direction.

Students support one another in groups, and two of the most important ways they do this are by calling each other by name and maintaining eye contact. They also cultivate a climate of trust in the group by expressing agreement, sharing feelings, voicing approval, and referring to comments that group members made earlier. Conflict is inevitable, but students need to learn how to deal with it so that it doesn't get out of control. They learn to accept that there will be differing viewpoints and to make compromises. Cintorino (1993) reported that her eighth graders used humor to defuse disagreements in small-group conversations.

At the end of a conversation, students reach consensus and conclude that they've finished sharing ideas, explored all dimensions of a question, or completed a project. Sometimes they create a product during the conversation; it may be a brainstormed list, a chart, or something more

FIGURE 5-5	Small-Group Conversations
Characteristic	**Description**
Size	Each group has three to six members. Some groups are permanent, but others are established for specific activities. Established groups often choose names to identify themselves.
Participants	Students are expected to form a cohesive group, be courteous to and supportive of their classmates, and assume responsibility for completing the task.
Purposes	Teachers clearly set the goal of the small-group conversation and explain the activities to be completed. Small-group conversations are used to create knowledge, organize information, and deepen interpretations, and the best activities are those that require collaboration and could not be done as effectively by students working independently.
Questions	Teachers pose questions to guide students' conversations; the most useful questions are meaningful, functional, and genuine, and they should require higher level thinking and critical analysis.
Strategies	Students apply strategies they've learned to begin the conversation, keep it focused, deal with disagreements, and conclude it.

elaborate, such as a set of puppets. Group members are responsible for collecting and storing materials they've used and for reporting on the group's work.

Teachers play an important role in making conversations successful, beginning with creating a community of learners in the classroom so that students understand that they're responsible group members (Kaufman, 2000). Teachers create a climate of trust by demonstrating to students that they trust them and their ability to learn. Similarly, students learn to socialize with classmates and to respect one another as they work together.

Discussions

Students participate in both teacher-led and student-led discussions that support their learning and promote their ability to think and solve problems. As they learn how to participate in discussions, students move beyond one-word and single-sentence responses, engage in speculative thinking, piggyback on classmates' ideas, and ask their own questions. And, as students become more active participants in discussions, teachers ask fewer questions and the questions they do ask require higher level, more critical thinking.

Grand Conversations About Stories. To dig into a story and deepen their comprehension, students talk about books they're reading in literature focus units and literature circles; these conversations are called *grand conversations* (Peterson & Eeds, 2007). They're different from traditional discussions because students take responsibility as they voice their opinions and support their views with examples from the text. They talk about what puzzles them, what they find interesting, their personal connections to the story, and connections they see between this book and others they've read. Students also encourage their classmates to contribute to the conversation and value their contributions. Even though teachers often sit in on conversations as a participant, not as a judge, the talk is primarily among the students.

Teachers often use a combination of small-group and whole-class groupings for grand conversations, but they can be held with the whole class or in small groups. When students meet in small groups, they have more opportunities to talk, and when they meet as a class, there's a feeling of community. Young children usually meet as a class, but students participating in literature circles meet in small groups because they're reading different books. When the teacher is reading aloud a novel, students often meet first in small groups and then come together as a class to respond to the book.

Grand conversations have two parts. The first part is open-ended: Students talk about their reactions to the book, and their comments determine the direction of the conversation. Teachers do participate, however, and share their responses, ask questions, and provide information. In the second part, the teacher focuses students' attention on one or two aspects of the book that they didn't talk about in the first part of the conversation. The steps are shown in the Step-by-Step feature on page 130.

After the grand conversation, students often write in their reading logs, or write again if they wrote before the grand conversation. Then they continue reading the book if they've read only part of it. Both participating in grand conversations and writing entries in reading logs help students think about and respond to what they've read.

PreK *Spotlight*

Which talk strategies do young children learn?

Even though young children come to school already knowing how to talk, they need to learn how to engage in meaningful academic talk activities—collaborating with partners, working in small groups at centers, participating in grand conversations about picture books and other discussions, and retelling stories, for instance. They learn to use these strategies:

Asking and Answering Questions. Children express their curiosity by asking genuine questions about a topic, and they also search for answers to questions that classmates ask.

Elaborating. Children explore topics and deepen their understanding by sharing information, thinking of examples, and making connections to past experiences.

Responding. Children respond to comments made by others—adding information, agreeing, offering opinions, and asking questions, for example.

Retelling. Children learn how to retell stories that include a beginning, middle, and end and move the plot along quickly enough to sustain the audience's interest.

Sticking to the Topic. Even though children have lots of ideas they'd like to share, they refrain from making comments that aren't related to the topic.

Taking Turns. Children share the spotlight and allow classmates to have opportunities to ask questions, share insights, and make other comments.

These strategies are action plans that children use to initiate and sustain meaningful talk activities. Roskos, Tabors, and Lenhart (2009) suggest that teachers should be "planful, purposeful, and playful" (p. 6) as they introduce and model the strategies during interactive read-alouds, circle time, storytelling, dramatic play activities, and other small-group and whole-class activities. Evans (2009) emphasizes the importance of playful talk activities using picture books. Children link oral, written, and visual language as they use these talk strategies to respond to the text and illustrations in books that teachers read aloud.

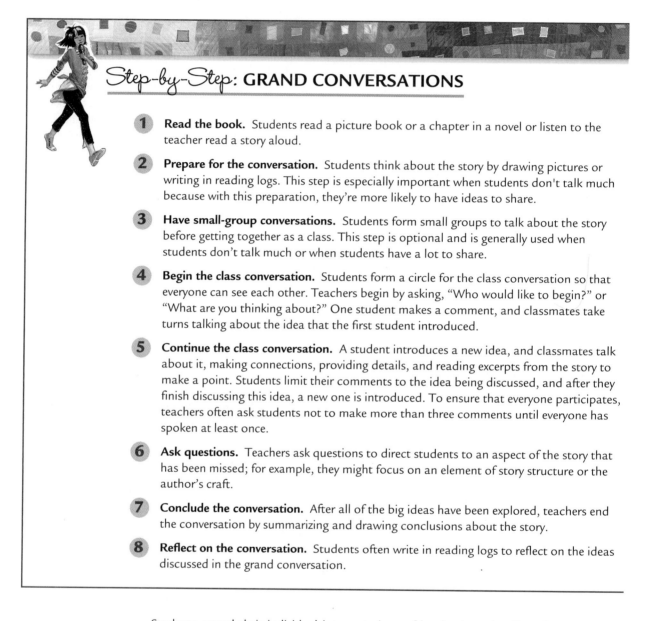

Step-by-Step: GRAND CONVERSATIONS

1 **Read the book.** Students read a picture book or a chapter in a novel or listen to the teacher read a story aloud.

2 **Prepare for the conversation.** Students think about the story by drawing pictures or writing in reading logs. This step is especially important when students don't talk much because with this preparation, they're more likely to have ideas to share.

3 **Have small-group conversations.** Students form small groups to talk about the story before getting together as a class. This step is optional and is generally used when students don't talk much or when students have a lot to share.

4 **Begin the class conversation.** Students form a circle for the class conversation so that everyone can see each other. Teachers begin by asking, "Who would like to begin?" or "What are you thinking about?" One student makes a comment, and classmates take turns talking about the idea that the first student introduced.

5 **Continue the class conversation.** A student introduces a new idea, and classmates talk about it, making connections, providing details, and reading excerpts from the story to make a point. Students limit their comments to the idea being discussed, and after they finish discussing this idea, a new one is introduced. To ensure that everyone participates, teachers often ask students not to make more than three comments until everyone has spoken at least once.

6 **Ask questions.** Teachers ask questions to direct students to an aspect of the story that has been missed; for example, they might focus on an element of story structure or the author's craft.

7 **Conclude the conversation.** After all of the big ideas have been explored, teachers end the conversation by summarizing and drawing conclusions about the story.

8 **Reflect on the conversation.** Students often write in reading logs to reflect on the ideas discussed in the grand conversation.

Students extend their individual interpretations of books through talk and even create a better understanding of them. They talk about their understanding of the story and sometimes change their opinions after listening to classmates' alternative views. Students share personal stories related to their reading in poignant ways that trigger classmates to identify with them. They also gain insights about how authors use the elements of story structure to develop their message.

Martinez and Roser (1995) researched students' grand conversations, and they found that students often talk about story events and characters or explore the themes but delve less often into the author's craft to explore the way he or she structured the book, the arrangement of text and illustrations on the page, or the author's use of figurative language. The researchers called these three conversation directions *experience, message,* and *object.* They suggest that stories help to shape students' talk about books and that some books lend themselves to conversation about message and others to talk about experience or object. Stories with dramatic plots or those that present a problem students can relate to, such as *Chrysanthemum* (Henkes, 1991) and *The Tale of Despereaux* (DiCamillo, 2003), focus the conversation on the book as experience. Multilayered stories or books in which main characters deal with dilemmas, such as *Smoky Night* (Bunting, 1999) and *Princess Academy* (Hale, 2007), focus the conversation on the message. Books with distinctive structures or language features, such as *Flotsam* (Wiesner, 2006) and *Witness* (Hesse, 2005), focus the conversation on the object.

Drawing students' attention to the "object" is important because they apply what they've learned about the author's craft when they write their own stories. Students who know more about leads, figurative language, point of view, imagery, surprise endings, voice, and flashbacks write better stories than those who don't. One way teachers can help students examine the author's craft is through the questions they ask during grand conversations.

Thematic Unit Discussions. Discussions deepen students' content-area knowledge and develop their academic language proficiency in these ways:

- Students deepen their knowledge about the topic.
- Students use technical and precise vocabulary and more complex sentence structures to express the ideas being discussed.
- Students learn to provide support for the ideas they present with information found in non-fiction books, content-area textbooks, and other classroom resources.
- Students ask inference and critical-level questions, those with more than one answer.
- Students participate actively and make comments that build on and expand classmates' comments.

Students participate in discussions to accomplish goals, learn information, and work out problems in thematic units. As they talk, students pose hypotheses, ask questions, provide information, and clarify ideas; recall ideas presented earlier; make personal, world, and literary connections; draw inferences; and evaluate the text and the information presented in it (Roser & Keehn, 2002). In contrast to grand conversations about stories in which students use primarily aesthetic talk to create and deepen their interpretations, here students use primarily efferent talk to create knowledge and understand relationships among the big ideas they're learning.

Researchers have compared the effectiveness of small-group conversations with other instructional approaches and have found that students' learning is enhanced when they relate what they're learning to their own experiences—especially when they do so in their own words (Wittrock & Alesandrini, 1990). Similarly, Pressley (1992) reported that students' learning was promoted when they had opportunities to elaborate ideas through talk.

Asking Questions. Asking and answering questions are common types of talk in classrooms. Researchers have found that teachers ask as many as 50,000 questions a year, but students ask as few as 10 (Watson & Young, 2003). The most common questions are literal questions, those that require simple recall, even though the most useful questions require students to analyze, interpret, evaluate, and offer opinions.

After reading *Amber Brown Is Not a Crayon* (Danziger, 2006), the story of two best friends and what happens as one of them moves to another state, a group of third graders wrote these questions:

 Why do you think Amber and Justin are best friends?
Do you think Mr. Cohn is sort of like Ms. Frizzle [in the Magic School Bus series]?
Do you think Mr. Cohn is a good teacher?

Did you know from the beginning that Justin was going to move away?
How can best friends fight and still be best friends?
Is Justin happy or sad about moving to Alabama?
Why is Amber so mean to Justin?
What do you think will happen to the friendship after Justin moves away?
Can they still be best friends after Justin moves away?

These questions involve higher level thinking and delve into the "best friends" theme of the book. They require students to think deeply about the story and even to go back and reread portions to support their answers. If students aren't going this deeply into a story, teachers should pose questions like these.

Questions can be grouped into three levels: literal, inferential, and critical. Literal or "on the page" questions have a single factual answer and can usually be answered with a few words or *yes* or *no*. When the questions refer to a story or other book that students are reading, the answers are directly stated in the text. The second level of questions is inferential or "between the lines"; to answer these questions, students synthesize information and form interpretations using both their background knowledge and clues in the text. The answers are implicitly stated in the text. The third, most complex level of questioning is critical or "beyond the page." These questions are open-ended; they require students to go beyond the text and think creatively and abstractly about global ideas, issues, and concerns. At this level, students apply information, make connections, evaluate and value the text, and express opinions. Figure 5–6 reviews the three levels of questioning.

Teachers use these three levels of questions for different purposes. They use literal questions to check that students have basic information and understand the meaning of words. Literal questions are easy to ask and to answer, but, because they're the most frequently asked questions, teachers need to be careful not to use too many of them. To help students think more deeply and to challenge their thinking, teachers use inferential and critical questions. When they're talking about literature, teachers ask inferential questions to probe students' understanding of a story and make interpretations, and when they ask students to analyze the ideas, make comparisons, and summarize information. Teachers ask critical questions to challenge students' thinking to go beyond the story to make connections, evaluate the story, reflect on the overall

FIGURE 5–6   Levels of Questioning

Level	Category	Description
3	Critical or "Beyond the Page" Questions	Critical questions go beyond the text and focus on global issues, ideas, and problems. Often there are no correct answers. To answer these questions, students think creatively; make personal, world, and literary connections; evaluate the text; and express opinions.
2	Inferential or "Between the Lines" Questions	Inferential questions require analysis and interpretation; the answers are implicitly stated in the text. To answer these questions, students use a combination of background knowledge and clues in the text.
1	Literal or "On the Page" Questions	Literal questions are factual; the answers to these questions are stated explicitly in the text. Students answer these questions with *yes* or *no* or with a few words taken directly from the text.

theme, and delve into the author's craft. They ask critical questions during thematic units for similar purposes: to consider different viewpoints, examine issues, and draw conclusions.

Oral Reports

Students prepare and give reports about topics they're studying in social studies and science. Giving a report orally helps students to deepen their knowledge as well as to develop their ability to speak in front of a group. Students need to learn how to prepare and present an oral report.

Students begin by brainstorming a list of possible topics related to the thematic unit, and then each student chooses a topic. Next, students inventory, or think over, what they know about their topic and decide what they need to learn about it. Teachers often help students identify several key questions to focus the report. Next, students gather information to answer the key questions using a variety of resources, including nonfiction books, content-area textbooks, the Internet, and encyclopedias. In addition, students can view videotapes and interview people in the community who have special expertise on the topic.

Students review the information they've gathered and decide how best to present it so that the report will be both interesting and well organized. They can transfer the notes they want to use for their reports from the graphic organizer onto note cards. Only key words—not sentences or paragraphs—should be written on the cards. Students also develop visuals, such as charts, diagrams, maps, pictures, models, and time lines. Visuals provide a crutch for the speaker and add interest for the listeners. Students choose an interesting fact to begin their presentation, review key points, and read over their note cards; however, they don't read the report verbatim from the note cards. Then they rehearse their presentations. Finally, students give their oral presentations, making sure they speak loudly enough for all to hear, look at the audience, keep to the key points, refer to note cards for important facts, and use the visuals they've prepared.

Interviews

Students refine their ability to ask questions as they conduct interviews as part of literature focus units and thematic units. They participate in these types of activities:

Students pose as book characters and are interviewed by classmates.
Students interview favorite authors and illustrators.
Students interview experts as they study thematic units.
Students participate in oral history projects and interview grandparents and older community members.

As part of a unit on school, for example, a first grade class invited their principal for an interview. The principal, who had been blinded several years earlier, brought his guide dog with him. The first graders asked him how he manages everyday tasks as well as how he performs his job as a principal. They also asked questions about his guide dog. Afterward, students drew pictures and wrote about the interview. A first grader's report is shown in Figure 5–7.

One way to introduce interviewing is to watch interviews conducted on television and discuss their purposes, the interviewer's activities before and after the interview, and the types of questions used. Interviewers use a variety of questions, some to elicit facts and

FIGURE 5-7   An Interview Report

Mr. Kirtley came down. We asked him questions. He answered them. He is blind. His dog's name is Milo.

others to probe for feelings and opinions, but most questions are open-ended. Rarely do interviewers ask questions that require only a single-word answer.

Students prepare for an interview by researching the topic, contacting the person to be interviewed, and generating a list of questions. They usually conduct the interview in person, but they can also use Skype, telephone, or email. During the interview, students establish rapport with the interviewee, ask questions, and take notes or videotape the interview. Afterward, students use the information they've learned in some way. For example, they might create a video of the interview, write an article for the classroom website, or create a photo collage interspersed with quotes from the interviewee and other resources.

Hot Seat. Students assume the persona of a character from a story or biography they're reading and sit in the "hot seat" to be interviewed by classmates. These informal interviews are called "hot seat" because students are expected to respond to their classmates' questions. Students are usually eager for their turn to sit in the hot seat. They answer the questions they're asked from the viewpoint of the character, and through this questioning, they deepen their comprehension as well as their classmates'. The steps in the procedure are listed in the Step-by-Step feature on the next page. Students often wear a costume they've created when they assume the character's persona and share information about the character with classmates. They also collect objects and make artifacts to share.

Debates

Students participate in debates when they're excited about an issue and when most of the students have taken positions on one side of the issue or the other. Students debate issues related to social studies and science topics, community issues, and current events. Middle and upper grade students also debate topics related to novels. For example, after reading *Tuck Everlasting* (Babbitt, 2007), they might debate whether people should live forever. Books that spark debates are presented in the Booklist feature on the next page. Students have strong feelings about the issues raised in many of these books, and debating provides a forum for thinking about important issues.

Step-by-Step: HOT SEAT

1. **Learn about the character.** Students prepare for the hot seat activity by reading a story or a biography to learn about the character they'll impersonate.

2. **Create a costume.** Students design a costume appropriate for the character. In addition, they often collect objects or create artifacts to use in their presentation.

3. **Prepare opening remarks.** Students think about the most important things they'd like to share about the character and plan what they'll say at the beginning of the activity.

4. **Introduce the character.** The student sits in front of classmates in a chair designated as the "hot seat," tells a little about the character he or she is role-playing using a first-person viewpoint (e.g., "I said, 'one small step for man, one giant leap for mankind'"), and shares artifacts.

5. **Ask questions.** Classmates ask thoughtful, higher level questions to learn more about the character, and the student remains in the role to answer them.

6. **Summarize the ideas.** The student doing the role-play selects a classmate to summarize the important ideas that were presented and adds any big ideas the classmate doesn't mention.

Booklist

BOOKS THAT SPARK DEBATES

Avi. (2003). *Nothing but the truth.* New York: Orchard Books. U
Babbitt, N. (2007). *Tuck everlasting.* New York: Square Fish Books. U
Bunting, E. (1997). *A day's work.* New York: Clarion Books. M
Bunting, E. (1999). *Smoky night.* San Diego: Harcourt Brace. M
Clements, A. (1998). *Frindle.* New York: Aladdin Books. M–U
Curtis, C. P. (2000). *The Watsons go to Birmingham—1963.* New York: Delacorte. M–U
Fox, P. (2003). *One-eyed cat.* New York: Simon & Schuster. M–U
Gantos, J. (2000). *Joey Pigza loses control.* New York: Farrar, Straus & Giroux. U
Haddix, M. P. (1998). *Among the hidden.* New York: Aladdin Books. U
Lowry, L. (2006). *The giver.* New York: Delacorte. U
Lowry, L. (2011). *Number the stars.* New York: Sandpiper. M–U
Naylor, P. R. (2000). *Shiloh.* New York: Aladdin Books. M
Ryan, P. M. (1998). *Riding Freedom.* New York: Scholastic. M–U
Sachar, L. (2008). *Holes.* New York: Farrar, Straus & Giroux. U
Staples, S. F. (1989). *Shabanu: Daughter of the wind.* New York: Knopf. U
Steig, W. (1990). *Doctor DeSoto.* New York: Farrar, Straus & Giroux. M

P = primary grades (preK–2); M = middle grades (3–5); U = upper grades (6–8)

As they participate in debates, students learn how to use oral language to persuade their classmates. They must articulate their viewpoints clearly, use logical and emotional appeals to support their viewpoints, and think on their feet to respond to questions raised by the opposing team. Students form supporting and opposing teams, and each team prepares by deciding on arguments and how they'll respond to the other team's arguments. Next, the teacher begins the debate by asking a student from the supporting side to state their position, and then a student on the opposing side makes a statement. From this point, students take turns speaking in support of or in opposition to the issue. Students who have just made a statement are often asked a question before the student for the other side makes a return statement. To conclude the debate, one student from each team makes a final statement, summing up their position. Students not participating in the debate often assess their classmates' performance and determine the winning team. Teachers work with students to develop a rubric or assessment form and award points based on the effectiveness of the team's arguments and manner of presentation.

EACHING ORAL LANGUAGE

Teachers teach oral language in conjunction with the other language arts. For example, they often teach aesthetic and critical listening during literature focus units and questioning and interviewing during thematic units. Students at each grade level are expected to meet oral language standards related to listening, talking, and working collaboratively in small groups. The Common Core State Standards for oral language are summarized here.

It's essential that students refine their oral language abilities because they're involved in listening and talk activities as part of all four patterns of practice. Students listen to teachers as they present minilessons and share books, and they participate in grand conversations and other discussions in each of the instructional patterns. They also use oral language as they work collaboratively in small groups. In literature circles, for example, students work in small groups as they respond to books they're reading, and in writing workshop, students participate in revising groups. The Patterns of Practice box on the next page describes additional ways oral language fits into the instructional patterns.

Minilessons

Researchers have repeatedly cited the need to teach listening strategies to help students become more effective listeners (Optiz & Zbaracki, 2004; Wolvin & Coakley, 1996). There are added benefits, too: Students use many of the same strategies for listening, reading, and viewing because these three language arts are receptive processes, and sometimes teachers are more successful when they teach strategies while students are listening instead of when they're reading. Teachers teach minilessons to introduce, practice, and review strategies, as well as procedures and other concepts related to listening and talking. A minilesson showing how a second grade teacher teaches her students to sustain a conversation is shown on page 138.

How Oral Language Fits Into the Patterns of Practice

Literature Focus Units

Students listen to the teacher read aloud and take part in small-group and whole-class grand conversations. They create oral projects, including podcasts and oral reports.

Literature Circles

Literature circles are essentially small-group conversations, so listening and talk take on special importance. Group members rely on classmates to participate willingly.

Reading and Writing Workshop

Students listen to teachers teach minilessons and read aloud, and they listen to classmates share their writing. Students also participate in revising groups during writing workshop.

Thematic Units

Students get into small groups to read and discuss nonfiction books and to work on projects. They also conduct interviews, participate in debates, and give oral reports.

Mentor Texts

Teachers often use mentor texts as they teach students to listen and talk more effectively. Many stories and informational books that teachers read aloud, for example, encourage critical thinking. Students use a combination of aesthetic and critical listening as they listen to stories such as *Flush* (Hiaasen, 2005) and *The True Story of the 3 Little Pigs!* (Scieszka, 1999); they use critical listening to evaluate the environmental theme and to determine whether the wolf's story is believable. When students listen to informational books such as *Rosa* (2005), in which Nikki Giovanni recounts Rosa Parks's act of civil disobedience, they confront important social issues. Through these activities, students think more deeply about controversial issues and challenge and expand their own beliefs. The Booklist on page 139 presents books that encourage critical listening.

Taking Notes

Students are more active listeners when they take notes to help them remember the big ideas while they listen to an oral presentation. Teachers introduce note taking by demonstrating the procedure. They set a clear purpose, and during the oral presentation, they stop periodically and ask students to identify the idea being presented and its relationship to other ideas that have been presented. Then teachers list students' responses on the whiteboard. Teachers often begin by writing notes in a list format, but the notes can also be written in an outline or diagram.

Middle and upper grade students often use a special kind of note taking in which they divide their papers into two columns, labeling the left column *Take Notes* and the right column *Make Notes*. They write notes in the left column, but, more importantly, they think about the notes, make connections, and personalize the notes in the right column (Berthoff, 1981). The right column should be more extensive than the left one because this column shows students' thinking. Figure 5–8 shows a fifth grader's note-taking and note-making sheet about illegal drugs. The student's comments in the "Make Notes" column are especially interesting because they show the connections she was making.

Minilesson

Ms. Shapiro Teaches Her Second Graders About Sustaining Conversations

1. Introduce the Topic

Ms. Shapiro explains to her second graders that she wants them to think about how they behave during grand conversations. She asks them to observe a grand conversation that she's planned with four students in the class. "We'll be doing some good things to help the conversation and some bad things that hurt the conversation," she says. "Watch carefully so you'll notice them."

2. Share Examples

Ms. Shapiro and four students have a grand conversation about a familiar story, *Hey, Al* (Yorinks, 1989). She chose a familiar story so everyone could focus on the conversation itself and not get caught up in the story. Group members take turns making comments, but they don't expand on each other's comments, nor do they call each other by name or look at classmates as they're talking. Also, some children are looking away from the group as though they aren't listening.

3. Provide Information

Ms. Shapiro's students are eager to identify the strengths and weaknesses of the grand conversation they've observed. The "good things" were that "everyone talked about the story and nothing else" and "everybody was nice." The "bad things" included that "some

people didn't pay attention and look at the person talking," "some people didn't say other people's names," and "some people just said things but they didn't go next to what other people said." Ms. Shapiro agrees with their assessment, and she explains that she's seen some of these same problems in their conversations. Together they make a chart of "Good Things to Do in a Grand Conversation."

4. Supervise Practice

Ms. Shapiro's students participate in grand conversations as part of literature circles and after she reads a book aloud to the class. She explains that she'll observe their grand conversations to make sure they're doing all the good things they listed on their chart. For the next 2 weeks, Ms. Shapiro briefly reviews the chart before each grand conversation and takes a few minutes afterward to talk about the changes in behavior she's observed.

5. Reflect on Learning

After 2 weeks of practice, Ms. Shapiro brings the children together to talk about their grand conversations, and she asks the second graders which of the good things from the chart they're doing better now. They mention various points and conclude that their grand conversations have improved.

INTEGRATING TECHNOLOGY

A variety of technology tools support students as they communicate with others: For example, they collaborate with classmates and use software to perform authentic oral language tasks, and they create multimedia projects, talk with outside resources, and develop technical skills. Here are three ways to integrate technology:

Booklist

BOOKS THAT ENCOURAGE CRITICAL LISTENING

Avi. (2003). *Nothing but the truth.* New York: Orchard Books. U
Babbitt, N. (2007). *Tuck everlasting.* New York: Square Fish Books. U
Bunting, E. (1999). *Smoky night.* San Diego: Harcourt Brace. M
Cohen, B. (1999). *Molly's pilgrim.* New York: Scholastic. M
Cowcher, H. (1990). *Antarctica.* New York: Farrar, Straus & Giroux. P–M
Creech, S. (2004). *Heartbeat.* New York: HarperCollins. M–U
Gantos, J. (2000). *Joey Pigza loses control.* New York: Farrar, Straus & Giroux. M–U
Giovanni, N. (2005). *Rosa.* New York: Henry Holt. M
Haddix, M. P. (1998). *Among the hidden.* New York: Aladdin Books. U
Hesse, K. (2005). *Witness.* New York: Scholastic. U
Hiaasen, C. (2002). *Hoot.* New York: Knopf. M–U
Hiaasen, C. (2005). *Flush.* New York: Knopf. M–U
Jeffers, S. (2002). *Brother eagle, sister sky.* New York: Dial Books. M
Lobel, A. (2004). *Potatoes, potatoes.* New York: Greenwillow. P–M
Naylor, P. R. (2000). *Shiloh.* New York: Aladdin Books. M–U
Scieszka, J. (1999). *The true story of the 3 little pigs!* New York: Viking. P–M
Spinelli, J. (1997). *Wringer.* New York: HarperCollins. M–U
Turner, A. (1987). *Nettie's trip south.* New York: Macmillan. M
Whelan, G. (2000). *Homeless bird.* New York: HarperCollins. U
Woodson, J. (2005). *Show way.* New York: Putnam. M–U

SKYPE. Skype is free, downloadable software that teachers use to conduct free voice and video calls from their classrooms. Students use Skype to interview authors and illustrators, scientists, politicians, and other prominent people; take virtual field trips with scientists and historians; participate in pen pal projects; and broadcast performances or projects for parents and community members. The website http://education.skype.com is a free online community to help teachers collaborate with colleagues around the world.

PODCASTS. Students listen to podcasts others have created on topics that interest them, and they record their own broadcasts on a wide range of topics. Check these podcast galleries: Inkless Tales: Podcasts for Kids (http://inklesstales.wordpress.com), The Story Home (http://thestoryhome.com), and Podcasts for Kids at Zencast (http://www.zencast.com). Students can also view vodcasts (video podcasts) on science concepts, including temperature and buoyancy, at the KidsKnowIt Network (http://www.kidsknowit.com). Creating podcasts provides an opportunity for students' voices to be heard in their community and around the world. They can create their own regularly scheduled broadcasts online using GarageBand, Audacity, or other software to capture the audio. Next, they delete awkward pauses or add embellishments, and then they upload and distribute the podcasts using RSS.

PRESENTATION SOFTWARE. Both teachers and students create multimedia presentations using Microsoft PowerPoint or another software program. These presentations include audio and video elements as well as text and art. Students often create PowerPoint presentations as part of oral reports and virtual museums, and teachers use them during lessons and for presentations to parents.

FIGURE 5–8   A Note-Taking Sheet

DRUGS

Take notes	Make Notes
pot affects your brain mariquania is a ilegal drug and does things to your lungs makes you forget things. affects your brain	How long does it take to affect your brain? how long does it last? Could it make you forget how to drive?
Crack and coacain is illegal a small pipeful can cause death. It can cause heart atachs. is very dangerous It doesent make you cool. It makes you a dummy. you and your friends might think so but others think your a dummy. People are stupid if they attemp to take drugs. The answer is no, no, no, no.	Like basketball players? Why do people use drugs? How do people get the seeds to grow drugs?

These technology-supported activities capture students' attention, sustain their interest, and enhance learning. ■

ENGAGING ENGLISH LEARNERS

Talk facilitates learning for all students, but it's especially important for English learners who are struggling to learn English at the same time they're grappling with grade-level content-area learning (Gibbons, 2002; Rothenberg & Fisher, 2007). In addition, school is the only place where some English learners have opportunities to hear and speak English. How does talk facilitate learning? As they talk, students focus on the big ideas, questioning, clarifying, and elaborating their thinking. They organize these big ideas, relate them to their background knowledge, and practice using newly introduced vocabulary words. English learners benefit from daily opportunities to talk in large groups, in small groups, and one-on-one with a classmate or the teacher (Fay & Whaley, 2004).

English learners use talk as a learning tool in all four patterns of practice. In thematic units, for example, students use talk as they're involved in meaningful oral, written, and visual activities and broaden their knowledge of the world. Teachers support English learners in these ways during thematic units and the other patterns of practice:

- Involve students in hands-on, active learning opportunities
- Have students work with classmates in small groups
- Link lessons to students' prior experiences, or build needed background knowledge
- Clarify meaning with objects, photos, and demonstrations
- Teach technical vocabulary related to the topic
- Use graphic organizers to emphasize the relationships among the big ideas
- Have students talk, read, create visuals, and write about the topic
- Teach students to recognize when they're confused and how to take action to solve the problem
- Demonstrate how to ask and answer higher level questions
- Teach students how to listen to informational books and content-area textbooks
- Involve students in making small-group projects to demonstrate their learning

With these instructional supports in place, students are better able to learn age-appropriate content knowledge along with their classmates. ■

Assessing Oral Language

Teachers often don't take time to assess students' listening and talk because they aren't graded, but students' ability to use oral language strategies affects their written language achievement. Teachers can assess students' use of oral language informally, in a variety of ways:

PLANNING. Teachers plan minilessons to teach oral language strategies and have students apply what they're learning in a variety of listening and talk activities. When planning oral language activities, it's critical that teachers anticipate which strategies and procedures might be unfamiliar so they can present minilessons as needed.

MONITORING. Teachers often use observation and anecdotal notes to monitor students' use of oral language strategies and their participation in small-group conversations and other talk activities. For instance, teachers judge students' aesthetic listening by the predictions and comments they make during grand conversations, and they check students'

Middle School Spotlight

What are digital discussions?

In digital discussions, students exchange ideas and participate in social-learning opportunities using electronic message boards. Larson (2009) conducted a study with older students to examine how they form online literature circles to read an ebook, craft and post prompts, and participate in online conversations. She taught students how to construct open-ended prompts that would spark their classmates' interest to initiate the discussions, how to craft elaborated responses with examples from the text, and how to post their responses. She classified students' prompts according to Hancock's (2008) categories:

Experiential Prompts. Experiential prompts ask students to share personal knowledge and experiences to make connections between the novel they're reading and their own lives. Examples: Have you ever been to Texas? Have you ever been that frightened?

Aesthetic Prompts. These prompts elicit students' feelings about the novel they're reading and provide opportunities for classmates to comfort each other. Examples: I am so mad. How about you? Do you agree?

Cognitive Prompts. Cognitive prompts invite students to make predictions, draw inferences, and use other comprehension strategies as they discuss the novel. Examples: Where do you think they'll find the clue? What do you think about . . .?

Interpretive Prompts. Interpretive prompts ask students to make moral judgments and personalize their reading. Examples: What would you do if you were . . .? Was he being patriotic?

Clarification Prompts. Students use these prompts when they're confused or when classmates' comments aren't clear. Examples: Why did he do that? This book is really confusing. What do you think?

Larson pointed out that the types of prompts that elicited the most discussion varied with the book students read and discussed; nonetheless, she concluded that students' digital discussions led to greater engagement with literature and increased comprehension and interpretation. Moreover, it seems reasonable that students will apply what they've learned about online discussions when they ask questions and make comments during grand conversations and other discussions.

FIGURE 5–9   A Self-Assessment Checklist for Oral Reports

	no	1	2	3	4	yes
1. Did I collect enough information?		—	—	—	—	
2. Did I make a useful chart or visual?		—	—	—	—	
3. Did I rehearse my presentation?		—	—	—	—	
4. Did I speak loudly so everyone could hear?		—	—	—	—	
5. Did I look at the audience?		—	—	—	—	
6. Did I use my visuals?		—	—	—	—	
7. Did I make my main points?		—	—	—	—	
8. Was my report successful?		—	—	—	—	
9. Did the audience like my report?		—	—	—	—	

---

application of efferent listening strategies as they take notes, ask questions, and take part in discussions. Teachers monitor students' critical listening as they critique debates, commercials, and other oral presentations.

EVALUATING. Teachers use checklists to assess students' interviews, oral reports, debates, and other oral presentations. Classmates also provide feedback to speakers about their presentations using a checklist or rubric, and at other times, students self-assess their presentations. Figure 5–9 shows a self-assessment rubric developed by a fourth grade class; it lists questions about the students' preparation for the presentation and about the presentation itself.

Even though oral language assessment is informal, it's important because both students and adults use the oral language arts so often.

SUMMING UP

Listening and talking are the most commonly used language arts. Despite their importance, however, oral language is often neglected because teachers assume that students already know how to listen and talk. The four types of listening are discriminative, aesthetic, efferent, and critical. Students use discriminative listening to recognize and manipulate sounds and aesthetic listening to enjoy stories, plays, and movies. They use efferent listening to remember information they're learning and critical listening to evaluate messages. Talk is a valuable instructional tool. Students talk about stories they're reading and information they're learning in thematic units, and they learn to ask thoughtful questions. Students refine their presentational skills when they give oral reports, and they develop their ability to persuade others when they participate in debates.

MyEducationLab™

Go to the topics Speaking and Listening, and Oral Language Development in the MyEducationLab (http://www.myeducationlab.com) for *Language Arts: Patterns of Practice*, where you can:

- Find learning outcomes for Speaking and Listening, and Oral Language Development, along with the national standards that connect to these outcomes.
- Complete Assignments and Activities that can help you more deeply understand the chapter content.
- Apply and practice your understanding of the core teaching skills identified in the chapter with the Building Teaching Skills and Dispositions learning units.
- Check your comprehension of the content covered in the chapter with the Study Plan. Here you will be able to take a chapter quiz, receive feedback on your answers, and then access Review, Practice, and Enrichment activities to enhance your understanding of chapter content.

On the **MyEducationLab** for this course, you'll also be able to:

- **A+RISE** Go to the topic A+RISE, an innovative and interactive database of strategies that differentiate instruction across the language arts and provide particular insight into research-based methods to meet the needs of English learners.
- Explore the topic Literacy Portraits—yearlong case studies of second graders, complete with student artifacts, teacher commentary, and student and teacher interviews, tracking the month-by-month language arts growth of five students.
- Gain practice with the Grammar Tutorial, online guided instruction to improve your own ability with grammar.

CHAPTER 6

Written Language: Reading and Writing

MS. KAKUTANI USES THE READING PROCESS During the first week of school, Ms. Kakutani reads aloud *Granny Torrelli Makes Soup* (Creech, 2003) to her class of 34 fourth graders. It's a story about friendship, which is her theme for the first month of school. In the story, Granny Torrelli helps her granddaughter Rosie smooth out her relationship with best friend Bailey. Ms. Kakutani makes connections between what Rosie learns about being a friend and how she wants the students to behave toward their classmates. It's her first step in creating a community of learners in the classroom.

After they finish the book, Ms. Kakutani and her students prepare spaghetti and meat-balls and invite parents, grandparents, and siblings to join them for lunch. The students write invitations, and parents volunteer to supply many of the ingredients and help prepare the food in the classroom. Others bring salad, bread, fruit, and dessert to complete the meal. It's a festive occasion where students introduce their families to Ms. Kakutani and show them around their classroom.

For the next 2 weeks, Ms. Kakutani and her students read *Amber Brown Goes Fourth* (Danziger, 1995), the third in a series of chapter-book stories about a spunky girl with a two-color name. This book, also with a friendship theme, is written at the third grade reading level; it's appropriate for this class because most students read a year below grade level. The teacher has a class set of this Amber Brown book that she distributes to students and a text set with multiple copies of the other books in the series that she places in the classroom library for students to read independently.

Ms. Kakutani reads this story using shared reading because she wants to ensure that everyone can read the story, and she wants to introduce the comprehension strategies

How do teachers use the reading process to organize literature focus units?

Good teaching isn't accidental! Teachers organize literature focus units to ensure that students comprehend what they're reading. Some activities introduce the book and activate background knowledge, some guide students as they interpret the story, and others provide opportunities to teach students about literature and for students to apply what they're learning. As you read this vignette, notice how Ms. Kakutani incorporates the prereading, reading, responding, exploring, and applying stages of the reading process in the unit.

that she'll emphasize this year. The students follow along in their copies as she reads the book aloud, chapter by chapter. The class spends 9 days reading the 14 chapters in the book; some days, they read one chapter; other days, they read two. As they read, Ms. Kakutani pauses off and on to think aloud about the comprehension strategies she's using—monitoring, visualizing, connecting, summarizing, and evaluating.

After they finish reading, the students participate in a grand conversation with Ms. Kakutani. Participating in a free-flowing discussion about the story is new to many students. The teacher explains the activity, models it, and teaches them how to ask questions, offer opinions, and make connections between their own lives and *Granny Torrelli Makes Soup*. They talk about the events in the story, the importance of having friends, and their own nervousness about beginning fourth grade.

When the grand conversation slows down, Ms. Kakutani returns to the book and rereads a sentence to redirect the conversation. After reading Chapters 6 and 7, for example, she rereads the bottom part of page 47 and asks, "What does Brandi mean when she says, 'I am NOT Justin'?" At first the students are unsure, but as they talk about how Brandi might feel, they recognize that one child cannot replace another one. Then the teacher asks, "Do you think Brandi and Amber will become best friends?" The students make predictions that guide their reading for the second half of the story.

After reading and discussing Chapter 14, Ms. Kakutani rereads Amber's comment, "I guess there will always be changes in my life" (p. 100), and asks students what they think it means. They reflect on the changes in Amber's life—her friend Justin moving away, her parents getting divorced, her father moving to Paris, her mother dating Max, and Amber starting fourth grade. Then Ms. Kakutani asks if they expect to have changes in their lives, and the conversation continues as students talk about the changes in their lives—parents who are soldiers in Afghanistan, new babies born into their families, mothers losing their jobs, families moving to a new community, grandparents dying, older siblings going to prison, and, of course, starting fourth grade.

After they talk about the story, the students write entries in their reading logs. Ms. Kakutani provides questions to guide their responses. She makes her questions open-ended to encourage students to continue to think more deeply about the story and make connections to their own lives. Here are Ms. Kakutani's questions:

Chapters 1 and 2	*What have you learned about Amber?*
	How do you think her life is going to change?
Chapter 3	*What's hard about starting fourth grade?*
Chapters 4 and 5	*How is Amber's fourth grade different from third grade?*
	How is fourth grade different for you?
Chapters 6 and 7	*Do you think Amber and Brandi will become best friends?*
	Do you agree with Amber that everyone should have a best friend?
Chapter 8	*What funny things have you done with your mom or dad?*
Chapter 9	*Do you think it was fair for the girls to get detention for laughing?*
Chapters 10 and 11	*Why do you think Brandi and Amber are getting to be better friends?*
	Would you want to be the Burp Queen or Burp King of fourth grade?
Chapters 12 and 13	*What should Amber do to be a good friend?*
	Do you think Amber is ever going to like Max?
Chapter 14	*Do you think Max was trying to bribe Amber with the mermaid?*
	What changes have you had in your life?

The students make small journals by stapling together sheets of lined paper and adding construction paper covers. They illustrate the covers to reflect the book they're reading. They begin each entry on a new page and add the chapter number, a title, and the date at the top of the page. Bella writes this entry after reading Chapters 6 and 7, in response to the question "Do you think Amber and Brandi will become best friends?":

> *I feel sorry for Amber Brown. She has too many changes in her life. She needs a new best friend. Her old best friend moved away and she is lonely. I am thinking Brandi will be her best friend because she needs one, too. I hope there are no more changes for her!*

Jordan writes this entry after reading Chapter 14 and adds this title—"The Change in My Life":

> *I'm having a change right now and it scares me. My Dad is in Afghanistan. He is a sergeant. I pray to God to watch over him. He says he's safe but I think he could get killed. I'm proud of him because he is brave. I pray he comes back safe.*

Ms. Kakutani also emphasizes the important vocabulary in the story. She posts a word wall—a large chart divided into alphabetized sections—and after reading each chapter or two, students choose the most important words to add to the word wall.

They take turns writing the words on the chart, and they refer to the word wall whenever they need help spelling or thinking of a word. The teacher also points out the word-play in the story. The students get interested in reading jokes after reading the ones in Chapter 1 and Chapter 6, and Ms. Kakutani locates several joke books in the classroom library to share with them.

Ms. Kakutani also shares information about author Paula Danziger and does a book talk to introduce the other Amber Brown books. Then students spend the last week in the unit reading other Amber Brown stories individually, with partners, and in small groups. Even after the unit ends, many students will trade books and continue reading about Amber Brown's adventures during independent reading time.

eading and writing involve similar processes. The reading process is a series of stages during which readers read, explore, and reflect on the text they're reading. The writing process is similar, involving a variety of activities as students gather and organize their ideas, write rough drafts, revise and edit the drafts, and, finally, publish their writings. The goal of both written language processes is making meaning. Readers create meaning through negotiation with the texts they're reading, and, similarly, writers create meaning through negotiation with the texts they're writing. Readers use their life and literature experiences and their knowledge of written language as they read, and writers bring similar knowledge and experiences to writing. It's quite common for two people to read a text and come away with differing interpretations and for two writers to write different accounts of the same event. Meaning doesn't exist on the pages of the book that a reader is reading or in the words of the composition that a writer is writing; instead, meaning is created through the transaction between readers and what they're reading or between writers and what they're writing.

The Common Core State Standards focus on written language and address the reading and writing processes; the reading standards emphasize developing comprehension, and the writing standards highlight developing effective compositions representing a variety of genres. This Standards box provides additional information about the written language standards.

COMMON CORE STATE STANDARDS

Written Language

The Common Core State Standards address reading and responding to texts, conducting research, and writing texts representing varied genres. The standards include these points:

- Students read and comprehend literature and informational texts.
- Students make inferences and draw conclusions from text.
- Students conduct research projects using information from multiple sources.
- Students use the writing process to develop and refine writing.
- Students write stories, informational texts, and arguments.
- Students use technology to produce and publish writing.

To learn more about the written language standards, go to http://www.corestandards.org, or check your state's language arts standards.

THE READING PROCESS

Reading is a process in which readers negotiate meaning in order to comprehend, or create an interpretation. During reading, the meaning does not go from the page to the readers. Instead, it involves a complex negotiation between the text and readers that's shaped by many factors: readers' knowledge about the topic; readers' purpose for reading; the language community readers belong to and how closely that language matches the language used in the text; readers' culturally based expectations about reading; and readers' expectations about reading based on their previous experiences.

Readers move through the five stages of the reading process: prereading, reading, responding, exploring, and applying. The components of each stage are summarized in Figure 6–1.

Stage 1: Prereading

The reading process begins before readers open a book to read. The first stage is prereading. As students prepare to read, they're involved in these activities:

- Activating background knowledge
- Setting purposes
- Planning for reading

FIGURE 6–1   The Reading Process

Stage 1: Prereading
Students activate or build background knowledge.
Students set purposes for reading.
Students preview the text.

Stage 2: Reading
Students read independently, with a buddy, using shared reading, or through guided reading, or listen to the text read aloud.
Students read the text from beginning to end or read one or more sections to learn specific information.
Students apply strategies.
Students read the illustrations, charts, and diagrams.

Stage 3: Responding
Students respond in reading logs.
Students discuss the text with classmates and/or the teacher.

Stage 4: Exploring
Students reread and think more deeply about the text.
Students examine the author's craft.
Students learn vocabulary words.
Students participate in minilessons.

Stage 5: Applying
Students create a project.
Students value the reading experience.

Activating Background Knowledge. Readers activate their background knowledge about the book before beginning to read; the topic of the book, the title, the author, the genre, the cover illustration, a comment someone makes about the book, or something else may trigger this activation. When students are reading independently—during reading workshop, for example—they choose the books they'll read and activate their background knowledge themselves. At other times, such as during literature focus units, teachers help students activate and build their background knowledge. They share information on a topic related to the book or introduce a book box with a collection of objects connected to the book. Or, they show a video, talk about the author, read the first paragraph aloud, or ask students to make a prediction about the book. For example, before reading *The Giver* (Lowry, 2006b), teachers build a concept of what a "perfect" society might be like by having students brainstorm a list of problems in today's society and think of possible remedies.

Setting Goals. The purpose guides students' reading. It provides motivation and direction for reading, as well as a mechanism for students to monitor their reading to see if they're meeting their goals. Sustaining a single purpose while students read the text is more effective than presenting students with a series of purposes (Blanton, Wood, & Moorman, 1990). Sometimes teachers set purposes for reading, and sometimes students set their own. During literature focus units, teachers set the goal, but in reading workshop, students set their own purposes because everyone's reading different books. As students develop as readers, they become more effective at choosing books and setting their own goals.

Planning for Reading. Once students activate their background knowledge and identify their purpose for reading, they take their first look at the text and plan for reading. Students vary how they make plans according to the type of selection they're preparing to read. For stories, they make predictions about the characters and events in the story. They often base their predictions on the book's title or the cover illustration. If they've read other stories by the same author or in the same genre, students also use this information in making their predictions. Sometimes students share their predictions orally, and at other times, they write predictions in their reading logs.

When students are preparing to read articles and nonfiction books, they preview the selection by flipping through the pages and noting section headings, illustrations, and diagrams. Sometimes they examine the table of contents to see the book's organization, or they consult the index to locate specific information they want to read. They also notice highlighted terminology that's unfamiliar to them.

Stage 2: Reading

Students do the actual reading in the second stage. Sometimes they read independently, but at other times, they listen to the teacher read aloud or read with classmates and the teacher. These types of reading are used in preK–8 classrooms:

- Shared reading
- Guided reading
- Independent reading
- Buddy reading
- Reading aloud to students

The type of reading that teachers choose depends on the text's difficulty level, students' reading levels, and the teacher's purpose. The advantages and disadvantages of each type of reading are outlined in Figure 6–2.

FIGURE 6–2 Types of Reading

Type	Advantages	Disadvantages
Shared Reading Teachers read aloud while students follow along using individual copies of a book, a class chart, or a big book.	• Students have access to books they can't read independently. • Teachers model fluent reading. • Teachers apply reading strategies. • Students become a community of readers.	• Multiple copies, a class chart, or a big book version of the text is needed. • The text may not be appropriate for all students. • Some students may not be interested in the text.
Guided Reading Teachers support students as they read texts at their reading levels. Students are grouped homogeneously.	• Teachers provide direction and scaffolding. • Students practice reading strategies. • Students read independently. • Students practice reading high-frequency words.	• Multiple copies of the text are needed. • Teachers control the reading experience. • Some students may not be interested in the text.
Independent Reading Students read a text independently and often choose the text themselves.	• Students develop responsibility and ownership. • Students self-select texts. • Readers have a more authentic experience.	• Students may need assistance to read the text. • Teachers have little involvement or control.
Buddy Reading Two students read or reread a text together.	• Students learn to collaborate. • Students reread familiar texts. • Students develop reading fluency. • Students talk about texts to deepen comprehension.	• Teachers' involvement and control are limited. • One student may depend on the other to do the reading.
Reading Aloud to Students Teachers or other fluent readers read aloud to students.	• Students have access to books they can't read independently. • Teachers model fluent reading. • Students become a community of readers. • Only one copy of the text is required.	• Students have no opportunity to read. • The text may not be appropriate for some students. • Some students may not be interested in the text.

Shared Reading. Students follow along as the teacher reads the selection aloud. Prekindergarten, kindergarten, and first grade teachers often use big books—enlarged versions of the selection—for shared reading (Holdaway, 1979). Children sit so that they can see the book, and they listen to the teacher read aloud and read along as the teacher reads refrains and other familiar words. The teacher or a child points to each line of text as it's read to draw children's attention to the words, to show the direction of print on a page, and to highlight important concepts about letters, words, and sentences.

Teachers in other grades also use shared reading when students have individual copies of the reading selection but it's too difficult for them to read independently (Fisher & Medvic, 2000). The teacher reads aloud as students follow along in their copies. Sometimes teachers read the first chapter or two of a chapter book together with the class, using shared reading, and then students use other types of reading as they read the rest of the book. Only those students for whom the book is too difficult continue to use shared reading and read along with the teacher.

Guided Reading. Teachers read with small groups of students who read at the same level or who use similar reading strategies and skills. They scaffold students' reading to enable them to develop and use reading strategies and skills in guided reading (Fountas & Pinnell, 1996, 2001). Selections used for guided reading should be written at students' instructional reading levels, that is, slightly beyond their ability to read the text independently. Teachers usually read the first page or two with students, and then the students read the rest of the selection silently. Teachers often group and regroup students for guided reading so that the book selected is appropriate for all students in a group.

Independent Reading. Students read silently by themselves and at their own pace (Taylor, 1993). Independent reading is the most authentic type of reading. This is what most people do when they read, and it's the way students develop a love of reading and come to think of themselves as readers. It's essential that the reading selection is either at an appropriate level of difficulty or very familiar so that students can read it independently; otherwise, teachers use one of the other types of reading to support students and make it possible for them to participate in the reading experience.

Buddy Reading. Students read or reread a selection with a classmate in buddy reading. Sometimes students read with buddies because it's an enjoyable social activity, and sometimes they read together to help each other. Often students can read selections together that neither one could read individually. By working together, they're often able to figure out unfamiliar words and talk out comprehension problems. Teachers show students how to support each other as they read together. Unless students know how to work collaboratively, buddy reading often deteriorates into the better reader reading aloud to the other student, but that isn't the intention of this activity. Students need to take turns reading aloud to each other or read in unison. They often stop and help each other identify unfamiliar words or take a minute or two at the end of each page to talk about what they've read. It's a valuable way of providing the practice that students need to become fluent readers or understand challenging texts.

Reading Aloud to Students. At every grade level, teachers read aloud to students for a variety of purposes each day. Teachers read aloud books that are appropriate for students' interest level but too difficult for them to read by themselves. When they read aloud, teachers do two things: They model what good readers do, and they actively engage students in the reading experience by asking them to make predictions and use other comprehension strategies.

Reading aloud to students isn't the same as round-robin reading, in which students take turns reading paragraphs aloud as the rest of the class listens. Round-robin reading has been used for reading chapter books aloud, but it's more commonly used for reading chapters in content-area textbooks, even though there are more effective ways to teach content-area information and read textbooks. Round-robin reading is no longer recommended because if the selection's easy enough for students to read aloud, they should be reading independently. Moreover, many students follow along only just before it's their turn to read, so they don't do much reading (Opitz, 2008).

Stage 3: Responding

Students respond to what they've read and continue negotiating meaning to deepen their comprehension. They make tentative and exploratory comments by writing in reading logs and participating in grand conversations immediately after reading.

Writing in Reading Logs. Students write and draw thoughts and feelings about what they've read in reading logs. Rosenblatt (2005) explains that as readers write about what they've read, they unravel their thinking and at the same time elaborate on and clarify their responses. Students often choose their own topics for reading log entries, but many teachers hang a list of open-ended prompts in the classroom to guide students' responses. Possible prompts include the following:

> I really don't understand . . .
> I like/dislike (character) because . . .
> This book reminds me of . . .
> (Character) reminds me of myself because . . .
> I think (character) is feeling . . .
> I wonder why . . .
> (Event) makes me think about the time I . . .
> If I were (character), I'd . . .
> I noticed that (the author) is . . .
> I predict that . . .

These open-ended prompts allow students to make connections to their own lives, the world, and other literature. At other times, teachers ask specific questions to direct students' attention to some aspect of a book, as Ms. Kakutani did in the vignette at the beginning of the chapter.

Participating in Grand Conversations. Students talk about the text with classmates in discussions called *grand conversations*. Peterson and Eeds (2007) explain that in this type of discussion, students share their personal responses and tell what they liked about the selection. After sharing personal reactions, they shift the focus to "puzzle over what the author has written and . . . share what it is they find revealed" (p. 61). Often students make connections between the selection and their own lives, the world around them, or other literature they've read. If they're reading a chapter book, they also make predictions about what will happen in the next chapter. Teachers often participate in grand conversations, but they act as interested participants, not as leaders.

Grand conversations can be held with the whole class or with small groups. Young children usually meet as a class, but older students often prefer to talk with classmates in small groups. When students get together as a class, there's a feeling of community, and the teacher can be part of the group. When students meet in small groups, students have more opportunities to participate in the discussion and share their responses, but fewer viewpoints are expressed in each group and teachers must move around, spending only a few minutes with each group. Some teachers compromise and have students begin their discussions in small groups and then come together as a class and have the groups share what they discussed.

Stage 4: Exploring

Teachers lead students back into the text to explore it more analytically in this stage. They're involved in these activities:

- Rereading the selection
- Examining the author's craft
- Focusing on new vocabulary words
- Participating in minilessons

Rereading the Selection. Students often reread picture books, articles, and other brief selections several times. If the teacher used shared reading for the first reading, then students might reread the selection once or twice with a buddy or with their parents, and after these experiences, they read it independently. Each time they reread, students benefit in specific ways (Yaden, 1988): They enrich their comprehension and make deeper connections between the selection and their own lives or between the selection and other literature they've read.

Examining the Author's Craft. Teachers plan exploring activities to focus students' attention on the genre, the structure of the text, and the literary language that authors use (Eeds & Peterson, 1995). Students sequence story events using story boards (pages of a picture book cut apart and glued on tagboard cards) and make story maps to visually represent the plot and other story elements. To focus on literary language, students often reread favorite excerpts in a read-around and write memorable quotes on charts. Teachers also share information about the author and introduce other books by that author. Sometimes teachers have students compare several books written by a particular author.

Focusing on Vocabulary. Students add "important" words related to the book to word walls posted in the classroom and then refer to the word walls for a variety of activities during the exploring stage. Researchers emphasize the importance of immersing students in words, teaching strategies for learning words, and personalizing word learning (Blachowicz & Fisher, 2006). Students make word maps and posters to highlight particular words and play word games.

Teaching Minilessons. Teachers present minilessons on reading strategies and skills. They introduce the topic and make connections between the topic and examples in the featured selection so that students can connect the information with their own reading process.

Stage 5: Applying

Readers continue to deepen their interpretations and value the reading experience in this final stage. Students build on their reading experiences, the responses they made immediately after reading, and the exploring activities as they create projects. These projects involve the productive language arts—talking, writing, or visually representing—and can take many forms, including writing sequels, developing a website about the book, researching the author, and making digital slide shows. A list of projects is presented in Figure 6–3. Students usually choose which projects they do rather than being assigned to work on a specific project, unless the class decides to work together on a project. Sometimes students work in small groups or with partners; at other times, they create individual projects.

Teaching the Reading Process

Teachers apply the five-stage reading process to teach reading, no matter whether they organize instruction into literature focus units, literature circles, reading workshop, or thematic units. Successful language arts instruction doesn't just happen; teachers cultivate a community of learners in their classrooms and teach students the procedures for various language arts activities. Each pattern of practice requires that teachers carefully structure activities, provide appropriate books and other materials, present instruction, create time and space for students to work, and plan for assessment.

Everyone—parents, teachers, and politicians—has an opinion about what's important in reading instruction. Often the debate centers on phonics: Some people believe that phonics is the most important factor because students need to be able to decode the words they're reading, but others consider phonics to be less important than comprehension because the purpose

---

FIGURE 6-3   Projects

Oral Language	Written Language	Visual Language
Present a book talk about the book.	Research the author or illustrator of the book online.	Create a collage to represent the book's theme.
Create and perform a song about a book.	Write a letter to the author.	Make a story box with objects and quotes from the book.
Share a poem related to the book.	Research a topic related to the book.	Develop a set of story boards about a book.
Dress as a book character and answer classmates' questions about the story.	Write a found poem about the book.	Draw a graphic representation of the big ideas in a nonfiction book.
Retell an episode from a book.	Read and compare two versions of a story.	Make a scrapbook about the book.
Give a presentation about the topic of a nonfiction book.	Write a prequel or sequel for a book.	Create a quilt about a book.
	Prepare a multigenre project.	View a film version of a book.
	Rewrite the story from another viewpoint.	Analyze the illustrator's craft.
	Write a simulated journal from the viewpoint of a character.	Videotape a commercial for a book.
	Compose a simulated letter from one character to another.	Create a slide presentation about a book.
		Present a dramatization of an episode from the book.

---

of reading is to make meaning from text. The view presented in this text is that there are four important factors in developing capable readers:

- Word identification
- Fluency
- Vocabulary
- Comprehension

Teachers address all of these factors through direct instruction, by reading aloud to students every day, and by providing daily opportunities for students to read books at their own reading level.

Word Identification. Capable readers have a large bank of words that they recognize instantly and automatically because they can't stop and analyze every word as they read. Students learn to read phonetically regular words, such as *baking* and *first,* and high-frequency words, such as *there* and *said.* In addition, they learn how to figure out unfamiliar words. They use phonic analysis to read *raid, strap,* and other phonetically regular words, syllabic analysis to read *jungle, election,* and other multisyllabic words, and morphemic analysis to read *omnivorous, millennium,* and other words with Latin and Greek word parts. Through a combination of instruction and reading practice, students' ability to identify words continues to grow.

Phonics, the set of phoneme-grapheme relationships, is an important part of word-identification instruction in the primary grades, but it's only one part of word identification because English isn't an entirely phonetic language. At the same time they're learning phonics, children also learn to recognize at least 300 high-frequency words, such as *what* and *come,* that can't be sounded out. Older students learn more sophisticated word-identification strategies about dividing words into syllables and recognizing root words and affixes.

Fluency. The components of fluency are reading speed, accuracy, and prosody (Rasinski, 2004). Students need to read at least 100 words per minute to be considered fluent readers, and most children reach this speed by third grade. Speed is important because it's hard for students to remember what they're reading when they read slowly. Word recognition is related to speed because readers who automatically recognize most of the words they're reading can read more quickly than those who don't. Prosody, the ability to read sentences with appropriate phrasing and intonation, is important because when readers read expressively, the text is easier to understand.

Developing fluency is critical because readers don't have unlimited cognitive resources, and both word identification and comprehension require a great deal of mental energy. During the primary grades, the focus is on word identification, and students learn to recognize hundreds of words, but in fourth grade—after most students have become fluent readers—the focus changes to comprehension. Students who are fluent readers have the cognitive resources available for comprehension, but students who are still word-by-word readers are focusing on word identification.

Vocabulary. Capable readers have larger vocabularies than less capable readers do (National Reading Panel, 2000b). They learn words at the amazing rate of 7 to 10 per day. Learning a word is developmental: Children move from recognizing that they've seen or heard the word before to learning one meaning, and then to knowing several ways to use the word (Allen, 1999). Strong vocabulary knowledge is essential because it's easier to decode words that you've heard before and to comprehend what you're reading when you're already familiar with some words related to the topic.

Reading is the most effective way that students expand their vocabularies. Capable readers do more reading than less capable students, so they learn more words. Not only do they do more reading, but the books capable students read contain more age-appropriate vocabulary than the easier books that lower performing students read.

Comprehension. Readers use their past experiences and the text to construct comprehension, a meaning that's useful for a specific purpose (Irwin, 2007). Comprehension is a complex process that involves both reader and text factors (Sweet & Snow, 2003). While they're reading, readers are actively thinking about what they already know about a topic. They set a purpose for reading, read strategically, and make inferences using clues in the text. Readers also use their knowledge about texts. They think about the genre and the topic of the text, and they use what they've learned about text structure to guide their reading.

Capable readers are strategic: They use predicting, visualizing, connecting, questioning, summarizing, and other strategies to think about and understand what they're reading (Pressley, 2002). They also learn to monitor whether they're comprehending and learn how to take action to solve problems and clarify confusions when they occur. Teaching comprehension involves introducing strategies through minilessons, demonstrating how capable readers use them, and involving students in supervised practice activities.

FIGURE 6–4   How the Reading Process Develops Successful Readers

Stage	Word Identification	Fluency	Vocabulary	Comprehension
Stage 1 **Prereading**	Teachers introduce new words and teach word-identification strategies.		Teachers introduce key vocabulary words as they build background knowledge.	Students activate their background knowledge, and teachers build knowledge when necessary. Also, students set purposes for reading.
Stage 2 **Reading**	Students use phonics and other word-identification strategies as they read.	Students read texts at their instructional reading level with teacher support.	Teachers read aloud books that students can't read on their own.	Students use comprehension strategies as they read.
Stage 3 **Responding**				Students deepen their comprehension as they write in reading logs and talk about the book or other text.
Stage 4 **Exploring**	Teachers teach phonics, high-frequency words, and word-identification strategies.	Students reread familiar texts to build fluency.	Students post words on word walls and participate in vocabulary activities.	Teachers teach comprehension strategies, genres, and text structure.
Stage 5 **Applying**			Students independently read texts at their reading levels.	Students extend their comprehension as they create and share projects.

Through these activities, teachers scaffold students and then gradually release responsibility to them (Pearson & Gallagher, 1983). Teachers withdraw support slowly once students show that they can use comprehension strategies independently. Of course, even when students apply strategies independently, they may need increased scaffolding when they're reading more difficult text, texts about unfamiliar topics, or different genres (Pardo, 2004).

Students develop into capable readers as they use the reading process. Activities are included in each stage to develop these four factors. Figure 6–4 shows how word identification, fluency, vocabulary, and comprehension are developed through the reading process.

THE WRITING PROCESS

The focus in the writing process is on what students think and do as they compose; it's writer centered. The five stages of the writing process are prewriting, drafting, revising, editing, and publishing; the components of each stage are shown in Figure 6–5. The labeling and numbering of the stages don't mean, however, that the writing process is a linear series of neatly packaged categories: Research has shown that the process involves recurring cycles, and labeling is only an aid to identifying and discussing writing activities (Barnes, Morgan, & Weinhold, 1997; D. Graves, 1994; Perl, 1994). In the classroom, the stages merge and recur as students write.

Stage 1: Prewriting

Prewriting is the getting-ready-to-write stage. Writers begin the writing process before they've completely thought out their topic. They begin tentatively—talking, reading, writing—to discover what they know and decide what direction they want to take (Flower & Hayes, 1994). Prewriting has probably been the most neglected stage in the writing process; however, it's as crucial to writers as a warm-up is to athletes. Murray (1982) believes that at least 70% of writing time should be spent in prewriting. Students are involved in these activities during this stage:

- Choosing a topic
- Considering purpose, audience, and genre
- Generating and organizing ideas for writing

Choosing a Topic. Students often choose their own topics so that they write about things they're interested in and knowledgeable about. It's the first step in helping students become responsible for their own writing. At other times, however, teachers supply topics for writing

---

FIGURE 6–5   The Writing Process

Stage 1: Prewriting
Students engage in rehearsal activities.
Students identify the audience and the purpose of the writing activity.
Students choose an appropriate genre or form based on audience and purpose.

Stage 2: Drafting
Students write a rough draft.
Students mark their writing as a rough draft.
Students emphasize content rather than mechanics.

Stage 3: Revising
Students reread their own rough draft.
Students share their writing in revising groups.
Students participate constructively in discussions about classmates' writing.
Students make changes in their compositions to reflect comments from classmates and the teacher.
Students make substantive rather than minor changes.

Stage 4: Editing
Students proofread their own compositions.
Students help proofread classmates' compositions.
Students increasingly identify and correct their own mechanical errors.
Students meet with the teacher for a final editing.

Stage 5: Publishing
Students make the final copy of their writing, often using word processing.
Students publish their writing in an appropriate form.
Students sit in the author's chair to share their writing.

assignments. They may ask students to write in response to a book they've read in a literature focus unit, for example, as Ms. Kakutani did in the vignette at the beginning of the chapter, or to do a writing project as part of a thematic unit. Whenever possible, teachers keep the topics general so that students can narrow them in a way that interests them.

Setting a Purpose. As students prepare to write, they think about their purpose for writing. Are they writing to entertain? to inform? to persuade? Understanding the purpose of a piece of writing is important because it influences other decisions students make about audience and form. When students have no purpose in mind other than to complete the assignment, their writing is usually lackluster—without a strong voice or controlling idea.

Considering Audience. Students' writing is influenced by their sense of audience. Britton, Burgess, Martin, McLeod, and Rosen (1975) define *sense of audience* as "the manner in which the writer expresses a relationship with the reader in respect to the writer's understanding" (pp. 65-66). Students may write primarily for themselves or for others. Possible audiences include classmates, younger children, parents, grandparents, and pen pals. Other audiences are more distant and less well known, such as when students write letters to businesses to request information. Students adapt their writing to fit their audience, just as they vary their speech to meet the needs of their listeners.

Choosing a Genre. One of the most important considerations is the form the writing will take: a story? a letter? a poem? a report? Five genres that students learn to use are informational writing, journals and letters, persuasive writing, poetry, and stories. Figure 6-6 reviews these genres and lists some writing activities exemplifying each one. Through reading and writing, students develop a strong sense of these genres and how they're structured. Langer (1985) found that by third grade, children responded in distinctly different ways to story- and report-writing assignments; they organized the writing differently and included varied kinds of information and elaboration. Because children are clarifying the distinctions between various genres, teachers should use the correct terminology and not call all writing "stories."

Gathering and Organizing Ideas. Students engage in activities to gather and organize ideas for writing. Graves (1994) calls what writers do to prepare for writing "rehearsal" activities. When students read books, take field trips, view DVDs, and dramatize events, for example, they're participating in rehearsal activities and building background knowledge. Young children generally use drawing to gather and organize ideas for writing, and older students often make diagrams to organize their ideas as they prepare for writing.

Stage 2: Drafting

Students get their ideas down on paper during the drafting stage. They write on every other line to leave space for revisions; teachers often make a small *x* on every other line of students' papers as a reminder to skip lines as students draft their compositions. Students label their drafts by writing "rough draft" in ink at the top of the paper or by stamping them with a ROUGH DRAFT stamp; this label indicates to the writer, other students, parents, and administrators that the composition is a draft in which the emphasis is on content, not mechanics. It also explains why the teacher hasn't graded the paper or marked mechanical errors.

Drafting is messy. Students write quickly, trying to capture the ideas they're thinking about. It's not uncommon for them to leave out a word here and there and make careless spelling errors. They cross out sentences that aren't working, use carets to insert new ideas, and draw arrows to rearrange text. As students write rough drafts, teachers shouldn't emphasize correct spelling

FIGURE 6-6	Writing Genres	
Genre	**Purpose**	**Activities**
Informational Writing	Students collect and synthesize information for informational writing; this writing is objective. Reports are the most common type of informational writing. Students use informational writing to give directions, sequence steps, compare one thing to another, explain causes and effects, or describe problems and solutions.	Autobiographies Biographies Directions Interviews Reports
Narrative Writing	Students retell familiar stories, develop sequels for stories they have read, write stories called *personal narratives* about events in their own lives, and create original stories. They organize their stories into three parts: beginning, middle, and end.	Original short stories Personal narratives Retellings of stories Sequels to stories Scripts of stories
Personal Writing	Students write to themselves and to specific, known audiences in journals and letters. Their writing is often less formal than for other genres. They share news, explore new ideas, and record notes. Letters and envelopes require special formatting, and children learn these formats during the primary grades.	Blogs Email Friendly letters Postcards Reading logs
Persuasive Writing	*Persuasion* is winning someone to your viewpoint or cause. The three ways people are persuaded are by appeals to logic, moral character, and emotion. Students present their position clearly and then support it with examples and evidence.	Advertisements Book and movie reviews Commercials Persuasive letters Persuasive posters
Poetry Writing	Students create word pictures and play with rhyme and other stylistic devices as they create poems. As students experiment with poetry, they learn that poetic language is vivid and powerful but concise, and they learn that poems can be arranged in different ways on a page.	Acrostic poems Five-senses poems Found poems Free verse "I Am…" poems

or neatness. In fact, pointing out mechanical errors during this stage sends a false message that mechanical correctness is more important than content (Sommers, 1994). Later, during editing, students can clean up mechanical errors before they put their composition into a neat, final form.

Stage 3: Revising

Revising is the time when writers clarify and refine the ideas in their compositions. Novice writers often break the writing process cycle as soon as they finish a rough draft, believing that once they've jotted down their ideas, the writing task is complete. Experienced writers, however, know that they must turn to others for reactions and revise on the basis of these comments (Sommers, 1994). Revision isn't just polishing; it's meeting the needs of readers by adding, substituting, deleting, and rearranging material. The word *revision* means "seeing again," and in this stage, students see their compositions more objectively with the help of classmates and the teacher. They participate in these activities:

- Rereading the rough draft
- Sharing the rough draft in a revising group

Step-by-Step: REVISING GROUPS

1. **The writer reads.** Students take turns reading their compositions aloud. Classmates listen politely, thinking about compliments they'll make after the writer finishes reading. Only the writer looks at the composition, because when others look at it, they quickly notice and comment on mechanical errors, even though the emphasis during revising is on content. Listening to classmates read their writing aloud keeps the focus on content.

2. **Listeners offer compliments.** Revising-group members say what they liked about the writing. These positive comments should be specific, rather than the often-heard "I liked it" or "It was good."

3. **The writer asks questions.** Writers ask for assistance with trouble spots they identified earlier when rereading their writing, or they ask questions that reflect more general concerns about how well they're communicating.

4. **Listeners offer suggestions.** Members of the revising group ask questions about things that were unclear to them and suggest changes. Because it's difficult for students to appreciate suggestions, it's important to teach them what kinds of suggestions are acceptable and how to word their comments in helpful ways.

5. **The process is repeated.** Students repeat the first four steps as they share their rough drafts.

6. **Writers plan for revision.** At the end of the revising-group session, students make a commitment to revise their writing. When students verbalize their planned revisions, they're more likely to complete the revision stage. After the group disbands, students make the revisions.

- Revising on the basis of feedback
- Conferencing with the teacher

Rereading the Rough Draft. After finishing the rough draft, writers need to distance themselves from it for a day or two, then reread it from a fresh perspective, as a reader might. As they reread, students make changes—adding, substituting, deleting, and moving—and place question marks by sections that need work. Students ask for help with these trouble spots in their revising groups.

Sharing in Revising Groups. Students meet in revising groups to share their compositions with classmates. Because writing must meet the needs of readers, feedback is crucial. These small groups provide a scaffold so teachers and classmates can talk about students' writing and make revising suggestions (Calkins, 1994). The Step-by-Step feature above describes the procedure for revising groups.

Teaching students how to work in revising groups takes patience and practice. Teachers explain the purpose of these groups and the steps in the procedure, and next, they model the steps using a rough draft they've written. Then small groups of students model the steps while their classmates watch, and teachers point out how to provide useful feedback to writers. Teachers often have students develop a list of meaningful comments and post it in the classroom for students to refer to during revising. Figure 6–7 shows a sixth grade class list of compliments, questions, and suggestions that students can offer to classmates. Teachers also coach students on how to accept their classmates' compliments and suggestions without getting upset.

Revising groups can form spontaneously when several students are ready to share their compositions, or they can be formal groupings with identified leaders. In some classrooms, revising groups form when four or five students finish their rough drafts. The students gather around a conference table or in a corner of the classroom. They take turns reading their rough drafts aloud, and classmates in the group listen and respond, offering compliments and suggestions for revision. Sometimes the teacher joins the group, but if the teacher's involved in something else, students work independently. In other classrooms, the revising groups are established, and students get together to share their writing when everyone in the group is ready. Sometimes the teacher participates in the group, providing feedback along with the students. At other times, revising groups function independently. Four or five students are assigned to each group, and a list of groups and their members is posted in the classroom. Students take turns serving as group leader.

FIGURE 6–7   Sixth Graders' Revising-Group Comments

Compliments	Questions	Suggestions
I liked the part where _____ .	Did my introduction grab your attention?	Could you add more about _____ ?
Your lead grabbed my attention because _____ .	What do you want to know more about?	I think the part about _____ is long, and you could delete some of that.
My favorite sentence is _____ .	Did you understand my organization?	Which part is your conclusion?
I like the way you described _____ .	What do you think the best part of my paper is?	I think you should substitute a better word for _____ , such as _____ .
I noticed this metaphor: _____ .	Are there some words that I need to change?	Your organization isn't clear because _____ .
I could hear your "voice" when you wrote _____ .	Did you like my title?	I think you might try moving the part about _____ to _____ .
I like your conclusion because _____ .	Does my dialogue sound "real" to you?	I think you used _____ too many times. Can you combine some sentences?
I liked your organization because _____ .	Is there something that isn't clear to you?	
Your sequence is _____ .	Is there something that I need to delete?	
Your writing is powerful because it made me feel _____ .	Is there something I should move from one part of my writing to another part?	

Making Revisions. Students make four types of changes—additions, substitutions, deletions, and moves—as they revise (Faigley & Witte, 1981). They add words, substitute sentences, delete paragraphs, and move phrases, sentences, and even paragraphs. Students often use a blue pen to cross out, draw arrows, and write in the space left between the double-spaced lines of their rough drafts so that revisions will show clearly. This way teachers can examine the types of revisions students make. Revisions are an important gauge of students' growth as writers.

Conferencing With the Teacher. Sometimes the teacher participates in revising groups and provides revision suggestions along with the students, and at other times, the teacher conferences individually with students about their rough drafts. The teacher's role during conferences is to help students make choices and identify directions for revision. Barry Lane (1993, 1999) offers these suggestions for talking with students about their papers:

- Have students come to a conference prepared to begin talking about their concerns. Students should talk first.
- Ask questions rather than give answers. Ask students what's working well for them, what problems they're having, and what questions they have.
- React to students' writing as a reader, not as a teacher. Offer compliments first; give suggestions later.
- Keep the conference short, and recognize that not all problems can be discussed.
- Limit the number of revision suggestions, and make all suggestions specific.
- Have students meet in revising groups before conferencing so they can share the feedback they received from classmates with the teacher.
- To conclude the conference, ask students to identify the revisions they plan to make.
- Take notes during conferences and summarize students' revision plans. These notes are a record of the conference, and revision plans can be used in assessing students' final copies.

It's time-consuming to meet with every student, but it's worth the time (Calkins, Hartman, & White, 2005). In a 5-minute conference, teachers listen to students talk about their writing processes, guide students as they make revision plans, and offer feedback during the writing process, when it's most usable.

Stage 4: Editing

Students polish their compositions during editing. Until this stage, the focus has been on the content, but now it changes to mechanics, and students try to correct spelling, punctuation, and capitalization errors so their writing will be easier to read. Writers who write for readers understand that if their compositions aren't readable, they've written in vain because their ideas will never be read.

Mechanics are the commonly accepted conventions of written Standard English; they include capitalization, punctuation, spelling, sentence structure, usage, and formatting considerations specific to poems, scripts, letters, and other writing forms. The use of these commonly accepted conventions is a courtesy to those who will read the composition.

Mechanical skills are best taught during editing. When students are editing a composition that will be shared with a genuine audience, they're more interested in using mechanical skills correctly so that they can communicate effectively. In a study of two third grade classes, Calkins (1980) found that the students who learned punctuation marks as a part of editing could explain more marks than the students in the other class, who were taught punctuation skills in a traditional manner, with instruction and practice exercises on each punctuation mark. In other words, the results of this research, as well as other studies (D. Graves, 1994), suggest that students learn mechanical skills better as part of the writing process than through practice exercises. Students participate in these activities during editing:

- Getting distance from the composition
- Proofreading to locate errors
- Correcting errors

Getting Distance. Students are more efficient editors if they set the composition aside for a few days before beginning to edit. After working so closely with a piece of writing during drafting and revising, they're too familiar with it to be able to locate many mechanical errors. With the distance gained by waiting a few days, students can approach editing with a fresh perspective and gather the enthusiasm necessary to finish the writing process.

Proofreading. Students proofread their rough drafts to locate and mark possible errors. *Proofreading* is a unique type of reading in which students read slowly, word by word, hunting for errors rather than reading quickly for meaning. Concentrating on mechanics is difficult because our natural inclination is to read for meaning. Even experienced proofreaders often find themselves reading for meaning and overlooking errors that don't inhibit meaning. It's important, therefore, to take time to explain proofreading and show how it differs from regular reading.

To demonstrate proofreading, the teacher projects a piece of student writing on a whiteboard. The teacher reads it several times, each time hunting for a particular type of error. During each reading, the teacher reads the composition slowly, softly pronouncing each word and touching the word with a pen to focus attention on it. The teacher circles possible errors as they're located.

Errors are marked or corrected with special proofreaders' marks. Students enjoy using these marks, the same ones that adult authors use. Proofreaders' marks that students can learn to use in editing their writing are presented in Figure 6–8. Editing checklists help students focus on particular types of errors. Teachers develop checklists with two to six items appropriate for the grade level. A first grade checklist, for example, might contain only two items—one about capital letters at the beginning of sentences and another about periods at the end. In contrast, a middle grade checklist might have items such as using commas in a series, indenting paragraphs, capitalizing proper nouns, and spelling homonyms correctly. Teachers can revise the checklist during the school year to focus attention on skills that have recently been taught.

A third grade editing checklist is presented in Figure 6–9. First, students proofread their own compositions, searching for errors in each category on the checklist; after proofreading, they check off each item. Then, after completing the checklist, students sign their names and trade checklists and compositions with a classmate: Now they become editors and complete each other's checklists. Having both writer and editor sign the checklist helps them take the activity seriously.

Correcting Errors. After students proofread their compositions, they correct the errors they've found individually or with an editor's assistance. Some errors are easy to correct, some require use of a dictionary, and others involve instruction from the teacher. It's unrealistic to expect students to locate and correct every mechanical error in their writing. Not even published books are error free! Once in a while, students change a correct spelling and make it incorrect, but they correct far more errors than they create.

Editing can end after students and their editors correct as many mechanical errors as possible, or after students conference with the teacher for a final editing. When mechanical correctness is crucial, this conference is important. Teachers proofread the composition with the

FIGURE 6-8	Proofreaders' Marks	
Delete	✶	There were cots to sleep on and food to eat or at the shelter.
Insert	∧	Mrs. Kim's cat is the color of carrots.
Indent paragraph	¶	¶ Riots are bad. People can get hurt and buildings can get burned down but good things can happen too. People can learn to be friends.
Capitalize	=	Daniel and his mom didn't like mrs. Kim or her cat.
Change to lowercase	/	People were Rioting because they were angry.
Add period	⊙	I think Daniel's mom and Mrs. Kim will become friends ⊙
Add comma	∧	People hurt other people, they steal things, and they burn down buildings in a riot.
Add apostrophe	∨	Daniel's cat was named Jasmine.

student, and they make the remaining corrections together, or the teacher makes checkmarks in the margin to note errors for the student to correct independently.

Stage 5: Publishing

Students bring their compositions to life by publishing them. When they share their writing with classmates, other students, parents, and community members, students come to think of themselves as authors. Students are involved in these activities during this stage:

- Making final copies of their writing
- Reading from the author's chair
- Sharing their writing

Making Final Copies. One of the most popular ways for students to publish their writing is by making books. Simple booklets can be made by folding a sheet of paper into quarters, like a greeting card. Students write the title on the front and use the three remaining sides for their compositions. They can also construct booklets by stapling sheets of writing paper together and adding construction paper covers. These stapled booklets can be cut into various shapes, too.

Students can make more sophisticated books by covering cardboard covers with contact paper, wallpaper, or cloth; pages are sewn or stapled together, and the first and last pages (endpapers) are glued to the cardboard covers to hold the book together.

Reading From the Author's Chair. Teachers designate a special chair in their classroom as "the author's chair" (Graves & Hansen, 1983). This chair might be a rocking chair, a lawn chair with a padded seat, a wooden stool, or a director's chair, and it should be labeled "Author's Chair." Students sit in the chair to read aloud books they've written, and this is the only time anyone sits there.

When students share their writing, one student sits in the author's chair, and a group of classmates sit on the floor or in chairs in front of the author's chair. The student sitting in the author's chair reads the writing aloud and shows the accompanying illustrations. After the reading, classmates who want to comment raise their hands, and the author chooses several classmates to ask questions and give compliments. Then the author chooses another student to share and takes a seat in the audience.

Most students really enjoy reading their writing aloud to their classmates, and they learn about the importance of audience as they watch for their classmates' reactions. And classmates benefit from the experience as well: They get ideas for their own writing as they listen to how other students use sentence patterns and vocabulary that they might not be familiar with. The process of sharing their writing brings closure to the writing process and energizes students for their next writing project.

Sharing Writing. In addition to reading their writing to classmates, students share their writing in other ways. They may share it with larger audiences through hardcover books placed in the

| FIGURE 6–9 | A Third Grade Editing Checklist |

Author	Editor	
☐	☐	1. I have circled the words that might be misspelled.
☐	☐	2. I have checked that all sentences begin with a capital letter.
☐	☐	3. I have checked that all sentences end with a punctuation mark.
☐	☐	4. I have checked that all proper nouns begin with a capital letter.

Signatures

Author: _____   Editor: _____

class or school library, plays performed for classmates, or poems posted on an ezine, and these other ways to share writing:

- Submit the piece to writing contests
- Contribute to a class anthology
- Submit it to a literary magazine
- Share at a read-aloud party
- Share with parents and siblings
- Send it to a pen pal
- Design a poster about the writing

Through this sharing, students communicate with audiences who respond to their writing in meaningful ways.

INTEGRATING TECHNOLOGY

The Internet offers unlimited opportunities for students to publish their writing online, share it with a global audience, and receive authentic feedback from readers (McNabb, 2006). When students create multimodal compositions that incorporate audio, video, animation, or graphics, online publication is essential so that readers can fully experience them (Labbo, 2005). These websites are some of the best:

CYBER KIDS (http://www.cyberkids.com). This site publishes original writing by 7- to 16-year-olds, including multimodal stories.

KIDSWWWRITE (http://www.kalwriters.com/kidswwwrite). Students' stories and poems are published in this ezine that's divided into sections for 5- to 8-year-olds, 9- to 12-year-olds, and 13- to 16-year-olds.

POETRY ZONE (http://www.poetryzone.woodshed.co.uk). This British website posts students' poetry in the Poetry Gallery and provides other poetry resources for teachers.

STORIES FROM THE WEB (http://www.storiesfromtheweb.org). This website accepts submissions of students' stories, play scripts, poems, raps, and songs.

Students can use Internet search engines to locate new ezines. It's inevitable that some online publication sites will shut down, but others will spring up to take their place.

Each electronic magazine posts its own submission information that students should read and follow. Most ezines specify that students' submissions must be original, and that writing dealing with violent or offensive topics or employing inappropriate language won't be published. Submissions must be ready for posting; editors don't format students' writing or correct errors. Students usually complete an online information sheet and email their writing to the ezine's website, and parents must submit a permission statement.

Students can also display their writing on the class website for others to read and respond to in guest books, blogs, and email messages. If the teacher doesn't have a class website, students can work with their teacher to create one and post their writing there. ■

Teaching the Writing Process

Students learn to use the writing process when they write compositions as projects in literature focus units and thematic units and when they participate in writing workshop. Learning to use the writing process is more important than any particular writing project students might be involved in, because the writing process is a tool. The feature below shows how the reading and writing processes fit into the patterns of practice.

One way to introduce the writing process is to write a collaborative composition. The teacher models the writing process and provides an opportunity for students to practice the process approach in a supportive environment. Students write a composition together with teacher guidance, moving through the writing process, just as writers do when they work independently. The teacher demonstrates the strategies that writers use and clarifies misconceptions during the group composition, and students offer ideas for writing as well as suggestions for tackling common writing problems.

The teacher introduces the idea of writing a group composition and explains the project. Students dictate a rough draft, which the teacher records on chart paper. The teacher notes any misunderstandings students have about the writing process and, when necessary, reviews concepts and offers suggestions. Then the teacher and students read the composition and identify ways to revise it. Some parts of the composition will need reworking, and other parts may be deleted or moved. More specific words will be substituted for less specific ones, and redundant words and sentences will be deleted. Students may also want to add new sections. Once students are satisfied with the content, they proofread the composition, checking for mechanical errors, paragraph breaks, and sentences to combine. They correct errors they locate. Then the teacher copies the completed composition for each student. Collaborative compositions are an essential part of many writing experiences, especially when students are learning to use the writing process because they serve as a dry run during which students' questions and misconceptions can be clarified.

Teachers also use minilessons to teach students how to gather and organize ideas for writing, how to participate in revising groups, how to proofread, and how to format their writing. Minilessons can be taught as part of class collaborations, during literature focus units and thematic units, and in writing workshop. A third grade minilesson on revising is presented on page 168.

How Written Language Fits Into the Patterns of Practice

Literature Focus Units

Teachers use the reading process to organize units: They build knowledge before reading, and afterward students respond, explore, and apply what they've learned. Students use the writing process to create projects during the applying stage of the reading process.

Literature Circles

Students use the reading process to read self-selected books. More emphasis is placed on the reading and responding stages, but students participate in other activities as well. The writing process isn't used because the focus here is on reading, not writing.

Reading and Writing Workshop

Although the focus is on independent reading during reading workshop, students activate background knowledge and participate in other activities, but to a lesser degree. And, they use the writing process to develop and refine compositions during writing workshop.

Thematic Units

Students read fiction and nonfiction books during thematic units, and teachers incorporate activities representing each stage of the reading process. Students often create projects to share what they've learned during the unit, and they use the writing process to develop them.

Minilesson

Ms. Yarborough Introduces Revising to Third Graders

1. Introduce the Topic

Ms. Yarborough names the five stages of the writing process as she points to the writing process charts hanging in the classroom. She explains that today's focus is on revising. She reminds students that the purpose of revising is to make their writing communicate better and explains that writers add, delete, substitute, and move words and sentences as they revise.

2. Share Examples

Ms. Yarborough shares this paragraph that she's written on chart paper and explains that she wrote it because they're studying about amphibians:

Amphibians live in water and on land. They live in water when they are babies. They live on land when they grow up. Frogs are some amphibians.

She reads the paragraph aloud and asks the class to help her make it better by adding, deleting, substituting, and moving words and sentences.

3. Provide Information

Students work with Ms. Yarborough to revise the paragraph. They add words and sentences and reorder sentences in the paragraph. As

students make suggestions, Ms. Yarborough writes the changes on the chart. Here's the revised paragraph:

Amphibians live part of their lives in water and part on land. Frogs, toads and salamanders are amphibians. They hatch from eggs in water, grow up, and live on land when they are adults. This process of changing is called metamorphosis.

4. Supervise Practice

Ms. Yarborough divides students into small groups and gives each group another paragraph about amphibians to revise. Students work together to make revisions, using blue pens and making marks as Ms. Yarborough demonstrated. Ms. Yarborough circulates as they work, and then students share their rough drafts and revised paragraphs with the class.

5. Reflect on Learning

Ms. Yarborough asks the students to compare the rough drafts and revised paragraphs and decide which communicate better. Then students brainstorm a list of reasons why revision is important. Their list includes: "The writing is more interesting," "It's more fun to read," and "The words are more scientific."

The Author's Craft

Vicki Spandel (2005, 2008) and her colleagues at the Northwest Regional Educational Laboratory examined student writing to identify the traits of effective writing. Through their research, they identified these traits: ideas, organization, voice, word choice, sentence fluency, and conventions. When students learn about these traits, they grow in their understanding of what effective writing looks like and develop a vocabulary for talking about writing. In a multiyear study, Culham (2003) found that teaching students about these traits improves the quality of their writing.

TRAIT 1: IDEAS. Ideas are the "heart of the message" (Culham, 2003, p. 11). When ideas are well developed, the writing is clear and focused. Effective details elaborate the big ideas and create images in readers' minds. As students examine this trait, they develop these abilities:

- Choosing original and interesting ideas
- Narrowing and focusing ideas
- Choosing details to develop an idea
- Using the senses to add imagery

Esperanza Rising (Ryan, 2000), the story of a girl and her mother who flee from Mexico and find work in California as migrant workers, demonstrates how effective authors develop ideas. The title emphasizes the theme: The main character's name is Esperanza, the Spanish word for *hope*, and she rises above her difficult circumstances. At the beginning, Pam Muñoz Ryan paints a vivid picture of Esperanza's comfortable life on her family's ranch in Mexico, and later in the story, she creates a powerful contrast as she describes Esperanza's harsh existence in a migrant labor camp. As the story ends, Esperanza remains hopeful, telling her good friend Isabel never to be afraid of starting over.

TRAIT 2: ORGANIZATION. Organization is the internal structure of a composition; its function is to enhance the central idea. Spandel (2001) explains that organization is putting "information together in an order than informs, persuades, or entertains" (p. 39). The logical pattern of the ideas varies according to genre; stories, for example, are organized differently than nonfiction or poetry. As students learn about organization, they develop these abilities:

- Using structural patterns in their writing
- Crafting leads to grab the reader's attention
- Using transition words to link ideas together
- Writing satisfying endings

Louis Sachar's award-winning novel *Holes* (2008) is a well-organized story about a hapless boy named Stanley Yelnats who is wrongly convicted of theft and sent to Camp Green Lake, a juvenile detention facility where he spends every day digging holes. The beginning, middle, and end of the story are easy to pick out: The beginning is before Stanley arrives at Camp Green Lake, the middle is while he's there, and the end is when he escapes and redeems himself. What makes this book unique is the second plot about a curse that has followed the Yelnats family for generations. As the book ends, Stanley fulfills his destiny by digging up the truth and unraveling the family curse.

TRAIT 3: VOICE. Voice is the writer's style; it's what breathes life into writing. Culham (2003) calls it "the soul of the piece" (p. 12). The writer's voice can be humorous or compelling, reflective or persuasive. What matters most is that the author connects with readers. Students develop their own voices in these ways:

- Retelling familiar stories from the viewpoints of different characters
- Assuming a persona and writing from that person's viewpoint
- Using strong verbs
- Avoiding redundancy and vague wording

Catherine, Called Birdy (Cushman, 2005), the fictional diary of a rebellious teenager in medieval England, has a compelling voice. In this witty first-person account of daily life, Birdy recounts how she avoids marrying the rich suitors that her father brings to meet her. Her journal entries have an authentic ring because they're infused with period details and sprinkled with exclamations, such as "corpus bones" and "God's thumbs," that sound plausible.

TRAIT 4: WORD CHOICE. Carefully chosen words have the power to clarify meaning or to create a mood. It's important for writers to choose words that fit both their purpose and the audience to whom their writing is directed. Students increase their word knowledge through literature focus units and lots of reading. As students experiment with word choice, they develop these abilities:

- Using precise nouns, vivid verbs, and colorful modifiers
- Consulting a thesaurus to consider options
- Avoiding tired words and phrases
- Using wordplay

Readers appreciate the importance of careful word choice in Pamela Duncan Edwards's collection of alliterative stories, including *Some Smug Slug* (1996), and *The Worrywarts* (2003). These tongue-twister books are fun to read aloud.

TRAIT 5: SENTENCE FLUENCY. Sentence fluency is "the rhythm and flow of carefully structured language that makes it both easy and pleasurable to read aloud" (Spandel, 2001, p. 101). Effective sentences vary in structure and length, and students are now encouraged to include some sentence fragments to add rhythm and energy to their writing (Culham, 2003). Teachers teach students about sentence structure so that they develop these abilities:

- Varying sentence structure and length
- Including some sentence fragments
- Beginning sentences in different ways
- Combining or expanding sentences

In *Old Black Fly* (Aylesworth, 1992), a pesky fly goes on an alphabetical rampage until he is finally stopped by a fly swatter. The rhythm and flow of the snappy couplets make this a popular read-aloud book, and after reading, students are eager to try their hand at creating an imitative poem featuring an old grinning grasshopper or an old slippery seal.

TRAIT 6: CONVENTIONS. Conventions guide readers through the writing. Mechanics, paragraphing, and design elements are three types. Writers check that they've used Standard English mechanics—spelling, punctuation, capitalization, and grammar—as a courtesy to readers. They verify that their division of the text into paragraphs enhances the organization of the ideas. They also create a design for their compositions and arrange the text on the page to enhance readability. Students learn to apply these conventions during the editing and publishing stages of the writing process:

- Proofreading to identify mechanical errors
- Using a dictionary to correct spelling errors
- Checking paragraphing
- Adding design elements to the final copy

The importance of punctuation is highlighted in *Punctuation Takes a Vacation* (Pulver, 2003). After reading the book, teachers can remove the punctuation in excerpts from a familiar book so students can see what happens when "punctuation takes a vacation." The page layout is important in many picture books. In Jan Brett's *The Umbrella* (2004), a story set in the rain forest, and in many of her other books, illustrations on the edge of the left-hand pages show what happened on the previous page, and illustrations on the edge of the right-hand pages show what will happen next.

Teaching the Six Traits. A good way to introduce the six traits is by having students examine what makes a favorite book effective. For example, in Janet Stevens and Susan Stevens Crummel's *Jackalope* (2003), the story of a jackrabbit who wishes to be feared so his fairy godrabbit gives him horns, there's a lot to like. A class of fourth graders identified these qualities:

- The story is told by an armadillo. (Ideas, Organization)
- Armadillo sounds like he's a cowboy. (Voice)
- The story mentions fairy tales and nursery rhymes. (Ideas)
- The beginning, middle, and end are easy to pick out. (Organization)
- Some of the sentences rhyme. (Sentence fluency)
- What the armadillo says is typed in colored boxes. (Conventions)
- The funny vegetable wordplays are italicized so you are sure to notice them. (Word choice, Conventions)
- Jack is a good character because he saved the fairy godrabbit. (Ideas)
- The theme is clear: You should be happy being yourself. (Ideas)
- We didn't find any spelling or punctuation or capitalization mistakes. (Conventions)

Later, the students reread their comments and classified them according to the traits they illustrate, and like many of the best books available for children today, *Jackalope* exemplifies all of them!

Teachers introduce the six traits one by one through a series of minilessons. They explain the characteristics of the trait using stories and other books as models. The Booklist on page 172 suggests mentor texts to use in teaching about each trait. Once students have some knowledge of the trait, they examine how other students applied it in sample compositions, and then they revise other sample compositions to incorporate the trait. Finally, they apply what they've learned in their own writing.

Linking the Six Traits to the Writing Process. The writing process is a cyclical series of activities that students use as they draft and refine their writing, but it doesn't specify how to make writing better. That's where the six traits come in: Students apply what they've learned about the traits to improve the quality of their writing, particularly during the revising and editing stages (Culham, 2003).

As students reread their rough drafts, they can check that their writing exemplifies each of the traits. Teachers can develop rubrics that focus on one or more traits that students can use to self-assess their writing. Students also ask classmates in a revising group for feedback about how they might improve their sentence fluency, organization, or another trait. The six traits provide another reason for students to carefully proofread their rough drafts. They learn that they correct mechanical errors and check paragraphing to improve the readability of their compositions. Students also think about the design for their published compositions. They decide how to arrange the text on the page in order to make their writing more understandable, and with word processing, students can make their writing look very professional.

Booklist

THE SIX TRAITS	
Ideas	Law, I. (2008). *Savvy*. New York: Dial Books. M–U Ryan, P. M. (2002). *Esperanza rising*. New York: Scholastic. M Willems, M. (2004). *Knuffle bunny*. New York: Hyperion Books. P Yolen, J. (2007). *Owl moon*. New York: Philomel. P–M
Organization	Fleischman, P. (2004). *Seedfolks*. New York: Harper Trophy. M Sachar, L. (2008). *Holes*. New York: Farrar, Straus & Giroux. U Schmidt, G. D. (2007). *The Wednesday wars*. New York: Clarion Books. U Steig, W. (2010). *Sylvester and the magic pebble*. New York: Atheneum. P–M
Voice	Cronin, D. (2007). *Diary of a fly*. New York: HarperCollins. P Cushman, K. (2005). *Catherine, called Birdy*. New York: HarperCollins. U Erickson, J. R. (2003). *Hank the cow dog*. New York: Puffin Books. M Scieszka, J. (1999). *The true story of the 3 little pigs!* New York: Puffin Books. P–M
Word Choice	Babbitt, N. (2007). *Tuck everlasting*. New York: Square Fish Books. U Horowitz, R. (2004). *Crab moon*. Cambridge, MA: Candlewick Press. P–M Rylant, C. (1991). *Night in the country*. New York: Atheneum. P Scieszka, J. (2001). *Baloney (Henry P.)*. New York: Viking. M
Sentence Fluency	Gray, L. M. (1999). *My mama had a dancing heart*. New York: Scholastic. P–M Schachner, J. (2005). *Skippyjon Jones*. New York: Puffin Books. P White, E. B. (2006). *Charlotte's web*. New York: HarperCollins. M–U Wisniewski, D. (1999). *Tough cookie*. New York: Lothrop, Lee & Shepard. M
Conventions	Holm, J. L. (2007). *Middle school is worse than meatloaf*. New York: Atheneum. M–U Klise, K. (2007). *Regarding the trees: A splintered saga rooted in secrets*. New York: Sandpiper. M–U Pulver, R. (2003). *Punctuation takes a vacation*. New York: Holiday House. P–M Stein, D. E. (2010). *Interrupting chicken*. Somerville, MA: Candlewick Press. P–M

P = primary grades (preK–2); M = middle grades (3–5); U = upper grades (6–8)

ENGAGING ENGLISH LEARNERS

English learners use the same writing process that native English speakers use, but it can be more challenging because ELs are learning to speak and write English at the same time. Teachers support ELs during each stage of the writing process, but as students become more fluent in English, they pay special attention to assisting students with English vocabulary words and sentence structure.

STAGE 1: PREWRITING. ELs identify words to express their ideas, use the words in sentences, and organize their ideas. Students often use drawing as a rehearsal activity and then teachers work with ELs to brainstorm ideas and vocabulary words. Teachers also assist ELs in organizing their ideas using a series of pictures or a diagram. Finally, students often "talk out" their compositions with a classmate before beginning to write.

STAGE 2: DRAFTING. Teachers scaffold English learners by helping them turn their ideas into phrases and sentences, and they reassure students that spelling and other mechanical skills aren't important during drafting.

STAGE 3: REVISING. English learners participate in revising just like their native English-speaking classmates, but at first ELs make only one or two revisions. It's helpful to have students share their rough drafts with a trusted classmate before meeting in a revising group or conferencing with the teacher so they can catch omitted words and incomplete ideas. This first sharing also provides practice so they can read their writing more fluently when they participate in a revising group.

STAGE 4: EDITING. This stage provides many teachable moments that teachers can take advantage of. It's often more effective to focus on one type of grammar/usage error at a time. A useful procedure is to have students proofread and mark possible errors and then fix them together. For longer compositions, teachers often have students identify and correct errors on the first page of their compositions, then they correct the remaining errors with students.

STAGE 5: PUBLISHING. Students' final copies are rarely error free even though they've been carefully edited. When teachers read students' published writing, they're tempted to correct the remaining errors, but it's not effective because it sends the message that mechanical correctness is more important than the content. In addition, English learners need opportunities to share their writing with classmates; depending on ELs' level of oral language development and their comfort being in front of the class, they can share their writing with a buddy, in a small group, or with the whole class.

The instruction and scaffolding that teachers provide ensure that English learners become capable writers. ∎

Reading and Writing Are Reciprocal Processes

Reading and writing are reciprocal; they're both constructive, meaning-making processes. Researchers have found that more reading leads to better writing, and more writing has the same effect on reading (Spivey, 1997). Not surprisingly, they've also learned that integrating instruction improves both reading and writing (Tierney & Shanahan, 1991). It's likely that students use the same kind of thinking in both reading and writing.

The reading and writing processes have comparable activities at each stage (Butler & Turbill, 1984); Figure 6–10 shows this comparison. For example, notice the similarities between the activities in the third stage of reading and writing—responding and revising, respectively. Fitzgerald (1989) analyzed these activities and concluded that they draw on similar processes of author-reader-text interactions. The same kind of analyses can be made for activities in the other stages as well.

Teachers help students appreciate the similarities between reading and writing and understand the importance of connecting the two when they follow these guidelines:

- Involve students in daily reading and writing activities.
- Introduce the reading and writing processes in kindergarten.
- Talk with students about the similarities between the reading and writing processes.
- Teach students about reading and writing strategies.
- Emphasize both the processes and the products of reading and writing.
- Emphasize the purposes for which students use reading and writing.
- Teach reading and writing using genuine literacy experiences.

FIGURE 6–10	A Comparison of the Reading and Writing Processes

Stage	What Readers Do	What Writers Do
Stage 1	**Prereading** Readers use knowledge about • the topic • reading • literature • language systems Readers' expectations are cued by • previous reading/writing experiences • genre • purpose for reading • audience for reading Readers preview the text and make predictions.	**Prewriting** Writers use knowledge about • the topic • writing • literature • language systems Writers' expectations are cued by • previous reading/writing experiences • genre • purpose for writing • audience for writing Writers gather and organize ideas.
Stage 2	**Reading** Readers • use word-identification strategies • use comprehension strategies • monitor reading • create meaning	**Drafting** Writers • use spelling strategies • use writing strategies • monitor writing • create meaning
Stage 3	**Responding** Readers • respond to the text • clarify misunderstandings • develop interpretations	**Revising** Writers • respond to the text • clarify misunderstandings • develop interpretations
Stage 4	**Exploring** Readers examine the text by • considering the impact of words and literary language • exploring structural elements • comparing the text to others	**Editing** Writers examine the text by • correcting mechanical errors • reviewing paragraph and sentence structure
Stage 5	**Applying** Readers • develop projects to extend knowledge • share projects with classmates • reflect on the reading process • value the piece of literature • feel success • want to read again	**Publishing** Writers • produce the final copy of their compositions • share their compositions with genuine audiences • reflect on the writing process • value the composition • feel success • want to write again

Based on Butler & Turbill, 1984.

Tierney explains: "What we need are reading teachers who act as if their students were developing writers and writing teachers who act as if their students were readers" (1983, p. 151). Reading contributes to students' writing development, and writing contributes to students' reading development (Schulze, 2006; Shanahan, 1988).

SUMMING UP

Reading and writing are similar processes of constructing meaning. Teachers organize reading and writing instruction using the reading and writing processes. The five stages of the reading process are prereading, reading, responding, exploring, and applying; and the five stages of the writing process are prewriting, drafting, revising, editing, and publishing. Students learn to use the reading and writing processes through literature focus units, literature circles, reading and writing workshop, and thematic units. The goal of both reading and writing is to construct meaning, and the two processes have comparable activities at each stage.

MyEducationLab™

Go to the topic Reading and Writing in the MyEducationLab (http://www.myeducationlab.com) for *Language Arts: Patterns of Practice*, where you can:

- Find learning outcomes for Reading and Writing, along with the national standards that connect to these outcomes.
- Complete Assignments and Activities that can help you more deeply understand the chapter content.
- Apply and practice your understanding of the core teaching skills identified in the chapter with the Building Teaching Skills and Dispositions learning units.
- Examine challenging situations and cases presented in the IRIS Center Resources.
- Use the Lesson Plan Builder Activities to practice lesson planning and integrating national and state standards into your planning.
- Check your comprehension of the content covered in the chapter with the Study Plan. Here you will be able to take a chapter quiz, receive feedback on your answers, and then access Review, Practice, and Enrichment activities to enhance your understanding of chapter content.

On the **MyEducationLab** for this course, you'll also be able to:

- **A+RISE** Go to the topic A+RISE, an innovative and interactive database of strategies that differentiate instruction across the language arts and provide particular insight into research-based methods to meet the needs of English learners.
- Explore the topic Literacy Portraits—yearlong case studies of second graders, complete with student artifacts, teacher commentary, and student and teacher interviews, tracking the month-by-month language arts growth of five students.
- Gain practice with the Grammar Tutorial, online guided instruction to improve your own ability with grammar.

CHAPTER 7

Visual Language: Viewing and Visually Representing

EIGHTH GRADERS LEARN ABOUT IRONY The eighth graders in Mr. Garibay's language arts class are viewing the first slide in a PowerPoint presentation on irony that he's projecting on a huge whiteboard on one wall of the classroom. It shows a flight of stairs and an escalator leading to a fitness center; several people are heading to the fitness center on the escalator, but no one's taking the stairs. "Take a look at this picture," Mr. Garibay begins, "and tell me what you see." Students partner with classmates to talk about it. Some immediately begin to snicker because they recognize the humor; others, however, examine the picture without noticing anything funny.

The teacher brings the class back together to discuss the photo. Ricardo begins, "I see some people on an escalator," and Alexis continues, "I think they're going up to a fitness center." "You know, it's ridiculous," Jamar comments, "that those people are riding up the escalator, even though they're going to exercise. They should be walking up the stairs!" Mr. Garibay agrees. He explains that this picture is an example of irony, and they're going to learn to identify and interpret the irony.

Mr. Garibay shows the next slide that asks, "What is irony?" and the students share their ideas. "It's different than what you expect," Tyrell says; and Shandra adds, "It's when you're surprised." Next, Dominic offers, "It's when you think one thing and what happens is different," and Kat says, "It's the opposite of what you think will happen." The next slide defines irony as a contrast between what's expected and what actually occurs. The teacher explains, "Irony is all around us—in pictures, speech, stories, poems, songs, movies, and music videos."

How does visual language support the other language arts?

The six language arts are listening, talking, reading, writing, viewing, and visually representing. Teachers make thoughtful choices about the language modes to use as they teach lessons based on difficulty level of the topic and their students' abilities. As you read this vignette, notice how Mr. Garibay integrates oral, written, and visual language and how he sequences them in his weeklong lesson on irony.

Next, Mr. Garibay displays the fitness center photo again and asks students to explain the irony. Ella offers, "It's ironic that people are on the escalator." Mr. Garibay asks the students to expand Ella's idea. Roshaun suggests, "It's ironic that people are riding the escalator to the fitness center." Reina expands the thought further: "People riding the escalator instead of walking the stairs to the fitness center to exercise— that's ironic!"

Mr. Garibay shows five additional photos containing irony, and the students divide into small groups to talk about each one and point out the irony. The first photo shows a sign that a beach is closed because of pollution that's been placed next to a waste can labeled "Keep your beach clean." In the second photo, there's a man in a shirt labeled "peace team" attacking people trying to force their way around a gate. A bald man who's shirtless and very hairy everywhere but on his head appears in the next photo. In the fourth photo, a dazed woman is sitting in a car from the Easy Method Driving School that's been involved in a crash. By the time the students examine the fifth photo—the class favorite—showing an elderly woman who's toothless standing in front of a Colgate toothpaste display, Mr. Garibay is confident that all 32 students can recognize irony in pictures.

The next day, Mr. Garibay focuses on examples of irony in speech. One by one, he displays these statements on the whiteboard:

A boy wrecks on his skateboard and his friend says, "Great trick."

A woman looks out the window on a rainy day and says, "Lovely day for a stroll around the park."

A boy picks up a girl for a date in a ratty old car, and the girl says, "Wow! Nice ride!"

A child shows his mom his test paper with a grade of F and says, "Mom, look how great I did on my test!"

The eighth graders work with partners to identify the irony in the statement and write an explanation that they share with the class. Tyrell and Dominic wrote this about the skateboard statement: *The friend's comment "great trick" is ironic because it's the opposite of what happened. He probably said it to make the boy feel better.* Latanya and Ella identified the irony in the statement about the boy's car this way: *The girl's comment is ironic. She probably said it because she was so surprised that her boyfriend had such a ratty old car, but she really did not mean it was a great car.*

Several days later, Mr. Garibay shares these four poems, and students discuss each one to identify the irony:

"The New Kid on the Block," by Jack Prelutsky

"Mean Maxine," by Jack Prelutsky

"Almost Human," by Pat Moon

"O Captain! My Captain!" by Walt Whitman

The first two poems are from Prelutsky's classic anthology, *The New Kid on the Block* (1984), and Mr. Garibay selected the other two from the students' eighth grade literature anthology. They read the first poem together as a class; quickly the students recognize that the new kid who's a bully is a girl. "I get it!" Ricardo confidently shouts out, "It's ironic because she's a girl." Next, the students divide into small groups to read and analyze the next two poems.

The following day, the eighth graders discuss the Civil War and Abraham Lincoln before reading Walt Whitman's tribute to the fallen president in their literature anthology, "O Captain! My Captain!" They read the poem several times, slowly grasping the meaning. Mr. Garibay asks about Lincoln's role as captain of the ship of state. The students pick out examples of symbolism: The president is the ship's captain, the ship is the country, and the voyage is the Civil War. Next, the teacher rereads the lines that mention bells ringing and asks about them. The students seem confused, so he explains that church bells are rung at big celebrations, but they're also rung during funerals. With that clue, the students figure out the irony: Even though Abraham Lincoln secured the country, he was assassinated. What was supposed to be a happy homecoming with bells ringing in celebration became a funeral with bells ringing in his memory. "Abraham Lincoln was the country's captain during the Civil War," Jamar concludes, "and it's ironic that he saved the country, but he couldn't save himself."

Now the students turn their attention to examples of irony in stories. Mr. Garibay reads aloud Chris Van Allsburg's stunning picture book, *The Sweetest Fig* (1993); it's the story of Monsieur Bibot, a Parisian dentist, who receives two supposedly magic figs as payment from a patient who tells him they have the power to make his dreams come true. He eats one but saves the second, planning to use it to make himself rich; however, his long-suffering dog eats it, and the next morning the dentist awakes to discover that he's been turned into a dog and his dog has become his master. The students quickly notice the twist at the story's end and agree that the dentist deserved this fate, but identifying the irony was more difficult. Alexis begins, "*The Sweetest Fig* is a story about a dentist who gets turned into a dog. He deserved it, but I don't think that's the irony." "I knew the dog was going to eat the second fig because I noticed the foreshadowing, so that wasn't a big surprise. I think the dog's wish—to trade places with the man—was the ironic part because that surprised me," Reina offers. "So, it's the surprising part that's the irony?" Cole asks. "Yes, that makes sense to me," Amee answers.

The next day, the students divide into small groups to read and discuss one of these picture-book stories:

> *Click Clack Moo: Cows That Type* (Cronin, 2011), the story of Farmer Brown's cows who go on strike
>
> *The Frog Prince, Continued* (Scieszka, 1991), a story that tells what happened after the princess kissed the frog
>
> *Goldilocks Returns* (Ernst, 2003), the story of Goldilocks's second visit to the bears' home she vandalized 50 years earlier
>
> *A Million Fish . . . More or Less* (McKissack, 1996), a bayou tale of a fisher boy's adventures
>
> *Walter the Farting Dog* (Kotzwinkle, 2010), the story of a stinky dog that keeps his family's home safe

For this activity, Mr. Garibay asked each group to write a paragraph collaboratively to explain the irony in the book they read. He met with each group to review their rough drafts and suggest revisions, and then students prepared a final copy of their paragraphs.

The culminating activity focuses on "The Gift of the Magi," by O Henry, the classic Christmas story about a young couple, Della and Jim, who don't have enough money to buy gifts for each other. Della cuts off her long hair and sells it to buy a gold chain for her husband's valuable watch, but he sells his watch to buy expensive combs for Della's hair. The eighth graders read the short story in their literature anthologies. They read the first section together as a class and in a grand conversation discuss the question Who is Della, and how does she live? Afterward, they write entries in their reading logs that address the question. Then they read the remaining three sections and discuss these questions:

> Section 2: *How does Della get the money to buy Jim a gift?*
>
> Section 3: *What will Jim do when he sees Della's hair?*
>
> Section 4: *What gift does Jim buy for Della?*

They also respond to the questions in journal entries.

Once Mr. Garibay is sure that the students understand the story events, he leads a discussion about O Henry's use of symbolism and irony in the story. They recognize that the wife's hair and the husband's watch are symbols of love, and they decide that the story's theme is mutual sacrifice. The irony: Della and Jim can't use the gifts they received because they sold their possessions to purchase gifts for each other. Were they wise? O Henry says they were in the last paragraph. Does he mean it, or is he being sarcastic?

Next, Mr. Garibay explores the story's theme. To begin, he writes the title on the whiteboard and says, "I've been wondering about the title of this story. Who were the Magi?" Tyrell answers, "They were the wise men who brought gifts to the Baby Jesus." "They started the tradition of giving gifts at Christmas; that's what my mom told me," Shandra adds. "So, what do the Magi, or wise men, have to do with this story?" the teacher wonders aloud. No one has an idea, so he displays the last paragraph of the story on the whiteboard, reads it aloud, and follows up with this question: "O Henry says that like the wise men, Della and Jim were wise. Do you think they were wise in choosing the gifts they gave each other?" The students are split in their comments. "No," Dominic offers, "they had almost no money at all, and their gifts were extravagant. I think I read that Jim needed a new winter coat, and I think that's what Della should have given him." "You're just being practical," Reina responds. "This is a story of love and sacrifice so it doesn't have to be sensible. And, there wouldn't be any irony if she gave him a coat!"

For their final project, students worked in small groups to create digital posters or videos using a combination of images, text, and sound to highlight the symbolism, the irony, or the theme of "The Gift of the Magi." Jamar and Reina created a video about irony. It begins with the definition of irony, continues through a series of scenes, juxtaposing Della and her gift with Jim and his gift, and ends with their conclusion, "If this story didn't have irony, it wouldn't be a story because it wouldn't have a message." For the sound track, they chose "Ironic," by Alanis Morissette, which led to a brief lesson about the popular song. Mr. Garibay shared the lyrics with the students, pointing out that Morissette was more familiar with the term *irony* than with its definition: Of her 11 attempts at irony, only two or three fit the definition.

 tudents are bombarded with visual language—picture books, 3-D animation, TV and movies, maps, billboards and commercials, monuments, diagrams and tables, and more. Visual texts use images, symbols, and meaningful patterns to create meaning (Moline, 1995). Students use visual language to understand images and to communicate more effectively; this ability to navigate and compose visual texts is indispensable in today's information age. Visual language is easier for many students to understand than written language. Students must learn to process both words and pictures; that is, "to move gracefully and fluently between text and images, between literal and figurative worlds" (Burmark, 2002, p. 1).

Visual language is a powerful way of learning, and it supports oral and written language, as Mr. Garibay demonstrated in the vignette. Although it seems obvious that oral and written language are related, the visual language modes are also linked to listening, talking, reading, and writing because all six language arts are used for communication (McDonald & Fisher, 2006). Some kinds of information are expressed more effectively orally, in writing, or visually; for instance, teachers often use images and graphics to explain complex concepts such as irony more effectively than they could with oral and written language. In addition, students often learn more easily using one or another of the modes. The language barrier is significantly reduced for English learners when they use visual language. The saying that "a picture is worth a thousand words" highlights the communicative power of images. Students use the viewing mode to navigate visual texts and the visually representing mode to compose visual texts: As they navigate, students use their knowledge about visual language to comprehend, interpret, and respond to images, symbols, and graphics; and when they compose, students design and construct visual and dramatic productions.

VISUAL ELEMENTS

Images have visceral power to convey information and emotions simultaneously. Burmark (2002) explains that "the effect of an image is virtually instantaneous and viewers respond without conscious thought" (p. vii). Visual texts are windows on reality, created using colors, symbols, humor, and fonts, and constructed from a viewpoint with a purpose in mind. Teachers teach students how to recognize visual elements and interpret the visual language that bombards them.

Color

Color evokes meaning. Valentines are red because red represents love and passion; school buses are yellow because yellow's an attention-getting color; and ninjas, judges, and Batman wear black because it signals power. Colors often evoke more than one meaning. Green, for instance, typically stands for life, nature, vitality, renewal, energy, growth, freshness, cleanliness, ecology and fertility, and gardeners are said to have a "green thumb." However, green also evokes these meanings:

- Immaturity: Unripe fruit is "green."
- Inexperience: An inexperienced person is often said to be "green" or a "greenhorn."
- Emotions: Jealousy is known as the "green-eyed monster."
- Money: Green represents prosperity; sometimes dollar bills are referred to as "greenbacks."
- Illness: A sick person is often described as looking "green."
- Deterioration: Rotten food turns "green" because of bacteria and mold.
- Go: The color green on traffic lights signifies "go."
- Good fortune: Green, four-leaf clovers are said to be lucky.

Idioms and familiar sayings emphasize some of these meanings. For example, astronauts get the green light before a space mission, and people often lament that grass is always greener on the other side. Figure 7–1 lists 13 colors and some of their associations and meanings.

In every culture, colors have powerful significance, but they often evoke different meanings than they do in the United States. In Japan, green represents eternal life, and it's a sign of respect in Islam, but in China, green means disgrace. Also, in mainstream American culture, red signals danger, but in Japan and China, brides wear red. Black is the American funeral color, but in India and Asia, white signifies death.

Color plays an essential role in visual language; for instance, it draws attention, calms us, communicates happiness, relaxes us, and stirs up excitement. Students need to learn about these basic concepts to understand how color influences them and know how to use it in their visual representations:

PRIMARY COLORS. The primary colors are red, yellow, and blue. They're the building blocks of the color wheel.

SECONDARY COLORS. The secondary colors are green, orange, and purple. They're made by mixing two primary colors: Blue and yellow produce green, yellow and red make orange, and blue and red create purple.

TERTIARY COLORS. The tertiary colors are yellow-orange, red-orange, red-purple, blue-purple, blue-green, and yellow-green. They're made by mixing a primary and a secondary color.

FIGURE 7–1   Color Meanings

Color Family	Color	Meanings	Images
Warm	Red	danger, warning, courage, vitality, love, embarrassment, heat, violence	stop sign heart fire truck
	Pink	beauty, sweetheart, romance, love	cotton candy bubble gum little girls
	Yellow	cheerful, hopeful, happy, joyous, cowardly	sunshine hazard sign yellow ribbons
	Gold	extravagance, grandeur, prosperity, praise, wealth	castles jewelry Olympic medal
	Orange	energetic, stimulating, warm, vibrant	autumn leaves setting sun pumpkins
Cool	Blue	calming, peaceful, truthful, tranquil	ocean sky police uniform
	Green	environment, envy, fertility, health, inexperience, jealousy, life, nature, renewal	trees four-leaf clover recycling containers
	Purple	magical, mysterious, noble, royalty	magician kings the Purple Heart
	Silver	distinguished, glamorous, modern, ornate, rich, sleek	coins silverware sports car
Neutral	Brown	earthy, simple, wholesome	soil dead leaves wood
	Gray	moodiness, sorrow, maturity, formality	gray hair cloudy days a sad person
	Black	death, mourning, sophistication, power	tuxedo funeral procession martial arts belt
	White	innocence, cleanliness	brides nurses snowflakes

ANALOGOUS COLORS. Analogous colors are three side-by-side colors on the color wheel, such as yellow, yellow-orange, and orange.

COMPLEMENTARY COLORS. Complementary colors are those that are directly opposite on the color wheel; red and green and yellow and blue are examples. These colors provide the most contrast and stability.

WARM COLORS. The warm colors are red, orange, and yellow. They're active, exciting, and enthusiastic.

COOL COLORS. The cool colors are green, blue, and purple. They evoke a calm and peaceful feeling and sometimes an air of mystery.

And a few terms need to be defined: *Hue* is a more sophisticated name for "color," *value* refers to a color's lightness or darkness, and *intensity* describes a color's level of brightness.

Color is relative; the way a color looks depends on the colors around it. The pleasing arrangement of colors is known as *color harmony*. When colors are harmonious, they establish a sense of balance or order, but when they aren't harmonious, the result is either a bland or a chaotic picture. Viewers aren't engaged when the color's bland, and they can't stand to look at a picture when the colors are too chaotic.

Preschoolers begin their study of colors as they learn to identify the colors and common objects representing each one. First they learn that bananas are yellow, and then they notice that the fruit is green before it's ripe and brown when it's old. Their awareness of color continues to develop as they carefully copy the colors and other details of their clothes when they draw pictures of themselves. At the same time, they begin to associate colors with meanings; for instance, red lights on traffic lights and red stop signs both mean stop.

Young children experiment with mixing primary colors to make secondary and tertiary colors, and they create tints by adding white to a color and shades by adding black. Teachers often introduce color mixing when they read *Green Eggs and Ham* (Dr. Seuss, 1960a) in kindergarten, and in third grade share *Amber Brown Is Not a Crayon* (Danziger, 2006) and other books in Paula Danziger's series that cleverly incorporate color words.

Students' color vocabularies mushroom through wide reading and a variety of language arts activities. They learn labels for a range of colors. For example, consider these brown tints and shades: tan, copper, chocolate, bronze, mahogany, camel, tawny, auburn, chestnut, burnt umber, rust, sandy, ecru, and fawn. At the same time students are increasing their color vocabularies, they're associating multiple meanings with each color. Idioms and other familiar sayings have contributed these meanings:

red tape (bureaucratic delay)
white elephant (useless possession)
roll out the red carpet (a big welcome)
in the black (successful)
out of the blue (unexpectedly)
tickled pink (delighted)
caught red-handed (during a crime)
white lie (harmless lie)
yellow-bellied (cowardly)

Students apply this knowledge when they examine art or compare the impact of black-and-white versus color photos, and as they choose colors to grab attention and send messages in the projects they create.

Line

Lines define objects, communicate ideas, and express feelings. They have both direction and weight and combine to create textures and patterns. Lines move in different directions—they're horizontal, vertical, diagonal, curved, and straight. Each line type expresses qualities and communicates emotions:

- Straight lines appear rigid or predictable.
- Curved lines create graceful bends that change direction; shallow lines are safe or comforting, but deep curves are dynamic or turbulent.
- Horizontal lines are quiet, calm, and peaceful.
- Vertical lines seem to reach up into the sky and suggest grandeur and spirituality.
- Diagonal lines suggest vitality and movement.
- Zigzag lines are a series of connected diagonal lines; they're dramatic and energetic.

Viewers are sensitive to line quality. Thick lines suggest stability or dominance, but thin lines suggest delicateness or elegance. Line quality contributes to the mood of a picture, particularly in drawings, photos, and paintings.

Various line arrangements provide unique types of information: Fonts add style to text messages, maps provide information about locations, and graphs present data visually so that they're easier to interpret. These are three types of lines that preK–8 students learn to use.

Fonts. Fonts give visual form to language, and viewers recognize visual representations of words, even in unfamiliar writing systems. These fonts conjure a variety of images, including soldiers' names on footlockers, pirates, teachers writing on chalkboards, college banners, and typewriters:

American Typewriter
CHALKDUSTER
Edwardian Script
HERCULANUM
Lucida Blackletter

Lucida Handwriting
Mistral
Princetown LET
STENCIL

The lines in some fonts are straight but in others, they're curved; some lines are thick and others are thin. Some fonts are serious; others are playful.

Maps. Maps use lines to present symbolic representations of places, and they help viewers understand how the places are related to each other. Road maps, weather maps, bus maps, airplane route maps, climate maps, and topographic maps show different types of information. Other maps are floor plans, describing the layout of a building—airports and shopping malls, for instance. Most maps include these three features:

COMPASS ROSE. The compass rose indicates north, south, east, and west directions on a map.

SCALE. The scale looks like a ruler and shows the ratio of the distance on the map to the corresponding distance on the ground.

KEY. A key explains the meaning of the symbols used in the map; it's usually set off in a box and placed in a corner of the map.

Students examine a variety of maps and identify the purpose of each type, and they learn to draw maps of locations in books they're reading and as part of thematic units.

Graphs. Graphs use lines to communicate information visually. Magazines, newspapers, and nonfiction books often present complex information in graphs, so it's essential that students learn to read and interpret the visual representations. Students learn to use these four types of graphs:

PICTURE GRAPHS. Picture graphs are the easiest type of graphs to read and interpret: They convey information using pictures as symbols to represent quantities. A key is needed to indicate the quantity represented by each symbol. For example, in a fifth grade picture graph showing how many novels each student has read, each book symbol might represent one book or five books; that's why the key is so important. First graders can interpret a picture graph showing the number of ducks, gulls, swans, and egrets at a wildlife refuge center.

LINE GRAPHS. Line graphs compare two variables that are plotted along the x and y axes. These graphs track changes over time, and they can be used for more than one group. For example, fifth graders can track high and low temperatures in their community from week to week.

BAR GRAPHS. Bar graphs compare groups or track changes over time, much like line graphs do. They're similar to line graphs because they're created using the x and y axes, but these graphs use horizontal or vertical bars that make comparisons easy to see. For example, third graders can graph the class's favorite movie or cupcake flavors.

PIE CHARTS. Pie charts are shaped like circles, and they're divided into fractional parts that look like slices of pie. These graphs are used to compare the parts of a whole, with the results presented as percentages. In contrast to line and bar graphs, pie charts don't show changes over time. For example, middle school students might be asked to interpret a pie chart showing the market shares of five national fast food restaurant chains.

Students learn how to choose the most appropriate type of graph, how to read and interpret the data, and how to construct graphs to present data visually.

Symbols

Students are surrounded by *symbols*; that is, objects used to stand for something else. Some symbols, such as the American flag and the Statue of Liberty, are patriotic; some, such as Nike's swoosh, are displayed on clothes students wear; and some—the Christian cross and the Jewish Star of David, for example—are religious. Other symbols, usually referred to as icons, are displayed on food packages, and others are found on stores and restaurants; the Keebler elves, the red-headed, smiling girl on the Wendy's restaurant sign, KFC's Colonel Sanders, and the Green Giant are immediately recognizable. Other logos are more abstract; details have been removed so that only the essential and most typical features remain. McDonald's golden arches, the International Red Cross's emblem, the Jolly Roger pirate flag, and the Zodiac signs are familiar examples. They're abstract images to which society has attached a shared meaning, and viewers must recognize the symbols to understand them. For example, if students don't recognize the Democratic Party's donkey symbol, they're unlikely to understand political cartoons, and they won't be able to interpret political charts and maps. Symbols are classified as pictograms, ideograms, and logograms:

PICTOGRAMS. *Pictograms* are simplified, self-explanatory pictorial representations used to present information and to guide people. Prehistoric cave paintings were pictograms, and contemporary pictograms include men's and women's restroom signs, handicapped parking signs, and map symbols, such as picnic tables, bicycles, and skiers.

IDEOGRAMS. *Ideograms* are graphic symbols that represent an idea or concept. Egyptian hieroglyphics were early ideograms. For example, the stylized image of a snake meant "snake" and the image of waves meant "water" or "liquid." Chinese characters, zodiac symbols, and musical notes are ideograms, as are Arabic numerals (e.g., *4, 5, 6*), religious symbols, and mathematical notation, including + (*plus*), ÷ (*divide*), ≠ (*unequal*), > (*more than*), ≈ (*appropriately the same*), and π (*pi*).

LOGOGRAMS. *Logograms* are visual symbols that represent words, including punctuation marks, ampersand (&), and these other symbols found on keyboards: % (*percent*), @ (*at*), # (*pound* or *number*), © (*copyright*), and $ (*dollar*). These symbols aren't related to the pronunciation of the words they represent, and they're arbitrary because they don't resemble what they stand for. Interestingly, most logograms began as abbreviations.

It isn't necessary to classify symbols according to these three categories; rather, this classification system emphasizes that symbols range from pictorial representations to abstract images.

Students are familiar with a variety of age-appropriate symbols—ranging from the ubiquitous yellow smiley face, Superman's *S* shield, and the handicapped access sign to Under Armour's linked *U*s logo, the U.S. Postal Service's speeding eagle logo, the peace sign, and the Olympic Games' five interlocking rings—but they may not understand their significance. As students examine symbols, teachers have them identify the images, describe what they represent, and explain why the images are memorable. Teachers often choose images from these categories:

ANIMAL SYMBOLS. Many animals symbolize human qualities; for example: dogs (loyalty), doves (peace), elephants (memory), foxes (cleverness), lions (nobility), owls (wisdom), sharks (remorselessness), squirrels (preparedness), tigers (power), and zebras (individuality).

CORPORATE LOGOS. McDonald's golden arches, Target's red-and-white concentric circles icon, Pepsi's red, white, and blue waves set in a circle, and Apple's bitten apple icon are familiar emblems of corporate identity. In addition, the triangular recycling symbol with three chasing arrows has become instantly recognizable over the past 25 years.

EMERGENCY SYMBOLS. A skull and crossbones on a label indicates poison, and other signs warn people about biohazards and radiation dangers. Street signs with an *H* provide directions to the nearest hospital, and signs with a hook and ladder fire truck indicate the location of fire stations.

ENTERTAINMENT LOGOS. Television networks are recognized by their logos; ABC's logo of the world with the letters *ABC* superimposed, CBS's black-and-white eye logo, NBC's multicolor peacock logo, and PBS's heads logo are familiar to everyone. Movie studios and television production companies also have recognizable logos; one example is Disney's mouse ears icon.

MONUMENTS. The Washington and Lincoln Memorials, the Statue of Liberty, the Gateway Arch, the Alamo, the Vietnam Veterans Memorial, and other monuments in Washington, DC and across the United States symbolize patriotism, courage, and other American values. World monuments, including the Eiffel Tower in Paris, the Great Wall of China, and the Great Pyramid of Giza, stand as symbols of ancient civilizations and modern technological achievements.

PEACE SYMBOLS. The olive branch and the white dove are traditional symbols of peace. The *V* hand sign that Winston Churchill waved during World War II represented victory, but now it's used to signify peace. The broken upside-down cross that's associated with the Hippie movement of the 1960s is used today as a peace symbol, but 50 years ago it was used to protest nuclear weapons.

POLITICAL SYMBOLS. American political symbols include Uncle Sam, the Democratic Party donkey, and the Republican Party elephant. Other familiar political symbols include the hammer and sickle, which represents Communism, and the Nazi swastika.

SPORTS LOGOS. The Dallas Cowboys, Minnesota Vikings, Cleveland Indians, Boston Bruins, and other professional sports franchises have identifiable logos that fans wear on shirts, hats, and other clothing to show their support, but it's not just professional teams that have familiar logos; Little League, high school, and college teams also have identifying logos: USC Trojans, University of Georgia Bulldogs, and Penn State Nittany Lions, for instance.

Young children notice different symbols than older students do, but because they're surrounded by images, all students are familiar with some of these symbols.

Teachers introduce students to visual symbols by having them find examples at home, in their communities, and in the media. They collect items with logos and draw pictures of other symbols. Figure 7–2 presents a symbols chart created by two seventh graders; the chart shows the range of symbols that middle school students understand.

Once students understand symbols, they're prepared to look for them in the books they're reading and critique the use of symbols in the media. They can also create their own symbols. A fifth grader created a personal symbol and explains it this way:

> *God holds me in His hands and I am blessed. I put that symbol in the middle because it's my center. On the top I have a heart. It means that I love my family. To the right is my Nintendo DS because I love to play video games. To the left is an apple. It represents health and I'm a healthy kid. On the bottom is a baseball because it's my favorite sport, and I'm a good player.*

Emoticons. *Emoticons* are sequences of punctuation marks and letters that create facial expressions. For example, : D is the emoticon for a big grin: A colon represents the eyes, and the capital

FIGURE 7–2   Two Seventh Graders' Symbols Chart

D is the smiling mouth. The word *emoticon* is a portmanteau, made by combining *emotion* and *icon*. Both children and adults use hundreds of emoticons to express excitement, sadness, and encouragement in email, instant messages, and other digital communication. These emoticons are among the most frequently used:

angry	:-@	sick	:-&
confused	:-/	surprise	:-o
crying	:'(	thinking	:-?
hurry up	:!!	thumbs up	:-bd
laughing	:))	winking	;)

These emotional graphics improve readers' interpretation of online texts because they add nuances to messages, just as facial expressions do during face-to-face conversations.

Humor

Humor—whimsy, irony, parody, satire, and comic nonsense, for example—typically involves the unexpected pairing of dissimilar words and the surprise juxtaposition of images (Burmark, 2002). Students notice visual humor in cartoons, comics, picture books, graphic novels, photographs, and advertisements: Young children laugh at the whimsical drawings and wordplay in Dr. Seuss books, second graders notice exaggerations about Batman and other superheroes, third graders recognize parody in *The True Story of the 3 Little Pigs!* (Scieszka, 1999), fifth graders draw pictures of mile-high ice cream sundaes and other exaggerations, and eighth graders identify irony in photographs. Teachers draw students' attention to examples of visual humor and ask them to analyze what makes the images funny.

Hyperbole is an exaggeration or overstatement, often used in a humorous way to make a point. Tall tales about larger-than-life heroes, including the giant lumberjack Paul Bunyan and the southwestern cowboy Pecos Bill, use hyperbole for heightened effect. Teachers share these tall tales with students: *A Million Fish . . . More or Less* (McKissack, 1996), about a fisher boy who tells an outlandish tale about his adventure on the bayou; *Tall Tales* (Sniegoski, 2010), the prequel to the Bone graphic-novel series featuring a Davy Crockett–like character; and Steven Kellogg's impressive series of picture-book tall tales, including *Johnny Appleseed* (1988), *Pecos Bill* (1992), *Paul Bunyan* (1985), *Sally Ann Crockett* (1995), and *Mike Fink* (1998). In addition to reading and discussing tall tales, students participate in these visual language activities:

- View video versions of tall tales on DVDs and online
- Examine story boards of a tall tale made by cutting apart the pages of a picture book, backing the pages with cardboard, and laminating them
- Visit websites to learn more about a tall tale hero
- Create a Venn diagram to compare two tall tale heroes
- Retell a tall tale as a comic strip or using another graphic format
- Dramatize a tall tale

These activities help deepen students' understanding of narrative devices.

Political Cartoons. Cartoonists comment on current events through cartoon images, and they try to influence viewers to agree with their viewpoint. Political cartoons feature a drawing, and sometimes the people or objects in the cartoon are labeled to make it easier for viewers to understand the message. Most cartoons also have a caption placed at the top or at the bottom of the drawing to hint at the message. Cartoonists tackle a wide variety of topics, including bullying, natural disasters, politics, airport security, drugs, oil spills, NASA, and immigration.

Ben Franklin is credited with publishing the first political cartoon in *The Pennsylvania Gazette* on May 9, 1754; his woodcut cartoon urged the colonists to unite against British rule. It showed a snake cut into eight pieces, each representing a colony or region in colonial America. Under the picture was the caption "Join, or Die." The picture was based on the superstition that if a snake with a severed head was rejoined before sunset, it would come back to life.

Cartoonists use three tools—caricature, symbols, and analogies—to communicate their messages:

> **CARICATURE.** A *caricature* is a portrait that exaggerates or distorts a person's appearance to make him or her easier to identify. Cartoonists draw caricatures of politicians and other personalities by exaggerating their unflattering physical characteristics, such as big teeth, a large forehead, frizzy hair, or glasses. For instance, Jay Leno is typically drawn with a big chin, and Barack Obama with protruding ears.
>
> **SYMBOLS.** A *symbol* is an object that represents something else. For example, cartoonists use a dove to stand for peace, a skull and crossbones as a poison warning, and an elephant to represent the Republican Party.
>
> **ANALOGIES.** An *analogy* is a comparison between two things to highlight a point of similarity. Cartoonists compare the familiar with the unfamiliar to emphasize their message; in Ben Franklin's cartoon, for instance, the American colonies are compared to a severed snake. When viewers recognize the analogy, it clarifies the cartoon's message; however, recognizing these comparisons is the most difficult part of interpreting political cartoons.

Students need to recognize and understand the caricatures, symbols, and analogies; otherwise, they won't understand the cartoonist's meaning.

Imagine a cartoon showing Little Red Riding Hood innocently walking through the woods on her way to Grandmother's house with a menacing wolf following her. Suppose the wolf was labeled "drug dealers" and the little girl was "middle school students." If viewers recognize the comparison to the familiar folktale and understand the dangers of illegal drugs, they'll grasp the message that drug dealers are targeting young people and, perhaps, draw the conclusion the community needs to take action to protect tweens from this menace. If the labels were changed, this cartoon would send a different message; for example, what if the wolf's label changed to "big oil" and Little Red Riding Hood became "America's coastlines"?

Teachers often introduce political cartoons as part of American history or U.S. government units. They begin by showing examples of political cartoons and comparing them with other graphica, such as newspaper comics, comic books, and graphic novels. Next, they teach students to recognize caricature, symbols, and analogies and to interpret political cartoons using the procedure described in the Step-by-Step feature on page 190. They also share several cartoons on the topic, but representing different viewpoints, for students to compare. Finally, students create their own cartoons, expressing their opinions about current events and school- and community-based issues. Teachers can find appropriate political cartoons in *Time for Kids* and online at Daryl Cagle's Political Cartoonists Index (http://www.cagle.com) and Creators: A Syndicate of Talent (http://www.creators.com/editorialcartoons.html). It's important to teach students to interpret political cartoons because standardized tests often ask older students to interpret primary source documents, including political cartoons.

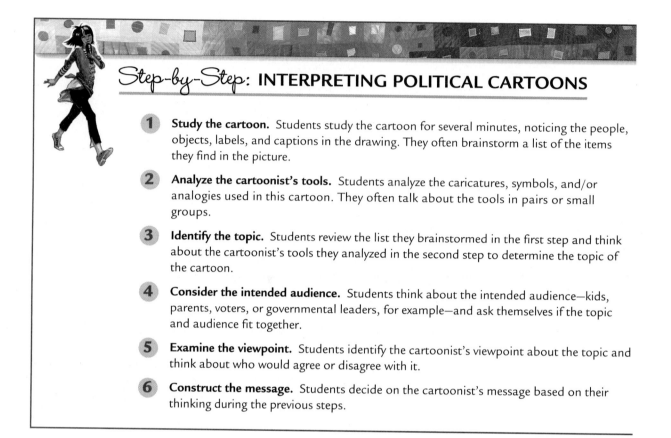

Step-by-Step: INTERPRETING POLITICAL CARTOONS

1 **Study the cartoon.** Students study the cartoon for several minutes, noticing the people, objects, labels, and captions in the drawing. They often brainstorm a list of the items they find in the picture.

2 **Analyze the cartoonist's tools.** Students analyze the caricatures, symbols, and/or analogies used in this cartoon. They often talk about the tools in pairs or small groups.

3 **Identify the topic.** Students review the list they brainstormed in the first step and think about the cartoonist's tools they analyzed in the second step to determine the topic of the cartoon.

4 **Consider the intended audience.** Students think about the intended audience—kids, parents, voters, or governmental leaders, for example—and ask themselves if the topic and audience fit together.

5 **Examine the viewpoint.** Students identify the cartoonist's viewpoint about the topic and think about who would agree or disagree with it.

6 **Construct the message.** Students decide on the cartoonist's message based on their thinking during the previous steps.

COMMON CORE STATE STANDARDS

Visual Language

The Common Core State Standards emphasize visual language. Students use visual language to comprehend stories, to gather information from nonprint sources, and to convey complex information visually. The standards highlight these points:

- Students use information from illustrations to comprehend literature.
- Students create visual displays about narrative texts.
- Students interpret information presented in charts, diagrams, and webpages.
- Students use visual displays of data to convey information.

To learn more about the visual language standards, go to http://www.corestandards.org, or check your state's language arts standards.

Teaching Visual Language

Visual language has become an important part of the language arts, and the Common Core State Standards expect students to use pictures and photos to comprehend stories, interpret information in maps, graphs, and diagrams, and communicate complex information visually. Check this Common Core State Standards box for more information about the visual language standards.

Teachers introduce the elements of visual language during minilessons and make connections to books students are reading and during thematic units. They teach about color, line, symbols, and humor so students can deepen their understanding of the books they're reading and the films they're viewing. Students also apply the elements they've studied in multimedia projects they develop as part of literature focus units and thematic units. Teaching the elements of visual language fits into the patterns of practice, as shown in the Patterns of Practice box on the next page.

How Visual Language Fits Into the Patterns of Practice

Literature Focus Units

During units on picture books, teachers teach about visual language and encourage students to experiment with the medium used in the book. Students compare book and film versions and use diagrams to examine story structure.

Literature Circles

When students read graphic novels and other books with visual features, teachers provide instruction about visual language. And students use visually representing when they draw diagrams and share them with members of their group.

Reading and Writing Workshop

Teachers teach minilessons about visual language and have students apply what they're learning as they read picture books, graphic novels, and nonfiction books. Students also use the elements of visual language when creating their own books.

Thematic Units

Students learn about the visual features of nonfiction texts and how to interpret images, diagrams, time lines, and maps. They also use graphics in the projects they create at the end of the unit to share their learning.

INTEGRATING TECHNOLOGY

The 21st century ushered in a technological revolution that has resulted in the development of new digital tools and visual language applications, many of them appropriate for preK–8 students. Three of the best are virtual field trips, art resources, and learning games:

VIRTUAL FIELD TRIPS. Students take virtual field trips to the CIA, National Weather Service, colonial Williamsburg, a coal mine, a veterinary clinic, an ancient Roman villa, the White House, a watershed, the solar system, and other locations online. Kentucky Educational Television (http://www.ket.org/trips) and the Utah Education Network (UEN) (http://www.uen.org/tours) are two extensive website galleries; at the UEN website, teachers can create and post their own virtual field trips. They can locate many other websites featuring virtual field trips using Google or another search engine.

ONLINE ART RESOURCES. Students learn about art, view demonstrations, and participate in interactive art activities at these websites:

- Art Babble (http://www.artbabble.org) is a video site dedicated to all kinds of art and contemporary artists. Students learn about African, ancient Roman, or Asian art, for instance, or view video clips on dance, textiles, robots, animation, ceramics, glass, and other media.

- The @rt Room (http://www.artjunction.org) is a collaborative art space for students and teachers with information about art and artists, activities, and a gallery of students' drawings.

Students can also view art masterpieces at the Metropolitan Museum of Art, National Gallery of Art, Guggenheim Museum, Museum of Modern Art, and other museum websites.

DIGITAL LEARNING GAMES. Eduweb (http://www.eduweb.com) is an award-winning educational website that presents an amazing collection of learning games with visual language components. The website includes interactive games on art, social studies, and science topics:

- A crime detection adventure, where students create composite portraits to help identify the culprits of a crime

- An architect studio experience, where students explore architecture with Frank Lloyd Wright as their guide
- An inside art game, where students imagine they're trapped inside a painting and have to solve a mystery to escape
- A study of George Washington, where students visit a 3-D Mount Vernon to collect artifacts to describe the "real" man
- A movie time exploration, where students make an animated film about life on a coral reef
- A pop studio experience, where students go behind the scenes of a television show to learn about media literacy
- An art adventure, where students step into the shoes of a detective named A. Pintura to try to solve a case

These innovative learning games were devised in collaboration with art and history museums.

There's a wide variety of outstanding websites that incorporate viewing and visually representing components. Check The Digital Classroom feature on page 204 to read about additional websites. ■

VIEWING

Viewing is more than looking at images, because visual language is complex and multilayered (Moline, 1995). Students use a process that's similar to reading: They activate their background knowledge and apply what they've learned about color, symbols, and other elements of visual language. They view images—art masterpieces, picture books, graphics in nonfiction books, films, and advertisements—and analyze them to comprehend their meaning and make judgments. The viewing procedure is described in the Step-by-Step feature on the next page, and it emphasizes that viewing involves more than simply looking at an image. Of course, teachers tweak the steps when viewing different types of images because viewing an art masterpiece requires a different emphasis than viewing a film, a political cartoon, or an advertisement.

Art Appreciation

Art appreciation is a broad topic, ranging from Stone Age cave paintings in Lascaux, France, Egyptian hieroglyphic cartouches, and Roman mosaics to Van Gogh's vibrant paintings, Rodin's sculptures, Matisse's paper cutouts, Calder's mobiles, and Dorothea Lange's photographs of life during the Great Depression. Students learn about color, line, and shape; examine masterpieces; study specific artists and art media; and visit art galleries. Art appreciation has been neglected in schools for several decades, but with the current emphasis on visual language, it's being revitalized.

Teachers approach art appreciation in different ways: Some hang reproductions of art masterpieces in their classrooms or read about the lives of artists during a biography unit, and others integrate works of art into literature focus units or coordinate art appreciation with thematic units. They often use mentor texts, such as those in the Booklist on page 194, to share information about artists and works of art.

Students deepen their understanding of visual language when they examine works of art; they sharpen their powers of observation and learn to interpret visual images. Art appreciation has other benefits, too: Not surprisingly, involvement in arts activities is associated with higher reading achievement and cognitive development.

Masterpieces to Examine. There's no consensus on what makes a work of art a masterpiece, or which works of art are most important to introduce to students; however, teachers often choose works that tell a story and evoke a feeling, such as curiosity or awe. Students interpret art masterpieces much like they do other types of texts. Teachers provide background knowledge about the artist and the subject of the masterpiece; then students apply their knowledge of visual language to examine the work of art, and teachers ask questions to guide their interpretation. These masterpieces are recommended:

Pilgrims Going to Church, by George Henry Boughton
The Boating Party, by Mary Cassatt
Mona Lisa, by Leonardo da Vinci
Dance Class, by Edgar Degas
Beautiful World, by Grandma Moses
Sailing the Catboat, by Winslow Homer
Nighthawks, by Edward Hopper
Washington Crossing the Delaware, by Emanuel Leutze
The Rooster, by Joan Miró
Water Lilies, by Claude Monet
The Smoke Signal, by Frederick Remington
A Girl With a Watering Can, by Pierre Auguste Renoir
The Flower Carrier, by Diego Rivera
The Golden Rule, by Norman Rockwell
George Washington, by Gilbert Stuart
Portrait of a Man in a Red Cap, by Titian
Starry Night, by Vincent Van Gogh
Big Campbell's Soup Can, 19¢, by Andy Warhol

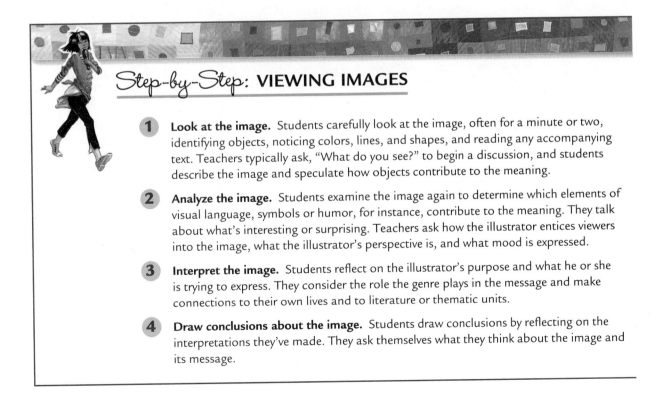

Step-by-Step: VIEWING IMAGES

1 **Look at the image.** Students carefully look at the image, often for a minute or two, identifying objects, noticing colors, lines, and shapes, and reading any accompanying text. Teachers typically ask, "What do you see?" to begin a discussion, and students describe the image and speculate how objects contribute to the meaning.

2 **Analyze the image.** Students examine the image again to determine which elements of visual language, symbols or humor, for instance, contribute to the meaning. They talk about what's interesting or surprising. Teachers ask how the illustrator entices viewers into the image, what the illustrator's perspective is, and what mood is expressed.

3 **Interpret the image.** Students reflect on the illustrator's purpose and what he or she is trying to express. They consider the role the genre plays in the message and make connections to their own lives and to literature or thematic units.

4 **Draw conclusions about the image.** Students draw conclusions by reflecting on the interpretations they've made. They ask themselves what they think about the image and its message.

Booklist

ART AND ARTISTS	
Artists	Anholt, L. (2007). *The magical garden of Claude Monet.* New York: Barron's. P–M Balliett, B. (2005). *Chasing Vermeer.* New York: Scholastic. U Balliett, B. (2007). *Wright 3.* New York: Scholastic. U Balliett, B. (2008). *The Calder game.* New York: Scholastic. U Cocca-Leffler, M. (2001). *Edgar Degas: Paintings that dance* (Smart About Art series). New York: Grosset & Dunlap. P–M Gherman, B. (2002). *Ansel Adams: America's photographer.* Boston: Little, Brown. U Greenberg, J., & Jordan, S. (2007). *Action Jackson.* New York: Square Fish Books. P–M Hill, L. C. (2010). *Dave the potter: Artist, poet, slave.* Boston: Little, Brown. P–M Holub, J. (2001). *Vincent Van Gogh: Sunflowers and swirly stars.* New York: Grosset & Dunlap. P–M O'Connor, J. (2002). *Henri Matisse: Drawing with scissors.* New York: Grosset & Dunlap. P–M O'Connor, J. (2003). *Mary Cassatt: Family pictures.* New York: Grosset & Dunlap. P–M Partridge, E. (2001). *Restless spirit: The life and work of Dorothea Lange.* New York: Puffin Books. U Rodriquez, R. V. (2006). *Through Georgia's eyes.* New York: Henry Holt. P–M Venezia, M. (1988). *Picasso.* Chicago: Children's Press. M–U Warhola, J. (2005). *Uncle Andy's: A faabbbulous visit with Andy Warhol.* New York: Puffin Books. M
Multiple Artists	Finger, B. (2010). *13 American artists children should know.* New York: Prestel. P–M Wenzel, A. (2009). *13 artists children should know.* New York: Prestel. P–M
Books With Works of Art	Burgan, M. (2011). *Raising the flag: How a photograph gave a nation hope in wartime.* Minneapolis: Compass Point Books. M–U DK Publishing. (2009). *Children's book of art.* New York: Dorling Kindersley. M–U Sayre, H. M. (2004). *Cave paintings to Picasso: The inside story on 50 art masterpieces.* San Francisco: Chronicle Books. M–U Weitzman, J. P. (1998). *You can't take a balloon into the Metropolitan Museum.* New York: Puffin Books. P–M Wenzel, A. (2009). *13 paintings children should know.* New York: Prestel. M Wenzel, A. (2010). *13 sculptures children should know.* New York: Prestel. M
Teaching Art Appreciation	Barbe-Gall, F. (2005). *How to talk to children about art.* Chicago: Chicago Review Press. P–M–U Kohl, M. F., & Solga, K. (1997). *Discovering great artists: Hands-on art for children in the styles of great masters.* Bellingham, WA: Bright Ring. P–M–U Kohl, M. F., & Solga, K. (2008). *Great American artists for kids: Hands-on art experiences in the styles of great American masters.* Bellingham, WA: Bright Ring. P–M–U

P = primary grades (preK–2); M = middle grades (3–5); U = upper grades (6–8)

American Gothic, by Grant Wood
The Giant, by N. C. Wyeth

In these paintings, artists wrestle with ideas, tell stories, evoke emotional responses, and record moments in time.

Although paintings receive the most attention, other art forms are important. Students examine sculpture in neighborhood parks, and they learn about notable sculptures, including the ancient Greek sculpture Winged Victory, Rodin's *The Thinker*, the Statue of Liberty, Calder's mobiles, and Saint Phalle's mosaic sculptures—*Ricardo Cat*, for example. In addition, African masks, wood carvings, pottery, quilts, cartoons, and 3-D animations are other artistic forms that interest preK–8 students.

Artistic styles are movements representing a philosophy followed by a group of artists during a specific time period. A style is a combination of medium, technique, and subject; it affects the appearance of art because artists change the way they apply color and use perspective. For example, Impressionism was a 19th-century art movement that originated with Claude Monet and other Paris-based artists who developed a fresh, new way of seeing, emphasizing color over lines and details. Figure 7–3 lists the artistic styles since 1700.

FIGURE 7–3   Artistic Styles

Style	Description	Artists
Realism	Artists painted accurate and objective representations of ordinary people involved in everyday activities.	John Singleton Copley Edgar Degas Winslow Homer
Impressionism	Artists captured the image of an object as if they just caught a glance of it and without attention to details. Most are outdoor scenes. Artists used bright, vibrant colors and often created a shimmering effect to their paintings.	Mary Cassatt Claude Monet Pierre Auguste Renoir
Postimpressionism	Artists pushed the Impressionists' ideas in new directions by using intense colors, outlines of shapes, and sharp edges in their paintings. Seurat depicted scenes using dots of color that blended together to form pictures when viewed from a distance.	Paul Cézanne Paul Gauguin Georges Seurat Vincent Van Gogh
Primitivism	Artists incorporated visual forms from non-Western and ancient peoples into their paintings. Gauguin, for example, incorporated Tahitian motifs in his work.	Paul Klee Henri Matisse Paul Gauguin
Expressionism	Artists used vivid colors and exaggerated lines to express their intense feelings through art. They often distorted or altered reality. Their paintings have been described as vivid, jarring, or dynamic.	Marc Chagall Edvard Munch Pablo Picasso
Cubism	At the beginning of the 20th century, artists used geometric, 3-D shapes to represent objects and scenes from different perspectives. Cubism was an avant-garde movement that ushered in abstract art.	Marc Chagall Salvador Dali Paul Klee Pablo Picasso
Surrealism	Artists depicted familiar objects so that they appeared strange and mysterious. Their paintings were dreamlike and contained unexpected juxtapositions. These artists wanted to stir up feelings in viewers' minds.	Salvador Dali Max Ernst Henri Rousseau
Abstract Art	Artists created nonrepresentational paintings emphasizing color and shape. They wanted to reflect the technological and scientific changes taking place in the world.	Piet Mondrian Jackson Pollock Mark Rothko
Pop Art	From 1955 to 1975, artists painted recognizable images—often consumer products and celebrities—drawn from popular culture using brash lines and bright colors. Pop art was inspired by comic strip art and newspaper photos.	Roy Lichtenstein Andy Warhol

Looking at Art. Students look at individual works of art, compare two masterpieces, or study one artist. They use the viewing procedure to study works of art and expand their vocabularies as they talk and write about the art. Sixth graders worked in small groups to study particular artists during a biography unit. One group choose Vincent Van Gogh, and they compared two of his paintings:

Vincent Van Gogh's "The Starry Night" is his best known painting. It is a picture of a French village at night. The sky filled with swirling clouds, exploding stars, and a very bright moon. Your eye goes to the top half of the painting because Van Gogh used color boldly. The village scene in the bottom half is peaceful if you compare it with the sky's exploding energy.

In contrast, Van Gogh's "The Potato Eaters" is a dark painting. The painting shows five people sitting around a table eating potatoes. You quickly notice the center of the painting where light from an oil lamp shines on the people's faces. They show different emotions like real people do. This painting emphasizes the difficult life of peasant farmers. We are drawn in, feeling like we are eavesdropping on their conversation.

Vincent Van Gogh was a post-impressionist painter. His paintings are emotionally charged. He painted with intense colors, and he used short brush strokes. Van Gogh rejected traditional ideas about art; he painted peasants instead of wealthy people.

The sixth graders also drew or painted pictures using bright colors, distorted shapes, and other Postimpressionistic techniques.

Visual Language in Books

In many books, illustrations and other visual texts provide different types of information to elaborate and extend the written text's message. Six types of books with visual texts are picture books, wordless picture books, graphic novels, novels, nonfiction books, and multigenre books; see the Booklist on the next page for mentor texts representing these types of books. Teachers share some of these books with students and show them how to apply what they've learned about the elements of visual language to comprehend visual texts.

Picture Books. Picture books are a unique genre in children's literature. These books combine visual and written narratives in book format; they're visual storytelling because illustrations are as much a part of the narrative as the text (Cianciolo, 1997). The art extends the story by adding visual information that's not presented in the text. The American Library Association annually presents the Caldecott Medal for the most distinguished illustrations in a children's book published that year. Winners of this prestigious award include *Smoky Night* (Bunting, 1999), *Owl Moon* (Yolen, 1988), *Black and White* (Macaulay, 2005), *The Polar Express* (Van Allsburg, 2005), *Kitten's First Full Moon* (Henkes, 2005), *Hey, Al* (Yorinks, 1989), and *Officer Buckle and Gloria* (Rathmann, 1995).

Some picture books such as *Kitten's First Full Moon*, the story of a kitten who thinks the moon is a bowl of milk, are intended for preschoolers and kindergartners, and some are appropriate for primary grade students, such as *Hey, Al*, the story of a man who leaves his day-to-day life to find paradise only to appreciate the life he left behind. Others, however, have more sophisticated story lines and themes that appeal to older students, such as *Black and White*. Barbara Kiefer (1994) talked with students about the illustrations in picture books; she learned that first graders could talk about artistic elements, including line, shape, texture, and color, and that older students could reflect on the expressive qualities of illustrations.

Booklist

BOOKS WITH VISUAL LANGUAGE

Graphic Novels	Cammuso, F. (2008). *The dodgeball chronicles.* New York: Graphix. M Denton, S. E., & Warner, G. C. (2009). *The boxcar children: A graphic novel.* New York: Whitman. (P–M) Holm, J. L., & Holm, M. (2005). *Babymouse: Queen of the world.* New York: Random House. M Krosoczka, J. (2009). *Lunch Lady and the cyborg substitute.* New York: Knopf. M Siegel, S. C. (2006). *To dance: A ballerina's graphic novel.* New York: Atheneum. M–U Smith, J. (2005). *Bone: Out of Boneville.* New York: Scholastic. M
Nonfiction Books	Bryant, J. (2008). *A river of words: The story of William Carlos Williams.* Grand Rapids, MI: Eerdmans Books. M–U Greenaway, T. (2005). *Jungle.* New York: Dorling Kindersley. M–U Jenkins, S. (2009). *Down, down, down: A journey to the bottom of the sea.* Boston: Houghton Mifflin. P–M Macaulay, D. (1998). *The new ways things work.* Boston: Houghton Mifflin. M–U Ross, S. (2005). *Egypt: In spectacular cross-section.* New York: Scholastic. M–U
Novels With Illustrations	Kinney, J. (2007). *Diary of a wimpy kid.* New York: Amulet Books. M Selznick, B. (2007). *The invention of Hugo Cabret.* Scholastic. M–U Stilton, G. (2004). *Lost treasure of the emerald eye.* New York: Scholastic. M Vernon, U. (2009). *Dragonbreath.* New York: Dial Books. M
Photo Essays	Halls, K. M. (2010). *Saving the Baghdad Zoo: A true story of hope and heroes.* New York: Greenwillow. M–U Knight, B. J. (1997). *From cow to ice cream.* Chicago: Children's Press. P–M Mitchell, D. (2010). *Driven: A photobiography of Henry Ford.* Washington, DC: National Geographic. M–U Robbins, K. (2010). *For good measure: The ways we say how much, how far, how heavy, how big, how old.* New York: Roaring Brook Press. P–M Sandler, M. W. (2009). *The Dust Bowl through the lens.* New York: Walker. U
Picture-Book Stories	Macaulay, D. (2005). *Black and white.* New York: Sandpiper. M–U Say, A. (1998). *The stranger in the mirror.* New York: Sandpiper. M–U Thomson, B. (2010). *Chalk.* New York: Marshall Cavendish. P Van Allsburg, C. (1991). *The wretched stone.* Boston: Houghton Mifflin. M–U Wiesner, D. (2001). *The three pigs.* New York: Clarion Books. M
Wordless Picture Books	Geisert, A. (2008). *Hogwash.* Boston: Houghton Mifflin. P–M Lehman, B. (2007). *Rainstorm.* Boston: Houghton Mifflin. P–M Mayer, M. (2003). *Frog goes to dinner.* New York: Dial Books. P–M Pinkney, J. (2009). *The lion and the mouse.* Boston: Little, Brown. P–M Wiesner, D. (2006). *Flotsam.* New York: Clarion Books. M–U
Multigenre Books	Cole, J. (1996). *The magic school bus inside a hurricane.* New York: Scholastic. P–M Fleming, C. (2003). *Ben Franklin's almanac: Being a true account of the good gentleman's life.* New York: Atheneum. M–U Holm, J. L. (2007). *Middle school is worse than meatloaf: A year told through stuff.* New York: Atheneum. M–U Olson, T. (2008). *How to get rich in the California gold rush.* Washington, DC: National Geographic. M–U Pipe, J. (2007). *Titanic.* Buffalo, NY: Firefly Books. U

As students examine picture-book illustrations, they identify some of the same styles they used to study famous paintings:

REALISM. Illustrators create accurate, lifelike depictions of their subjects with attention to details. Examples include *Make Way for Ducklings* (McCloskey, 2004), *Rapunzel* (Zelinsky, 2002), and *Grandfather's Journey* (Say, 2008).

IMPRESSIONISM. Illustrators provide an impression of the subject the way they see it at the moment. They emphasize light and color as they create an impression of reality. Examples include *Mirette on the High Wire* (McCully, 1997), *The Napping House* (A. Wood, 2004), and *Miss Rumphius* (Cooney, 1985).

EXPRESSIONISM. Illustrators convey emotional responses to subjects. Their art often uses bold lines, distorted shapes, or strong colors. Examples include *Smoky Night* (Bunting, 1999), *Hey, Al* (Yorinks, 1989), and *Lon Po Po: A Red-Riding Hood Story From China* (Young, 1996).

SURREALISM. Illustrators present startling and shocking images, the kinds experienced in dreams and nightmares. Examples include *Jumanji* (Van Allsburg, 1981) and *Tuesday* (Wiesner, 1997).

FOLK ART. Illustrators model their art on the style of a region, country, or cultural group. They often incorporate ethnic decorative designs and patterns in their illustrations. Examples include *The Mitten* (Brett, 2009), *Abuela* (Dorros, 1997), and *Strega Nona* (dePaola, 2010).

NAÏVE ART. Illustrators employ a simple style that resembles folk art. The art is often two-dimensional or flat. Examples include *Tar Beach* (Ringgold, 1996) and *Ox-Cart Man* (Hall, 1983).

CARTOON ART. Illustrators create simplified line drawings, either black-and-white or colored, that are often humorous. Examples include *Martha Speaks* (Meddaugh, 1995), *Goldilocks and the Three Bears* (J. Marshall, 1998), and *Don't Let the Pigeon Drive the Bus!* (Willems, 2003).

COLLAGE. Illustrators glue paper, cloth, wood, glass, and photos to a flat surface to create a picture. (The word *collage* comes from a French word meaning "to paste.") Even though the collage has been photographed and reproduced in books, the feeling of texture is still apparent. Examples include *Smoky Night* (Bunting, 1999), *The Very Hungry Caterpillar* (Carle, 2001), and *Lunch* (Fleming, 1996).

COMPUTER-GENERATED ART. Illustrators use 21st-century digital technology and software programs to create art. Examples include *Knuffle Bunny: A Cautionary Tale* (Willems, 2004) and *Cook-a-Doodle-Do!* (Stevens & Crummel, 2005).

When illustrating picture books, artists decide which style and media they'll use.

Illustrators use a variety of art media in picture-book illustrations. Some specialize in one medium, but others work with an assortment of art materials. Paint is the most commonly used: Paul O. Zelinsky used oils for the illustrations in *Rapunzel* (2002), Faith Ringgold painted the illustrations in *Tar Beach* (1996) with acrylics, Maurice Sendak painted the illustrations for *Where the Wild Things Are* (1988) using tempera and ink, and Jerry Pinkney chose watercolors for *The Ugly Duckling* (1999). Other illustrators use pencils and colored pencils. For example, Brian Selznick created pencil illustrations for *Amelia and Eleanor Go for a Ride* (Ryan, 1999), and Stephen Gammel used colored pencils for the illustrations in *Song and Dance Man* (Ackerman, 2003). Illustrators also create collages using layers of tissue paper, cut textured paper, and common objects, and a few artists make prints using wood blocks, as Erin Stead did in *A Sick Day for Amos McGee* (Stead, 2010). Teachers can often find out about the art media used in the illustrations on the copyright page or in the information about the illustrator at the back of the book or on the book jacket flap.

Illustrators also use color, line, shape, texture, and other elements of art in creating their artwork. In *The Very Hungry Caterpillar* (2001), Eric Carle used bold color and strong lines in his collage illustrations, and Kevin Henkes used thick black lines, soft shading, and monochromatic colors in *Kitten's First Full Moon* (2005). John Schoenherr used cool colors to accentuate the cold winter night in *Owl Moon* (Yolen, 1988), and David Diaz's dark, textured collage with heavy black lines in *Smoky Night* (Bunting, 1999) evokes the fear caused by the riots.

The design, or arrangement of art on the page, is another consideration. Illustrators work to achieve a unified design, a coherent whole that conveys meaning through balance, rhythm, repetition, variety, and emphasis. They understand, for instance, that diagonal lines are dynamic and suggest movement, and that images placed in the upper half of a scene imply triumph, happiness, or freedom. Also, light-colored backgrounds feel safer than dark ones, and rounded shapes or curves add comfort, in contrast to pointed shapes that frighten (Bang, 2000). Artists use these principles to compose their illustrations so the viewer's eye is guided by the art as they intend. To learn more about illustrators, check *Artist to Artist: 23 Major Illustrators Talk to Children About Their Art* (Eric Carle Museum of Picture Book Art, 2007), *Show and Tell: Exploring the Fine Art of Children's Book Illustration* (D. Evans, 2008), and *A Caldecott Celebration: Seven Artists and Their Paths to the Caldecott Medal* (Marcus, 2008).

Students explore the illustrations in a picture book once they're familiar with the story. If teachers don't have multiple copies, they can make story boards, cards on which the pages of a picture book have been attached, so students can really study the illustrations. Teachers make them by cutting apart two copies of a picture book and attaching the pages to pieces of tagboard; the Step-by-Step feature below describes the procedure. Students examine individual illustrations carefully, sequence the story by lining the cards up on a whiteboard tray or hanging them on a clothesline, and once the pages are laid out, students visualize the story and study its structure in new ways. They examine the illustrations more closely to notice how colors change, lines extend or move in new directions, and the placement of images changes.

Step-by-Step: STORY BOARDS

1 **Collect two copies of a book.** Teachers use two copies of a picture book for the story boards; paperbacks are preferable because they're less expensive. In a few picture books, all of the illustrations are on either the right-hand or the left-hand pages, so only one copy is needed.

2 **Cut the books apart.** Teachers remove the covers and separate the pages, evening out the cut edges.

3 **Attach the pages to pieces of cardboard.** Teachers glue each page or double-page spread to a piece of cardboard, making sure that the pages from each book are alternated so that every illustration is included.

4 **Laminate the cards.** Teachers laminate the cards so they can withstand use by students.

5 **Use the cards.** Teachers use the story-board cards for a variety of activities, including visual language, story structure, and word-study activities.

Teachers often begin by asking, "What did you notice?" and students talk about their impressions as they develop their individual responses. For example, when second graders examined the illustrations in *Roller Coaster* (Frazee, 2003), they noticed Marla Frazee's use of lines to express speed, and they spotted the two men who weren't enjoying the thrilling ride. Sometimes teachers build on students' comments, but at other times, they ask students to focus on artistic styles, elements of art, or art media. Or, they talk about how the illustrations extend the text or emphasize the story's message. Teachers plan author/illustrator studies and ask students to examine the illustrations in a collection of books. For example, as fifth graders examined Chris Van Allsburg's surrealistic illustrations, they located the bull terrier hiding in each book. Students also experiment with artistic elements themselves and create pictures using the same techniques the illustrator used in a favorite picture book.

Wordless Picture Books. Wordless picture books are just what the name suggests: They're picture books where the story is told entirely through illustrations. Most wordless picture books are intended for young children, such as *The Snowman* (Briggs, 1997) and *Picnic* (McCully, 2003); kindergartners can "read" these stories without needing to decode any words. The books introduce the concept that images are visual language, and they build children's sense of story and their storytelling abilities.

Other wordless picture books are intended for primary grade students. *Hogwash* (Geisert, 2008), *The Lion & the Mouse* (Pinkney, 2009), and *Rainstorm* (Lehman, 2007) are more detailed stories that appeal to first and second graders. David Wiesner's wordless and nearly wordless books, including *June 29, 1999* (1995), *Tuesday* (1997), and *Flotsam* (2006), intrigue older students; these books feature stunning visuals, wacky humor, skewed perspectives, and illogical events that challenge students to think deeply and make creative interpretations. Shaun Tan's surrealistic wordless story, *The Arrival* (2007), requires students to assume the viewpoint of a newly arrived immigrant as he creates a new life for himself and his family.

Graphic Novels. Graphic novels are chapter-book stories told using a series of cartoons. They're written and illustrated in comic-book format, but they have the length and depth of novels. Authors incorporate story structures to create complex plots and embed narrative devices, including dialogue, flashbacks, and suspense. These book-length stories have a beginning, middle, and end. They're complete stories, but they're often part of an ongoing series, including Babymouse, Magic Pickle, Bone, Lunch Lady, Big Nate, Knights of the Lunch Table, and Stink.

Typical categories of graphic novels are superheroes, fantastic worlds, adventure, crime fighting, or traditional literature. The stories often contain elements of fantasy, technology, and humor—especially puns. For example, *Magic Pickle* (Morse, 2008) features an energy-blasting flying pickle who fights for "dill" justice. In the first story in this series designed for second through fourth graders, Magic Pickle teams up with a sassy girl to take down scientifically advanced super-veggies before they wreak havoc. *Meanwhile: Pick Any Path* (Shiga, 2010) is a mind-boggling choose-your-own-adventure story. On the first page, readers are asked to choose vanilla or chocolate ice cream, and that first choice begins their adventure. Readers don't read the panels from left to right on each page; instead, they follow color-coded tubelike lines to the panels they should read, and when the tube splits in two, readers must choose which scenario to follow. The author claims 3,856 possible stories, depending on the choices that readers make.

Other graphic novels retell chapter-book stories using pictures. One example is *Artemis Fowl* (Colfer, 2009), the first in a series of stories about a 12-year-old criminal mastermind, and *Artemis Fowl: The Graphic Novel* (Colfer & Donkin, 2007). Most readers say that the graphic novel captures the story and the graphic format enhances it. Some say that the graphics are amazing, that they bring the story to life, but others are disappointed; they complain that the illustrations don't fit the images they created in their mind when they read the text version, or they say that the plot was condensed, and their favorite scenes were de-emphasized.

Graphic novels appeal to nearly all students, and they're especially popular with reluctant readers. Graphic novels accelerate students' reading development because the illustrations provide clues to meaning and foster comprehension (Thompson, 2008). In addition, because students enjoy reading these books, they do more reading and are more motivated to read.

Novels. Most novels have no illustrations or include only a few small drawings; however, in some novels, drawings are integral to the story. One of the best known is *The Invention of Hugo Cabret* (Selznick, 2007), the story of a remarkable boy who lives in the walls of a Paris train station at the turn of the 20th century. Brian Selznick received the 2008 Caldecott Medal for his artful blending of narrative, illustration, and cinematic techniques in this 550-page novel. Other authors create multigenre novels by including letters, charts, photos, newspaper clippings, maps, email messages, time lines, lists, recipes, and other images in their stories. Scholastic's Geronimo Stilton easy-to-read chapter-book series about the editor of "The Rodent's Gazette" on Mouse Island is one example; and Kate Klise's series, *Regarding the Fountain* (1999), *Regarding the Sink* (2006), *Regarding the Trees* (2007), *Regarding the Bathrooms* (2008), and *Regarding the Bees* (2009), is another.

Nonfiction Books. Most nonfiction books incorporate visual components because complex information can often be presented more clearly and concisely as images, diagrams, and other graphic representations. Plus, many students say that information presented in visual texts is more memorable. In *The Magic School Bus Explores the Senses* (Cole, 2001) and other books in the popular Magic School Bus series, author Joanna Cole and illustrator Bruce Degen effectively place visual texts, often in chart form, in side panels; and author/illustrator David Macaulay presents complex, detailed information through pen-and-ink diagrams in his acclaimed nonfiction books, including *Built to Last* (2010), *Pyramid* (1982), and *City: A Story of Roman Planning and Construction* (1983).

Images, diagrams, time lines, and maps are four types of visual texts used in nonfiction books (Moline, 1995):

IMAGES. Images in nonfiction books include paintings, drawings, and photographs. In *Our Country's Presidents* (Bausum, 2009), the author presents short biographies of each president, George Washington to Barack Obama, accompanied by official portraits done in oil paint and drawings and photos of the presidents and their families. These images amplify the text and breathe life into the book. Detailed drawings in *Pharaoh's Boat* (Weitzman, 2009) show how ancient Egyptian shipwrights constructed huge ships. And illustrator Andy Comins took stunning photos to show the step-by-step process of scientific experiments examining the effect of pesticide on frogs for *The Frog Scientist* (P. Turner, 2009), a biography of Tyrone Hayes, a scientist who's devoted his life to saving frogs from pesticide contamination and improving the health of our environment.

DIAGRAMS. Diagrams graphically represent information, helping to structure the way students think about a topic. There are many different types of diagrams, but these are commonly used in nonfiction books:

- Clusters are nonlinear diagrams used to generate and organize ideas about a topic.
- Cross-sections illustrate the components inside an object.
- Cutaways show the internal structure of a three-dimensional model.
- Flow charts graphically represent the steps in a process.
- How-to diagrams demonstrate how to make or do something.
- Matrix diagrams condense and organize data about a topic.

- Pie charts display information about parts of a whole or about percentages.
- Venn diagrams highlight the similarities and differences between two topics.

Flow charts, for instance, are used effectively in *Who Eats What? Food Chains and Food Webs* (Lauber, 1995). The food chains follow one path as predators eat prey, but food webs show how animals and plants are interconnected by different paths. Arrows point out the direction of the flow.

TIME LINES. Time lines are a tool for examining events across a period of time. In *Look at the Stars* (Aldrin, 2009), the astronaut-author uses a time line to highlight events in space exploration, beginning with Copernicus in 1543. Autobiographical and biographical life lines are time lines that focus on events in a person's life. Sometimes personal events on a life line are compared and contrasted with historical events on an accompanying time line.

MAPS. Maps provide information on locations, and most maps have a compass rose to indicate which way is north and a scale to estimate distances. Students learn to read a variety of maps, including climate maps with weather information; physical maps with the geographic features of an area; political maps with state boundaries and capital cities; road maps with highways, roads, and points of interest in an area; and topographic maps with contour lines to show the shape and elevation of an area. There's a map of the pony express route on the inside cover of *Off Like the Wind! The First Ride of the Pony Express* (Spradlin, 2010). This map resembles a road map because it highlights points of interest along the route.

Figure 7–4 shows the variety of visual texts used in nonfiction books.

Multigenre Books. In the past decade, a number of multigenre books have appeared that incorporate more than one genre—journals, letters, menus, newspaper articles, and postcards, for example—as well as a rich visual display, including images, diagrams, time lines, and maps. *Lincoln Shot: A President's Life Remembered* (Denenberg, 2008), for instance, is a biography that's written and illustrated in a newspaper format. This simulated 1865 newspaper includes articles, letters, poems, quotes, advertisements, drawings, photos, wanted posters, and maps. Similarly,

FIGURE 7–4   Visual Texts in Nonfiction Books

Type	Description	Examples			
Diagrams	Diagrams graphically represent information about a topic and provide a visual structure.	Clusters Cross-sections Cutaway diagrams Flow charts		How-to diagrams Matrix charts Pie charts Venn diagrams	
Images	Realistic images convey information to clarify and extend the text.	Drawings Paintings		Photographs Movies	
Maps	Maps provide information about locations.	Weather maps Airplane route maps Bus maps		Road maps Topographical maps Floor plans	
Time Lines	Time lines present a chronological sequence of related events.	Autobiographical life lines Biographical life lines		Historical time lines	

Based on Moline, 1995.

How to Get Rich on the Oregon Trail (Olson, 2009)—the purported journal of William Reed, who traveled to Portland, Oregon, in 1852—includes journal entries, labeled drawings, diagrams, a ledger, letters, postcards, photos, wanted posters, and a map. Together the varied genres and illustrations provide comprehensive information about the topic.

ISUALLY REPRESENTING

Students visually represent ideas and communicate information for a variety of purposes using art, graphics, and drama. They develop and organize ideas, explore ideas they're learning, demonstrate knowledge, share information, and try to persuade others. Students often work collaboratively with classmates and incorporate digital technology. They apply the elements of visual language as they create visual projects and multimedia texts that integrate images and text and often include sound and movement as well.

Artistic Representations

Students use art to support their learning and create artistic projects to demonstrate their learning (Burmark, 2002). As they create artistic representations, they use observing, scanning, translating, and other visual language strategies (Riddle, 2009). Students create both paper and digital artistic representations:

DRAWING PICTURES. Young children commonly draw pictures, but older students also make sketches and drawings and use digital drawing programs.

CONSTRUCTING COLLAGES. Students create collages from a variety of papers, photos, and objects. They use colors, lines, symbols, images, and words to express ideas.

MAKING QUILTS. Students make quilt squares from paper or fabric and arrange them to create a quilt that celebrates a book, commemorates a person or an event, or is the culminating project in a thematic unit. They choose colors and symbols to represent important ideas.

DESIGNING TABLETOP DISPLAYS. Students make maps and design visually complex scenes of stories and historical events.

CREATING POSTERS. Students use words and images to make posters that present information about a big idea or persuade viewers about a topic.

DRAWING CARTOONS. Students draw cartoons or use software programs such as ToonDoo (http://www.toondoo.com) to make them. They apply what they've learned about symbols and other visual elements.

CONSTRUCTING PUPPETS. Students construct puppets to use in retelling stories from a variety of materials, including paper plates, paper cups, and toilet paper rolls.

TAKING PHOTOGRAPHS. Students use digital cameras to take photos that communicate ideas, feelings, and opinions, and they refine their pictures with photo-editing software.

PRESENTING SLIDE SHOWS. Students sequence a series of drawings or photos to create digital slide shows on a variety of topics.

SHOOTING MOVIES. Students use digital video cameras to create movies that tell stories and share information. They make storyboards, shoot the movie, and do the editing using iMovie or another movie-making software application.

The Digital Classroom feature on page 204 lists a number of software programs that students can use to create artistic projects and other visual representations.

DIGITAL CLASSROOM

Visual Language Software

▶ **Animoto**
http://www.animoto.com
Students use this web application to generate high-quality videos with user-selected images and music.

▶ **AuthorSTREAM**
http://www.authorstream.com
Students share their PowerPoint presentations on the web, and they can convert them to video presentations. This site allows students to keep their presentations private, if desired.

▶ **Dabbleboard**
http://www.dabbleboard.com
This online collaboration application calls itself "the whiteboard reinvented." Teachers and students can draw pictures and create graphics with their powerful, easy-to-use, flexible tools.

▶ **Flickr**
http://www.flickr.com
Students tell stories with photos, add notes to explain or comment on the photos, insert tags to categorize their photos, and share them with friends and family.

▶ **Gliffy**
http://www.gliffy.com
Students make, share, and collaborate on diagrams, including Venn diagrams, flow diagrams, and floor plans. The site's name comes from glyph, a word meaning a symbol that imparts visual information.

▶ **Glogster**
http://www.edu.glogster.com
Students create multimedia, interactive posters, and class projects that they can share with online audiences.

▶ **Inspiration**
http://www.inspiration.com
Upper grade students create concept maps and graphic organizers at this website, and there's another version, Kidspiration, for students in kindergarten through fifth grade.

▶ **Pixton**
http://www.pixton.com
Students use this online software to make comics that they can download, imbed into projects, or share on the web.

▶ **Prezi**
http://prezi.com
Students use this presentation editor to showcase work and share ideas using images and video clips.

▶ **ToonDoo**
http://www.toondoo.com
Students design, draw, and publish their own cartoons, comic strips, and comic books at this website.

▶ **Visuwords**
http://www.visuwords.com
Students check word meanings and associations in this online graphical dictionary. Information is displayed in a clusterlike diagram with color-coded lines connecting the words that indicate parts of speech and relationships between words.

Graphic Representations

Graphic representations involve charts, graphs, and diagrams, and they're different than pictures. Riddle (2009) explains that students use graphic representations as visual organizers "to record, organize, prioritize, and synthesize information" (p. 13). Students create graphic representations as learning tools and to demonstrate learning (Burke, 2002). They generate and compare ideas, explain relationships among ideas, and synthesize information from various sources. Sometimes the graphic representations that students create are informal learning log entries, but at other times, they create these visual presentations as projects, usually during literature focus units and thematic units. Students use web applications to create many graphic representations.

Students investigate clusters, Venn diagrams, time lines, flow charts, and other graphics as they learn about the elements of visual language—line, in particular—and as they read nonfiction books. They learn to choose the most appropriate graphic for the information they're presenting; for instance, time lines show the sequence of events, Venn diagrams compare ideas, and clusters describe ideas.

When they're viewing graphics, many students have difficulty deciphering them because the supporting text doesn't provide much explanation, and the graphic lacks a caption or labels. Too often, students take only a quick look at the graphic; they don't analyze the information and learn from it. McTigue and Flowers (2011) point out that it's essential to teach students how to interpret graphic representations so they can use them effectively and because high-stakes achievement tests often include a number of questions about information that's provided visually. Students need to learn to determine the relationship between the graphic and the surrounding text, examine the graphic, read and analyze the information provided in the graphic, and draw conclusions. McTigue and Flowers conclude that "although graphics can provide important information, they can also add complexity to the task of comprehension" (p. 580).

Students apply what they've learned about graphics when they make their own, but, not surprisingly, it's easier to view and analyze a graphic than to construct one. They begin by determining their purpose in making a graphic so they can select the most appropriate one. They use paper and pencil or software to make the chart or diagram and list the information with images, symbols, words, or numbers.

Dramatic Representations

Drama provides a medium for students to use visual language in an imaginative and meaningful context (Edmiston, 2011). It's not only a powerful form of communication but also a valuable way of knowing (McDonald & Fisher, 2006). When students participate in dramatic activities, they interact with classmates, share experiences, and explore their own understanding. They stimulate their imaginations, solve problems, and negotiate with classmates. According to Dorothy Heathcote, a highly acclaimed British drama teacher, drama "cracks the code" so that messages can be understood (Wagner, 1999). Drama has this power for three reasons: It involves a combination of logical and creative thinking, it requires active experience, and it integrates the language arts. Research confirms that drama has a positive effect on students' oral and written language development (McMaster, 1998; Wagner, 2003). Too often, however, teachers ignore drama because it seems unimportant.

Dramatic activities range from quick improvisations that are student centered to polished theatrical performances that are audience centered. Instead of encouraging students to be spontaneous and use drama to explore ideas, theatrical performances require that students memorize lines and rehearse their presentations. Our focus here is on student-centered dramatizations that are used to enhance learning.

Improvisation. Students step into someone else's shoes and view the world from that perspective as they reenact stories. These activities are usually quick and informal because the emphasis is on learning, not performance. Students assume the roles of characters and then role-play as the teacher narrates or guides the dramatization. They usually don't wear costumes, and there's little or no rehearsal; it's the spontaneity that makes improvisation so effective.

Students often reenact stories during literature focus units. Sometimes they dramatize episodes while they're reading to examine a character, understand the sequence of events, or delve into the theme. As students dramatize an episode, teachers often direct the class's attention by asking questions, such as "What's [character's name] thinking?" and "Why is [character's name] making him do this?" For example, while seventh graders read *Holes* (Sachar, 2008), the story of a boy named Stanley Yelnats who's sent to a juvenile detention center for a crime he didn't

Middle School Spotlight

Does drama-infused instruction improve middle school students' learning?

In a yearlong study of four urban schools, Walker, Tabone, and Weltsek (2011) examined whether drama-infused instruction would improve learning for low-income sixth and seventh graders. Fourteen teachers in four schools participated in the study, and an equal number of teachers in four other schools in the district served as the control group. At the comparison schools, students read the same literature selections, but they didn't participate in drama activities. During the study, students participated in a variety of drama activities to explore *A Single Shard* (Park, 2011), *Tuck Everlasting* (Babbitt, 2007), *Maniac Magee* (Spinelli, 2002), *The Midwife's Apprentice* (Cushman, 1996b), and other novels. Teachers led activities to teach students about these components of drama:

- Scenery design and setting
- Acting and understanding the characters
- Directing and understanding the theme
- Plot and character relationships
- Script writing and dialogue

They taught students how to use their voices, body movements, and visual representations to interpret novels they were reading in class. Each activity was based on a section of text taken from one of the novels; the students used improvisation, process drama, and script-writing techniques as they participated in the activities. Afterward, the researchers analyzed students' scores on the standardized achievement tests, and they found that students in the drama-infused classrooms were more likely to pass the language arts section of the standardized achievement test. In fact, students in the drama-infused classes amazingly "increased the odds of … passing the state assessment by 77%" (p. 370)! The researchers also found that they significantly increased their scores on the math section of the standardized test. The results were powerful enough that students sustained their learning gains the following year, even without continued drama-infused instruction. This study provides strong evidence that drama can significantly contribute to students' academic achievement, and it underscores the necessity of integrating drama into language arts instruction.

commit, they often reenact Stanley digging a hole on his first day at Camp Green Lake to analyze the effect of the experience on him. Later, as they continue reading, they focus on pivotal points in the story: when Stanley finds the small, gold lipstick tube while he's digging a hole, when he claims he stole a bag of sunflower seeds and is taken to the warden's office, when he escapes from the camp and meets up with another escaped boy, nicknamed "Zero," and finally, when the two boys return to camp and find the "treasure" suitcase. Through these improvisations, students understand individual episodes as well as the overall structure of the story.

At other times, students, especially young children, dramatize an entire story after they finish reading it or listening to the teacher read it aloud. Teachers often break stories into three parts—beginning, middle, and end—to organize the dramatization and provide more opportunities for children to participate in the activity. Through improvisation, children review and sequence the story events and develop their concept of story. Folktales, such as *The Gingerbread Boy* (Galdone, 2008), *Little Red Riding Hood* (Pinkney, 2007), and *The Empty Pot* (Demi, 2007), are easy for younger children to dramatize.

Process Drama. British educator Dorothy Heathcote developed an imaginative and spontaneous dramatic activity called *process drama* to help students explore stories they're reading, social studies topics, and current events from a variety of viewpoints (Tierney & Readence, 2005; Wagner, 1999). Teachers create an unscripted dramatic context about a story episode or a historical event, and the students assume roles to experience and reflect on the episode or event (Schneider & Jackson, 2000).

For example, when eighth graders are studying the Underground Railroad, teachers might create a dramatic context on the moment when the escaped slaves reach the Ohio River. They'll be safe once they cross the river, but they're not safe yet. It's important to focus on a particular critical moment—one that's tension filled or that creates challenges. Most students play the role of escaped slaves, but others are conductors guiding the slaves to safety or Quakers risking their lives to hide the slaves. Other students play bounty hunters or plantation owners trying to capture the escaped slaves.

With everyone participating in a role, the class dramatizes the event, examining the critical moment from their viewpoints. The teacher moves the action forward by recounting the event and asking questions. After reliving the experience, students reflect on it by writing simulated journal entries or simulated letters; they write in the persona of their character, sharing information about the experience and reflecting on it. Afterward, students step out of their roles to discuss the experience and share what they've learned. The steps in process drama are summarized in the Step-by-Step feature below.

Process drama goes beyond improvisation: Not only do the students reenact the episode or event, but they explore the topic from the viewpoint of their character as they respond to the teacher's questions and when they write simulated journal entries or letters. The discussion that follows the reenactment also deepens students' understanding. Heathcote believes that process drama is valuable because it stimulates students' curiosity and makes them want to read books and learn more about historical or current events.

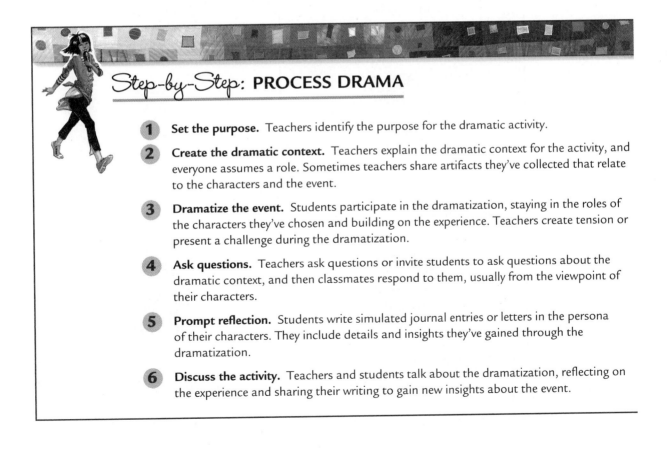

Step-by-Step: PROCESS DRAMA

1. **Set the purpose.** Teachers identify the purpose for the dramatic activity.

2. **Create the dramatic context.** Teachers explain the dramatic context for the activity, and everyone assumes a role. Sometimes teachers share artifacts they've collected that relate to the characters and the event.

3. **Dramatize the event.** Students participate in the dramatization, staying in the roles of the characters they've chosen and building on the experience. Teachers create tension or present a challenge during the dramatization.

4. **Ask questions.** Teachers ask questions or invite students to ask questions about the dramatic context, and then classmates respond to them, usually from the viewpoint of their characters.

5. **Prompt reflection.** Students write simulated journal entries or letters in the persona of their characters. They include details and insights they've gained through the dramatization.

6. **Discuss the activity.** Teachers and students talk about the dramatization, reflecting on the experience and sharing their writing to gain new insights about the event.

Playing With Puppets. Students become characters from their favorite stories when they put puppets on their hands. Second graders pull on worm, fly, and spider finger puppets, and *Diary of a Worm* (Cronin, 2003), *Diary of a Spider* (Cronin, 2005), and *Diary of a Fly* (Cronin, 2007), amusing adventures of three friends, come to life. Children talk in the voices of the tiny characters and use the puppets to retell events from the books as well as to create new stories. Even though many adults feel self-conscious with puppets, children don't.

Students can create puppet shows with commercially manufactured puppets, or they can construct their own. When students make their own puppets, they're limited only by their imaginations, their ability to construct things, and the materials at hand. Simple puppets provide students with the opportunity to develop both creative and dramatic ability. The simpler the puppet, the more is left to the imagination of the audience and the puppeteer. Six kinds of hand and finger puppets that students can make are shown in Figure 7-5.

FIGURE 7-5   Puppets

Stick Puppets
Attach pictures students have drawn or pictures cut from magazines to sticks, tongue depressors, or popsicle sticks to make these simple puppets.

Paper Bag Puppets
Place the puppet's mouth at the fold of the paper bag and draw or paint on faces, add clothes and yarn for hair, and attach arms and legs.

Cylinder Puppets
Paint faces on cardboard tubes, add yarn for hair, and decorate with clothing. Insert fingers in the bottom of the tube to manipulate the puppet.

Cup Puppets
Glue facial features, hair, wings, and other decorations on a styrofoam cup. Then attach a stick or heavy-duty straw to the inside of the cup as the handle.

Paper Plate Puppets
Use crayons or paint to make a face on the paper plate and add junk materials for decorations. Tape a stick or ruler to the back of the plate as the handle.

Finger Puppets
Draw, color, and cut out small figures, add tabs to either side of the figure and tape the tabs together to fit around a finger. Or, cut a finger section from a glove and add decorations.

After students make puppets, they can create and perform puppet shows almost anywhere; they don't even need a script or a stage. Several students can sit together on the floor holding their puppets and invent a story that they tell to classmates who sit nearby, listening intently. Or, students can make a stage from an empty appliance packing crate and climb inside to present their show. What matters is that students use their puppets to share a story with an appreciative audience. Simple puppets provide the opportunity to develop both creative and dramatic ability.

SUMMING UP

Visual language is a powerful way of learning, and it's likely to become even more important as new digital tools are developed and technological applications increase. Viewing and visually representing are the two visual language arts. Students apply their knowledge about the visual elements—color, line, symbols, and humor—to comprehend, interpret, and respond to images, symbols, and graphics, and they design and construct graphic and dramatic productions.

MyEducationLab™

Go to the topic Visual Literacy in the MyEducationLab (http://www.myeducationlab.com) for *Language Arts: Patterns of Practice*, where you can:

- Find learning outcomes for Visual Literacy, along with the national standards that connect to these outcomes.
- Complete Assignments and Activities that can help you more deeply understand the chapter content.
- Apply and practice your understanding of the core teaching skills identified in the chapter with the Building Teaching Skills and Dispositions learning units.
- Check your comprehension of the content covered in the chapter with the Study Plan. Here you will be able to take a chapter quiz, receive feedback on your answers, and then access Review, Practice, and Enrichment activities to enhance your understanding of chapter content.

On the **MyEducationLab** for this course, you'll also be able to:

- **A+RISE** Go to the topic A+RISE, an innovative and interactive database of strategies that differentiate instruction across the language arts and provide particular insight into research-based methods to meet the needs of English learners.
- Explore the topic Literacy Portraits—yearlong case studies of second graders, complete with student artifacts, teacher commentary, and student and teacher interviews, tracking the month-by-month language arts growth of five students.
- Gain practice with the Grammar Tutorial, online guided instruction to improve your own ability with grammar.

CHAPTER 8

Building Vocabulary

EIGHTH GRADERS STUDY WORDS   During a unit on the Middle Ages, Ms. Boland's eighth graders identify words to put on the word wall as they read books about the Middle Ages, including *Catherine, Called Birdy* (Cushman, 2005), *Castle Diary: The Journal of Tobias Burgess, Page* (Platt, 1999), *Ms. Frizzle's Adventures: Medieval Castle* (Cole, 2002), and *Castle* (Macaulay, 1977). Students choose 10 important words and draw word clusters on index cards, and they also write the words in their learning logs so that they can refer more easily to them during the thematic unit. The word wall is shown on page 212.

Ms. Boland uses the words on the word wall for a series of minilessons. To review the meaning of the words, she uses a semantic feature analysis chart with the categories "castle," "knights," "peasants," "crusades," and "cathedral" and 20 words for students to categorize. For *villein,* they check the "peasants" category, and for *fortress,* they check the "castle" category, for example. For other words, such as *Black Death,* more than one category is checked. She demonstrates how to fill in the chart, and then students complete it in small groups.

In the second minilesson, Ms. Boland focuses on etymology, or word history, and students learn that words about the Middle Ages come from English, French, Latin, and Greek. Ms. Boland shares guidelines for determining the language source, such as that compound words are usually English, words in which *ch* is pronounced /sh/ are French, words that end in *-tion* are Latin, and words in which *ch* is pronounced /k/ are Greek. Then students sort these words according to language:

English: *freeman, drawbridge, knight, forenoon, heathen, scabbard,* and *king*
French: *chivalry, heraldry, garderobe, lute, troubadour,* and *tournament*

Latin: *apprentice, illumination, joust, entertainment, cathedral,* and *Renaissance*

Greek: *alchemy, monk,* and *monastery*

*W*hat's the best way to teach vocabulary?

Students are expected to learn many technical words in thematic units, but too often having students look up the definition of words and write sentences using the words substitutes for really teaching vocabulary. Researchers tell us that students learn many words incidentally through multiple exposures and others through word-study activities that go beyond looking up definitions. As you read this vignette, notice how Ms. Boland involves students in a variety of meaningful word-study activities.

Next, students examine root words and affixes to determine the meaning of *Renaissance* (rebirth), *monk* and *monastery* (alone), *manuscript* (handwritten), *medieval* (Middle Ages), *Crusades* (cross), *solar* (sun), *unicorn* (one horn). They also compare related English and Latin words—for example, *church* and *cathedral, Middle Ages* and *medieval, kingly* and *royal,* and *Black Death* and *plague*—to discover that the more common words are English and the more sophisticated ones are Latin.

In the fourth minilesson, Ms. Boland compares the English word *hand* with the Latin word *manus* ("hand") and words made from these two root words. Students brainstorm words with the root word *hand: handwriting, handle, handy, handmade, handshake, handsome, handicraft, right-* (or *left-*) *handed,* and *handbag.* Then Ms. Boland introduces the Latin root word *manus,* which is used in *manuscript* and a "handful" of other words, including *manufacture, manual,* and *manicure.* Students make root-word clusters for the two words in their learning logs.

Finally, Ms. Boland focuses on synonyms: Together as a class, students use thesauri to locate appropriate synonyms for *knight,* including *warrior, defender, protector, gallant,* and *cavalier.* Next, students work in small groups to identify appropriate synonyms for other words on the word wall.

After reading about the Middle Ages, students divide into research teams to learn more about a particular aspect of life at that time. One group researches the building of a castle, and other groups investigate medical practices, the Crusades, knighthood, the feudal social system, food and drink, and the life of a serf. The students in each group research their topic and develop a display with artifacts and a PowerPoint presentation to document what they've learned. Then at the end of the thematic unit, students transform their classroom into a museum. They dress in costumes and set up their displays. Parents, other students, and community members visit the displays, and Ms. Boland's students share what they've learned about the Middle Ages.

Visit the **MyEducationLab** for *Language Arts: Patterns of Practice* to enhance your understanding of chapter concepts with a personalized Study Plan. You'll also have the opportunity to hone your teaching skills through video- and case-based Assignments and Activities, and Building Teaching Skills and Dispositions lessons.

Word Wall on the Middle Ages

A		B		C		D E
archery	alchemy	Black Death	bailey	cathedral	castle	estate
acre	archer	battlements	barter	chain mail	crusade	dub
apprentice	armorer	battering ram	barron	coat of arms	chivalry	drawbridge
		bloodletting		constable	clergy	earl

F		G		H		I J K	
fairs	fortress	gatehouse		heraldry	harvest	illumination	keep
feudal system	fanfare	garderobe		heathen	humors	knight	king
forenoon	fresco	guilds		huntsman	herbs	knighthood	Jerusalem
flying buttress	freeman	great hall					

L		M		N O		P	
lance	landlord	Magna Carta	moat	Notre Dame		pagan	pillory
lord	lute	mercenary	minstrel	nave		peasant	plague
leprosy		monastery	merchant	nobles		parchment	pilgrim
		missionary	monk			portcullis	poacher

Q R		S		T U		V W X Y Z
royal	quartering	scabbard	siege	tournament	turret	watchtower
reeve	quill pen	steward	serf	unicorn	trencher	villein
Renaissance	queen	suit of armor	squire	troubadour	transept	yeoman
		shield	solar	twelvemonth		vernacular

ord knowledge plays a critical role in students' academic success. High-achieving students know many more words than low achievers do; in fact, researchers report that the vocabularies of high-achieving third graders equal the lowest achieving high school seniors (Beck, McKeown, & Kucan, 2002). Differences in children's word knowledge are apparent in kindergarten and first grade, and these differences appear to relate to the families' socioeconomic status (SES). Researchers have noticed that children from high SES homes know twice as many words as those from low SES homes (Beck et al., 2002). High SES children's vocabulary is enhanced in these ways:

BACKGROUND KNOWLEDGE. High SES children participate in a broader array of vocabulary-enriching experiences with their families.

BOOK EXPERIENCES. High SES children are more likely to be read to every day, regularly visit the library and check out books, and have their own collection of books.

PARENTS' VOCABULARY LEVEL. High SES parents use more sophisticated vocabulary when they talk with their children.

One way to demonstrate these differences is by comparing kindergartners' knowledge of color words. Some 5- and 6-year-olds know 25 color words or more, including *silver, magenta, turquoise, navy,* and *tan;* however, others can't identify the eight basic colors.

It's difficult for students with less vocabulary knowledge to catch up with their classmates because high achievers learn more words and acquire them more quickly than lower achievers. High SES students' vocabularies grow at an astonishing rate of 3,000 to 4,000 words a year, but low SES students learn words at a slower rate. By the time they graduate from high school, high-achieving students' vocabularies reach 50,000 words or more!

ISTORY OF THE ENGLISH LANGUAGE

Understanding the history of English and how words entered the language contributes greatly to understanding words. English is a historical language, which accounts for word meanings and some spelling inconsistencies (Tompkins & Yaden, 1986). English has a number of words for a single concept, and the etymology of the words explains many apparent duplications. Consider these words related to water: *aquatic, hydrant, aquamarine, waterfall, watery, aquarium, waterproof, hydraulic,* and *hydrogen.* These words come from three root words, each meaning "water": *water* is English, of course, *aqua* is Latin, and *hydro* is Greek. The choice of root word depends on the people who created the word, the word's purpose, and when the word entered English.

The development of the English language is divided into three periods: Old English, Middle English, and Modern English. The beginning and end of each period are marked by a significant event, such as an invasion or an invention.

Old English (A.D. 450–1100)

The recorded history of English begins in A.D. 449, when Germanic tribes, including the Angles and Saxons, invaded Britain. The invaders pushed the original inhabitants, the Celts, to the northern and western corners of the island; this annexation is romanticized in the King Arthur legends. Arthur is believed to have been a Celtic military leader who fought against the Germanic invaders.

The English language began as an intermingling of the dialects spoken by the Germanic tribes in Britain. Many people assume that English is based on Latin, but it has Germanic roots and was brought to Britain by these invaders. Although 85% of Old English words are no longer used, many everyday words remain (e.g., *child, foot, hand, house, man, mother, old,* and *sun*). In contrast to Modern English, Old English had a highly developed inflectional system for indicating number, gender, and verb tense. The Anglo-Saxons added affixes to existing words, including *be-, for-, -ly, -dom,* and *-hood.* They also invented vividly descriptive compound words; the Old English word for "music," for example, was *ear-sport.* The folk epic *Beowulf,* the great literary work of the period, illustrates the poetic use of words; for instance, the sea is described as a "whale-path" and a "swan's road."

Foreign words also made their way into the predominantly Germanic word stock. The borrowed words came from two main sources: Romans and Vikings. The missionaries who reintroduced Christianity to Britain in 597 contributed religious words, including *angel, candle,* and *hymn.* In 787, the Vikings began raiding English villages, and for several centuries, they occupied much of England. The Vikings' contributions to English were significant: They provided the pronouns *they, their, them;* introduced the /g/ and /k/ sounds (e.g., *get, kid*); contributed most of our *sk-* words (e.g., *skin, sky*) and some of our *sc-* words (e.g., *scalp, score*); and enriched our vocabulary with more than 500 everyday words, including *husband* and *window.*

The structure, spelling, and pronunciation of Old English were significantly different from those of Modern English, so much so that we wouldn't understand an Old English text or someone speaking Old English. Some consonant combinations were pronounced that aren't heard today, including the /k/ in words such as *knee.* The letter *f* represented both /f/ and /v/, resulting in the Modern English spelling pattern of *wolf* and *wolves.* The pronunciation of the vowel sounds was very different, too; for example, the Old English *stan* (*a* as in *father*) became our word *stone.*

Middle English (1100–1500)

The Norman Conquest in 1066 changed the course of the English language and ushered in the Middle English period. William, Duke of Normandy defeated King Harold at the Battle of Hastings and claimed the English throne. For more than 200 years, French was the official language, spoken by the nobility, even though the lower classes continued to speak English, but before the end of the 14th century, English was restored as the official language. Chaucer's *Canterbury Tales,* written in the late 1300s, provides evidence that English was replacing French. Political, social, and economic changes contributed to this reversal.

Tremendous changes occurred during the Middle English period. Many Old English words were lost as 10,000 French words were added to the language, reflecting the Norman impact on English life, including military words (e.g., *soldier, victory*), political words (e.g., *government, princess*), medical words (e.g., *physician, surgeon*), and words related to the arts (e.g., *comedy, music, poet*) (Baugh & Cable, 2002). Many of the new loan words duplicated Old English words. Typically, the Old English word was eventually lost. If both words remained, they developed slightly different meanings. For example, *hearty* (Old English) and *cordial* (French) were originally synonyms, meaning "from the heart," but in time they differentiated, and they now have different but related meanings.

In addition, there was a significant reduction in the use of inflections, or word endings. Many irregular verbs were lost, and others developed regular past and past-participle forms (e.g., *climb, talk*), although Modern English retains some irregular verbs (e.g., *sing, fly, be, have*) that contribute to our usage problems. By 1000, *-s* had become the accepted plural marker, although the Old English plural form *-en* was used in some words. This artifact remains in a few plurals, such as *children*.

Modern English (1500–Present)

William Caxton's introduction of the printing press in England marks the beginning of the Modern English period. It was a powerful force in standardizing English spelling, and from this point the lag between pronunciation and spelling began to widen. The tremendous increase in exploration during the 1600s and 1700s resulted in borrowing words from more than 50 languages, including *alcohol* (Arabic), *chocolate* (Spanish), *cookie* (Dutch), *czar* (Russian), *hallelujah* (Hebrew), *hurricane* (Spanish), *kindergarten* (German), *smorgasbord* (Swedish), *tycoon* (Chinese), and *violin* (Italian).

Many Latin and Greek words were added during the Renaissance to increase the language's prestige; for example, *congratulate, democracy,* and *education* from Latin, and *catastrophe, encyclopedia,* and *thermometer* from Greek. Many modern Latin and Greek borrowings are scientific words (e.g., *aspirin, vaccinate*), and some of the more recently borrowed forms (e.g., *criterion, focus*) have retained their native plural forms, adding confusion about how to spell them. Also, some French loan words kept their native spellings and pronunciations, such as *hors d'oeuvre* and *cul-de-sac.*

Extensive sound changes occurred during this period. The short vowels remained relatively stable, but there's been a striking change in the pronunciation of long vowels. This change, known as the Great Vowel Shift, was gradual, occurring during the 1500s. Because spelling became fixed before the shift, spellings no longer corresponded to the sounds. For example, the word *name* had two syllables and rhymed with *comma* during Middle English, but because of the Great Vowel Shift, the pronunciation of *name* changed to rhyme with *game* (Hook, 1975).

The Modern English period brought changes in syntax, particularly the disappearance of double negatives and double comparatives and superlatives. Eliminations came about slowly; for instance, Shakespeare wrote, "the most unkindest cut of all." Also, the practice of using *-er* or *-est* to form comparatives and superlatives in shorter words and *more* or *most* with longer words wasn't standardized until after Shakespeare's time.

Learning About Word Histories

The best source of information about word histories is an unabridged dictionary, which provides etymological information about words: the language the word was borrowed from, the spelling of the word in that language or the transliteration of the word into the Latin alphabet, and its original meaning. Etymologies are enclosed in square brackets and appear at the end of a dictionary entry. They're written in a shortened form to save space, using abbreviations for language names, such as *Ar* for *Arabic* and *L* for *Latin*. Look at these etymologies for three words derived from very different sources: *king, kimono,* and *thermometer.* Each etymology is elaborated, beginning with *king:*

> *king* [bef. 900; ME, OE *cyng*]
> *Elaboration:* The word *king* is an Old English word originally spelled *cyng.* It was used in English before the year 900. In the Middle English period, the spelling changed to its current form.

The next word is *kimono:*

> *kimono [1885–1890;* < Japn clothing, garb, equiv. to *ki* wear + *mono* thing]
> *Elaboration:* Our word *kimono* comes from Japanese, and it entered English between 1885 and 1890. *Kimono* means "clothing" or "garb," and it's equivalent to the Japanese words *ki*, meaning "wear," and *mono*, meaning "thing."

Finally, take a look at *thermometer:*

> *thermometer* [1615-1625; thermo < Gr *thermos,* hot + meter < *metron,* measure]
> *Elaboration:* The first recorded use of the word *thermometer* in English was between 1615 and 1625. Our word was created from two Greek words meaning "hot" and "measure."

Teachers use mentor texts to teach students about the history of English and share stories about individual words and sayings. Recommended books are presented in the Booklist below.

Booklist

WORD HISTORIES

American Heritage. (2004). *Word histories and mysteries: From abracadabra to Zeus.* Boston: Houghton Mifflin. U

American Heritage. (2006). *More word histories and mysteries: From aardvark to zombie.* Boston: Houghton Mifflin. U

Brook, D. (1998). *The journey of English.* New York: Clarion Books. M

Funk, C. E. (2002). *Heavens to Betsy! And other curious sayings.* New York: HarperCollins. U

Funk, C. E. (2002). *Horsefeathers and other curious words.* New York: HarperCollins. U

Funk, C. E. (2002). *Thereby hangs a tale: Stories of curious word origins.* New York: HarperCollins. U

Metcalf, A. (1997). *America in so many words: Words that have shaped America.* Boston: Houghton Mifflin. U

Metcalf, A. (1999). *The world in so many words: A country-by-country tour of words that have shaped our language.* Boston: Houghton Mifflin. U

Morris, E. (2004). *From altoids to zima: The surprising stories behind 125 famous brand names.* Palmer, AK: Fireside Books. U

Raschka, C. (2005). *New York is English, Chattanooga is Creek.* New York: Atheneum. M–U

Terban, M. (2006). *Scholastic dictionary of idioms.* New York: Scholastic. M–U

Terban, M. (2007). *In a pickle and other funny idioms.* New York: Sandpiper. M

Terban, M. (2007). *Mad as a wet hen! And other funny eponyms.* New York: Sandpiper. M

Terban, M. (2008). *Guppies in tuxedos: Funny eponyms.* New York: Sandpiper. M

P = primary grades (preK–2); M = middle grades (3–5); U = upper grades (6–8)

WORDS AND THEIR MEANINGS

Five-year-olds have approximately 5,000-word vocabularies, and their vocabularies grow at a rate of at least 3,000 words a year (M. Graves, 2006). Through literature focus units, literature circles, reading and writing workshop, and thematic units, students experiment with words and concepts, and their knowledge of words and meanings grows. Young children assume that every word has only one meaning, and words that sound alike, such as *son* and *sun*, confuse them. Through continued experiences with language, students' word knowledge becomes more sophisticated. They learn about root words and affixes, words that mean the same thing and opposites, words that sound alike, words with multiple meanings, idioms, and how words have been borrowed from languages around the world.

Morphological Information

A root word is a *morpheme*, the basic part of a word to which affixes are added. Many words are developed from a single root word; for example, the Latin word *portare* ("to carry") is the source of at least nine Modern English words: *deport, export, import, port, portable, porter, report, support,* and *transportation.* Latin is one source of English root words, and Greek and Old English are other sources. Some root words are whole words, and others are word parts. For instance, the word *act* comes from the Latin word *actus,* meaning "doing." English uses part of the word and treats it as a root word that can be used independently or in combination with affixes, as in *actor, activate, react,* and *enact.* In the words *alias, alien, inalienable,* and *alienate,* the root word *ali* comes from the Latin word *alius,* meaning "other"; it isn't used as an independent root word in English. A list of English, Latin, and Greek root words appears in Figure 8–1.

Students draw root word clusters to illustrate the relationship of the root to the words developed from it. Figure 8–2 shows a seventh grade class's root word cluster for the Greek root *graph,* meaning "write." Students use morphological information to unlock the meaning of words by identifying root words and peeling off affixes. Recognizing basic elements from word to word helps students cut down on the amount of memorizing necessary to learn meanings and spellings.

Affixes are bound morphemes that are added to words. They're either prefixes or suffixes: *Prefixes* are added to the beginnings of words, such as *re-* in *reread,* and *suffixes* are added to the ends of words, such as *-ing* in *singing* and *er* in *player.* Like root words, affixes come from English, Latin, and Greek, and they often change a word's meaning, such as adding *un-* to *happy* to make *unhappy.* Sometimes they change the part of speech; for example, when *-tion* is added to *attract* to form *attraction,* the verb *attract* becomes a noun.

When an affix is "peeled off," or removed from a word, the remaining word is usually a real word. For example, when the prefix *pre-* is removed from *preview,* the word *view* can stand alone; and when the suffix *-able* is removed from *lovable,* the word *love* can stand alone (when the final *e* is added, anyway). Some words include letter sequences that might look like affixes, but because the remaining word can't stand alone, they aren't. For example, the *in-* at the beginning of *include* isn't a prefix because *clude* isn't a word, and the *-ic* at the end of *magic* isn't a suffix because *mag* can't stand alone as a word, but the *-ic* at the end of *atomic* is a suffix because *atom* is a word. Here's the confusing part: Sometimes, however, the root word can't stand alone. One example is *legible:* The *-ible* is a suffix and *leg-* (meaning *read*) is the root word even though it can't stand alone.

Some affixes have more than one form. The prefixes *il-, im-,* and *ir-* are forms of the prefix *in-,* with the meanings of "in," "into," and "on"; these prefixes are used with verbs and nouns. The prefixes *il-, im-, ir-,* and *ig-* are also forms of the prefix *in-,* with the meaning "not"; these prefixes are used with adjectives. Both *in-* prefixes are borrowed from Latin. The prefix *a-* and its alternate form *an-* are borrowed from Greek and also mean "not"; the alternate form is used when the word it's being added to begins with a vowel. Similarly, some suffixes have alternate forms; for

FIGURE 8-1   Root Words

Root	Language	Meaning	Examples
ann/enn	Latin	year	anniversary, annual, centennial, millennium, perennial
arch	Greek	ruler	anarchy, archbishop, architecture, hierarchy, monarchy
astro	Greek	star	aster, asterisk, astrology, astronaut, astronomy, disaster
auto	Greek	self	autobiography, automatic, automobile, autopsy
bio	Greek	life	biography, biohazard, biology, biodegradable, bionic
capit/capt	Latin	head	capital, capitalize, capitol, captain, decapitate, per capita
cent	Latin	hundred	bicentennial, cent, centigrade, centipede, century, percent
circ	Latin	around	circle, circular, circus, circuit, circumference, circumstance
corp	Latin	body	corporal, corporation, corps, corpuscle
cosmo	Greek	universe	cosmic, cosmopolitan, microcosm
cred	Latin	believe	credit, credible, creed, discredit, incredulity
cycl	Greek	wheel	bicycle, cycle, cyclist, cyclone, recycle, tricycle
dict	Latin	speak	contradict, dictate, dictator, prediction, verdict
graph	Greek	write	autobiography, biographer, cryptograph, graphic, paragraph
gram	Greek	letter	cardiogram, diagram, grammar, monogram, telegram
jus/jud/jur	Latin	law	injury, injustice, judge, juror, jury, justice, justify, prejudice
lum/lus/luc	Latin	light	illuminate, lucid, luminous, luster
man	Latin	hand	maneuver, manicure, manipulate, manual, manufacture
mar/mer	Latin	sea	aquamarine, Margaret, marine, marshy, mermaid, submarine
meter	Greek	measure	centimeter, diameter, speedometer, thermometer
mini	Latin	small	miniature, minimize, minor, minimum, minuscule, minute
mort	Latin	death	immortal, mortality, mortuary, postmortem
nym	Greek	name	anonymous, antonym, homonym, pseudonym, synonym
ped	Latin	foot	biped, pedal, pedestrian, pedicure
phono	Greek	sound	earphone, microphone, phonics, saxophone, symphony
photo	Greek	light	photograph, photographer, photosensitive, photosynthesis
pod/pus	Greek	foot	octopus, podiatry, podium, tripod
port	Latin	carry	exporter, import, port, portable, reporter, support, transportation
quer/ques/quis	Latin	seek	inquisitive, query, quest, question
scope	Latin	see	horoscope, kaleidoscope, microscope, periscope, telescope
scrib/scrip	Latin	write	describe, inscription, postscript, prescribe, scribble, script
sphere	Greek	ball	atmosphere, atmospheric, hemisphere, sphere, stratosphere
struct	Latin	build	construction, destruction, indestructible, instruct, reconstruct
tele	Greek	far	telecast, telegram, telephone, telescope, telethon, television
terr	Latin	land	subterranean, terrace, terrain, terrarium, terrier, territory
vers/vert	Latin	turn	advertise, anniversary, controversial, divert, reversible, versus
vict/vinc	Latin	conquer	convict, convince, evict, invincible, victim, victory
vis/vid	Latin	see	improvise, invisible, revise, television, video, visitor
viv/vit	Latin	live	revive, survive, vital, vitamin, vivacious, vivid, viviparous
volv	Latin	roll	convolutions, evolution, involve, revolutionary, revolver, volume

FIGURE 8-2   A Cluster for the Root Word *Graph*

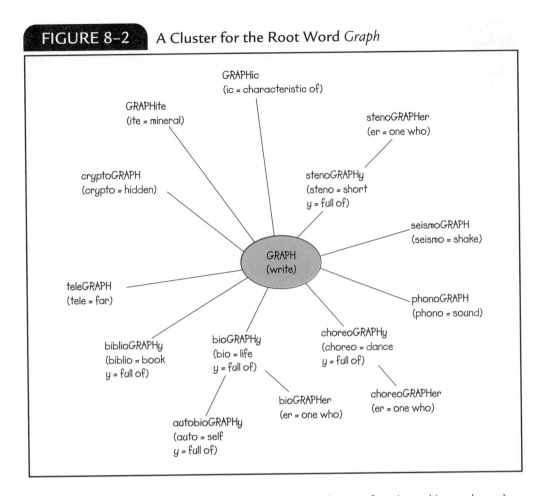

GRAPHic
(ic = characteristic of)

GRAPHite
(ite = mineral)

stenoGRAPHer
(er = one who)

cryptoGRAPH
(crypto = hidden)

stenoGRAPHy
(steno = short
y = full of)

seismoGRAPH
(seismo = shake)

GRAPH
(write)

teleGRAPH
(tele = far)

phonoGRAPH
(phono = sound)

biblioGRAPHy
(biblio = book
y = full of)

bioGRAPHy
(bio = life
y = full of)

choreoGRAPHy
(choreo = dance
y = full of)

bioGRAPHer
(er = one who)

choreoGRAPHer
(er = one who)

autobioGRAPHy
(auto = self
y = full of)

example, the suffix *-ible* is an alternate form of *-able*. The alternate form is used in words, such as *legible,* whose roots can't stand alone. There are exceptions, however, such as *collectible.*

A list of prefixes and suffixes is presented in Figure 8-3. White, Sowell, and Yanagihara (1989) identified the affixes most commonly used in English words; these are marked with an asterisk in the figure. White and his colleagues recommend that the commonly used affixes be taught because of their usefulness. Some of the most commonly used prefixes are confusing because they have more than one meaning. The prefix *in-,* for instance, can mean either "not" or "in," and *un-* can mean "not" or it can reverse the meaning of the word (e.g., *tie—untie*).

Synonyms and Antonyms

Synonyms are words that have the same or nearly the same meaning. English has many synonyms because so many words have been borrowed from other languages. Synonyms provide options, allowing us to express ourselves precisely. Think of the synonyms for *cold: cool, chilly, frigid, icy, frosty,* and *freezing,* for example. Each word has a unique shade of meaning: *Cool* means moderately cold; *chilly* is uncomfortably cold; *frigid* is intensely cold; *icy* means very cold; *frosty* means covered with frost; and *freezing* is so cold that water changes into ice. Our language would be limited if we had only the word *cold.*

Many synonyms entered English during the Norman occupation of Britain. Compare these pairs of synonyms: *end—finish, clothing—garments, forgive—pardon, buy—purchase, deadly—mortal.* The

FIGURE 8–3   Affixes

Language	Prefixes	Suffixes
English	*over- (too much): overflow self- (by oneself): self-employed *un- (not): unhappy *un- (reversal): untie under- (beneath): underground	-ed (past tense): played -ful (full of): hopeful -ing (participle): eating, building -ish (like): reddish -less (without): hopeless -ling (young): duckling *-ly (in the manner of): slowly *-ness (state or quality): kindness -s/-es (plural): cats, boxes *-y (full of): sleepy
Greek	a-/an- (not): atheist, anaerobic amphi- (both): amphibian anti- (against): antiseptic di- (two): dioxide hemi- (half): hemisphere hyper- (over): hyperactive hypo- (under): hypodermic micro- (small): microfilm mono- (one): monarch omni- (all): omnivorous poly- (many): polygon sym-/syn-/sys- (together): symphony, synonym, system	-ism (doctrine of): communism -ist (one who): artist -logy (the study of): zoology
Latin	bi- (two, twice): bifocal, biannual de- (away): detract *dis- (not): disapprove * dis- (reversal): disinfect ex- (out): export *il-/im-/in-/ir- (not): illegible, impolite, inexpensive, irrational *in- (in, into): indoor inter- (between): intermission milli- (thousandth): millisecond *mis- (wrong): mistake multi- (many): multimillionaire post- (after): postwar pre- (before): precede quad-/quart- (four): quadruple, quarter re- (again): repay *re-/retro- (back): replace, retroactive *sub- (under): submarine trans- (across): transport tri- (three): triangle	-able/-ible (worthy of, can be): lovable, audible *-al/-ial (action, process): arrival, denial -ance/-ence (state or quality): annoyance, absence -ant (one who): servant -ary/-ory (person, place): secretary, laboratory -cule (very small): molecule -ee (one who is): trustee *-er/-or/-ar (one who): teacher, actor, liar -ic (characterized by): angelic -ify (to make): simplify -ment (state or quality): enjoyment -ous (full of): nervous *-sion/-tion (state or quality): tension, attraction -ure (state or quality): failure * = most common affixes

first word in each pair comes from Old English; the second was borrowed from the Normans. The English words are common, but the French loan words are sophisticated. Perhaps that's why both words have survived—they express slightly different meanings. Other pairs of synonyms come from different languages, such as *comfortable-cozy. Comfortable* is a Latin loan word, but *cozy* is English, probably of Scandinavian origin.

Students check a dictionary or a thesaurus to locate synonyms. A fifth grade class examined the word *wretched* after reading Chris Van Allsburg's picture-book fantasy *The Wretched Stone* (1991), the story of a strange, glowing stone picked up on a sea voyage that transforms the ship's crew. They guessed that the word meant something "bad" or "evil," but they didn't know the exact meaning. One student checked a dictionary and found three meanings for the word— "unfortunate," "causing misery," and "of poor quality." He reported back to his classmates who immediately recognized that the second meaning—"causing misery"—was the most appropriate. Then they checked the word in a thesaurus and found seven synonyms. The students divided into seven groups and each group studied one of the synonyms, checking its meaning in a dictionary and thinking about how the word was used in the story. Then the groups reported back that *terrible, miserable,* and *dreadful* were appropriate synonyms, but the others weren't. Finally, the students collaborated to make a class chart for *wretched,* which is shown in Figure 8–4. They used a T-chart to indicate the synonyms' appropriateness in this context.

Antonyms are words that express opposite meanings. Antonyms for *loud* include *soft, subdued, quiet, silent, inaudible, sedate, somber, dull,* and *colorless.* These words express shades of meaning, just as synonyms do, and some opposites are more appropriate for one meaning of *loud* than for another. When *loud* means *gaudy,* for instance, appropriate opposites are *somber, dull,* and *colorless.*

Students use dictionaries and thesauri to examine the meanings of words. Dictionaries focus on presenting definitions and explaining shades of meaning of related words. Series of dictionaries published by American Heritage, Merriam-Webster, and other publishing companies are available for students. Most series include a first dictionary for young children, a children's dictionary for

FIGURE 8–4	Students' T-Chart of Synonyms

Wretched

The captain threw the [wretched] stone overboard.

yes	no
terrible	lousy
miserable	rotten
dreadful	horrid
	unfortunate

grade 4–6 students, and a student's dictionary for older students. The *Merriam-Webster Children's Dictionary* (DK Publishing, 2008), with more then 32,000 entries and 3,000 striking photo-illustrations, is an excellent reference. This dictionary takes into account students' interests and was designed with visually exciting illustrations and diagrams that expand word definitions. In addition, synonym boxes suggest word choices, and word-history boxes present interesting information about how words entered English and have changed in meaning over the centuries.

An easy-to-use thesaurus is *A First Thesaurus* (Wittels & Greisman, 2001), which contains more than 2,000 entry words. Synonyms are printed in black type for each entry word, and the antonyms follow in red type. Another good thesaurus is the *Scholastic Children's Thesaurus* (Bollard, 2006). More than 2,500 synonyms are grouped under 500 entries in the thesaurus. Under the entry *common,* for example, the synonyms *ordinary, typical, familiar, everyday,* and *widespread* are listed along with a brief definition and sample sentence for each. Online versions of print dictionaries that have electronic features, including a pronunciation sound file, multiple definitions, etymological information, word games, and word-of-the-day, are available. These online dictionaries are recommended for students in grades 4–8:

Fact Monster (http://dictionary.factmonster.com)
Word Central (http://wordcentral.com)
Yahoo! Kids Dictionary (http://kids.yahoo.com/reference)

Word Central offers both a dictionary and a thesaurus at its site.

Homonyms

Homonyms, words with sound and spelling similarities, are divided into three categories: homophones, homographs, and homographic homophones. *Homophones* are words that sound alike but are spelled differently, such as *sun–son, it's–its,* and *to–two–too.* Most homophones developed from entirely different root words, and it's only by accident that they've come to sound alike; for example, the homophones *right* and *write* entered English before the year 900 and were pronounced differently. *Right* was spelled *riht* in Old English, but during the Middle English period French scribes changed the spelling. The verb *write* was spelled *writan* in Old English and *writen* in Middle English. *Write* is an irregular verb, suggesting its Old English heritage, and the silent *w* was pronounced a millennium ago. In contrast, a few words were derived from the same root word, such as *flea–flee, flower–flour, stationary–stationery,* and *metal–medal–mettle,* and the similar spellings demonstrate semantic relationships.

Homographs are words that are spelled the same but pronounced differently. Examples of homographs are *bow, close, lead, minute, record, read,* and *wind. Bow* is a homograph that has three unrelated meanings. The verb form, meaning "to bend in respect," was spelled *bugan* in Old English; the noun form, meaning "a gathering of ribbon" or "a weapon for propelling an arrow," is of Old English origin and was spelled *boga.* The other noun form of *bow,* meaning "forward end of a ship," entered English from German in the 1600s.

Homographic homophones are words that are spelled and pronounced alike, such as *bark, bat, bill, box, fair, fly, hide, jet, mine, pen, ring, row, spell, toast,* and *yard.* Some are related words; others are linguistic accidents. The different meanings of *toast,* for example, came from the same Latin source word, *torrere,* meaning "to bake." The derivation of the noun *toast* as heated and browned slices of bread is obvious. However, the relationship between the source word and *toast* as a verb, "drink to someone's honor or health," isn't immediately apparent; the connection is that toasted bread flavored the drinks that Angles and Saxons used in making toasts. In contrast, *bat* is a linguistic accident: *Bat* meaning "a cudgel" comes from the Old English word *batt;* the verb *bat* is derived from the Old French word *batre;* and the nocturnal animal called a *bat* derives its

FIGURE 8-5   A Page From a Homophone Book

name from an unknown Viking word and was spelled *bakke* in 1200. Not only do the three forms have unrelated etymologies, they were borrowed from different languages!

Many books of homonyms are available for students, including Gwynne's *The King Who Rained* (1988), *A Chocolate Moose for Dinner* (2005), and *A Little Pigeon Toad* (1998). Students enjoy reading these books and making their own word books. Figure 8–5 shows a page from a second grader's homophone book.

Multiple Meanings

Many, many words have more than one meaning, and some words have more than five or six meanings. The word *bank,* for example, may refer to a piled-up mass of snow or clouds, the slope of land beside a lake or river, the slope of a road on a turn, the lateral tilting of an airplane in a turn, to cover a fire with ashes for slow burning, a business establishment that receives and lends money, a container in which money is saved, a supply for use in emergencies (e.g., blood bank), a place for storage (e.g., computer's memory bank), to count on, similar things arranged in a row (e.g., a bank of elevators), or to arrange things in a row. You may be surprised that there are at least 12 meanings for the common word *bank.* These meanings come from three sources. The first five come from a Viking word, and they're related because they all deal with something slanted or making a slanted motion. The next five meanings come from the Italian word *banca,* a money changer's table; these meanings deal with financial banking except for the 10th meaning, "to count on," which requires a bit more thought. The saying "to bank on" means "to depend on," but it began more literally from the actual counting of money on a table. The last two meanings come from the Old French word *banc,* meaning "bench."

Words acquired multiple meanings as society became more complex and finer shades of meaning were necessary; for example, the meanings of *bank* as an emergency supply and a storage place are fairly new. As with many words with multiple meanings, it's a linguistic accident that three words from three languages, with unrelated meanings, came to be spelled the same way. Students create word clusters to show multiple meanings of words (Bromley, 1996). Figure 8–6 shows a cluster with 10 meanings for *hot* that several seventh graders created. They drew rays and wrote the meanings, listed examples, and drew illustrations.

Words assume additional meanings when an affix is added or when they're combined with another word, or compounded. Think about the word *fire* and these words and phrases that incorporate *fire: fire hydrant, firebomb, fireproof, fireplace, firearm, fire drill, under fire, set the world on fire, fire away,* and *open fire.* Students often compile lists of words made from a common word or make booklets illustrating words. Other common words with many variations include *short, key, water, book, rain, shoe, head, make, walk, cat,* and *side.*

FIGURE 8–6 A Multiple Meanings Poster

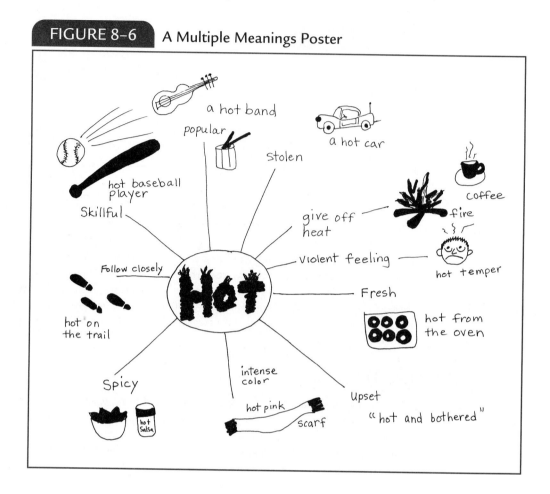

Idioms

Idioms are phrases with figurative meanings, such as "spill the beans." They can be confusing because they must be interpreted figuratively rather than literally. "Spill the beans" dates back to ancient Greece. Many men belonged to secret clubs where they held secret votes to decide whether to admit new members. They voted by each placing a white or brown bean in a special jar; a white bean was a *yes* vote, and a brown bean a *no* vote. The club leader would empty the jar and examine the beans, and if they were all white, the person was admitted. Sometimes during the voting, one member would accidentally (or not so accidentally) knock the jar over, spilling the beans to see how members had voted. The Greeks turned this real event into a saying that's still used today. Another idiom with a different history but a similar meaning is "let the cat out of the bag."

Children and adults use hundreds of idioms to create word pictures. "Out in left field," "a skeleton in the closet," "stick your neck out," "a chip off the old block," and "don't cry over spilt milk" are familiar idioms. Some of them have been created recently, but others are hundreds or thousands of years old; some are American in origin, and others come from around the world.

Three excellent books of idioms are the *Scholastic Dictionary of Idioms, Phrases, Sayings, and Expressions* (Terban, 2006), *Punching the Clock: Funny Action Idioms* (Terban, 1990), and *In a Pickle and Other Funny Idioms* (Terban, 2007). Because idioms are figurative sayings, many students—especially

English learners—have difficulty using them. It's crucial that students move beyond the literal meanings and learn to use language creatively. Students often create idiom posters to highlight the literal and figurative meanings of words.

Borrowed Words

English often borrows words from other languages; in fact, nearly 75% of English words have been borrowed from other languages. Word borrowing began when the Angles and Saxons borrowed more than 400 words from the Romans, and the Vikings contributed approximately 900 words. The Norman conquerors introduced thousands of French words into English, reflecting every aspect of life; for example, *adventure, fork, juggler,* and *quilt.* Later, during the Renaissance, scholars borrowed many words from Latin and Greek to enrich English, including *chaos, encyclopedia, pneumonia,* and *skeleton.* More recently, words from at least 50 languages have been added to English through exploration, colonization, and trade. These loan words have been borrowed from other languages (Tompkins & Yaden, 1986):

Aboriginal Australian: *kangaroo, kiwi*
African (many languages): *banjo, cola, gumbo, safari, zombie*
Arabic: *alcohol, apricot, assassin, magazine*
Chinese: *chop suey, kowtow, tea, wok*
Dutch: *caboose, easel, pickle, waffle*
French: *ballet, beige, chauffeur*
German: *kindergarten, poodle, pretzel, waltz*
Greek: *atom, cyclone, hydrogen*
Hebrew: *cherub, kosher, rabbi*
Hindi: *dungaree, juggernaut, jungle, shampoo*
Italian: *broccoli, carnival, macaroni, opera, pizza*
Japanese: *honcho, judo, kimono, origami*
Persian: *bazaar, divan, khaki, shawl*
Portuguese: *cobra, coconut, molasses*
Russian: *czar, sputnik, steppe, troika, vodka*
Scandinavian: *egg, fjord, husband, ski, sky*
Spanish: *alligator, guitar, mosquito, potato*
Turkish: *caviar, horde, khan, kiosk, yogurt*

Native Americans have also contributed a number of words to English. Colonists encountered unfamiliar animals, plants, and foods so they borrowed the Native American terms and tried to spell them phonetically; they also borrowed words to describe the Native Americans and their activities. Loan words include *chipmunk, hickory, moccasin, moose, muskrat, opossum, papoose, powwow, raccoon, skunk, toboggan, tomahawk,* and *tepee.*

 ## TEACHING STUDENTS ABOUT WORDS

Learning a word isn't as simple as you might think. It's not that you either know a word or you don't; instead, there's a continuum of word knowledge, moving from never having seen or heard the word to being able to use it effectively in a variety of contexts (Allen, 1999). Beck and her colleagues (2002) suggest this continuum of word knowledge that moves from not knowing a word at all to knowing it well:

LEVEL 1: *NO KNOWLEDGE.* Students aren't familiar with the word.

LEVEL 2: *INCIDENTAL KNOWLEDGE.* Students have seen or heard the word, but they don't know its meaning.

LEVEL 3: *PARTIAL KNOWLEDGE.* Students know one definition for the word or can use it in one context.

LEVEL 4: *FULL KNOWLEDGE.* Students have a deep understanding of the word's multiple meanings and are able to use it effectively in multiple contexts.

It takes time for students to move from having little or no knowledge of a word to full knowledge. During a week's study of a word, for example, students may move one or two levels, but it's unlikely they'll reach the fourth level. In fact, it may take several years of using a word to develop a rich, decontextualized understanding of its meaning and related words.

To reach the full-knowledge level, students develop "ownership" of the word, meaning that they can do these things:

- Pronounce the word correctly
- Understand the word's multiple meanings
- Use the word appropriately in sentences
- Identify related noun, verb, and adjective forms
- Recognize related words that come from the same root word
- Name synonyms and antonyms

With this knowledge, students will be able to understand the word when they're listening and reading and use it to express ideas in talk and writing. This Common Core State Standards box highlights the importance of vocabulary instruction.

Even though students learn hundreds or thousands of words incidentally through reading and content-area study each year, teaching high-utility vocabulary explicitly is an essential part of language arts instruction for all students, even prekindergartners, and especially for struggling students and English learners (M. Graves, 2006). Blachowicz and Fisher (2006) have reviewed the research on effective vocabulary instruction and identified these guidelines for teaching vocabulary:

WORD-RICH ENVIRONMENT. Teachers create a word-rich environment in the classroom because when teachers display words, students are more likely to learn them incidentally and through direct instruction.

INDEPENDENT WORD LEARNERS. Teachers prepare students to become independent word learners. When teachers involve students in choosing some of the words they'll study and teach word-learning strategies, such as how to use root words to analyze words and how to use a dictionary, students are more likely to take control of their own learning.

WORD-LEARNING STRATEGIES. Teachers explicitly teach students how to use context clues, morphology, and other word-learning strategies to figure out the meaning of words, and they also model word-learning strategies when they come across words that students don't know.

COMMON CORE STATE STANDARDS

Vocabulary

The Common Core State Standards emphasize that vocabulary development is essential for success in the six language arts. K–8 students must learn grade-appropriate academic vocabulary as well as strategies to figure out the meaning of unfamiliar words that they encounter. The standards highlight these points:

- Students determine the meaning of grade-appropriate academic vocabulary words.
- Students recognize multiple meanings of words and shades of meaning.
- Students analyze unfamiliar words using word-learning strategies.

To learn more about the vocabulary standards, go to http://www.corestandards.org, or check your state's language arts standards.

PreK Spotlight

Do young children really need explicit vocabulary instruction?

You might be surprised that vocabulary instruction is an essential component of the preschool language arts program. Word knowledge is necessary for reading comprehension, and children's level of word knowledge predicts their later literacy achievement (Cunningham & Stanovich, 1997). PreK teachers typically teach vocabulary as they read aloud picture books. In *One Duck Stuck* (Root, 2003), teachers can target *stuck, deep*, and *slither*, and in *Lunch* (Fleming, 1996), they can focus on *crisp, tend*, and *tart*, for instance. Read-aloud sessions are often recommended as the best way to teach vocabulary because the expressive language and rich illustrations in picture books facilitate word learning. Recently, Silverman and Crandell (2010) examined vocabulary instruction during both read-aloud and non-read-aloud times and concluded that a focus on words should be infused throughout the school day. They recommended these instructional techniques:

Acting Out and Illustrating Words. Teachers dramatize and show pictures of targeted words as they're reading aloud or during other language arts activities. This technique is effective for children with low levels of vocabulary development but not for those with higher levels.

Defining Words Explicitly in Rich Context. Teachers explicitly define targeted words as they're reading aloud or during a discussion so children understand what the word means and how to use it. This technique is effective for everyone, but more useful for children with higher levels of word knowledge. The researchers speculated that children with less vocabulary development need more scaffolding than conversations provide.

Viewing Words. Teachers write targeted words on a whiteboard and draw children's attention to some of the sounds and letters in them. This technique is effective for all children during both read-aloud and non-read-aloud sessions.

Applying Words in New Contexts. Teachers encourage children to use targeted words and to make personal connections to them. This technique is effective for all children, but especially for those with higher levels of vocabulary knowledge.

The researchers' most far-reaching conclusion is that children's level of vocabulary knowledge influences the effectiveness of instructional techniques. In particular, children with less vocabulary knowledge need more scaffolding than those with higher levels of development.

ASSESSMENT. Teachers assess both the depth and the breadth of students' vocabulary knowledge. When teachers choose assessment techniques based on their instructional goals, they can evaluate both how well students understand the words they've studied and the range of words they learned.

Vocabulary instruction fits into all four patterns of practice, as shown in the box on page 228. Teachers apply Blachowicz and Fisher's guidelines as they teach vocabulary. During thematic units, for example, teachers, like Ms. Boland in the vignette at the beginning of the chapter, highlight important words on word walls and teach minilessons using these words.

The goal of vocabulary instruction is to develop students' *word consciousness*, their interest in learning and using words (Graves & Watts-Taffe, 2008). According to Scott and Nagy (2004), word consciousness is "essential for vocabulary growth and comprehending the language of schooling" (p. 201). Students who have word consciousness exemplify these characteristics:

- Students use words skillfully, understanding the nuances of word meanings.
- Students gain a deep appreciation of words and value them.
- Students are aware of differences between social and academic language.
- Students understand the power of word choice.
- Students are motivated to learn the meaning of unfamiliar words.

Developing students' word consciousness is important because vocabulary knowledge is generative—that is, it enhances their learning of other words.

Targeting Words to Teach

Teachers often feel overwhelmed when they think about all of the unfamiliar words in a book students are reading or in a thematic unit they're teaching. Of course, it's not possible to teach every unfamiliar word. Teachers need to target high-utility words—those that are most important to understand the book or the big ideas in the unit and common enough that students can use them in other contexts.

Words have different levels of usefulness. Some words, such as *comfortable* and *lonely,* are words that we use frequently; others, such as *brawny, frolic,* and *tolerate,* are less common but still useful. In contrast, other words, such as *bailey* and *nebula,* are more specialized and used infrequently. Beck, McKeown, and Kucan (2002) classified words into three tiers:

TIER 1 WORDS. This tier includes basic, everyday words that don't usually have to be taught in school.

TIER 2 WORDS. This tier includes academic words that students need to learn in school.

TIER 3 WORDS. This tier includes specialized words related to thematic units and uncommon words that students may not need to learn before high school.

Teachers target Tier 2 words because they're academic vocabulary—words that students need to learn to be successful in school.

How Vocabulary Fits Into the Patterns of Practice

Literature Focus Units

Students post key words on the word wall and participate in activities, including word maps and word sorts, during the exploring stage of the reading process.

Literature Circles

Students identify key words in books they're reading, check their meanings in a dictionary, and talk about them as they participate in literature circle discussions.

Reading and Writing Workshop

Students learn hundreds of new words incidentally as they use word-learning strategies while reading books and listening to the teacher read books aloud.

Thematic Units

Students post key words on a word wall and participate in a variety of activities, including tea party, word chains, and semantic feature analysis.

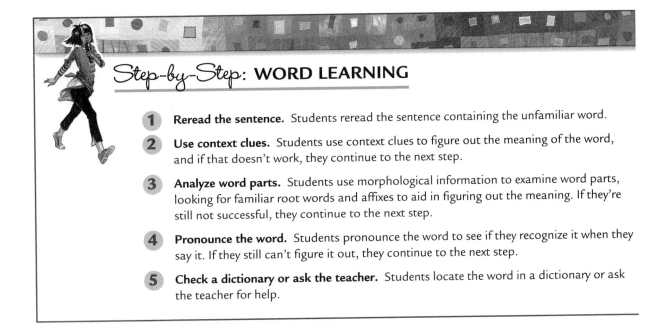

Step-by-Step: **WORD LEARNING**

1 **Reread the sentence.** Students reread the sentence containing the unfamiliar word.

2 **Use context clues.** Students use context clues to figure out the meaning of the word, and if that doesn't work, they continue to the next step.

3 **Analyze word parts.** Students use morphological information to examine word parts, looking for familiar root words and affixes to aid in figuring out the meaning. If they're still not successful, they continue to the next step.

4 **Pronounce the word.** Students pronounce the word to see if they recognize it when they say it. If they still can't figure it out, they continue to the next step.

5 **Check a dictionary or ask the teacher.** Students locate the word in a dictionary or ask the teacher for help.

Instead of teaching 50 or more unfamiliar words from a book or a thematic unit, teachers focus on Tier 2 words. These questions help teachers choose appropriate words for instruction:

- Is the word necessary to understand the book or the big idea?
- Do students already understand the concept?
- Can students explain the unfamiliar word using words they already know?
- Can students use the word in other contexts?

After considering these questions, teachers target 5 to 10 words or more, depending on the grade level, to teach.

Word-Learning Strategies

If you ask students what they do when they're reading and come across an unfamiliar word, they're likely to report sounding it out, looking for context clues in the surrounding sentence, skipping over it, and asking the teacher. Some techniques, however, work better than others. Graves (2006) identified these effective strategies:

- Use context clues
- Analyze word parts
- Check a dictionary

Students need to learn what to do when they encounter an unfamiliar word. Graves recommends the procedure for identifying unfamiliar words outlined in the Step-by-Step feature above.

Using Context Clues. Students learn many words from context. The surrounding words and sentences offer context clues; some provide information about the meaning of a word, and others provide information about the part of speech and how the word is used in a sentence. This contextual information helps students infer the meaning of the unfamiliar word. Illustrations also provide useful contextual information. Students use six types of context clues to identify words:

DEFINITION. Students use the definition in the sentence to understand the unfamiliar word.

EXAMPLE-ILLUSTRATION. Students use an example or illustration to understand the unfamiliar word.

COMPARISON-CONTRAST. Students understand the unfamiliar word because it's compared or contrasted with another word in the sentence.

LOGIC. Students think about the rest of the sentence to understand the unfamiliar word.

MORPHOLOGY. Students use their knowledge of root words and affixes to figure out the unfamiliar word.

GRAMMAR. Students use the word's function in the sentence or its part of speech to figure out the unfamiliar word.

Interestingly, two or three types of contextual information are often found in the same sentence.

The best way to teach context clues is by modeling. When teachers are reading aloud, they stop at an unfamiliar word and do a think-aloud to show students how they use context clues to figure out its meaning. When the context provides enough information, teachers use the information and continue reading, but when the rest of the sentence or paragraph doesn't provide enough information, teachers use another strategy to figure out the word.

Analyzing Word Parts. Students use their knowledge of morphology (i.e., affixes and root words) to unlock many multisyllabic words when they understand how word parts function. Teaching derivational prefixes and suffixes and non-English root words in fourth through eighth grades improves students' ability to unlock the meaning of unfamiliar words (Baumann, Font, Edwards, & Boland, 2005; Kieffer & Lesaux, 2010). For example, when students recognize that the Latin roots *quad* and *quart* mean "one fourth" or "four," they can figure out the meanings of these words: *quart* (one-fourth of a gallon), *quadruple* (four times), *quartet* (group of four), *quadrennial* (once every four years), *quarter* (one of four equal parts), and *quadruped* (having four feet). Graves (2006) recommends that teachers teach morphemic analysis when non-English root words appear in books students are reading and during thematic units.

Checking a Dictionary. Looking up unfamiliar words in the dictionary is often frustrating because the definitions don't provide enough useful information or because words used in a definition are forms of the word being defined. And, sometimes the definition that students choose—usually the first one—is the wrong one. Or, the definition doesn't make sense. Dictionary definitions are most useful when students are vaguely familiar with the word's meaning, so teachers play an important role in dictionary work: They teach students how to read a dictionary entry and decide which definitions make sense, and they model the strategy when they're reading aloud and come across a word that's unfamiliar to most students. They also assist students by explaining the definitions that students locate, providing sample sentences, and comparing the word to related words and opposites.

Word Walls

The best way to focus students' attention on words is to write important words on word-wall charts and post them in the classroom. Teachers hang blank word walls made from large sheets

Step-by-Step: WORD WALLS

1. **Prepare the word wall.** Teachers hang a long sheet of butcher paper on a wall in the classroom, divide it into 12 to 16 boxes, and label the boxes with letters of the alphabet.

2. **Introduce the word wall.** Teachers introduce the word wall and write several key words on it as part of preparing activities before reading.

3. **Add words to the word wall.** After reading a picture book or a chapter in a longer book, students suggest "important" words for the word wall. Students and the teacher write the words on the word wall, making sure to write large enough so that most students can see them. If a word is misspelled, it should be corrected because students will be using the word in various activities. Sometimes the teacher adds a small picture or writes a synonym for a difficult word, puts a box around the root word, or writes the plural form or other related words nearby.

4. **Use the word wall for exploring activities.** Students use the word wall for a variety of activities, and teachers expect them to spell the words correctly. During literature focus units, students refer to the word wall when they're writing in reading logs, doing word sorts, or working on projects. During thematic units, students use the word wall in similar ways.

5. **Write the words on word cards.** Teachers transfer the words from the word wall to word cards at the end of the unit. They can write the words on index cards, sentence strips, or small sheets of decorated paper that reflect the unit's topic. They punch holes in one corner of the cards and use metal rings or yarn to make a booklet. They place the word booklets in the vocabulary center for students to refer to as needed.

of butcher paper that have been divided into alphabetized sections. Students and the teacher write key terms on the word wall, either from books they're reading or topics they're learning during thematic units. Usually students choose the words to add to the word wall, and they may even do the writing themselves. Teachers add any important words that students don't choose. Words are added as they come up rather than in advance. The procedure for creating a word wall is described in the Step-by-Step feature above.

The words written on word walls during literature focus units are usually Tier 2 words. They're essential to understanding the book, as well as words students will need to read other books. During thematic units, the focus is on Tier 3 technical terms. Even though 50 to 100 words are often added to the word wall, not all will be directly taught. As they plan, teachers create lists of words that they anticipate will be written on word walls during the unit; they identify which words will be recognizable sight words for their students and which words represent new concepts, new words, and new meanings for them. From this list, teachers target the key words—the ones that are critical to understanding the book or the unit—and these are the words they plan to teach. They also identify any words that must be introduced before reading or at the beginning of the unit. According to Vygotsky's notion of a "zone of proximal development," teachers need recognize that some students have more background knowledge and are familiar with more words on a topic so they differentiate instruction to meet students' needs and provide a minilesson when students are most interested in learning about words.

Identifying some words on the word wall as key words doesn't mean the others aren't important. Students have many opportunities to use all the word wall words as they write and talk about what they're learning. For example, students often refer to the word wall to locate a specific word they want to use to make a point during a discussion or to check the spelling of a word they're writing in a reading log or in a report. Teachers also use the words listed on the word wall for word-study activities.

Word-Study Activities

Word-study activities provide opportunities for students to explore the meanings of words listed on word walls, other words related to books they're reading, and words they're learning during social studies or science units. In these activities, students explore the word meanings and make associations among words:

WORD POSTERS. Students choose a word from the word wall and write it on a small poster. Then they draw a picture to illustrate the word and write a sentence using the word to describe their drawing.

WORD MAPS. Students create diagrams known as *word maps* to highlight a word and its meanings. They present information about the word, including its etymology, word forms, related words, and meanings. The information that's included depends on students' knowledge of the word and the word itself. Figure 8–7 shows two word maps; a fourth grader created the *alien* word map, and a fifth grader created the *repel* map.

DRAMATIZING WORDS. Students play a guessing game that's similar to charades. One student chooses a word from the word wall and acts it out for classmates to guess. Through dramatization, students use physical activity rather than language to convey the word's meaning.

WORD SORTS. Students sort a collection of words taken from the word wall into two or more categories (Bear, Invernizzi, Templeton, & Johnston, 2008). Usually students choose

FIGURE 8–7   Two Students' Word Maps

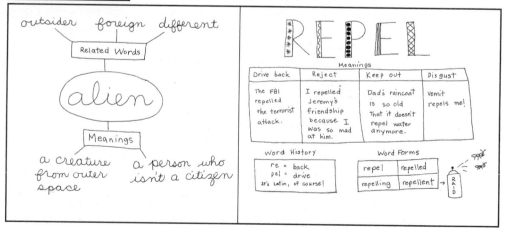

FIGURE 8–8   A Word Sort on the American Colonies

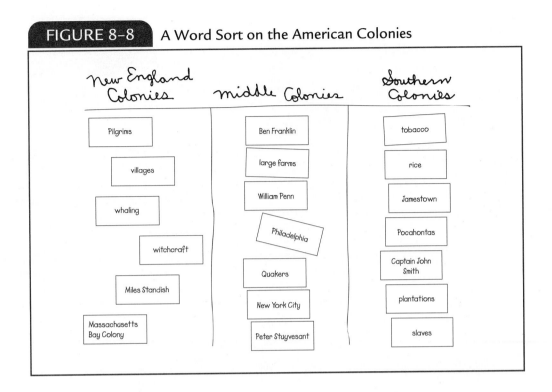

the categories for the sort, but sometimes the teacher chooses. For example, words from a story might be sorted by character, or words from a thematic unit on machines might be sorted according to type of machine. The words can be written on cards, and then students sort the words into categories and paste them on a sheet of paper. Figure 8–8 shows fifth graders' word sort about the 13 colonies. They identified the categories—New England colonies, middle colonies, and Southern colonies—and sorted word cards for each category. Then they glued the word cards onto a large sheet of paper.

MENTOR TEXTS. Teachers use books to teach vocabulary. *Zin! Zin! Zin! A Violin* (Moss, 2005), for instance, explains words for groups of musicians (e.g., *solo, duo, trio, quartet*), and Ruth Heller introduces *batch, school, fleet, bevy,* and *flock* in *A Cache of Jewels and Other Collective Nouns* (1998). Other useful mentor texts are presented in the Booklist on page 234.

TEA PARTY. Teachers prepare a set of cards with text (sentences or paragraphs) from a book students are reading. At least one word from the word wall is included in each excerpt, and the word is highlighted. Students have a "tea party": They read the cards to classmates and talk about the highlighted word and its meaning. Sometimes teachers write the definition of the word or a synonym on the back of the card.

WORD CHAINS. Students choose a word from the word wall and then identify three or four related words to make a chain. For example, the word *tadpole* can be chained this way: *egg, tadpole, frog;* and the word *aggravate* can be chained like this: *irritate, bother, aggravate, annoy.* Students write their chains on a sheet of paper or make a construction paper chain and write the words on each link.

Booklist

VOCABULARY	
PreK–Grade 2	DeGross, M. (1998). *Donovan's word jar*. New York: HarperCollins. Mammano, J. (2001). *Rhinos who play soccer*. San Francisco: Chronicle Books. (Check other books in the series.) Moss, L. (2005). *Zin! Zin! Zin! A violin*. New York: Aladdin Books. O'Connor, J. (2008). *Fancy Nancy's favorite fancy words: From accessories to zany*. New York: HarperCollins.
Grades 3–5	Barretta, G. (2007). *Dear deer: A book of homophones*. New York: Henry Holt. Cleary, B. P. (2007). *How much can a bare bear bear? What are homonyms and homophones?* New York: First Avenue Editions. Clements, A. (1998). *Frindle*. New York: Atheneum. Falwell, C. (2006). *Word wizard*. New York: Sandpiper. Frasier, D. (2000). *Miss Alaineus: A vocabulary disaster*. San Diego: Harcourt Brace. Heller, R. (1998). *A cache of jewels and other collective nouns*. New York: Putnam. Melmed, L. K. (2009). *Heart of Texas: A lone star ABC*. New York: HarperCollins. Napier, M. (2002). *Z is for Zamboni: A hockey alphabet*. Farmington Hills, MI: Sleeping Bear Press. Pallotta, J. (2006). *The construction alphabet book*. Watertown, MA: Charlesbridge. (See other alphabet books by this author.)
Grades 6–8	Agee, J. (2009). *Palindromania!* New York: Farrar, Straus & Giroux. (See other books by this author.) Bauer, P. (2009). *B is for battle cry: A Civil War alphabet*. Farmington Hills, MI: Sleeping Bear Press. Evans, D. (2004). *MVP**. Blodgett, OR: Hand Print Press. Fine, E. H. (2004). *Cryptomania! Teleporting into Greek and Latin with the Cryptokids*. Berkeley, CA: Tricycle Press. Lederer, R., & Morice, D. (1998). *Word circus: A letter-perfect book*. Springfield, MA: Merriam Webster. Terban, M. (2006). *Building your vocabulary and making it great!* New York: Scholastic. Terban, M. (2006). *The Scholastic dictionary of idioms*. New York: Scholastic.

SEMANTIC FEATURE ANALYSIS. Teachers select a group of related words, such as characters in a novel or names of birds, and make a grid to classify them according to distinguishing characteristics. A semantic feature analysis that Ms. Boland's class created during their thematic unit on medieval life is presented in Figure 8–9. This activity reinforces students' organization of knowledge and related words into schemata (Pittelman, Heimlich, Berglund, & French, 1991).

Traditional vocabulary instruction involved assigning students to look up the definitions of a list of words in a dictionary and use the words in sentences, but this approach often failed to produce in-depth understanding.

Minilessons

Teachers teach minilessons about specific words as well as word-learning strategies (Baumann & Kame'enui, 2004). Teachers provide in-depth information about specific words, including one or more meanings, root words, related words, and the word's etymology, and they provide multiple opportunities for students to actively investigate the word. To teach word-learning strategies, they explain and demonstrate strategies for unlocking word meanings, such as peeling off affixes or using the root to determine the word's meaning. A minilesson showing how a sixth grade teacher explains how related words developed from English, Latin, and Greek root words is presented on page 236.

FIGURE 8–9 A Semantic Feature Analysis on Medieval Life

	castle	knights	peasants	Crusades	cathedral
apprentice	O	✓	O	O	O
bailey	✓	O	O	O	O
Black Death	O	✓	✓	O	O
chivalry	O	✓	O	O	O
clergy	O	O	O	?	✓
flying buttress	O	O	O	O	✓
jousts	O	✓	O	O	O
mercenary	O	?	O	✓	O
moat	✓	O	O	O	O
pilgrims	O	?	O	✓	O
portcullis	✓	O	O	O	O
serf	O	O	✓	O	O
siege	✓	O	O	O	O
tournament	O	✓	O	O	O
villein	O	O	✓	O	O

Code: ✓ = yes   O = no   ? = don't know

Minilesson

Mrs. Monroe Teaches Her Sixth Graders About Word Histories

1. Introduce the Topic

Sixth graders brainstorm a list of words about teeth, including *teeth, toothbrush, floss, dentist, cavities, cleaning, tooth fairy, dental, orthodontist, braces,* and *dentures,* and then Mrs. Monroe points out that it seems odd that *toothbrush, dentist,* and *orthodontist* are related to teeth but look so different.

2. Share Examples

Mrs. Monroe explains that many words about teeth come from three root words—*tooth* (English), *dent* (Latin), and *dont* (Greek). Students sort the words from the brainstormed list into four columns:

tooth	dent	dont	other
teeth	dentist	orthodontist	floss
toothbrush	dental		cavities
tooth fairy	dentures		braces

She points out that Latin and Greek words are likely to be medical or scientific.

3. Provide Information

Mrs. Monroe explains that there are other trios of related words:

star (E), *stell* (L), and *astr* (Gr)
sound (E), *sono* (L), and *phon* (Gr)
people (E), *pop* (L), and *demo* (Gr)
foot (E), *ped* (L), and *pod* (Gr)
water (E), *aqua* (L), and *hydro* (Gr)

The students brainstorm some examples of the trios and ask why words come from different root words. The teacher explains that many English words were borrowed from other languages because people wanted to be able to express various ideas, and that at different historical times, the English liked to invent new words from other languages, especially Latin and Greek.

4. Supervise Practice

Mrs. Monroe divides the class into five groups and gives each group a set of word cards representing a different trio of words. The students read the word cards, check the meanings of any unfamiliar words, sort the words, glue the sorted words on a poster, and add other related words.

5. Reflect on Learning

Students share their posters with the class and marvel at the complexity of English.

INTEGRATING TECHNOLOGY

Teachers use digital tools to interest and engage students in vocabulary activities. Not surprisingly, students overwhelmingly prefer looking up words using online dictionaries rather than using print resources, for example. Here are a variety of free web-based programs and other digital tools for teaching vocabulary:

VOCABULARY CLOUDS. Students use Wordle (http://www.wordle.net) to make word clouds with text they provide. The clouds give greater prominence to more frequently used words. Students can tweak the clouds using a variety of fonts, layouts, and color schemes.

Students make Wordles featuring a targeted vocabulary word, its definition, synonyms and antonyms, and related words. Or, as an alternative, teachers prepare a Wordle with the targeted vocabulary words in one color and their synonyms or antonyms in another; then students match the words.

CROSSWORD PUZZLES. Students and teachers use free software to create crossword puzzles using targeted vocabulary words and their definitions. Check these sites: Create Your Own Crossword (http://www.armoredpenguin.com/crossword), Eclipse Crossword (http://www.eclipsecrossword.com), and Puzzlemaker (http://www.discoveryeducation.com/free-puzzlemaker).

VIRTUAL WORD WALLS. Teachers generate virtual word walls using Wallwisher (http://www.wallwisher.com), and students post virtual sticky notes with photos, diagrams, and definitions for each word.

COMIC STRIPS. Students use ToonDoo (http://www.toondoo.com), a free web-based comics maker, to develop cartoons with targeted vocabulary words. This website bills itself as the "fastest way to create comics," and it's easy to do with just a few clicks and drag and drops needed to create a cartoon.

VIDEO CLIPS. Students use digital video cameras to film classmates dramatizing targeted words, and then classmates view the video clips.

SCAVENGER HUNTS. Students search the Internet to find photos and clip art to illustrate targeted words. Teachers often bookmark Photos8 (http://www.photos8.com), Pics4Learning (http://pics4learning.com), or other public domain image sites for students to use. This activity is a good way for less computer-savvy students to learn how to access websites.

Because these technology resources make word study more fun, students are likely to spend more time studying targeted words and to deepen their level of vocabulary knowledge. ■

Differentiating Instruction

Teachers have two purposes for differentiating vocabulary instruction: First, to increase students' interest and engagement in expanding their knowledge of academic vocabulary, and second, to tailor instruction to accommodate students' needs. They provide students with different routes to learn academic vocabulary by varying instructional techniques, activities, grouping patterns, and pacing:

TALK. Teachers encourage students to talk about words they're learning and related words.

GAMES. Teachers involve students in vocabulary games, such as word sorts, to provide needed practice with academic vocabulary.

ROLE-PLAYING. Teachers involve students in role-playing to demonstrate meanings of targeted vocabulary words and to apply new vocabulary knowledge.

TECHNOLOGY. Teachers use digital tools to interest students in studying vocabulary words.

READING ALOUD. Teachers teach targeted vocabulary words and demonstrate word-learning strategies while reading aloud.

MINILESSONS. Teachers provide additional instruction and guided practice activities.

VISUALLY REPRESENTING. Teachers have students use images to define words and create graphics and posters to share information about them.

WIDE READING. Teachers provide opportunities for students to do independent reading.

Middle School Spotlight

How do teachers teach academic vocabulary to struggling middle school students?

Most struggling middle school students, including those who are English learners or who come from low-income backgrounds, have gaps in their vocabulary knowledge and lack the academic language that they need for school success. These students can't rely on learning words through wide reading as their higher achieving classmates do because they read less often, encounter less grade-level academic vocabulary, and apply only a limited number of word-learning strategies. In addition, they can't use surrounding known words to figure out the meaning of an unknown word because their ratio of known to unknown words is too low. Kelley, Lesaux, Kieffer, and Faller (2010) urge teachers to provide vocabulary instruction to struggling middle school students that embodies these five principles:

Target High-Utility Academic Words for Instruction. Teachers choose the most useful academic vocabulary to teach rather than less frequently used words. Many school districts have developed grade-level lists of academic vocabulary, or teachers can consult another academic word list, such as Marzano's (2004).

Teach a Small Number of Words in Depth. Teachers develop lessons using the six language modes to build full word knowledge, including multiple meanings, semantically related words, and other morphological forms (e.g., *explode–explosion–explosive*).

Anchor the Words in Engaging Text. Teachers use appropriate and appealing nonfiction texts written at appropriate reading levels to introduce academic vocabulary. For example, the researchers used articles from *Time for Kids* in their study.

Provide Multiple Exposures to Each Word. Teachers focus on a set of words for a week and plan several activities involving the words. The researchers used each word approximately 10 times during the week.

Balance Instructional Time Between Teaching Individual Words and Word-Learning Strategies. In addition to teaching individual words, teachers teach struggling students how to use context clues and other word-learning strategies to figure out the meaning of unfamiliar words.

By following these principles, teachers can increase the quality and quantity of struggling students' vocabulary knowledge.

Teachers often choose word-study activities using oral, written, and visual language to accommodate students' interests, preferred modalities, and instructional needs. The Differentiated Instruction box on the next page organizes vocabulary activities according to language mode.

ENGAGING ENGLISH LEARNERS

Many English learners have smaller vocabularies than their classmates, and their limited word knowledge impedes their school success. Nonetheless, it's wrong to assume that all English learners have limited vocabularies: Students who have rich vocabularies in their first language learn English words fairly easily because translating words from one language to another is much easier than learning new words and concepts. Teachers differentiate instruction and support ELs' vocabulary development in a variety of ways.

Meaningful Contexts for Learning. Graves and Fitzgerald (2006) advise teachers to provide rich, meaningful language experiences for English learners so that they can acquire new vocabulary just like native English speakers do. One way to accomplish this is by reading aloud stories, nonfiction books, and books of poetry. Another way is through independent reading of interesting, age-appropriate books at students' reading levels (Akhavan, 2006). A third way is through thematic units where students expand their background knowledge as they develop concepts and related words (Peregoy & Boyle, 2009).

Useful Words. English learners need explicit instruction to rapidly expand their vocabularies and to develop both conversational English and academic English (M. Graves, 2006). Teachers have to be selective in choosing words to teach because they can't possibly teach all unfamiliar words related to a book students are reading or to a thematic unit. Akhavan (2006) recommends using the word's usefulness as a guide in determining which words to teach; Coxhead's (2000) list of academic vocabulary is a useful tool in choosing words to teach. Whenever possible, teachers group the words they've chosen to teach thematically and focus on related words and the concepts underlying them. Words are posted on the wall so students can read and think about them.

Teaching a word involves more than looking it up in a dictionary and explaining its meanings. Teachers also demonstrate how to pronounce the word, use it in sentences, and spell it. English learners learn best when they're actively engaged in learning words using all six language arts (Peregoy & Boyle, 2009). They can use improvisation, for example, to dramatize how they would use a word in informal conversation, or they can create a diagram to explain its connection to related words.

Word-Learning Strategies. Word-learning strategies are especially important for English learners because they have so many words to learn (Graves & Fitzgerald, 2006; Kieffer & Lesaux, 2010).

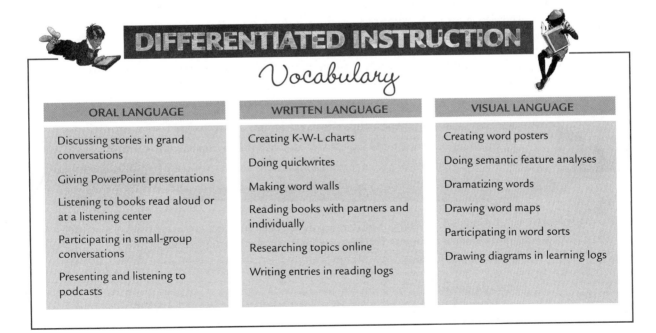

DIFFERENTIATED INSTRUCTION
Vocabulary

ORAL LANGUAGE	WRITTEN LANGUAGE	VISUAL LANGUAGE
Discussing stories in grand conversations	Creating K-W-L charts	Creating word posters
Giving PowerPoint presentations	Doing quickwrites	Doing semantic feature analyses
Listening to books read aloud or at a listening center	Making word walls	Dramatizing words
Participating in small-group conversations	Reading books with partners and individually	Drawing word maps
Presenting and listening to podcasts	Researching topics online	Participating in word sorts
	Writing entries in reading logs	Drawing diagrams in learning logs

Students learn these strategies so that they can independently unlock the meaning of unfamiliar words:

CONTEXT CLUES. Students use context to infer the meaning of an unfamiliar word.

MORPHOLOGY. Students apply knowledge of root words and affixes to deduce the meaning of a word and to transform related words.

MULTIPLE MEANINGS. Students consider alternative meanings of a word.

DICTIONARIES. Students use the dictionary to check the meaning of an unfamiliar word.

COGNATES. Students recognize that an English word is similar to a word in their native language (Carlo et al., 2004). Cognates are especially useful for native Spanish speakers because so many English words have Spanish cognates.

Too often, vocabulary instruction is equated with giving students lists of words to look up in the dictionary, but this isn't a worthwhile instructional practice. Instead, Beck, McKeown, and Kucan (2002) emphasize that teaching vocabulary to English learners involves teaching concepts about words so students can make sense of the new information and expand their background knowledge. ■

Assessing Vocabulary Knowledge

Because of the importance of academic vocabulary knowledge, teachers focus on teaching vocabulary and assessing students' learning while they're preparing for instruction, monitoring students' progress during instruction, and evaluating their learning afterward. They also monitor students' use of word-learning strategies and their developing word consciousness.

Planning for Instruction. Teachers identify targeted academic vocabulary when they plan for instruction and incorporate a variety of vocabulary activities to teach words and word-learning strategies. At the beginning of the unit, teachers often check students' knowledge of these words by distributing lists of targeted vocabulary words and asking students to indicate their level of knowledge for each word, ranging from "I don't know this word" and "I've heard this word before, but I don't really know it" to "I know several ways to use this word."

Monitoring Progress. Teachers monitor how students incorporate targeted words in activities involving all six language arts, using these techniques:

- Check students' reading logs, learning logs, or simulated journals for targeted words
- Examine students' word maps or other diagrams about targeted words
- Listen for students to use targeted words when they participate in discussions
- Ask students to talk about and write reflections about their use of word-learning strategies
- Notice students' enthusiasm for adding words to the word wall and participating in vocabulary activities

These formative assessment techniques assure that students are progressing; when they aren't making adequate progress, teachers modify instruction, and if that doesn't work, they implement classroom-based and schoolwide interventions.

Evaluating Learning. Teachers evaluate students' learning of targeted vocabulary by examining how they incorporate targeted words in the projects they create and asking them to self-assess their vocabulary. They often ask students to reflect on their word knowledge, strategy use, and word consciousness in self-assessment letters that they write at the end of a unit of study. It's rarely beneficial to administer tests to evaluate students' knowledge of vocabulary because correct answers on a test don't indicate whether students are applying words in meaningful and genuine ways or developing word consciousness.

SUMMING UP

English is a historical language, and its diverse origins account for many meaning and spelling inconsistencies. Few words have only one meaning, and students gradually learn multiple meanings as well as root words and affixes, homonyms, synonyms, antonyms, and idioms. The fact that students' vocabularies grow at a rate of about 3,000 to 4,000 words a year suggests that they learn many words incidentally; reading and writing are the most important ways students learn vocabulary, but direct instruction is also important. Words are not all equally difficult or easy to learn; the degree of difficulty depends on what students already know. Teachers also teach word-learning strategies; their goal is to develop students' word consciousness. The best measure of vocabulary development is students' ability to use the words in meaningful ways.

MyEducationLab™

Go to the topic Vocabulary in the MyEducationLab (http://www.myeducationlab.com) for *Language Arts: Patterns of Practice*, where you can:

- Find learning outcomes for Vocabulary, along with the national standards that connect to these outcomes.
- Complete Assignments and Activities that can help you more deeply understand the chapter content.
- Apply and practice your understanding of the core teaching skills identified in the chapter with the Building Teaching Skills and Dispositions learning units.
- Examine challenging situations and cases presented in the IRIS Center Resources.
- Use the Lesson Plan Builder Activities to practice lesson planning and integrating national and state standards into your planning.
- Check your comprehension of the content covered in the chapter with the Study Plan. Here you will be able to take a chapter quiz, receive feedback on your answers, and then access Review, Practice, and Enrichment activities to enhance your understanding of chapter content.

On the **MyEducationLab** for this course, you'll also be able to:

- **A+RISE** Go to the topic A+RISE, an innovative and interactive database of strategies that differentiate instruction across the language arts and provide particular insight into research-based methods to meet the needs of English learners.
- Explore the topic Literacy Portraits—yearlong case studies of second graders, complete with student artifacts, teacher commentary, and student and teacher interviews, tracking the month-by-month language arts growth of five students.
- Gain practice with the Grammar Tutorial, online guided instruction to improve your own ability with grammar.

CHAPTER 9

Comprehending and Composing Stories

FIFTH GRADERS READ A NOVEL Mrs. Ochs teaches a literature focus unit on *Number the Stars* (Lowry, 2011), a Newbery award–winning story of two girls, one Christian and one Jewish, set in Denmark during World War II. In the unit, she wants to help her fifth grade students use their knowledge of genre and story structure to deepen their comprehension of the story. She rereads the story, analyzes the elements of story structure in the book, and considers how she wants to teach the unit. The box on page 244 shows her analysis of the novel.

To begin, Mrs. Ochs asks about friendship: "Would you help your friend if he or she needed help?" The students talk about friendship and what it means to them. They agree that they would help their friends in any way they could—helping them get medical treatment if they were ill, and sharing their lunch if they were hungry, for example. One student volunteers that he's sure that his mom would let his friend's family stay at his house if the friend's house burned down. Then Mrs. Ochs asks, "What if your friend asked you to hold something for him or her, something so dangerous that 70 years ago you could be killed for having it?" Many say they would, but doubt they'd ever be called on to do that. Then she shows them a broken Star of David necklace, similar to the one on the cover of *Number the Stars,* and one student says, "You're talking about the Nazis and the Jews in World War II." The prereading stage continues for several days as students share what they know about the war, and Mrs. Ochs presents information, reads several picture books about the war, and shows a video.

Mrs. Ochs reads the first chapter of *Number the Stars* aloud as students follow along in individual copies. She begins this way because she wants to get all students off to

How can teachers facilitate students' comprehension of stories?

Teachers include activities at each stage of the reading process to ensure that students comprehend what they're reading. This attention to comprehension is essential because when students don't understand, the experience has been wasted. As you read this vignette, notice how Mrs. Ochs involves her fifth graders in language arts activities to deepen their understanding of World War II and facilitate their comprehension of *Number the Stars*.

a good start and because many difficult concepts, such as Resistance fighters, are introduced early in the novel. After the first chapter, most students read independently, but some read with buddies, and Mrs. Ochs continues reading with a group of struggling readers.

Next, Mrs. Ochs brings the class together for a grand conversation. The students make connections between the information they've learned about World War II and the story events. Mrs. Ochs reads aloud *The Yellow Star: The Legend of King Christian X of Denmark* (Deedy, 2000), a picture-book story about the Danish king who defies the Nazis, because the king is the focus of the second chapter. The students predict that the Nazis will take Ellen and her family to a concentration camp even though Annemarie and her family try to hide them. After the grand conversation, the students write in reading logs. For this entry, Mrs. Ochs asks them to write predictions about what will happen in the story based on what they know about World War II and what they've read in the first two chapters.

Mrs. Ochs continues having the students read and respond to the chapters. Some read independently, but many form groups so that they can read and talk about the story as they're reading. Mrs. Ochs continues reading with the struggling readers. The whole class comes together after reading each day to talk about the story in a grand conversation. Afterward, they write in journals.

During the grand conversations, Mrs. Ochs probes students' understanding and asks them to think about the role of plot, characters, setting, and other elements of story structure. Mrs. Ochs's students know about the elements, so they're able to apply their knowledge to whichever story they're reading. One day, she asks about the conflict situation. At first the students say that the conflict is between people—Nazis and Danes—but as they continue talking, they realize that the conflict is not between individual people, but within society.

Another day, Mrs. Ochs talks about the setting. She asks if this story could have happened in the United States. At first the students say no, because the Nazis never invaded the United States, and they use maps to make their point. But as they continue talking,

Mrs. Ochs's Story Analysis		
Element	**Story Analysis**	**Teaching Ideas**
Plot	The beginning is before Ellen goes into hiding; the middle is while Ellen is hiding; and the end is after Ellen and her family leave for the safety of Sweden. The problem is saving Ellen's life.	Build background knowledge about World War II, the Nazis, Jews and the holocaust, and Resistance fighters before reading. There are many details, so it's important to focus on the problem and how to solve it.
Characters	Annemarie and Ellen are the main characters. Through their actions and beliefs, readers learn that the girls are more alike than different. They're both courageous, one because she has to be, the other because she chooses to be.	Even though one girl is Christian and one is Jewish, the girls are more alike than they are different. Use a Venn diagram to emphasize this point. Students can make open-mind portraits showing one girl's viewpoint.
Setting	The story is set in Denmark during World War II. The setting is integral to the plot and based on actual events, including fishermen ferrying Jews to safety in Sweden.	Use maps of Europe to locate the setting. Students can draw maps and mark story locations, and they can mark the spread of the German and Japanese forces on a world map.
Point of View	The story is limited omniscient. It's told from the third-person viewpoint, and readers know only what Annemarie is thinking.	Have students retell important events from Ellen's perspective or from the parents' or the Nazis' viewpoints.
Theme	This story deals with courage: the Jews; the Resistance fighters; King Christian X, who wore a yellow star on his clothes; and Annemarie and her family. One theme is that people choose to be courageous when others are mistreated.	Ask students to focus on the theme as they talk in grand conversations and collect favorite quotes from the story. Students might also read about other courageous people to examine the qualities of courage.

students broaden their discussion to the persecution of minorities, including the mistreatment of Native Americans and internment of Japanese Americans during World War II, and conclude that persecution can happen anywhere.

During the grand conversation after students finish reading *Number the Stars,* Mrs. Ochs asks about the theme. "Did Lois Lowry have a message in her book? What do you think about the theme?" Several students comment that the theme was that the Nazis were bad people. Others said "innocent people get killed in wars" and "peace is better than war." To move the students forward in their thinking, Mrs. Ochs suggests that one theme is about courage. She reads two sentences from the book: "That's all that *brave* means—not thinking about the dangers. Just thinking about what you must do" (p. 123). The students agree that both girls and their families were brave. Mrs. Ochs asks students to think back through the story and help her brainstorm a list of the times they were brave. Together, they brainstormed more than 30 instances of courage!

Mrs. Ochs and her students continue their discussion about the theme for several more days. Finally, she asks them, "Do you think you're brave? Would you be brave if you were Annemarie or Ellen?" They talk about war and having to be brave in a war. "What about Ellen?" Mrs. Ochs asks. "Did she *have* to be brave?" The students agree that she did. "But what about Annemarie? Couldn't she and her family have stayed safely in Copenhagen?" The students are surprised by the question, but through their discussion, they realize that Annemarie, her family, and the other Resistance fighters chose to be brave.

As the students read *Number the Stars,* Mrs. Ochs also involves them in exploring-stage activities focusing on the story's structure. For example, to compare characters, they make Venn diagrams and conclude that Annemarie and Ellen are more alike than they are different; one student's Venn diagram is shown below. They also make open-mind portraits of one character, showing what that girl is thinking at pivotal points in the novel. The portrait and one page from a student's open-mind portrait of Ellen are shown on page 246.

The students plan an applying-stage activity after one student brings his great-grandfather to school to talk about his remembrances of World War II. Afterward, students decide to each interview a great-grandparent or an elderly neighbor who was alive during the war. They develop this set of interview questions:

- *What did you do during the war?*
- *How old were you?*

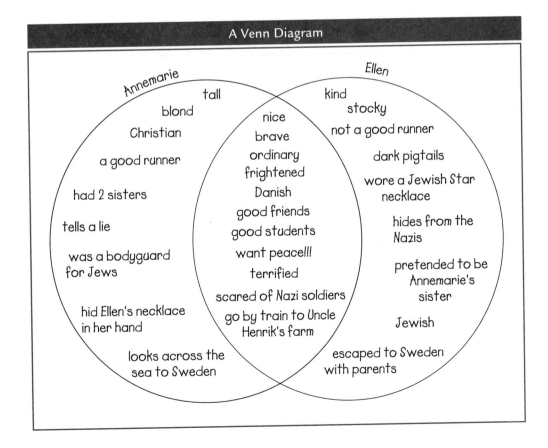

A Venn Diagram

Annemarie — tall, blond, Christian, a good runner, had 2 sisters, tells a lie, was a bodyguard for Jews, hid Ellen's necklace in her hand, looks across the sea to Sweden

Both (center) — nice, brave, ordinary, frightened, Danish, good friends, good students, want peace!!!, terrified, scared of Nazi soldiers, go by train to Uncle Henrik's farm

Ellen — kind, stocky, not a good runner, dark pigtails, wore a Jewish Star necklace, hides from the Nazis, pretended to be Annemarie's sister, Jewish, escaped to Sweden with parents

---

An Open-Mind Portrait

Ellen Rosen

Can the Nazis smell me? I am SO scared I can hear there boots on the deck. Now what do I hear? Its my friend Annemarie! My mom squeezes my hand to be still. She hears her too. She must think I will call her name, but I won't. Someday when the war is over I will come back to Copenhagen and be your best friend again. I will come home when it is safe and I am free once again.

- *Were you on the home front or the war front?*
- *Did you know about the Holocaust then?*
- *What do you remember most from World War II?*

Each student conducts an interview and writes a report about the person's wartime experiences. They word process their reports so that they have a professional look. Here's one student's essay:

> *My great-grandfather Arnold Ott was in college at the time the war started. All of a sudden after Pearl Harbor was attacked, all his classmates started to join the army. He did also and became an engineer that worked on B-24 and B-25 bombers. The military kept sending him to different schools so he would be able to fix all the bombers. He never had to fight because of that. He earned some medals, but he said the real ones were only given to those who fought. He said that he was glad that he did not fight because he had friends that never came back.*

Mrs. Ochs duplicates the reports and collates them to make books. The students are so excited about the people they interviewed and the reports they wrote that they decide to celebrate. They invite the interviewees to the party and introduce them to their classmates, and they ask the interviewees to autograph the reports they've written.

Stories give meaning to the human experience, and they're a powerful way of knowing and learning. Preschoolers listen to family members tell and read stories aloud, and through these experiences, they develop an understanding or concept of story by the time they come to school. Students' knowledge about stories is refined as they learn about plot, characters, and the other elements of story structure; folktales, historical fiction, and other story genres; and imagery, symbolism, and other narrative devices. Developing students' concept of story is crucial because it plays an important role in learning to comprehend and compose stories (Golden, Meiners, & Lewis, 1992; Rumelhart, 1975). Story knowledge is dynamic, growing continuously in students' minds, and as they respond to stories they're reading and develop stories they're writing.

CONCEPT OF STORY

Researchers have documented that children's knowledge about stories begins in the preschool years (Applebee, 1978). Children acquire a concept of story gradually, by listening to stories read aloud, by reading stories themselves, and by telling and writing stories. Not surprisingly, older students have a better understanding than younger children do. Similarly, the stories older students tell and write are increasingly more complex; the plot structures are more tightly organized, and the characters are more fully developed. Yet, Applebee found that by the time children who have been read to begin kindergarten, they've already developed a basic concept of story, and this knowledge guides them in telling their own stories. He found, for example, that kindergartners could use three story markers: "Once upon a time . . . " to begin a story; the past tense in telling a story; and formal endings such as "The End" or " . . . and they lived happily ever after."

Elements of Story Structure

Stories have unique structural elements that distinguish them from other forms of literature. In fact, the structure of stories is quite complex—plot, characters, setting, and other elements interact to produce a story. Authors manipulate the elements to make their stories complex and interesting. The five most important elements of story structure are plot, characters, setting, point of view, and theme.

Plot. The sequence of events involving characters in conflict situations is the *plot*. The plot is based on the goals of one or more characters and the processes they go through to attain them (Lukens, 2006). The main characters want to achieve a goal, and other characters are introduced to oppose the main characters or prevent them from being successful. The story events are put in motion by characters as they attempt to overcome conflict, solve problems, and reach their goals.

FIGURE 9–1   A Beginning-Middle-End Map

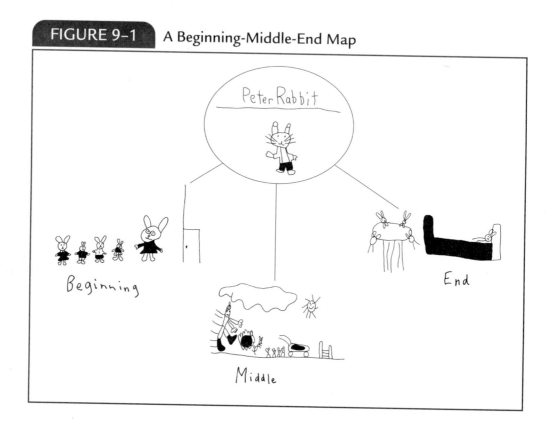

The most basic aspect of plot is the division of a story into three parts—beginning, middle, and end. Sometimes older students substitute the terms *introduction, development* or *complication,* and *resolution.* In *The Tale of Peter Rabbit* (Potter, 2006), for instance, the three story parts are clear: As the story begins, Mrs. Rabbit sends her children out to play after warning them not to go into Mr. McGregor's garden; in the middle, Peter goes to Mr. McGregor's garden and is almost caught; then Peter finds his way out of the garden and gets home safely—the end. Students can cluster the beginning-middle-end of a story using words or pictures, as the map for *The Tale of Peter Rabbit* in Figure 9–1 shows.

Each story part serves a function. In the beginning, the author introduces the characters, describes the setting, and presents a problem; together, the characters, setting, and events develop the plot and sustain the theme throughout the story. In the middle, the author adds to events presented in the beginning, with each event preparing readers for what comes next. Conflict heightens as the characters face roadblocks that keep them from solving their problems. Seeing how the characters tackle these problems adds suspense to keep readers interested. In the end, the author reconciles all that has happened, and readers learn whether the characters' struggles were successful. Mentor texts exemplifying the elements of story structure are presented in the Booklist on the next page.

The plot is developed through the problem that's introduced in the beginning, expanded in the middle, and finally resolved at the end. Plot development involves four components:

A PROBLEM. A problem is presented at the beginning of a story.

ROADBLOCKS. In the middle of the story, characters face roadblocks in attempting to solve the problem.

THE HIGH POINT. The high point in the action occurs when the problem is about to be solved. It separates the middle and the end of the story.

SOLUTION. The problem is solved and the roadblocks are overcome at the end of the story.

The problem is introduced at the beginning, and the main character is faced with trying to solve it; this problem determines the conflict. For example, the problem in Hans Christian Andersen's heartfelt story *The Ugly Duckling* (Pinkney, 1999) is that the big, gray duckling doesn't fit in with the other ducklings, and conflict develops between the ugly duckling and the other ducks.

After the problem's been introduced, authors use conflict to throw roadblocks in the way of an easy solution. As characters remove one roadblock, the author devises another to further

Booklist

STORY STRUCTURES	
Plot	Dahl, R. (2004). *Charlie and the chocolate factory.* New York: Knopf. M Lowry, L. (2011). *Number the stars.* New York: Sandpiper. M Paulsen, G. (2007). *Hatchet.* New York: Simon & Schuster. U Sachar, L. (2008). *Holes.* New York: Farrar, Straus & Giroux. U Soto, G. (1993). *Too many tamales.* New York: Putnam. P Willems, M. (2004). *Knuffle bunny: A cautionary tale.* New York: Hyperion Books. P
Characters	Avi. (2005). *Poppy.* New York: HarperCollins. M Cushman, K. (2005). *Catherine, called Birdy.* New York: HarperCollins. U Henkes, K. (1991). *Chrysanthemum.* New York: Greenwillow. P Marino, N. (2009). *Neil Armstrong is my uncle and other lies Muscle Man McGinty told me.* New York: Roaring Brook Press. M Spinelli, J. (2002). *Maniac Magee.* New York: Scholastic. U Zelinsky, P. O. (1996). *Rumpelstiltskin.* New York: Puffin Books. P–M
Setting	Bunting, E. (1999). *Smoky night.* San Diego: Harcourt. M Curtis, C. P. (2000). *The Watsons go to Birmingham—1963.* New York: Delacorte. M–U Hale, S. (2007). *Princess Academy.* New York: Bloomsbury. M–U Kajikawa, K. (2009). *Tsunami!* New York: Philomel. P–M Patron, S. (2006). *The higher power of lucky.* New York: Atheneum. U Polacco, P. (1997). *Thunder cake.* New York: Putnam. P
Point of View	Creech, S. (2000). *The wanderer.* New York: Scholastic. M–U Fleischman, P. (2004). *Seedfolks.* New York: Harper Trophy. M–U Meddaugh, S. (1995). *Hog-eye.* Boston: Houghton Mifflin. P Ryan, P. M. (2000). *Esperanza rising.* New York: Scholastic. M Schachner, J. (2003). *Skippyjon Jones.* New York: Puffin Books. P Selznick, B. (2007). *The invention of Hugo Cabret.* New York: Scholastic. U
Theme	Avi. (2003). *Nothing but the truth: A documentary novel.* New York: Orchard Books. U Babbitt, N. (2007). *Tuck everlasting.* New York: Square Fish Books. U Hesse, K. (2005). *Witness.* New York: Scholastic. U Law, I. (2009). *Savvy.* New York: Dial Books. M Pinkney, J. (1999). *The ugly duckling.* New York: Morrow. P Steig. W. (2010). *Sylvester and the magic pebble.* New York: Atheneum. P

P = primary grades (preK–2); M = middle grades (3–5); U = upper grades (6–8)

thwart the characters. Postponing the solution by introducing roadblocks is the core of plot development. In *The Ugly Duckling*, the first conflict comes in the yard when the ducks make fun of the main character. The conflict is so great that the duckling goes out into the world and spends a miserable, cold winter in the marsh.

The high point of the action occurs when the solution of the problem hangs in the balance. Tension is high, and readers continue reading to learn whether the main characters solve the problem. With *The Ugly Duckling*, readers are relieved that the duckling has survived the winter, but tension continues because he's still an outcast. Then he flies to a pond and sees some beautiful swans. He flies near to them even though he expects to be scorned.

As the story ends, the problem is solved and the goal is achieved. When he joins the other swans at the pond, they welcome him. He sees his reflection in the water and realizes that he's a swan and is happy at last!

Students make a chart called a *plot profile* to track the tension in a story (Johnson & Louis, 1987). Figure 9-2 presents a plot profile for *Stone Fox* (Gardiner, 2003), a story about a boy who wins a dogsled race to save his grandfather's farm. A class of fourth graders met in small groups to talk about each chapter, and after these discussions, the whole class came together to decide how to mark the chart. At the end of the story, students analyzed the chart and rationalized the tension dips in Chapters 3 and 7: They decided that the story would be too stressful without these dips. Also, students were upset about the abrupt ending to the story and wished it had continued a chapter or two longer so that their tension would have been reduced.

Characters. *Characters*, the people or personified animals in the story, are often the most important element of story structure because many stories are centered on a character. In *Catherine, Called Birdy* (Cushman, 2005), for example, the story focuses on Birdy and her determination

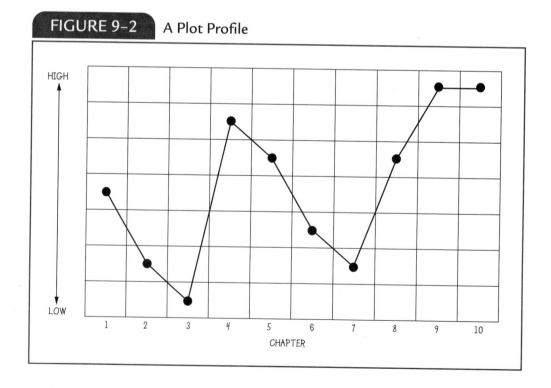

FIGURE 9–2 A Plot Profile

to outwit her father and not be married off to a revolting, shaggy-bearded suitor. Usually, one or two well-rounded characters and several supporting characters are created in a story. Fully developed main characters have many personality traits, both good and bad—that is, they have all the characteristics of real people—and it's essential to understand these traits to comprehend a story. Smith (2005) emphasizes that teachers should introduce their students to character-rich stories. The Booklist on page 249 includes stories with fully developed main characters.

Birdy is the main character in *Catherine, Called Birdy,* and readers get to know her as a real person. Although she's shaped by the culture of medieval England, she challenges the traditional role of "a lady" and is determined to marry someone she cares for, not some rich lord of her father's choosing. Through Birdy's journal entries, readers learn about her activities at the manor, how she helps her mother care for sick and injured people, and her beliefs and superstitions. Readers view events in the story through her eyes and sense her wit as she recounts her daily activities. In contrast, the author tells us little about the supporting characters in the story: Birdy's parents, her brothers, the servants, and the peasants who live and work on her father's lands.

Characters are developed in four ways—through appearance, action, dialogue, and monologue. Authors present the characters to involve readers in the story's experiences. Similarly, readers notice these four types of information as they read in order to understand the characters. Authors generally provide some physical description of the characters when they're introduced. Readers learn about characters by the description of their facial features, body shapes, habits of dress, mannerisms, and gestures. Little emphasis is placed on Birdy's appearance, but Birdy writes that she's unattractive. She squints because of poor eyesight and describes herself as tanned and with gray eyes. She often blackens her teeth and crosses her eyes to make herself more unattractive when her father introduces her to potential suitors.

The second way to learn about characters is through their actions; what a character does is often the best way to know him or her. Birdy writes about picking fleas off her body, doctoring with her mother, keeping birds as pets, traveling to a fair and to a friend's castle, and learning how to sew and embroider. She tells how she prefers being outside and how she sneaks away to visit the goat-boy and other friends who work at the manor.

Dialogue is the third way characters are developed. What characters say is important, but so is how they speak. The register of the characters' language is determined by the social situation: A character might speak less formally with friends than with respected elders or characters in positions of authority. The geographic location of the story, the historical period, and the characters' socioeconomic status also determine how they speak. The language in Birdy's journal entries is often archaic:

"Mayhap I could be a hermit." (p. 130)

"I am full weary tonight . . . " (p. 131)

"Corpus bones. I utterly loathe my life." (p. 133)

Authors also provide insight into characters by revealing their thoughts through monologue. Birdy shares her innermost thoughts in her journal. Readers know how she attempts to thwart her father's plans to marry her off to a rich lord, her worries about her mother's miscarriages, her love for the goat-boy, and her guilt over meddling in Uncle George's love life.

As students examine the main character, they draw conclusions about his or her defining traits. Birdy, for example, is witty, defiant, determined, clever, kindhearted, and superstitious. Teachers work with students to develop a list of character traits, and then students write about one or more of the traits, providing examples from the story to show how the character exemplified the trait. Students can write about character traits in a reading log entry or make

FIGURE 9–3   An Eighth Grader's Character Traits Chart

Will the Real Birdy Please Stand Up?

Trait	Explanation
Defiant	Birdy is defiant because she does not obey her parents. She doesn't want to marry any of the rich men that her father wants her to marry. She does not want to do the needlework that her mother wants her to do. Because she is rebellious, disobedient, and obstinate, she is defiant.
Kindhearted	Birdy is very kindhearted. She is compassionate to the servants and the peasants who are her friends. She treats them like they are as good as her. She is humane because she is like a doctor making medicines and treating sick people. Birdy has a charitable manner; therefore, she is kindhearted.
Clever	Birdy is a clever girl. She manages to get rid of her suitors with ingenious plans. She avoids her mother because she is quick-witted. She is smart for someone in the Middle Ages, but not for someone now. She can even read and write which is unusual for a girl back then. Because she gets her way most of the time, I think she is clever.

a chart. Figure 9–3 shows an eighth grader's chart about Birdy's character traits. Another way students can examine characters and reflect on story events from the character's viewpoint is to draw open-mind portraits, as Mrs. Ochs's students did in the vignette at the beginning of the chapter. These portraits have two parts: The face of the character is on one page, and his or her mind is on the second page. The two pages are stapled together, with the mind page under the face page.

Setting. In some stories, the setting is barely sketched; these settings are *backdrop settings*. The setting in many folktales, for example, is relatively unimportant, and these tales may simply use the convention "Once upon a time . . ." to set the stage. In other stories, the setting is elaborated and is integral to the story's effectiveness; these settings are *integral settings* (Lukens, 2006). Stories with integral settings are included in the Booklist on page 249. The setting is specific, and authors take care to ensure the authenticity of the historical period or geographic location in which the story is set. Four dimensions of setting are location, weather, time period, and time.

Location is an important dimension in many stories. For example, the Boston Public Garden in *Make Way for Ducklings* (McCloskey, 2004) and the Alaskan North Slope in *Julie of the Wolves* (George, 2005) are integral to the effectiveness of those stories. The settings are artfully described and add something unique to the story. In contrast, many stories take place in predictable settings that don't contribute to their effectiveness.

Weather is a second dimension of setting and, like location, it's crucial in some stories. A rainstorm is essential to the plot development in *Bridge to Terabithia* (Paterson, 2006), but at other times, weather isn't mentioned because it doesn't affect the outcome of the story. Many stories take place on warm, sunny days. Think about the impact weather can have on a story; for example, what might have happened if a snowstorm had prevented Little Red Riding Hood from reaching her grandmother's house?

The third dimension is the time period, an important element in stories set in the past or future. If *The Witch of Blackbird Pond* (Speare, 2003), for example, were set in a different era, it would lose much of its impact; today, few people would believe that Kit Tyler is a witch. In stories that take place in the future, such as *A Wrinkle in Time* (L'Engle, 2007), things happen that aren't possible today.

The fourth dimension, time, includes both time of day and the passage of time. Most stories ignore time of day, except for scary stories that take place after dark. In nighttime stories, time is a more important dimension than in stories that take place during the day, because night makes things scarier. Many picture-book stories span a brief period of time, often less than a day, and sometimes less than an hour. Other stories, such as *Charlotte's Web* (White, 2006) and *The Ugly Duckling* (Pinkney, 1999), span a long enough period for the main character to grow to maturity.

Students can draw maps to show the setting of a story; these maps may show the path a character traveled or the passage of time in a story. Figure 9–4 shows a setting map for *Number the Stars* (Lowry, 2011) that indicates where the families lived in Copenhagen, their trip to a fishing village in northern Denmark, and the ship Ellen's family hid away on for the trip to Sweden.

Point of View. Stories are written from a particular viewpoint, and this focus determines to a great extent readers' understanding of the story. The four points of view are first-person viewpoint, omniscient viewpoint, limited omniscient viewpoint, and objective viewpoint (Lukens, 2006). The Booklist on page 249 includes stories written from different viewpoints.

The first-person viewpoint tells a story through the eyes of one character using the first-person pronoun *I*. In this point of view, the reader experiences the story as the narrator tells it. The narrator, usually the main character, speaks as an eyewitness to and a participant in the events. For example, in *Shiloh* (Naylor, 2000), Marty tells how he works for Judd Travers in order to buy the puppy Travers has mistreated, and in *Abuela* (Dorros, 1991) and the sequel, *Isla* (Dorros, 1995), a girl describes magical flying adventures with her grandmother. Many stories are written from the first-person viewpoint, and the narrator's voice is usually very effective. However, one limitation is that the narrator must remain an eyewitness.

In the omniscient viewpoint, the author is godlike, knowing all. The author tells readers about the thought processes of each character without worrying about how the information is obtained. Most stories told from the omniscient viewpoint are novels, because revealing the thought processes of each character makes a story longer. One notable exception is *Doctor De Soto* (Steig, 1990), a picture-book story about a mouse dentist who outwits a fox with a toothache. Steig lets readers know that the fox wants to eat the dentist as soon as his toothache is cured and that the mouse dentist is planning to trick the fox.

The limited omniscient viewpoint is used so readers can know the thoughts of one character. The story is told in the third person, and the author concentrates on the thoughts and feelings of the main character or another important character. Many stories are told from this viewpoint. Lois Lowry uses this viewpoint in *The Giver* (2006b). She concentrates on the main character, Jonas, using his thoughts to explain the "perfect" community to readers. Later, Jonas's thoughts reveal his growing dissatisfaction with the community and his decision to escape with little Gabe.

In the objective viewpoint, readers are eyewitnesses and are confined to the immediate scene. They learn only what they can see and hear, without knowing what any character thinks. Many folktales, such as *The Little Red Hen* (Pinkney, 2006), are told from this viewpoint. Other picture-book stories, such as *Martha Speaks* (Meddaugh, 1995), are also told from the objective viewpoint. The focus is on recounting events, not on developing the personalities of the characters.

Most teachers postpone introducing the four viewpoints until the upper grades, but younger children can experiment with point of view to understand how the author's viewpoint affects a story. One way to demonstrate point of view is to contrast *The Three Little Pigs* (Galdone, 2006b), the traditional version told from an objective viewpoint, with *The True Story of the 3 Little Pigs!* (Scieszka, 1999), a self-serving narrative told by Mr. A. Wolf. In this satirical retelling, the wolf

FIGURE 9–4   A Setting Map

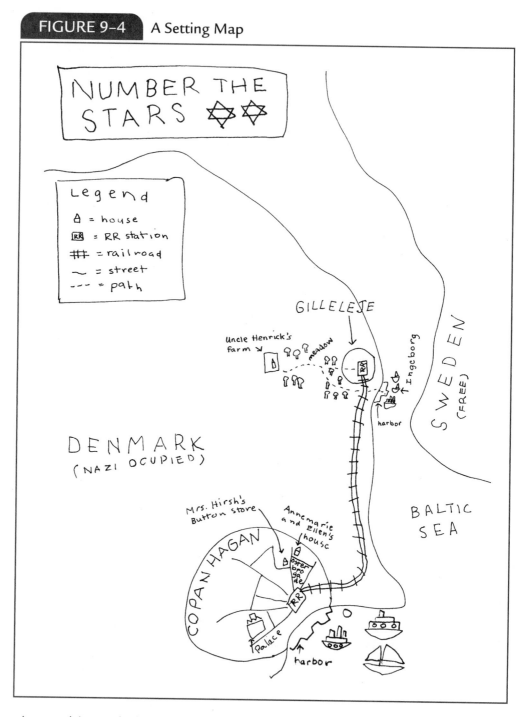

tries to explain away his bad image. Even first graders are struck by how different the two versions are and how the narrator filters the information.

Theme. The underlying meaning of a story is the *theme*, and it embodies general truths about human nature (Lehr, 1991). It usually deals with the characters' emotions and values. Themes can be stated either explicitly or implicitly. *Explicit themes* are stated openly and clearly in the story. Lukens (2006) uses *Charlotte's Web* to point out how one theme of friendship—the giving of one-self for a friend—is expressed as an explicit theme:

> Charlotte has encouraged, protected, and mothered Wilbur, bargained and sacrificed for him, and Wilbur, the grateful receiver, realizes that "Friendship is one of the most satisfying things in the world." And Charlotte says later, "By helping you perhaps I was trying to lift up my life a little. Anyone's life can stand a little of that." Because these quoted sentences are exact statements from the text they are called explicit themes. (p. 94)

In contrast, *implicit themes* are suggested rather than explicitly stated in the story. The theme emerges through the thoughts, speech, and actions of the characters as they seek to resolve their conflicts. Lukens also uses *Charlotte's Web* to illustrate implicit themes:

> Charlotte's selflessness—working late at night to finish a new word, expending her last energies for her friend—is evidence that friendship is giving oneself. Wilbur's protection of Charlotte's egg sac, his sacrifice of first turn at the slops, and his devotion to Charlotte's babies—giving without any need to stay even or to pay back—leads us to another theme: True friendship is naturally reciprocal. As the two become fond of each other, still another theme emerges: One's best friend can do no wrong. In fact, a best friend is sensational! Both Charlotte and Wilbur believe in these ideas; their experiences verify them. (p. 95)

Charlotte's Web has several friendship themes, one explicitly stated and others inferred from the story. Teachers ask questions during grand conversations to guide students' thinking as they strive to identify themes (Au, 1992). Students need to go beyond one-word labels in describing a theme.

Sketch-to-stretch is a visually representing activity that moves students beyond literal comprehension to think more deeply about the theme (Harste, Short, & Burke, 1988; Whitin, 1996). Students work in small groups or individually to draw pictures or diagrams that represent what the story means to them, not pictures of their favorite character or episode. In their sketches, students use lines, shapes, colors, symbols, and words to express their interpretations. Because students work in a social setting with the support of classmates, they share ideas, extend their understanding, and generate new insights. The steps in sketch-to-stretch are described in the Step-by-Step feature on page 256.

Students need many opportunities to experiment with this activity before they can think symbolically. Teachers introduce the activity through a minilesson and draw several sketches together as a class before students make their own. As they create symbolic illustrations, students probe their understanding of the story and what it means to them (Whitin, 2002). *The Ballad of Lucy Whipple* (Cushman, 1996a), for example, is the story of a girl who reluctantly comes with her family to Lucky Diggins, California, during the 1849 Gold Rush. Even though she wants nothing more than to return home to Massachusetts, Lucy makes a new home for herself and finally becomes a "happy citizen" (p. 187) in Lucky Diggins. Figure 9–5 shows a fourth grader's sketch-to-stretch drawing about *The Ballad of Lucy Whipple* that reflects the "home" theme.

In a yearlong study of two seventh grade language arts classes, Whitin (1996) found that students' use of sketching helped deepen their understanding of theme; however, she warns that some upper grade students view this activity as an easy form of response and suggests that teachers clarify this misconception early in the school year. Students explored new avenues of expression, such as using color to signify meaning and pie charts to signify feelings. Whitin also had her students write reflections to accompany their sketches.

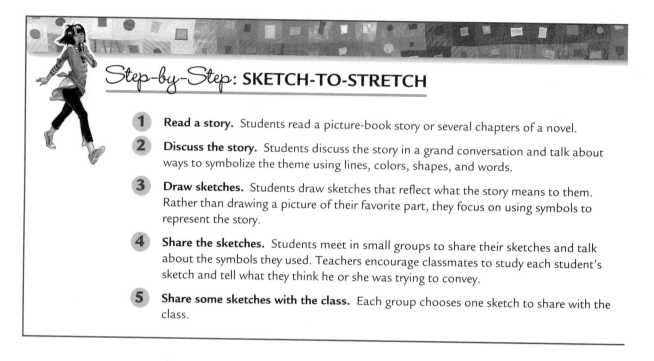

Step-by-Step: SKETCH-TO-STRETCH

1 **Read a story.** Students read a picture-book story or several chapters of a novel.

2 **Discuss the story.** Students discuss the story in a grand conversation and talk about ways to symbolize the theme using lines, colors, shapes, and words.

3 **Draw sketches.** Students draw sketches that reflect what the story means to them. Rather than drawing a picture of their favorite part, they focus on using symbols to represent the story.

4 **Share the sketches.** Students meet in small groups to share their sketches and talk about the symbols they used. Teachers encourage classmates to study each student's sketch and tell what they think he or she was trying to convey.

5 **Share some sketches with the class.** Each group chooses one sketch to share with the class.

Story Genres

Stories can be categorized in different ways, and one is according to genres (Buss & Karnowski, 2000). Three broad categories are folklore, fantasies, and realism. Traditional stories, including fables, fairy tales, myths, and legends, are *folklore*. Many of these stories, such as "The Gingerbread Man," "The Tortoise and the Hare," and "Cinderella," were told for centuries before they were written down. *Fantasies* are make-believe stories, set in imaginary worlds or in future worlds where characters do impossible things. In some fantasies, such as *Bunnicula: A Rabbit-Tale of Mys-*

FIGURE 9–5   A Sketch-to-Stretch Drawing

tery (Howe & Howe, 2006), animals can talk, and in others, the characters travel through time. *Realistic stories*, in contrast, are believable. Some stories take place in the past, such as *Crispin: The Cross of Lead* (Avi, 2002), set in medieval England, and *Rodzina* (Cushman, 2003), an orphan train story set in the 1800s. Other stories are set in the contemporary world, such as *Joey Pigza Loses Control* (Gantos, 2000) and *Amber Brown Is Not a Crayon* (Danziger, 2006). Figure 9–6 presents an overview of the story genres.

Some researchers are currently looking at genres in a broader way: They've moved beyond the idea of genres as simply categories of literature to examine the different patterns or genres of

FIGURE 9–6   Story Genres

Category	Genre	Description and Examples
Folklore	Fables	Brief tales told to point out a moral. For example: *Aesop's Fables* (Pinkney, 2000) and *Head, Body, Legs: A Story From Liberia* (Paye & Lippert, 2002).
	Folktales and Fairy Tales	Stories in which heroes and heroines demonstrate virtues to triumph over adversity. For example: *Beautiful Blackbird* (Bryan, 2003), *The Girl Who Spun Gold* (Hamilton, 2000), and *The Sleeping Beauty* (Hyman, 2000).
	Myths	Stories created by ancient peoples to explain natural phenomena. For example: *King Midas: The Golden Touch* (Demi, 2002), *A Gift From Zeus: Sixteen Favorite Myths* (Steig, 2001), and *The Star-Bearer: A Creation Myth From Ancient Egypt* (Hofmeyr, 2001).
	Legends	Stories, including tall tales, that recount the courageous deeds of people as they struggled against each other or against gods and monsters. For example: *Mystic Horse* (Goble, 2003), *Mike Fink* (Kellogg, 1998), *The Boy Who Drew Cats* (Hodges, 2002), and *Master Man: A Tall Tale of Nigeria* (Shepard, 2001).
Fantasy	Modern Literary Tales	Stories written by modern authors that exemplify the characteristics of folktales. For example: *The Runaway Tortilla* (Kimmel, 2000), *Gingerbread Baby* (Brett, 1999), and *Sylvester and the Magic Pebble* (Steig, 2010).
	Fantastic Stories	Imaginative stories that explore alternate realities and contain one or more elements not found in the natural world. For example: *Princess Academy* (Hale, 2007) and *Charlotte's Web* (White, 2006).
	Science Fiction	Stories that explore scientific possibilities. For example: *Commander Toad in Space* (Yolen, 1980), *The Giver* (Lowry, 2006b), and *Stinker From Space* (Service, 1988).
	High Fantasy	These stories focus on the conflict between good and evil and often involve quests. For example: *The Lion, the Witch and the Wardrobe* (Lewis, 2005) and *Harry Potter and the Chamber of Secrets* (Rowling, 1999).
Realism	Contemporary Stories	Stories that portray the real world and contemporary society. For example: *Hatchet* (Paulsen, 2007), *Joey Pigza Loses Control* (Gantos, 2000), and *Locomotion* (Woodson, 2003).
	Historical Fiction	Realistic stories set in the past. For example: *The Watsons Go to Birmingham—1963* (Curtis, 2000), *Sarah, Plain and Tall* (MacLachlan, 2005), and *A Single Shard* (Park, 2011).

text that young children interact with at home or at school. These genres include magazines, lists, recipes, books, newspapers, and greeting cards. Through their examination of young children's interaction with genres, Duke and Purcell-Gates (2003) concluded that during the preschool years, children develop the understanding that texts have different patterns or genres. Duke and Kays (1998) also found that kindergartners demonstrate their knowledge of genres when they vary how they pretend-read unfamiliar wordless books; they pretend-read informational books differently than stories. These studies suggest that students come to school with a concept of genre and that through reading and writing experiences and minilessons, they refine and apply their understanding of genres.

Narrative Devices

Narrative devices breathe life into stories, making them more vivid and memorable, and without them, writing can be dull (Lukens, 2006). These devices employ words to create images in readers' minds. Students learn about these narrative devices and apply what they learn in comprehending and composing stories:

COMPARISON. Authors use comparison in creating descriptions of events and people. When the comparison uses the word *like* or *as*, it's a simile, but when the comparison is stated directly, it's a metaphor. For example, "His muscles were as hard as a rock" is a simile; "She cried a river of tears" is a metaphor. Metaphors are stronger because the comparison is more direct.

HYPERBOLE. Authors stretch the truth and add humor using outlandish exaggerations to their stories. This type of figurative language help readers visualize the words they're reading. American tall tales have rich examples of hyperbole; Paul Bunyan, for example, as an eight-foot-tall lumberjack credited with digging the Grand Canyon and creating the Great Lakes.

IMAGERY. Authors use descriptive language to appeal to readers' senses and create pictures in readers' minds. They often use words representing one or more of the five senses to evoke vivid images. For example, a third grader described dandelions as "stars in the grass."

PERSONIFICATION. Authors use personification when they attribute human characteristics to animals or objects because readers find it easier to relate to people than to things that aren't human. For example, "the trees danced in the breeze" is personification.

SYMBOLISM. Authors use a person, place, or thing as a symbol to represent something else; for example, a dove symbolizes peace and the statue of Liberty symbolizes freedom. In addition, sometimes authors use symbolism to represent the story's theme with an object.

TONE. Authors create an overall emotional feeling in the story through their choice of words. Tones include humorous, cautionary, comical, depressed, heartwarming, scary, persuasive, earnest, fanciful, apologetic, cynical, sad, and joyful.

Young children focus on events and characters as they read and write stories, but gradually students become more sophisticated readers and writers as they apply what they've learned about narrative devices.

Teaching Students About Stories

Teachers support students as they expand their knowledge of stories in three ways. First, teachers read aloud mentor texts and provide opportunities for students to examine stories closely and respond to them. Next, they teach minilessons about the elements of story structure, story genres, and narrative devices to expand students' knowledge about fiction, and finally, they provide opportunities for students to write a variety of stories, including written retellings of familiar stories, genre stories, and original stories. This Common Core State Standards box outlines what students are expected to learn about composing and comprehending stories.

Students read stories as they participate in literature focus units, literature circles, reading workshop, and thematic units, and in the process, their concept of story informs and supports their reading. Teachers provide guidance and support for students as they participate in a variety of reading activities, including guided reading and readers theatre, and they can assess students' comprehension through retelling stories. The Patterns of Practice feature below shows the important role of stories in the instructional approaches.

COMMON CORE STATE STANDARDS

Stories

The Common Core State Standards emphasize concept of story. Students need to develop an understanding of literature and apply their knowledge about story structure, genre, and narrative devices to comprehending and composing stories. The standards address these points:

- Students identify the elements of story structure.
- Students recognize story genres.
- Students analyze how narrative devices contribute to the meaning of stories.
- Students retell stories.
- Students write well-organized and effective stories.

To learn more about the literature, reading, and writing standards, go to http://www .corestandards.org, or check your state's language arts standards.

Minilessons. Teachers teach minilessons to develop students' knowledge about story structure, genres, and narrative devices. They're usually taught during the exploring stage of the reading process, after students have had an opportunity to read and respond to a story and share their reactions. This sequence is important because students need to understand the events of the story before they try to analyze the story at a more abstract level. A second grade teacher's minilesson about theme is presented on page 260.

How Stories Fit Into the Patterns of Practice

Literature Focus Units

Students read stories and respond using reading logs and grand conversations. Teachers teach concept of story topics through minilessons, and students apply what they're learning as they create projects at the end of the units.

Literature Circles

Students apply what they've learned about stories as they read and respond to books in small, student-led groups. Sometimes each group reads a book representing the same genre, or each group focuses on an element of story structure.

Reading and Writing Workshop

Students learn about story structure, genres, and narrative devices through minilessons and mentor texts that teachers read aloud. Students apply their concept of story as they comprehend books they're reading and compose stories.

Thematic Units

Teachers often read aloud stories, especially historical fiction, as part of thematic units, and students apply what they've learned to comprehend the story. Students also tell and write stories as projects.

Minilesson

Mrs. Levin's Second Graders Learn About Theme

1. Introduce the Topic

Mrs. Levin's second grade class has just read *Martha Speaks* (Meddaugh, 1995), the story of a talking dog. Mrs. Levin rereads the last paragraph of the story, which exemplifies the theme, and says, "I think this is what the author, Susan Meddaugh, is trying to tell us—that sometimes we should talk and sometimes we should be quiet. What do you think?" The children agree, and Mrs. Levin explains that the author's message or lesson about life is called the *theme*.

2. Share Examples

Mrs. Levin shows the class *Little Red Riding Hood* (Galdone, 1974), a story they read earlier in the year, and after briefly reviewing the story, she asks children about the theme of this story. One child quickly responds, "I think the author means that you shouldn't talk to strangers." Another child explains, "Little Red Riding Hood's mom probably tried to teach her to not talk to strangers but Little Red Riding Hood must have forgotten because she talked to the wolf and he was like a stranger." It's a message every child has heard, but they agree that they, too, sometimes forget, just like Little Red Riding Hood.

3. Provide Information

The next day, Mrs. Levin shares three other familiar books and asks children to identify the theme. The first book is *The Three Bears* (Galdone, 1972), and children easily identify the "don't intrude" theme. The second book is *Chrysanthemum* (Henkes, 1991), the story of a young mouse named Chrysanthemum who doesn't like herself after her classmates make fun of her name. The children identify two variations of the theme: "you should be nice to everyone and not hurt their feelings," and "kids who aren't nice get in trouble." The third book is *Miss Nelson Is Missing!* (Allard, 1985), the story of a sweet teacher who transforms herself into a mean teacher after her students refuse to behave. The children identify the theme as "teachers are nice when you behave but they are mean when you are bad."

4. Supervise Practice

Mrs. Levin asks children to choose one of the five stories they've examined and to draw pictures showing the theme. For example, they could draw a picture of Martha using the telephone to report burglars in the house or a picture of themselves ringing the doorbell at a friend's house. Mrs. Levin walks around as children work, helping them add titles to their pictures that focus on the theme of the story.

5. Reflect on Learning

Children share their pictures with the class and explain how they illustrate the theme of the various stories.

Booklist

NARRATIVE DEVICES	
Comparison	Ackerman, K. (2003). *Song and dance man*. New York: Viking. P Babbitt, N. (2007). *Tuck everlasting*. New York: Square Fish Books. U O'Dell, S. (2010). *Island of the blue dolphins*. New York: Sandpiper. M–U Ringgold, F. (1996). *Tar beach*. New York: Dragonfly. P–M
Hyperbole	Kellogg, S. (1992). *Pecos Bill*. New York: HarperCollins. M Lester, J. (1999). *John Henry*. New York: Puffin Books. M Scieszka, J. (1999). *The true story of the 3 little pigs!* New York: Viking. P–M Steig, W. (1990). *Shrek!* New York: Farrar, Straus & Giroux. M
Imagery	Almond, D. (1998). *Skellig*. New York: Delacorte. U MacLachlan, P. (2005). *Sarah, plain and tall*. New York: Scholastic. M Paulsen, G. (2007). *Hatchet*. New York: Simon & Schuster. U Yolen, J. (1987). *Owl moon*. New York: Philomel. P–M
Personification	Martin, B., Jr., & Archambault, J. (2009). *Chicka chicka boom boom*. New York: Beach Lane Books. P Rathmann, P. (1995). *Officer Buckle and Gloria*. New York: Putnam. P Steig, W. (2010). *Sylvester and the magic pebble*. New York: Atheneum. P–M Tolkien, J. R. R. (2007). *The hobbit*. Boston: Houghton Mifflin. U
Symbolism	Bunting, E. (1993). *Fly away home*. New York: Sandpiper. P–M Rowling, J. K. (2008). *Harry Potter and the sorcerer's stone*. New York: Scholastic. U Sachar, L. (2008). *Holes*. New York: Farrar, Straus & Giroux. U Van Allsburg, C. (1991). *The wretched stone*. Boston: Houghton Mifflin. M
Tone	Cushman, K. (2005). *Catherine, called Birdy*. New York: HarperCollins. U Howe, D., & Howe, J. (2006). *Bunnicula: A rabbit-tale of mystery*. New York: Atheneum. M–U King-Smith, D. (2005). *Babe the gallant pig*. New York: Knopf. M Martin, B., Jr., & Archambault, J. (1988). *The ghost-eye tree*. New York: Henry Holt. P

Mentor Texts. Teachers use mentor texts to examine the structure of stories, illustrate the characteristics of genres, realize the power of narrative devices that authors use, and provide models for stories that students write. The Booklist on page 249 recommends picture-book stories and novels to use in teaching about the elements of story structure, Figure 9–6 lists books representing the story genres, and the Booklist above shares stories that illustrate the narrative devices. Sometimes teachers read these books aloud or have students read them themselves during literature focus units, and they focus students' attention on concept of story topics during minilessons. They also ask students to apply what they've learned about stories as they read books in literature circles and reading workshop.

INTEGRATING TECHNOLOGY

Students use the Internet and other digital tools as they read and write stories. They research information about authors online, respond to stories using online reading logs and blogs, complete WebQuests related to the books, and publish the projects they create on classroom websites. When they're composing stories, they use word processing programs with editing software, create

DIGITAL CLASSROOM

Digital Storytelling

Digital storytelling combines composing stories with technology. Students create short, first-person multimedia narratives by combining still and moving images, text, music, and sound effects, and tell them using their own voice (Miller, 2010). They compose stories from their own lives, retell folktales, create original short stories, and recount historical events, and they can use other genres, including biography, poetry, and persuasive writing, too. These digital stories are often compelling and emotionally engaging.

A variety of software applications can be used to create digital stories. Students with PCs use Microsoft Photostory 3, Windows Movie Maker, or QuickTime; students with Macs use iMovie, iDVD, or QuickTime Pro; and everyone uses Adobe PhotoShop Elements. For young children, teachers can try Tech4Learning's Pixie3 software. Digital still and movie cameras, digital microphones, and scanners are also needed.

Students use the writing process to create 2- to 3-minute movies that they can upload to the Web for audiences around the world to view. As they're developing their stories, students also apply their knowledge of the six traits—imaginative ideas, elements of story structure, narrative voice, and eye-catching layout, for example. In addition, students are learning to use technology to craft their movies. They choose relevant and engaging images that extend meaning, sounds to create mood and emotional impact, and a confident personal style that enhances the message.

To learn more about digital storytelling, teachers check these resources:

▶ **Make Me a Story**
Make Me a Story: Teaching Writing Through Digital Storytelling *(Miller, 2010) shows how to teach students to create digital stories, and the accompanying CD has samples of students' stories.*

▶ **Center for Digital Storytelling**
http://www.storycenter.org
The Center for Digital Storytelling provides information and builds partnerships to develop digital storytelling initiatives. It's a nonprofit project dedicated to assisting people in using digital media to tell meaningful stories from their lives.

▶ **DigiTales**
http://www.digitales.us
DigiTales has a variety of resources, including a section that describes how to create digital stories, assessment rubrics, and a gallery of digital stories.

▶ **Educational Uses of Digital Storytelling**
http://digitalstorytelling.coe.uh.edu
Educational Uses of Digital Storytelling is a comprehensive website developed by faculty and students at the University of Houston, with information about how to create and assess digital stories and sample stories.

podcasts of their stories, do digital storytelling projects, and publish their writing online. Here's more information about three ways to integrate technology with reading and writing stories:

WEBQUESTS. WebQuests are online inquiry projects related to books; to complete them, students assume roles and search the Internet to find answers, solve problems, and produce technology-enhanced group projects. Teachers have posted online a wide variety of Web-Quests that they've developed for picture-book stories and novels, including *Olivia* (Falconer, 2000), *The Keeping Quilt* (Polacco, 2001), *Charlie and the Chocolate Factory* (Dahl, 2011), *Hatchet* (Paulsen, 2007), *Catherine, Called Birdy* (Cushman, 2005) *Dragonwings* (Yep, 1977), *The Giver* (Lowry, 2006b), and *Roll of Thunder, Hear My Cry* (Taylor, 2004). Teachers can easily adapt these WebQuests or develop their own for students to complete during literature focus units, literature circles, and thematic units.

DIGITAL STORYTELLING. Students use movie-making software to create multimedia versions of their stories (Miller, 2010); they combine text with still and moving images, voiceovers, and sound effects to create powerful brief narratives. To learn more about digital storytelling, check the Digital Classroom feature on the previous page.

LITERATURE FOCUS UNIT WEBSITES. Students can post the projects they create during literature focus units on classroom websites to share their learning with worldwide audiences. Check Mrs. Taverna's second grade class website about *Charlotte's Web* (White, 2006) (http://www2.lhric.org/pocantico/charlotte/index) to view great examples of literature-based projects. The website includes a collaborative ABC book, chapter summaries, puzzles, poems, and a collaborative book about the lessons learned from reading E. B. White's classic story of friendship.

It's essential that teachers integrate new technology into the language arts curriculum to prepare students for the new literacies of the 21st century, and reading and writing stories offer many opportunities for preK–8 students to use computers and other digital tools. ■

ENGAGING ENGLISH LEARNERS

When English learners understand about how stories are structured, their comprehension improves, and they're better able to write well-crafted, entertaining stories. Three ways that teachers help English learners learn about stories are through providing opportunities for students to do extensive reading, teaching them about the elements of story structure, and nurturing their responses to literature:

EXTENSIVE READING. All students need daily opportunities to enjoy good literature. Teachers regularly read stories to students using interactive read-aloud procedures, and students read stories themselves as they participate in guided reading, literature circles, and reading workshop. As they listen and read, students expand their background knowledge, build their vocabularies, and become more interested in literature. It's essential that teachers put together a large collection of multicultural books at a variety of reading levels that their students will find interesting. Students need to know how to select books at their reading levels; if older students read at lower levels, then books at those levels need to be age-appropriate.

ELEMENTS OF STORY STRUCTURE. To deepen their understanding of stories, English learners need to learn about the elements of story structure (Peregoy & Boyle, 2009). They'll acquire some basic understanding about the structure of stories through reading, but they also need direct instruction about the story elements. In addition to minilessons, English learners benefit from activities that include nonverbal components. Graphic organizers, such as diagrams of the beginning, middle, and end of a story or open-mind portraits, help students visually represent the structure of a story. Dramatic activities are also useful: To examine the plot of a story, students can reenact beginning, middle, and end events; to explore a character, they can participate in a hot seat activity; and to understand the importance of setting, they can draw a setting map.

RESPONSE TO LITERATURE. English learners negotiate meaning through social interaction, just like their classmates do (Samway & McKeon, 1999). As they share their own reactions to a story and listen to their classmates' ideas about plot, characters, and setting, they deepen their comprehension. It's important that English learners know how to talk about the stories they're reading and that they're able to apply what they've learned about story structure through conversation. They need to learn how to reflect on stories they're reading, write in reading logs, and participate in grand conversations in small, comfortable groups with their classmates.

Because stories are often at the center of the language arts program, it's crucial that English learners develop their concept of story so that they can read and write them more successfully. ■

Assessing Students' Knowledge About Stories

Teachers assess students' growing concept of story because their knowledge affects how well they comprehend and compose stories. Assessment begins as teachers plan for instruction and continues as they monitor students' progress and evaluate their learning:

PLANNING. Teachers plan grade-appropriate minilessons about the elements of story structure, genres, and narrative devices as part of their language arts instruction, and they also incorporate opportunities to talk informally about the topic being taught as they read and discuss mentor texts.

MONITORING. Teachers informally monitor students' understanding of the topic being taught during minilessons and grand conversations, and as they conference with students about the stories they're drafting.

EVALUATING. Teachers evaluate students' concept of story by determining whether they understand the topic being taught and can apply what they've learned to comprehend and compose stories. Teachers ask these questions as they evaluate students' learning:

- Can students define or identify the characteristics of the topic being taught?
- Can students explain how the topic was used in a particular story?
- Did students apply the topic in stories they've written?

Teachers often address these questions in the rubrics they use to evaluate students' comprehension of stories they've read and stories they've written.

COMPREHENDING STORIES

Students read stories during literature focus units, literature circles, reading workshop, and thematic units, and their concepts of story inform and support their reading. Teachers provide guidance and support for students as they participate in a variety of reading activities, including guided reading and readers theatre.

Guided Reading

Teachers scaffold students' reading to enable them to develop and use reading strategies in guided reading (Fountas & Pinnell, 1996, 2001). This type of reading is teacher directed and is usually done in small groups with students who read at the same level or who use similar reading strategies and skills. Teachers listen to individual students read during guided reading, noticing how they use meaning, structure, and phonological cues. When a student makes an error, the teacher quickly determines the source of the error and decides what type of immediate instruction or other support to use so that the student can be successful (Schwartz, 2005). Teachers often use guided reading with young children and with older students who need direct instruction.

Stories used for guided reading should be written at students' instructional reading levels, that is, slightly beyond their ability to read the text independently, or at their level of proximal development. They usually read the story silently so if it's too difficult, shared reading is a better procedure. If the story is too easy, then independent reading is a better choice because teacher support isn't needed. Teachers often group and regroup students for guided reading so that the

PreK *Spotlight*

How do teachers develop young children's comprehension of stories?

"Storybook reading is the cornerstone of early literacy instruction," according to Vukelich and Christie (2009, p. 12). Teachers regularly read aloud picture-book stories to small groups, whole classes, and individual children in preschool classrooms; they use a procedure known as *shared storybook reading*, based on the traditional bedtime story ritual, in which teachers read aloud a picture-book story, pausing to engage children in conversation about the story (Ezell & Justice, 2005). In their study, Beauchat, Blamey, and Walpole (2009) researched the value of embedding questions before, during, and after reading to develop students' comprehension as they named the main characters, described story events, related book experiences to their own lives, and recognized the relationship between the characters' feelings and their actions. They used these types of comprehension questions to elicit children's responses (with sample questions about Jan Brett's *The Mitten* [2009]):

Completion Questions. Teachers ask children to provide one word to complete a phrase or sentence taken directly from the text. Example: Then Baba said, "I will look to see if you still have your snow-white _____."

Recall Questions. Teachers ask children to recall a series of events in order. Example: Which animal crawled into the mitten after the owl?

Open-Ended Questions. Teachers ask open-ended questions without right or wrong answers; and children make predictions and offer other comments and opinions. Examples: What do you think happened to the animals after they tumbled out of the mitten? What do you think Baba thought when she saw the enormous mitten?

W Questions. Teachers ask *who, what, when, where,* and *why* questions, and these questions usually require only one- or two-word answers. Examples: What made the bear sneeze? Why didn't Baba want to knit white mittens?

Distance Questions. Teachers ask children to make connections between the story and their lives. Example: Have you ever lost a mitten? What do you think happened to it?

The researchers concluded that shared storybook reading results in increased understanding of stories and provides opportunities for teachers to develop young children's phonemic awareness, vocabulary, and written-language concepts.

book selected is appropriate for all students in a group. The steps in guided reading are shown in the Step-by-Step feature on page 266.

Readers' Theatre

Readers theatre is a dramatic presentation of a story by a group of readers; students develop reading fluency through this dramatic activity (Black & Stave, 2007; Worthy & Prater, 2002). Stories are rewritten as scripts, and students each assume a role and read that character's lines. Readers interpret a story without using much action; they may stand or sit, but they carry the whole communication of the plot, characterization, mood, and theme through their voices, gestures, and facial expressions.

Students begin by reading the book and thinking about its theme, characters, and plot. Next, they choose an episode to script, make copies of it, and use felt-tip pens to highlight the dialogue.

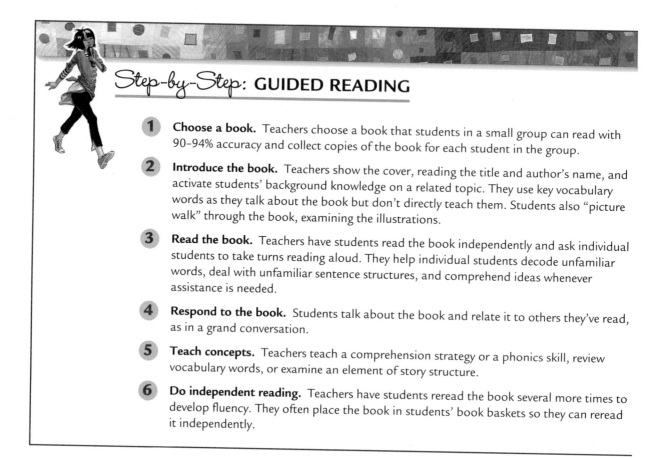

Step-by-Step: GUIDED READING

1 Choose a book. Teachers choose a book that students in a small group can read with 90–94% accuracy and collect copies of the book for each student in the group.

2 Introduce the book. Teachers show the cover, reading the title and author's name, and activate students' background knowledge on a related topic. They use key vocabulary words as they talk about the book but don't directly teach them. Students also "picture walk" through the book, examining the illustrations.

3 Read the book. Teachers have students read the book independently and ask individual students to take turns reading aloud. They help individual students decode unfamiliar words, deal with unfamiliar sentence structures, and comprehend ideas whenever assistance is needed.

4 Respond to the book. Students talk about the book and relate it to others they've read, as in a grand conversation.

5 Teach concepts. Teachers teach a comprehension strategy or a phonics skill, review vocabulary words, or examine an element of story structure.

6 Do independent reading. Teachers have students reread the book several more times to develop fluency. They often place the book in students' book baskets so they can reread it independently.

They then adapt the scene by adding narrators' lines to bridge gaps, set the scene, and summarize. Students assume roles and read the script aloud, revising and experimenting with new text until they're satisfied with the script. The final version is typed, duplicated, and stapled into booklets.

A few collections of readers theatre scripts are available for young children, including *Getting Ready to Read With Readers Theatre* (Barchers & Pfeffinger, 2007) and *Readers Theater for Building Fluency* (Worthy, 2008). However, very few quality scripts are available for older students, so they usually prepare their own scripts using episodes from books they've read, such as *Amber Brown Is Not a Crayon* (Danziger, 2006) and *The Giver* (Lowry, 2006b). Karen Hesse's *Witness* (2005), a story told from multiple voices, is very powerful when performed as a readers theatre presentation.

Responding to Stories

When you're reading a novel, do you imagine yourself as one of the characters? Do you laugh out loud or cry? Do you wish the story wouldn't end because you're enjoying it so much? If so, it's because you're having a dynamic engagement with literature. This powerful feeling of pleasure and desire to do more reading is reader response, and it's what teachers want their students to experience. Hancock (2008) describes response to literature as "the unique interaction that occurs within the mind and heart of the individual reader through the literature event" (p. 9).

Many responses that students make are spontaneous, but others are planned. For example, kindergartners laugh—a spontaneous response—while listening to their teacher read Thacher Hurd's hilarious picture book *Moo Cow Kaboom!* (2003). In the story, Moo Cow is cownapped by a space cowboy named Zork and taken to Planet 246 for the InterGalactic Rodeo. Afterward, children take turns dressing up as Farmer George wearing a nightshirt, Moo Cow wearing a cow mask, and Zork wearing a black cowboy hat, while classmates become a cast of supporting characters to reenact the story; this is a planned response. Similarly, as eighth graders read *Crispin: The Cross of Lead* (Avi, 2002), the story of Crispin, a 13-year-old peasant boy who is falsely accused of being a thief and declared a "wolf's head" (which gives everyone in the country permission to kill him on sight), they compare Crispin's life to their own and comment on their compassion for him; this is a spontaneous response. Students also make entries in reading logs to explore story ideas and make connections to what they're learning about the Middle Ages; this is a planned response. And when students reach the end of the story, where Crispin redeems himself, they cheer loudly—another spontaneous response.

Spontaneous responses are those that students make without any prompting. They make these responses because they're engaged in the story. Young children, for example, clap their hands and tap their feet to the rhythm of Bill Martin and John Archambault's *Chicka Chicka Boom Boom* (2009) and chant along as the teacher rereads the book. They spot the dangers facing two bugs named Frieda and Gloria in the illustrations in *Absolutely Not!* (McElligott, 2004) and call out warnings. Older students take action in their own neighborhood after reading Paul Fleischman's *Seedfolks* (2004b), a timeless story about a blighted community that's transformed after a girl plants some seeds and her neighbors are stirred to take action.

Teachers plan responses that are appropriate for the books students are reading, and it's possible to design responses that address any of the language arts, as shown in the Differentiated Instruction box below. Students often listen to a book on tape, view the film version of a story, or examine the illustrations in a picture book; they talk about the story in a grand conversation, invent sequels, perform puppet shows, and dramatize the story while their classmates watch; they write in reading logs and write letters to the author, or compose new stories using the story as a model.

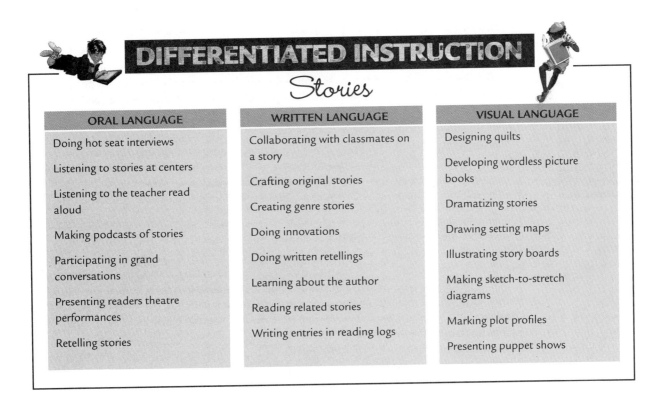

DIFFERENTIATED INSTRUCTION
Stories

ORAL LANGUAGE	WRITTEN LANGUAGE	VISUAL LANGUAGE
Doing hot seat interviews	Collaborating with classmates on a story	Designing quilts
Listening to stories at centers	Crafting original stories	Developing wordless picture books
Listening to the teacher read aloud	Creating genre stories	Dramatizing stories
Making podcasts of stories	Doing innovations	Drawing setting maps
Participating in grand conversations	Doing written retellings	Illustrating story boards
Presenting readers theatre performances	Learning about the author	Making sketch-to-stretch diagrams
Retelling stories	Reading related stories	Marking plot profiles
	Writing entries in reading logs	Presenting puppet shows

Retelling Stories

Students often retell familiar stories they've read or watched on TV; and when they retell a story, students organize the information they remember and provide a personalized summary (Hoyt, 1999). Teachers can capitalize on students' interest in retelling stories and use it to assess their comprehension (McKenna & Stahl, 2003). As they listen to students retell a story, teachers use a scoring sheet or rating scale to evaluate the cohesiveness and completeness of the retellings. This activity is especially valuable for English learners because teachers can assess both students' comprehension and their oral language fluency (O'Malley & Pierce, 1996).

Once teachers begin listening to students retell stories, they notice that the ones who understand a story retell it differently than those who don't. Capable readers' retellings make sense: Their retellings reflect the organization of the story, and they incorporate all of the important story events. In contrast, less capable readers often recall events haphazardly or omit important events, especially those in the middle of the story.

Three Retellings. A first grade teacher read aloud *Hey, Al* (Yorinks, 1989), the award-winning picture-book story about Al, a hardworking janitor, and his loyal dog, Eddie, who yearn for a better life. At the beginning, Al is discouraged because he has to work so hard, and then a bird offers him an easy life. Al accepts the bird's offer, and in the middle, the bird flies Al and Eddie to an island paradise where they have a wonderful time—until they start turning into birds. They escape and fly toward their home in the city. Al reaches home safely, but Eddie almost drowns. At last Al and Eddie are reunited, and they realize that it's up to them to make their own happiness. After the teacher finishes reading the story, the children draw pictures of their favorite parts and talk about the story in a grand conversation. Afterward, they individually retell the story, but they aren't prompted to add more information. Here are the children's retellings:

- **Retelling #1.** *The story is about Al and Eddie. A bird took them to Hawaii and they had a lot of fun there. They were swimming and playing a lot. Then they came back home because they didn't like being birds.*

- **Retelling #2.** *Al and Eddie are at the island. They like it and they are changing into birds. They have wings and feathers and stuff that made them look funny. That makes them scared so they fly back to their old home. I think Eddie crashed into the ocean and drowned. So Al buys a new dog and they have lots of fun together.*

- **Retelling #3.** *This man named Al and his puppy called Eddie wanted more excitement so they went to an island. It was wonderful at first, but then they started changing into birds and they hated that. They wanted to go back home. They started flying home, and they were flying, and they were changing back into their real selves. Al made it home, but Eddie almost drowned because he was smaller. All in all, they did learn an important lesson: You should be happy with yourself just the way you are.*

These retellings show children's differing levels of comprehension. The first child's brief retelling is literal: It includes events from the beginning, middle, and end of the story but lacks any interpretation. Many details are missing; in fact, this child doesn't mention that Al's a man (or a janitor) or that Eddie's a dog. Even though the second retelling is longer than the first one, it shows only partial comprehension. It's incomplete because it lacks a beginning: This child focuses most of the retelling on the middle and misunderstands the end of the story because Eddie doesn't drown. With some prompting from the teacher, this child might have added more information about the beginning of the story or corrected the ending. The third child's retelling, in contrast, is quite complete. This child retells the beginning, middle, and end and explains the characters' motivation for going to the island. Most importantly, this child establishes a purpose for the story by explaining its theme—making your own happiness.

After examining the strengths and weaknesses of each retelling, teachers use what they learn to plan instruction. For example, the first child might benefit from learning to add more details in a retelling, and the second one to learn more about organizing the retelling into beginning, middle, and end parts. They both need to learn more about how to recognize the theme. Because the third child's retelling was so complete, this child might be interested in reading more challenging stories where the theme is less obvious.

Retelling Guidelines. Teachers sit one-on-one with individual students in a quiet area of the classroom and ask them to retell a familiar story. While the student is retelling, teachers use a scoring sheet to mark the components included in the retelling. If the student hesitates or doesn't finish retelling the story, teachers ask questions, such as "What happened next?" The steps in the procedure are explained in the Step-by-Step feature below.

Although many students already know how to retell stories, teachers can't assume that all students do. Through a series of minilessons and demonstrations, students learn what's expected of them. They need to practice retelling stories before they'll be good at it; they can retell stories with a classmate and to their parents at home. Students who have difficulty may need to learn more

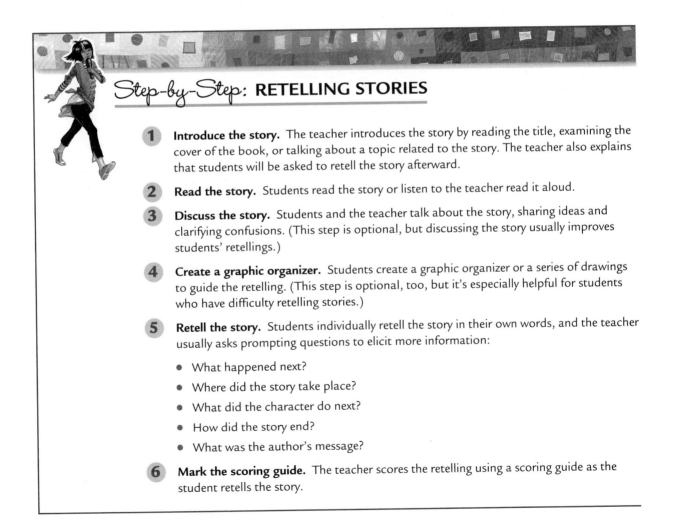

Step-by-Step: RETELLING STORIES

1. **Introduce the story.** The teacher introduces the story by reading the title, examining the cover of the book, or talking about a topic related to the story. The teacher also explains that students will be asked to retell the story afterward.

2. **Read the story.** Students read the story or listen to the teacher read it aloud.

3. **Discuss the story.** Students and the teacher talk about the story, sharing ideas and clarifying confusions. (This step is optional, but discussing the story usually improves students' retellings.)

4. **Create a graphic organizer.** Students create a graphic organizer or a series of drawings to guide the retelling. (This step is optional, too, but it's especially helpful for students who have difficulty retelling stories.)

5. **Retell the story.** Students individually retell the story in their own words, and the teacher usually asks prompting questions to elicit more information:

   - What happened next?
   - Where did the story take place?
   - What did the character do next?
   - How did the story end?
   - What was the author's message?

6. **Mark the scoring guide.** The teacher scores the retelling using a scoring guide as the student retells the story.

FIGURE 9–7   Retelling Stories Rubric

Name _Cassie_   Date _Mar. 1_

Book _Ruby Lu, Brave and True_

4	__ Names and describes all characters.
	__ Includes specific details about the setting.
	__ Explains the problem.
	__ Describes attempts to solve the problem.
	__ Explains the solution.
	__ Identifies the theme.
③	✓ Names all characters and ^P_describes_ some of them.
	__ Identifies more than one detail about the setting (location, weather, time).
	✓ Recalls events in order.
	✓ Identifies the problem.
	✓ Includes the beginning, ^P_middle_, and end.
2	__ Names all characters.
	✓ Mentions the setting.
	__ Recalls most events in order.
	__ Includes the beginning and end.
1	__ Names some characters.
	__ Recalls events haphazardly.
	__ Includes only beginning or end.

P = prompted

---

about story structure, especially beginning, middle, and end. It's often helpful to have them draw pictures to scaffold their retellings. As their comprehension improves, so will their retelling abilities.

Figure 9–7 presents a rubric for scoring third graders' retellings. Some students, however, are shy or uncomfortable talking with teachers, so their scores may underestimate how well they comprehend (McKenna & Stahl, 2003). The same is true for English learners.

 # RITING STORIES

Students draw from stories they've read as they create their own stories, intertwining several story ideas and adapting story elements and genres to meet their own needs. Cairney (1990) found that students weave bits of the stories they've read into the stories they write; they share their compositions, and then bits of these compositions make their way into classmates' compositions. Students make intertextual links in these ways:

- Use specific story ideas without copying the plot
- Copy the plot, but add new events, characters, and settings
- Use a specific genre they've studied for a story
- Use a character borrowed from a story read previously
- Retell a story
- Incorporate content from an informational book into a story
- Combine several stories into a new story

The first two strategies were the ones most commonly used in Cairney's study of sixth graders. The next-to-the-last strategy was used only by less capable readers, and the last one only by more capable readers.

The type of stories that students read also affects the quality of their writing. When students read stories in traditional basal reading textbooks, they write stories that reflect the short, choppy linguistic style of the textbooks, but when they read trade-book stories, their writing reflects the more sophisticated language structures and literary style of the trade books. Dressel (1990) found that the quality of fifth graders' writing was dependent on the quality of the stories they read or listened to someone read aloud, regardless of their reading levels.

Writing Retellings

Students often write retellings of stories they've read and enjoyed. As they retell a story, they internalize its structure and play with the language the author used. Sometimes students work together to write a collaborative retelling, and at other times, they write their own individual retellings. Students can work together as a group to write or dictate the retelling, or they can divide the story into sections or chapters and have each student or pair of students write a small part. Then the parts are compiled. A class of second graders worked together to dictate their retelling of *I, Doko: The Tale of a Basket* (Young, 2004), which they published as a big book.

Page 1: *I am a basket, and my name is Doko. A good man named Yeh-yeh bought me at a market many years ago.*

Page 2: *Yeh-yeh's wife used to carry her precious baby inside me. I was a safe basket.*

Page 3: *In the blink of an eye the baby grew and became a boy. I was always with him and I helped him carry the wood for the cooking fire. I was a protective basket.*

Page 4: *Then a bad time came and Yeh-yeh's wife died. Yeh-yeh put her dead body in my basket, and I carried her to the grave. I was a trusted basket.*

Page 5: *By now the boy was all grown up and he got married. I got a good scrubbing before the wedding, and I got to carry the bride's presents to her new home. I was a handsome basket.*

Page 6: *Next the boy and his wife had a baby. They called him Wangal and I carried him in my basket. I was a proud basket.*

Page 7: *Finally Yeh-yeh got old and so did I. We stayed home by the fire, and Yeh-yeh told me wonderful stories. I was a listening basket.*

Page 8:   *One day Yeh-yeh let the fire go out of the fireplace and almost burned down the house. People said it was time to get rid of Yeh-yeh. They told Yeh-yeh's son to take him to the temple steps and leave him there for the priests to take care of. I was a worried basket.*

Page 9:   *The next day Yeh-yeh's son put the old man in my basket to take him to the temple steps, but Wangal said something very important. He said, "Don't forget to bring Doko back home because I will need it to get rid of you when you get old." That made Yeh-yeh's son understand that he was doing something very bad. I was a sad basket.*

Page 10:   *Yeh-yeh's son learned a good lesson: He learned to respect old people and not want to get rid of them. So Yeh-yeh lived at home with his son and Wangal and me for many happy years. I was a respectful basket.*

As the second graders dictated the retelling, their teacher wrote it on chart paper. Then they read the story over several times, making revisions. Next, the children divided the text into sections for each page. Then they recopied the text onto each page for the big book, drew pictures to illustrate each page, and added a cover and a title page. Children also wrote their own books, including the major points at the beginning, middle, and end of the story.

Sometimes students change the point of view in their retellings and tell the story from a particular character's viewpoint. A fourth grader wrote this retelling of "Goldilocks and the Three Bears" from Baby Bear's perspective:

One day mom got me up. I had to take a bath. I hate to take baths, but I had to. While I was taking my bath, Mom was making breakfast. When I got out of the tub breakfast was ready. But Dad got mad because his breakfast porridge was too hot to eat. So Mom said, "Let's go for a walk and let it cool." I thought, "Oh boy, we get to go for a walk!" My porridge was just right, but I could eat it later.

When we got back our front door was open. Dad thought it was an animal so he started to growl. I hate it when Dad growls. It really scares me. Anyway, there was no animal anywhere so I rushed to the table. Everybody was sitting down to eat. I said, "Someone ate my porridge." Then Dad noticed someone had tasted his porridge. He got really mad.

Then I went into the living room because I did not want to get yelled at. I noticed my rocking chair was broken. I told Dad and he got even madder.

Then I went into my bedroom. I said, "Someone has been sleeping in my bed and she's still in it." So this little girl with long blond hair raises up and starts to scream. Dad plugged his ears. She jumped up like she was scared of us and ran out of the house. We never saw that little girl again.

Story Innovations

Many stories have a repetitive pattern or refrain, and students can use this structure to write their own stories. A first grade class read *If You Give a Mouse a Cookie* (Numeroff, 1985) and talked about the circular structure of the story: The story begins with giving a mouse a cookie and ends with the mouse getting a second cookie. Then the first graders wrote stories about what they would do if they were given a cookie. A child named Michelle drew the circle diagram shown in Figure 9–8 to organize her ideas and then composed this story, which has been transcribed into conventional spelling:

If you gave Michelle a cookie she would probably want some pop. Then she would want a napkin to clean her face. That would make her tired and she would go to bed to take a nap. Before you know it, she will be awake and she would like to take a swim in a swimming pool. Then she would watch cartoons on T.V. And she would be getting hungry again so she would probably want another cookie.

FIGURE 9–8   A Circle Diagram

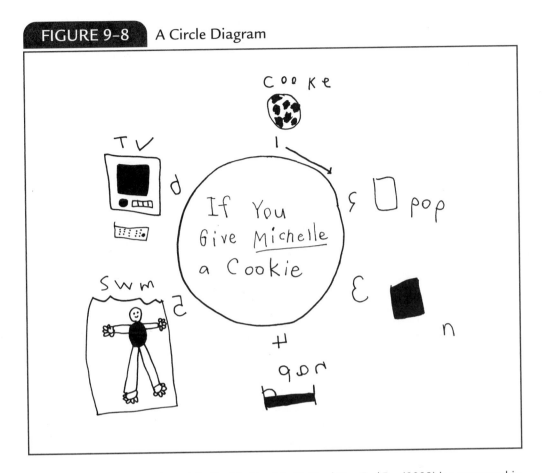

Judith Viorst's *Alexander and the Terrible, Horrible, No Good, Very Bad Day* (2009) is a more sophisticated pattern story. After reading the book, students often write about their own bad days. A fifth grader named Jacob wrote his version, entitled "Jacob and the Crummy, Stupid, Very Bad Day":

> One day I was riding my bike and I fell off and broke my arm and sprained my foot. I had to go to the hospital in an ambulance and get my arm set in a cast and my foot wrapped up real tight in a bandage. I knew it was going to be a crummy, stupid, very bad day. I think I'll swim to China.
> Then I had to go to the dentist with my sister Melissa. My sister had no cavities, but guess who had two cavities. I knew it was going to be a crummy, stupid, very bad day. I think I'll swim to China.
> My mom felt bad for me because it was such a bad day so she went and bought me a present—two Nintendo games. But my sister started fighting with me and my mom blamed me for it even though it wasn't my fault. So my mom took the games away. I wonder if there are better sisters in China?
> Then I went outside and found out that someone had stolen my bike. It was gone without a trace. It really was a crummy, stupid, very bad day. Now I am going to swim to China for sure.

Genre Stories

During some literature focus units, students read books and learn about a particular genre, such as folktales, historical fiction, myths, or fables. After learning about the genre, they try their hand at writing stories that incorporate its characteristics. A seventh grade class read and examined myths and compared myths from various cultures. Then they applied what they had learned about myths in this class collaboration myth, "Suntaria and Lunaria: Rulers of the Earth," about the origin of the sun and the moon:

> *Long ago when gods still ruled the earth, there lived two brothers, Suntaria and Lunaria. Both brothers were wise and powerful men. People from all over the earth sought their wisdom and counsel. Each man, in his own way, was good and just, yet the two were as different as gold and coal. Suntaria was large and strong with blue eyes and brilliantly golden hair. Lunaria's hair and eyes were the blackest black.*
>
> *One day Zeus, looking down from Mount Olympus, decided that Earth needed a ruler—someone to watch over his people whenever he became too tired or too busy to do his job. His eyes fell upon Suntaria and Lunaria. Both men were wise and honest. Both men would be good rulers. Which man would be the first ruler of the earth?*
>
> *Zeus decided there was only one fair way to solve his problem. He sent his messenger, Postlet, down to earth with ballots instructing the mortals to vote for a king. There were only two names on the ballot—Suntaria and Lunaria.*
>
> *Each mortal voted and after the ballots were placed in a secure box, Postlet returned them to Zeus. For seven years Zeus and Postlet counted and recounted the ballots. Each time they came up with the same results: 50% of the votes were for Suntaria and 50% were for Lunaria. There was only one thing Zeus could do. He declared that both men would rule over the earth.*
>
> *This is how it was, and this is how it is. Suntaria still spreads his warm golden rays to rule over our days. At night he steps down from his throne, and Lunaria's dark, soft night watches and protects us while we dream.*

The students incorporated three characteristics of myths in their story. First, their myth explained a phenomenon that has more recently been explained scientifically. Second, the setting is backdrop and barely sketched, and finally, the characters in their myth are heroes with supernatural powers.

Original Stories

Students move into writing original stories through writing personal narratives and writing retellings of familiar stories they've read, movies and TV programs they've watched, and video games they've played. Their first stories are typically action driven. Jorgensen (2001) explains that many children's stories resemble a fast-paced TV commercial: There's action, more action, and still more action; sometimes with a high point, but other times without one. Other young writers' stories lack focus; they're either endless conversations or a series of unrelated events.

In contrast, more knowledgeable writers craft character-driven stories that exemplify these characteristics:

- The plot is logical with a beginning, middle, and end, and the focus is on the conflict between the characters.

- The characters seem like real people: They come to life through their appearance, dialogue, and actions.

- The setting is carefully described so that readers can visualize it, and it's usually important to the story.

- The narrator's viewpoint is consistent throughout the story.

- A worthwhile theme or message is expressed through the story's characters and events.

Students learn to write more effective stories by examining the elements of story structure, reading lots of stories, and writing stories themselves.

Students' stories represent a variety of genres, especially realistic stories based on events drawn from their own lives and fantasy stories describing imaginary worlds, talking animals, and events that couldn't really happen in today's world. Books, such as the Harry Potter series (Rowling, 2007), give students ideas for their fantasies. Increasingly, both boys and girls include violence in their stories, and it's essential that teachers set guidelines to avoid offensive language and gratuitous bloodthirstiness and brutality.

Karen Jorgensen (2001) taught her fifth graders to write well-crafted stories through a writing workshop approach she calls "fiction workshop." They spend time writing stories independently, and they also conference with classmates and the teacher to get feedback on their stories. When students finish writing a story, they publish it by making a book and reading it to classmates. Then they ceremoniously place the book in the classroom library. Jorgensen also teaches minilessons about the elements of story structure and how to solve common fiction-writing problems, such as ineffective settings and excessive dialogue.

SUMMING UP

Students develop a concept of story as they learn that stories have unique structural elements; that stories are categorized according to genre, and each genre has distinguishing characteristics; and that narrative devices make stories more memorable. Teachers introduce these topics using minilessons and mentor texts, and students apply what they're learning to comprehend and compose stories more effectively.

MyEducationLab™

Go to the topics Reading, Writing, and Literature in the MyEducationLab (http://www.myeducationlab.com) for *Language Arts: Patterns of Practice*, where you can:

- Find learning outcomes for Reading, Writing, and Literature along with the national standards that connect to these outcomes.
- Complete Assignments and Activities that can help you more deeply understand the chapter content.
- Apply and practice your understanding of the core teaching skills identified in the chapter with the Building Teaching Skills and Dispositions learning units.
- Examine challenging situations and cases presented in the IRIS Center Resources.
- Use the Lesson Plan Builder Activities to practice lesson planning and integrating national and state standards into your planning.
- Check your comprehension of the content covered in the chapter with the Study Plan. Here you will be able to take a chapter quiz, receive feedback on your answers, and then access Review, Practice, and Enrichment activities to enhance your understanding of chapter content.

On the **MyEducationLab** for this course, you'll also be able to:

- **A+RISE** Go to the topic A+RISE, an innovative and interactive database of strategies that differentiate instruction across the language arts and provide particular insight into research-based methods to meet the needs of English learners.
- Explore the topic Literacy Portraits—yearlong case studies of second graders, complete with student artifacts, teacher commentary, and student and teacher interviews, tracking the month-by-month language arts growth of five students.
- Gain practice with the Grammar Tutorial, online guided instruction to improve your own ability with grammar.

CHAPTER 10

Investigating Nonfiction

KINDERGARTNERS LEARN ABOUT FISH   Mrs. LaRue's kindergartners are studying fish. The thematic unit began when the teacher brought in two goldfish to be class pets. The children were excited and immediately named them; they named the orange one Goldie and the white one Moon. So that the children would know how to care for them, the teacher read aloud *Pet Fish* (Nelson, 2002). After listening to the book, the class wrote about their new pets using interactive writing. The children usually write one sentence on chart paper, but because they had more to write, they wrote the first sentence interactively and then Mrs. LaRue wrote their dictated sentences. Here's their completed chart about "Our New Pets":

> *We have 2 goldfish named Goldie and Moon. We will take good care of them. We will feed them goldfish food and keep their bowl clean. We will look at them but we will not touch them.*

They posted the chart near the fish bowl and reread it daily. With practice, the children learned to pick out familiar words on the chart, such as *we, good, goldfish, Goldie,* and *Moon.*

Mrs. LaRue began a K-W-L chart at the beginning of the unit to record what the children knew about fish and what they wanted to learn. Looking for answers to their questions helped direct the children's attention as they participated in unit-related activities. Today, they're completing the right column of the chart about what they've learned; they know so much information to list on the chart that it takes Mrs. LaRue 30 minutes to write their dictated sentences. The completed chart is shown on page 278.

The children are curious about the parts of a fish, so Mrs. LaRue shows them a drawing of a goldfish in *Fish: Pet Care Guides for Kids* (Evans & Caras, 2001), and they identify the fish's body parts—mouth, eyes, scales, gills, fins, tail. Afterward, she draws a picture of goldfish on chart paper, and the children use interactive writing to label the parts. Later, the children draw or paint their own pictures of fish, and Mrs. LaRue helps them label two or more body parts on their pictures.

Each day, Mrs. LaRue reads aloud a book about fish. The kindergartners' favorite one is *The Rainbow Fish* (Pfister, 2002), the story of a vain and selfish fish who learns the value of friendship. The children talk about this story in a grand conversation, and later they draw pictures about their favorite part of the story and dictate a sentence for Mrs. LaRue to add to them. The children share their pictures from the author's chair, and then the teacher binds the pictures into a book that's placed in the classroom library for children to "read."

The next day, this question is posted on their sign-in chart: *What did the rainbow fish learn?* The children choose from among these three answers: *To be selfish. To be a friend. To look pretty.* Mrs. LaRue reads the three possible answers to the first few children who arrive in the classroom, and then they read them to the next group and so on until everyone has signed in. The teacher uses the sign-in chart to check her students' comprehension as well as to take attendance and encourage socialization and sharing.

The children learn more about fish at learning centers. They spend 30 minutes each day working at centers. Mrs. LaRue has set up these centers in the classroom:

SCIENCE CENTER. Children use magnifying glasses to observe the goldfish and draw pictures of them in their science journals. Charts about fish and several informational books about fish are also available for children to examine.

BOOK-MAKING CENTER. After reading Lois Ehlert's *Fish Eyes: A Book You Can Count On* (2001), the children make their own

Can kindergartners read and write information?

Some teachers think that stories are more appropriate for young children and that reading and writing information should be postponed until the middle grades. Nothing could be further from the truth! Many kindergartners, especially boys, are very curious about science topics. In fact, they prefer to read and write about information. As you read this vignette, notice how Mrs. LaRue's students listened to informational books read aloud and wrote their own informational books.

The Kindergartners' K-W-L Chart About Fish

What We Know About Fish	What We Wonder About Fish	What We Learned About Fish
Fish live in water.	Are sharks fish?	Sharks are fish.
Fish can swim.	How does a fish breathe underwater?	Eels are fish.
Tuna is a fish.	How long does a fish live?	Sea horses are fish, too.
My Grandpa likes to fish.	Why don't fish have arms and legs?	Whales are not fish.
There are different kinds of fish.	Are whales fish?	Jellyfish and starfish are not fish either.
Fish are slippery if you hold them.	Where do fish live?	Fish breathe through gills.
You can eat fish.	Do fish sleep?	Fish live any place there is water.
Fish are pretty.	What do they eat?	Fish eyes don't have eyelids.
	Can fish hear me talk?	Fish swim by moving their tails.
		Fish will die if they are not in the water because they cannot breathe.
		Fish hatch from eggs in the water.
		Fishes' skin is covered with scales.
		Yes, fish can hear.

fish counting books. Some kindergartners make books to count to 5, and others with more interest in writing and knowledge about numbers make books to count to 10. They use a familiar sentence starter, "I see . . . ," and Mrs. LaRue has introduced the words *big* and *little*. Children choose a word card with one of the words to add to their sentence; they write the other words themselves with the assistance of a parent volunteer.

LISTENING CENTER. Children listen to cassette tapes of Dr. Seuss's *One Fish Two Fish Red Fish Blue Fish* (1960b) and *Fish Is Fish* (Lionni, 2005) and follow along in individual copies of the books.

STORYTELLING CENTER. Children use story boards (pictures from the story backed with cardboard and laminated) from *The Rainbow Fish* (Pfister, 2002) and puppets of the rainbow fish and other fish to retell the story and create new adventures for the rainbow fish.

SEQUENCING CENTER. Kindergartners arrange a set of life-cycle photos of fish in sequence from egg to adult.

SORTING CENTER. Children sort picture cards of fish and other water animals and place the cards with pictures of fish in one pocket chart labeled "Fish," and pictures of other animals in the "Not Fish" pocket chart. Fish pictures include goldfish, swordfish, trout, shark, eel, catfish, and seahorse; other animal pictures include dolphin, octopus, crab, turtle, whale, jellyfish, lobster, sea otter, and starfish. Mrs. LaRue introduced this center after teaching that fish have backbones and breathe with gills. The children practiced identifying and sorting the picture cards with the teacher before working at the center.

WORD WORK CENTER. Mrs. LaRue teaches phonemic awareness, phonics, and spelling lessons here. The children read and recite rhymes about fish, match objects that rhyme, such as *fish* and *dish,* and sort pictures and objects that begin with /f/, such as a fish, a fan, and a feather. They also write letters and words on whiteboards as Mrs. LaRue teaches handwriting skills at the same time she's teaching phonics and spelling.

LIBRARY CENTER. Children look at fish books from the text set. Each day, a fifth grade student comes to help out at the center; this student rereads one of the books Mrs. LaRue has already read to interested children while other kindergartners look at books independently.

The highlight of the unit is a field trip to a nearby aquarium to observe the fish they've been learning about. Mrs. LaRue takes many photos with her digital camera, and when they get back to school, she prints out copies of the photos for the children to examine and discuss. Then each child chooses one photo to use in making a square

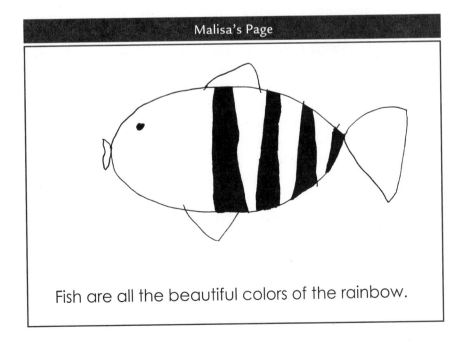

Malisa's Page

Fish are all the beautiful colors of the rainbow.

for their paper fish quilt. They glue their photos to the center of 8 by 8-inch squares of light blue construction paper and add a sentence under the photo. Joshua dictates, "Sharks are very dangerous!" Miriam dictates, "I saw lots of shiny sardine fish." Anthony writes, "Jellyfish are beautiful but they're not fish." Some children dictate their sentence for Mrs. LaRue to write, and others write interactively with her assistance. Because these sentences will be read and reread, Mrs. LaRue emphasizes that they should be written with "grown-up" spelling so that everyone can read them. Finally, the kindergartners help the teacher place the photo squares on a bulletin board that she has covered with wrapping paper decorated with fish. They add a title: Our Field Trip to the Aquarium.

Now the unit is coming to an end. After finishing the K-W-L chart, the children work on their culminating project—a collaborative book about fish. Each child dictates one fact about fish, and Mrs. LaRue types their facts on the computer. Children then add a picture to illustrate their fact. Malisa's page is shown in the box on page 279. The teacher compiles and laminates the pages, adds a cover, and binds the book together. Everyone eagerly watches as Mrs. LaRue shares the book with the class, clapping with excitement after each page is read. The book is ceremoniously added to their classroom library, and children take turns checking it out and taking it home to share with their families. Mrs. LaRue included three blank pages at the back of the book, and families write notes to the class on these pages, congratulating them on making such an informative book. These kindergartners are proud authors!

hildren are curious about the world—why dinosaurs became extinct, Neil Armstrong's moon landing, how to decipher secret codes, threats to the rain forest, why snakes shed their skins, and how skyscrapers are built—and nonfiction books provide this information. These books are more than collections of facts, and once students start reading, they get interested and continue reading because they're curious. They broaden their background knowledge by reading nonfiction books and become interested in learning more about content-area topics (Moss & Hendershot, 2002). Nonfiction books are visually appealing, blending textual and visual information, and students often pick them up to look at the photos and graphic presentations of information. Because so many high-quality nonfiction books are available today, preschool through eighth grade teachers incorporate more nonfiction books into their instruction (Palmer & Stewart, 2003).

Students like to read nonfiction texts, and they're able to understand these books as well as they do stories (Kristo & Bamford, 2004). Many times, they pick up a nonfiction book to check a fact, and then they continue reading because the information is fascinating (S. Read, 2001; Robb, 2004). Students also write nonfiction texts to share what they're learning, and the books they've read serve as models for their writing (Stead, 2002).

NONFICTION BOOKS

Nonfiction books are different than stories. They provide factual information about a variety of topics, use special text-structure patterns, and incorporate reader-friendly features, such as headings, glossaries, and indexes. Consider these nonfiction books:

Team Moon: How 400,000 People Landed Apollo 11 on the Moon (Thimmesh, 2006), the behind-the-scenes stories of the men and women at the Kennedy Space Center who put the first human being on the moon

Off to War: Voices of Soldiers' Children (Ellis, 2008), a collection of interviews with kids whose lives have been upended by their military parents' deployment to the Middle East

Dave the Potter: Artist, Poet, Slave (Hill, 2010), an inspiring picture biography of an extraordinary potter who lived in 19th-century South Carolina, told through poetry, with an author's note that provides more information

Down, Down, Down: A Journey to the Bottom of the Sea (Jenkins, 2009), a stunning top-to-bottom look at the ocean using paper collage illustrations of sea creatures at each depth

Lincoln Shot: A President's Life Remembered (Denenberg, 2008), an invented newspaper memorial of Lincoln's death, illustrated with period portraits, photos, and maps

The Way We Work: Getting to Know the Amazing Human Body (Macaulay, 2008b), a presentation of complex and technical information about the body systems

These books point out the differences between fiction and nonfiction. The topics are factual, and the information presented in these books is current and objective. The authors use nonfiction organizational patterns to organize the information and reader-friendly features to enhance readability.

The best nonfiction books exemplify these characteristics:

ACCURACY. The information is factual, objective, and current, avoiding stereotypes and anthropomorphism—that is, attributing human characteristics to animals and inanimate objects. The text distinguishes between fact and opinion. The author's qualifications are emphasized through evidence of research, information about how the author studied the topic, and suggestions for further reading and related websites.

ORGANIZATION. Ideas are developed logically using sequence, cause and effect, or another expository pattern, and the author's purpose is clear. Reader-friendly nonfiction features, including table of contents, diagrams, and margin notes, make the information more accessible.

DESIGN. The design is appealing, and illustrations complement the text, making the book more engaging. Margin notes, headings, feature boxes, and other reader-friendly nonfiction features make the book easier to comprehend.

STYLE. The style reveals the author's curiosity and enthusiasm for the topic. The tone suits the topic, and the text is written at appropriate interest and reading levels for the intended audience.

Each year, the National Council of Teachers of English presents the Orbis Pictus Award to the most outstanding nonfiction book published the previous year; these award winners embody the characteristics of good nonfiction books. Recent winners include *Ballet for Martha* (Greenberg & Jordan, 2010), about the extraordinary collaboration among Aaron Copeland (musical score), Martha Graham (choreography), and Isamu Noguchi (set design) for the 1944 production of "Appalachian Spring"; and *Amelia Earhart: The Legend of the Lost Aviator* (Tanaka, 2008), a well-written profile of the famous flier with archival photos and full-page paintings that add authenticity and vitality.

There are many types of nonfiction books, ranging from alphabet books and autobiographies to question-and-answer books and reference books; their formats as well as the information they provide vary from one type to another. The Booklist on the next page presents a variety of nonfiction books.

Alphabet Books. The text and visual information in alphabet books are organized around key words beginning with each letter. Some alphabet books are intended for young children, such as *The Sleepy Little Alphabet* (Sierra, 2009), where K stands for "kiss good night"; but other alphabet books appeal to older students, such as *A Is for Abigail: An Almanac of Amazing American Women* (Cheney, 2003), which celebrates the achievements of American women. Each letter celebrates a group, such as "O is for Sandra Day O'Connor and others who were first" and "R is for Rosie the Riveter and women who went to war." Sleeping Bear Press has also published a wide variety of alphabet books, including *G Is for Golden: A California Alphabet* (Domeniconi, 2002), *M Is for Masterpiece: An Art Alphabet* (Domeniconi, 2006), and *Z Is for Zeus: A Greek Mythology Alphabet* (Wilbur, 2008).

Autobiographies. *Autobiographies* are life stories written by the featured person; these books provide insight into people's lives from their own subjective viewpoints. Many popular children's authors, including Gary Paulsen (1999, 2001), Sid Fleischman (1998), Tomie dePaola (2006), Lois Lowry (2000), and Dick King-Smith (2002), have written autobiographies that appeal to readers who enjoy their books. In addition, many upper grade students read Francisco Jiménez's moving books about his family's experiences as migrant farm workers, *The Circuit* (1997) and *Breaking Through* (2001).

Biographies. *Biographies* are accounts of a person's life written by someone else, such as *Leonardo: Beautiful Dreamer* (Byrd, 2003) and *Eleanor, Quiet No More: The Life of Eleanor Roosevelt* (Rappaport, 2009). These life stories feature well-known people such as astronauts, prophets, and entertainers, as well as "common" people who have endured hardship and shown exceptional courage. As students read about these people's lives, they're also learning about personal qualities such as courage and determination that they can apply to their own lives to help them fulfill their dreams.

Many biographies span the featured person's entire life, including *Theodore Roosevelt: Champion of the American Spirit* (Kraft, 2003) and *Martin's Big Words: The Life of Dr. Martin Luther King, Jr.* (Rappaport, 2001), but others revolve around particular events or phases in the person's life. *Duel! Burr and Hamilton's Deadly War of Words* (Fradin, 2008) explains the causes and events culminating in the famous duel, and *John Muir: America's First Environmentalist* (Lasky, 2006) focuses on Muir's reverence for the natural world and his drive to preserve it.

Concept Books. Many nonfiction books are concept books—they explore a topic, such as opposites, penguins, gravity, or discrimination. There's no single definition of concept books, but many people think of them as picture books designed for very young children to help them understand their world. *The Quiet Book* (Underwood, 2010), designed for 4- and 5-year olds, explores the concept of "quiet." More detailed concept books for primary grade students include *What Do You Do With a Tail Like This?* (Jenkins & Page, 2003) and *The Vegetables We Eat* (Gibbons, 2008), but others such as *Hurricanes* (Simon, 2003) and *Mosque* (Macaulay, 2008a) are sophisticated concept books intended for older students.

Booklist

NONFICTION	
Alphabet Books	McArthur, M. (2010). *An ABC of what art can be.* Los Angeles: Getty Museum. M Shoulders, C., & Shoulders, M. (2010). *G is for gladiator: An ancient Rome alphabet.* Farmington Hills, MI: Sleeping Bear Press. M–U Spradlin, M. P. (2010). *Baseball from A to Z.* New York: HarperCollins. P–M
Autobiographies	Aldrin, B. (2005). *Reaching for the moon.* New York: HarperCollins. P–M Bryan, A. (2009). *Ashley Bryan: Words to my life's song.* New York: Atheneum. M–U Cohen, S., & Maciel, A. (2006). *Sasha Cohen: Fire on ice.* New York: HarperCollins. M–U
Biographies	Brown, D. (2010). *A wizard from the start: The incredible boyhood and amazing inventions of Thomas Edison.* Boston: Houghton Mifflin. P–M Fleischman, S. (2010). *Sir Charlie: Chaplin, the funniest man in the world.* New York: Greenwillow. M–U McCarthy, M. (2010). *Pop! The invention of bubblegum.* New York: Simon & Schuster. P–M
Concept Books	Demi. (2008). *Marco Polo.* New York: Marshall Cavendish. M Goin, M. B. (2009). *Storms!* Washington, DC: National Geographic. P–M Pfeffer, W. (2009). *Life in a coral reef.* New York: HarperCollins. P–M
Directions	Bell-Rehwoldt, S. (2009). *The kids' guide to building cool stuff.* Mankato, MN: Capstone Press. M–U Bucholz, D. (2010). *The unofficial Harry Potter cookbook.* Avon, MA: Adams Media. M–U Moss, M. (2008). *Amelia's guide to babysitting.* New York: Simon & Schuster. M
Journals, Letters, and Speeches	Doubilet, D., & Hayes, J. (2009). *Face to face with sharks.* Washington, DC: National Geographic. M–U Frank, A. (1995). *Anne Frank: The diary of a young girl* (New ed.). New York: Doubleday. U Obama, B. (2009). *Yes, we can! A salute to children from President Obama's victory speech.* New York: Orchard Books. P–M
Multigenre Books	Cole, J. (2010). *The magic school bus and the climate challenge.* New York: Scholastic. P–M Herbert, J. (2000). *Lewis and Clark for kids.* Chicago: Chicago Review Press. M–U Kerley, B. (2010). *The extraordinary Mark Twain (according to Susy).* New York: Scholastic. M
Photo Essays	Halls, K. M. (2010). *Saving the Baghdad zoo: A true story of hope and heroes.* New York: Greenwillow. M–U Mitchell, D. (2010). *Driven: A photobiography of Henry Ford.* Washington, DC: National Geographic. M–U Robbins, K. (2010). *For good measure: The ways we say how much, how far, how heavy, how big, how old.* New York: Roaring Brook Press. P–M
Question-and-Answer Books	Crisp, M. (2004). *Everything dolphin: What kids really want to know about dolphins.* Minnetonka, MN: NorthWord Press. M Kaner, E. (2009). *Have you ever seen a duck in a raincoat?* Tonawanda, NY: Kids Can Press. P–M Ransom, C. F. (2010). *Who wrote the U.S. Constitution? And other questions about the Constitutional Convention of 1787.* Minneapolis: Lerner. M–U
Reference Books	*First human body encyclopedia.* (2005). New York: DK. M King, D. C. (2003). *Children's encyclopedia of American history.* New York: DK. M–U *National Geographic beginner's world atlas* (Updated ed.). (2005). Washington, DC: National Geographic. M

P = primary grades (preK–2); M = middle grades (3–5); U = upper grades (6–8)

Directions. Cookbooks, how-to guides, and other guidebooks provide step-by-step instructions that help readers accomplish a task, from baking cupcakes and drawing animals to conducting science experiments. Three examples of technical writing are *Ed Emberley's Drawing Book of Animals* (2006), *Show Off: How to Do Absolutely Everything. One Step at a Time* (Hines-Stephens, 2009), and *The Everything Kids' Cookbook* (Nissenberg, 2008). Students can compare the format of a traditional recipe with *Sopa de Frijoles/Bean Soup* (Argueta, 2009), a recipe-poem.

Journals, Letters, and Speeches. Journals written by real people, collections of letters, and illustrated speeches are other types of nonfiction. Many books written as journals or collections of letters are fiction, but one nonfiction example is *Of Thee I Sing: A Letter to My Daughters*, by Barack Obama (2010). Other picture books are richly illustrated versions of speeches: *I Have a Dream* (King, 1997) presents the civil rights leader's eloquent speech, with award-winning children's illustrators' interpretations of his words on each page; and in *We the Kids: The Preamble to the Constitution of the United States* (Catrow, 2005), well-known political cartoonist David Catrow uses illustrations to explain each line of the introductory statement.

Multigenre Books. Multigenre books present information using more than one genre. The Magic School Bus series of science-related books, including *The Magic School Bus in the Rain Forest* (Cole, 1998), and the social studies–related books in the Ms. Frizzle's Adventures series, including *Ms. Frizzle's Adventures: Medieval Castle* (Cole, 2003), are the best known multigenre books. The main text is presented as a narrative, and the side panels and other special boxes provide information—questions and answers, notes, and brief reports written by Ms. Frizzle's students as well as charts, maps, and other diagrams. *The 5,000-Year-Old Puzzle: Solving a Mystery of Ancient Egypt* (Logan, 2002) presents information about the discovery of King Tut's tomb through journal entries, photos, maps, postcards, sidebars, and newspaper articles. By using a combination of genres, the author and the illustrator provide multiple viewpoints and enrich their presentation of information. In *Leonardo: Beautiful Dreamer* (Byrd, 2003), boxes with notes, explanations, and excerpts from Leonardo da Vinci's own journals amplify the text.

Multigenre books are richly layered texts, often presented in picture-book form. Because of the complexity of the page layout, Chapman and Sopko (2003) compare reading a multigenre book to peeling an onion and recommend that teachers read these books three or four times over a period of several days so that students can fully comprehend and appreciate them. First, they suggest taking a picture walk to examine the illustrations. Then teachers read the book, focusing on the nonfiction text, and for the second reading, they focus on the narrative text. Finally, they focus on the sketches and borders. Of course, the number of readings depends on students' interests and the complexity of the book.

Photo Essays. Nonfiction books in which concepts are explored mainly using a collection of photographs are known as *photo essays. Cubes, Cones, Cylinders and Spheres* (Hoban, 2000) and *City Signs* (Milich, 2005) are wordless books that present their topics using artistic photographs, and in *Extra Cheese, Please: Mozzarella's Journey From Cow to Pizza* (Peterson, 2004), the author describes how mozzarella cheese is produced, using photos complemented with brief texts.

Question-and-Answer Books. As the name suggests, authors pose a question on each page and then provide a detailed answer. Scholastic has published an extensive collection of question-and-answer books on social studies topics, including ... *If You Lived When There Was Slavery in America* (Kamma, 2004), ... *If You Lived When Women Won Their Rights* (Kamma, 2008), ... *If You Lived*

With the Indians of the Northwest Coast (Kamma, 2002), and ... *If You Lived in the Days of the Knights* (McGovern, 2001). These books serve as useful models for students who want to write their own question-and-answer books.

Reference Books. Students use reference books, including almanacs, encyclopedias, dictionaries, and atlases, to track down information and research topics. *The World Almanac for Kids* (Janssen, 2011) is an eye-catching fact book, filled with kid-friendly information about fashion, games, disasters, Native Americans, movies, prizes and contests, technology, geography, mythology, and census data, for example. This almanac is completely updated each year, so the topics included in the book vary. Other reference books are handy guidebooks, including *My First Pocket Guide: Seashore Life* (Kinghorn, 2002) and *First Field Guide: Reptiles* (Behler, 1999).

The World Book Encyclopedia is a commonly used reference book in middle and upper grade classrooms. It's a 22-volume set with articles organized in alphabetic order and supplemented with thousands of photographs, illustrations, and diagrams to extend the text and provide information visually. Recently added topics include crime scene investigations, doping, tsunamis, fossil fuel, hip hop, and martial arts. The encyclopedia is also available online with reference articles, multimedia, games, interactive tools, activities, and links to primary source documents, newspapers, and ebooks.

Expository Text Structures

Nonfiction books are organized in patterns called *expository text structures*. Five of the most common organizational patterns are description, sequence, comparison, cause and effect, and problem and solution (Meyer & Freedle, 1984). Figure 10–1 gives an overview of these patterns and lists mentor texts illustrating each one. Students learn about these expository text patterns:

DESCRIPTION. Writers describe a topic by listing characteristics, features, and examples in this organizational pattern. Phrases such as *for example* and *characteristics are* cue this structure. When students delineate any topic, such as tigers, submarines, or Alaska, they use description.

SEQUENCE. Writers list items or events in numerical or chronological order in this pattern. Cue words include *first, second, third, next, then,* and *finally.* Students use sequence to write directions for completing a math problem, the stages in an animal's life cycle, or events in a biography.

COMPARISON. Writers explain how two or more things are alike or different in this structure. *Different, in contrast, alike, same as,* and *on the other hand* are cue words and phrases that signal this structure. When students compare and contrast book and video versions of a story, reptiles and amphibians, or life in ancient Greece with life in ancient Egypt, they use this organizational pattern.

CAUSE AND EFFECT. Writers describe one or more causes and the resulting effect or effects in this pattern. *Reasons why, if . . . then, as a result, therefore,* and *because* are words and phrases that cue this structure. Explanations of why dinosaurs became extinct, the effects of pollution on the environment, or the causes of the Civil War use the cause-and-effect pattern.

PROBLEM AND SOLUTION. Writers present a problem and offer one or more solutions in this expository structure. A variation is the question-and-answer format, in which the

FIGURE 10-1   The Expository Text Structures

Structure	Description	Books
Description	A topic is delineated using attributes and examples.	Arnosky, J. (2002). *All about frogs*. New York: Scholastic. P–M Gibbons, G. (2007). *Vegetables we eat*. New York: Holiday House. P Guiberson, B. Z. (2010). *Disasters*. New York: Henry Holt. M–U
Sequence	Steps, events, or directions are presented in numerical or chronological order.	Arnold, C. (2010). *A bald eagle's world*. Mankato, MN: Capstone Press. P–M Burton, V. (2009). *Life story*. Boston: Houghton Mifflin. P–M Minor, W. (2006). *Yankee Doodle America: The spirit of 1776 from A to Z*. New York: Putnam. M–U
Comparison	Two or more things are compared or contrasted.	Bidner, J. (2007). *Is my cat a tiger? How your cat compares to its wild cousins*. New York: Lark Books. M Schanzer, R. (2007). *George vs. George: The American Revolution as seen from both sides*. Washington, DC: National Geographic. M Spier, P. (1991). *We the people*. New York: Doubleday. M–U
Cause and Effect	Causes and the resulting effects are described.	Brown, C. L. (2006). *The day the dinosaurs died*. New York: HarperCollins. P–M Burns, L. G. (2007). *Tracking trash: Flotsam, jetsam, and the science of ocean movement*. Boston: Houghton Mifflin. M–U Pfeffer, W. (2004). *Wiggling worms at work*. New York: HarperCollins. P–M
Problem and Solution	A problem and one or more solutions are presented. Also uses question-and-answer format.	Allen, T. B. (2004). *George Washington, spymaster: How the Americans outspied the British and won the Revolutionary War*. Washington, DC: National Geographic. M–U Montgomery, S. (2010). *Kakapo rescue: Saving the world's strangest parrot*. Boston: Houghton Mifflin. M Sayre, A. P. (2010). *Turtle, turtle: Watch out!* Watertown, MA: Charlesbridge. P–M

P = primary grades (pre K–2); M = middle grades (3–5); U = upper grades (6–8)

writer poses a question and then answers it. Cue words and phrases include *the problem is, the puzzle is, solve,* and *question . . . answer*. Students use this structure when they write about why money was invented, saving endangered animals, or building dams to stop flooding. They often use the problem-solution pattern in writing advertisements and in other persuasive writing.

Some nonfiction books are organized around a single pattern, but often they incorporate several patterns. Gail Gibbons's picture book *Owls* (2006), for example, is basically a book that describes owls, their behavior, and their habitat (descriptive), but it also includes information on their life cycle (sequence), different species (comparison), and environmental hazards threatening some species (cause and effect).

Students use graphic organizers to organize and visually represent ideas for the organizational patterns. Students might use a cluster for description, a Venn diagram or T-chart for comparison, or a series of boxes and arrows for cause and effect (Yopp & Yopp, 2005). Most of the research on expository text structures has focused on older students' use of these patterns in reading; however, primary grade students also use the patterns and cue words in their writing (Raphael, Englert, & Kirschner, 1989).

Nonfiction Features

Nonfiction books have unique text features that stories don't normally have, such as margin notes and indexes; their purpose is to make text easier to read and understand. These features are found in many nonfiction books:

- Table of contents to assist readers in locating chapters or sections of the text
- Headings and subheadings to direct readers' attention
- Photographs and drawings to illustrate big ideas
- Figures, maps, and tables to present detailed information visually
- Margin notes to provide supplemental information or direct readers to additional information
- Highlighted vocabulary words to identify key terms
- Glossaries to assist readers in pronouncing and defining key terms
- Review sections to provide summaries of big ideas at the end of chapters or the entire book
- Indexes to assist readers in locating specific information

In addition, different font sizes and colors are used to highlight key points, technical vocabulary, and other features. Researchers have found that using these nonfiction features improves students' comprehension and the effectiveness of their writing (Harvey & Goudvis, 2007).

Some excellent nonfiction books look more like stories than informational books. One example is *Listen to the Wind: The Story of Dr. Greg and Three Cups of Tea* (Mortenson & Roth, 2009), the inspiring true story of Greg Mortenson's first school-building project in Korphe, Pakistan, told from the viewpoint of the village children who will attend the school. The illustrations accompanying the text are collages, but at the back of the book, there's a section called "A Korphe Scrapbook" with photos documenting the project, an artist's note, and a bibliography. Most informational books, however, incorporate many nonfiction features. Books in the DK Eyewitness and Eye Wonder series are great examples; Dorling Kindersley is known for its spectacular page layouts that integrate text with photos. In *DK Eyewitness Books: Soccer* (Hornby, 2010), for instance, you'll find a table of contents, chapter titles, photo illustrations with captions and labels, text boxes, a question-and-answer section, a glossary, an index, a resources list including useful websites and places to visit, and an index. The book's divided into two- and four-page chapters on topics such as soccer balls, game rules, the goalkeeper, and the World Cup, and each chapter includes a succinct text supplemented with 7 to 10 photographs. The Booklist on page 288 presents books incorporating a variety of nonfiction features.

Comparing Fiction and Nonfiction Books

Because fiction and nonfiction are different, it's important to teach students about the differences so that they can read informational books effectively. To examine these differences, pick up a story and a nonfiction book on the same topic. *Mythology* (Steer, 2007) and its companion, *The Mythology Handbook* (Steer, 2009), and other books in Candlewick Press's "Ologies" series for

Booklist

NONFICTION FEATURES	
PreK–Grade 2	Adler, D. A. (2009). *Money madness*. New York: Holiday House. Gibbons, G. (2009). *Tornadoes!* New York: Holiday House. Hayward, L. (2001). *DK readers: A day in the life of a builder*. New York: DK. Mugford, S. (2005). *Sharks and other dangers of the deep*. New York: Priddy Books. Page, R., & Jenkins, S. (2010). *How to clean a hippopotamus: A look at unusual animal partnerships*. Boston: Houghton Mifflin.
Grades 3–5	Bingham, C. (2004). *DK eye wonder: Rocks and minerals*. New York: DK. Cole, J. (2010). *The magic school bus and the climate challenge*. New York: Scholastic. Herbert. K. (2002). *The American Revolution for kids*. Chicago: Chicago Review Press. Stewart. M. (2009). *Snakes!* Washington, DC: National Geographic. Turner, P. S. (2009). *The frog scientist*. Boston: Houghton Mifflin.
Grades 6–8	Bausum, A. (2009). *Our country's presidents*. Washington, DC: National Geographic. Fleischman, S. (2008). *The trouble begins at 8: A life of Mark Twain in the wild, wild west*. New York: Greenwillow. Twist, C. (2010). *The oceanology handbook: A course for underwater explorers*. Somerville, MA: Candlewick Press. Walker, S. M. (2009). *Written in bone: Buried lives of Jamestown and colonial Maryland*. Minneapolis: Carolrhoda. Weitzman, D. (2009). *Pharaoh's boat*. Boston: Houghton Mifflin.

upper grade students are great examples; and Mary Pope Osborne's popular Magic Tree House series includes storybooks and companion nonfiction research guides for middle grade students. The differences between fiction and nonfiction are easy to pick out when students read *Monday With a Mad Genius* (Osborne, 2009b) and *Leonardo da Vinci: A Nonfiction Companion to Monday With a Mad Genius.* (Osborne, 2009a), for example. A class of fourth graders noticed these differences after reading the two books about the great artist:

- Nonfiction books are true, but stories are invented.
- You can start reading anywhere in a nonfiction book, but you read stories from beginning to end.
- Nonfiction books have photos and drawings, but stories just have drawings.
- Nonfiction books have a table of contents, but only some stories have it.
- Nonfiction books have indexes at the back, but stories don't.
- Nonfiction books have extra things: notes in the margin, highlighted words, pronunciation guides, and diagrams with labels.
- At the end of nonfiction books, the author tells you how to learn more.

In addition, upper grade students can compare Jean Craighead George's award-winning survival story, *My Side of the Mountain* (2004), and its nonfiction companion book, *Pocket Guide to the Out-doors* (George, 2009).

As they examine nonfiction books, students learn how authors use expository text structures to organize the text and special features to enhance readability. They learn how to use an index to locate specific information and to use diagrams and margin notes to learn more about topics presented in the regular text. Plus, they apply what they're learning as they organize and craft their own nonfiction books and projects.

RESEARCH

Children are naturally inquisitive, and they like to explore nonfiction topics. They enthusiastically pursue special interests and show genuine engagement as they participate in research projects. They identify an important question that drives the research (McMackin & Siegel, 2002). Asking questions seems to be as empowering for students as for adults, and the process helps them become more thoughtful learners. As students explore topics they're passionate about and search for answers to questions that puzzle them, they learn the research process. Their understanding of the world deepens as they uncover answers, write reports, and share what they've learned with classmates (Harvey, 1998).

The Research Process

Students use the research process to identify topics they're interested in studying; locate information using books, online materials, and other resources; and then use what they learn to create a project to share with classmates and wider audiences. They learn to use authentic research procedures and work collaboratively with classmates to find answers and solve problems that matter to them. The research process is participatory, collaborative, and creative (Boss & Kraus, 2007), and the procedure is described in the Step-by-Step feature on page 290. It's similar to the writing process in that students are involved in a sequence of activities as they develop and refine their knowledge and share what they've learned with authentic audiences.

Plagiarism isn't a big problem when students use the research process, but they still need to understand what plagiarism is and why it's wrong. Students are less likely to plagiarize because they've collected information to answer questions they care about, and because they've developed their projects step-by-step. The two best ways to avoid having students copy from another source and pass it off as their own are to use the research process and to have students do research projects at school rather than as homework.

Research Tools

Students often find it challenging to take notes and organize information they're gathering to answer research questions. As they gather information from Internet resources and books, they take notes, but sometimes the information they record is confusing or incomplete. Also, the amount of information students collect can be overwhelming, or they spend several days gathering information without realizing that they've dealt with only one part of their topic. To address these problems, teachers teach students to use these research tools:

NOTE TAKING. Students have traditionally taken notes on note cards: They organize the information they find according to their research questions, writing one idea on each card and paraphrasing the ideas they're recording. Sometimes students also record a few direct quotes, but they're careful to use quotation marks to indicate a quotation, copy the words exactly as they appear in the reference, and include the page the quote appeared on. On other index cards, students record all necessary bibliographic information for their reference lists, including the title, author, publisher, and copyright date. Increasingly, students are using NoteStar, Notefish, and other online note-taking tools to take notes. To learn more about online note-taking tools, check the Digital Classroom feature on the next page.

DATA CHARTS. *Data charts* are grids that students make to organize the information they're gathering about a topic (McMackin & Siegel, 2002). They make a data chart by drawing a grid and labeling the columns with big ideas or questions and the rows with bibliographic information about the print and digital resources they've consulted. Then they fill in the boxes with information from each resource to complete the chart. This organizing procedure is useful whenever the topic can be divided into four or more big ideas or questions.

POCKET CHARTS. Students make pocket charts to organize the notes they're taking. Before beginning to take notes, students write each research question on an envelope and attach the envelopes to the inside of a file folder. Then students take notes on small slips of paper or note cards and file them in the envelopes. Not only are students' notes neatly organized, but they can quickly notice if they need additional information about one of their questions.

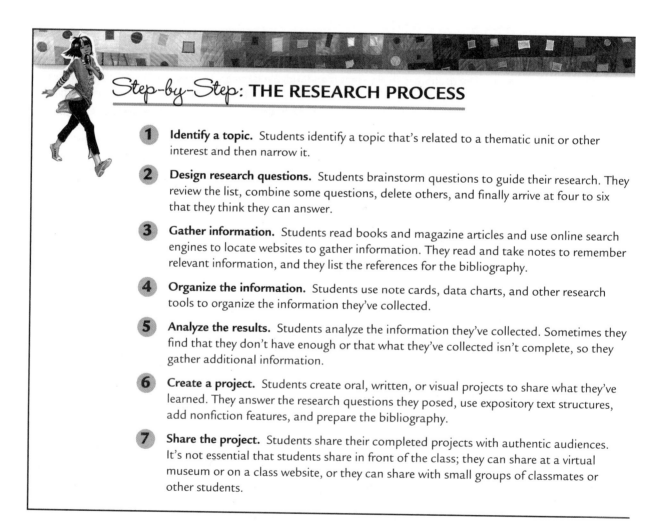

Step-by-Step: THE RESEARCH PROCESS

1 **Identify a topic.** Students identify a topic that's related to a thematic unit or other interest and then narrow it.

2 **Design research questions.** Students brainstorm questions to guide their research. They review the list, combine some questions, delete others, and finally arrive at four to six that they think they can answer.

3 **Gather information.** Students read books and magazine articles and use online search engines to locate websites to gather information. They read and take notes to remember relevant information, and they list the references for the bibliography.

4 **Organize the information.** Students use note cards, data charts, and other research tools to organize the information they've collected.

5 **Analyze the results.** Students analyze the information they've collected. Sometimes they find that they don't have enough or that what they've collected isn't complete, so they gather additional information.

6 **Create a project.** Students create oral, written, or visual projects to share what they've learned. They answer the research questions they posed, use expository text structures, add nonfiction features, and prepare the bibliography.

7 **Share the project.** Students share their completed projects with authentic audiences. It's not essential that students share in front of the class; they can share at a virtual museum or on a class website, or they can share with small groups of classmates or other students.

DIGITAL CLASSROOM

Online Note-Taking Tools

Online note-taking tools are quickly replacing the stacks of colored note cards students compile when they're gathering and organizing data during research projects. Online notes are easier to make, and students can access them easily. Note-taking tools are platform independent, so whether they're using a PC or a Mac, students need only a browser to access their notes. These free note-taking tools support students in fourth through eighth grades as they gather and organize information during the research process:

▶ **NoodleTools**

http://www.noodletools.com
Students record, organize, and synthesize information on online note cards at this website, and they can also create and format the bibliography.

▶ **Notefish**

http://www.notefish.com
Students use this application to simplify Internet research. Note taking involves three steps: saving snippets of webpages, *annotating and organizing the information, and sharing the notes.*

▶ **NoteStar**

http://notestar.4teachers.org
NoteStar is a collaborative note-taking application. Small groups of students organize their research projects with subtopics, and then students each take notes about one subtopic and organize them. This tool also helps students collect references and prepare their bibliography.

▶ **Yahoo! NotePad**

http://yahoo.com
Students use this popular tool to write and organize notes in folders.

In these note-taking tools, students take notes, organize them, and then share them. Most applications allow students to revise and edit their notes and tag important ideas.

CLUSTERS. Students organize information they've collected on weblike diagrams called *clusters*. They draw clusters with one ray for each research question or big idea and add details to each ray. Students can also create clusters online. The best known program is Inspiration (http://www.inspiration.com); Kidspiration is a version for younger children.

These tools simplify the task of gathering and organizing information during the research process.

Reporting

Students share what they learn by creating oral, written, and visual projects. The Differentiated Instruction box on page 292 shows the possible projects that students pursue. Creating projects offers an opportunity for teachers to differentiate instruction because they suggest project and grouping options for students according to their interests and abilities. Sometimes students work together as a class to create a virtual museum or write an alphabet book, for instance, or they work with partners or in teams to create websites or multigenre projects; at other times, students work independently to create a PowerPoint presentation or a written report.

Boxes of Artifacts. Students collect artifacts and make items related to a research topic, write cards to explain each artifact, and put the collection in a decorated box. Artifact boxes can be used to share information about almost any topic. For example, kindergartners learning about the life cycle of butterflies make an egg, a caterpillar, a chrysalis, and an adult butterfly using craft materials; write cards describing each artifact; attach the cards to the artifacts; and put the collection into a decorated tin. Or, fifth graders studying their state make artifact boxes with a map of the state, small items representing agricultural or industrial products, postcards showing major cities, charts with data about the state, a small state flag, and a time line showing key events in the state's history.

Posters. Students present the information they've learned through a research project using a combination of drawings and writing on a poster. Sometimes students write the question they've researched at the top of the poster and use drawings or pictures downloaded from the Internet to answer the question. They add labels to the pictures or write a summary sentence at the bottom of the poster to make sure the answer is clear.

Charts. Students create visual reports to share the answers they've found in charts, maps, flowcharts, and other diagrams (Stead, 2006). Charts are used when the information can be presented more effectively through a diagram than through an oral or written project. Formats for visual reports include clusters, diagrams, data charts, maps, time lines, and cubes. Moline (1995) explains that visual presentations are sophisticated, multilayered reports. At first thought, these formats might seem easier to produce than written reports, but when they're done properly, they're just as challenging.

Students consider the layout, how the words and drawings are integrated, as they create charts (Moline, 1995). They think about the arrangement of the diagram on the page; the use of lines, boxes, and headings to organize information; and pictures to highlight key points. Students also consider how they use type styles: They might print some words in capital letters or use color to highlight key terms, or they might choose a type style that emphasizes the concept. For example, students creating a chart about ancient Egypt use a type style that resembles hieroglyphics for the title. Word processing programs allow students to experiment with a variety of fonts and to use size and boldface for emphasis.

DIFFERENTIATED INSTRUCTION
Nonfiction

ORAL LANGUAGE	WRITTEN LANGUAGE	VISUAL LANGUAGE
Conduct interviews	Compose "All About . . ." books	Collect boxes of artifacts
Give PowerPoint presentations	Craft poems	Create virtual museums
Participate in hot seat activities	Create brochures	Develop slide shows
Perform songs and raps	Develop websites and wikis	Draw charts and diagrams
Present oral reports	Make alphabet books	Make life lines/time lines
Read poems aloud	Read and write feature articles	Perform plays and puppet shows
Record and listen to podcasts	Write reports and essays	Present information on posters
		View videos and DVDs

FIGURE 10-2   A Cluster About Eagles

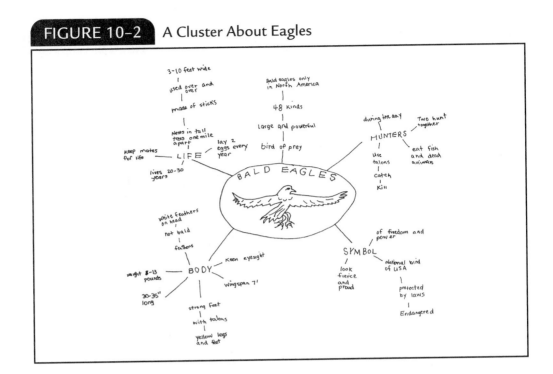

Two charts that students make are clusters and cubes. *Clusters* are weblike diagrams that students use to gather and organize information (Rico, 2000). The topic is written in a circle centered on a sheet of paper or a poster. Main ideas are written on rays drawn out from the circle, and branches with details and examples are added to complete each main idea. Figure 10–2 presents a cluster that a sixth grader developed during a thematic unit about birds to share what he learned about bald eagles. The information is divided into four categories: life, hunters, symbol, and body; other facts are listed at the top of the figure.

On a *cube*, students explore a topic from six dimensions or viewpoints (Neeld, 1990). The name comes from the fact that cubes have six sides. Students explore the topic from these perspectives:

DESCRIPTION. Students describe the topic, including its colors, shapes, and sizes.

COMPARISON. Students compare the topic to something else. They consider how it is similar to or different from this other thing.

ASSOCIATION. Students associate the topic to something else and explain why the topic makes them think of this other thing.

ANALYSIS. Students analyze the topic and tell how it's made or what it's composed of.

APPLICATION. Students apply the topic and tell how it can be used or what can be done with it.

ARGUMENTATION. Students argue for or against the topic. They take a stand and list reasons to support it.

The steps in creating a cube are described in the Step-by-Step feature on page 294.

What's especially valuable about cubing is that students apply the information they've been learning about a topic in new ways as they analyze, associate, and consider the other perspectives.

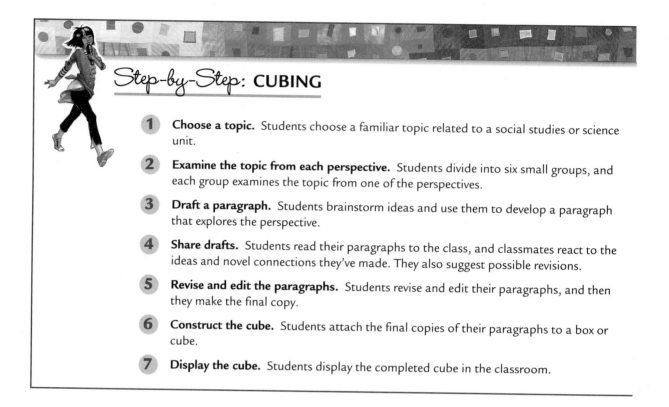

Step-by-Step: **CUBING**

1   **Choose a topic.** Students choose a familiar topic related to a social studies or science unit.

2   **Examine the topic from each perspective.** Students divide into six small groups, and each group examines the topic from one of the perspectives.

3   **Draft a paragraph.** Students brainstorm ideas and use them to develop a paragraph that explores the perspective.

4   **Share drafts.** Students read their paragraphs to the class, and classmates react to the ideas and novel connections they've made. They also suggest possible revisions.

5   **Revise and edit the paragraphs.** Students revise and edit their paragraphs, and then they make the final copy.

6   **Construct the cube.** Students attach the final copies of their paragraphs to a box or cube.

7   **Display the cube.** Students display the completed cube in the classroom.

Figure 10–3 presents a cubing written by small groups of fifth graders at the end of a thematic unit on the American Revolution.

"All About . . . " Books. Young children write or dictate "All About . . . " books on nonfiction topics. Usually one piece of information and an accompanying illustration appear on each page. A kindergarten class compiled this book-length report on police officers:

Page 1: *Police officers help people who are in trouble. They are nice to kids. They are only mean to robbers and bad people. Police officers make people obey the laws. They give tickets to people who drive cars too fast.*

Page 2: *Men and women can be police officers. They wear blue uniforms like Officer Jerry's. But sometimes police officers wear regular clothes when they work undercover. They wear badges on their uniforms and on their hats. Officer Jerry's badge number is 3407. Police officers have guns, handcuffs, whistles, sticks, and two-way radios. They have to carry all these things.*

Page 3: *Police officers drive police cars with flashing lights and loud sirens. The cars have radios so the officers can talk to other police officers at the police station. Sometimes they ride on police motorcycles or on police horses or in police helicopters or in police boats.*

Page 4: *Police officers work at police stations. The jail for the bad people that they catch is right next door. One police officer sits at the radio to talk to the police officers who are driving their cars. The police chief works at the police station, too.*

Page 5: *Police officers are your friends. They want to help you so you shouldn't be afraid of them. You can ask them if you need some help.*

Page 6: *How We Learned About Police Officers for Our Report*

 1. *We read these books:*
    Police by Ray Broekel
    What Do They Do? Policemen and Firemen by Carla Greene
 2. *We interviewed Officer Jerry.*
 3. *We visited the police station.*

The teacher read two books aloud to the children, and Officer Jerry visited the classroom and talked to the class about his job. The kindergartners also took a field trip to the police station. The teacher took photos of Officer Jerry, his police car, and the police station to illustrate the report. With this background, the teacher helped the kindergartners develop a cluster with these five main ideas: what police officers do, what equipment police officers have, how police officers travel, where police officers work, and police officers are your friends. The children added details to the main ideas, and then each main idea was used to create one page of the report. Afterward, the children created a bibliography—"How We Learned About Police Officers for Our

FIGURE 10-3   A Cubing on the American Revolution

Describe	The American Revolution was fought from 1775 to 1783 between Britain's Lobster Backs and the young American patriots. From the first major battle of Bunker Hill in 1775 to the battle of Yorktown in 1781, there were many hardships and deaths. The brave Americans continued on in spite of Britain's better supplied army because they wanted freedom, justice, and independence from King George.
Compare	The American Revolution and the Civil War were alike in many ways. They were both fought on American soil. Both wars were fought for people's rights and freedoms. With families fighting against families, these wars were very emotional. The winning side of each war had commanding generals who became presidents of the United States: George Washington and Ulysses S. Grant. The soldiers in the war rallied to the song "Yankee Doodle."
Associate	We celebrate the American Revolution on the 4th of July with fireworks and parades. Fireworks are spectacular things for spectacular days! Rockets shoot into the air like cannonballs! Great big booms and sparkles fall from the sky as people celebrate! Parades remind us of soldiers marching into battle led by flutes, drums, and flags! The 4th of July is a celebration of history.
Analyze	The American Revolution began when King George taxed the colonists too much and did not ask them if they wanted to pay or not. In five years, the Stamp Act, the Townsend Act, the Quartering Act, and the Intolerable Acts were forced on the colonists. This money was to pay for the French and Indian War. This made the colonists angry. One time the colonists dressed up like Indians and threw tea into the Boston Harbor. King George kept on pushing until the colonists revolted and started a war.
Apply	The most important outcome of the American Revolution was the beginning of our 200-year-old country. We enjoy the freedom of speech, religion, and the press. The Constitution grants us a lot of other freedoms, too. This living document has given us the opportunity to be anything we want to be.
Argue for	If we had not fought and won the American Revolution, there would be no United States of America. We would not have the right to speak our minds. We might all have to go to the same church. We would not have freedom or equality. There would be no Liberty Bell or Statue of Liberty. Although war is scary, painful, and violent, if we had the chance to go back, we would go and fight with all our might. We would rather do math problems all day than be ruled by a king.

Report"—and inserted the photographs; then the completed book was ceremoniously presented to the school library.

News Articles. Students write nonfiction articles like those found in newspapers on current events and other newsworthy topics. They research the topic and gather information to answer the five *W* questions—*who, what, when, where,* and *why*—from multiple sources, including interviews, when possible. News articles are usually 150–300 words long, and in the first paragraph, students write a lead to grab readers' attention and make them want to keep reading. In the next two to five paragraphs, students build on the information they introduced in the first paragraph. They present the big ideas to answer the five *W* questions and include quotes and details. In the last paragraph, often called the *kicker*, students sum up the big ideas, referring to the first paragraph. Sometimes they add illustrations, including drawings, photos, and diagrams.

Both the *Weekly Reader* and Scholastic's classroom news magazines are available in print and digital formats for preK–8 students. These magazines contain articles about current events; students read them to learn about recent news, and they serve as mentor texts. As they examine news articles, students learn how to organize ideas, write effective leads and kickers, use quotes, and format writing in this genre. In addition, students can check out Scholastic's Kids Press Corps; they go to http://teacher.scholastic.com and search for Kids Press Corps. At the website, students view video versions of news reports on current events, entertainment, and sports topics; read writing tips; meet the student reporters; and even apply to join the team of reporters.

Feature Articles. Feature articles are creative compositions that address real events, issues, and trends. They're longer than news stories and address a topic in more depth. Students write from a more personal viewpoint, providing commentary as well as information (Morgan, 2010). They organize their articles into short paragraphs with two or three sentences that include statistics and quotes as well as Internet links to more in-depth information and related topics. These characteristics highlight the differences between feature articles and news articles:

- Storytelling techniques to grab readers' attention
- Quotes and anecdotes to add color
- Sensory details to make images more vivid
- Subheadings to highlight big ideas

Students also include nonfiction features, such as charts, maps, and illustrations, to provide additional information.

Students write different types of feature articles, which usually fall into one of these five categories:

HUMAN INTEREST ARTICLES. Students describe a person's triumph over a continuing struggle or a tragic event. This is the most common type of feature article.

PERSONALITY ARTICLES. Students focus on a contemporary or historical personality who's done something interesting. These articles are similar to character sketches.

HOW TO . . . ARTICLES. Students describe how to do something, and they explain why it's important.

INFORMATIONAL ARTICLES. Students explain a topic, adding a personal connection with it.

HISTORICAL EVENT ARTICLES. Students recount a historical event, putting a human face on it.

Students' strong personal voice is evident in each of these categories.

Teachers collect feature articles to use as mentor texts from newspapers, magazines, and websites for students to read and examine. Three Internet sources of feature articles are Kids. LibraryPoint (http://kids.librarypoint.org), Scholastic's Heads Up archive of feature articles (http://headsup.scholastic.com/articles/feature-article-archive), and National Geographic Kids (http://news.nationalgeographic.com/kids).

Collaborative Reports. Teachers often introduce the research process by writing a collaborative report. They introduce a broad "umbrella" topic, and then students brainstorm subtopics and identify research questions. Students choose questions, and those who are interested in the same questions gather in small groups to work together. Before they begin working, however, the teacher models the process by choosing one of the remaining questions and having the class research that question and write the answer together. Then the groups work together to research their questions and write their sections of the report. They follow the writing process to develop and refine their sections before preparing the final copies. Afterward, the teacher collects the completed sections, compiles them, and makes copies for each student.

A second grade class researched crabs as part of a thematic unit, and students wrote this chapter as a collaborative report:

  How Are Crabs Like Us?

We don't look anything like crabs, but people and crabs are alike in some ways. The most important thing is that crabs and people are both alive. Crabs eat, but they eat different food than we do. Crabs have arms but they look different. They have pincers instead of fingers. They have legs, but they have 6 more legs than we do. We can walk, run, and swim, and that's what crabs can do.

Then the second graders divided into small groups to research and write answers to these questions:

Where Do Crabs Live?

Crabs live in lots of different places. Some crabs live in shallow pools. They also like to live under the sand and in the ocean. Each place is just perfect for the crabs to live and grow.

How Do Crabs Move?

Crabs have eight legs. There are four on each side. We think that so many legs probably makes it hard to move. Crabs don't walk or run like we do. They actually move sideways.

Do You Know Why Crabs Have Pincers?

Crabs have two claws called pincers. They use their pincers to catch food, and they use their pincers to fight predators like seagulls. The pincers are powerful.

How Do Crabs Grow?

Crabs have hard shells. They grow and grow inside their shells. When they outgrow their shells, crabs shed it and grow a new one.

Can Crabs Grow New Legs?

Yes! Crabs really can grow new legs. They can get new claws and new antennas, too. So if an animal bites off their leg, crabs grow new ones. They are small at first but they keep growing until they are normal. It's just remarkable!

FIGURE 10–4   The "U" Page From an Alphabet Book

Unbearable

Some of the Indians thought life was UNBEARABLE at the missions. They thought this because they couldn't hunt or do the things they were used to. Once they were at the missions they couldn't leave. They were sometimes beaten if they did.

Students organize reports in a variety of formats—formats they see used in mentor texts. One possibility is a question-and-answer format; another is an alphabet book. A fourth grade class wrote an alphabet book about the California missions, with one page for each letter of the alphabet. The "U" page appears in Figure 10–4.

Individual Reports. After students learn to conduct research and share what they learn in collaborative reports, they're prepared to write individual reports. Writing an individual report is similar to writing a collaborative report, except that students assume the responsibility for writing the entire report themselves. To begin, students identify several research questions, and then they conduct the research to find the answers. Each question and answer usually become a chapter. Students use a variety of techniques as they conduct research: They interview experts, collect data through surveys, conduct experiments, make observations, consult Internet sources, and read nonfiction books (Kristo & Bamford, 2004).

As students consult the books and other resources, they collect lots of information that they need to remember. Students often use self-stick notes to mark important information in books as they're reading. Then they go back and write short phrases, paraphrasing the information, on note cards, or they complete graphic organizers. They don't try to take notes about everything they read, only about the big ideas. In addition, they're careful not to get distracted by other interesting information in the resources they're reading. Next, students organize the information they've collected. Choosing an appropriate organizational structure is key because it influences which information is most important. Students complete graphic organizers, design charts, or write informal outlines.

As students begin to draft, they write sentences and paragraphs to present the information they collected. They also think about which special features to include to aid readers, such as chapter titles, headings, and charts. As they write, they summarize and synthesize the big ideas, being careful to distinguish between fact and opinion. They write leads to engage readers and summarize the big ideas in the conclusion. Students also create visuals to display other information, and sometimes they identify additional information to highlight in sidebars (Kristo & Bamford, 2004).

When students revise their rough drafts, their first concern is whether they've answered their questions. They share their rough drafts with classmates and get feedback on how well they're communicating. They also double-check their notes to ensure the accuracy of their information and statistics, add details, revise their leads, and check transitions. Next, students continue the writing process by editing their reports to correct misspelled words, capitalization and punctuation errors, and nonstandard English usage.

Students usually word process the final copies of their reports, and they carefully format them, taking advantage of what they know about nonfiction features. They include a title page, a table of contents, chapter titles, illustrations with captions, photos downloaded from the Internet, a bibliography, and an index. They compile the pages and bind them into a book or display them on a chart.

Multigenre Projects

Students create multigenre projects to explore a topic through several genres (C. Allen, 2001; Romano, 2000). "Research comes alive when students explore a range of alternate genres instead of writing the traditional research report" (Grierson, Anson, & Baird, 2002, p. 51). Figure 10–5 lists genres that students use to share knowledge in multigenre projects. Tom Romano (1995) explains, "Each genre offers me ways of seeing and understanding that others do not" (p. 109). Students collect a variety of nonfiction materials, including books, textbooks, Internet articles, charts, diagrams, and photos, and then they study them. Students write several pieces, including feature articles, letters, journal entries, stories, and poems; collect photos, charts, and other visual representations; and compile them in a book or display them on a poster. For example, for a multigenre project on the planet Mars, fourth graders included these pieces:

- A feature article about the planet written collaboratively by the class
- A data chart comparing Mars to other planets taken from a nonfiction book
- A photograph of the planet downloaded from the NASA website
- A found poem about Mars with phrases taken from a book students have read
- A simulated journal written from the perspective of an astronaut who's exploring the planet

Through these five pieces, students presented several kinds of information, written from varied viewpoints. The project was much more complete than it would have been with just one genre.

| FIGURE 10–5 | Genres for Multigenre Projects |

Artifacts	Students gather or create a collection of objects, photos, postcards, time lines, and other items about a topic.
Biographical Sketches	Students write biographical sketches of people related to the topic.
Cartoons	Students draw cartoons or copy published cartoons from a book or Internet site.
Clusters	Students draw clusters or other diagrams to display information concisely.
Cubes	Students examine a topic from six perspectives.
Data Charts	Students create data charts to present and compare information.
Essays	Students write essays to describe a topic, examine an issue, or persuade readers to a course of action.
Feature Articles	Students bring a human-interest slant to the news or a nonfiction topic in these creative compositions.
Found Poems	Students collect words and phrases from a book or article and arrange them to make poems.
Games	Students create cardboard or digital games and puzzles about a topic for classmates to play.
Letters	Students write simulated letters or make copies of real letters related to the topic.
Life Lines	Students draw life lines and mark important dates related to a person's life.
Maps	Students make copies of actual maps or draw maps related to a topic.
Newspaper Articles	Students make copies of actual newspaper articles or write simulated articles related to the topic.
Open-Mind Portraits	Students draw open-mind portraits of people related to the topic.
Photos	Students download photos from the Internet.
Podcasts	Students create podcasts to share information they've learned or stories and poems they've written.
Poems	Students write list poems, poems for two voices, "I Am . . . " poems, and other types of poems about the topic.
Postcards	Students create picture postcards related to the topic.
PowerPoint Presentations	Students prepare a set of pages or slides for a PowerPoint presentation.
Quotes	Students collect quotes about the topic from materials they're reading.
Simulated Journals	Students write simulated journal entries from the viewpoint of a person related to the topic.
Slide Shows	Students prepare slide shows with photos and other images related to the topic.
Time Lines	Students draw time lines to sequence events related to the topic.
Venn Diagrams	Students draw Venn diagrams to compare two components of the topic or the topic with something else.
WebQuests	Students create digital inquiry projects called WebQuests.
Websites and Wikis	Students display information they've collected about a topic in an online database.
Word Clouds	Students create word clouds related to the topic at http://www.wordles.net.

Life Stories

Biographies and autobiographies are life stories. They're true accounts of people's lives that provide insight into the subject's accomplishments and personality. Most life stories are structured like stories with a beginning, a middle, and an end, and authors often sequence events in chronological order. Students craft these types of life stories:

PERSONAL NARRATIVES. *Personal narratives* are first-person accounts of single events from students' own lives. Students focus on one experience, and as they become more sophisticated writers, they explain how the event has affected them. They set a dramatic tone so readers live through the event vicariously and understand what the experience means to the author. These life stories are usually the first sustained writing that young children do: They write about themselves, their families, and experiences in their community. One reason why students are so successful with personal narratives is that they draw on what they know best—themselves!

MEMOIRS. *Memoirs* are stories to interpret events in the writer's life. Older children move from writing personal narratives to crafting memoirs to recount and interpret significant life events. They create engaging narratives by developing powerful images, incorporating vivid details, and linking the episodes with a unifying theme.

AUTOBIOGRAPHIES. *Autobiographies* are more complete than memoirs, usually spanning the writer's entire life and with the events presented in chronological order. In the autobiographies that students create, they describe memorable events, the ones needed to understand their personalities. Sometimes teachers ask students to craft autobiographies that focus on one aspect of their lives, such as their life as a reader, writer, or technology user.

BIOGRAPHIES. *Biographies* focus on selected events in a person's life or the person's entire life, written by someone else. To make these accounts as accurate and authentic as possible, students consult a variety of sources of information. The best source, of course, is the person himself or herself, and through interviews students can learn many things about the person. Other primary sources include diaries and letters, photographs, mementos, and historical records. In contrast, books, websites, and films are secondary sources.

Students use a combination of oral, written, and visual projects to tell these four types of life stories.

Bio Boxes. Students make bio boxes with items that represent the person they've researched. A fifth grader created a bio box for Paul Revere and decorated it with aluminum foil, explaining that it looked like silver because Paul Revere was a silversmith. He placed these items in the box:

- A spoon to represent Paul Revere's career as a silversmith
- A toy horse to represent his famous midnight ride
- A tea bag to represent his involvement in the Boston Tea Party
- A copy of Longfellow's poem "The Midnight Ride of Paul Revere"
- An advertisement for Revere pots and pans along with an explanation that Paul Revere is credited with inventing the process of layering metals
- A portrait of the patriot
- Photos of Boston, Lexington, and Concord downloaded from the Internet
- A life line marking important events in Paul Revere's life

The student wrote a card describing the relationship of each object to Paul Revere and attached it to the item.

Students also make "me" boxes to share information about themselves (Duthie, 1996). Students collect objects and pictures representing events in their lives, their families, their hobbies, and special accomplishments and write cards to accompany each object. Then they decorate the outside of a shoe box, coffee can, or other container and place the objects inside.

Hot Seat. Students participate in an oral activity called *hot seat* to share information they've learned about a person they've researched. They sit in a special chair designated as the "hot seat" to be interviewed. Students have to think quickly and respond to their classmates' questions. Wilhelm (2002) explains that through this activity, students analyze and interpret the historical figure's or contemporary celebrity's life events. Students aren't intimidated by the interactive oral performance; in fact, in most classrooms, it's very popular.

FIGURE 10–6   A Biography Poster About Martin Luther King Jr.

FIGURE 10-7   Two Pages From a First Grader's "All About Me" Book

This is me wen I'm, five. I'm, reading a book. MY MOM comes in and puts out my cloths for me to wear but I didn't, wat to wear them. I became very picky about my cloths my dad said.

This is my Grammy's house. I have my own room in it. Sometimes I sleep on the love seat. I like to see papa, Sometimes my papa takes me fishing. I love to go fishing. My Grammy makes me feel special.

Life Lines. When students are working on biographies and autobiographies, they sequence the information on life lines. They can use clotheslines and actually hang artifacts, photos, drawings, and information cards about milestone events on them, or they can draw life lines on long paper rolls and write and draw the information on them (Fleming & McGinnis, 1985). Students also create time lines about historical events using either clotheslines or paper time lines.

Biography Posters. Students often create posters as part of biography projects. The posters present a portrait of the person along with information about his or her life and accomplishments. Students in an eighth grade class made a biography quilt with paper squares, and each square was modeled after the illustrations in *My Fellow Americans,* by Alice Provensen (1995). One student's square about Martin Luther King Jr. is presented in Figure 10-6. This student drew a portrait of the civil rights leader set in Washington, DC, on August 28, 1963, the day he delivered his famous "I Have a Dream" speech. The student also added well-known sayings and other phrases related to Martin Luther King Jr. around the outside.

"All About Me" Books. Children in kindergarten and first grade often compile "All About Me" books that are similar to "All About . . . " books. These autobiographies usually list information such as the child's birthday, family members, friends, and favorite activities, with drawings as well as text. Figure 10-7 shows two pages from a first grader's "All About Me" book. To write these books, the children first decide on a topic for each page; then, after brainstorming possible ideas for the topic, they draw a picture and write about it. Children may also need to ask their parents for information about their birth and events during their preschool years.

Multigenre Biographies. Multigenre biography projects are similar to nonfiction projects. Students collect and create some of the following items for a multigenre biography:

life line	collection of objects	biographical sketch
quotations	simulated journal	found poem
photographs	feature article	poster
simulated letters	open-mind portrait	box of artifacts

Each item is a complete piece by itself and contributes to the overall impact of the biography. Students compile their biographies on posters or in notebooks. Seventh graders created multigenre biographies. To begin, they read a biography and located additional information about the person from two other sources, one print and one online resource. Then they created the following pieces for their biography project:

- A life line of the person's life, indicating the dates of the person's birth and death and at least 10 key events in his or her life

- A simulated journal with 10 entries spanning the person's entire life

- An open-mind portrait with a portrait of the person and additional pages showing what the person was thinking about three key events in his or her life

- A collection of three quotes that illustrate what the person believed

- A heart map with a heart filled with pictures and words representing things that really mattered to the person

Figure 10–8 presents excerpts from a seventh grader's multigenre biography project on Maya Angelou.

TEACHING NONFICTION

For students to become capable researchers, teachers need to establish a research climate in their classrooms and teach students how to conduct research and share the results. They scaffold students' first research experiences to help them understand the process and develop the knowledge, strategies, and tools to be successful. Perry and Drummond (2002) describe this process as moving from teacher-regulated to student self-regulated learning. They have identified these characteristics of classrooms that promote responsible, independent researchers:

- The classroom is a community of learners where students collaborate and cooperate with classmates.

- Students are involved in meaningful research activities that require them to think strategically and reflectively.

- Students increasingly assume responsibility for their learning by making choices, dealing constructively with challenges, and evaluating their work.

- The teacher scaffolds students' learning by providing direct instruction about doing research, modeling the process, having students do research in groups, and gradually releasing responsibility to the students to work independently.

- Evaluation emphasizes both the research process that students use and the quality of their projects.

It's essential that teachers establish a research climate in their classrooms and teach students how to find answers to questions that interest them rather than just assigning students to

FIGURE 10–8   Excerpts From a Seventh Grader's Multigenre Project

Maya Angelou

In Maya's Heart

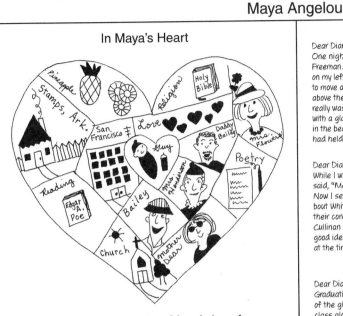

- The pineapple expresses Maya's love for pineapples.
- Ms. Flowers is the woman who gave Maya her first book of poetry.
- Mother Dear is Maya's mother and even though she didn't really raise her, Maya looked up to her.
- Bailey was Maya's brother and they had a strong bond being that they were only one year apart in age.
- Guy is her son and her entire life.

Dear Diary,
One night I was scared and momma let me sleep in the bed with her and Mr. Freeman. Then when momma left early to run an errand, I felt a strange pressure on my left leg. I knew it wasn't a hand because it was much too soft. I was afraid to move and I didn't budge. Mr. Freeman's eyes were wide open with both hands above the covers. He then said, "Stay right here, Rite, I'm not gonna hurt you." I really wasn't afraid, a little curious, but not afraid. Then he left and came back with a glass of water and poured it on the bed. He said, "see how you done peed in the bed." Afterwards, I was confused and didn't understand why Mr. Freeman had held me so gently, then accused me of peeing in the bed.

Marguerite

Dear Diary,
While I was sitting talking to Miss Glory, Mrs. Cullinan called for someone. She said, "Mary P." We didn't know who she was calling, but my name is Marguerite. Now I settled for Margaret, but Mary was a whole nother name. Bailey told me bout Whites and how they felt like they had the power to shorten our names for their convenience. Miss Glory told me her name used to be Hallelujah and Mrs. Cullinan shortened it to Glory. Mrs. Cullinan sent me on an errand, which was a good idea because I was upset and anything was bound to come out of my mouth at the time.

Marguerite

Dear Diary,
Graduation day was a big event in Stamps. The high school seniors received most of the glory. I'm just a twelve year old 8th grader. I'm pretty high-ranked in my class along with Henry Reed. Henry is also our class valedictorian. The tenth grade teacher helped him with his speech. Momma was even going to close the store. Our graduation dresses are a lemon yellow, but momma added ruffles and cuffs with a crocheted collar. She added daisy embroideries around the trim before she considered herself finished. I just knew all eyes were going to be on me when graduation day came.

Marguerite

Quotes

"Cleanliness is next to Godliness."

"God blessed everyone with an intelligent mind. Only we can decide how we use it."

write reports on a topic. The Common Core State Standards emphasize the importance of nonfiction; the Standards feature on page 306 highlights the role of nonfiction in the language arts curriculum. Teachers share nonfiction books with students in all four patterns of practice and encourage them to ask questions and search for answers to their queries. The Patterns of Practice feature, also on page 306 describes some of the ways that nonfiction fits into language arts instruction.

Research Workshop

Research workshop is a 60- to 90-minute period where students identify questions and use the research process to find answers to the questions they've posed. Sometimes students choose questions that interest them; at other times, research workshop is connected to thematic units where teachers identify an umbrella topic, and then students choose subtopics and pose questions.

COMMON CORE STATE STANDARDS

Nonfiction

The Common Core State Standards make non-fiction a priority. K–8 students are expected to read and comprehend grade-level nonfiction texts, conduct research projects, and write nonfiction texts to convey complex ideas. The standards highlight these points:

- Students identify main ideas and details.
- Students analyze expository text structures.
- Students use nonfiction text features.
- Students conduct research and report the results.
- Students write nonfiction texts.
- Students gather information from multiple print and digital sources.

To learn more about the nonfiction standards, go to http://www.corestandards.org, or check your state's language arts standards.

In addition to providing a large chunk of time for students to gather information and write a report or do another project, teachers teach minilessons on research procedures and model how to do research as the class works together on collaborative projects. At the end of the workshop, students come together as a class to share what they've learned.

When Rogovin (2001) conducts research workshops, she chooses broad topics for her students to study, and then they choose subtopics, ask questions, and do research in small groups. The students collect information and create projects to share what they've learned, such as writing reports and giving oral presentations. Christine Duthie (1996) also has her primary grade students conduct research during their writing workshop periods.

Minilessons

Teachers teach minilessons about the nonfiction genre, the research process, and how to share information students have learned (Portalupi & Fletcher, 2001). Students learn to pose questions, search for answers, and share what they've learned in artifact boxes, reports, multigenre projects, and other types of oral, written, and visual reports. The Minilesson feature on the next page shows how Mr. Uchida introduces data charts, an effective tool for gathering and organizing information.

Mentor Texts

Teachers use mentor texts as models for reading and writing nonfiction. The Booklist on page 283 presents a wide variety of nonfiction books, including alphabet books, biographies, multigenre books, and question-and-answer books, and Figure 10–1 lists books illustrating each of

How Nonfiction Fits Into the Patterns of Practice

Literature Focus Units

Sometimes teachers feature nonfiction books during literature focus units, and they teach minilessons on the nonfiction genre, expository text structures, and nonfiction features.

Literature Circles

Students read nonfiction books during literature circles, and they analyze genre characteristics, organizational patterns, and nonfiction features in the books they're reading.

Reading and Writing Workshop

Students read nonfiction books during reading workshop, and during writing workshop they write personal narratives, reports, and informational books.

Thematic Units

Students read many nonfiction books during thematic units. They conduct research to find answers to questions and write reports to share what they've learned.

Minilesson

Mr. Uchida Teaches His Fifth Graders How to Write Data Charts

1. Introduce the Topic

Mr. Uchida's fifth graders are preparing to write state reports. They've each chosen a state to research, and they developed this list of research questions:

Who are the people in the state?
What are the physical features of the state?
What are the key events in the state's history?
What is the economy of the state?
What places should you visit in the state?

Mr. Uchida explains that students need to collect information to answer each of these questions, and he has a neat tool to use to collect the data: It's called a *data chart*.

2. Share Examples

Mr. Uchida shares three sample data charts that his students made to collect information for their state reports last year. He unfolds the large sheets of construction paper that have been folded into many cells or sections; each cell is filled with information. The students examine the data charts and read the information in each cell.

3. Provide Information

Mr. Uchida folds a clean sheet of construction paper into four rows and five columns to create 20 cells. Then he unfolds the paper, shows it to the students, and counts the 20 cells. He explains how he folded the paper and traces over the folded lines so that students can see the cells. Then he writes the five research questions in the cells in the top row. He explains that students will write the information they locate to answer each question in the cells under that question. He demonstrates how to paraphrase information and take notes in the cells.

4. Supervise Practice

Mr. Uchida passes out large sheets of white construction paper and assists students as they divide the sheet into 20 cells and write the research questions in the top row. Then the fifth graders take notes using resources they've collected. Mr. Uchida circulates in the classroom, helping students to locate information and take notes.

5. Reflect on Learning

After several days, Mr. Uchida brings the class together to check on the progress students are making. They show their partially completed charts and talk about their data collection. They ask what to do when they can't find information or when the information won't fit into one box. Several students comment that they know how they'll use their data charts when they begin writing their reports: They'll use all the information in one column for one chapter of the report. They're amazed to have made this discovery!

the five expository text structures. The Booklist on page 288 includes examples of books that incorporate margin notes, glossaries, and other nonfiction features effectively. Teachers also locate other print texts—newspapers, maps, magazines, and menus, for instance—as well as online articles.

During minilessons, teachers use mentor texts when they're teaching about the nonfiction genre. They share books illustrating the expository text structures, point out nonfiction features, and highlight the differences between fiction and nonfiction. They also use mentor texts when they're teaching about research tools, including demonstrating how to identify big ideas, take notes, and complete data charts. In addition, teachers use mentor texts as models for nonfiction texts students are writing.

INTEGRATING TECHNOLOGY

Students use digital technology both as a learning tool and to create projects to demonstrate learning. Here are five nonfiction applications:

DIGITAL MOVIES. Students create biography projects using iMovie or Photo Story 3 integrating text; diagrams, including life lines and maps; photos and other illustrations; and sound components about family members, contemporary personalities, or historical figures. They often include several genres in their movies, making their projects more powerful than they would be if they contained only written text.

ONLINE NOTE-TAKING TOOLS. Instead of taking notes on note cards, students can use online note-taking tools to take notes when they're gathering information during the research process. To learn more about online note-taking tools, check the Digital Classroom feature on page 291.

PUBLIC PADS. Public pads are web-based word processing applications that allow teachers and students to work together on reports and other writing projects in real time. Students can collaborate on documents and revise or edit them at the same time; the changes are instantly displayed on everyone's screen. Primary Pad (http://primarypad.com) was designed by a teacher and can be used in the primary grades as well as with older students; Ether-Pad (http://ietherpad.com), Writeboard (http://writeboard.com), and Titan Pad (http://titanpad.com) are other word processing applications used in fourth through eighth grade classrooms.

CAPTIONED MEDIA. Teachers can use captioned videos and PBS television programs on nonfiction topics to teach the expository text structures (Strassman, MacDonald, & Wanko, 2010). These captioned media can serve as mentor texts, because they're organized using the same patterns found in nonfiction books. Students view the media presentations several times, study the transcript of the program, and produce their own captioned digital media.

VIRTUAL MUSEUMS. Students create virtual museums on nonfiction topics using wiki software to connect to webpages to share what they've learned. They create categories within the wiki where viewers can contribute to it or participate in activities.

Students also use a variety of other digital applications, including blogs, podcasts, and Power-Point presentations, as they investigate nonfiction. ■

ENGAGING ENGLISH LEARNERS

English learners use writing to understand and remember the big ideas and important details they're learning. Students are more apt to understand connections among big ideas when they write about them, both in learning logs and through projects. Peregoy and Boyle (2009) recommend that teachers have English learners use writing to facilitate learning in these ways: write in learning logs, conduct research, and create projects. They've found that even young English learners can use writing as a learning tool and to report their learning:

WRITING IN LEARNING LOGS. As English learners make entries in learning logs, they use the technical vocabulary that teachers have introduced and posted on word walls. They learn the meanings of these words and how to spell them, and they practice stringing words together and manipulating sentences to clarify and extend the meaning. As they write, students summarize the big ideas they're learning, make connections to their background knowledge and personal experiences, and think about ways to apply the information. Sometimes students self-select topics for journal entries, but teachers often provide prompts to direct students' attention to the big ideas and technical vocabulary words.

CONDUCTING RESEARCH. English learners often participate in small groups to conduct research on nonfiction topics related to thematic units. Like their classmates, English learners should select and shape their own research topics. They work together to learn about a topic using nonfiction books, Internet resources, and other classroom resources. By working together with their classmates, English learners share the work and learn from each other. Students use writing as they take notes and record information on graphic organizers and drawings.

CREATING PROJECTS. English learners create projects to share the results of their research. They can work with classmates to create traditional written reports, but multigenre reports are often more successful because they integrate written and visual reports of information. Peregoy and Boyle (2009) suggest that English learners create photo essays by organizing a set of photographs into a useful sequence and adding captions. Or, students can draw a series of pictures and use them in creating a pictorial essay. Afterward, students do brief oral presentations to share their projects with classmates.

All three of these ways are effective because they encourage students to think about the big ideas they're studying. As an added benefit, teachers can monitor students' writing to assess their understanding. ■

Assessing Nonfiction Projects

Assessment goes hand in hand with instruction, and teachers assess students while they research answers to questions they've posed and develop nonfiction projects. They assess students' knowledge of the nonfiction genre, their ability to apply the research process, and the quality of the projects they develop through planning, monitoring, and evaluation activities.

Planning. Teachers plan for assessment before students begin research projects because it's essential that students understand what they're expected to accomplish and how they'll be evaluated. Many teachers distribute a checklist to students before they begin working so they can take responsibility for completing each step. Students staple the checklist to the inside cover of the folder in which they keep all the work for the project and check off each requirement as they complete it. Figure 10–9 shows a second grade checklist for an autobiography project. Students keep checklists in their research folders and check off each item as it's completed; at the end of the project, they submit the folders as well as the completed

| FIGURE 10-9 | Checklist for an Autobiography Project |

_____ Collect or make 5 or more artifacts to represent your life.
_____ Write a card to explain each artifact.
_____ Put the artifacts and cards in a box you've decorated.
_____ Write a book about one of the artifacts.
       What's your topic? _____
_____ Use the writing process:
       ☐ 1. Prewriting: Brainstorm ideas.
       ☐ 2. Drafting: Write a rough draft.
       ☐ 3. Revising: Meet in a revising group and make 3 changes.
       ☐ 4. Editing: Proofread and fix mistakes.
       ☐ 5. Publishing: Make a title page and recopy your writing.
       Don't forget to keep all of your work!
_____ Add covers to make a book.

project to be graded. This approach gives students a better understanding of why they receive a particular grade.

Monitoring. Teachers monitor students' use of the research process as they narrow topics, identify research questions, search for answers, and develop projects. This monitoring is usually informal; teachers observe students as they work, check their use of research tools, and conference with students individually and in small groups about the progress they're making.

Evaluating. Teachers often use rubrics to evaluate the quality of students' reports, biographies, autobiographies, and other nonfiction projects. Evaluating is also the time when students self-evaluate their achievement and effort. In particular, teachers ask them to evaluate how they applied the research process and to examine the quality of the projects they've created. Sometimes students complete rubrics, and at other times, they write reflections. No matter which format students use, they consider how they used the research process, whether they understood the answers they found, the usefulness of the project they developed, how hard they worked, and the effectiveness of their collaboration with classmates.

SUMMING UP

Students enjoy reading nonfiction books, and as they examine these books, they learn about the five expository text patterns—description, sequence, comparison, cause and effect, and problem and solution—that authors use to organize nonfiction and the features they include to improve readability. Students' knowledge about this genre supports their reading and writing. Teachers teach students to use the research process to find answers to questions that interest them and to share what they learn in oral, written, and visual projects. They create multigenre projects using a combination of reports, stories, poems, photographs, and other materials, and they also write autobiographies about their own lives and biographies about historical and contemporary personalities.

MyEducationLab™

Go to the topics Reading, Writing, and Literature in the MyEducationLab (http://www.myeducationlab .com) for *Language Arts: Patterns of Practice*, where you can:

- Find learning outcomes for Reading, Writing, and Literature along with the national standards that connect to these outcomes.
- Complete Assignments and Activities that can help you more deeply understand the chapter content.
- Apply and practice your understanding of the core teaching skills identified in the chapter with the Building Teaching Skills and Dispositions learning units.
- Examine challenging situations and cases presented in the IRIS Center Resources.
- Use the Lesson Plan Builder Activities to practice lesson planning and integrating national and state standards into your planning.
- Check your comprehension of the content covered in the chapter with the Study Plan. Here you will be able to take a chapter quiz, receive feedback on your answers, and then access Review, Practice, and Enrichment activities to enhance your understanding of chapter content.

On the **MyEducationLab** for this course, you'll also be able to:

- **A+RISE** Go to the topic A+RISE, an innovative and interactive database of strategies that differentiate instruction across the language arts and provide particular insight into research-based methods to meet the needs of English learners.
- Explore the topic Literacy Portraits—yearlong case studies of second graders, complete with student artifacts, teacher commentary, and student and teacher interviews, tracking the month-by-month language arts growth of five students.
- Gain practice with the Grammar Tutorial, online guided instruction to improve your own ability with grammar.

Exploring Poetry

SIXTH GRADERS PARTICIPATE IN POETRY WORKSHOP   Mrs. Harris holds a weeklong poetry workshop in her sixth grade classroom several times each year. The first hour is devoted to reading poetry and the second to writing poetry; her students read and respond to poems during the reading workshop component and write poems during the writing workshop component. The box on page 314 shows her schedule.

During class meetings this week, Mrs. Harris draws students' attention to poetic devices. On Monday, she asks them to think about their favorite poems: What makes a poem a good poem? She reads aloud some favorite poems, and the students mention these poetic elements: rhyme, alliteration, repetition, and onomatopoeia, which they call "sound effects." The next day, Mrs. Harris focuses on metaphors and similes. She reads aloud these poems from *The Random House Book of Poetry for Children* (Prelutsky, 2000): "The Toaster," "Steam Shovel," "The Dandelion," and "The Eagle." As she reads, students they notice these comparisons: The toaster is compared to a dragon, the steam shovel to a dinosaur, the dandelion to a soldier, and the eagle's dive to a bolt of lightning. On Wednesday, students come to the class meeting to share poems they've found that have comparisons, and classmates identify the comparisons. After they discuss the poems, Mrs. Harris explains the terms *metaphor* and *simile* and asks students to classify the comparisons in the poems they've shared.

On Thursday, Mrs. Harris reads aloud "The Night Is a Big Black Cat" (Prelutsky, 2000), a brief, four-line poem comparing night to a black cat, the moon to the cat's eye, and the stars to mice she's hunting in the sky. The students draw pictures illustrating the poem and add the lines or paraphrases of the lines to them. One student's drawing is

How does poetry fit into the four patterns of practice?

Teachers incorporate poetry into all four instructional patterns. They share poems with students on topics related to literature focus units and thematic units, and in literature circles and reading workshop, students read books of poetry as well as other books. Students write poems as projects, and once they learn how to write poetry, they often choose to do so during writing workshop. As you continue reading, notice how Mrs. Harris adapts the reading and writing workshop approach for her poetry workshop.

shown on page 314. On Friday, students finish their pictures and share them with the class.

Mrs. Harris points out the poetry section in the classroom library that's been infused with 75 more books of poetry. Students select books from the library to read during the independent reading time. Next, she introduces some of her favorite poetry books. *Love That Dog* (Creech, 2001), *Locomotion* (Woodson, 2003), and *A Bird About to Sing* (Montenegro, 2003) are stories written in poetic form about how children use poetry to write about their feelings. She also shares Janet Wong's book of poetry with advice about writing poems, *You Have to Write* (2002), and three books about how to write poems, *Poetry Matters: Writing a Poem From the Inside Out* (Fletcher, 2002), *A Kick in the Head: An Everyday Guide to Poetic Forms* (Janeczko, 2005), and *Troy Thompson's Excellent Peotry* [sic] *Book* (Crew, 1998). She has several copies of each book for students to read during the week.

During independent reading time, students read poems and pick their favorites to share with classmates. They list the books they read in their poetry folders. They also choose their three favorite poems, and Mrs. Harris makes copies of them for their poetry folders. For each poem, students write a brief reflection explaining why they like the poem, mentioning poetic elements whenever possible in their explanations. After reading, students get into small groups to share poems, and they rehearse the poem they'll read aloud to the class. Five or six students share one poem each day. During a previous poetry workshop, Mrs. Harris taught the students how to read poetry expressively, or as she says, "like a poet." They know how to vary the speed and loudness of their voices, how to emphasize the rhyme or other important words, and how to pause at the ends of lines or within lines. Mrs. Harris expects her students to apply what they've learned when they read poetry aloud.

During the writing workshop minilessons this week, Mrs. Harris focuses on "unwriting," a strategy students use to revise their poems. On Monday, she shares the rough draft of a color poem she's written. She explains that she thinks it has too many unnecessary words and asks the students to help her unwrite it. They make suggestions, and she crosses out words and substitutes stronger words for long phrases.

Poetry Workshop Schedule

15 minutes	**Class Meeting** Mrs. Harris leads a class meeting to give a book talk about a new poetry book, talk about a poet, read several poems using choral reading, or discuss a difficult or confusing poem.
30 minutes	**Independent Reading** Students choose books of poetry and read poems independently. As they read, students mark favorite poems with small self-stick notes.
15 minutes	**Sharing** Students form small groups and share favorite poems with classmates. Then several students read their favorites aloud to the whole class. They rehearse before reading aloud to "read like a poet" with good expression.
15 minutes	**Minilesson** Mrs. Harris teaches minilessons on how to use poetic devices, arrange the lines of a poem on a page, and use "unwriting" to revise poems. She also introduces and reviews poetry formulas.
45 minutes	**Writing** Students write lots of rough-draft poems and choose their best to take through the writing process. They meet in revising groups and editing conferences with Mrs. Harris as they polish their poems. On Friday, students have a poetry reading where they read aloud one of the poems they've written.

A Student's Drawing of a Poem

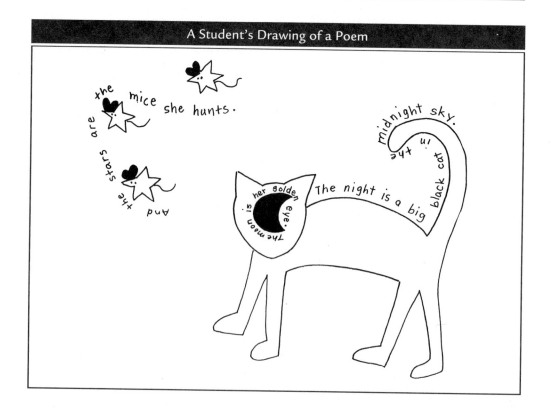

Together they revise the poem to make it tighter. Mrs. Harris explains that poems are powerful because they say so much using only a few words and encourages students to use unwriting as they craft their poems. On Tuesday and Wednesday, Mrs. Harris shares students' rough-draft poems, and students suggest ways to unwrite their classmates' poems.

Several students ask to learn more about limericks, so on Thursday, Mrs. Harris reviews the limerick form and shares limericks from a book in the classroom library and other limericks that her students wrote in previous years. Then on Friday, students divide into small groups to try their hand at writing limericks. Mrs. Harris moves from group to group, providing assistance as needed. Afterward, they share their limericks with classmates.

Mrs. Harris's students keep writing notebooks in which they record collections of words, quotes from books they've read, interesting sentences and descriptions, lists of writing topics, and rough drafts of stories, poems, and other writings. They also have a paper describing the poetic forms that Mrs. Harris has taught. During the independent writing time, they often write ideas, words and sentences, and even rough-draft poems in their writing notebooks. Students write lots of rough drafts and then choose the most promising ones to take through the writing process and publish. Throughout the week, they meet in revising groups and editing conferences with Mrs. Harris and with classmates; during the first half of the writing time, Mrs. Harris holds a revising group, and during the second half, she holds an editing group. Students sign up for the groups in advance. They keep all drafts of the poems they publish to trace the development of their poems and document their use of the writing process.

On the last day, the students word process final copies of their poems, which they contribute to the class book that Mrs. Harris compiles. The students move their desks into a circle and have a poetry reading: They read around, taking turns to read aloud one of their poems.

Mrs. Harris sets out her expectations at the beginning of the poetry workshop: Students will read and write lots of poems. She wants them to choose at least three favorite poems from those they read and to take at least one poem that they write through the writing

---

Poetry Workshop Grading Sheet

Student's Check		Teacher's Grade
_____	1. Read lots of poems. Keep a list of poetry books that you read. (15)	_____
_____	2. Make copies of three favorite poems and write why you like the poems. (15)	_____
_____	3. Read one poem aloud to the class. Be sure to read like a poet. (10)	_____
_____	4. Write rough drafts of at least five poems. (25)	_____
_____	5. Take one poem through the writing process to publication. (15)	_____
_____	6. Read one of your poems during the poetry reading on Friday. (10)	_____

_____	7. Other (10)
	  Draw a "night cat" picture.
	  Write a limerick in a small group.
		_____

process. She passes out copies of the grading sheet they'll use that week and that they keep in their writing folders; this way students know from the first day of the workshop what they're expected to accomplish. A copy of Mrs. Harris's poetry workshop grading sheet is shown on page 315. As students complete the assignments, they add checkmarks in the left-hand column. After they finish the unit, they turn in their writing folders with the grading sheet and the papers they completed during the workshop. Mrs. Harris reviews their assignments and awards points to determine the grade using a 100-point grading scale.

Poetry "brings sound and sense together in words and lines," according to Donald Graves, "ordering them on the page in such a way that both the writer and reader get a different view of life" (1992, p. 3). Our concept of poetry has broadened to include songs and raps, word pictures, memories, riddles, observations, questions, odes, and rhymes. Adult and child poets write about every imaginable subject—fire trucks, boa constrictors, spaghetti and meatballs, Jupiter, and grandfathers. These poems tell stories, create images and moods, make readers laugh or cry, develop a sense of wonder, and show the world in a new way (Cullinan, Scala, & Schroder, 1995; M. K. Glover, 1999).

Siemens (1996) describes how her primary grade students are immersed in reading and writing poetry. She makes poetry the core of her language arts program, and her students respond enthusiastically. She shares her students' descriptions of poetry (p. 239):

> A poem is like a big green dragon waiting to blow fire at the knight who seeks the treasure.

> Poems are words that you feel and mumble jumble words too, also words that float around in your head.

> I think poetry is when you wake up and see the sun racing above from the clouds. Poetry is when sunlight and moon shines up together. Poetry is when you go to Claude Monet's garden for the first time and everything is breathtaking. That is what I think poetry is.

With the current emphasis on standards, poetry is sometimes considered to be a frill, but for these children, it's essential! Other teachers, too, know that reading and writing poetry can be an effective way to meet state standards (Holbrook, 2005). The Common Core State Standards for poetry are highlighted in the box on the next page.

PLAYING WITH WORDS

As children experiment with words, they create images, play with words, and evoke feelings. They laugh with language, experiment with rhyme, and invent new words. These activities provide a rich background of experiences for reading and writing poetry, and children gain confidence in choosing the "right" word to express an idea, emphasizing the sounds of words, and expressing familiar ideas with fresh comparisons. The Booklist on the next page presents a collection of wordplay books.

Laughing With Language

As children learn that words have the power to amuse, they enjoy reading, telling, and writing riddles and jokes. Geller (1985) researched children's humorous language and identified two stages of riddle play: Primary grade students experiment with the riddle form and its content, and beginning in third or fourth grade, students explore the paradoxical constructions in riddles. Riddles are written in a question-and-answer format, but young children at first may only ask questions, or ask questions and offer unrelated answers. As they gain experience, children learn to provide questions and give related answers, and their answers may be either descriptive or nonsensical. Here's an example of a descriptive answer:

> Why did the turtle go out of his shell?
> Because he was getting too big for it.

A nonsensical answer might involve an invented word. For example:

> Why did the cat want to catch a snake?
> Because he wanted to turn into a rattlecat.
> (Geller, 1981, p. 672)

Children's riddles seem foolish by adult standards, but wordplay is an important precursor to creating true riddles.

COMMON CORE STATE STANDARDS

Poetry

Although the Common Core State Standards emphasize reading and writing nonfiction, poetry is included as a type of literature. K–8 students must learn about figurative language and to identify themes and interpret poems. The standards highlight these points:

- Students interpret poems through oral presentations and audio recordings.
- Students read and comprehend grade-appropriate poems.
- Students examine how poetic devices and figurative language enhance meaning.
- Students use the writing process and technology to craft a variety of texts.

To learn more about the poetry standards, go to http://www.corestandards.org, or check your state's language arts standards.

Booklist

WORDPLAY BOOKS

PreK–Grade 2	Bayer, J. (1992). *A my name is Alice*. New York: Dial Books. Cerf, B. (1999). *Riddles and more riddles*. New York: Random House. Eiting, M., & Folsom, M. (2005). *Q is for duck: An alphabet guessing game*. New York: Clarion Books. Ernst, L. C. (2004). *The turn-around, upside-down alphabet book*. New York: Simon & Schuster. Hall, K., & Eisenberg, L. (2002). *Kitty riddles*. New York: Puffin Books.
Grades 3–5	Cobb, R. (2006). *Tongue twisters to tangle your tongue*. London: Marion Boyars. Cole, J. (1994). *Why did the chicken cross the road?* New York: HarperCollins. Gwynne, F. (2006). *The king who rained*. New York: Aladdin Books. Schwartz, A. (1992). *Busy buzzing bumblebees and other tongue twisters*. New York: HarperCollins. Terban, M. (1992). *Funny you should ask: How to make up jokes and riddles with wordplay*. New York: Clarion Books. Terban, M. (1997). *Time to rhyme: A rhyming dictionary*. Honesdale, PA: Wordsong. Terban, M. (2007). *Eight ate: A feast of homonym riddles*. New York: Clarion Books. Terban, M. (2007). *In a pickle and other funny idioms*. New York: Clarion Books. Wilbur, R. (2006). *Opposites, more opposites, and a few differences*. San Diego: Harcourt.
Grades 6–8	Agee, J. (1994). *Go hang a salami! I'm a lasagna hog! and other palindromes*. New York: Farrar, Straus & Giroux. Agee, J. (2002). *Palindromania!* New York: Farrar, Straus & Giroux. Carroll, L. (2003). *Jabberwocky*. Cambridge, MA: Candlewick Press. Gwynne, F. (2005). *A chocolate moose for dinner*. New York: Aladdin Books.

Riddles depend on using metaphors and on manipulating words with multiple meanings or similar sounds. The Opies (1967) identified five riddle strategies that students learn to use:

- Using multiple referents for a noun: *What has an eye but cannot see? A needle.*
- Combining literal and figurative interpretations for a single phrase: *Why did the kid throw the clock out the window? Because he wanted to see time fly.*
- Shifting word boundaries to suggest another meaning: *Why did the cookie cry? Because its mother was a wafer (away for) so long.*
- Separating a word into syllables to suggest another meaning: *When is a door not a door? When it's ajar (a jar).*
- Creating a metaphor: *What are polka dots on your face? Pimples.*

Children begin riddle play by telling familiar riddles and reading riddles written by others, and soon they're composing their own by adapting riddles they've read and turning jokes into riddles. A third grader wrote this riddle using two meanings for Milky Way:

Why did the astronaut go to the Milky Way?
Because he wanted a Milky Way bar.

A fifth grader wrote this riddle using the homophones *hair* and *hare*:

What is gray and jumpy and on your head? A gray hare!

The juxtaposition of words is important in many jokes and riddles.

Creating Word Pictures

Students create word pictures by arranging words to make a picture. These word pictures can be single-word pictures or a string of words or a sentence arranged in a picture. Figure 11–1 shows two word pictures. In the box on the left, the word *nervous* is written concretely, and on the right, descriptive sentences about an ice cream cone have been arranged in that shape. An asterisk indicates where to start reading the sentence picture. To make word pictures, students sketch a picture. Next, they place a second sheet of paper over the drawing and replace all or most of the lines with descriptive words so that the arrangement, size, and intensity of the letters illustrate the meaning.

Experimenting With Rhyme

Because of their experience with Dr. Seuss stories and nursery rhymes, children enjoy creating rhymes. When it comes naturally, rhyme adds a delightful quality to children's writing, but when it's equated with poetry, rhyme can get in the way of wordplay and vivid images. The following three-line poem, "Thoughts After a 40-Mile Bike Ride," shows a fifth grader's effective use of rhyme:

My feet
And seat
Are beat.

A group of first graders created their own version of *Oh, A-Hunting We Will Go* (Langstaff, 1991). They identified the refrain (lines 1, 2, and 5) and added rhyming couplets, as this excerpt shows:

Oh, a-hunting we will go,
a-hunting we will go.

We'll catch a little bear
and curl his hair,
and never let him go.

Oh, a-hunting we will go,
a-hunting we will go.
We'll catch a little bug
and give him a big hug
and never let him go.

Oh, a-hunting we will go,
a-hunting we will go.
We'll catch a little bunny
and fill her full of honey,
and never let her go.

Oh, we'll put them in a ring
and listen to them sing
and then we'll let them go.

The first graders created this collaborative rhyme with the teacher taking their dictation, and then each child chose a stanza to copy and illustrate. Later, the teacher collected the pages and compiled them to make a book. Finally, the first graders shared the book with classmates.

Hink-pinks are short rhymes that take the form of an answer to a riddle or describe something. These rhymes are composed with two one-syllable rhyming words; they're called *hinky-pinkies*

FIGURE 11–1   Students' Word Pictures

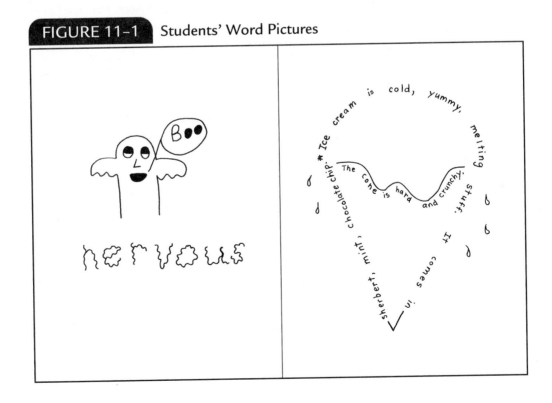

when two two-syllable words are used, and *hinkity-pinkities* with two three-syllable words (Geller, 1981). These two examples are hink-pinks:

Ghost
White
Fright

What do you call an astronaut?
A sky guy.

THE POETRY GENRE

Children have a natural affinity to verse, songs, riddles, jokes, chants, and puns. Preschoolers are introduced to poetry when their parents repeat Mother Goose rhymes, read *The House at Pooh Corner* (Milne, 2001) and the Dr. Seuss books, and sing songs to them. And, children often create jump-rope rhymes and other ditties on the playground.

Poems Students Read

Poems assume many forms. The most common type is rhymed verse, such as John Ciardi's "Mummy Slept Late and Daddy Fixed Breakfast" (Prelutsky, 2000). Other poems such as Clement Moore's *The Night Before Christmas* (1998) and Henry Wadsworth Longfellow's *Hiawatha* (1996) tell a story; they're narrative poems. A Japanese form, haiku, is popular in anthologies for children. *Haiku* is a three-line poem that contains 17 syllables. Because of its brevity, haiku has been deemed appropriate for children to read and write. *Free verse* has lines that don't rhyme, rhythm is less important than in other types of poetry, and images take on greater importance. Carl Sandburg's "Fog" and William Carlos Williams's "This Is Just to Say" (Prelutsky, 2000) are two examples of free verse. Other forms include *limericks*, a short, five-line, rhymed verse form popularized by Edward Lear (1995), and word pictures called *concrete poems*.

Three types of poetry books are available today. Some are picture-book versions of single poems in which one line or stanza is illustrated on a page, such as *The Midnight Ride of Paul Revere* (Longfellow, 2001). Others are specialized collections, either written by a single poet or related to a one topic, such as dinosaurs or flight. Comprehensive anthologies are the third type; they feature 50 or more poems arranged by category. One of the best anthologies is *The Random House Book of Poetry for Children* (Prelutsky, 2000). The Booklist on the next page includes books representing each type.

Students have definite preferences about which poems they like best. Years ago, Fisher and Natarella (1982) surveyed the poetry preferences of first, second, and third graders; Terry (1974) investigated fourth, fifth, and sixth graders' preferences; and Kutiper (1985) researched seventh, eighth, and ninth graders' preferences. The results of these studies are worth considering when teachers select poems. The most popular forms were limericks and narrative poems; least popular were haiku and free verse. In addition, students preferred humorous poems, poems about animals, and poems about familiar experiences; they disliked poems with visual imagery and figurative language. The most important elements were rhyme, rhythm, and sound. Primary grade students preferred traditional poetry, middle graders preferred modern poetry, and upper grade students preferred rhyming verse. The researchers found that students in all three studies liked poetry, enjoyed listening to poetry read aloud, and could explain why they liked or disliked particular poems.

Booklist

POETRY BOOKS

Comprehensive Anthologies	Driscoll, M. (2003). *A child's introduction to poetry*. New York: Black Dog & Leventhal. P–M Paschem, E., & Raccah, D. (Sels.). (2005). *Poetry speaks to children*. Naperville, IL: Sourcebooks MediaFusion. M–U Prelutsky, J. (Ed.). (2000). *The Random House book of poetry for children*. New York: Random House. P–M–U
Picture-Book Versions of Single Poems	Bates, K. L. (2003). *America the beautiful*. New York: Putnam. M Carroll, L. (2003). *Jabberwocky*. Cambridge, MA: Candlewick Press. M–U Frost, R. (2002). *Birches*. New York: Henry Holt. U Hoberman, M. A. (2003). *The lady with the alligator purse*. Boston: Little, Brown. P Howitt, M. (2002). *The spider and the fly*. New York: Simon & Schuster. P Thayer, E. L. (2006). *Casey at the bat*. Tonawanda, NY: Kids Can Press. M–U
Specialized Collections	Ehlert, L. (2010). *Lots of spots*. New York: Simon & Schuster. P Florian, D. (2010). *Poetrees*. New York: Simon & Schuster. P–M Hopkins, L. B. (Ed.). (2002). *Hoofbeats, claws and rippled fins: Creature poems*. New York: HarperCollins. P Issa, K. (2007). *Today and today*. New York: Scholastic. M–U Kuskin, K. (2003). *Moon, have you met my mother? The collected poems of Karla Kuskin*. New York: HarperCollins. M Myers, W. D. (2003). *blues journey*. New York: Holiday House. M–U Prelutsky, J. (2006). *Behold the bold umbrellaphant*. New York: Greenwillow. M Raczka, B. (2010). *Guyku: A year of haiku for boys*. Boston: Houghton Mifflin. P–M Sidman, J. (2010). *Ubiquitous: Celebrating nature's survivors*. Boston: Houghton Mifflin. P–M Soto, G. (2006). *A fire in my hands*. Orlando, FL: Harcourt. U Swados, E. (2002). *Hey you! C'mere: A poetry slam*. New York: Scholastic. M–U

P = primary grades (preK–2); M = middle grades (3–5); U = upper grades (6–8)

Poems Students Write

Students write funny verses, vivid word pictures, powerful comparisons, and expressions of deep sentiment. The key to successful poetry is poetic formulas, which serve as scaffolds, or temporary writing frameworks, so that students focus on ideas rather than on the mechanics of writing poems. In some formula poems, students begin each line with particular words; in some, they count syllables; and in others, they follow rhyming patterns. Many types of poetry don't use rhyme, and rhyme is the sticking point for many would-be poets. In searching for a rhyming word, children often create inane verse, for example:

> I see a funny little goat
> Wearing a blue sailor's coat
> Sitting in an old motorboat.

Of course, students should be allowed to write rhyming poetry, but rhyme should never be imposed as a criterion for acceptable poetry. They should use rhyme when it fits naturally into their writing. When students write poetry, they're searching for their voices, and they need freedom to do that.

Five types of poetic forms are formula poems, free-form poems, syllable- and word-count poems, rhymed poems, and model poems. The Booklist feature below presents books of poetry with examples of different poetic forms.

Formula Poems. Poetic formulas may seem like recipes to be followed rigidly, but that's not how they're intended; rather, they provide a skeleton for students' poems. Kenneth Koch (2000) worked in New York City schools and developed some simple formulas that make it easy for nearly every student to become a successful poet.

ACROSTIC POEMS. Students use a key word to structure acrostic poems. They choose a key word and write it vertically on a sheet of paper. Then they create lines of poetry, each one beginning with a letter in the key word they've chosen. For example, after reading *Officer*

Booklist

POETIC FORMS	
Acrostics	Harley, A. (2009). *African acrostics: A word in edgeways.* Cambridge, MA: Candlewick Press. P–M Schnur, S. (2001). *Summer: An alphabet acrostic.* New York: Clarion Books. (And books about the other seasons.) P–M
Apology Poems	Sidman, J. (2007). *This is just to say: Poems of apology and forgiveness.* Boston: Houghton Mifflin. M
Color Poems	Larios, J. (2006). *Yellow elephant: A bright bestiary.* Orlando: Harcourt. P–M O'Neill, M. (1990). *Hailstones and halibut bones.* New York: Doubleday. P–M Sidman, J. (2009). *Red sings from treetops: A year in colors.* Boston: Houghton Mifflin. P–M
Concrete Poems	Grandits, J. (2004). *Technically, it's not my fault: Concrete poems.* New York: Sandpiper. M–U Janeczko, P. B. (2001). *A poke in the I.* Cambridge, MA: Candlewick Press. M Roemer, H. (2004). *Come to my party and other shape poems.* New York: Henry Holt. P–M
Haiku	Clements, A. (2009). *Dogku.* New York: Atheneum. P–M Gollub, M. (2004). *Cool melons—Turn to frogs!* New York: Lee & Low. M–U Prelutsky, J. (2004). *If not for the cat.* New York: Greenwillow. P–M Raczka, B. (2010). *Guyku: A year of haiku for boys.* Boston: Houghton Mifflin. P–M Rosen, M. J. (2009). *The cuckoo's haiku and other birding poems.* Cambridge, MA: Candlewick Press. M–U
Limericks	Brooks, L. (2009). *Twimericks: The book of tongue-twisting limericks.* New York: Workman. M Marshall, J. (2003). *Pocketful of nonsense.* Boston: Houghton Mifflin. M
List Poems	Heard, G. (Ed.). (2009). *Falling down the page: A book of list poems.* New York: Roaring Brook Press. M–U
Model Poems	Koch, K. (1990). *Rose, where did you get that red?* New York: Vintage Books. M–U
Odes	Bennett, K. (2010). *Dad and Pop: An ode to fathers & stepfathers.* Cambridge, MA: Candlewick Press. P–M Soto, G. (2005). *Neighborhood odes.* Orlando: Harcourt. M
Poems for Two Voices	Fleischman, P. (2004). *Joyful noise: Poems for two voices.* New York: HarperCollins. P–M–U Franco, B. (2009). *Messing around on the monkey bars: And other school poems for two voices.* Cambridge, MA: Candlewick Press. M

Buckle and Gloria (Rathmann, 1995), the story of a police officer and his dog who give safety speeches at schools, a group of first graders wrote this acrostic using the dog's name, *Gloria*, as the key word:

Gloria
Loves to do tricks.
Officer Buckle tells safety
Rules at schools.
I wish I had
A dog like Gloria.

Other students composed this acrostic using the same key word:

Good dog Gloria
Likes to help
Officer Buckle teach safety
Rules to boys and girls.
I promise to remember
All the lessons.

COLOR POEMS. Students begin each line or stanza with a color word when they write color poems (Koch, 2000). For example, seventh graders wrote couplets about yellow:

Yellow is shiny galoshes
splashing through mud puddles.

Yellow is a street lamp
beaming through a dark, black night.

Yellow is the egg yolk
bubbling in a frying pan.

Yellow is the lemon cake
that makes you pucker your lips.

Yellow is the sunset
and the warm summer breeze.

Yellow is the tingling in your mouth
after a lemon drop melts.

Students also write more complex poems by expanding each line into a stanza, as this poem about black illustrates:

Black is a deep hole
sitting in the ground
waiting for animals
that live inside.

Black is a beautiful horse
standing on a high hill
with the wind
swirling its mane.

Black is a winter night sky
without stars or a moon
and only the cold wind
to keep it company.

Black is a panther
creeping around a jungle
never making a sound
searching for its prey.

FIVE-SENSES POEMS. Students write about a topic using the senses in five-senses poems. These poems are usually brief, with one line for each sense, as this sixth grader's poem, "Being Heartbroken," demonstrates:

 Sounds like thunder and lightning
Looks like a carrot going through a blender
Tastes like sour milk
Feels like a splinter in your finger
Smells like a dead fish
It must be horrible!

It's often helpful to have students develop a five-senses cluster and collect ideas for each sense before beginning to write. Then they select the most vivid idea for each sense to expand into a line of the poem.

"I AM . . . " POEMS. Students write "I Am . . . " poems about themselves or from the viewpoint of a book character or historical figure. They begin and end each stanza with "I am" and start the lines in between with "I." First graders wrote this collaborative poem after reading *Where the Wild Things Are* (Sendak, 2003), the story of a boy who imagines that he travels to the land of the wild things after being sent to his bedroom for misbehaving:

 I am Max
wearing my wolf suit
and making mischief.
I turned into a Wild Thing.
I became the king of the Wild Things.
But I got homesick
so I sailed home.
I am Max,
a hungry little boy
who wants his mommy.

"IF I WERE . . . " POEMS. Students write about how they'd feel and what they'd do if they were something else—a Tyrannosaurus Rex, a hamburger, or sunshine (Koch, 2000). They can also write poems from the viewpoint of a book character. Fifth graders, for example, wrote this poem after reading *Number the Stars* (Lowry, 2011):

 If I were Annemarie,
I'd be brave.

I'd hide my friends,
and trick those Nazi soldiers.
I would lie if I had to.
If I were Annemarie,
I'd be brave.

PREPOSITION POEMS. Students write preposition poems by beginning each line with a preposition, often producing a delightful poetic effect. A seventh grader wrote this poem about Superman:

Within the city
In a phone booth
Into his clothes
Like a bird
In the sky
Through the walls
Until the crime
Among us
Is defeated!

It's helpful to have a list of prepositions available for students to refer to when they're writing. Some students need to ignore the formula for a line or two to give the content of their poems top priority, or they may mistakenly begin a line with an infinitive (e.g., *to say*) rather than a preposition. This poetic form provides a structure, but it should be adapted as necessary.

WISH POEMS. Students begin each line with the words "I wish" and complete the line with a wish (Koch, 2000). In this second grade class collaboration, children simply listed their wishes:

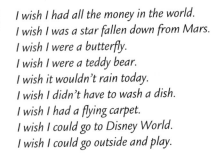

I wish I had all the money in the world.
I wish I was a star fallen down from Mars.
I wish I were a butterfly.
I wish I were a teddy bear.
I wish it wouldn't rain today.
I wish I didn't have to wash a dish.
I wish I had a flying carpet.
I wish I could go to Disney World.
I wish I could go outside and play.

Then children choose one of the wishes and expand on it in several more lines. Brandi expanded her wish this way:

I wish I were a teddy bear
Who sat on a beautiful bed
Who got a hug every night
By a little girl or boy.
Maybe tonight I'll get my wish
And wake up on a little girl's bed
And then I'll be as happy as can be.

Some of these formulas may seem more like sentences than poems, but the line between poetry and prose is blurry, and these experiences move students toward authentic poetic expression.

Free Verse. Unrhymed poetry is called *free verse*. Word choice and visual images take on great importance, and rhythm is de-emphasized. Students use free verse to describe an idea, express a thought, or tell a story. The number of words in a line and the use of punctuation marks vary. In this poem, an eighth grader describes loneliness poignantly and concisely, using only 15 well-chosen words:

> *A lifetime*
> *of broken dreams*
> *and promises*
> *Lost love*
> *hurts*
> *My heart*
> *cries*
> *in silence*

Students use several methods for writing free-form poems: They can select words and phrases from brainstormed lists, or they can write a paragraph and then "unwrite" it by deleting unnecessary words; then they arrange the remaining words to look like a poem.

BILINGUAL POEMS. Students write bilingual poems by inserting words from other languages into their poems (Cahnmann, 2006). Pat Mora's *Confetti: Poems for Children* (1999), Gary Soto's *Neighborhood Odes* (2005), and Juan Felipe Herrera's *Laughing Out Loud, I Fly* (1998) are examples of Spanish-English bilingual poems. In other books, the poems are printed side by side in Spanish and English, such as *Sol a Sol: Bilingual Poems* (Carlson, 1998), *Poems to Dream Together/Poemas para Soñar Juntos* (Alarcón, 2005), and *The Tree Is Older Than You Are* (Nye, 1998). Students can read these poems in either language, or alternate reading one stanza in English and the next in Spanish. When bilingual students and English learners read and write bilingual poems, they move between the linguistic and cultural communities of home and school, and the poems they create are often very powerful.

COMPARISON POEMS. Students compare something to something else and then expand on the comparison in the poem (Koch, 2000). A third grader wrote this poem after brainstorming a list of humorous explanations of thunder:

> *Thunder is a brontosaurus sneezing,*
> *that's all it is.*
> *Nothing to frighten you—*
> *just a dinosaur with a cold.*

This student's comparison is a metaphor. She could have written "Thunder is like a brontosaurus sneezing"—a simile—but the metaphor creates a stronger comparison.

CONCRETE POEMS. Students create concrete poems through the careful arrangement of words on a page (Fletcher, 2002). Words, phrases, and sentences can be written in the shape of an object, or word pictures can be inserted within poems written left to right and top to bottom (Janeczko, 2005). Figure 11–2 shows two concrete poems. In "Ants," the words *ants, cake,* and *frosting* create the image of a familiar picnic scene, and in "Cemetery," repetition and form create a reflection of peace.

FIGURE 11-2 Students' Concrete Poems

FOUND POEMS. Students create poems by culling words from stories, newspaper and magazine articles, and nonfiction books and arrange them to make a poem. A sixth grader wrote this poem after reading *Hatchet* (Paulsen, 2007), the story of a boy who survives in the wilderness after his plane crashes:

He was 13.
Always started with a single word:
Divorce.
An ugly word,
A breaking word, an ugly breaking word.
A tearing ugly word that meant fights and yelling.
Secrets.
Visitation rights.
A hatchet on his belt.
His plane.
The pilot had been sighted.
He rubbed his shoulder.
Aches and pains.
A heart attack.
The engine droned.
A survival pack which had emergency supplies.
Brian Robeson
Alone.
Help, p-l-e-a-s-e.

When they write found poems, students experiment with more sophisticated words and language structures than they might write themselves, and they also document their understanding of the stories and other texts they've read.

LIST POEMS. Students create poems using words and phrases from a list they've brainstormed about a topic, following models in Georgia Heard's (2009) book of list poems. Each line in the poem follows the same structure, and the last line presents a twist or sums up the topic. Third grade Jeremy wrote this list poem, titled "Jeremy's Favorite Pizza":

Crispy crust
Tomato sauce
Italian seasoning
Pepperoni slices
Sausage meatballs
Mushrooms—OK
NO olives
Mozzarella cheese
PIPING HOT!

Jeremy proudly pointed out that each of his lines has two words, and he used uppercase letters to indicate which words should be emphasized when reading the poem aloud.

ODES. Students write odes to celebrate everyday objects, especially those things that aren't usually appreciated. The poem, written directly to an object, tells what's good about it and why it's valued. Traditionally, odes were sophisticated lyrical verses, such as Keats's "Ode to a Nightingale," but Chilean poet Pablo Neruda (2000) introduced an informal contemporary version. Gary Soto's *Neighborhood Odes* (2005) is a very approachable collection of odes that celebrate everyday things, including water sprinklers and tennis shoes.

POEMS FOR TWO VOICES. Poems for two voices are a unique form. They're written in two columns, side by side, and the columns are read together by two readers: One reader reads the left column, and the other reads the right column. When both readers have words—either the same words or different ones—written on the same line, they read them simultaneously so that the poem sounds like a duet. Students' poems are often written from two characters' viewpoints. For example, after reading *Officer Buckle and Gloria* (Rathmann, 1995), second graders wrote this poem. The voice on the left is Officer Buckle's and the one on the right is Gloria's:

I am Officer Buckle

                                                          I am Gloria,
                                                          a police dog in the K-9.
I teach safety tips   *I teach safety tips*
to boys and girls.   *to boys and girls.*
I say,
"Keep your shoelaces tied."

                                                          I do a trick.
I say,
"Do not go swimming
during electrical storms."

                                                          I do a trick.
I say,
"Stay away from guns."

                                                          I do a trick.

Bravo!	*Bravo!*
Everyone claps.	*Everyone claps.*
Do the kids love me?	
	Yes, they do.
No, the kids love you more.	
	The kids love both of us.
We're buddies!	*We're buddies!*
Always stick with your buddy.	*Always stick with your buddy.*

Two books of poems for two readers are Paul Fleischman's *I Am Phoenix: Poems for Two Voices* (1985), about birds, and the Newbery Medal–winning *Joyful Noise: Poems for Two Voices* (2004a), about insects. And, if two voices aren't enough, check *Big Talk: Poems for Four Voices* (Fleischman, 2000).

Syllable- and Word-Count Poems. Haiku and other syllable- and word-count poems provide a structure that helps students succeed; however, adhering to a formula can restrict students' expression. The exact syllable or word counts force students to search for just the right words to express their ideas and feelings, but at the same time it provides a valuable opportunity for students to use thesauri.

CINQUAIN. A *cinquain* (SIN-cane) is a five-line poem containing 22 syllables in a 2-4-6-8-2 syllable pattern that usually describe something but may tell a story. This is the formula:

Line 1: a one-word subject with two syllables
Line 2: four syllables describing the subject
Line 3: six syllables showing action
Line 4: eight syllables expressing a feeling or an observation about the subject
Line 5: two syllables describing or renaming the subject

A seventh grade student wrote this cinquain poem:

Wrestling
skinny, fat
coaching, arguing, pinning
trying hard to win
tournament

If you compare this poem to the cinquain formula, you'll notice that some lines are short a syllable or two. The student bent some of the rules in choosing words to create a powerful image of wrestling; however, the message of the poem is always more important than adhering to the formula.

DIAMANTE. Tiedt (2002) invented the *diamante* (dee-ah-MAHN-tay), a seven-line contrast poem written in the shape of a diamond. This poetic form helps students apply their knowledge of opposites and parts of speech. Here's the formula:

Line 1: one noun as the subject
Line 2: two adjectives describing the subject
Line 3: three participles (ending in *-ing*) telling about the subject
Line 4: four nouns (the first two related to the subject and the second two related to the opposite)
Line 5: three participles telling about the opposite
Line 6: two adjectives describing the opposite
Line 7: one noun that is the opposite of the subject

A third grade class wrote this diamante poem about the stages of life:

Baby
wrinkled tiny
crying wetting sleeping
rattles diapers money house
caring working loving
smart helpful
Adult

The students created a contrast between *baby,* the subject represented by the noun in the first line, and *adult,* the opposite in the last line. The third word in the fourth line, *money,* begins the transition from *baby* to its opposite, *adult.*

HAIKU. The most familiar syllable-count poem is *haiku* (high-KOO), a Japanese form consisting of 17 syllables arranged in three lines of 5, 7, and 5 syllables. Haiku poems focus on nature and present a single, clear image. Haiku is a concise form, much like a telegram. A fourth grader wrote this haiku poem about a spider web she saw one morning:

Spider web shining
Tangled on the grass with dew
Waiting quietly.

Books of haiku to share with students include *Cool Melons—Turn to Frogs!* (Gollub, 2004), *Fold Me a Poem* (George, 2005), *If Not for the Cat* (Prelutsky, 2004), and *Don't Step on the Sky: A Handful of Haiku* (Chaikin, 2002). An added benefit is that the artwork in these books provides ideas for illustrating haiku poems.

Rhymed Verse. Although rhymed verse is the most common type of poetry that students read, they're less likely to write rhymed verse. Older students do write several rhymed verse forms, such as limericks and clerihews; however, it's important that teachers try to prevent the forms and rhyme schemes from restricting students' creative expression.

LIMERICKS. The limerick is a form of light verse that uses both rhyme and rhythm. The poem consists of five lines; the first, second, and fifth lines rhyme, and the third and fourth lines rhyme with each other and are shorter than the other three. The last line often contains a funny or surprise ending, as in this eighth grader's limerick:

There once was a frog named Pete
Who did nothing but sit and eat.
He examined each fly
With so careful an eye
And then said, "You're dead meat."

Edward Lear popularized limericks in the 19th century, and it's easy to find collections of limericks to share with students.

CLERIHEWS. *Clerihews* (KLER-i-hyoos), rhymed verses that describe a person, were named for Edmund Clerihew Bentley (1875–1956), a British detective writer who invented the form. This formula has four lines:

Line 1: the person's name
Line 2: the last word rhymes with the last word in the first line
Lines 3 and 4: the last words in these lines rhyme with each other

Clerihews can be written about anyone—historical figures, characters in stories, and even the students themselves. A sixth grader wrote this clerihew about Albert Einstein:

Albert Einstein
His genius did shine.
Of relativity and energy he did dream
And scientists today hold him in high esteem.

Students often write clerihews as part of autobiography and biography units.

Model Poems. Students model their poems on poems composed by adult poets, as Kenneth Koch suggested in *Rose, Where Did You Get That Red?* (1990). They read and examine a poem written by an adult poet and write their own, using the structure, some of the words, or the theme expressed in the model poem.

APOLOGIES. Using William Carlos Williams's "This Is Just to Say" as the model, students write poems in which they apologize for something they're secretly glad they did (Koch, 1990). Middle and upper graders are familiar with offering apologies and enjoy writing humorous ones. A seventh grader wrote this apology poem, "The Truck," to his dad:

Dad,
I'm sorry
that I took
the truck
out for
a spin.
I knew it
was wrong.
But . . .
the exhilarating
motion was
AWESOME!

Apology poems aren't always humorous; they may be sensitive, genuine apologies, as another seventh grader's poem, "Open Up," demonstrates:

I didn't
open my
immature eyes
to see
the pain
within you
a death
had caused.
Forgive me,

I misunderstood
your anguished
broken heart.

INVITATIONS. Students write poems in which they invite someone to a magical, beautiful place full of sounds and colors and where all kinds of marvelous things happen. The model is Shakespeare's "Come Unto These Yellow Sands" (Koch, 1990). A seventh grader wrote this invitation poem:

Come unto the golden shore
Where days are filled with laughter,
And nights filled with whispering winds.
Where sunflowers and sun
Are filled with love.
Come take my hand
As we walk into the sun.

Poetic Devices

Poets choose words carefully. They craft powerful images when they use unexpected comparisons, repeat sounds within a line or stanza, imitate sounds, and repeat words and phrases; these techniques are *poetic devices*. As students learn about them, they appreciate the poet's ability to manipulate a device in poems they read and then apply it in their own writing. The terminology is also helpful when students talk about poems they've read; and in revising groups, they use the terms to compliment classmates on the use of a device or suggest that they try a particular technique when they revise their poems.

Comparison. One way to describe something is to compare it to something else. Students compare images, feelings, and actions to other things using two types of comparisons—similes and metaphors. A *simile* is an explicit comparison of one thing to another—a statement that one thing is like something else. Similes are signaled by the use of *like* or *as*. In contrast, a *metaphor* compares two things by implying that one thing is something else, without using *like* or *as*. Differentiating between the two is less important than using them to make poems more vivid; for example, students might compare anger to a natural occurrence: Using a simile, they write, "Anger is like a thunderstorm, screaming with thunder-feelings and lightning-words." Or, as a metaphor, they write, "Anger is a volcano, erupting with poisonous words and hot-lava actions."

Students begin by learning traditional comparisons and idioms; then, they learn to avoid stale comparisons, such as "high as a kite," "butterflies in your stomach," and "light as a feather." Finally, they invent fresh, unexpected comparisons. A sixth grader uses a combination of expected and unexpected comparisons in this poem, "People":

People are like birds
who are constantly getting their feathers ruffled.
People are like alligators
who find pleasure in evil cleverness.
People are like bees
who are always busy.
People are like penguins
who want to have fun.
People are like platypuses—unexplainable!

| FIGURE 11-3 | Two Pages From a Fourth Grade Class Book |

Alliteration. *Alliteration* is the repetition of the initial consonant sound in consecutive words or in words in close proximity. Repeating the initial sound makes poetry fun to recite, and primary grade students enjoy reading alliterative verses, such as *A My Name Is Alice* (Bayer, 1992) and *The Z Was Zapped* (Van Allsburg, 1998). After reading one of these books, students can create their own versions. A fourth grade class created its own version of Van Allsburg's book, which they called *The Z Was Zipped*. Students divided into pairs, and each group composed two pages for the class book. Students illustrated their letter on the front of the paper and wrote a sentence on the back to describe their illustration, following Van Allsburg's pattern. Two pages are shown in Figure 11–3. Examine the illustrations before reading these sentences:

    The D got dunked by the duck.

The T was totally terrified.

Tongue twisters are an exaggerated type of alliteration in which almost every word in the twister begins with the same letter. Dr. Seuss compiled an easy-to-read collection of tongue twisters for primary grade students in *Oh Say Can You Say?* (2004). *Tongue Twisters to Tangle Your Tongue* (Cobb, 2006) and *Alison's Zinnia* (Lobel, 1996) are two good books of tongue twisters for middle grade students. Practice with tongue twisters and alliterative books increases students' awareness of alliteration. Only a few students consciously think about adding alliteration to a poem, but they get high praise from classmates when they do.

Onomatopoeia. Poets use *onomatopoeia*, or sound words, to make their writing more sensory and more vivid. Sound words include *crash, slurp, varoom,* and *meow*. Two books of sound words are *Slop Goes the Soup: A Noisy Warthog Word Book* (Edwards, 2001) and *Achoo! Bang! Crash! The Noisy Alphabet* (MacDonald, 2003). Students can compile a list of sound words they find in poems and display the list on a classroom chart to refer to when they're writing poems.

In *Wishes, Lies, and Dreams* (2000), Kenneth Koch recommends having students write noise poems that include a noise or sound word in each line. These first poems often sound contrived (e.g., "A dog barks bow-wow"), but the experience helps them learn to use onomatopoeia, as this poem, "Elephant Noses," dictated by a kindergartner, illustrates:

Elephant noses
Big noses
Elephants have big noses
Big noses
Elephants have big noses
through which they drink
SCHLURRP

Repetition. Repetition of words and phrases is another device writers use to structure poems as well as to add interest. Poe's use of the word *nevermore* in "The Raven" is a well-known example. In this riddle, a fourth grader uses a refrain effectively:

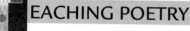

I am a little man standing all alone
In the deep, dark wood.
I am standing on one foot
In the deep, dark wood.
Tell me quickly, if you can,
What to call this little man
Standing all alone
In the deep, dark wood.
Who am I?

(Answer: a mushroom)

TEACHING POETRY

Teachers share poems and invite students to write poems as part of the patterns of practice. It's easy to find poems to accompany most featured books for literature focus units and thematic unit topics, and many students often choose to write poetry during writing workshop. The box on the next page shows how poetry fits into the patterns of practice. Teachers also create poetry workshops, combining reading and writing workshop, as Mrs. Harris did in the vignette at the beginning of the chapter.

How to Read Poems

In her poem "How to Eat a Poem," Eve Merriam (American Poetry and Literacy Project, 2006) provides useful advice for students who read poetry: She compares reading a poem to eating a piece of fruit and advises biting right in and letting the juice run down your chin. The focus is on enjoyment: Students read poems and listen to them read aloud because they're pleasurable activities. With so many books of poetry available today, it's easy to find poems that appeal to every student and poems that teachers like, too. Figure 11–4 presents guidelines for reading and responding to poems.

Poetry is intended to be shared orally because the words and phrases lose much of their music when they're read with the eyes and not with the voice. As teachers and students read poems aloud, they read expressively, stressing and elongating words, adjusting reading speeds, and using musical instruments or props to accompany the reading (Elster & Hanauer, 2002). Readers consider these four aspects of expressive reading:

- Tempo—how fast or slowly to read the lines
- Rhythm—which words to stress or say loudest
- Pitch—when to raise or lower the voice
- Juncture—when and how long to pause

Students experiment with tempo, rhythm, pitch, and juncture as they read poems in different ways and learn how to vary their reading to make their presentations more interpretive. They also learn that in some poems, reading speed may be more important and that in others, pausing is more important. These considerations reinforce the need to rehearse a poem several times before reading it aloud for classmates.

Interpreting Poems. Some poems are very approachable, and students grasp their meaning during the first reading. For example, Jack Prelutsky's poem "The New Kid on the Block" (1984) is about a bully, and in the last line of the poem, students learn that the bully is a girl. What a kicker! Students laugh as they realize that they'd assumed the bully was a boy. They reread the poem to figure out how the poet set them up, and they pick out the words in the poem that created the image of a boy bully in their minds. As they talk about the poem, students discuss their assumptions about bullies and point out words in the text that led them astray. Some students also insist that the poet used the words *and boy* as an interjection early in the poem to intentionally mislead them.

Other poems are more difficult to understand. It might be helpful to think that understanding a poem is like peeling an onion: It requires multiple readings (Wood, 2006). From the first reading, students come away with an initial impression. Words and images stick in their minds: They giggle over silly rhymes, repeat alliterations and refrains, and ask questions about things that puzzle them.

Students' comprehension grows as they explore the poem. In the primary grades, students often explore poems together as a class, but Dias (1996) recommends that older students work in small groups to reread and talk about a poem. At this point, it's important that students remain

How Poetry Fits Into the Patterns of Practice

Literature Focus Units

Teachers often share poems in conjunction with featured books, and they teach author units that focus on poets. Also, sometimes students choose to write poems as projects after reading a featured book.

Literature Circles

Students rarely read books of poetry during literature circles, but sometimes they read novels written in poetic form. Also, during poetry workshop, students read and respond to books of poetry written by a particular poet.

Reading and Writing Workshop

Sometimes students choose books of poetry to read during reading workshop. Many students write poems during writing workshop, especially when they've learned to use a variety of poetic formulas.

Thematic Units

Teachers often read aloud poems related to the thematic unit, and students also write poems. Sometimes they use the poems they've read as models, incorporate a line from a familiar poem, or choose a formula they've learned.

FIGURE 11–4	Guidelines for Reading and Responding to Poems

Reading Aloud
Read poetry aloud, not silently, in order to appreciate the cadence of the words. Even if students are reading independently, they should speak each word, albeit softly or in an undertone.

Expression
Teach students how to read a poem expressively, how to emphasize the rhythm and feel of the words, and where to pause.

Song Tunes
Have children sing poems to familiar tunes, such as "Twinkle, Twinkle Little Star" or "I've Been Working on the Railroad," that fit the line structure of the poem.

Rehearsal
Have readers rehearse poems several times before reading aloud so that they can read fluently and with expression. In other words, encourage students to read "poetically."

Poetry Books
Include a collection of poetry books in the classroom library for students to read during reading workshop and other independent reading times.

Memorization
Rarely assign students a particular poem to memorize; rather, encourage students who are interested in learning a favorite poem to do so and to share it with class members.

Author Units
Teach author units to focus on a poet, such as Dr. Seuss, Jack Prelutsky, or Gary Soto. Have students read the poet's poems and learn about his or her life through biographies and Internet resources.

Display Poems
Copy and display poems on chart paper or on sentence strips in pocket charts for students to read and enjoy.

flexible and recognize that a fuller meaning is possible. They reread the poem, drawing on their personal experiences and their knowledge of poetry to look for clues to meaning. Sometimes they wonder about the title of the poem and why the poet chose it. They also identify favorite lines, divide the poem into parts to understand its organization, examine line breaks, and discuss one or more of these points:

- Structure of the poem
- Order of words in a line
- Rhythm and rhyme
- Shape of the poem
- Imagery in the poem

Students share their ideas, and as they listen to classmates' comments, their understanding grows. Teachers support students as they delve into a poem; they don't simply tell them what it means. They do provide information and ask questions to nudge students toward becoming independent, responsible readers. Poems often mean different things to students because they approach the poem with individual background knowledge and past experiences. Even so, a poem can't mean just anything; students' interpretations must be supported by the words in the text.

Performing Poems. Students share their understanding of a poem as they perform it for class-mates. One way is using choral reading, in which students take turns reading a poem together. Students arrange the poem for choral reading so that individual students, pairs of students, and small groups read particular lines or stanzas using one of these arrangements:

ECHO READING. The leader reads each line, and the group repeats it.

LEADER AND CHORUS READING. The leader reads the main part of the poem, and the group reads the refrain or chorus in unison.

SMALL-GROUP READING. The class divides into two or more groups, and each group reads one part of the poem.

CUMULATIVE READING. One student or one group reads the first line or stanza, and another student or group joins in as each line or stanza is read so that a cumulative effect is created.

Then students rehearse their parts and, finally, read the poem as an oral presentation. Students also add props or play music in the background to enhance the presentation. The Step-by-Step feature below describes the procedure for choral reading.

What about memorizing poems? Memorization can be a useful mental exercise, but it's not a good idea to assign a particular poem for all students to learn. Children vary in their poetry preferences, and requiring them to learn a poem that they don't like risks killing their interest in poetry. Patrice Vecchione (2002) advocates having students memorize special poems that speak to them. She explains that things "we commit to memory we know differently than the things we don't. The way to really know a poem, to befriend it, is to learn it by heart. Then, it's yours for always" (p. xvi). Her anthology of memorable poems, *Whisper and*

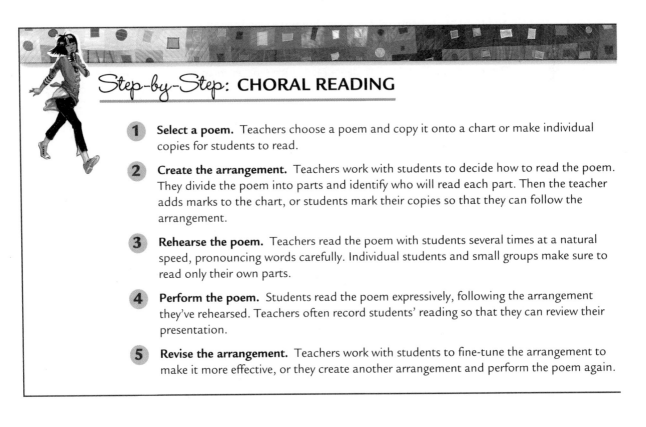

Step-by-Step: CHORAL READING

1. **Select a poem.** Teachers choose a poem and copy it onto a chart or make individual copies for students to read.

2. **Create the arrangement.** Teachers work with students to decide how to read the poem. They divide the poem into parts and identify who will read each part. Then the teacher adds marks to the chart, or students mark their copies so that they can follow the arrangement.

3. **Rehearse the poem.** Teachers read the poem with students several times at a natural speed, pronouncing words carefully. Individual students and small groups make sure to read only their own parts.

4. **Perform the poem.** Students read the poem expressively, following the arrangement they've rehearsed. Teachers often record students' reading so that they can review their presentation.

5. **Revise the arrangement.** Teachers work with students to fine-tune the arrangement to make it more effective, or they create another arrangement and perform the poem again.

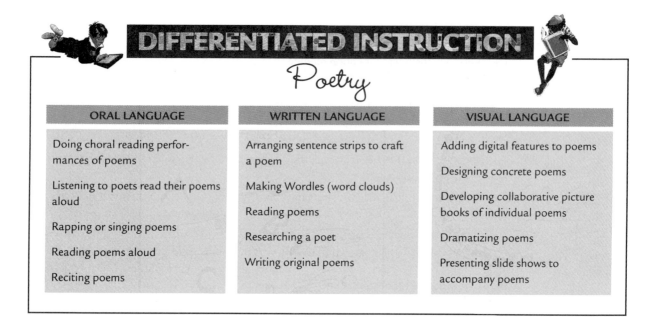

DIFFERENTIATED INSTRUCTION
Poetry

ORAL LANGUAGE	WRITTEN LANGUAGE	VISUAL LANGUAGE
Doing choral reading performances of poems	Arranging sentence strips to craft a poem	Adding digital features to poems
Listening to poets read their poems aloud	Making Wordles (word clouds)	Designing concrete poems
Rapping or singing poems	Reading poems	Developing collaborative picture books of individual poems
Reading poems aloud	Researching a poet	Dramatizing poems
Reciting poems	Writing original poems	Presenting slide shows to accompany poems

Shout: Poems to Memorize (2002), includes "The Road Not Taken," by Robert Frost, "Song," by Ashley Bryan, "Louder Than a Clap of Thunder!" by Pack Prelutsky, and "Dream Deferred," by Langston Hughes. When teachers encourage students to memorize a favorite poem and recite it for the class, memorizing poems quickly becomes a popular response activity. In addition, as students rehearse for choral reading presentations, they often memorize poems without even trying.

Response Activities. As students read poems or listen to them read aloud, they participate spontaneously in response actions: They move their bodies, tap their feet, or clap to the poem's rhythm, and repeat words, rhymes, and refrains, savoring word choice and rhyme. Teachers also plan response activities to enhance students' understanding and appreciation of poems. The Differentiated Instruction box above lists a variety of oral, written, and visual response activities.

One way students explore a poem is by sequencing the lines. Teachers copy the lines of the poem on long strips of chart paper, and students sequence them in a pocket chart or by lining up around the classroom. Through this sequencing activity, students investigate the syntactic structure of poems and get ideas for poems they write.

A second way students respond to poems is by singing them. They pick a tune that fits the rhythm of the poem and sing it instead of reading it. Many teachers report that students quickly memorize poems when they sing them again and again. Alan Katz's hilarious book *Take Me Out of the Bathtub and Other Silly Dilly Songs* (2001) shows students how to fit new words to familiar tunes.

Students can celebrate a favorite poem by creating a class collaboration book of the poem. They each prepare one page by writing a line or stanza of the poem on it and then add an illustration to complement the text. One student also makes a cover for the book with the title of the poem and the poet's name. The teacher compiles the pages and binds the book, and then the book is placed in the classroom library. Students enjoy rereading their illustrated version of the poem. A page from a third grade class book illustrating Shel Silverstein's "Hug O' War" (2004) is shown in Figure 11–5.

FIGURE 11–5 A Page From a Third Grade Class Book

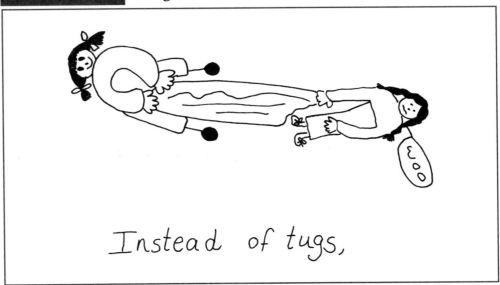

Instead of tugs,

Writing is another way students respond to poems. They can write new poems following the format of the poem they've read. In this poem, a second grader uses "My Teacher" (Dakos, 1995) as a model:

> *My Mom*
> *She loves to exercise at the gym*
> *And watch romantic movies*
> *And eat Mexican food*
> *And get flowers painted on her nails*
> *And sing in the choir at church*
> *And most of all*
> *ME!*

Students also write poems by choosing a favorite line from a poem and incorporating it in a poem they write.

Teaching Students to Write Poems

Students apply what they've learned about poetry as they write poems. Too often they have misconceptions that interfere with their ability to write poems. It's important to help students develop a concept of poetry and experiment with poetic devices as they begin writing poems.

Introducing Poetry Writing. One way to introduce students to writing poetry is to read excerpts from the first chapter of *Anastasia Krupnik* (Lowry, 1995), in which 10-year-old Anastasia writes a poem as a homework assignment. She works for eight nights to craft her poem. Lowry does an excellent job of describing how poets search long and hard for words to express meaning and the delight that comes when they realize their poems are finished. Then Anastasia and her classmates bring their poems to class. One student reads aloud his four-line rhymed verse:

> I have a dog whose name is Spot.
> He likes to eat and drink a lot.
> When I put water in his dish,
> He laps it up just like a fish. (p. 10)

Anastasia isn't impressed. She knows the boy who wrote the poem has a dog named Sputnik, not Spot! But her teacher, Mrs. Westvessel, gives it an A. Soon it's Anastasia's turn, and she's nervous because her poem is very different. She reads her poem about tiny creatures that move about in tidepools at night:

> hush   hush   the sea-soft night is aswim
>   with wrinklesquirm creatures
>   listen (!)
> to them   move   smooth   in the moistly dark
>   here in the   whisperwarm   wet (pp. 11–12)

In this free-form poem without rhyme or capital letters, Anastasia has created a marvelous picture with invented words. Regrettably, her teacher has an antiquated view that poems should be about serious subjects, incorporate rhyme, and use conventional capitalization and punctuation. She doesn't understand Anastasia's poem and gives her an F because she didn't follow directions.

Although this first chapter presents a depressing picture of teachers' lack of knowledge about poetry, it's a dramatic introduction about what poetry is and what it isn't. After reading excerpts from the chapter, teachers often develop a chart with their students comparing what poetry is in Mrs. Westvessel's class and what poetry really involves. A seventh grade class developed the chart in Figure 11–6.

FIGURE 11–6   Rules About Writing Poetry

Mrs. Westvessel's Rules	Our Rules
1. Poems must rhyme.	1. Poems don't have to rhyme.
2. The first letter in each line must be capitalized.	2. The first letter in each line doesn't have to be capitalized.
3. Each line must start at the left margin.	3. Poems can take different shapes and be anywhere on a page.
4. Poems must have a certain rhythm.	4. You hear the writer's voice in a poem--with or without rhythm.
5. Poems should be written about serious topics.	5. Poems can be about anything--serious or silly topics.
6. Poems should be punctuated like other types of writing.	6. Poems can be punctuated in different ways or not be punctuated at all.
7. Poems are failures if they don't follow these rules.	7. There are no real rules for poems, and no poem is a failure.

After this introduction, teachers teach minilessons about the poetic formulas, poetic devices, and how to write poems, and they provide opportunities for students to write poems. Jack Prelutsky's *Read a Rhyme, Write a Rhyme* (2005) also provides "poemstarts" to help students start writing poetry.

Publishing Students' Poems. The most common way that students share their poems is by reading them aloud—and with expression—from the author's chair. Classmates listen and then offer compliments about what they liked about the poem—word choice, topic, or poetic devices. Another way that students share their poems with classmates is through a read-around, as Mrs. Harris's students did in the vignette at the beginning of the chapter.

Students compile their poems into anthologies that they place in the classroom library for classmates to read. Teachers also display copies of students' poems, often accompanied by an illustration, on a wall of the classroom and then have a gallery walk for students to read and respond to the poems. If there isn't enough classroom space to display the students' work, teachers can post them in the hallway or on students' desks. Students move from poem to poem and read and respond using small self-stick notes that they attach to the edge of the student's paper. The Step-by-Step feature below lists the steps in conducting a gallery walk. This activity is quick; it can be completed much faster than if students were to each share their poems in front of the class.

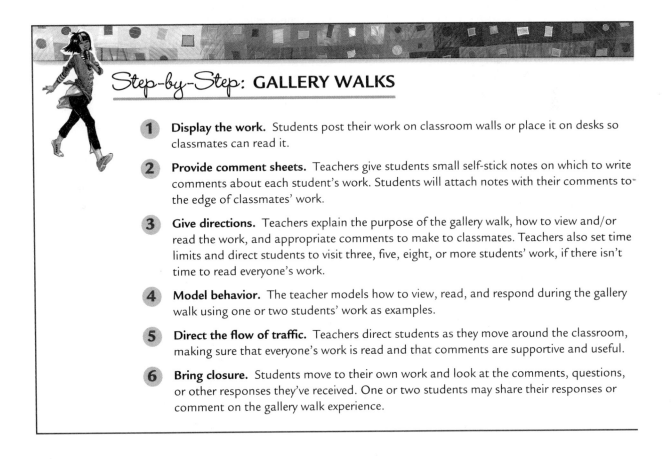

Step-by-Step: GALLERY WALKS

1. **Display the work.** Students post their work on classroom walls or place it on desks so classmates can read it.

2. **Provide comment sheets.** Teachers give students small self-stick notes on which to write comments about each student's work. Students will attach notes with their comments to the edge of classmates' work.

3. **Give directions.** Teachers explain the purpose of the gallery walk, how to view and/or read the work, and appropriate comments to make to classmates. Teachers also set time limits and direct students to visit three, five, eight, or more students' work, if there isn't time to read everyone's work.

4. **Model behavior.** The teacher models how to view, read, and respond during the gallery walk using one or two students' work as examples.

5. **Direct the flow of traffic.** Teachers direct students as they move around the classroom, making sure that everyone's work is read and that comments are supportive and useful.

6. **Bring closure.** Students move to their own work and look at the comments, questions, or other responses they've received. One or two students may share their responses or comment on the gallery walk experience.

Minilessons

Teachers use minilessons to teach students how to read and respond to poems. Minilessons cover procedures and strategies about reading poems expressively. They also teach students to identify and appreciate rhymes, word pictures, and other types of wordplay. A minilesson about how to read a poem expressively is presented below.

Teachers use minilessons to introduce students to poetic forms and write collaborative poems for practice before they write poems independently. Collaborative compositions are crucial because they're a practice run for students who aren't sure what to do; the 5 minutes it takes to write a class collaboration poem can be the difference between success and failure. Teachers also teach other topics related to writing poetry. They teach minilessons on the poetic devices

Minilesson

Mr. Johnston Teaches His Third Graders to Read Poems Expressively

1. Introduce the Topic

Mr. Johnston projects a copy of "A Pizza the Size of the Sun," by Jack Prelutsky (1996), on the interactive whiteboard and reads it aloud in a monotone voice. He asks his third graders if he did a good job reading the poem, and they tell him that his reading was boring.

2. Share Examples

Mr. Johnston asks what he could do to make his reading better, and they suggest that he read with more expression. He asks the students to tell him which words he should read more expressively and marks their changes on his copy. He reads the poem again, and the students agree that it's better. Then they suggest he vary his reading speed, and he reads the poem a third time, incorporating more changes. The students agree that his third reading is the best!

3. Provide Information

Mr. Johnston praises his students for their suggestions; they did help him make this reading better. Then he asks what he can do to make

his reading more interesting, and they make these suggestions:

- Read some parts loud and some parts soft.
- Read some parts fast and some parts slow.
- Change your voice for some words.

4. Supervise Practice

Mr. Johnston divides the class into small groups and passes out copies of other poems. Students in each group decide how to read the poem and mark parts they'll read in special ways. Mr. Johnston circulates around the classroom, providing assistance as needed. Then students display their poems on the whiteboard and read them aloud with expression.

5. Reflect on Learning

Mr. Johnston asks the third graders to talk about what they've learned. One student explains that there are two ways of reading: One is boring and the other is fun. They've learned how to read the fun way so that they can share their enjoyment of poems with others.

and how to incorporate them into the poems that students write, how to arrange lines of poetry for the greatest impact, and how to punctuate and capitalize poems, for example.

It isn't enough to provide opportunities for students to experiment with poetry; students also need to learn about the poetry genre and how to read and write poems. The Common Core State Standards address poetry, with an emphasis on interpretation; for more information, check the Standards box on page 317. Even young children can learn about this genre. Georgia Heard (1999), for example, emphasizes the importance of teaching students about line breaks and white space on the page. Kindergartners and first graders often write poems with the same page arrangement as stories, but as they experiment with line breaks, they shape their poems to emphasize rhythm and rhyme, images, and poetic devices. With practice, students learn that the way the lines are broken affects both how the poem looks and how it sounds when it's read aloud.

Mentor Texts

Teachers share poems from mentor texts as they teach students about wordplay, poetic forms, and poetic devices. Booklists with wordplay books, books with poems in varied formats, and books with poems representing different poetic forms are included in this chapter. During minilessons, teachers use poems from mentor texts as models, to demonstrate reading and writing strategies, and for guided practice activities. Students choose favorite poems for choral reading performances and multimedia presentations, and they use these poems as models for those they write.

INTEGRATING TECHNOLOGY

Students use technology to enhance their poems with images and sound, and they use other applications to learn about poetry and to write their own poems:

ONLINE POETRY GENERATORS. Online poetry generators are interactive tools that students use to learn about poetic forms and write their own poems. Students choose a poetry form, such as "I Am . . ." poems or limericks, read information that explains the formula, and view one or two sample poems. Next, they type words in a poetry frame to compose their poems. Once they're satisfied with their work, students click one button to view their finished poems and another to print them. Online poetry generators are available at Instant Poetry Forms (http://ettcweb.lr.k12 .nj.us/forms/newpoem.htm), ReadWriteThink (http://www.readwritethink.org), Poetry Idea Engine (http://teacher.scholastic.com/writewit/poetry/poetry_engine.htm), and other websites.

DIGITAL POETRY. Students create multimedia versions of familiar poems using digital images, sounds, and text, and they also produce digital versions of poems they write. To read more about digital poetry, check the Digital Classroom feature on the next page and the Middle School Spotlight on page 345.

CONNECTING WITH POETS. Students learn about poets and listen to them reading and discussing their own writing online. Many poets, such as Jack Prelutsky (http://www .jackprelutsky.com), Joyce Sidman (http://www.joycesidman.com), and Janet Wong (http:// www.janetwong.com), have their own websites, with biographical information, interviews, information about their books, and other activities. In addition, in its Writing With Writers section, Scholastic (http://www.scholastic.com) features video clips of Karla Kuskin and other poets talking about how they write and reading their poems.

The power of technology to engage students becomes clear when they use online resources to write poems and create multimedia projects. ■

DIGITAL CLASSROOM

Digital Poetry

Digital poetry combines the text with images and sounds to extend the poem's meaning. Students view digital poems and talk about their initial impressions and how the multimedia presentation helps them interpret the poem. Once they gain experience viewing these poems, students create their own digital poetry using poems they've read, or they can compose their own poems and then make choices about the interpretation and add photographs and other images, varied fonts for the text, and music, sound effects, and a voice track to deepen the meaning. Calo (2011) explains that digital poetry integrates bold visual images with the poet's words to breathe life into poetry. The genre of digital poetry is evolving; it's sometimes called *graphic poetry*, and a decade ago it included almost any poems available online, but today it's limited to multimedia poems that combine text, image, and sound components to enhance meaning.

Tarasiuk's (2009) middle school students created digital poems that she called "extreme poetry": Her students each chose a poem; then they added images, music, a voice track, and sound effects to interpret its meaning. Poetry can be daunting to many students, but Tarasiuk found that her students were motivated to complete this project, even those who claimed they didn't like poetry. They reported that they enjoyed the opportunity to represent words with a variety of media.

One way to introduce digital poetry is using "Your Three Words" (http://abcnews.go.com/GMA/Your3Words), a feature on ABC Television's Good Morning America as a model. Viewers submit multimedia messages using images and just three words, and the program shows them with musical accompaniment. A street poet named MadV came up with the idea for these public digital poems: He invited people to write three words on the palms of their hands and film themselves showing their hands. Both children and adults have submitted three-word digital poems that have appeared on Good Morning America, including a man about to jump from an airplane who shares "hope it opens," a smiling child who's lost a tooth holding up a sign that reads "lost first tooth," and a portrait of a wife and kids with the words "proud Army family."

ENGAGING ENGLISH LEARNERS

You might argue that there's so much language arts instruction that English learners need that they don't have time for poetry, but that's just plain wrong. Poetry offers English learners a unique opportunity for success, and when they're successful, their self-confidence increases, and they're more willing to take risks with other language arts activities.

There are specific benefits for reading, too. Students develop reading fluency and learn vocabulary words as they practice reading a favorite poem in preparation for a choral reading performance (Peregoy & Boyle, 2009). Students refine their oral presentation skills as they read and respond to poetry: They might memorize a favorite poem and recite it expressively, adding background music or pictures to accompany it. Or, they might share a poem written in their native language and then translate it for the class.

There are benefits for writing as well. Many English learners have difficulty with long writing assignments, but because poems are short, they're often easier to write. English learners' poems are usually better organized than other compositions because they structure their writing with familiar poetic forms, and the quality of their poems is often remarkable. They draw powerful images with words, combine words in fresh, unexpected ways, and create a strong voice through their writing; in fact, students often surprise themselves with the poems they write. ■

Middle School Spotlight

How can students use poetry for social action?

As part of a schoolwide focus on the global changes affecting the Earth, a sixth and seventh grade class decided to speak for the environment: They created digital poems combining text, images, and sound to share at the school's environmental fair to teach students, parents, and the community about the natural beauty that surrounds them (Hughes & John, 2009). The teacher wanted her students to move beyond poetic forms and "experiment with language, to climb inside a poem, and to play with it from within" (p. 16). To begin, the class took a field trip to a nearby forest, where students found a tree with a story to share. They each chose a tree and sat with it, creating descriptions, recording details, and taking digital photos. Students worked independently and collaboratively with classmates on the project, and the teacher reported a palpable excitement in the classroom because students had an authentic and meaningful goal. They wrote rough drafts of their poems and shared them with classmates to get feedback; at the same time, they thought about how they'd arrange and perform the poem. They used PhotoStory3 or MovieMaker to create the digital performance and experimented with how to present text, and they examined fonts, adjusting their size, color, and style. The teacher taught minilessons about three performance tools—paint, punch, and pause—so viewers could see as well as hear the poem. Students learned to pronounce words for effect, to pause before or after words and phrases, and to vary the tempo. The teacher also taught students how to use the poem's arrangement on the page, including line breaks and punctuation, to provide direction to viewers. The students practiced reading their poems using choral reading techniques because they knew that tone of voice, emphasis, pace, and volume shape viewers' understanding. The students presented their digital poems at the school's environmental fair, and the audience's response was overwhelmingly positive. The teacher concluded that her students experienced poetry in new ways through this multimedia project, and digital media allowed them to give voice to their poems.

Assessing Poetry

Teachers assess students' experiences with poetry in several ways, beginning when they plan for instruction, and continuing as they monitor students' progress and evaluate their learning. Graves (1992) recommends that teachers focus on the passion and wonder in students' writing and on their unique ability to make the common seem uncommon. Teachers notice the specific details, strong images, wordplay, comparisons, onomatopoeia, alliteration, and repetitions of words and lines that students incorporate in their poems.

Planning. Teachers consider how they'll monitor students' progress and assess their learning as they plan poetry workshops and other poetry units. They identify the poetry reading and writing activities they'll use, the poets they'll introduce, and the poetry forms and poetic devices they'll teach in minilessons. As they develop checklists and rubrics, teachers focus on the poetry concepts they're teaching.

Monitoring. Teachers observe students as they participate in poetry activities, keep anecdotal notes of students as they respond to poems, and examine the poems students are writing. They hold revising and editing conferences with students to monitor their application of poetry forms they've introduced and poetic devices students have studied in the poems they're writing.

Evaluating. Assessing the quality of students' poems is especially difficult, because poems are creative combinations of wordplay, poetic forms, and poetic devices. Instead of giving a grade for quality, teachers can ask these questions:

- Has the student experimented with the poetic form presented in a minilesson?
- Has the student used the process approach in writing, revising, and editing the poem?
- Has the student used wordplay or another poetic device in the poem?

Teachers also ask students to assess their own poems. Students choose their best efforts and poems that show promise. They explain which writing strategies they used in particular poems and which poetic forms they used.

SUMMING UP

Poetry isn't a frill; it's an essential part of the language arts program. Students explore poetry as they participate in wordplay, read and respond to poems, and write their own poems. PreK–8 students have definite opinions about the types of poems they like best, and they enjoy participating in oral, written, and visual language activities involving poetry. They write poems successfully using poetic formulas in which they begin each line with particular words, count syllables, or create word pictures. Because rhyme is a sticking point for many, students should be encouraged to experiment with comparison, repetition, and other poetic devices.

MyEducationLab™

Go to the topics Reading, Writing, and Literature in the MyEducationLab (http://www.myeducationlab.com) for *Language Arts: Patterns of Practice*, where you can:

- Find learning outcomes for Reading, Writing, and Literature along with the national standards that connect to these outcomes.
- Complete Assignments and Activities that can help you more deeply understand the chapter content.
- Apply and practice your understanding of the core teaching skills identified in the chapter with the Building Teaching Skills and Dispositions learning units.
- Examine challenging situations and cases presented in the IRIS Center Resources.
- Use the Lesson Plan Builder Activities to practice lesson planning and integrating national and state standards into your planning.
- Check your comprehension of the content covered in the chapter with the Study Plan. Here you will be able to take a chapter quiz, receive feedback on your answers, and then access Review, Practice, and Enrichment activities to enhance your understanding of chapter content.

On the **MyEducationLab** for this course, you'll also be able to:

- **A+RISE** Go to the topic A+RISE, an innovative and interactive database of strategies that differentiate instruction across the language arts and provide particular insight into research-based methods to meet the needs of English learners.

- Explore the topic Literacy Portraits—yearlong case studies of second graders, complete with student artifacts, teacher commentary, and student and teacher interviews, tracking the month-by-month language arts growth of five students.

- Gain practice with the Grammar Tutorial, online guided instruction to improve your own ability with grammar.

Learning to Spell Conventionally

FOURTH GRADERS STUDY SPELLING WORDS   The 28 fourth graders in Mr. Martinez's classroom participate in a 30-minute spelling lesson sandwiched between reading and writing workshop. During this time, Mr. Martinez assigns spelling words, and students practice them for the Friday test. He uses the words from a textbook spelling program, and each week's list of words focuses on a topic—*r*-controlled vowels or compound words, for example. The teacher introduces the concept through a series of lessons a week in advance so that his students understand the concept and are familiar with the words before they study them for the spelling test.

During the first semester, students studied vowel patterns (e.g., *strike, each*), *r*-controlled vowels (e.g., *first*), diphthongs (e.g., *soil*), more sophisticated consonant spellings (e.g., *edge, catch*), words with silent letters (e.g., *climb*), and homophones (e.g., *one–won*). Now in the second semester, they're learning two-syllable words. They've studied compound words (e.g., *headache*) and words with inflectional suffixes (e.g., *get–getting*), and this week's topic is irregular verbs. It's a difficult one because students need to know the verb forms as well as how to spell the words.

Because the students' spelling levels range from second to sixth grade, Mr. Martinez has divided them into three groups. Each month, the groups choose new food-related names for themselves. This month, the names are types of pizza; earlier in the year, they chose fruit names, Mexican food names, vegetable names, cookie names, and snack names. Of course, at the end of the month, they sample the foods. Mr. Martinez calls these food names his secret classroom management tool because students work hard in order to participate in the tasting.

How can teachers incorporate textbooks into their spelling programs?

Teaching spelling is more than having students memorize a list of words and take a test on Friday. Students need to learn spelling concepts—not just practice words—in order to become competent spellers. Also, a single list of words usually isn't appropriate for everyone. As you read this vignette about Mr. Martinez's spelling program, notice how he teaches spelling concepts, incorporates the textbook's weekly lists of spelling words, and takes into account students' levels of spelling development.

Students in the Pepperoni Pizza group spell at the second grade level, and they're studying *r*-controlled vowels. They've already studied two-letter spelling patterns, and now they're learning three-letter patterns. This week, the focus is on *ear* and *eer* patterns. Students in the Sausage Pizza group are almost at grade level; they're reviewing ways to spell /ou/. Students in the Hawaiian Pizza group are above-grade-level spellers; they're studying Latin root words and examining noun and verb forms of these words. This week's focus is spelling /shun/. Mr. Martinez meets with each group twice a week, and each group has a folder of activities to work on between meetings. Some meetings are held during the spelling period (usually on Thursdays), and others are squeezed into reading and writing workshop. The teacher also encourages students to hunt for words representing the concept they're studying in the books they're reading and to use them in their writing. They bring their examples to share at these meetings.

This week's spelling list is shown on page 350. The irregular verbs in the "All Pizzas" column are taken from the spelling textbook. All students study the words in the "All Pizzas" column, and students in each group also study their own list of words. Students study between 15 and 20 words each week, and they spell 15 words on the Friday test. When they're studying more than 15 words, as they are this week, students don't know which words will be on the test, but the asterisks in the box indicate the words Mr. Martinez plans to use.

Mr. Martinez and his students are involved in three types of activities during the 30-minute spelling period: He teaches lessons on the weekly topic, students study words for the weekly spelling test, and they meet in small groups to study other spelling concepts. Here's the schedule:

Monday	15 min.	Introduce the topic for the week
	15 min.	Have students take the pretest and self-check it
Tuesday	20 min.	Teach a lesson on the week's topic
	10 min.	Have students practice spelling words

Wednesday	15 min.	Teach a lesson on the week's topic
	15 min.	Have students take the practice test and self-check it
Thursday	20 min.	Work with small groups on other spelling concepts
	10 min.	Have students practice spelling words
Friday	10 min.	Administer the spelling test
	20 min.	Review topic for the week and/or meet with small groups

This is the fourth week that Mr. Martinez has been teaching verbs. During the first week, students brainstormed verbs and Mr. Martinez listed them on one of four charts: verbs that don't change form (e.g., *set, hurt*), regular verbs (e.g., *walk–walked*), irregular verbs with three forms (e.g., *do–did–done*), and irregular verbs with two forms (e.g., *sell–sold*). The students reviewed verbs that don't change form and regular verbs whose past and past-participle forms are created by adding *-ed*. That week, students were tested on words with inflectional suffixes, the concept taught the previous week. Regular verbs were tested the week after they were taught. For the next 2 weeks, students studied irregular verbs with three forms; because it was a difficult concept for many students, Mr. Martinez took a second week to teach it. Students sorted the words into present, past, and past participle columns, practiced spelling the words on whiteboards, and created posters using the words in sentences. One student chose *eat–ate–eaten* and wrote this paragraph:

I like to EAT m & ms. They are my favorite candy. I ATE a whole bag of m & ms yesterday. Now I have a stomachache because I have EATEN too much candy.

The students created their posters during writing workshop. They used the writing process to draft and refine their sentences, word processed them, enlarged them to fit their posters, and printed them out. After sharing them during a spelling lesson, the students posted them on a classroom wall.

This week, the focus changes to irregular verbs with two forms, such as *sleep–slept*, *leave–left*, and *buy–bought*. On Monday, they review the list of verbs they created several

This Week's Spelling List

All Pizzas	Pepperoni Pizzas	Sausage Pizzas	Hawaiian Pizzas
*forget	*year	*smooth	educate
*forgot	fear	*group	*education
*forgotten	deer	soup	observe
*know	beard	*moving	*observation
*knew	*cheer	food	admit
*known	*hear	through	*admission
*throw			
*threw			
*thrown			
*break			
*broke			
*broken			

* = words on the spelling test

Irregular Verbs			
*sleep-slept	meet-met	*leave-left	*bring-brought
shine-shone	fight-fought	*wind-wound	*buy-bought
*catch-caught	pay-paid	mean-meant	hang-hung
bleed-bled	*teach-taught	creep-crept	*build-built
dig-dug	tell-told	*think-thought	sell-sold
make-made	keep-kept	*sweep-swept	say-said

* = word (past-tense form) on next week's spelling list

weeks ago that's shown above. Mr. Martinez observes that students are already familiar with these irregular verbs; the only difficult one is *wind–wound*. They know the nouns *wind* and *wound*, but not the verbs *wind* and *wound*. Mr. Martinez explains each word:

Wind (noun; pronounced with a short *i*): air in motion
Wind (verb; pronounced with a long *i*): to coil or wrap something or to take a bending course
Wound (noun; the *ou* is pronounced as in *moon*): an injury
Wound (verb—past tense of *wind*; the *ou* is pronounced as in *cow*): having coiled or wrapped something or to have taken a bending course

To clarify the words, he sets out a small alarm clock to wind, a map showing a road that winds around a mountain, wind chimes to show the wind's motion, a skein of yarn to wind, and an elastic bandage to wind around a wound. The students examine each item and talk about how it relates to one or more of the words. Clayton explains the bandage and manages to include all four words:

> OK. Let's say it is a windy day. The wind could blow you over and you could sprain your ankle. I know because it happened to me. A sprain is an injury like a wound but there's no blood. Well, then you get a bandage and you put it around your ankle like this [he demonstrates as he talks]: You wind it around and around to give your ankle some support. Now [he says triumphantly], I have wound the bandage over the wound.

On Tuesday, the students play the "I'm thinking of . . ." game to practice the words on the Irregular Verbs With Two Forms chart; they're familiar with the game and eager to play. Mr. Martinez begins, "I'm thinking of a word where you delete one vowel to change the spelling from present to past tense." The students identify *bleed–bled* and *meet–met.* Next, he says, "I'm thinking of a word where you add one letter to the present-tense verb to spell the past-tense form," and the students identify *mean–meant.* Then the students take turns being the leader. Simone begins, "I'm thinking of a word where you change one vowel for the past tense." The students identify *dig–dug, hang–hung,* and *shine–shone.* Next, Erika says, "I'm thinking of a word where you change one consonant to make past tense," and the students answer *build–built* and *make–made.* Joey offers, "I'm thinking of a verb where you change the *i* to *ou* to get the past tense." The students identify four pairs: *wind–wound, think–thought, bring–brought,* and *fight–fought.* Then Camille says, "I'm thinking of a verb where you take away an *e* and add a *t* to make the past tense," and the students reply *keep–kept, sweep–swept, sleep–slept,* and *creep–crept.* They continue the game until they've practiced all the verbs.

Today, Mr. Martinez distributes whiteboards to students. He says the past-tense form of an irregular verb (e.g., *slept, taught*), and students write both the present- and the past-tense forms, without looking at the chart unless they need help. Many of the words he chooses are the ones that will be on next week's spelling list, but he also includes other words from the list. After they write each pair of words, students hold up their boards so that Mr. Martinez can check their work. When necessary, he reviews how to form a letter or points out an illegible letter.

After 15 minutes of practice, the students return to their desks to take the practice test on this week's words. Mr. Martinez reads the list aloud while the students write using blue pens, and then he projects the list of words on the interactive whiteboard so students can check their own tests. The students put away their blue pens and get out red pens to check their papers, so cheating is rarely a problem.

 pelling is a tool for writers that allows them to communicate conventionally with readers. As Donald Graves explains: "Spelling is for writing. Children may achieve high scores on phonic inventories or weekly spelling tests, but the ultimate test is what the child does under 'game conditions,' within the process of moving toward meaning" (1983, pp. 193–194). Rather than equating spelling development with scores on weekly spelling tests, students need to learn to spell words conventionally so that they can communicate effectively through writing. English spelling is complex, and attempts to teach spelling through weekly lists haven't been very successful. Too often, students spell words correctly on the weekly test but misspell them in their writing.

SPELLING DEVELOPMENT

The alphabetic principle suggests a one-to-one correspondence between phonemes and graphemes, but English spelling is phonetic only about half the time. Other spellings reflect the languages words were borrowed from. For example, *alcohol,* like most words beginning with *al-,* is an Arabic word, and *homonym,* like most words with *y* where *i* would work, is a Greek word. Other words are spelled to reflect semantic relationships, not phonological ones; the spelling of *national* and *nation* and of *grade* and *gradual* indicate related meanings even though there are vowel or consonant changes in the pronunciations of the word pairs. If English were a purely phonetic language, words would be easier to spell, but at the same time, the language would lose much of its sophistication.

Students learn to spell the phonetic elements of English as they learn about phoneme-grapheme correspondences, and they continue to refine their spelling knowledge through a combination of instruction and reading and writing experiences. Students' spelling reflects their growing awareness of English orthography, and they move from using scribbles and single letters to represent words through a series of stages until they adopt conventional spellings.

Invented Spelling

Children create unique spellings, called *invented spellings*, based on their knowledge of English orthography. Charles Read (1975), one of the first researchers to study preschoolers' efforts to spell words, discovered that they used their knowledge of phonology to invent spellings. These young children used letter names to spell words, such as U (*you*) and R (*are*), and they used consonant sounds rather consistently: GRL (*girl*), TIGR (*tiger*), and NIT (*night*). The preschoolers used several unusual but phonetically based spelling patterns to represent affricates: They spelled *tr* with *chr* (e.g., CHRIBLES for *troubles*) and *dr* with *jr* (e.g., JRAGIN for *dragon*), and they substituted *d* for *t* (e.g., PREDE for *pretty*). Words with long vowels were spelled using letter names: MI (*my*), LADE (*lady*), and FEL (*feel*). The children used several ingenious strategies to spell words with short vowels. The 3-, 4-, and 5-year-olds rather consistently selected letters to represent short vowels on the basis of place of articulation in the mouth: Short *i* was represented with *e* as in FES (*fish*), short *e* with *a* as in LAFFT (*left*), and short *o* with *i* as in CLIK (*clock*). These spellings may seem odd to adults, but they're based on phonetic relationships. The children often omitted nasals in words (e.g., ED for *end*) and substituted *-eg* or *-ig* for *-ing* (e.g., CUMIG for *coming*). Also, they often ignored the vowel in unaccented syllables, as in AFTR (*after*) and MUTHR (*mother*).

These children developed spelling strategies based on their knowledge of the phonological system and of letter names, their judgments of phonetic similarities and differences, and their ability to abstract phonetic information from letter names. Read suggested that from among the many phonetic properties in the phonological system, children abstract certain phonetic details and preserve others in their invented spellings.

Stages of Spelling Development

Based on Read's seminal work, other researchers began to systematically study how children learn to spell. After examining students' spelling errors and determining that their errors reflected their knowledge of English orthography, Bear, Invernizzi, Templeton, and Johnston (2008) identified these five stages of spelling development that students move through as they learn to read and write: Emergent spelling, Letter Name-Alphabetic spelling, Within-Word spelling, Syllables and Affixes spelling, and Derivational Relations spelling. The characteristics of each of the stages are summarized in Figure 12–1.

As they continued to study students' spelling development, Bear and his colleagues also noticed three principles of English orthography that students master as they move through the stages of spelling development:

- The alphabetic principle, which explains that letters represent sounds.
- The pattern principle, which explains that letters are combined in predictable ways to spell sounds.
- The meaning principle, which explains that related words have similar spellings even when they're pronounced differently.

Young children focus on the alphabetic principle as they learn to represent sounds with letters. They pronounce words and record letters to represent sounds they hear, spelling *are* as *r* and *bed* as *bad*, for example. Children learn the pattern principle next, as they study phonics. They spell consonant and vowel patterns; for example, they learn to spell the /k/ at the end of short-vowel words with *ck* so that they spell *luck* correctly, not as *luk*. They also learn the pattern for adding inflectional suffixes, so that they spell the plural of *baby* as *babies*, not *babys*. The third principle focuses on meaning; students learn, for example, that the words *oppose* and *opposition* are related in both spelling and meaning. Once students understand the meaning principle, they're less confused by irregular spellings because they don't expect words to be phonetically regular.

FIGURE 12–1 The Stages of Spelling Development

Stage 1: Emergent Spelling
Children string scribbles, letters, and letterlike forms together, but they don't associate the marks they make with any specific phonemes. This stage is typical of 3- to 5-year-olds who learn these concepts:

- The difference between drawing and writing
- The direction of writing on a page
- Some letter-sound matches
- The formation of letters

Stage 2: Letter Name-Alphabetic Spelling
Children represent phonemes in words with letters. At first, their spellings are quite abbreviated, but they learn to use consonant blends and digraphs and short-vowel patterns to spell words. Spellers are 5- to 7-year-olds who learn these concepts:

- The alphabetic principle
- Short vowel sounds
- Consonant sounds
- Consonant blends and digraphs

Stage 3: Within-Word Spelling
Students learn long-vowel patterns and *r*-controlled vowels, but they may confuse spelling patterns and spell *meet* as METE and reverse the order of letters, such as FORM for *from* and GRIL for *girl*. Spellers are 7- to 9-year-olds who learn these concepts:

- Long-vowel spelling patterns
- Complex consonant patterns
- *r*-controlled vowels
- Diphthongs

Stage 4: Syllables and Affixes Spelling
Students learn to spell multisyllabic words. They also add inflectional endings, use apostrophes in contractions, and differentiate between homophones, such as *your–you're*. Spellers are often 9- to 11-year-olds who learn these concepts:

- Inflectional endings
- Homophones
- Syllabication
- Possessives

Stage 5: Derivational Relations Spelling
Students explore the relationship between spelling and meaning and learn that words with related meanings are often related in spelling despite sound changes (e.g., *wise–wisdom*). They also learn Latin and Greek root words and derivational affixes (e.g., *amphi-, -tion*). Spellers are 11- to 14-year-olds who learn these concepts:

- Consonant and vowel alternations
- Greek affixes and root words
- Latin affixes and root words
- Etymologies

Based on Bear, Invernizzi, Templeton, & Johnston, 2008.

Emergent Spelling. Young children, typically ages 3 to 5, string scribbles, letters, and letterlike forms together, but they don't associate the marks with any specific phonemes. Emergent spelling represents a natural, early expression of the alphabet and other concepts about writing. Children write from left to right, right to left, top to bottom, or randomly across the page. Some Emergent spellers have a large repertoire of letterforms to use, but others repeat a small number of letters over and over. Children use both upper- and lowercase letters, but they show a distinct preference for uppercase letters. Toward the end of this stage, children begin to discover how spelling works and that letters represent sounds in words.

Letter Name-Alphabetic Spelling. Children learn to represent phonemes in words with letters, indicating they have a rudimentary understanding of the alphabetic principle—that a link exists between letters and sounds. Spellings are quite abbreviated and represent only the most prominent features in words. Examples of this stage spelling are DA (*day*), KLZ (*closed*), BAD (*bed*), and CLEN (*clean*). Many children continue to write mainly with capital letters. These spellers use a letter-name strategy: They slowly pronounce words they want to write, listening for familiar letter names and sounds. Spellers at this stage are 5- to 7-year-olds.

Within-Word Spelling. Children's understanding of the alphabetic principle is further refined in this stage as they learn to spell long-vowel patterns, diphthongs and the less common vowel patterns, and *r*-controlled vowels (Henderson, 1990). Examples of Within-Word spelling include LIEV (*live*), SOPE (*soap*), HUOSE (*house*), and BERN (*burn*). Children, typically 7- to 9-year-olds, experiment with long-vowel patterns and learn that words such as *come* and *bread* are exceptions. Children often confuse spelling patterns and spell *meet* as METE, and they reverse the order of letters, such as FORM for *from* and GRIL for *girl*. They also learn about complex consonant sounds, including *-tch* (*match*) and *-dge* (*judge*), and about diphthongs (*oi/oy*) and other less common vowel patterns, including *au* (*caught*), *aw* (*saw*), *ou* (*house*), and *ow* (*cow*). Children also compare long- and short-vowel combinations (*hop–hope*) as they experiment with vowel patterns.

Syllables and Affixes Spelling. The focus in this stage is on two-syllable words and the spellings used where syllables join together. Students, generally 9- to 11-year-olds, apply what they've learned about one-syllable words to longer words, and they learn to break words into syllables. They learn about inflectional endings (*-s, -es, -ed,* and *-ing*) and rules about consonant doubling, changing the final *y* to *i*, or dropping the final *e* before adding an inflectional suffix. They also learn about compound words, possessives, homophones, and contractions, as well as some of the more common derivational prefixes and suffixes. Examples of syllables and affixes spelling include EAGUL (*eagle*), MONY (*money*), GETING (*getting*), BABYIES (*babies*), THEIR (*there*), CA'NT (*can't*), and BE CAUSE (*because*).

Derivational Relations Spelling. Older students explore the relationship between spelling and meaning during the Derivational Relations stage, and they learn that words with related meanings are often related in spelling despite changes in vowel and consonant sounds (e.g., *wise–wisdom, sign–signal, nation–national*). Examples of spelling errors include CRITISIZE (*criticize*), APPEARENCE (*appearance*), and COMMITTE or COMMITEE (*committee*). The focus in this stage is on morphemes, and students learn about Greek and Latin root words and affixes. They also begin to examine etymologies and the role of history in shaping how words are spelled. They learn about eponyms (words from people's names), such as *maverick* and *sandwich.* Some students reach this stage at age 11 or 12, but others don't attain it until age 14 or 15.

Teachers do many things to scaffold students' learning as they move through the stages of spelling development, and the kind of support they provide depends on students' developmental level. As young children scribble, for example, teachers encourage them to use pencils, not crayons, for writing, to differentiate between drawing and writing. Letter Name-Alphabetic spellers notice words in their environment, and teachers help children use these familiar words to choose letters to represent the sounds in the words they're writing. As students enter the Syllables and Affixes stage, teachers teach syllabication rules, and in the Derivational Relations stage, they teach students about root words and the variety of words created from a single Latin or Greek root word. For example, from the Latin root word *-ann* or *-enn,* meaning "year," students learn these words: *annual, centennial, biannual, millennium, anniversary, perennial,* and *sesquicentennial.* Figure 12–2 presents suggestions for supporting students' spelling development.

FIGURE 12–2 Ways to Support Students' Spelling Development

Stage 1: Emergent Spelling
- Allow the child to experiment with making and placing marks on the paper.
- Suggest that the child write with a pencil and draw with a crayon.
- Model how adults write.
- Point out the direction of print in books.
- Encourage the child to notice letters in names and environmental print.
- Ask the child to talk about what he or she has written.

Stage 2: Letter Name-Alphabetic Spelling
- Sing the ABC song and name letters of the alphabet with children.
- Show the child how to form letters in names and other common words.
- Demonstrate how to say a word slowly, stretch it out, and isolate beginning, middle, and ending sounds in the word.
- Use Elkonin boxes to segment words into beginning, middle, and ending sounds.
- Post high-frequency words on a word wall.
- Teach lessons on consonants, consonant digraphs, and short vowels.
- Write sentences using interactive writing.

Stage 3: Within-Word Spelling
- Teach lessons on long-vowel spelling rules, vowel digraphs, and *r*-controlled vowels.
- Encourage students to develop visualization skills in order to recognize whether a word "looks" right.
- Teach students to spell irregular high-frequency words.
- Focus on silent letters in one-syllable words (e.g., *know, light*).
- Have students sort words according to spelling patterns.
- Have students make words using magnetic letters and letter cards.
- Introduce proofreading so students can identify and correct misspelled words in compositions.
- Write sentences using interactive writing.

Stage 4: Syllables and Affixes Spelling
- Teach how to divide words into syllables and the rules for adding inflectional endings.
- Teach the schwa sound and spelling patterns (e.g., *handle*).
- Teach homophones, contractions, compound words, and possessives.
- Sort two-syllable words and homophones.
- Have students make words using letter cards.
- Teach proofreading skills, and encourage students to proofread all writings.

Stage 5: Derivational Relations Spelling
- Teach root words and derivational affixes.
- Make clusters with a root word in the center and related words on rays.
- Teach students to identify words with English, Latin, and Greek spellings.
- Sort words according to roots or language of origin.
- Have students check the etymologies of words in a dictionary.

Analyzing Students' Spelling Development

Teachers analyze students' spelling development by classifying the errors in their compositions according to the stages of spelling development. This analysis provides information about students' current level of spelling development and the kinds of errors they make. Knowing students' level of spelling development helps teachers determine the appropriate type of instruction.

Figure 12–3 shows personal journal entry written by a first grader named Marc. He reverses *d* and *s,* and these two reversals make his writing more difficult to decipher. Here is Marc's composition using conventional spelling:

Today a person at home called us and said that a bomb was in our school and made us go outside and made us wait a half of an hour and it made us waste our time on learning. The end.

Marc was writing about a traumatic event, and it was appropriate for him to use invented spelling in his journal entry. Primary grade students write using invented spelling, but teachers help students use conventional spelling when the composition will "go public." Prematurely differentiating between "kid" and "adult" spelling interferes with children's natural spelling development and makes them dependent on adults to supply the conventional spelling.

Spelling can be categorized on a chart, also shown in Figure 12–3, to gauge students' spelling development and to anticipate upcoming changes in their spelling strategies. Teachers write the stages of spelling development across the top of the chart and list each misspelled word in the student's composition under one of the categories, ignoring proper nouns. When teachers are scoring young children's spellings, they often ignore capitalization errors and poorly formed or reversed letters, but when scoring older students' spellings, these errors are considered.

Perhaps the most interesting thing about Marc's writing is that he spelled half the words correctly even though at first reading it might seem that he spelled very few words correctly. Marc wrote this paper in January of his first grade year, and his spellings are typical of first graders. Of his misspellings, eight were categorized as Letter Name-Alphabetic spellings, and another eight were Within-Word spellings; this score suggests that Marc's moving into the Within-Word stage. He's clearly using a sounding-out strategy, which is best typified by his spelling of the word *learning.* His errors suggest that he's ready to learn CVCe and other long-vowel spelling patterns and *r*-controlled vowels. Marc spells some high-frequency words phonetically, so he would benefit from more exposure to high-frequency words, such as *was* and *of.* He also spelled *today* and *outside* as separate words, so he's ready to learn about compound words. Marc pronounced the word MAKBE as "maked," and the DE is a reversal of letters, a common characteristic of Within-Word spelling. His teacher should also monitor his *b/d* and *s/z* reversal problem to see if it disappears with more writing practice. It's important, of course, to base instructional recommendations on more than one writing sample; teachers should look at three or more samples to be sure the recommendations are valid.

Older students' spelling can also be analyzed the same way. Fifth grade Eugenio wrote the "Why My Mom Is Special" essay shown in Figure 12–4. Eugenio is Hispanic; his native language is Spanish, but he's now fully proficient in English. His writing is more sophisticated than Marc's, and the spelling errors he makes reflect both his use of longer, more complex words and his pronunciation of English sounds.

All but one of Eugenio's spelling errors are classified at either the Within-Word stage or the Syllables and Affixes stage. His other error, classified at the Letter Name-Alphabetic stage, is probably an accident because when he was asked, he could spell the word correctly. Eugenio's Within-Word spelling errors involve more complex consonant and vowel spelling patterns. He's moved beyond spelling *because* as BECUZ, but he still must learn to replace the *u* with *au* and the *z* with *s.* His spelling of *shoes* as SHOSE is interesting because he's reversed the last two letters. He didn't recognize that, however, when he was questioned. Instead, his focus is on representing the /sh/ and the /oo/ sounds correctly. His spellings of *school* and *career* seem to be influenced by his pronunciation. The /sh/ sound is difficult for him, as it is for many Spanish speakers, and

FIGURE 12–3   An Analysis of a First Grader's Spelling

Tobay a perezun at home kob
uz anb seb that a bome wuz in
or skuwl anb mab uz go at zib
anb makbe uz wat a haf uf
a awn anb it mab uz wazt on
time on loren ee ing.

THE eNb

Emergent	Letter Name-Alphabetic	Within-Word	Syllables and Affixes	Derivational Relations
	KOB/called	BOME/bomb	TO BAY/today	
	SEB/said	OR/our	PEREZUN/person	
	WUZ/was	SKUWL/school	MAKBE/maked	
	MAB/made	AT SIB/outside		
	WAT/wait	UF/of		
	HAF/half	AWR/hour		
	MAB/made	OR/our		
	WAZT/waste	LORENEEING/learning		

Data Analysis		Conclusions
Emergent	0	Marc's spelling is between Letter Name-Alphabetic and Within-Word stages. From his misspellings, he is ready for the following instruction:
Letter Name-Alphabetic	8	
Within-Word	8	• high-frequency words
Syllables and Affixes	3	• CVCe spellings
Derivational Relations	0	• r-controlled vowels
Correctly spelled words	22	• compound words
Total words in sample	41	He also reverses b/d and s/z.

he doesn't recognize that *school* begins with /sk/, not /sh/. Eugenio pronounces the first syllable of *career* as he spelled it, and he explains that it's a hard word but it looks right to him. These comments suggest that Eugenio understands that spelling has both phonetic and visual properties. In the word *policeman*, Eugenio used *s* rather than *ce* to represent the /s/. Even though it's a

FIGURE 12–4	An Analysis of a Fifth Grader's Spelling

My mom is special to me. she gave me everething when I was small. When she gets some mony she byes me pizza. My mom is specil to me becuze she taks me anywhere I want to get some nike shose. She byes me some.

My mom changed my life. She is so nice and loveble. She cares what I am doing in shool. She cares about my grades. I will do anything for mom. I would get a ceriar. Maybe I could be a polisman. That is why I think she is so nice.

Emergent	Letter Name–Alphabetic	Within-Word	Syllables and Affixes	Derivational Relations
	TAKS/takes	BECUZE/because	SPECIL/special	
		SHOSE/shoes	EVERETHING/everything	
		SHOOL/school	MONY/money	
		CERIAR/career	BYES/buys	
		POLISMAN/policeman	SPECIL/special	
			BYES/buys	
			LOVEBLE/lovable	

Data Analysis		Conclusions
Emergent	0	Eugenio's spelling is at the Syllables and Affixes stage. Based on this sample, this instruction is suggested:
Letter Name–Alphabetic	1	• dividing words into syllables
Within-Word	5	• compound words
Syllables and Affixes	7	• using y at the end of 1- and 2-syllable words
Derivational Relations	0	• homophones
Correctly spelled words	82	• suffixes
Total words in sample	95	

compound word, this word is classified at this level because the error involves spelling a complex consonant sound.

The largest number of Eugenio's spelling errors fall into the Syllables and Affixes stage. Most of his errors deal with spelling multisyllabic words. In SPECIL, Eugenio has misspelled the schwa sound, the vowel sound in unaccented syllables of multisyllabic words. In *everything*, Eugenio wrote *e* instead of *y* at the end of *every*; what he doesn't understand is that the long *e* sound at the end of a two-syllable word is usually represented by *y*. Eugenio spelled *money* as MONY; it's interesting that he used *y* to represent the long *e* sound here, but in this case, *ey* is needed. BYES for *buys* is a homophone error, and all homophone errors are classified as this stage even though they're one-syllable words. Eugenio's other spelling error is LOVEBLE. Here he added the suffix *-able* but misspelled it; he wasn't aware that he added a suffix. When asked about it, he explained that he sounded it out and wrote the sounds he heard. It's likely that he also knows about the *-ble* end-of-word spelling pattern because if he had spelled the suffix phonetically, he probably would have written LOVEBUL.

Even though Eugenio has a number of errors at both the Within-Word and Syllables and Affixes stages, his spelling level is at the Syllables and Affixes stage because most of his errors are at this stage. Based on this one writing sample, it appears that he'd benefit from instruction on dividing words into syllables, compound words, using *y* at the end of one- and two-syllable words, homophones, and suffixes. These instructional recommendations shouldn't be based on only one writing sample; they should be validated by examining several samples.

TEACHING SPELLING

The goal of spelling instruction is to help students develop what Gentry (1997) and Turbill (2000) call a *spelling conscience*—a desire to spell words conventionally. A spelling conscience requires that students understand that conventional spelling is a courtesy to readers and that they develop the ability to proofread to identify and correct misspellings. Spelling is important to effective writing, but it's a means to an end, not the end in itself. Dull, uninspired writing, no matter how well spelled, has little communicative effect. The box on this page lists the Common Core State Standards for spelling.

The question is how to best teach spelling because we know that reliance on spelling textbooks and rote memorization of words is inadequate. The widely held assumption that children learn how to spell through weekly spelling tests has been challenged by research (Rymer & Williams, 2000). Studies raise questions about the transfer of spelling skills learned through weekly spelling tests to students' writing. There's more to the development of conventional spellers than rote memorization of a thousand words between first and eighth grades. The Patterns of Practice feature on the next page describes how to fit spelling instruction into various instructional approaches. Sometimes it's integrated but at other times, spelling is taught separately and teachers make what connections they can, as Mr. Martinez did in the vignette at the beginning of the chapter.

COMMON CORE STATE STANDARDS

Spelling

The Common Core State Standards view spelling as a language tool and expect students to spell grade-appropriate words correctly. Primary grade students apply phonics knowledge to spell phonetically regular words, and older students use additional spelling strategies. The standards emphasize these points:

- Students generalize phonics patterns and rules to spell words.
- Students spell high-frequency words conventionally.
- Students use morphological information to spell words.
- Students consult dictionaries to check and correct spelling errors.

To learn more about the spelling standards, go to http://www.corestandards.org, or check your state's language arts standards.

Spelling Strategies

As they move through the stages of spelling development, students become increasingly more sophisticated in their use of phonological, semantic, and historical knowledge to spell words; that is, they become more strategic. They learn how to use these spelling strategies:

SOUND IT OUT. Students segment the word into sounds and spell each one.

SPELL BY ANALOGY. Students spell unknown words by analogy to familiar words.

How Spelling Fits Into the Patterns of Practice

Literature Focus Units
Teachers post words from books students are reading on word walls, choose some words for weekly spelling lists, use these words in spelling activities, and expect students to use the word wall as a tool to spell most words correctly.

Literature Circles
Teachers teach spelling separately from literature circles using an individualized spelling program or textbook approach. They understand that good readers tend to be good spellers and explain the relationship between reading and spelling.

Reading and Writing Workshop
Teachers teach spelling separately but make connections between the words students are studying and those they're reading and writing. They expect students to spell words they've studied correctly in their writing projects.

Thematic Units
Teachers post words related to thematic units on word walls and expect students to refer to the word wall to spell most words correctly in writing projects. They also include some words, when appropriate, in weekly spelling lists.

APPLY AFFIXES. Students apply affixes to root words.

PROOFREAD. Students use a special kind of reading called *proofreading* to locate spelling errors in a rough draft.

CHECK A DICTIONARY. Students locate the spelling of unfamiliar words in a dictionary.

Teachers often give the traditional "sound it out" advice when young children ask how to spell an unfamiliar word, but they provide more useful information when they suggest a strategic "think it out" approach. This advice reminds students that spelling involves more than phonological information and encourages them to think about spelling patterns, inflectional endings, and what the word looks like.

Components of the Spelling Program

Daily reading and writing opportunities are the best spelling activities (Hughes & Searle, 1997, 2000). Students use their knowledge of English orthography to spell unfamiliar words, and in the process they move closer and closer toward conventional spelling. Through the writing process, students learn to recognize spelling for what it is—a courtesy to readers. As they write, revise, edit, and share their writing, students understand that they need to spell conventionally so that their audience can read their compositions. Similarly, reading plays an enormous role in students' learning to spell because as they read, students store their memories of the visual shapes of words. The ability to recall how words look helps students decide when words are spelled correctly.

Word Walls. Teachers direct students' attention to words in books they're reading or during thematic units with word walls, large sheets of paper divided into alphabetical sections that hang in the classroom. Students and the teacher write important words on word walls, and then students refer to these word walls for word-study activities and when they're writing. Seeing the words posted in the classroom and using them in their writing help students learn to spell the words.

Teachers also hang word walls with high-frequency words (Cunningham, 2009). Researchers have identified the most commonly used words and recommend that children learn to spell these words because of their usefulness. The 100 most frequently used words represent more than 50% of all the words children and adults write (Horn, 1926)! Figure 12–5 presents the 100 most frequently used words that students should learn to spell by third grade.

Proofreading. *Proofreading* is a special kind of reading that students use to locate misspelled words and other mechanical errors in their rough drafts. As students learn about the writing process, they're introduced to proofreading. In the editing stage, they receive more in-depth instruction about how to proofread to locate spelling errors and then correct these misspelled words. In minilessons, students proofread sample student papers and mark misspelled words. Then, working in pairs, students correct them. Proofreading activities are more valuable for teaching spelling than dictation activities, in which teachers dictate sentences for students to write and correctly capitalize and punctuate. Few people use dictation in their daily lives, but students use proofreading skills every time they polish a piece of writing.

FIGURE 12–5 **The 100 Most Frequently Used Words**

A	B	C	D E
a and	back	came	day do
about are	be	can	did don't
after around	because	could	didn't down
all as	but		
am at	by		
an			

F G	H	I J	K L
for	had his	I is	know
from	have home	if it	like
get	he house	in just	little
got	her how	into	
	him		

M N	O	P Q R	S
man no	of our	people	said she
me not	on out	put	saw so
mother now	one over		school some
my	or		see

T	U V	W X	Y Z
that think	up	was when	you
the this	us	we who	your
them time	very	well will	
then to		went with	
there too		were would	
they two		what	
things			

Dictionaries. Teachers teach students how to locate the spelling of unknown words in the dictionary. Of the approximately 750,000 entry words in an unabridged dictionary, students typically learn to spell 3,000 through weekly spelling tests by the end of eighth grade—leaving 747,000 words unaccounted for! Obviously, students must learn how to locate the spellings of some additional words. Although it's relatively easy to find a "known" word in the dictionary, it's hard to locate an unfamiliar one, so students need to learn what to do when they don't know how to spell a word. The best approach is to predict possible spellings for unknown words, then check the most probable ones in a dictionary. The procedure involves these steps:

1. Identify root words and affixes.
2. Consider related words (e.g., *medicine–medical*).
3. Determine the sounds in the word.
4. Generate a list of possible spellings.
5. Select the most probable alternatives.
6. Consult a dictionary to check the correct spelling.

The fourth step, during which students develop a list of possible spellings using their knowledge of both phonology and morphology, is undoubtedly the most difficult: Phoneme-grapheme relationships may rate primary consideration in generating spelling options for some words, but root words and affixes or related words may be more important in determining how other words are spelled.

Spelling Options. In English, alternative spellings exist for many sounds because so many words borrowed from other languages retain their native spellings. There are many more options for vowel sounds than for consonants; even so, *f, ff, ph,* and *gh* are spelling options for /f/. Spelling options sometimes vary according to position in a syllable or word. For example, *ff* and *gh* are used to represent /f/ only at the end of a syllable or word, as in *cuff* and *laughter.* Figure 12–6 lists common spelling options for phonemes. Teachers point out spelling options as they write words on word walls, during minilessons, and when students ask about the spelling of a word. Students often develop lists of the various ways sounds are spelled in English, giving examples of each spelling. A sixth grade chart on long *i* is presented in Figure 12–7 with lists of one-syllable and multisyllable words. The location of the long *i* sound in the word is also marked on the chart.

Root Words and Affixes. Students learn about roots and affixes as they read and spell longer, multisyllabic words. Teaching about root words helps students unlock meaning when they read and spell the words correctly when they write. Consider the Latin root word *terra,* meaning "earth." Middle and upper grade students learn to read and spell these *terra* words and phrases: *terrarium, all-terrain vehicles, subterranean, territory, terrace,* and *terrier dogs.* Lessons about root words merge instruction about vocabulary and spelling.

Students learn to spell inflectional suffixes, such as the plural *-s* marker and the past-tense *-ed* marker, in the primary grades, and in the middle and upper grades, they learn about derivational prefixes and suffixes and how they affect meaning. They learn to recognize the related forms of a root word, for example: *educate, uneducated, educator, education, educational.* Students also learn rules for spelling suffixes. For example, the *-able* suffix is added to *read* to spell *readable,* but the *-ible* suffix is added to *leg-* (a Latin root word that is not a word in English) to spell *legible.* The rule is that *-able* is added to complete words and *-ible* is added to word parts. In other words, such as *lovable,* the final *e* in *love* is dropped before adding *-able* because *a* serves the same function in the word, and in *huggable,* the *g* is doubled before adding *-able* because the *u* in *hug* is short.

Teachers also use a variety of word-study activities to differentiate instruction and provide opportunities for students to practice the spelling concepts they're learning. These activities are flexible; students can do them together as a class, in small groups, or individually:

FIGURE 12-6 Common Spelling Options for Phonemes

Sound	Spellings	Examples	Sound	Spellings	Examples
long a	a-e	date	short oo	oo	book
	a	angel		u	put
	ai	aid		ou	could
	ay	day		o	woman
ch	ch	church	ou	ou	out
	t(u)	picture		ow	cow
	tch	watch	s	s	sick
	ti	question		ce	office
long e	ea	each		c	city
	ee	feel		ss	class
	e	evil		se	else
	e-e	these		x(ks)	box
	ea-e	breathe	sh	ti	nation
short e	e	end		sh	she
	ea	head		ci	ancient
f	f	feel		ssi	admission
	ff	sheriff	t	t	teacher
	gh	cough		te	definite
	ph	photograph		ed	furnished
j	ge	strange		tt	attend
	g	general	long u	u	union
	j	job		u-e	use
	dge	bridge		ue	value
k	c	call		ew	few
	k	keep	short u	u	ugly
	ck	black		o	company
l	l	last		ou	country
	ll	allow	y	y	yes
	le	automobile		i	onion
m	m	man	z	z	zoo
	me	come		s	present
	mm	comment		se	applause
n	n	no		ze	gauze
	ne	done	syllabic l	le	able
long o	o	go		al	animal
	o-e	note		el	cancel
	ow	own		il	civil
	oa	load	syllabic n	en	written
short o	o	office		on	lesson
	a	all		an	important
	au	author		in	cousin
	aw	saw		contractions	didn't
oi	oi	oil		ain	certain
	oy	boy	r-controlled	er	her
long oo	u	cruel		ur	church
	oo	noon		ir	first
	u-e	rule		or	world
	o-e	lose		ear	heard
	ue	blue		our	courage
	o	to			
	ou	group			

FIGURE 12-7 | Spelling Options for Long *i*

Spelling	Examples	Location		
		Initial	Medial	Final
i	child, climb, blind, wild, hire		x	
	idea, Friday, microwave, lion, gigantic, rhinoceros, variety, triangle, siren, liar, rabbi	x	x	x
i-e	smile, bride, drive, write		x	
	criticize, impolite, beehive, paradise, valentine, capsize, ninety, sniper, united, decide		x	x
ie	pies, lie, die		x	x
	untie			x
ei	none			
	feisty, seismograph		x	
igh	high, sight, knight, bright		x	x
	knighthood, sunlight		x	
eigh	height		x	
	none			
y	why, my, by, try, fly			x
	July, nylon, crying, xylophone, unicycle, notify, dynamite, skyscraper, hydrogen		x	x
y-e	byte, types, hype, rhyme		x	x
	paralyze, stylist		x	x
ye	dye, rye			x
	goodbye			x
eye	eye			x
	eyeball, eyelash	x		
ui	none			
	guidance		x	
ui-e	guide			x
	none			
uy	guy, buy			x
	buyer		x	

Making Words. Students arrange and rearrange a group of letter cards to spell words (Cunningham & Cunningham, 1992). Primary grade students can use the letters *s, p, i, d, e,* and *r* to spell *is, red, dip, rip, sip, side, ride,* and *ripe.* With the letters *t, e, m, p, e, r, a, t, u, r,* and *e,* a class of fifth graders spelled these words:

2-letter words: *at, up*
3-letter words: *pet, are, rat, eat, ate, tap, pat*
4-letter words: *ramp, rate, pare, pear, meat, meet, team, tree*
5-letter word: *treat*
6-letter words: *temper, tamper, mature, repeat, turret*
7-letter words: *trumpet, rapture*
8-letter word: *repeater*
9-letter words: *temperate, trumpeter*

The procedure for making words is explained in the Step-by-Step feature below. Teachers often introduce making words as a whole-class lesson and then set the cards and the word list in a center for students to use again independently or in small groups. Teachers can use almost any words for making-words activities, but those related to literature focus units and thematic units work best.

Word Sorts. Students compare and contrast spelling patterns as they sort a pack of word cards. Teachers prepare word cards for students to sort into two or more categories according to vowel patterns, affixes, root words, or another spelling concept (Bear et al., 2008). Sometimes teachers tell students what categories to use, making it a *closed sort.* At other times, students determine the

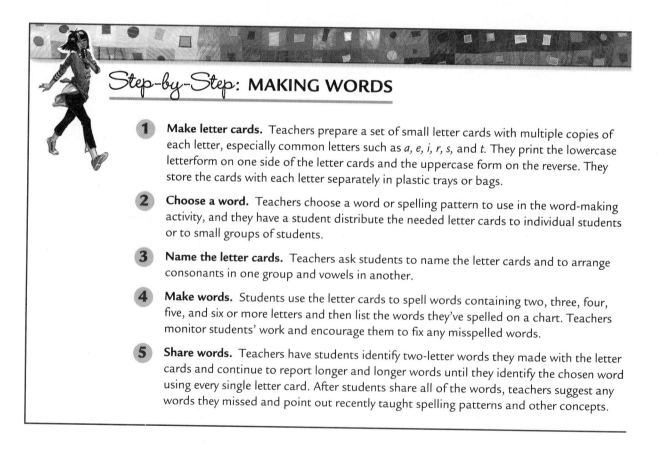

Step-by-Step: MAKING WORDS

1 **Make letter cards.** Teachers prepare a set of small letter cards with multiple copies of each letter, especially common letters such as *a, e, i, r, s,* and *t.* They print the lowercase letterform on one side of the letter cards and the uppercase form on the reverse. They store the cards with each letter separately in plastic trays or bags.

2 **Choose a word.** Teachers choose a word or spelling pattern to use in the word-making activity, and they have a student distribute the needed letter cards to individual students or to small groups of students.

3 **Name the letter cards.** Teachers ask students to name the letter cards and to arrange consonants in one group and vowels in another.

4 **Make words.** Students use the letter cards to spell words containing two, three, four, five, and six or more letters and then list the words they've spelled on a chart. Teachers monitor students' work and encourage them to fix any misspelled words.

5 **Share words.** Teachers have students identify two-letter words they made with the letter cards and continue to report longer and longer words until they identify the chosen word using every single letter card. After students share all of the words, teachers suggest any words they missed and point out recently taught spelling patterns and other concepts.

FIGURE 12–8   An /oo/ Word Ladder

The teacher says:	Students write:
Write the word *good*. We're practicing words with *oo* today.	good
Change the beginning sound to write the past tense of *stand*.	stood
Change the ending sound to write a word that means "a seat without arms or a back."	stool
Change the beginning sound to write a word that means the opposite of *warm*.	cool
Add two letters—one before and one after the c—to spell where we are right now.	school
Change the beginning sound to spell *tool*.	tool
Drop a letter to make a word that means *also*.	too
Change the first letter to write a word that means "a place where people can go to see wild animals."	zoo
Add a letter to *zoo* to spell the sound a car makes.	zoom
Change the beginning sound—use two letters for this blend—to spell something we use for sweeping.	broom
Change one letter to spell a word that means "a creek."	brook
Change the beginning sound to make a word that means "a dishonest person."	crook

categories themselves; then it's an *open sort*. Students can sort word cards and then return them to an envelope for future use, or they can glue the cards onto a sheet of paper.

Word Ladders. Students spell words and learn word meanings when they make word ladders (Rasinski, 2006). In this word-building game, teachers direct the whole class or a small group to write a word and then change it into another by substituting, adding, deleting, or rearranging letters. Figure 12–8 presents a fourth grade word ladder using short and long sounds of /oo/, and the procedure is explained in the Step-by-Step feature on page 368.

Minilessons

Teachers provide explicit instruction on spelling concepts and strategies that are developmentally appropriate. Children who are Letter Name-Alphabetic spellers, for example, are taught about consonant and short vowel sounds because these are the concepts they're attempting to represent with letters; they're also ready to learn the "sound it out" strategy. Instruction on these topics wouldn't be appropriate, however, for Syllables and Affixes spellers because they've already learned them. A second grade teacher's minilesson on the "think it out" strategy is presented on page 369. Sometimes teachers find that developmentally appropriate instruction conflicts with directives about focusing instruction on grade-level standards. Differentiated instruction is the best way to address students' needs while presenting lessons on grade-level topics.

Weekly Spelling Tests

Many teachers question the use of spelling tests to teach spelling, because research on children's spelling development suggests that spelling is best learned through authentic reading and writing activities (Gentry & Gillet, 1993). Teachers often complain that lists of spelling words aren't related to the words students are reading and writing, and that the 30 minutes of instructional

Step-by-Step: WORD LADDERS

1. **Create the word ladder.** Teachers create a word ladder with 5 to 15 words, choosing words from spelling lists, and write a clue for each word incorporating a combination of spelling and meaning clues.

2. **Pass out supplies.** Teachers generally have students use whiteboards and marking pens for this activity, but they can also use blank paper or paper with word ladders already drawn on them.

3. **Complete the word ladder.** Teachers read the clues they've prepared and have students write the words. When necessary, teachers provide additional clues and explain any unfamiliar words or spelling patterns.

4. **Review the word ladder.** Once students complete the word ladder, they reread the words and talk about any words they had difficulty writing.

time spent each day in completing practice activities is excessive. Instead, weekly spelling tests should be individualized so students learn to spell the words they need for their writing.

In an individualized approach, students may choose the words they'll study, and many of the words they choose are ones they use in their writing projects. Students study 5–15 words during the week using a study procedure. This approach places more responsibility on students for their own learning.

Teachers develop a weekly word list of 25 to 50 words of varying levels of difficulty from which students select words to study. Words for the master list are drawn from words students needed for their writing projects during the previous week, high-frequency words, and words related to literature focus units and thematic units ongoing in the classroom. Words from spelling textbooks can also be added to the list, but they should never make up the entire list. The master word list can be used for minilessons during the week. Students can look for phoneme-grapheme correspondences, add words to charts of spelling options, and note root words and affixes.

On Monday, the teacher administers the pretest using the master list of words, and students spell as many of the words as they can. They correct their own pretests, and from the words they misspell, each student chooses 5–15 words to study. They make two copies of their study list. Students number their spelling words using the numbers on the master list to make it easier to take the final test on Friday. Students keep one copy of the list to study, and the teacher keeps the other.

The pretest is a critical component in learning to spell, because it eliminates words that students already know how to spell so they can focus on the ones they can't spell. Almost a century ago, Ernest Horn recommended that the best way to improve students' spelling was for them to get immediate feedback by correcting their own pretests. His advice is still sound today.

Students spend approximately 5 to 10 minutes studying the words on their study lists each day. Research shows that instead of busywork activities, such as using their spelling words in sentences or gluing yarn on paper in the shape of the words, it's more effective for students to use this procedure for practicing spelling words:

1. Look at the word and say it to yourself.
2. Say each letter in the word to yourself.

3. Close your eyes and spell the word to yourself.
4. Write the word, and check that you spelled it correctly.
5. Write the word again, and check that you spelled it correctly.

This procedure focuses on the whole word rather than breaking it apart into sounds or syllables. During a minilesson early in the school year, teachers explain how to use the procedure, and then

Minilesson

Mrs. Hamilton Teaches the "Think It Out" Strategy

1. Introduce the Topic

Mrs. Hamilton asks her second graders how to spell the word *because,* and they suggest these options: *beecuz, becauz, becuse,* and *becuzz.* She asks the children to explain their spellings. Aaron explains that he sounded the word out and heard *bee* and *cuz.* Molly explains that she knows there is no *z* in *because* so she spelled it *becuse.* Other students explain that they say the word slowly, listening for all the sounds, and then write the sounds they hear. Mrs. Hamilton explains that this is a good first grade strategy, but now she is going to teach them an even more important second grade strategy called "think it out."

2. Share Examples

Mrs. Hamilton asks the class to observe as she spells the word *make.* She says the word slowly and writes *mak* on the whiteboard. Then she explains, "I sounded the word out and wrote the sounds I heard, but I don't think the word is spelled right because it looks funny." The children agree and eagerly raise their hands to supply the right answer. "No," she says, "I want to 'think it out.' Let's see. Hmmm. Well, there are vowel rules. The *a* is long so I could add an *e* at the end of the word." The students clap, happy that she's figured out the spelling of the word. She models the process two more times, spelling *great* and *running.*

3. Provide Information

Mrs. Hamilton shares a chart she's made with the steps in the "think it out" strategy:

1. *Sound the word out and spell it the best you can.*
2. *Think about spelling rules to add.*
3. *Look at the word to see if it looks right.*
4. *If it doesn't look right, try to change some letters, ask for help, or check the dictionary.*

The children talk about how Mrs. Hamilton used the strategy to spell *make, great,* and *running.*

4. Supervise Practice

Mrs. Hamilton passes out whiteboards and pens for the children to use as they practice the strategy. They write *time, what, walked, taking, bread,* and *people* using the "think it out" strategy. As they move through each step, they hold up their boards to show Mrs. Hamilton their work.

5. Reflect on Learning

Mrs. Hamilton ends the minilesson by asking children what they learned, and they explain that they learned the grown-up way to spell words. They explain the steps this way: First they sound it out, then they look it out, and then they think it out.

FIGURE 12–9   Individualized Spelling Tests

Master List
Teachers prepare a master list of 20–50 words, depending on students' grade level and the range of spelling levels in the classroom. Words on the list are drawn from spelling textbooks, words students misspell in their writing, and spelling skills being taught.

Pretest
On Monday, students take a pretest of the 20–50 words on the master list, and they self-correct their pretests immediately afterward using red pens.

Words to Study
Students choose 5 to 10 words to study from the words they misspelled on the pretest.

Study Lists
Students make two study lists, one to take home and one to use at school.

Study Strategy
Students use an effective strategy to study the words each day during the week. They study their spelling words this way rather than by writing sentences or stories using the words.

Practice Test
Students work with a partner to give each other a practice test during the week to check their progress in learning to spell the words.

Posttest
On Friday, students take a posttest of the words they've practiced. Teachers collect the tests and grade them themselves.

Next Week's Words
Teachers make a list of words that students misspell to include on their master list for the following week.

they post a copy of the steps in the classroom. In addition to this word-study procedure, students often trade word lists with a partner on Wednesday or Thursday and give each other a practice test.

A final test is administered on Friday. The teacher reads the master list, and students write only those words they've practiced during the week. To make it easier to administer the test, students first list the numbers of the words they've practiced from their study lists on their test papers. Any words that students misspell should be included on their lists the following week.

Figure 12–9 outlines the components of an individualized approach to spelling instruction. This approach is more effective than a textbook approach because textbooks are arranged in weeklong units, with lists of 10 to 20 words and practice activities that often require at least 30 minutes per day to complete. Research indicates that only 60 to 75 minutes per week should be spent on spelling instruction, however; greater periods of time don't result in improved spelling ability (Johnson, Langford, & Quorn, 1981).

The words in each unit are often grouped according to spelling patterns or phonetic generalizations, even though researchers question this approach unless teachers teach students about the pattern and provide practice activities, as Mr. Martinez did in the vignette at the beginning of the chapter. Otherwise, students memorize the rule or spelling pattern and score perfectly on the spelling test but later are unable to choose among spelling options in their writing. For example, after learning the *i-e* vowel rule and the *-igh* spelling pattern in isolation, students are often stumped about how to spell a word such as *light*. They've learned two spelling options for / ī /, *i-e* and *-igh,* and *lite* is an option, one they see in their community. Instead of organizing words according to phonetic generalizations and spelling rules, teachers should teach minilessons and point out the rules as they occur when writing words on word walls.

ENGAGING ENGLISH LEARNERS

English learners move through the same five stages of spelling development that native English speakers do (Helman, Bear, Templeton, Invernizzi, & Johnston, 2012). How quickly and easily they learn to spell English words depends on what they already know about how words are spelled. Students have more orthographic knowledge when their home language is similar to English, when they're literate in their home language, and when their parents are literate.

Helman and her colleagues recommend that in addition to determining students' level of spelling development, teachers do the following as they plan spelling instruction for English learners:

COMPARE ORAL LANGUAGES. Teachers analyze the sounds and grammar structures used in students' native language and compare them to English because it's important to point out the similarities and differences to make it easier for students to learn English words.

COMPARE WRITTEN LANGUAGES. Teachers examine the writing system—including its characters or letters and directionality—in students' native language, investigate how sounds are spelled and other spelling patterns, and compare them to English to explain the similarities and differences to students as they learn to spell English words.

INVESTIGATE STUDENTS' LANGUAGE AND LITERACY EXPERIENCES. Teachers learn about students' experience using their native language and English because students come to school with a range of language and literacy experiences, and they use what they know about their native language as they learn to speak, read, and write in English.

With this information, teachers set goals for their English learners, taking into account that students' differing levels of language and literacy experiences will affect their success, and plan spelling activities to support students as they become more conventional spellers.

The best way to teach spelling to English learners is through a combination of explicit and systematic instruction, opportunities to practice new spelling concepts through word-study activities, and authentic opportunities for students to apply through writing what they're learning about spelling. First, teachers teach minilessons on spelling concepts that are appropriate for students' level of spelling development, taking care to point out similarities and differences between students' home language and English. They emphasize the pronunciation of English words because the way students pronounce a word often influences their spelling. If the words are unfamiliar to students, teachers explain their meaning and model how to use them in English sentences. Next, they involve students in interactive writing activities and have them work in small groups to participate in word-study activities, including making words and word sorts. Third, teachers involve students in a wide variety of reading and writing activities every day so that they can apply their spelling knowledge. Just like their classmates, English learners write books and other compositions in writing workshop, read and discuss books with classmates in literature circles, and create projects as part of literature focus units and thematic units.

Weekly spelling tests aren't generally considered to be a good way to teach spelling, and they're even less effective for English learners. These students need to learn the sound, pattern, and meaning layers of words rather than simply memorize the sequence of letters in words. The words on a grade-level spelling list may be too difficult for English learners who might not be familiar with the words or understand their meaning. When teachers have to use weekly spelling tests, they should select several words from grade-level lists and others that are more appropriate for students' developmental level, including some high-frequency words. ◼

Assessing Students' Spelling Development

Grades on weekly spelling tests are the traditional measure of progress in spelling, and the individualized approach to spelling instruction provides this convenient way to assess students. This method of assessing student progress is somewhat deceptive, however, because the goal of spelling instruction is not simply to spell words correctly on weekly tests but to use the words, spelled conventionally, in writing. Samples of student writing should be collected periodically to determine whether words that were spelled correctly on tests are correct in writing projects. If students aren't applying in their writing what they've learned through the weekly spelling instruction, they haven't learned to spell the words after all.

When students perform poorly on spelling tests, consider whether faulty pronunciation or poor handwriting is to blame. Ask students to pronounce words they habitually misspell to see if their pronunciation or dialect differences may be contributing to spelling problems. Students need to recognize that pronunciation doesn't always predict spelling. For example, in some parts of the United States, people pronounce the words *pin* and *pen* as though they were spelled with the same vowel, and sometimes we pronounce *better* as though it were spelled *bedder* and *going* as though it were spelled *goin'*. Also, ask students to spell orally the words they misspell in their writing to see whether handwriting difficulties are contributing to spelling problems. Sometimes a minilesson on how to connect two cursive letters (e.g., *br*) or a reminder about the importance of legible handwriting will solve the problem.

It's essential that teachers keep anecdotal information and samples of students' writing to monitor their overall progress in spelling. Teachers can examine error patterns and spelling strategies in these samples. Checking to see if students have spelled their spelling words correctly in writing samples provides one type of information, and examining writing samples for error patterns and spelling strategies provides additional information. Fewer misspellings don't necessarily indicate progress, because to learn to spell, students must experiment with spellings of unfamiliar words, which will result in errors from time to time. Students often misspell a word by misapplying a newly learned spelling pattern. The word *extension* is a good example: Fifth graders spell the word EXTENSHUN; then they change their spelling to EXTENTION after they learn the suffix *-tion*. Although they're still misspelling the word, they've moved from using sound-symbol correspondences to using a spelling pattern—from a less sophisticated spelling strategy to a more sophisticated one.

Students' behavior as they proofread and edit their compositions also provides evidence of spelling development. They should become increasingly able to spot misspelled words in their compositions and to locate the spelling of unknown words in a dictionary. It's easy for teachers to calculate the number of spelling errors students have identified in proofreading their compositions and to chart their progress in learning to spot errors. Locating errors is the first step in proofreading; correcting the errors is the second step. It's fairly simple for students to correct the spelling of known words, but to correct unknown words, they must consider spelling options and predict possible spellings before they can locate the words in a dictionary. Teachers can document students' growth in locating unfamiliar words in a dictionary by observing their behavior when they edit their compositions.

Teachers can use the writing samples they collect to document students' spelling development. They monitor primary grade students' progression through the stages of invented spelling by analyzing writing samples using a chart such as the ones in Figures 12–3 and 12–4 to determine their stage of development. Students in the middle and upper grades can use this chart to analyze their own spelling errors.

SUMMING UP

Spelling is a language tool, and through instruction in spelling, students learn to communicate more effectively. Students move through five stages of spelling development. In the first stage, Emergent spelling, students string scribbles, letters, and letterlike forms together with little or no understanding of the alphabetic principle. In the second stage, Letter Name-Alphabetic spelling, students learn to represent phonemes in the beginning, middle, and end of words with letters. In the third stage, Within-Word spelling, students learn to spell long-vowel patterns, r-controlled vowels, and complex consonant combinations. In the fourth stage, Syllables and Affixes, students learn to spell two-syllable words and add inflectional endings. In the fifth stage, Derivational Relations, students learn that multisyllabic words with related meanings are often related in spelling despite changes in vowel and consonant sounds. Teachers analyze students' misspellings to determine their stage of spelling development and plan appropriate instruction. Spelling instruction includes daily opportunities to read and write; word walls; word-making and word-sort activities; proofreading; dictionary use; and instruction in spelling options, root words and affixes, and other spelling concepts. Weekly spelling tests, when they're used, should be individualized so that students learn to spell words they don't already know how to spell.

MyEducationLab™

Go to the topic Writing in the MyEducationLab (http://www.myeducationlab.com) for *Language Arts: Patterns of Practice*, where you can:

- Find learning outcomes for Writing, along with the national standards that connect to these outcomes.
- Complete Assignments and Activities that can help you more deeply understand the chapter content.
- Apply and practice your understanding of the core teaching skills identified in the chapter with the Building Teaching Skills and Dispositions learning units.
- Examine challenging situations and cases presented in the IRIS Center Resources.
- Use the Lesson Plan Builder Activities to practice lesson planning and integrating national and state standards into your planning.
- Check your comprehension of the content covered in the chapter with the Study Plan. Here you will be able to take a chapter quiz, receive feedback on your answers, and then access Review, Practice, and Enrichment activities to enhance your understanding of chapter content.

On the **MyEducationLab** for this course, you'll also be able to:

- **A+RISE** Go to the topic A+RISE, an innovative and interactive database of strategies that differentiate instruction across the language arts and provide particular insight into research-based methods to meet the needs of English learners.
- Explore the topic Literacy Portraits—yearlong case studies of second graders, complete with student artifacts, teacher commentary, and student and teacher interviews, tracking the month-by-month language arts growth of five students.
- Gain practice with the Grammar Tutorial, online guided instruction to improve your own ability with grammar.

CHAPTER 13

Language Tools: Grammar and Handwriting

FIFTH GRADERS LEARN GRAMMAR THROUGH LITERATURE Mr. Keogh's fifth graders are reading *Poppy* (Avi, 1995), the story of a little deer mouse named Poppy who outwits Mr. Ocax, a great horned owl. Mr. Keogh introduced the novel to the class, and they read the first chapter together. Then the students continued reading and talking about the book in small groups that operate like literature circles. The teacher brings the class back together for response activities and grammar lessons.

The students list important words from the story on the word wall posted in the classroom after reading each chapter or two, and as the words are listed, the teacher asks them to identify their parts of speech. Even though the book is rich with adverbs, few are chosen for the word wall, so Mr. Keogh begins adding some, including *profoundly, sufficiently,* and *ravenously.*

For the first grammar activity, Mr. Keogh has students work in small groups to list 10 nouns, 10 adjectives, 10 verbs, and 10 adverbs from the word wall. The teacher walks around the classroom, monitoring students' progress and referring them to the novel to see how a word was used or to the dictionary to check the part of speech. Some of the words are tricky because they're written in isolation on the word wall. An example is *fake*, which can be used in two ways: as an adjective, in *the fake owl*, and as a noun, in *it was a fake.* Mr. Keogh allows the students to list it either way, but they have to defend their choice.

Next, Mr. Keogh creates a word-sort activity using words from the groups' lists. Students cut the word cards apart and sort them into noun, adjective, verb, and adverb categories. Pairs of students practice several times before they glue the cards down. One student's completed word sort is shown on page 376.

How can teachers teach grammar as part of literature focus units?

Traditionally, teachers taught grammar by having their students complete exercises in a textbook; the problem was that students didn't apply what they were practicing orally or in writing. A newer approach is to teach grammar more authentically through books students are reading and through their own writing. The focus on grammar fits into the exploring stage of the reading process and the editing stage of the writing process. In this vignette, you'll see how Mr. Keogh incorporates grammar instruction into a literature focus unit.

The next day, the students create sentences using one or more words from each category on their word sort. The first sentences they create, *Mr. Ocax shrieked furiously from the abandoned tree* and *Mr. Ocax shrieked harshly under the crescent moon,* are predictable. Mr. Keogh encourages the fifth graders to experiment with more creative ways to use the words, the way Avi did in *Poppy*. The students work with partners to create these sentences:

> *Delicate little Poppy swiveled nervously on one foot, searching the sky for Mr. Ocax.*
> *Harshly Mr. Ocax snatched the appetizing little mouse named Poppy from the slippery moss-covered rock.*

They write their sentences on sentence strips and post them in the classroom to reread. The next day, Mr. Keogh has them reread the sentences and mark the nouns with green crayons and the verbs with blue crayons.

After this review of the parts of speech, Mr. Keogh changes his focus to sentences. He has created a pack of word and phrase cards to use in reviewing simple sentences, sentence fragments, and compound sentences. He also includes *as* and *when* cards in the pack so his students can build complex sentences, even though they aren't expected to learn this concept in fifth grade. Students cut apart a sheet of cards to use in making sentences about Mr. Ocax. A copy of the sheet of cards is shown on page 376.

The fifth graders use the cards to create these simple sentences:

> *The great horned owl ruled Dimwood Forest.*
> *He swiveled his head from right to left.*
> *The great horned owl smiled into the night air.*
> *Soundlessly, the great horned owl soared into the night air.*
> *With his piercing gaze, Mr. Ocax ruled Dimwood Forest triumphantly.*

After they create each sentence, Mr. Keogh asks them to identify the subject and the verb. To simplify the process, students color their subject cards green and their verb cards blue. They continue to sort the cards and identify the adverbs and prepositional phrases and the one conjunction card in the pack.

Grammar Word Sort

Nouns	Adjectives	Verbs	Adverbs
Mr. Ocax	crescent	shrieked	enormously
whirligig	charred	hunched	cautiously
dignity	appetizing	roosting	furiously
Poppy	motionless	luxuriating	harshly
porcupine	perplexed	saunter	desperately
notion	porcupine-quill	surveyed	deftly
Ereth	wary	skittered	stately
privacy	abandoned	swiveling	profoundly
effrontery	delicate	plunged	nervously
camouflage	fake	snatch	entirely

The students save their packs of cards in small plastic bags, and they continue this activity the next day. Mr. Keogh asks them to use the *and* card in their sentences, and they create these sentences with compound predicates:

Mr. Ocax swiveled his head from right to left and surveyed Dimwood Forest.

The great horned owl called a long, low cry of triumph, spread his wings, and soared back into the air.

Cards for Making Sentences

spread his wings	on a branch	triumphantly	with his piercing gaze
soundlessly	a long, low cry of triumph	surveyed	called
from right to left	and	of an old charred oak	he
back into the air	perched	Mr. Ocax	into the night air
swiveled his head	when	smiled	Dimwood Forest
ruled	the great horned owl	as	soared

The students identify the subjects and verbs in the sentences to figure out that these sentences have compound predicates. They try to make a sentence with a compound subject but find that they can't with the word cards they have.

Next, Mr. Keogh asks them to craft compound sentences using two subjects and two verbs, and they arrange these sentences:

The great horned owl called a long, low cry of triumph, and he soared soundlessly into the night air.

Mr. Ocax surveyed Dimwood Forest triumphantly, and he smiled.

After they share each sentence, Mr. Keogh asks the students to identify the subjects and verbs. Several students make additional word cards so they can create the compound sentences they want:

The great horned owl spread his wings, and he flew up high into the night sky.

Mr. Ocax blinked his large round eyes, and he watched a little mouse named Poppy.

"Let's make some even more interesting sentences," Mr. Keogh suggests as he asks them to use the *as* or *when* card in their sentences. They create these complex sentences:

Mr. Ocax smiled triumphantly as he ruled Dimwood Forest.

As the great horned owl called a long, low cry of triumph, he perched on a branch of an old charred oak.

Mr. Ocax smiled as he soundlessly spread his wings and soared back into the air.

The students identify the subjects and verbs in the sentences, and at first they assume the sentences are compound sentences. Mr. Keogh explains that these sentences are called *complex sentences*: They have one independent clause and one dependent clause. He explains that the clauses beginning with *as* or *when* are called *dependent clauses* because they can't stand alone as sentences. The students color these two cards red so that they'll stand out in a sentence.

Several days later, Mr. Keogh repeats the process with a pack of cards with words and phrases about Poppy. The students practice arranging the cards to make simple, compound, and complex sentences, and they keep a list of the sentences they make in their reading logs.

For one of the projects at the end of the book, the students write a character sketch about Mr. Ocax or Poppy. Mr. Keogh explains that in a character sketch, students do three things:

- Describe what the character looks like
- Describe what the character did
- Identify one trait the character exemplified, such as being smart, brave, or determined

This writing project grows out of the grammar activities. The students are encouraged to use words they've been arranging as well as other words from the word wall in their character sketches. They don't plagiarize because they're using newly learned words and phrases from charts in the classroom in their writing. Here's Darla's character sketch about Poppy; the underlined words and phrases in her writing came from the novel and were collected on charts or sentence strips posted in the classroom:

> Poppy was a <u>dainty</u> little girl mouse. She looked like a mouse. Her fur was <u>orange-brown</u>, and she had a <u>plump belly</u> that was white. She had a <u>tiny nose, pink toes</u>, and a very long <u>tail</u>. On her nose was a scar made by a <u>great horned owl</u> named Mr. Ocax. <u>Her ears were long</u>, and <u>her eyes were dark, almost round</u>.

> Mr. Ocax <u>ruled</u> over the entire <u>territory</u> where Poppy lived. He controlled them <u>with pure power and fury</u>. They had to get his <u>permission</u> to do anything or else they were his <u>dinner</u>. He said he protected them from the <u>vicious</u> porcupine who lived in Dimwood Forest, but he was lying. One day Poppy met Ereth, the porcupine. He told her that he eats bark, not mice. Mr. Ocax had to stop Poppy or she would tell everyone that he was <u>a liar and a bully</u>. He would not be <u>king</u> anymore. Many times the owl tried to catch Poppy, but she always escaped. Then he tricked her and caught her. <u>Bravely</u> she stuck her <u>porcupine-quill</u> sword into his <u>left claw</u>. That's how she escaped. Mr. Ocax was not so lucky. His flying was <u>totally out of control</u> because of the pain in his claw, and he <u>slammed into the salt lick</u>. It was the violent death he deserved.

> Poppy was a brave little mouse. I think she was a hero. That might surprise you because she <u>was trembling with fear</u> every time she confronted the owl who <u>looked like death</u> to her. What she did was she pretended to be brave. To be a coward was bad. She said it is <u>hard to be brave, but harder to be a coward</u>. She risked her life, but now her whole family was safe.

Through these grammar activities, Darla's writing has become stronger with more sophisticated language and sentence patterns.

hildren learn the structure of the English language—its grammar—intuitively as they learn to talk; the process is an unconscious one, and they've almost completed it by the time they enter kindergarten. The purpose of grammar instruction, then, is to make this intuitive knowledge about the English language explicit and to provide labels for words within sentences, parts of sentences, and types of sentences. Children speak the dialect—either Standard English or nonstandard English—that their parents and community members speak. Nonstandard English is informal and differs to some degree from the written Standard English, or book language, that students will read and write in school (Edelsky, 1989; Pooley, 1974).

Handwriting is a tool for writers. Students need to develop legible and fluent handwriting so they can communicate their ideas effectively though writing. Although nearly everyone would agree that the message is more than the formation of letters, handwriting instruction can't be ignored—not even in the 21st century. Donald Graves (1994) urges teachers to keep handwriting in perspective and to remember that it's a tool, best taught and applied through authentic writing activities.

GRAMMAR

Grammar is the most controversial language arts topic. Teachers, parents, and the community disagree about the content of grammar instruction, how to teach it, and when to begin teaching it. Some people believe that formal instruction in grammar is unnecessary—if not harmful—during the elementary grades; others believe that grammar instruction should be a key component of language arts instruction. Before getting into the controversy, let's clarify the terms *grammar* and *usage*. *Grammar* is the description of the syntax or structure of a language and prescriptions for its use (Weaver, 1996). It involves principles of word and sentence formation. In contrast, *usage* is correctness, or using the appropriate word or phrase in a sentence. It is the socially preferred way of using language within a dialect. *My friend, she; the man brung;* and *hisself* are examples of Standard English usage errors that students sometimes make.

Grammar Concepts

Five grammar concepts that students learn are parts of speech, parts of sentences, types of sentences, capitalization and punctuation, and usage.

Parts of Speech. Grammarians have sorted words into eight groups, called *parts of speech*: nouns, pronouns, verbs, adjectives, adverbs, prepositions, conjunctions, and interjections. Words in each group are used in essentially the same way in all sentences. Consider this sentence: *Hey, did you know that it rains more than 200 days a year in a tropical rain forest and that as much as 240 inches of rain fall each year?* All eight parts of speech are represented. *Rain forest, days, year, inches,* and *rain* are nouns, and *you* and *it* are pronouns. *Tropical* is an adjective describing *rain forest,* and *each* is an adjective describing *year.* The verbs are *did know, rains,* and *fall. More than* is an adverb modifying *200 days,* and *as much as* is an adverb modifying *240 inches;* they both answer the question "how much." *Of* and *in* are prepositions, and they introduce prepositional phrases. The conjunction *and* joins the two dependent clauses. The first word in the sentence, *hey,* is an interjection, and it's set off with a comma. Figure 13–1 presents an overview of the eight parts of speech.

Parts of a Sentence. A sentence is made up of one or more words to express a complete thought and, to express the thought, must have a subject and a predicate (one-word sentences have understood subjects—"Help!"—or predicates—"You!"). The subject names who or what the sentence is about, and the predicate includes the verb and anything that completes or modifies it. In a simple sentence with one subject and one predicate, everything that isn't part of the subject is part of the predicate. Consider this sentence about the rain forest: *Most rain forests are found in warm, wet climates near the equator.* The subject is *most rain forests,* and the rest of the sentence is the predicate.

Types of Sentences. Sentences are classified in two ways. First, they're classified according to structure, or how they're put together. The structure may be simple, compound, complex, or compound-complex, according to the number and type of clauses in the sentence. A clause consists of a subject and a predicate, and there are two types of clauses. If the clause presents a complete thought and can stand alone, it's an independent clause. If the clause isn't a complete thought and can't stand alone as a sentence, it's a dependent clause because it depends on the meaning expressed in the independent clause. An example of an independent clause is *Tropical rain forests are the most complex ecosystems on earth,* and an example of a dependent clause is *Because tropical rain forests are the most complex ecosystems on earth.* This dependent clause can't stand alone as a sentence; it must be attached to an independent clause. For example: *Because tropical rain*

FIGURE 13–1	The Eight Parts of Speech		
Part of Speech	**Definition**	**Examples**	
Noun	A word used to name something—a person, a place, or a thing. A proper noun names a particular person, place, or thing and is capitalized. In contrast, a common noun doesn't name a particular person, place, or thing and isn't capitalized.	United States Kleenex pilot	sandwich courage
Pronoun	A word used in place of a noun.	I me	you who
Adjective	A word used to describe a noun or a pronoun. Adjectives are common or proper, and proper adjectives are capitalized. Some words can be either adjectives or pronouns; they're adjectives if they come before a noun and modify it, and they're pronouns if they stand alone.	the fastest	American slippery-fingered
Verb	A word used to show action or state of being. A verb's form varies depending on its number (singular or plural) and tense (present, past, future). Some verbs are auxiliary, or helping, verbs; they're used to help form some tenses or voice. Voice is either active or passive.	eat think will have	saw is can would
Adverb	A word used to modify a verb, an adjective, or another adverb. An adverb tells how, when, where, why, how often, or how much.	quickly outside loudly	now well
Preposition	A word or group of words used to show position, direction, or how two words or ideas are related to each other.	at to between	with from
Conjunction	A word used to connect words and groups of words. These are the three types: coordinating conjunctions, which connect equivalent words, phrases, or clauses; correlative conjunctions, which are used in pairs; and subordinating conjunctions, which connect two clauses that aren't equally important.	and or because	but either-or when
Interjection	A word or phrase used to express strong emotion and set off by commas or an exclamation point.	wow hey	How are you? Cool, dude!

forests are the most complex ecosystems on earth, scientists are interested in studying them. The independent clause, which could stand alone as a sentence, is *scientists are interested in studying them.*

A simple sentence contains only one independent clause, and a compound sentence has two or more. A complex sentence contains one independent clause and one or more dependent clauses. A compound-complex sentence has two or more independent clauses and one or more dependent clauses. Can you identify which of these sentences are simple, compound, complex, and compound-complex?

Although a tropical rain forest is a single ecosystem, it's composed of four layers.
The tallest trees in the rain forest grow to be about 300 feet tall, and they form the top, emergent layer.

The next level is the canopy, and it's alive with activity as hummingbirds, woodpeckers, tree frogs, and monkeys go from flower to flower and branch to branch.

Vines, ferns, and palms grow in the understory.

Few flowers bloom in the understory because sunlight doesn't shine through the leaves of the canopy.

The bottom layer is the forest floor; mosses, fungi, and other parasitic plants grow here.

The fourth sentence is simple, the second and sixth sentences are compound, the first and fifth sentences are complex, and the third sentence is compound-complex.

Sentences are also classified according to their purpose or the type of message they contain. Sentences that make statements are declarative, those that ask questions are interrogative, those that make commands are imperative, and those that communicate strong emotion or surprise are exclamatory. The purpose of a sentence is often signaled by the punctuation mark placed at the end: Declarative sentences and some imperative sentences are marked with periods, interrogative sentences are marked with question marks, and exclamatory sentences and some imperative sentences are marked with exclamation points.

Capitalization and Punctuation. Students learn that capital letters divide sentences and signal important words within sentences. Think about how capital letters affect the meaning conveyed in these sentences:

They were going to the white house for dinner.

They were going to the White house for dinner.

They were going to the White House for dinner. (Wilde, 1992, p. 18)

Capital letters also express loudness of speech or intensity of emotion because they stand out visually.

Children often begin writing during the preschool years using only capital letters; during kindergarten and first grade, they learn the lowercase forms. They learn to capitalize *I*, the first word in a sentence, and names and other proper nouns and adjectives. By sixth grade, the most common problem is overcapitalization, or capitalizing too many words in a sentence, as in this example: *If the Tropical Rain Forest is destroyed, the Earth's climate could get warmer, and this is known as the Greenhouse Effect.* This problem persists because students have trouble differentiating between common and proper nouns. Too often, students assume that important words should be capitalized.

It's a common assumption that punctuation marks signal pauses in speech, but punctuation plays a greater role than that (Wilde, 1992). Punctuation marks signal grammatical boundaries, and they express meaning; some punctuation marks indicate sentence boundaries as well. Periods, question marks, and exclamation points mark sentence boundaries; in contrast, commas, semicolons, and colons mark grammatical units within sentences.

Quotation marks and apostrophes express meaning within sentences. Quotation marks are commonly used to indicate talk, but a more sophisticated use is to express irony, as in *My son "loves" to wash the dishes.* Apostrophes are used in contractions to join two words and in possessive nouns to show relationships. Notice how the punctuation changes the meaning of these phrases:

The monkey's howling (and it's running around the cage).

The monkey's howling (annoyed us; we wanted to kill it).

The monkeys' howling (annoyed us; we wanted to kill them).

(We listened all night to) the monkeys howling. (Wilde, 1992, p. 18)

Researchers have documented that learning to use punctuation is a developmental process. Beginning in the preschool years, children notice punctuation marks and begin to realize that they're different than letters (Clay, 1991). In kindergarten and first grade, they're formally introduced to the end-of-sentence punctuation marks and learn to use them conventionally about half the time (Cordeiro, Giacobbe, & Cazden, 1983). Many beginning writers use punctuation marks in more idiosyncratic ways, such as between words and at the end of each line of writing, but over time, children's usage becomes more conventional. English learners exhibit similar developmental patterns.

Usage. Children come to school speaking the dialects or varieties of English that their parents speak, and when these dialects differ from Standard English, they're called *nonstandard English*. Children may use double negatives, so that they say *I ain't got no money* instead of *I don't have any money*. Or they may use objective pronouns instead of subjective pronouns so that they say *Me and him have dirt bikes* instead of *He and I have dirt bikes*.

Students who speak nonstandard English learn Standard English as an alternative to the forms they already know. Rather than trying to substitute standard forms for students' nonstandard forms, teachers explain that Standard English is the language of school. It's the language used in books, and students can easily locate Standard English examples in books they're reading. Calling Standard English "book language" also helps to explain the importance of proofreading to identify and correct usage errors in students' writing. Figure 13–2 lists 10 types of usage errors that older students can learn to correct.

Teaching Grammar

For many years, grammar was taught using language arts textbooks. Students read rules and definitions, copied words and sentences, and marked them to apply the concepts presented in the text, but this type of activity often seemed meaningless to students. Researchers suggest that integrating grammar study with reading and writing produces the best results (Beers, 2001; Weaver, McNally, & Moerman, 2001). They view grammar as a language tool and recommend integrating grammar instruction with reading and writing. In the vignette at the beginning of the chapter, Mr. Keogh viewed grammar as a language tool and taught grammar concepts as part of a literature focus unit. This Patterns of Practice feature shows how grammar instruction fits into language arts instruction.

How Grammar Fits Into the Patterns of Practice

Literature Focus Units
Students use words and sentences from focus books during minilessons and for word sorts, sentence manipulation, and other grammar activities.

Literature Circles
Students use words and sentences from books they're reading during minilessons and for grammar activities, much like they do in literature focus units.

Reading and Writing Workshop
Students choose sentences from books they're reading for grammar activities, and they apply the grammar concepts they've learned when they edit their drafts during the writing process.

Thematic Units
Students apply their knowledge about sentences and other the grammar concepts when they write reports and create written and multigenre projects during thematic units.

FIGURE 13–2   Usage Errors

Irregular Verb Forms
Students form the past tense of irregular verbs as they would a regular verb; for example, some students use *catch + ed* to make *catched* instead of *caught*, or *swim + ed* to make *swimmed* instead of *swam*.

Past-Tense Forms
Students use present-tense or past-participle forms in place of past-tense forms, such as *I ask* for *I asked*, *she run* for *she ran*, or *he seen* for *he saw*.

Nonstandard Verb Forms
Students use *brung* for *brought* or *had went* for *had gone*.

Double Subjects
Students use both a noun and a pronoun in the subject, such as *My mom she...*

Nonstandard Pronoun Forms
Students use nonstandard pronoun forms, such as *hisself* for *himself*, *them books* for *those books*, and *hisn* for *his*.

Objective Pronouns for the Subject
Students use objective pronouns instead of subjective pronouns in the subject, such as *Me and my friend went to the store* or *Her and me want to play outside*.

Lack of Subject-Verb Agreement
Students use *we was* for *we were* and *he don't* for *he doesn't*.

Double Negatives
Students use two negatives when only one is needed; for example, *I don't got none* and *Joe don't have none*.

Confusing Pairs of Words
Some students confuse word pairs, such as *learn–teach*, *lay–lie*, and *leave–let*. They might say *I'll learn you to read*, instead of *I'll teach you to read*, *go lay down* instead of *go lie down*, and *leave me do it* instead of *let me do it*. Other confusing pairs include *bring–take*, *among–between*, *fewer–less*, *good–well*, *passed–past*, *real–really*, *set–sit*, *than–then*, *who–which–that*, *who–whom*, *it's–its*, and *your–you're*.

I as an Objective Pronoun
Students incorrectly use *I* instead of *me* as an objective pronoun, saying or writing *It's for Bill and I* instead of *It's for Bill and me*.

Based on Pooley, 1974, and Weaver, 1996.

Why Teach Grammar? Teachers, parents, and the community at large cite many reasons for teaching grammar. First, using Standard English is the mark of an educated person, and students should know how to use it. Many teachers believe that teaching grammar will help students understand sentence structure and form sentences to express their thoughts. Another reason is that parents expect that grammar will be taught, and teachers must meet these expectations. Other teachers explain that they teach grammar to prepare students for the next grade or for instruction in a foreign language. Others pragmatically rationalize grammar instruction because it's included in the language arts standards and included on norm-referenced achievement tests mandated by state departments of education. The box on page 384 highlights the role of grammar in the Common Core State Standards.

COMMON CORE STATE STANDARDS

Grammar

The Common Core State Standards expect students to demonstrate command of Standard English grammar and usage in talk and writing; they focus on the essential "rules" of Standard English and expect students to make informed choices among language alternatives for meaning or style. The standards emphasize these points:

- Students identify and understand the purpose of the parts of speech.
- Students use parts of speech correctly.
- Students compare and contrast varieties of English in literature.
- Students expand, combine, and reduce different types of sentences.

To learn more about the grammar standards, go to http://www.corestandards.org, or check your state's language arts standards.

Conventional wisdom is that knowledge about grammar and usage should improve students' oral language and writing, but research for more than 75 years hasn't confirmed this assumption. In 1936, for example, the National Council of Teachers of English (NCTE) passed a resolution against the formal teaching of grammar, and based on their review of research conducted before 1963, Braddock, Lloyd-Jones, and Schoer concluded that "the teaching of formal grammar has a negligible or, because it usually displaces some instruction and practice in actual composition, even a harmful effect on the improvement of writing" (1963, pp. 37–38). Since then, other studies have reached the same conclusion, and the NCTE resolution has been reaffirmed again and again (Hillocks & Smith, 2003).

Despite the controversy about teaching grammar and its value for students, grammar is a part of the language arts program and will undoubtedly remain so. Given this fact, it's only reasonable that grammar should be taught in the most beneficial manner possible.

Teaching Grammar Through Reading. Students learn about the structure of the English language through reading. They learn more sophisticated academic language, a more formal register than they speak, and sophisticated ways of phrasing ideas and arranging words into sentences. Students often read sentences that are longer than the ones they speak and learn new ways to string words into sentences. In *Chrysanthemum* (Henkes, 1991), the story of a mouse named Chrysanthemum who loves her name until she starts school and is teased by her classmates, the author uses a combination of long and short sentences very effectively: "Chrysanthemum could scarcely believe her ears. She blushed. She beamed. She bloomed" (n.p.).

Students read sentences exemplifying all four sentence types in many books. One example is the Caldecott Medal–winning *Officer Buckle and Gloria* (Rathmann, 1995), the story of a police officer and his dog, Gloria. "Officer Buckle loved having a buddy" and "That night Officer Buckle watched himself on the 10 o'clock news" (n.p.) are statements, or declarative sentences. "How about Gloria?" and "Could she come?" (n.p.) are questions, or interrogative sentences. Officer Buckle's safety tips, such as "Keep your shoelaces tied" and "Do not go swimming during electrical storms!" (n.p.), are imperative sentences. The children loved Gloria and her tricks, and they cheered, "Bravo!" (n.p.)—an example of an exclamation, or exclamatory sentence.

Similarly, students read simple, compound, complex, and compound-complex sentences in books. On the first page of *The Giver* (Lowry, 2006b), for instance, there are examples of simple, compound, and complex sentences:

Simple Sentence: "But the aircraft a year ago had been different."
Compound Sentence: "It was almost December, and Jonas was beginning to be frightened."
Complex Sentence: "Frightened was the way he had felt a year ago when an unidentified aircraft had overflown the community twice."

And on the second page, there's an example of a compound-complex sentence: "His parents were both at work, and his little sister, Lily, was at the Childcare Center where she spent her after-school hours."

One way to help students focus on sentences in stories is sentence collecting (Speaker & Speaker, 1991). Students collect favorite sentences and share them with classmates. They copy the sentences on chart paper or on long strips of tagboard and post them in the classroom. Students and the teacher talk about the merits of each sentence, focus on word choice, and analyze the sentence types. Sometimes students also cut the words in the sentences apart and rebuild them, either in the author's original order or in another that appeals to them.

Teaching the Parts of Speech. Students learn about parts of speech through reading and writing activities as well as through minilessons. They can locate examples of the parts of speech in books they're reading and experiment with words to see how the parts of speech are combined to form sentences. They read grammar concept books, including the popular books by author-illustrator Ruth Heller, and make their own books, too. Teachers use these activities to differentiate instruction:

COLLECTING PARTS OF SPEECH. Students work in small groups to identify words representing one or all eight parts of speech from a book they're reading. A group of fifth graders identified words representing the parts of speech in Van Allsburg's popular book *The Polar Express* (2005):

> Nouns: *train, children, Santa Claus, elves, pajamas, roller coaster, conductor, sleigh, hug, Sarah*
> Pronouns: *we, they, he, it, us, you, his, I, me*
> Verbs: *filled, ate, flickered, raced, were, cheered, marched, asked, pranced, stood, shouted*
> Adjectives: *melted, white-tailed, quiet, no, first, magical, cold, dark, polar, Santa's*
> Adverbs: *soon, faster, wildly, apart, closer, alone*
> Prepositions: *in, through, over, with, of, in front of, behind, at, for, across, into*
> Conjunctions: *and, but*
> Interjections: *oh, well, now*

After identifying the parts of speech, teachers make word cards and have students sort the words according to the part of speech. Because some words, such as *melted* and *hug*, can represent more than one part of speech, depending on how the word is used in a sentence, teachers must choose words for this activity carefully or use the words in a sentence on the word card so that students can classify them correctly.

After collecting words representing one part of speech from books they're reading or from books they've written, students can create a book using some of these words. Figure 13–3 shows the cover and a page from an alphabet book focusing on adjectives that second graders developed.

READING AND WRITING GRAMMAR CONCEPT BOOKS. Students examine concept books that focus on parts of speech or other grammar concepts. For example, Brian Cleary describes adjectives and lists many examples in *Hairy, Scary, Ordinary: What Is an Adjective?* (2000). After students read the book and identify the adjectives, they can make posters or write their own books about the parts of speech. Mentor texts for teaching parts of speech are presented in the Booklist on page 387.

Students in an eighth grade class divided into small groups to read Ruth Heller's books about parts of speech, including *Up, Up and Away: A Book About Adverbs* (1991), *Mine, All Mine: A Book About Pronouns* (1997), *Behind the Mask: A Book of Prepositions* (1995), and *Merry-Go-Round: A Book About Nouns* (1990). After reading, students made posters with information about the parts of speech, which they presented to the class. The students' poster for adverbs is shown in Figure 13–4. Later, students divided into small groups to do a word sort. In this activity, students cut apart a list of words and sorted them into groups according to the part of speech. All the words had been taken from posters that students created, and they could refer to the posters, if needed.

FIGURE 13–3 An Excerpt From a Class Book on Adjectives

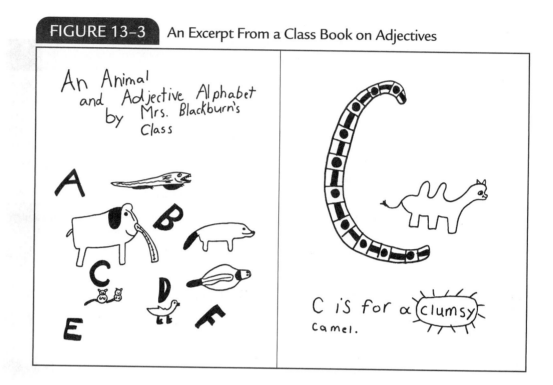

FIGURE 13–4 A Poster on Adverbs

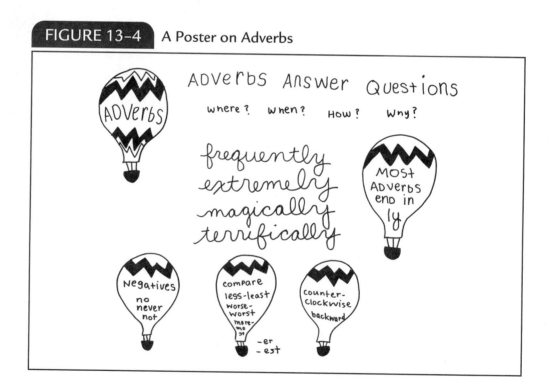

Booklist

PARTS OF SPEECH

Nouns	Cleary, B. P. (1999). *A mink, a fink, a skating rink: What is a noun?* Minneapolis: Carolrhoda. M
	Heller, R. (1998). *Merry-go-round: A book about nouns.* New York: Grosset & Dunlap. M–U
	Pulver, R. (2007). *Nouns and verbs have a field day.* New York: Holiday House. M
Pronouns	Cleary, B. P. (2004). *I and you and don't forget who: What is a pronoun?* Minneapolis: Carolrhoda. M
	Heller, R. (1999). *Mine, all mine: A book about pronouns.* New York: Grosset & Dunlap. M–U
Adjectives	Cleary, B. P. (2000). *Hairy, scary, ordinary: What is an adjective?* Minneapolis: Carolrhoda. M
	Heller, R. (1998). *Many luscious lollipops: A book about adjectives.* New York: Grosset & Dunlap. M–U
Verbs	Cleary, B. P. (2001). *To root, to toot, to parachute: What is a verb?* Minneapolis: Carolrhoda. M
	Heller, R. (1998). *Kites sail high: A book about verbs.* New York: Grosset & Dunlap. M–U
	Pulver, R. (2007). *Nouns and verbs have a field day.* New York: Holiday House. M
	Schneider, R. M. (1995). *Add it, dip it, fix it: A book of verbs.* Boston: Houghton Mifflin. M
Adverbs	Cleary, B. P. (2003). *Dearly, nearly, insincerely: What is an adverb?* Minneapolis: Carolrhoda. M
	Heller, R. (1998). *Up, up and away: A book about adverbs.* New York: Grosset & Dunlap. M–U
Prepositions	Cleary, B. P. (2002). *Under, over, by the clover: What is a preposition?* Minneapolis: Carolrhoda. M
	Heller, R. (1995). *Behind the mask: A book of prepositions.* New York: Grosset & Dunlap. M–U
Conjunctions	Cleary, B. P. (2010). *But and for, yet and nor: What is a conjunction?* Minneapolis: Millbrook Press. M
	Heller, R. (2000). *Fantastic! Wow! And unreal! A book about interjections and conjunctions.* New York: Penguin. M–U
Interjections	Heller, R. (2000). *Fantastic! Wow! And unreal! A book about interjections and conjunctions.* New York: Penguin. M–U

P = primary grades (preK–2); M = middle grades (3–5); U = upper grades (6–8)

Teaching Students to Manipulate Sentences. Students experiment with or manipulate sentences when they rearrange words and phrases in a sentence, combine several sentences to make a single, stronger sentence, or write sentences following a particular sentence pattern. Through these activities, students learn about the structure of sentences and experiment with more sophisticated sentences than they might otherwise write.

Primary grade students often create new books or "innovations" using the sentence structure in repetitive books. For example, young children write their own versions of *Brown Bear, Brown Bear, What Do You See?* (Martin, 2010) and the sequel, *Polar Bear, Polar Bear, What Do You Hear?* (Martin, 1992). Similarly, middle grade students write new verses following the rhyming pattern in Laura Numeroff's *Dogs Don't Wear Sneakers* (1993) and the sequel, *Chimps Don't Wear Glasses* (1995). Third graders used Numeroff's frame to write verses, including this verse that rhymes *TV* and *bumblebee*:

FIGURE 13–5 Killgallon's Four Types of Sentence Manipulation

Sentence Unscrambling
Teachers choose a long sentence from a book students are reading and break it into phrases. Then students reassemble the sentence to examine how the author structures sentences. Sometimes students duplicate the author's sentence, but other times, they create an original sentence that they like better.

Sentence Imitating
Teachers choose a sentence with an interesting structure to imitate from a book students are reading. Then students create a new sentence on a new topic that imitates the structure and style of the original sentence.

Sentence Combining
Teachers choose a conceptually dense sentence from a book students are reading and break the sentence into three or more simple sentences. Then students combine and embed the simple sentences to re-create the author's original sentence. They compare their sentence with the original one.

Sentence Expanding
Teachers choose a sentence from a book students are reading and shorten it to make an abridged version. Then students expand the abridged sentence, trying to re-create the author's original sentence, or write a new sentence, trying to match the author's style.

Based on Killgallon, 1997, 1998.

Ducks don't have tea parties,
Lions don't watch TV,
And you won't see a salamander
being friends with a bumblebee.

Older students often choose a favorite sentence from a book they're reading and imitate its structure by plugging in new words, a procedure Stephen Dunning calls "copy changes" (Dunning & Stafford, 1992). For example, eighth graders chose sentences from *The Giver* (Lowry, 2006b) for copy changes. One original sentence was "Dimly, from a nearly forgotten perception as blurred as the substance itself, Jonas recalled what the whiteness was" (p. 175). A student created this sentence using the sentence frame: "Softly, from a corner of the barn as cozy and warm as the kitchen, the baby kitten mewed to its mother."

Killgallon (1997, 1998) recommends that teachers help students examine how authors write sentences through four types of activities: sentence unscrambling, sentence imitating, sentence combining, and sentence expanding. Sentence imitating is like the innovations and copy changes just discussed. Through sentence manipulation, students learn new syntactic structures and practice ways to vary the sentences they write. These four types of sentence manipulation are summarized in Figure 13–5.

SENTENCE UNSCRAMBLING. Teachers choose a sentence from a book students are reading and divide it into phrases. They present the phrases in a random order, and students unscramble the sentence and rearrange the phrases, trying to duplicate the author's original order. Then students compare their rearrangement with the author's; sometimes they discover that they've created a new sentence that they like better. Here's a sentence from E. B. White's *Charlotte's Web* (2006), broken into phrases and scrambled:

in the middle of the kitchen

teaching it to suck from the bottle

a minute later

with an infant between her knees

Fern was seated on the floor

Can you unscramble the sentence? The original is "A minute later Fern was seated on the floor in the middle of the kitchen with an infant between her knees, teaching it to suck from the bottle" (pp. 6–7).

SENTENCE IMITATING. Students choose a sentence from a book they're reading and then write their own sentence imitating its structure. Here's an original sentence from *Charlotte's Web:* "Avery noticed the spider web, and coming closer, he saw Charlotte" (p. 71). Can you create a sentence on a new topic that imitates E. B. White's sentence structure, especially the "and coming closer" part? A class of sixth graders created this imitation: *The fox smelled the poultry, and coming closer, he saw five juicy chickens scratching in the dirt.* Here's another sentence from *Charlotte's Web:* "His medal still hung from his neck; by looking out of the corner of his eye he could still see it" (p. 163). Sixth graders also created this imitation: *The message was still stuck in the keyhole; using a magnifying glass the little mouse could still read those awful words.*

SENTENCE COMBINING. Students combine and rearrange words in sentences to make the sentences longer and more conceptually dense (Strong, 1996). The goal of sentence combining is for students to experiment with different ways to join and embed words. Teachers choose a sentence from a book students are reading and break it into short, simple sentences. Then students combine the sentences, trying to recapture the author's original sentence. Try your hand at combining these short sentences that were made from a more complex sentence in *Charlotte's Web:*

No one ever had such a friend.

The friend was so affectionate.

The friend was so loyal.

The friend was so skillful.

The original sentence is "No one ever had such a friend—so affectionate, so loyal, and so skillful" (p. 173). You might wonder whether the *and* before *so skillful* is necessary; students often wonder why E. B. White added it.

SENTENCE EXPANDING. Teachers choose a rich sentence from a book students are reading and present an abridged version. Then students expand it, taking care that the words and phrases they add blend in with the author's style. An abridged sentence from *Charlotte's Web* is "There is no place like home. . . ." and the original is "There is no place like home, Wilbur thought, as he placed Charlotte's 514 unborn children carefully in a safe corner" (p. 172). A sixth grader wrote this expansion: *There is no place like home, like his home in the barn, cozy and warm straw to sleep on, the delicious smell of manure in the air, Charlotte's egg sac to guard, and his friends Templeton, the goose, and the sheep nearby.* Even though it isn't the same as E. B. White's sentence, the student's sentence retains the character of White's writing style.

Minilessons. Teachers teach minilessons on grammar topics. They explain grammar concepts, have students make charts and posters, and involve them in examining sentences from books they're reading and in writing their own sentences. Finally, students apply what they're learning in their own writing. Teachers choose topics for grammar minilessons in two ways: They identify concepts by examining students' writing and noting what types of grammar errors they're making, and they choose topics from state standards for their grade level.

ENGAGING ENGLISH LEARNERS

The goal of grammar instruction is to increase students' ability to structure and manipulate sentences and to expand their repertoire of sentence patterns. Teaching grammar is a controversial issue, and it's especially so for English learners, but learning Standard English is crucial for these students' success in school.

CORRECTING STUDENTS' GRAMMAR ERRORS. The best way to promote students' language development is to encourage all students to talk freely in the classroom. In the past, researchers have recommended that teachers not correct students' talk so as not to embarrass them; however; teachers are now finding that many English learners want to be corrected so that they can learn to speak Standard English correctly in order to do well in school (Scarcella, 2003). The same is true with writing. During the editing stage of the writing process, teachers teach proofreading and help students identify and correct grammar and usage errors. After teachers explain grammar concepts in minilessons, students should become responsible for identifying and correcting the errors themselves.

TEACHING GRAMMAR CONCEPTS. Teachers also provide direct instruction about grammar concepts through minilessons for English learners and other students who don't speak and write Standard English. The rationale for providing direct instruction is that many English learners haven't been successful in acquiring Standard English through naturalistic approaches alone.

TOPICS FOR MINILESSONS. The best way to choose minilesson topics is to identify the kinds of errors students are making and then teach lessons on those topics. Also, teachers choose topics from state language arts standards. Here are 10 of the most common topics:

plurals	prepositions
verb tenses	possessives
irregular verbs	negatives
contractions	comparatives
subject-verb agreement	articles

Teachers use the same procedure for grammar minilessons that they use for lessons on other topics.

Learning to speak, read, and write Standard English takes time, and it's unrealistic to assume that students will learn a grammar topic through a single minilesson. What's important is that teachers regularly teach Standard English to their English learners and expect them to assume responsibility for learning it. ■

Assessing Students' Knowledge About Grammar

Teachers might think about administering a test to assess students' knowledge of grammar, but the best gauge is how they arrange words into sentences as part of genuine writing projects. As teachers examine students' compositions, they note errors, plan and teach minilessons based on these observed needs, note further errors, and plan and teach other minilessons. Teachers follow these steps:

PLANNING. Teachers plan for grammar instruction within their instructional program. They identify goals and plan instruction to achieve them. They choose mentor texts to share, and differentiate instruction to meet the needs of their students.

MONITORING. Teachers observe students as they teach minilesssons to check their progress, and they monitor students' ability to apply what they're learning as they participate in guided practice activities. Through this monitoring, teachers know which students aren't successful so they can provide additional instruction.

EVALUATING. Teachers can administer tests to evaluate students' learning, but it's more effective to assess their ability to apply grammar concepts in their writing. Teachers often have students identify grammar errors in the editing stage of the writing process.

HANDWRITING

The goal in handwriting instruction is to help students develop legible forms to communicate effectively through writing. Legibility and fluency are the two most important criteria in determining handwriting quality: Legible handwriting can be easily and quickly read, and fluent handwriting can be effortlessly and quickly produced. Very few students take great pleasure in developing flawless handwriting skills, and most feel that handwriting instruction is boring and unnecessary. It's imperative, therefore, to convey to students the importance of developing legible and fluent handwriting. Writing for genuine audiences is the best way to convey the importance of legibility. A letter sent to a favorite author that is returned by the post office because the address isn't decipherable or a child's published hardcover book that sits unread on the library shelf because the handwriting is illegible make clear the importance of legibility. Illegible writing means a failure to communicate—a harsh lesson for a writer!

Handwriting Forms

Two forms of handwriting are currently used in K–8 schools: manuscript, or printing, and cursive, or connected writing. Typically, young children use the manuscript form, and they switch to cursive handwriting in third grade. In the upper grades, students use both handwriting forms.

Manuscript Handwriting. Until the 1920s, students learned only cursive handwriting. Marjorie Wise is credited with introducing the manuscript form for young children in 1921 (Hildreth, 1960). Manuscript handwriting is considered better for young children because they lack the eye-hand coordination necessary for cursive handwriting. In addition, manuscript handwriting is similar to the type style in books and other reading materials. Only two lowercase letters, *a* and *g*, are usually different in typed and handwritten forms. The similarity may actually facilitate young children's introduction to reading because it simplifies letter recognition (Adams, 1990).

Despite its advantages, the manuscript form has been criticized. A major complaint is the reversal problem caused by some similar lowercase letters; *b* and *d* are particularly confusing. Detractors also argue that using both the manuscript and the cursive forms requires teaching students two totally different kinds of handwriting within several years. They also complain that the "circle and stick" style of manuscript handwriting requires frequent stops and starts, thus inhibiting a smooth and rhythmic flow of writing.

Cursive Handwriting. When most people think of handwriting, it's the cursive or connected form that comes to mind. The letters in cursive handwriting are joined together to form a word with one continuous movement. Children often view cursive handwriting as the grown-up type. Primary grade students often attempt to imitate this form by connecting the manuscript letters in their names and other words before they're taught how to form and join the letters. Awareness of cursive handwriting and interest in imitating it are indicators that children are ready for instruction.

D'Nealian Handwriting. D'Nealian handwriting is an alternative manuscript and cursive handwriting program developed by Donald Neal Thurber, a teacher in Michigan, to mitigate some of the problems associated with the traditional manuscript form. D'Nealian manuscript uses the same basic letterforms that students will need for cursive handwriting, as well as the slant and rhythm required for cursive. In the manuscript form, letters are slanted and formed with a continuous stroke; in the cursive form, the letters are simplified, without the flourishes of traditional cursive. Both forms were designed to increase legibility and fluency and to ease the transition from manuscript to cursive handwriting. Another advantage is that the transition from manuscript to cursive involves adding only connective strokes to most manuscript letters. Only five letters—*f, r, s, v,* and *z*—are shaped differently in the cursive form. Research has not yet documented that D'Nealian is better than the traditional manuscript form even though many teachers prefer it (Graham, 1992).

Students' Handwriting Development

Young children begin preschool and kindergarten with differing backgrounds of handwriting experience: Some 4-year-olds have never held a pencil, but others have learned to print their names and some other letters. Handwriting in prekindergarten and kindergarten typically includes three types of activities: stimulating children's interest in writing, developing their ability to hold writing instruments, and printing letters of the alphabet. Adults are influential role models in stimulating children's interest in writing. They record children's talk and write labels on signs. They can also provide paper, pencils, and pens so that children can experiment with writing. Children learn to hold a pencil by watching adults and through numerous opportunities to experiment with pencils, paintbrushes, and crayons. Instruction is necessary so that children don't learn bad habits that later must be broken. They often devise bizarre ways to form letters when they haven't been shown how to form them, and these bad habits can cause problems as children need to develop greater writing speed.

Formal handwriting instruction begins in first grade. Students learn how to form manuscript letters and space between them as well as other elements of legibility. A common handwriting activity requires students to copy short writing samples from the whiteboard, but this type of activity isn't recommended. For one thing, young children have great difficulty with far-to-near copying; a piece of writing should be placed close to the child for copying. Children can recopy interactive writing compositions and Language Experience stories, but other types of copying should be avoided. It's far better for children to create their own writing than to copy words and sentences they may not even be able to read!

Special pencils are often provided for handwriting instruction. Young children have commonly been given "fat" beginner pencils because it's been assumed that these pencils are easier to hold; however, most children prefer to use regular-sized pencils that adults use. Moreover, regular pencils have erasers! Plus, there's research that indicates that beginner pencils aren't better than regular-sized pencils for young children (Graham, 1992). Likewise, there's no evidence that specially shaped pencils and small writing aids that slip onto pencils to improve children's grips are effective.

Students' introduction to cursive handwriting typically occurs in the first semester of third grade. Parents and students often attach great importance to the transition from manuscript to cursive, thus adding unnecessary pressure for the students. Beverly Cleary's *Muggie Maggie* (1990) describes the pressure some children feel. The time of transition is usually dictated by tradition rather than by sound educational theory: All students in a school or school district are usually intro-duced to cursive handwriting at the same time, regardless of their interest in making the change.

Some students indicate an early interest in cursive handwriting by trying to connect manuscript letters or by asking their parents to demonstrate how to write their names. Because of individual dif-ferences in motor skills and levels of interest in cursive writing, it's better to introduce some students to cursive handwriting in first or second grade while providing other students with additional time to refine their manuscript skills. These students then learn cursive handwriting in third or fourth grade.

The practice of changing to cursive handwriting only a year or two after children learn the manuscript form is receiving increasing criticism. The argument has been that students need to learn cursive handwriting as early as possible because of their growing need for handwriting speed. Because of its continuous flow, cursive handwriting was believed to be faster to write than manuscript; however, research suggests that manuscript handwriting can be written as quickly as cursive handwriting (Jackson, 1971). The controversy over the benefits of the two forms and the best time to introduce cursive handwriting is likely to continue.

When teachers introduce students to cursive handwriting, they begin with the basic strokes that make up the letters (e.g., slant stroke, undercurve, downcurve). Next, the lowercase letters are taught in isolation, and then the connecting strokes are introduced. Uppercase letters are taught later because they're used far less often and are more difficult to form. Which cursive let-ters are most difficult? The lowercase *r* is the most troublesome letter. The other lowercase letters students frequently form incorrectly are *k, p,* and *z*.

Cursive handwriting shouldn't replace manuscript handwriting; students continue to use manuscript handwriting part of the time. Because manuscript handwriting is easier for them to form and to read, many students often continue to use the manuscript form when they're writing informally, saving cursive handwriting for projects and final copies of their writing. Teachers need to review both forms periodically. By this time, too, students have firmly established handwriting habits, both good and bad; now the emphasis is on helping students diagnose and correct their handwriting trouble spots so that they can develop a legible and fluent handwriting style. Older students both simplify their letterforms and add unique flourishes to their handwriting to develop their own trademark styles. Figure 13–6 reviews of the sequence of handwriting development.

Teaching Handwriting

Handwriting is best taught in separate periods of direct instruction and teacher-supervised practice. As soon as skills are taught, students should apply them in real-life writing activities; busywork assignments, such as copying sentences from the whiteboard, aren't effective. More-over, students often develop poor handwriting habits or learn to form letters incorrectly if they practice without direct supervision. It's much more difficult to correct bad habits and errors in letter formation than to teach correct handwriting in the first place.

Elements of Legibility. For students to develop legible handwriting, they need to know what qualities determine legibility and then to analyze their own handwriting according to these ele-ments (Hackney, 2003). Here are the six elements of legible handwriting:

LETTER FORMATION. Letters are formed with specific strokes. Letters in manuscript hand-writing are composed of vertical, horizontal, and slanted lines plus circles or parts of circles. The letter *b*, for example, is composed of a vertical line and a circle, and *M* is composed of vertical and slanted lines. Cursive letters are composed of slanted lines, loops, and curved lines. The lowercase cursive letters *m* and *n*, for instance, are composed of a slant stroke, a loop, and an undercurve stroke. An additional component in cursive handwriting is the con-necting stroke used to join letters.

SIZE AND PROPORTION. Students' handwriting gradually becomes smaller, and the proportional size of uppercase to lowercase letters increases. First graders' uppercase manuscript letters are twice the size of their lowercase letters. When second and third grade students begin cursive handwriting, the proportional size of letters remains 2:1; later, the proportion increases to 3:1 for middle and upper grade students.

SPACING. Students should leave adequate space between letters in words and between words in sentences. Spacing between words in manuscript handwriting should equal one lowercase letter *o*, and spacing between sentences should equal two lowercase *o*'s. The most important aspect of spacing within words in cursive handwriting is consistency. To correctly space between words, writers make the beginning stroke of the new word directly below the end stroke of the preceding word. Spacing between sentences should equal one uppercase letter *O*, and the indent for a new paragraph should equal two uppercase letter *O*'s.

SLANT. Letters should be consistently parallel. Letters in manuscript handwriting are vertical, and in the cursive form, letters slant slightly to the right. To ensure the correct slant, right-handed students tilt their papers to the left, and left-handed students tilt their papers to the right.

ALIGNMENT. For proper alignment in both manuscript and cursive handwriting, all letters should be uniform in size and consistently touch the baseline.

LINE QUALITY. Students should write at a consistent speed and hold their writing instruments correctly and in a relaxed manner to make steady, unwavering lines of even thickness.

Correct letter formation and spacing receive the major focus in handwriting instruction. Although the other elements usually receive less attention, they're important in developing legible handwriting.

FIGURE 13-6   Sequence of Handwriting Development

Handwriting Before First Grade
Four- and five-year-olds learn basic handwriting skills.
- Children learn how to hold a pencil.
- Children learn to form upper- and lowercase letters.
- Children learn to write their names and other common words.

Handwriting in the Primary Grades
Primary-grade students develop legible manuscript handwriting.
- Children learn to form upper- and lowercase manuscript letters and to space between letters.
- Children often use "fat" beginner pencils even though research doesn't support this practice.
- Children use wide, lined paper with a dotted midline to guide them in forming lowercase letters.

Transition to Cursive Handwriting in the Middle Grades
Students learn to read and write cursive handwriting.
- Students are introduced to cursive handwriting in third grade.
- Students learn to read cursive writing.
- Students learn to form upper- and lowercase letters and to join letters.

Handwriting in the Upper Grades
Students use both manuscript and cursive handwriting in daily writing activities.
- Students have learned both manuscript and cursive handwriting forms.
- Students develop their own trademark styles.
- Students vary the legibility and neatness of their handwriting for private and public writing.

Minilesson

Ms. Thomas Teaches Manuscript Letter Formation

1. Introduce the Topic

Ms. Thomas brings her first graders together on the rug for handwriting practice and passes out a small whiteboard, pen, and eraser to each child. They begin by rereading the class news chart that they wrote the day before using interactive writing. Ms. Thomas explains that she wants to practice three lowercase letters—*m, n,* and *u*—that the children had difficulty writing the previous day.

2. Share Examples

Ms. Thomas rereads the chart and asks children to point out the three letters when they notice them in the class news chart. She asks one child to underline each word the children point out. They mention these words: *and, made, not, when, never, some, then, you, your,* and *wanted.* After reading the entire chart, the children agree that these letters are important because they're used so often in their writing.

3. Provide Information

Ms. Thomas demonstrates how to form each of the letters by writing the letter on a whiteboard and verbalizing the strokes she's making. Then the children practice writing the letters on their boards as Ms. Thomas observes them. She assists several children in holding their pens correctly, and she demonstrates again for several children who are continuing to have trouble writing the letters.

4. Supervise Practice

Once she's satisfied that each child can form the three letters and differentiate among them, Ms. Thomas asks children to write several of the underlined words on their whiteboards as she observes. She provides immediate feedback to those who aren't forming the letters correctly or who make the letters too large.

5. Reflect on Learning

After this brief review, Ms. Thomas asks children to remember what they learned about forming these letters when they're writing. The children name all the occasions they have during the day to remember how to form the letters—when they write books at the writing center, when they write in journals, and when they do interactive writing.

Minilessons. Teachers use minilessons to teach handwriting. Brief lessons and practice sessions taught several times a week are more effective than a single, lengthy period weekly or monthly. Regular handwriting instruction is necessary when teaching the manuscript form in kindergarten and first grade and the cursive form in third grade. In the upper grades, instruction focuses on specific handwriting problems that students demonstrate and periodic reviews of both handwriting forms. A minilesson on teaching manuscript letter formation in first grade is shown above.

Teachers' active involvement in handwriting instruction and practice is crucial. Observing "moving" models—that is, having students watch the teacher write the handwriting sample—is of far greater value than copying models that have already been written. Moving models are possible when the teacher circulates around the classroom, stopping to demonstrate how to form a letter for one student and moving to assist another; circling incorrectly formed letters and marking other errors with a red pen on completed handwriting sheets are of little value.

Working With Left-Handed Writers. Approximately 10% of the U.S. population is left-handed, which means two or three students in most classrooms are left-handed. Until 1950 or so, teachers insisted that left-handed students use their right hands for handwriting because left-handed writers were thought to have inferior handwriting skills. Parents and teachers are more realistic now and accept children's natural tendencies for left- or right-handedness.

Most young children develop handedness—the preference for using either the right or the left hand for fine-motor activities—by age 4 or 5. After age 5, teachers must help those children who haven't developed handedness to consistently use one hand for handwriting and other fine-motor activities. Teachers observe the child's behavior and hand preference over a period of days and note which hand he or she uses in activities such as building with blocks, throwing balls, cutting with scissors, holding a paintbrush, manipulating clay, and pouring water. Teachers may find that a child uses both hands interchangeably. For example, a child may first reach for several blocks with one hand and then reach for the next block with the other. During drawing activities, the child may switch hands every few minutes. In this situation, the teacher asks the child's parents to observe his or her behavior at home, noting hand preferences when the child eats, brushes teeth, turns on the television, opens drawers, and so on. Then the teacher, the child, and the child's parents confer and—based on the results of joint observations, the handedness of family members, and the child's wishes—make a tentative decision about hand preference. At school, teacher and child will work closely together so that the child uses the chosen hand. As long as the child continues to use both hands interchangeably, neither hand will develop the prerequisite fine-motor control for handwriting.

Teaching handwriting to left-handed students isn't simply the reverse of teaching it to right-handed students: Left-handed students have unique handwriting problems, so special adaptations of the procedures for teaching right-handed students are necessary. In fact, many of the problems that left-handed students have can actually be made worse by using the procedures designed for right-handed writers. Special adjustments are necessary to enable left-handed students to write legibly, fluently, and with less fatigue.

The basic difference between right- and left-handed writing is physical orientation: Right-handed students pull their arms toward their bodies as they write, but left-handed writers push away. As left-handed students write, they move their left hand across what they've just written, often covering it. Consequently, many children adopt a "hook" position to avoid covering and smudging what they've written. Because of their different physical orientation, left-handed writers need to make three major types of adjustments:

HOLDING PENCILS. Left-handed writers should hold pencils an inch or more farther back from the tip than right-handed writers do; this change helps them see what they've just written and avoid smearing their writing. Left-handed writers need to work to avoid hooking their wrists: They should keep their wrists straight and elbows close to their bodies to avoid the awkward hooked position. Practicing handwriting on the whiteboard is one way to help them develop a more natural style.

FIGURE 13-7   Manuscript Handwriting Checklist

_____ 1.   Did I form my letters correctly?
_____ 2.   Did my lines touch the midline or top line neatly?
_____ 3.   Did I space evenly between letters?
_____ 4.   Did I leave enough space between words?
_____ 5.   Did I make my letters straight up and down?
_____ 6.   Did I make all my letters sit on the baseline?

TILTING PAPER. Left-handed students should tilt their writing papers slightly to the right, in contrast to right-handed students, who tilt their papers to the left. Sometimes it's helpful to place a piece of masking tape on the student's desk to indicate the proper amount of tilt.

SLANTING LETTERS. Right-handed students are encouraged to slant their cursive letters to the right, but left-handed writers often write vertically or even slant their letters slightly backward. Some handwriting programs recommend that left-handed writers slant their cursive letters slightly to the right as right-handed students do, but others advise teachers to permit any slant between vertical and 45 degrees to the left of vertical.

Correcting Handwriting Problems. Students use the elements of legibility to diagnose their handwriting problems. Primary grade students, for example, can check to see that they've formed a particular letter correctly, that the round parts of letters are joined neatly, and that slanted letters are joined in sharp points. Older students can examine a piece of handwriting to see if their letters are parallel and if the letters touch the baseline consistently. Figure 13–7 presents a checklist for evaluating manuscript handwriting; checklists can also be developed for cursive handwriting. It's important to involve students in developing the checklists so that they appreciate the need to make their handwriting more legible.

Another reason students need to diagnose and correct their handwriting problems is that handwriting quality influences teacher evaluation and grading. Researchers have found that teachers consistently grade papers with better handwriting higher than those with poor handwriting, regardless of the content (Graham, 1992). Children aren't too young to learn that poor or illegible handwriting may lead to lower grades.

INTEGRATING TECHNOLOGY

Keyboarding is an alternative to handwriting. In the 21st century, students need to develop keyboarding skills so they can use computers more easily for word processing. Keyboarding is also faster than writing by hand: By sixth or seventh grade, students can type 20 to 25 words per minute, but they handwrite only 10 to 15 words in the same amount of time (National Business Education Association, 1997).

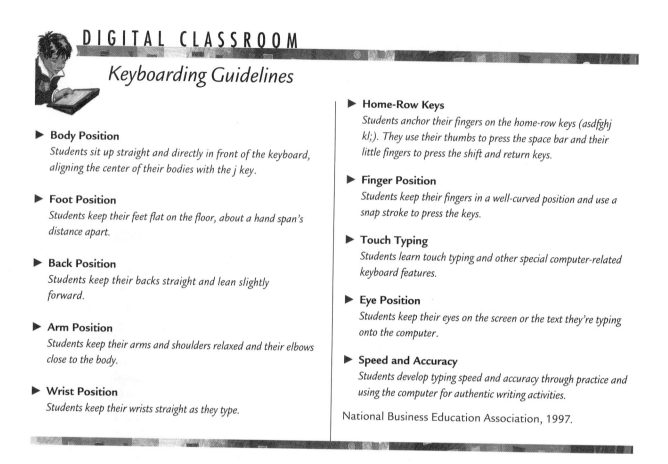

DIGITAL CLASSROOM

Keyboarding Guidelines

▶ **Body Position**

Students sit up straight and directly in front of the keyboard, aligning the center of their bodies with the j key.

▶ **Foot Position**

Students keep their feet flat on the floor, about a hand span's distance apart.

▶ **Back Position**

Students keep their backs straight and lean slightly forward.

▶ **Arm Position**

Students keep their arms and shoulders relaxed and their elbows close to the body.

▶ **Wrist Position**

Students keep their wrists straight as they type.

▶ **Home-Row Keys**

Students anchor their fingers on the home-row keys (asdfghj kl;). They use their thumbs to press the space bar and their little fingers to press the shift and return keys.

▶ **Finger Position**

Students keep their fingers in a well-curved position and use a snap stroke to press the keys.

▶ **Touch Typing**

Students learn touch typing and other special computer-related keyboard features.

▶ **Eye Position**

Students keep their eyes on the screen or the text they're typing onto the computer.

▶ **Speed and Accuracy**

Students develop typing speed and accuracy through practice and using the computer for authentic writing activities.

National Business Education Association, 1997.

Informal keyboarding instruction begins in the primary grades. Students become familiar with the keyboard and learn basic hand positioning. They learn to keep their right hand on the right side of the keyboard and their left hand on the left side. They learn simple keyboarding skills, such as keeping their fingers on the home-row keys (*asdfghjkl;*) and typing with more than one finger. Students also learn proper posture: They sit directly in front of the computer and keep their feet on the floor. The Digital Classroom feature above lists guidelines for successful keyboarding.

In third or fourth grade, students receive formal keyboarding lessons; they learn touch typing and to look mainly at the screen rather than at their fingers while typing. It's crucial that students develop good touch-typing skills and avoid bad habits that inhibit efficient keyboard use. Students often practice keyboarding using AlphaSmart or another portable keyboard because a full computer isn't needed.

Students can learn keyboarding through teacher-directed lessons or using software programs. The Kid Keys software, which is recommended for primary students, includes lessons on becoming familiar with the letter positions on the keyboard and games using keyboarding skills to make music. The Mavis Beacon Teaches Typing software is recommended for students in third grade and above; the lessons teach fundamental keyboarding skills at several levels of difficulty and offer games to reinforce the skills. Even though voice-recognition systems may someday replace the need for computer keyboards, keyboarding skills are still essential. ■

SUMMING UP

Grammar and handwriting are language tools. Grammar is the description of the structure of a language and the principles of word and sentence formation. Even though grammar is a controversial topic, it should be taught within the context of authentic reading and writing activities. Handwriting is a tool for writers, and students learn both manuscript and cursive handwriting. The emphasis in handwriting instruction is on legibility rather than on imitating handwriting models perfectly; students need to learn how to write so that their writing can be easily read. Students also learn keyboarding as an alternative to handwriting.

MyEducationLab™

Go to the topic Writing in the MyEducationLab (http://www.myeducationlab.com) for *Language Arts: Patterns of Practice*, where you can:

- Find learning outcomes for Writing, along with the national standards that connect to these outcomes.
- Complete Assignments and Activities that can help you more deeply understand the chapter content.
- Apply and practice your understanding of the core teaching skills identified in the chapter with the Building Teaching Skills and Dispositions learning units.
- Examine challenging situations and cases presented in the IRIS Center Resources.
- Use the Lesson Plan Builder Activities to practice lesson planning and integrating national and state standards into your planning.
- Check your comprehension of the content covered in the chapter with the Study Plan. Here you will be able to take a chapter quiz, receive feedback on your answers, and then access Review, Practice, and Enrichment activities to enhance your understanding of chapter content.

On the **MyEducationLab** for this course, you'll also be able to:

- **A+RISE** Go to the topic A+RISE, an innovative and interactive database of strategies that differentiate instruction across the language arts and provide particular insight into research-based methods to meet the needs of English learners.
- Explore the topic Literacy Portraits—yearlong case studies of second graders, complete with student artifacts, teacher commentary, and student and teacher interviews, tracking the month-by-month language arts growth of five students.
- Gain practice with the Grammar Tutorial, online guided instruction to improve your own ability with grammar.

CHAPTER 14

Putting It All Together

FIRST GRADERS STUDY THE SOLAR SYSTEM   At the beginning of the first graders' thematic unit, the children listed what they knew about the planets on a K-W-L chart, and at the end of the unit, they'll finish the chart by adding what they've learned. A word wall also went up at the beginning of the unit, and children added the names of the planets, *astronaut, moon, ring, asteroid, alien, comet,* and other new words to the word wall. They also added small illustrations to make identifying the words easier.

Each morning, the first graders sign in when they arrive in the classroom. Their teacher, Mrs. McNeal, makes daily sign-in sheets on a large sheet of drawing paper by writing a unit-related question at the top of the paper and two or three possible answers at the bottom. The children read the question and possible answers and sign in by writing their names in the column above the answer they think is correct. Today's question is *What makes the moon shine?* These are three possible answers: *The sun makes it shine, It has its own light,* and *The earth makes it shine.* Most of the students think that it has its own light, but they aren't sure. The purpose of the question is to pique children's interest, and then Mrs. McNeal reads aloud Gail Gibbons's *The Moon Book* (1997). They learn, of course, that the moon reflects the sun's light.

Mrs. McNeal has been reading aloud stories, nonfiction books, and poems from a text set of books about the solar system. After reading each book, the children have been writing paragraphs to define and explain concepts they're learning. They choose the three most important pieces of information, arrange them into sentences, and combine the sentences to make a paragraph. Here are several of their paragraphs:

How do students use the six language arts during thematic units?

Students use all six language arts as tools for learning and to document their learning during thematic units. For example, they talk and listen as they participate in discussions, read text sets of books, write in learning logs and create reports, view photos and maps, and make posters. As you continue reading, notice how Mrs. McNeal provides opportunities for her students to use the language arts as they learn about the solar system.

Moon

The moon is a ball of rock. It goes around the earth. It has no air or atmosphere.

Asteroids

Asteroids are chunks of rock and metal. They orbit around the sun. Many asteroids are in the asteroid belt between Mars and Jupiter.

The Inner Planets

The inner planets are Mercury, Venus, Earth, and Mars. They are closest to the sun. All four are made of rock.

The children write the paragraphs on chart paper using interactive writing, and Mrs. McNeal supervises their work, making corrections and teaching spelling, capitalization, and punctuation skills as needed. It's important that the paragraphs are written conventionally because they're posted in the classroom for children to read and reread.

The first graders participate in other unit-related activities at eight centers. They visit all of the centers, with certain ones assigned each day. They go to some centers only once a week and others, such as the research center, more often. Mrs. McNeal has these centers in her classroom:

ART CENTER. Children use paint to create a map of the solar system with a parent volunteer's assistance at this center. They dip nine round sponges of varying sizes (one for the sun and eight for the planets) into paint and stamp them on a wide sheet of construction paper. After the paint dries, the students label the planets, add moons, rings, and the asteroid belt using marking pens.

LISTENING CENTER. Each week, the children listen to a different book from the text set of books and draw pictures and write words to complete a chart about the book. This week, they're listening to Frank Asch's *The Sun Is My Favorite Star* (2000).

WRITING CENTER. The children make a pattern book based on Pat Hutchins's *Rosie's Walk* (2005), a story the first graders know well. Mrs. McNeal writes one line on each page of the book, omitting the last word or phrase. She compiles the pages and binds the

book together so that all children have to supply only the underlined word or phrase and add an illustration. Here is Jacky's completed book:

> My star and I traveled through <u>space</u>
> Across the <u>clouds</u>
> Around the <u>moon</u>
> Over the <u>stars</u>
> Past the <u>space shuttle</u>
> Under the <u>meteors</u>
> Through the <u>milky way</u>
> And I got back in time for my <u>birthday</u>.

The underlined words are the ones that Jacky chose for her book. After she finished her book, she put it in her personal box of books to read and reread at home and during the first 10 minutes of the school day.

WORD WALL CENTER. Children use a pointer to reread the words on the solar system word wall. Then they participate in other activities, including writing the words on whiteboards, spelling them with magnetic letters, and matching word cards to pictures.

RESEARCH CENTER. Children write and illustrate books about the solar system at the research center. Every other day, Mrs. McNeal focuses on one of the planets and records information about it on a large data chart hanging on the wall next to the center. The completed data chart is shown on the next page. Then children each write a paragraph-long report about the planet that contains three facts. They refer to the chart as they write their reports; through this activity, they're practicing what they've been learning about writing paragraphs with three facts. Alex's report about Jupiter is shown on page 404. He has incorporated three facts from the data chart, and most of the words are spelled correctly because he could check the spellings on the data chart.

COMPUTER CENTER. Children use the Internet to check the NASA website for photos of the planets taken by Voyager and other spacecraft, and the National Geographic site for a virtual tour of the solar system. Mrs. McNeal has bookmarked these two sites, and children navigate the World Wide Web with the assistance of a Tech Liaison from the local high school.

LIBRARY CENTER. Children read books from the solar system text set at this center. They're especially interested in reading and rereading the leveled books and in poring over the photos in the nonfiction books.

POETRY CENTER. Children reread poems about the sun, moon, and planets written on chart paper that they've practiced reading as a class. They also take the poems written on sentence strips out of pocket charts and rearrange the lines to create new versions. This is a popular center because one child gets to pretend to be Mrs. McNeal and use a pointer to direct the other children in the group as they read the poems.

Mrs. McNeal uses a magnetized whiteboard to direct children to centers, and they check off the centers they complete on a chart hanging near the board so that Mrs.

Data Chart on the Planets

Planet	Where is it?	How big is it?	Does it have moons or rings?	Is it hot or cold?	What does it look like?	Is there life?	Other facts
Mercury	first, closest to the sun	second smallest	no	roasting hot or freezing cold	dry, airless, rocky, lots of craters	no	about the size of our moon
Venus	second	about the size of earth	no	hotter than an oven	thick, yellow clouds and tall mountains	no	air is poisonous, easiest planet to see in the sky
Earth	third	a middle-sized planet	1 moon	just right for life	made of rock and mostly covered with oceans	yes	we live here
Mars	fourth	half the size of earth	2 tiny moons	colder than earth	red dirt desert and pink sky	no	nickname is the Red Planet because of rusty iron in the soil
Jupiter	fifth, outside the asteroid belt	biggest planet, the "king"	16 moons 2 rings	cold	giant ball of gas, has a great red spot, covered with clouds	no	all the other planets could fit inside it
Saturn	sixth	second biggest planet	17 moons thousands of rings	very cold	giant ball of gas, covered with clouds	no	most beautiful planet
Uranus	seventh	third biggest planet	15 moons 10 rings	freezing cold	giant ball of gas, bluish-green color	no	lies on its side, spins differently
Neptune	eighth	fourth biggest planet	8 moons 4 rings	freezing cold	giant ball of gas, also bluish-green color, has a great dark spot	no	takes a rocket 8 years to go from Neptune to the sun

McNeal can keep track of their work. At the end of each week, children are expected to have completed six of the eight centers, including the art, writing, and research centers.

As they approach the end of the unit, Mrs. McNeal brings the class together to talk about their final project to demonstrate all they've learned. They talk about several possibilities, but they decide to invite their parents to come to the classroom on Friday afternoon to listen to oral presentations about the planets and see their work. They divide into groups of two or three, and each group chooses one planet to report on. They make posters with drawings of the planet and three facts about it. They check the information on the data chart and practice what they'll say. They also ask Mrs. McNeal to take the parents on a tour of the classroom, showing them their books, charts, centers, and other activities. Many parents, grandparents, and friends come to the after-school presentation, and they're impressed with all that the first graders have learned, especially the new information that the NASA spacecraft have discovered.

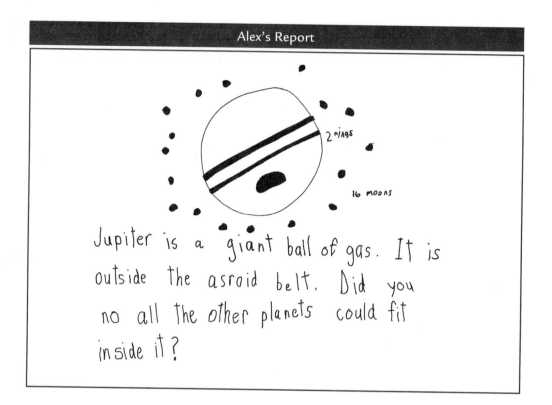

Alex's Report

Jupiter is a giant ball of gas. It is outside the asroid belt. Did you no all the other planets could fit inside it?

eachers often search for the single best way to develop units or design language arts instruction, but there isn't just one way. Instead, teachers pick and choose from thousands of books, activities, and assignments as they plan literature focus units, literature circles, reading and writing workshop, and thematic units. In this text, you've read about these components of language arts instruction:

- Creating a community of learners
- Language arts strategies
- Word walls and vocabulary activities
- Journals and other ways to use writing as a learning tool
- Listening and talking
- Reading and writing processes
- Viewing and visually representing
- Language arts centers
- Technology tools
- Reading and writing stories and learning about the structure of stories
- Reading and writing nonfiction and learning about expository text structures
- Reading and writing poetry and learning about poetic forms and stylistic devices
- Spelling, handwriting, and grammar

Teachers choose among these components as they plan for instruction. Choosing to have students write in reading logs or create a story quilt isn't necessarily better than having them write sequels or collect sentences from a book to examine sentence structure. Teachers use the instructional approaches as frameworks and then select literature, activities, and projects based on their instructional goals and beliefs about how children learn.

As teachers gain experience developing units, they often go beyond the "What shall I do with this book?" or "What shall I teach in this unit?" questions to think about the choices they make as they plan instruction and teach (McGee & Tompkins, 1995). Teachers need to think about why students should choose many of the books they read and why strategy instruction should be taught in context. Through this reflection, teachers realize how theories about how children learn, along with their instructional goals, provide the foundation for language arts instruction.

LITERATURE FOCUS UNITS

Teachers plan literature focus units featuring popular and award-winning stories for children and adolescents. Some literature focus units feature a single book, either a picture book or a chapter book, but others feature a text set of books for a genre unit or an author study unit. During these units, students move through the five stages of the reading process as they read and respond to stories, learn reading and writing strategies, and engage in language arts activities.

How to Develop a Literature Focus Unit

Teachers develop a literature focus unit through a seven-step series of activities, beginning with choosing the literature for the unit, continuing to identify and schedule activities, and ending with deciding how to assess students' learning. No matter whether teachers are using stories or nonfiction books, they follow the steps outlined in Figure 14–1. Teachers need to make the plans themselves because they're the ones who know their students, the standards their students are expected to meet, the reading materials they have available, the time available for the unit, the skills and strategies their students need to learn, and the language arts activities they want to use.

Literature focus units featuring a picture book are usually completed in 1 week, and units featuring a chapter book are completed in 2, 3, or 4 weeks. Genre and author units may last 2, 3, or 4 weeks. Rarely, if ever, do literature focus units continue for more than a month; when teachers drag a unit out for 6 weeks, 2 months, or longer, they risk killing students' interest in the particular book or, worse yet, their love of reading.

Step 1: Select the Featured Book. Teachers begin by selecting the featured book for the unit. The book may be a story—either a picture book or a chapter book—or a nonfiction book. The reading materials should be high-quality literature and should often include multicultural selections. Sometimes teachers select several related books representing the same genre for a genre study or books written by the same author for an author study. Teachers collect multiple copies of the book or books for the unit. In some school districts, class sets of selected books are available; in other school districts, however, teachers have to request that administrators purchase multiple copies of books or buy them themselves, often through book clubs.

Once the book (or books) is selected, teachers collect related books for the text set, including other versions of the same story, other books written by the same author, books with the same theme or representing the same genre, or related nonfiction books or books of poetry. Teachers collect one or more copies of each book for the text set, which they place on a special shelf or in a crate in the

---

FIGURE 14–1 Steps in Developing a Literature Focus Unit

1. Book Selection

Teachers select the book to be featured in the literature focus unit, obtain a class set of books, and collect a text set of related books.

2. Instructional Focus

Teachers identify the focus for the unit and the standards to address.

3. Reading Process Activities

Teachers plan activities representing all five stages of the reading process.

4. Differentiation

Teachers design instruction, plan a variety of activities, and choose grouping patterns to meet students' needs and ensure their success.

5. Technology Resources

Teachers locate digital tools related to the featured book.

6. Assessment

Teachers plan how students' work will be assessed, and make rubrics, checklists, or grading sheets.

7. Schedule

Teachers create a time schedule and lesson plans.

---

library center. At the beginning of the unit, teachers introduce the books and encourage students to read them during independent reading time.

Step 2: Identify the Instructional Focus. Teachers identify the instructional focus by matching the book's strengths with the language arts standards they'll teach. Some standards, such as interpreting words with multiple meanings, can be taught using almost any book, but others, such as comparing and contrasting tales from different cultures, are book-specific. Teachers also identify standards that focus on writing and other language arts to teach as students participate in the unit. For example, when teachers plan to read the featured book aloud, they identify listening comprehension standards to address, and when students will write sequels to the story, teachers identify standards dealing with the writing process and writing mechanics to teach. They decide what they want students to know and be able to do at the end of the unit, and then these standards become the focus of both instruction and assessment.

Step 3: Plan Reading Process Activities. Teachers decide which activities to include in the unit; the activities they choose need to fit into the five stages of the reading process. They ask themselves these questions about the prereading stage:

> What background knowledge do students need before reading?
> How will I introduce the story?
> What information will I share about the author or author's craft?

These questions address the reading stage:

> How will students read this story?
> Which reading strategies will I model or ask students to apply?
> How can I make the book more accessible for English learners or struggling readers?

These questions address the responding stage:

> Will students write entries in reading logs?
> Will students participate in grand conversations or other discussions?
> Will students dramatize some scenes from the book?

These questions address the exploring stage:

> Which Tier 2 words will be targeted?
> Which topics will I teach in minilessons?
> How will I use mentor texts?
> How will I focus students' attention on sentences in the book?

And these questions address the applying stage:

> What oral, written, and visual language projects might students pursue?
> How will students share their projects?

Teachers also make sure that students have opportunities to engage in listening, talking, reading, writing, viewing, and visually representing activities during the literature focus unit. Of course, not all six language arts fit into every unit, but for most units they do.

Step 4: Decide How to Differentiate Instruction. Teachers think about how to differentiate instruction and incorporate whole-class, small-group, buddy, and individual activities into their unit plans. It's important that students have opportunities to read and write independently as well as to work with small groups and to come together as a class. Small groups are especially effective for English learners because they feel more comfortable in these settings, and classmates help to clarify confusions and support their learning (Brock & Raphael, 2005).

Step 5: Locate Technology Resources. Teachers locate technology resources to use in the unit, including websites with author information and information on related topics, video versions of stories for students to view and compare to the book version, and audiotapes of stories to use at listening centers. Teachers also plan how they'll use computers and software programs for writing and creating projects.

Step 6: Plan for Assessment. Teachers plan how they'll monitor students' work during the unit and evaluate students' learning at the end of the unit. They provide opportunities for students to create standards-based projects rather than paper-and-pencil tests. Students usually choose the projects from a list of suggestions, and they often get involved in the assessment process when they self-assess their work and what they've learned. Students keep all work, reading logs, reading materials, and related materials in unit folders, which makes the unit management easier for both teachers and students. Teachers also plan ways to monitor students' work at centers. Figure 14–2 shows a centers checklist prepared in booklet form for a first grade unit on *The Mitten* (Brett, 2009). Students color the mitten on each page when they complete work at that center.

Teachers also plan ways to document students' learning and to assign grades. Many teachers use assignment checklists that they develop with students at the beginning of the unit. Students keep track of their work during the unit and sometimes negotiate to change the sheet as the unit evolves. They keep the checklists in unit folders, and they mark off each item as it's completed. At the end of the unit, students turn in their completed assignment checklist with their unit folders. Figure 14–3 shows an assignment checklist for an upper grade unit on *The Giver* (Lowry, 2006b), a story about a "perfect" community that isn't. Although this list doesn't include every activity students are involved in, it shows the assignments that the teacher holds them accountable for.

FIGURE 14–2 An Assessment Booklet

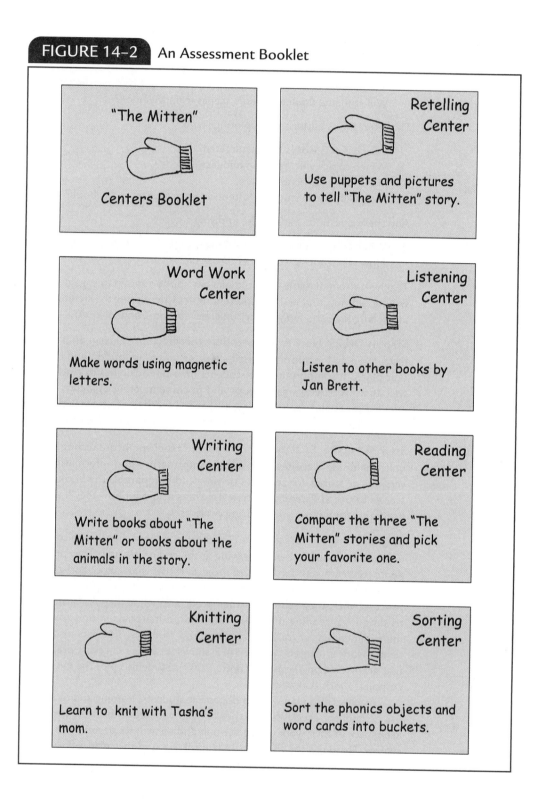

"The Mitten"

Centers Booklet

Retelling Center

Use puppets and pictures to tell "The Mitten" story.

Word Work Center

Make words using magnetic letters.

Listening Center

Listen to other books by Jan Brett.

Writing Center

Write books about "The Mitten" or books about the animals in the story.

Reading Center

Compare the three "The Mitten" stories and pick your favorite one.

Knitting Center

Learn to knit with Tasha's mom.

Sorting Center

Sort the phonics objects and word cards into buckets.

FIGURE 14–3	An Assessment Checklist

Student's
Check   Points

_____ 1. Read <u>The Giver</u>. (20)   _____

_____ 2. Write at least ten entries in your reading log. Use a double-entry   _____
            format with quotes and your connections. (20)

_____ 3. Participate in small-group grand conversations. (5)   _____

_____ 4. Create a story board. Chapter # _____ (5)   _____

_____ 5. Make an open-mind portrait of Jonas with four mind pages. (5)   _____

_____ 6. Write an essay about the theme of the book. (10)   _____

_____ 7. Choose and analyze ten words from the word wall according to prefix,   _____
            root word, and suffix. (5)

_____ 8. Read one book from the text set. Write a brief summary in your reading   _____
            log to compare what you learned about societies with <u>The Giver</u>. (5)

            Title _____

            Author _____

_____ 9. Make a square for the class story quilt. (5)   _____

_____ 10. Create a project and share it with the class. (20)   _____

            Project _____

            Date shared _____

                                                                                   Total _____

Students complete the checklist on the left side of the sheet and the teacher awards points—up to the number given in parentheses—on the right side and totals the number of points on the bottom of the page. Teachers often translate the total score into a letter grade.

Step 7: Create a Time Schedule. Teachers create a schedule that allows students sufficient time to move through the reading process and to complete the activities planned for the unit. Literature focus units require large blocks of time each day, at least 2 hours, in which students read, listen, talk, and write about the featured book.

A Primary Grade Unit on The Mitten

Jan Brett's *The Mitten* (2009), a cumulative picture-book story about a series of animals that climb into a mitten a little boy has dropped in the snow on a cold winter day, is the featured selection in literature focus units taught in many primary grade classrooms. A planning chart for a literature focus unit on *The Mitten* is shown on page 410. Teachers use the big-book version of *The Mitten* to introduce the unit and to examine Brett's innovative use of borders. Children retell the story with the teacher's collection of stuffed animals and puppets representing the animals in the story—a mole, a rabbit, a hedgehog, an owl, a badger, a fox, a bear, and a mouse. They read the story several

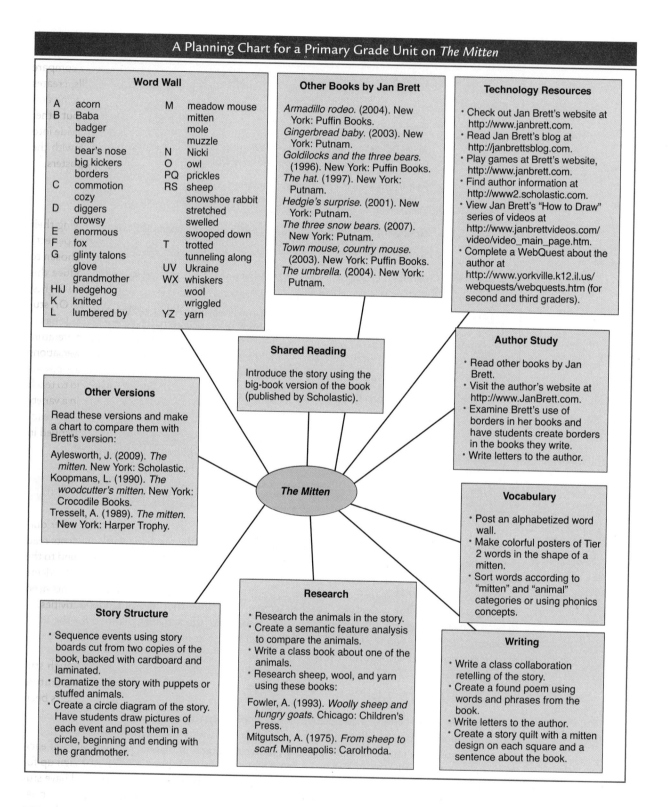

A Planning Chart for a Primary Grade Unit on *The Mitten*

Word Wall

A	acorn	M	meadow mouse
B	Baba		mitten
	badger		mole
	bear		muzzle
	bear's nose	N	Nicki
	big kickers	O	owl
	borders	PQ	prickles
C	commotion	RS	sheep
	cozy		snowshoe rabbit
D	diggers		stretched
	drowsy		swelled
E	enormous		swooped down
F	fox	T	trotted
G	glinty talons		tunneling along
	glove	UV	Ukraine
	grandmother	WX	whiskers
HIJ	hedgehog		wool
K	knitted		wriggled
L	lumbered by	YZ	yarn

Other Books by Jan Brett

Armadillo rodeo. (2004). New York: Puffin Books.
Gingerbread baby. (2003). New York: Putnam.
Goldilocks and the three bears. (1996). New York: Puffin Books.
The hat. (1997). New York: Putnam.
Hedgie's surprise. (2001). New York: Putnam.
The three snow bears. (2007). New York: Putnam.
Town mouse, country mouse. (2003). New York: Puffin Books.
The umbrella. (2004). New York: Putnam.

Technology Resources

- Check out Jan Brett's website at http://www.janbrett.com.
- Read Jan Brett's blog at http://janbrettsblog.com.
- Play games at Brett's website, http://www.janbrett.com.
- Find author information at http://www2.scholastic.com.
- View Jan Brett's "How to Draw" series of videos at http://www.janbrettvideos.com/video/video_main_page.htm.
- Complete a WebQuest about the author at http://www.yorkville.k12.il.us/webquests/webquests.htm (for second and third graders).

Shared Reading

Introduce the story using the big-book version of the book (published by Scholastic).

Author Study

- Read other books by Jan Brett.
- Visit the author's website at http://www.JanBrett.com.
- Examine Brett's use of borders in her books and have students create borders in the books they write.
- Write letters to the author.

Other Versions

Read these versions and make a chart to compare them with Brett's version:

Aylesworth, J. (2009). *The mitten*. New York: Scholastic.
Koopmans, L. (1990). *The woodcutter's mitten*. New York: Crocodile Books.
Tresselt, A. (1989). *The mitten*. New York: Harper Trophy.

The Mitten

Vocabulary

- Post an alphabetized word wall.
- Make colorful posters of Tier 2 words in the shape of a mitten.
- Sort words according to "mitten" and "animal" categories or using phonics concepts.

Story Structure

- Sequence events using story boards cut from two copies of the book, backed with cardboard and laminated.
- Dramatize the story with puppets or stuffed animals.
- Create a circle diagram of the story. Have students draw pictures of each event and post them in a circle, beginning and ending with the grandmother.

Research

- Research the animals in the story.
- Create a semantic feature analysis to compare the animals.
- Write a class book about one of the animals.
- Research sheep, wool, and yarn using these books:

Fowler, A. (1993). *Woolly sheep and hungry goats*. Chicago: Children's Press.
Mitgutsch, A. (1975). *From sheep to scarf*. Minneapolis: Carolrhoda.

Writing

- Write a class collaboration retelling of the story.
- Create a found poem using words and phrases from the book.
- Write letters to the author.
- Create a story quilt with a mitten design on each square and a sentence about the book.

times—in small groups with the teacher, with partners, and independently. The teacher also reads aloud several other versions of the story, such as *The Woodcutter's Mitten* (Koopmans, 1990), *The Mitten* (Aylesworth, 2009), and *The Mitten* (Tresselt, 1989), and children make a chart to compare the versions. The teacher presents minilessons on phonemic awareness and phonics skills, creates a word wall, and involves the children in word-study activities. They participate in sequencing and writing activities and learn about knitting from a parent volunteer. The teacher also sets out other books by Jan Brett and reads some of them aloud. As their application project, children divide into small groups to research one of the animals mentioned in the story. Fifth graders work with the primary grade students as they research the animals and share what they learn on large posters.

An Upper Grade Unit on The Giver

Upper grade students spend 3 or 4 weeks reading, responding to, exploring, and applying their understanding of Lois Lowry's Newbery Medal book, *The Giver* (2006b). Lowry creates a "perfect" community in which the people are secure but regulated. Jonas, the main character, is chosen to be a leader in the community, but he rebels against the society and escapes. To introduce this book, teachers might connect the book to the United States Constitution and the Bill of Rights, or discuss the problems in U.S. society today and ask students to create a perfect society. Or, students might think about how their lives would be different in a world without colors, like Jonas's.

Students can read the story together as a class, in small groups with the teacher or in literature circles, with buddies, or independently. They come together to discuss the story in grand conversations and deal with the complex issues presented in the book in both small groups and whole-class discussions. They also write in reading logs. Teachers identify strategies to model during reading and to teach in minilessons. Students write important words from the story on the word wall and engage in a variety of vocabulary activities. They also learn about the author and examine the story's structure. After reading, they do a choral reading, create a story quilt, compare U.S. society with the society described in the book, and create other projects. The planning chart for *The Giver* is shown on page 412.

ITERATURE CIRCLES

Students divide into small groups, and they read and respond to self-selected books together during literature circles (Daniels, 2001; Evans, 2001; Frank, Dixon, & Brandts, 2001). Students read independently, and then they come together to participate in grand conversations to respond to the book. Sometimes they also write in reading logs or create projects related to the book. For students to be successful in literature circles, a classroom community of learners is essential. Students need to develop responsibility, learn how to work in small groups, and participate in group activities.

How to Organize Literature Circles

Teachers move through a series of steps as they prepare for literature circles. Even though students assume leadership roles and make a number of decisions as they participate in literature circles, the success depends on the teacher's planning and the classroom community that's been created. Figure 14–4 outlines the steps in organizing literature circles.

Step 1: Choose Books. Teachers choose five to seven books and then collect six copies of each one. To introduce the books, teachers give a book talk about each one, and students sign up for the book they want to read. One way to do this is to set each book on the pen tray and have students sign their names on the whiteboard above the book they want to read. Or, teachers can set the books on a table and place a sign-up sheet beside each one. Students preview the books, and

A Planning Chart for an Upper Grade Unit on *The Giver*

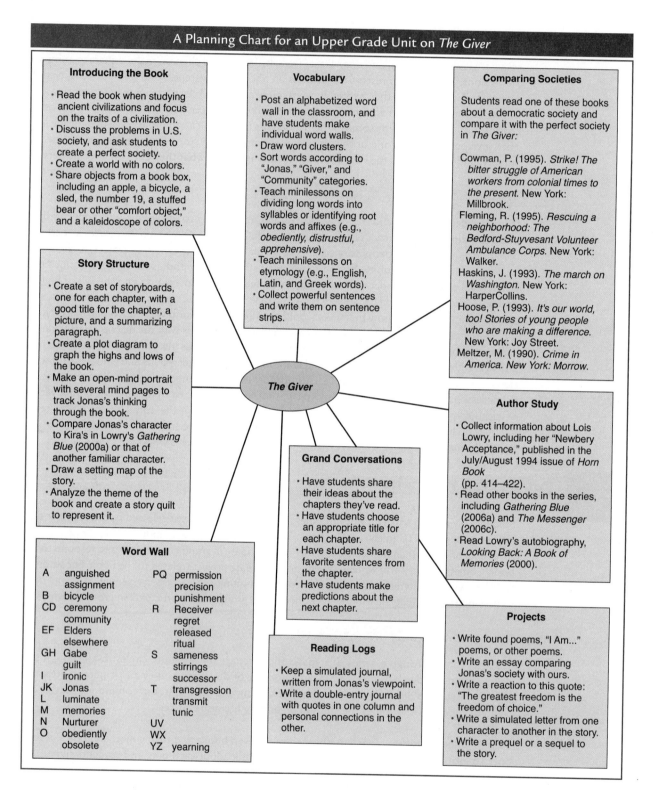

Introducing the Book

- Read the book when studying ancient civilizations and focus on the traits of a civilization.
- Discuss the problems in U.S. society, and ask students to create a perfect society.
- Create a world with no colors.
- Share objects from a book box, including an apple, a bicycle, a sled, the number 19, a stuffed bear or other "comfort object," and a kaleidoscope of colors.

Story Structure

- Create a set of storyboards, one for each chapter, with a good title for the chapter, a picture, and a summarizing paragraph.
- Create a plot diagram to graph the highs and lows of the book.
- Make an open-mind portrait with several mind pages to track Jonas's thinking through the book.
- Compare Jonas's character to Kira's in Lowry's *Gathering Blue* (2000a) or that of another familiar character.
- Draw a setting map of the story.
- Analyze the theme of the book and create a story quilt to represent it.

Vocabulary

- Post an alphabetized word wall in the classroom, and have students make individual word walls.
- Draw word clusters.
- Sort words according to "Jonas," "Giver," and "Community" categories.
- Teach minilessons on dividing long words into syllables or identifying root words and affixes (e.g., *obediently, distrustful, apprehensive*).
- Teach minilessons on etymology (e.g., English, Latin, and Greek words).
- Collect powerful sentences and write them on sentence strips.

Comparing Societies

Students read one of these books about a democratic society and compare it with the perfect society in *The Giver*:

Cowman, P. (1995). *Strike! The bitter struggle of American workers from colonial times to the present.* New York: Millbrook.

Fleming, R. (1995). *Rescuing a neighborhood: The Bedford-Stuyvesant Volunteer Ambulance Corps.* New York: Walker.

Haskins, J. (1993). *The march on Washington.* New York: HarperCollins.

Hoose, P. (1993). *It's our world, too! Stories of young people who are making a difference.* New York: Joy Street.

Meltzer, M. (1990). *Crime in America.* New York: Morrow.

Author Study

- Collect information about Lois Lowry, including her "Newbery Acceptance," published in the July/August 1994 issue of *Horn Book* (pp. 414–422).
- Read other books in the series, including *Gathering Blue* (2006a) and *The Messenger* (2006c).
- Read Lowry's autobiography, *Looking Back: A Book of Memories* (2000).

The Giver

Grand Conversations

- Have students share their ideas about the chapters they've read.
- Have students choose an appropriate title for each chapter.
- Have students share favorite sentences from the chapter.
- Have students make predictions about the next chapter.

Reading Logs

- Keep a simulated journal, written from Jonas's viewpoint.
- Write a double-entry journal with quotes in one column and personal connections in the other.

Projects

- Write found poems, "I Am..." poems, or other poems.
- Write an essay comparing Jonas's society with ours.
- Write a reaction to this quote: "The greatest freedom is the freedom of choice."
- Write a simulated letter from one character to another in the story.
- Write a prequel or a sequel to the story.

Word Wall

A	anguished
	assignment
B	bicycle
CD	ceremony
	community
EF	Elders
	elsewhere
GH	Gabe
	guilt
I	ironic
JK	Jonas
L	luminate
M	memories
N	Nurturer
O	obediently
	obsolete

PQ	permission
	precision
	punishment
R	Receiver
	regret
	released
	ritual
S	sameness
	stirrings
	successor
T	transgression
	transmit
	tunic
UV	
WX	
YZ	yearning

FIGURE 14–4   Steps in Organizing Literature Circles

1. Books
Teachers choose six or seven titles and collect five or six copies of each book for students to read.

2. Instructional Focus
Teachers identify the standards to address and the language arts strategies and skills related to the standards to teach.

3. Circles
Teachers organize the circles by giving book talks and having students sign up for the book they want to read.

4. Roles
Teachers decide on roles for group members and clearly explain the responsibilities of each role.

5. Schedule
Teachers set the schedule for literature circles and have students in each group decide how they'll schedule reading, discussion, and other work times.

6. Group Meetings
Teachers arrange group meetings so students can respond to and deepen their understanding of the book they're reading.

7. Assessment
Teachers plan ways to monitor students as they read and respond to the book in small groups.

---

then they select the one they want to read. Once in a while, students don't get their first-choice book, but they can always read it later during another literature circle or during reading workshop.

Traditionally, students read stories during literature circles, but teachers have found that students also enjoy reading nonfiction books (Heller, 2006/2007; Stien & Beed, 2004). Students read and discuss nonfiction much the same way they do stories, talking about what they liked about the book as well as the big ideas and what they learned. In fact, teachers report that literature circles are an effective way to increase students' interest in nonfiction.

Step 2: Identify Standards. Teachers identify the standards to address as students participate in literature circles. Sometimes the standard is specific, but at other times, teachers analyze the standards to decide which ones their students can meet through literature circles. Teachers plan the roles students will assume or plan questions for grand conversations. They also think about how they can monitor whether the standards are being met as they interact with the students in the literature circles.

Step 3: Organize the Circles. The books in the text set often vary in length and difficulty, but students aren't placed in groups according to their reading levels. Students choose the books they want to read and, as they preview the books, they consider how good a fit the book is, but that's not their only consideration: They often choose to read the book they find most interesting or the one their best friend has chosen. Students can usually manage whatever book they choose because of support and assistance from their group and through plain and simple determination. Once in a while, teachers counsel students to choose another book or provide an additional copy of the book to practice at home or to read with a tutor at school.

Step 4: Decide on Roles. Teachers decide how to structure the literature circles and what roles students will assume. Sometimes students choose their own group leader, or a natural leader emerges when they first get together; at other times, however, teachers identify the group leader. In addition to the leadership role, each group member assumes a role, which students also select during their first meeting. When teachers have students assume roles, they clearly outline the responsibilities and duties of each role. Teachers often spend a great deal of time at the beginning of the school year teaching students how to fulfill the responsibilities of each role.

Students assume roles to facilitate the group's understanding of the book they're reading: One student becomes the Passage Master, and other group members assume the roles of Word Wizard, Connector, Summarizer, Artist, and Investigator. When students are reading nonfiction books, some roles remain the same, but teachers and students create other roles that focus on the unique characteristics of nonfiction. Stien and Beed's (2004) students added a Time Line Traveler, who creates a time line of historical events, and a Fantastic Fact Finder, who shares interesting facts; and when students read biographies, an additional role was Vital Statistics Collector, who shares personal information about the person being profiled.

Some teachers have students use the same roles for each literature circle during the school year, but others find that after students learn to use each of the roles they can assume them flexibly as they read and think about the book. One way to do this is by "tabbing" (Stien & Beed, 2004): Teachers pass out packs of small self-stick notes, and students use them to make notes applying what they've learned about the different roles as they read. On some notes, students ask a question, choose an interesting passage to read aloud, note an interesting word to look up in the dictionary, or jot a personal, world, or text connection, for example.

Step 5: Set the Schedule. Teachers set a time schedule for the literature circle, and then each small group decides how to use the time to read and participate in grand conversations. During group meetings, teachers often participate in grand conversations and add their ideas to the discussion. They also check that students are completing reading assignments and fulfilling the responsibilities of their roles. While the teacher meets with one group, the other groups read independently or participate in other activities.

Step 6: Organize Group Meetings. Students alternate reading and discussing the book in grand conversations. At the beginning of the literature circle, students decide how often to have group meetings and how much of the book to read before each grand conversation. Sometimes teachers participate in the discussions; they behave as fellow readers who share joys and difficulties, insights and speculations. They also help students develop literary insights by providing information and asking thought-provoking questions.

Step 7: Plan for Assessment. The assessment focuses on students' comprehension of the book they've read and the quality of their group participation. The standards that teachers select guide the assessment. When teachers choose a standard that focuses on analyzing the theme of the story, for example, they listen to students' comments in grand conversations. They also plan how they'll assess students' participation in the literature circle. Most teachers move around the classroom, stopping to spend a few minutes each day with each group. Many teachers also use an assignment sheet to assess students' work.

EADING AND WRITING WORKSHOP

Nancie Atwell (2007) introduced reading workshop as an alternative to traditional reading instruction. In reading workshop, students read books that they choose themselves and respond to them through writing in reading logs and conferencing with teachers. This approach represents a change in what we believe about how children learn and how literature is used in classrooms. Atwell developed reading workshop with her middle school students, but it's been adapted and used successfully at every grade level, first through eighth. There are several versions of reading workshop, but they usually contain these components: reading, sharing, minilessons, and reading aloud to students (Serafini, 2001).

Writing workshop is similar to reading workshop, except that the focus is on writing. Students write on topics that they choose themselves, and they assume ownership of their writing (Atwell, 1998; Calkins, 1994; Fletcher & Portalupi, 2001). The classroom becomes a community of writers who write and share their writing, and a spirit of pride and acceptance is evident. Writing workshop is a 60- to 90-minute period scheduled each day. During this time, students are involved in these three components: writing, sharing, and minilessons. Sometimes a fourth activity, reading aloud to students, is added to writing workshop when it's not used in conjunction with reading workshop.

Establishing a Workshop Environment

Teachers begin to establish the workshop environment in their classroom from the first day of the school year by providing students with choices, time to read and write, and opportunities for response (Overmeyer, 2005). Through their interactions with students, the respect they show to students, and the way they model reading and writing, teachers establish the classroom as a community of learners.

Teachers develop a schedule for reading and writing workshop with time allocated for each component, or they alternate between the two types of workshops. They allot as much time as possible in their schedules for students to read and write. After developing the schedule, teachers post it in the classroom, talk about the activities, and discuss their expectations with students. Teachers teach the workshop procedures and continue to model them as students become comfortable with the routines (Kaufman, 2001). As students share what they're reading and writing at the end of workshop sessions, their enthusiasm grows.

Students keep two folders—one for reading workshop and one for writing workshop. In the reading workshop folder, students keep a list of books they've read, notes from minilessons, reading logs, and other materials. In the writing workshop folder, they keep the rough drafts and other papers related to their current writing project. They also keep a list of all compositions, topics for future pieces, and notes from minilessons.

How to Set Up a Reading Workshop

Teachers move through a series of steps as they set up their classroom, prepare students to work independently, and provide instruction. These steps are summarized in Figure 14–5.

Step 1: Collect Books for Reading Workshop. Students read all sorts of books during reading workshop, including stories, nonfiction books, and books of poetry. Most of their reading materials are selected from the classroom library, but students also bring books from home and borrow others from the public library, the school library, and classmates. Students read many award-winning books, but they also read series of popular books and technical books related to their hobbies and special interests. These books aren't necessarily the same ones that teachers use for literature focus units, but students often choose to reread books they read earlier in the school year or during the previous year in literature focus units and literature circles. Teachers need to have literally hundreds of books in their class libraries, including books written at a range of reading levels, in order to meet the needs of English learners, advanced readers, and struggling readers.

Teachers introduce students to the books in the classroom library so that they can more effectively choose books to read during reading workshop. The best way to preview books is using a very brief book talk to interest students in the book. In book talks, teachers tell students a little about the book, show the cover, and perhaps read the first paragraph or two (Prill, 1994/1995). Teachers also give book talks to introduce text sets of books, and students give book talks as they share books they've read with the class during the sharing part of reading workshop.

FIGURE 14–5	Steps in Setting Up Reading Workshop

1. Books

Teachers collect a wide variety of books at varying reading levels for students to read, including stories, nonfiction books, poems, and other resources, and place them on a special shelf in the classroom library.

2. Workshop Procedures

Teachers teach reading workshop procedures so that students know how to choose and respond to books, participate in conferences, and share books they've read.

3. Minilessons

Teachers present minilessons on topics drawn from standards as well as other strategies and skills that students are using but confusing.

4. Read-Aloud Books

Teachers choose read-aloud books to introduce students to new genres, authors, literary elements, or series stories that they might want to continue reading on their own.

5. Schedule

Teachers design a reading workshop schedule that incorporates reading, sharing, minilessons, and reading aloud to students.

6. Conferences

Teachers plan a schedule for conferences so that they can talk with students individually or in small groups about the books they're reading, and monitor their comprehension.

7. Assessment

Teachers monitor students' work and assess their reading with status-of-the-class charts, observations, and conferences.

Step 2: Teach Reading Workshop Procedures. Students need to learn how to choose books, write responses to books they're reading, share books they've finished reading, and conference with the teacher, as well as other procedures related to reading workshop. Some of these procedures need to be taught before students begin reading workshop, and others can be introduced and reviewed in minilessons during reading workshop.

Step 3: Identify Topics for Minilessons. Minilessons are an important part of reading workshop because the workshop approach is more than reading practice. Instruction is important, and minilessons are the teaching step. Teachers present minilessons on reading workshop procedures and on reading concepts, strategies, and skills. They identify topics for minilessons based on the standards they're addressing and students' observed needs. Teachers use examples from mentor texts they're reading aloud and books students are reading.

Step 4: Choose Books to Read Aloud to Students. When teachers include the reading-aloud component with reading workshop, they carefully choose the books they'll read. These books may be more difficult than those students can read independently, or they may be chosen to introduce students to a genre, an author, or a literary element. Sometimes teachers read aloud the first book in a series and then invite students to continue reading the sequels themselves. Teachers choose books to read aloud for a variety of specific instructional purposes.

Step 5: Design a Schedule for Reading Workshop. Teachers examine their daily schedule, consider the other language arts activities their students are involved in, decide how much time is available for reading workshop, and allocate time to each of the reading workshop components. Some teachers make reading and writing workshop their entire language arts program. They begin by reading aloud a book, chapter by chapter, to the class and talking about the book in a grand conversation for the first 30 minutes of reading workshop. During this time, teachers focus on modeling reading strategies and talking about elements of story structure. For the next 45 to 50 minutes, students read self-selected books independently. The teacher conferences with small groups of students as they read and presents minilessons to small groups of students as needed. Then students spend the next 15 to 20 minutes writing about their reading in reading logs. Sharing is held during the last 15 minutes, and students do book talks about books they've finished reading.

Other teachers coordinate reading workshop with literature focus units. For example, they decide to allocate one hour to reading workshop at the beginning of their language arts block. Students begin with 30 minutes of independent reading and then use the next 10 minutes to share books they've finished reading with the class. The last 20 minutes are used for a minilesson. Then students move into a literature focus unit for the next 90 minutes. In some classrooms, teachers alternate reading and writing workshop, either by month or by grading period.

Step 6: Plan for Conferencing. During reading workshop, students are reading independently, and teachers must find ways to monitor their progress. Many teachers begin each reading period by moving around the classroom to check that students have chosen books and are reading purposefully and then use the rest of the reading period for individual and small-group conferences. Teachers create conference schedules and meet with students on a regular basis, usually once a week, to talk about their reading and reading skills and strategies, listen to them read excerpts aloud, and make plans for the next book. Teachers take notes during these conferences in folders they keep for each student.

Step 7: Plan for Assessment. Teachers use a classroom chart to monitor students' work on a daily basis. At the beginning of reading workshop, students or the teacher records on a class chart what book students are reading and the activity they're currently involved in. Atwell (1998) calls this chart "the status of the class." Teachers can review students' progress and note who needs to meet with the teacher or receive additional attention. When students fill in the chart themselves, they develop responsibility for their actions and a stronger desire to accomplish tasks they set for themselves. To monitor primary grade students, teachers often use a pocket chart. They have children place a card in their pocket, indicating whether they're reading or responding during reading workshop or at which stage of the writing process they're working during writing workshop.

Teachers take time during reading workshop to observe students as they interact and work together in small groups. Researchers who have observed in reading and writing workshop classrooms report that some students, even as young as first graders, are excluded from group activities because of gender, ethnicity, or socioeconomic status (Henkin, 1995; Lensmire, 1992); the socialization patterns in classrooms seem to reflect society's patterns. Henkin recommends that teachers be alert to the possibility that boys might share books only with other boys or that some students won't find anyone willing to be their editing partner. If teachers see instances of discrimination in their classrooms, they should confront them directly and work to foster a classroom environment where students treat each other equitably.

How to Set Up a Writing Workshop

As teachers set up a writing workshop classroom, they collect writing supplies and materials for making books for the writing center. They set out different kinds of paper—some lined and some unlined—and various writing instruments, including pencils and red and blue pens. Bookmaking supplies include cardboard, contact paper, cloth, and wallpaper for book covers; stencils; stamps; art supplies; and a saddleback stapler and other equipment for binding books. Teachers also set up a bank of computers with word processing programs and printers or arrange for students to have access to the school's computer lab. Teachers encourage students to use the classroom library, and many times, students' writing grows out of favorite books they've read.

Teachers also think about the classroom arrangement. Students sit at desks or tables arranged in small groups as they write. The teacher circulates around the classroom, conferencing briefly with students, and the classroom atmosphere is free enough that students converse quietly with classmates and move around the classroom to collect materials at the writing center, assist classmates, or share ideas. There's space for students to meet for revising groups, and often a sign-up sheet for revising groups is posted in the classroom. A table is available for the teacher to meet with individual students or small groups for conferences, revising groups, proofreading, and minilessons.

In addition to collecting supplies and arranging the classroom, teachers need to prepare students for writing workshop and make plans for the instruction. Figure 14–6 summarizes the steps in setting up a writing workshop.

Step 1: Review the Writing Process. Teachers often begin writing workshop by reviewing the five stages of the writing process and taking students through one writing activity together.

Step 2: Teach Writing Workshop Procedures. Teachers need to explain how students will meet in groups to revise their writing, how to sign up for a conference with the teacher, how to

---

FIGURE 14–6   Steps in Setting Up Writing Workshop

1. Writing Process
Teachers review the stages of the writing process so that students understand how to develop and refine a composition.

2. Workshop Procedures
Teachers teach writing workshop procedures so that students know how to meet in revising groups, sign up for conferences, and publish their writing, for example. For students to be successful, it's essential that they know the procedures they'll be expected to use.

3. Minilessons
Teachers identify topics for minilessons to teach during writing workshop while anticipating that other topics will arise from strategies and skills that students are using but confusing.

4. Schedule
Teachers design a writing workshop schedule that includes writing, sharing, and teaching minilessons. Consistency is important so that students know what's expected of them and can develop a routine.

5. Conferences
Teachers plan how to conference in small groups and individually with students so they can monitor their work, provide feedback about their writing, and assess their progress.

6. Sharing
Teachers include opportunities for students to share their published writing with classmates.

7. Assessment
Teachers plan to monitor and assess students' work using status-of-the-class charts, conferences, writing-process checklists, and rubrics.

proofread, how to use the publishing center, and other procedures used in writing workshop (Ray & Laminack, 2001).

Step 3: Identify Topics for Minilessons. As with reading workshop, teachers teach minilessons during writing workshop related to the standards they've identified, and other topics for minilessons come from teachers' observations of students as they write and the questions students ask. Teachers also share information about authors and how they write. For students to think of themselves as writers, they need to know what writers do. Each year, more authors write autobiographies. Tomie dePaola, for example, has written a popular series of autobiographical picture-book stories for young children, including *For the Duration: The War Years* (2009), and Lois Lowry has written *Looking Back: A Book of Memories* (2000). Each chapter focuses on a memory prompted by a photo; this is a format students can imitate when they write autobiographies. A number of well-known authors and illustrators are profiled in the Meet the Author series published by Richard C. Owen, including *Can You Imagine*, by Patricia McKissack (1997), *If You Give an Author a Pencil*, by Laura Numeroff (2003), *From Paper Airplanes to Outer Space*, by Seymour Simon (2000), and *Firetalking*, by Patricia Polacco (1994). Students like these picture-book autobiographies because the authors come to life through the color photographs on each page. These books can be read aloud to primary students, and older students can read them independently. Video productions about authors and illustrators are also available. For example, in the 27-minute DVD *Eric Carle: Picture Writer* (2008), Eric Carle demonstrates how he uses paint and collage to create the illustrations for his popular picture books.

Step 4: Design a Writing Workshop Schedule. Teachers decide how to organize their daily schedule and what portion of the language arts block to allocate to reading and writing workshop. Some teachers make reading and writing workshop the focus of their language arts program. During the writing workshop portion, students move through the writing process as they write on self-selected topics for 45 or 50 minutes. The teacher meets with small groups of students or with individual students as they draft, revise, and edit their compositions during this writing time. Next, teachers use a 15- to 30-minute block of time during which they present minilessons on writing workshop procedures and writing strategies to the whole class, small groups of students, or individual students as needed. Sharing is held during the last 15 minutes, and students read their finished compositions aloud to classmates, often sitting in the author's chair. Other teachers coordinate writing workshop with literature focus units or literature circles. For example, they may allocate the last hour of their language arts block for reading and writing workshop, and alternate reading workshop and writing workshop by month or by grading period.

Step 5: Plan for Conferencing. Teachers conference with students as they write (Calkins, Hartman, & White, 2005). Many teachers prefer moving around the classroom to meet with students rather than having the students come to a table to meet with them because too often, a line forms as students wait to meet with the teacher, and students lose precious writing time. Some teachers move around the classroom in a regular pattern, meeting with one-fifth of the students each day. In this way, they can talk with every student during the week.

Other teachers spend the first 15 to 20 minutes of writing workshop stopping briefly to check on 10 or more students each day. Many use a zigzag pattern to get to all parts of the classroom each day. These teachers often kneel down beside students, sit on the edge of students' desks, or carry their own stool from desk to desk. During the 1- or 2-minute conferences, teachers ask students what they're writing, listen to students read a paragraph or two, and then ask what they plan to do next. Then these teachers use the remaining time during the workshop to conference more formally with students who are revising and editing their drafts. Teachers ask questions and make comments to identify strengths and discover possibilities. Some teachers like to read the pieces

FIGURE 14–7   A Status-of-the-Class Chart

Names	Dates 10/21	10/22	10/23	10/24	10/25	10/28	10/29	10/30
Antonio	4 5	5	5	6	7	8	8	8 9
Bella	2	2	2 3	2	2	4	5	6
Charles	8 9 1	3 1	1	2	2 3	4	5	6 7
Dina	6	6	6	7 8	8	9 1	1	2 3
Dustin	7 8	8	8	8	8	8	9 1	1
Eddie	2 3	2	2 4	5 6	8	9 1	1 2	2 3
Elizabeth	7	6	7	8	8	8	9	1 2
Elsa	2	3	4 5	5 6	6 7	8	8	9 1

Code:

1 = Prewrite   4 = Writing Group   7 = Conference

2 = Draft   5 = Revise   8 = Make Final Copy

3 = Conference   6 = Edit   9 = Publish

themselves, but others prefer to listen to students read their papers aloud. As they interact with students, teachers model the kinds of responses that students are learning to give to each other.

Step 6: Include Sharing. For the last 10 to 15 minutes of the workshop, students gather together as a class to share their new publications. Younger students often sit in a circle or gather together on a rug for sharing time, and students sit in the author's chair to read their compositions. Afterward, classmates clap and offer compliments.

Step 7: Plan for Assessment. Teachers monitor students' progress from day to day with a status-of-the-class chart; an excerpt from a fifth grade chart is shown in Figure 14–7. Teachers can also use the chart to award weekly effort grades, to have students request a conference with the teacher, or to have students announce that they're ready to share their writing. Many teachers have students use checklists to track their progress through the stages of the writing process, and they use rubrics to assess the quality of students' published compositions.

HEMATIC UNITS

Thematic units are interdisciplinary units that integrate reading and writing with social studies, science, and other curricular areas (Kucer, Silva, & Delgado-Larocco, 1995). Students take part in planning the thematic units and identifying some of the questions they want to explore and activities that interest them (Lindquist & Selwyn, 2000). They're involved in authentic and meaningful learning activities, not simply reading chapters in content-area textbooks in order to answer the questions at the end of the chapter. Textbooks might be used as a resource, but only as one of many available resources. Students explore topics that interest them and research answers to questions they've posed and are genuinely interested in answering. They share their learning at the end of the unit and are assessed on what they've learned as well as on the processes they used in learning and working in the classroom.

How to Develop a Thematic Unit

To begin planning a thematic unit, teachers choose the general topic and then identify three or four big ideas that they want to develop through the unit. The goal of a thematic unit is not to teach a collection of facts, but to help students grapple with several big understandings (Tunnell & Ammon, 1993). Next, teachers identify the resources that they have available for the unit and develop their teaching plan. Figure 14–8 summarizes the steps in developing a thematic unit.

Step 1: Identify Standards. Teachers identify the language arts standards they'll address and plan minilessons to teach strategies, expository text structures, report writing, and interviewing techniques. Minilessons are taught so that students can apply what they're learning in unit activities.

Step 2: Collect a Text Set. Teachers collect stories, poems, nonfiction books, magazines, and reference books for the text set related to the unit. The text set is placed in the special area in the classroom library. Teachers identify some books to read aloud, and some for students to read independently. These materials can also be used for minilessons and as models for writing projects.

FIGURE 14–8   Steps in Developing a Thematic Unit

1. Standards
Teachers identify language arts standards and decide how they'll address them in the unit.

2. Text Set
Teachers collect a text set of books to use in the unit. They set the books out on a special shelf in the classroom library.

3. Textbooks
Teachers coordinate content-area textbook readings with other activities in the unit.

4. Technology Resources
Teachers locate WebQuests, other technology resources, and digital tools; then they plan ways to integrate them into the unit.

5. Word Walls
Teachers identify potential words for the word wall and activities to teach those words.

6. Learning Logs
Teachers plan how students will use learning logs during the unit.

7. Differentiation
Teachers devise ways to differentiate instruction so that all students can be successful.

8. Projects
Teachers brainstorm possible oral, written, and visual projects students can create to apply their learning, but usually allow students some choice in which projects they develop.

9. Assessment
Teachers plan ways to monitor and assess students' learning with assignment checklists, rubrics, and other assessment tools.

Step 3: Coordinate Content-Area Textbook Readings. Teachers review the chapters in content-area textbooks related to the unit and identify the big ideas and technical vocabulary presented in the chapters. Next, they decide how to coordinate the textbook chapters and related resource materials with the unit. Sometimes, for example, students divide into small groups and each group reads one section of the chapter about one big idea and presents the information to the class, or students read the chapter as a review at the end of the unit.

Step 4: Locate Technology Resources. Teachers locate the CDs, DVDs, WebQuests, charts, maps, models, and other displays to use during the unit. Students complete WebQuests and explore websites to develop background knowledge at the beginning of the unit, and they use other materials to highlight the big ideas. To learn more about WebQuests, check the Digital Classroom feature below.

Step 5: Identify Words for the Word Wall. Teachers preview books in the text set and chapters in content-area textbooks to identify potential words for the word wall. This list is useful in planning vocabulary activities, but teachers don't just copy their word lists on the classroom word wall: Students and the teacher develop the word wall together as they participate in unit activities.

DIGITAL CLASSROOM

WebQuests

WebQuests are inquiry-oriented online projects that enhance students' learning by involving them in meaningful tasks. These projects foster students' ability to use the Internet to search and retrieve information from websites and understand multimodal presentations (Ikpeze & Boyd, 2007). Too often, students waste time searching for online resources, but in WebQuests, the resources are bookmarked so students can locate them easily. Bernie Dodge of San Diego State University invented these online inquiry projects in 1995; his website at http://webquest.org provides useful information about locating teacher-made WebQuests and creating your own.

WebQuests have these components:

▶ **Introduction**

An engaging scenario is presented with background information and descriptions of the roles that students will assume, such as botanist, superhero, or archaeologist.

▶ **Task**

The task explains the activity that students will complete, including open-ended questions to answer. Possible activities include making brochures or maps, writing newspaper articles or letters, and creating board games or video diaries.

▶ **Process**

The process describes the steps students will follow to complete the task.

▶ **Resources**

Bookmarked websites plus any other needed materials are listed.

▶ **Evaluation**

A rubric is provided for students to self-assess their work. Teachers also use it to assess students' work.

▶ **Conclusion**

Opportunities are presented for students to share their experience, reflect on learning, and pursue extensions.

WebQuests should include these components, and resource links must be active, or teachers need to replace them.

Teachers have created hundreds of WebQuests on a wide range of literature, social studies, and science topics that are available online. For example, in one WebQuest, students who are studying ancient Egypt travel back to 1250 B.C. to find King Tut's burial mask and decode the message hidden inside it. Other WebQuest topics include biomes, voting, polygons, World War II, and hurricanes.

Step 6: Consider How to Use Learning Logs. Teachers plan for students to keep learning logs in which they take notes, write questions, make observations, clarify their thinking, and write reactions to what they're learning during thematic units.

Step 7: Plan for Differentiation. Teachers think about how they'll differentiate instruction by planning for instruction, brainstorming a variety of oral, written, and visual activities, and considering grouping patterns.

Step 8: Brainstorm Possible Projects. Teachers think about projects students may choose to develop to apply and personalize their learning. This advance planning makes it possible for teachers to collect needed supplies and to have suggestions ready to offer to students who need assistance in choosing a project. Effective projects often integrate oral, written, and visual language.

Step 9: Plan for Assessment. Teachers consider how they'll monitor and assess students' learning. In this way, they can explain at the beginning of the thematic unit how students will be assessed, and they can check that their assessment will emphasize students' learning of the big ideas. Figure 14–9 shows an assignment checklist for a fourth grade unit about flight.

Using Content-Area Textbooks

Content-area textbooks are often difficult for students to read—more difficult, in fact, than many nonfiction books. One reason textbooks are difficult is that they mention many topics briefly without developing any of them. A second reason is that content-area textbooks are read differently than stories. Teachers need to show students how to approach content-area textbooks and teach them how to use specific expository-text reading strategies and procedures to make comprehension easier.

FIGURE 14–9   An Assessment Checklist

	Excellent	Good	Fair	Poor
1. Make a K-W-L chart on flight.	___	___	___	___
2. Read five books on flight and write a note card on each one.	___	___	___	___
3. Write 10 pages in your learning log.	___	___	___	___
4. Make a word wall on flight with 50 words.	___	___	___	___
5. Make a cluster about birds.	___	___	___	___
6. Make a time line about flight.	___	___	___	___
7. Write a compare-contrast essay on birds and airplanes.	___	___	___	___

_____ Prewriting
_____ Drafting
_____ Revising
_____ Editing
_____ Publishing

8. Make a report poster on flight. Choose four ways to share information.	___	___	___	___

_____ report   _____ diagram   _____ photo
_____ poem   _____ picture   _____ quote
_____ story   _____ Internet   _____ other

Teachers can make content-area textbooks more readable and show students ways to remember what they've read (Robb, 2003). Some activities are used before reading and others afterward: The before-reading activities help students activate prior knowledge, set purposes for reading, or build background knowledge; the after-reading activities help them identify and remember big ideas and details; and other activities are used when students want to locate specific information. These activities make content-area textbooks more readable:

PREVIEW. Teachers introduce the reading assignment by asking students to note main headings in the chapter and then skim or rapidly read the chapter to get a general idea about the topics covered.

ANTICIPATION GUIDES. Teachers present a set of true and false statements on the topic students will read about; students agree or disagree with each statement and then read the assignment to see if they were right (Head & Readence, 1992). The Step-by-Step feature below describes the procedure, and Figure 14–10 presents an eighth grade anticipation guide for a textbook reading assignment about atomic structure that's part of a chemistry unit on atomic structure, bonding concepts, and element placement in the periodic table.

EXCLUSION BRAINSTORMING. Teachers distribute a list of words, most of which are related to the key concepts to be presented in the reading assignment. They ask students to circle the words that are related to a key concept and then read the assignment to see if they circled the right words (Johns, Van Leirsburg, & Davis, 1994).

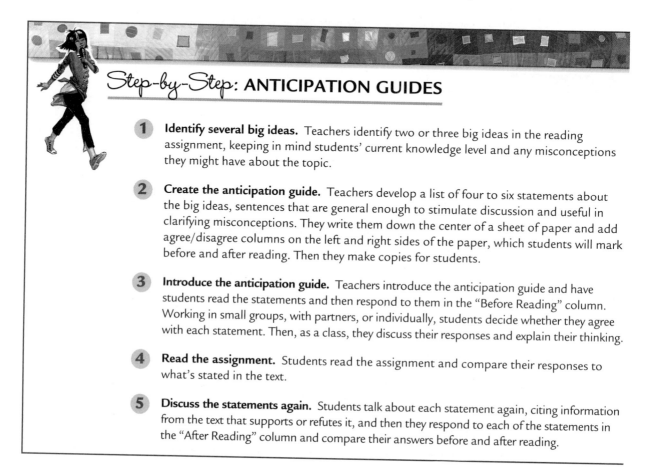

Step-by-Step: ANTICIPATION GUIDES

1 **Identify several big ideas.** Teachers identify two or three big ideas in the reading assignment, keeping in mind students' current knowledge level and any misconceptions they might have about the topic.

2 **Create the anticipation guide.** Teachers develop a list of four to six statements about the big ideas, sentences that are general enough to stimulate discussion and useful in clarifying misconceptions. They write them down the center of a sheet of paper and add agree/disagree columns on the left and right sides of the paper, which students will mark before and after reading. Then they make copies for students.

3 **Introduce the anticipation guide.** Teachers introduce the anticipation guide and have students read the statements and then respond to them in the "Before Reading" column. Working in small groups, with partners, or individually, students decide whether they agree with each statement. Then, as a class, they discuss their responses and explain their thinking.

4 **Read the assignment.** Students read the assignment and compare their responses to what's stated in the text.

5 **Discuss the statements again.** Students talk about each statement again, citing information from the text that supports or refutes it, and then they respond to each of the statements in the "After Reading" column and compare their answers before and after reading.

| FIGURE 14-10 | Anticipation Guide for a Chemistry Lesson |

Before Reading		Atomic Structure	After Reading	
Agree	Disagree		Agree	Disagree
✓		1. Electrons occupy an electron cloud surrounding the nucleus in different energy levels.	✓	
✓		2. The electrons are stationary; they do not move around the electron cloud.		✓
	✓	3. Each energy level in the electron cloud holds four electrons.		✓
✓		4. The electrons in the outer energy level are called valance electrons.	✓	
	✓	5. When the outer energy level is not filled, the atom can gain or lose electrons.	✓	

GRAPHIC ORGANIZERS. Teachers distribute a cluster, map, or other graphic organizer with the big ideas marked, and students complete it by adding details after reading each section.

NOTE TAKING. Students take notes because they can't remember everything the teacher says during a presentation or everything they read in a textbook chapter. They focus on the big ideas, writing phrases, inventing their own system of abbreviations, and adding pictures and diagrams when it's more effective to present information visually. The two hardest parts in note taking are deciding what to write down and how to record the information. Students can complete graphic organizers, draw clusters, write in learning logs, or create outlines. Teachers teach note-taking techniques and provide opportunities for guided practice during oral presentations and textbook reading assignments so that students learn how to identify the big ideas before they're expected to take notes on their own.

SKIMMING AND SCANNING. Skimming and scanning are two fast reading strategies, and the terms are often incorrectly used interchangeably. Students use skimming to preview and review texts. They don't read the entire text word by word; instead, they read to identify the big ideas or get the gist of the text. They focus on the titles, headings, illustrations, charts, and summaries, and often read the first and last sentences in paragraphs. In contrast, students use scanning to locate specific information to complete a task, find the answer to a question, or make a decision. They move their eyes quickly down a page, searching for specific words or phrases. As in skimming, students notice headings, boldface type, boxes, margin notes, and other features to find the information they're searching for. They also use scanning to locate words in dictionaries and encyclopedia entries, to use an index, to find phone numbers in telephone directories, and to browse TV guides and bus schedules.

A Fourth Grade Unit on Flight

Fourth graders and other middle grade students connect science and language arts in a thematic unit on flight. To begin the unit, students and the teacher create a K-W-L chart and students write facts about how birds and airplanes fly, space flight, and famous aviators. They also identify questions they'll investigate during the unit. The teacher provides a text set of stories, poems, and nonfiction books about flight for the students to read. Some of the books are on tape or CD, which students can listen to at the listening center. Students list important words about flight on a word wall and participate in a variety of vocabulary activities. They research flight-related questions using books and Internet resources and through interviews with a pilot, flight attendant, astronaut, or other knowledgeable person, and then they present oral reports or prepare multigenre projects to share what they learn. A planning chart for a thematic unit on flight is shown on page 426.

A Planning Chart for a Middle Grade Unit on Flight

Text Set

Borden, L. (1998). *Good-bye, Charles Lindbergh: Based on a true story*. New York: McElderry.

Busby, P. (2003). *First to fly: How Wilbur and Orville Wright invented the airplane*. New York: Crown.

Carson, M. K. (2003). *The Wright brothers for kids*. Chicago: Chicago Review Press.

Johnston, S. A. (1995). *Raptor rescue: An eagle flies free*. New York: Dutton.

Kalman, B. (1998). *How birds fly*. New York: Crabtree.

Lopez, D. (1995). *Flight*. New York: Time-Life.

Maynard, C. (1995). *Airplane*. London: Dorling Kindersley.

Priceman, M. (2005). *Hot air: The (mostly) true story of the first hot-air balloon ride*. New York: Atheneum.

Ryan, P. M. (1999). *Amelia and Eleanor go for a ride: Based on a true story*. New York: Scholastic.

Sandler, M. W. (2004). *Flying over the USA*. New York: Oxford University Press.

Weiss, H. (1995). *Strange and wonderful aircraft*. Boston: Houghton Mifflin.

Yolen, J. (2003). *My brothers' flying machine: Wilbur, Orville, and me*. Boston: Little, Brown.

Word Wall

AB	airflow	G	glide
	airfoil	H	helicopters
	airplane	I	instruments
	airport	JK	jet stream
	altitude	L	landing
	Amelia Earhart		lift
	astronauts	MNO	migration
	aviation	PQ	passengers
	aviator		pilot
C	Charles Lindbergh		pitch
	Chuck Yeager		propeller
	controls	RS	roll
D	drag		rudder
E	engine	TUV	takeoff
F	FAA		thrust
	flapping wings		tilt
	flight attendant	WX	weight
	flightless		wing
	flyways		Wright brothers
	fuselage	YZ	yaw

Graphics

- Make a time line of the history of flight.
- Draw diagrams of birds' wings or airplanes.
- Make a Venn diagram comparing birds and airplanes.
- Make a data chart with information about animals that fly, including birds, bats, insects, and fish.

Learning Logs

- Have students keep learning logs with notes, drawings, maps, diagrams, vocabulary words, and other information.

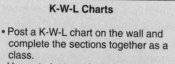

Flight

Technology

- Have students consult yahooligans.com or another search engine to learn about flight.
- Have students participate in a Skype interview with a pilot, astronaut, or other person involved with flight.
- View the DVD *Fly Away Home*, the story of a girl and her dad who try to teach geese to fly.

K-W-L Charts

- Post a K-W-L chart on the wall and complete the sections together as a class.
- Have students make individual flip book K-W-L charts.

Multigenre Projects

- Prepare a multigenre project about flight.
- Prepare a multigenre biography of an aviator, such as Chuck Yeager, Charles Lindbergh, or Amelia Earhart.

Oral Presentations

- Have students present oral reports or podcasts about an airplane, bird, or aviator.
- Have students do oral presentations of poems from Fleischman, P. (1985). *I am Phoenix: Poems for two voices*. New York: HarperCollins.

Vocabulary

- Post words on an alphabetized word wall hanging in the classroom.
- Use words on the word wall for a minilesson on dividing words into syllables.
- Make word clusters and hang them on airplane and bird mobiles.

Interviews

- Interview a pilot, flight attendant, astronaut, zookeeper, ornithologist, or someone else knowledgeable about flight.
- Participate in an online interview of a pilot or astronaut.

SUMMING UP

Designing language arts instruction that reflects the theory and research about language and how students learn is an important responsibility. Teachers develop literature focus units featuring high-quality, grade-appropriate books, and they organize for literature circles so that students can read and respond to self-selected books in small groups. They set up reading and writing workshop with plenty of time for reading and writing and teach minilessons on procedures, strategies, and other topics. Teachers also develop thematic units to teach social studies and science topics; sometimes they use content-area textbooks as one resource, but they should never be the only books that students read. Not surprisingly, teachers adapt and combine the patterns of practice to fit the needs of their students and their curriculum.

MyEducationLab™

Go to the topics Reading, Writing, Speaking and Listening, and Visual Literacy in the MyEducationLab (http://www.myeducationlab.com) for *Language Arts: Patterns of Practice*, where you can:

- Find learning outcomes for Reading, Writing, Speaking and Listening, and Visual Literacy, along with the national standards that connect to these outcomes.
- Complete Assignments and Activities that can help you more deeply understand the chapter content.
- Apply and practice your understanding of the core teaching skills identified in the chapter with the Building Teaching Skills and Dispositions learning units.
- Examine challenging situations and cases presented in the IRIS Center Resources.
- Use the Lesson Plan Builder Activities to practice lesson planning and integrating national and state standards into your planning.
- Check your comprehension of the content covered in the chapter with the Study Plan. Here you will be able to take a chapter quiz, receive feedback on your answers, and then access Review, Practice, and Enrichment activities to enhance your understanding of chapter content.

On the **MyEducationLab** for this course, you'll also be able to:

- **A+RISE** Go to the topic A+RISE, an innovative and interactive database of strategies that differentiate instruction across the language arts and provide particular insight into research-based methods to meet the needs of English learners.
- Explore the topic Literacy Portraits—yearlong case studies of second graders, complete with student artifacts, teacher commentary, and student and teacher interviews, tracking the month-by-month language arts growth of five students.
- Gain practice with the Grammar Tutorial, online guided instruction to improve your own ability with grammar.

References

Ackerman, K. (12003). *Song and dance man*. New York: Knopf.

Ada, A. F. (2001). *With love, Little Red Hen*. New York: Atheneum.

Adams, M. J. (1990). *Beginning to read: Thinking and learning about print*. Cambridge, MA: MIT Press.

Akhavan, N. (2006). *Help! My kids don't all speak English: How to set up a language workshop in your linguistically diverse classroom*. Portsmouth, NH: Heinemann.

Alarcón, F. X. (2006). *Poems to dream together/poemas para soñar juntos*. New York: Greenwillow.

Aldrin, B. (2009). *Look at the stars*. New York: Putnam.

Allard, H. (1985). *Miss Nelson is missing!* New York: Sandpiper.

Allen, C. A. (2001). *The multigenre research paper: Voice, passion, and discovery in grades 4–6*. Portsmouth, NH: Heinemann.

Allen, J. (1999). *Words, words, words*. Portsmouth, NH: Heinemann.

Allington, R. L. (2006). *What really matters for struggling readers: Designing research-based programs* (2nd ed.). Boston: Allyn & Bacon/Pearson.

Allington, R. L. (2009). *What really matters in Response to Intervention*. Boston: Allyn & Bacon/Pearson.

American Poetry and Literacy Project. (2006). *How to eat a poem: A smorgasbord of tasty and delicious poems for young readers*. Mineola, NY: Dover.

Anderson, T. H., & Armbruster, B. B. (1984). Studying. In P. D. Pearson, R. Barr, M. L. Kamil, & P. Mosenthal (Eds.), *Handbook of reading research* (pp. 657–679). New York: Longman.

Applebee, A. N. (1978). *The child's concept of story: Ages 2 to 17*. Chicago: University of Chicago Press.

Argueta, J. (2009). *Sopa de frijoles/bean soup*. Toronto, ON: Groundwood Books.

Asch, F. (2000). *The sun is my favorite star*. New York: Scholastic.

Ashton-Warner, S. (1965). *Teacher*. New York: Simon & Schuster.

Atwell, N. (1998). *In the middle: New understandings about writing, reading, and learning*. Portsmouth, NH: Heinemann/Boynton/Cook.

Atwell, N. (2007). *The reading zone: How to help kids become skilled, passionate, habitual, critical readers*. New York: Scholastic.

Au, K. H. (1992). Constructing the theme of a story. *Language Arts, 69*, 106–111.

Avi. (1995). *Poppy*. New York: Orchard Books.

Avi. (2002). *Crispin: The cross of lead*. New York: Hyperion Books.

Aylesworth, J. (1992). *Old black fly*. New York: Henry Holt.

Aylesworth, J. (2009). *The mitten*. New York: Scholastic.

Babbitt, N. (2007). *Tuck everlasting*. New York: Square Fish Books.

Ball, E., & Blachman, B. (1991). Does phoneme segmentation training in kindergarten make a difference in early word recognition and developmental spelling? *Reading Research Quarterly, 26*, 49–86.

Bandura, A. (1997). *Self-efficacy: The exercise of control*. New York: W. H. Freeman.

Bang, M. (2000). *Picture this: How pictures work*. San Francisco: Chronicle Books.

Barchers, S. I., & Pfeffinger, C. R. (2007). *Getting ready to read with readers theatre*. Portsmouth, NH: Teacher Ideas Press.

Barnes, D. (2008). Exploratory talk for learning. In N. Mercer & S. Hodgkinson (Eds.), *Exploring talk in school* (pp. 1–6). Thousand Oaks, CA: Sage.

Barnes, D., Morgan, K., & Weinhold, K. (Eds.). (1997). *Writing process revisited: Sharing our stories*. Urbana, IL: National Council of Teachers of English.

Barrentine, S. J. (1996). Engaging with reading through interactive read-alouds. *The Reading Teacher, 50*, 36–43.

Barone, D. M., & Morrow, L. M. (2003). *Literacy and young children: Research-based practices*. New York: Guilford Press.

Bates, K. (2003). *America the Beautiful*. New York: Putnam.

Baugh, A. C., & Cable, T. (2002). *The history of the English language*. Oxford, UK: Routledge.

Baumann, J. F., Font, G., Edwards, E. C., & Boland, E. (2005). Strategies for teaching middle-grade students to use word-part and context clues to expand reading vocabulary. In E. Hiebert & M. L. Kamil (Eds.), Teaching and learning vocabulary: Bringing research to practice (pp. 179–205). Mahwah, NJ: Erlbaum.

Baumann, J. F., & Kame'enui, E. J. (Eds.). (2004). *Vocabulary instruction: Research to practice*. New York: Guilford Press.

Bausum, A. (2009). *Our country's presidents*. Washington, DC: National Geographic.

Bayer, J. (1992). *A my name is Alice*. New York: Dial Books.

Bear, D. R., Invernizzi, M., Templeton, S., & Johnston, F. (2008). *Words their way: Word study for phonics, vocabulary, and spelling instruction* (4th ed.). Upper Saddle River, NJ: Merrill/Prentice Hall.

Beauchat, K. A., Blamey, K. L., & Walpole, S. (2009). Building preschool children's language and literacy one storybook at a time. *The Reading Teacher, 63,* 26–39.

Beck, I. L., McKeown, M. G., & Kucan, L. (2002). *Bringing words to life: Robust vocabulary instruction.* New York: Guilford Press.

Beers, K. (2001). Contextualizing grammar. *Voices From the Middle, 8*(3), 4.

Behler, J. L. (1999). *First field guide: Reptiles.* New York: Scholastic.

Bender, W. N., & Shores, C. (2007). *Response to Intervention: A practical guide for every teacher.* Thousand Oaks, CA: Corwin Press and the Council for Exceptional Children.

Bennett-Armistead, V. S., Duke, N. K., & Moses, A. M. (2005). *Literacy and the youngest learner: Best practices for educators of children from birth to 5.* New York: Scholastic.

Berne, J. I., & Clark, K. F. (2008). Focusing literature discussion groups on comprehension strategies. *The Reading Teacher, 62,* 74–79.

Berthoff, A. E. (1981). *The making of meaning.* Montclair, NJ: Boynton/Cook.

Blachowicz, C., & Fisher, P. (2006). *Teaching vocabulary in all classrooms* (3rd ed.). Upper Saddle River, NJ: Merrill/Prentice Hall.

Black, A., & Stave, A. M. (2007). *A comprehensive guide to readers theatre.* Newark, DE: International Reading Association.

Blanchard, J., & Moore, T. (2010). *The digital world of young children: Impact on emergent literacy.* Pearson Foundation. Retrieved from http://www.pearsonfoundation.org/downloads/EmergentLiteracy-WhitePaper.pdf

Blanton, W. E., Wood, K. D., & Moorman, G. B. (1990). The role of purpose in reading instruction. *The Reading Teacher, 43,* 486–493.

Block, C., Oakar, M., & Hurt, N. (2002). The expertise of literacy teachers: A continuum from preschool–grade 5. *Reading Research Quarterly, 37,* 178–206.

Bode, B. A. (1989). Dialogue journal writing. *The Reading Teacher, 42,* 568–571.

Bollard, J. K. (2006). *Scholastic children's thesaurus.* New York: Scholastic.

Boss, S., & Krauss, J. (2007). *Reinventing project-based learning: Your field guide to real-world projects in the digital age.* Eugene, OR: International Society for Technology in Education.

Boyd, M. P., & Galda, L. (2011). *Real talk in elementary classrooms: Effective oral language practice.* New York: Guilford Press.

Boyd-Batstone, P. (2004). Focused anecdotal records assessment: A tool for standards-based, authentic assessment. *The Reading Teacher, 58,* 230–239.

Braddock, R., Lloyd-Jones, R., & Schoer, L. (1963). *Research in written composition.* Champaign, IL: National Council of Teachers of English.

Brett, J. (1999). *Gingerbread baby.* New York: Putnam.

Brett, J. (2004). *The umbrella.* New York: Putnam.

Brett, J. (2009). *The mitten.* New York: Putnam.

Briggs, R. (1997). *The snowman.* New York: Random House.

Britton, J., Burgess, T., Martin, N., McLeod, A., & Rosen, H. (1975). *The development of writing abilities, 11–18.* London: Schools Council Publications.

Brock, C. H., & Raphael, T. E. (2005). *Windows to language, literacy, and culture.* Newark, DE: International Reading Association.

Bromley, K. D. (1996). *Webbing with literature: Creating story maps with children's books* (2nd ed.). Boston: Allyn & Bacon.

Brown, M. W. (1990). *The important book.* New York: HarperCollins.

Brownell, J. (2006). *Listening: Attitudes, principles, and skills.* Boston: Allyn & Bacon.

Bruchac, J. (2001). *The journal of Jesse Smoke: A Cherokee boy.* New York: Scholastic.

Bruner, J. S. (2004). *Toward a theory of instruction.* Cambridge, MA: Harvard University Press.

Bryan, A. (2003). *Beautiful blackbird.* New York: Atheneum.

Bunting, E. (1999). *Smoky night.* San Diego: Harcourt Brace.

Burke, J. (2002). *Tools for thought: Graphic organizers for your classroom.* Portsmouth, NH: Heinemann.

Burmark, L. (2002). *Visual literacy: Learn to see, see to learn.* Alexandria, VA: Association for Supervision and Curriculum Development.

Burns, S., Griffin, P., & Snow, C. E. (1999). *Starting out right: A guide to promoting children's reading success.* Washington, DC: National Academy Press.

Buss, K., & Karnowski, L. (2000). *Reading and writing literary genres.* Newark, DE: International Reading Association.

Butler, A., & Turbill, J. (1984). *Towards a reading-writing classroom.* Portsmouth, NH: Heinemann.

Byrd, R. (2003). *Leonardo: Beautiful dreamer.* New York: Dutton.

Cahnmann, M. (2006). Reading, living, and writing bilingual poetry as scholARTistry in the language arts classroom. *Language Arts, 83*(4), 341–351.

Cairney, T. (1990). Intertextuality: Infectious echoes from the past. *The Reading Teacher, 43,* 478–484.

Calkins, L. M. (1980). When children want to punctuate: Basic skills belong in context. *Language Arts, 57,* 567–573.

Calkins, L. M. (1994). *The art of teaching writing* (2nd ed.). Portsmouth, NH: Heinemann.

Calkins, L., Hartman, A., & White, Z. (2005). *One to one: The art of conferring with young writers.* Portsmouth, NH: Heinemann.

Calo, K. M. (2011). Comprehending, composing, and celebrating graphic poetry. *The Reading Teacher, 64,* 351–357.

Cambourne, B., & Turbill, J. (1987). *Coping with chaos.* Rozelle, NSW, Australia: Primary English Teaching Association.

Carle, E. (2001). *The very hungry caterpillar.* New York: Philomel.

Carle, E. (2008). *Eric Carle: Picture writer* (DVD). Amherst, MA: The Eric Carle Museum of Picture BookArt.

Carlo, M. S., August, D., McGlaughlin, B., Snow, C. E., Dressler, C., Lippman, D. N., Lively, T. J., & White, C. E. (2004). Closing the gap: Addressing the vocabulary needs of English-language learners in bilingual and mainstream classes. *Reading Research Quarterly, 39,* 188–215.

Carlson, L. M. (Ed.). (1998). *Sol a sol: Bilingual poems.* New York: Henry Holt.

Caserta-Henry, C. (1996). Reading buddies: A first-grade intervention program. *The Reading Teacher, 49,* 500–503.

Casey, K. (2006). *Literacy coaching: The essentials.* Portsmouth, NH: Heinemann.

Castek, J., Bevans-Mangelson, J., & Goldstone, B. (2006). Reading adventures online: Five ways to introduce the new literacies of the Internet through children's literature. *The Reading Teacher, 59,* 714–728.

Catrow, D. (2005). *We the kids: The Preamble to the Constitution of the United States.* New York: Puffin Books.

Caverly, D. C., & Orlando, V. P. (1991). Textbook study strategies. In D. C. Caverly & V. P. Orlando (Eds.), *Teaching reading and study strategies at the college level* (pp. 86–165). Newark, DE: International Reading Association.

Cazden, C. B. (2001). *Classroom discourse: The language of teaching and learning* (2nd ed.). Portsmouth, NH: Heinemann.

Chaikin, M. (2002). *Don't step on the sky: A handful of haiku.* New York: Henry Holt.

Chapman, V. G., & Sopko, D. (2003). Developing strategic use of combined-text trade books. *The Reading Teacher, 57,* 236–239.

Cheney, L. (2003). *A is for Abigail: An almanac of amazing American women.* New York: Simon & Schuster.

Cianciolo, P. J. (1997). *Picture books for children.* Chicago: American Library Association.

Cintorino, M. A. (1993). Getting together, getting along, getting to the business of teaching and learning. *English Journal, 82,* 23–32.

Clay, M. M. (1991). *Becoming literate: The construction of inner control.* Portsmouth, NH: Heinemann.

Cleary, B. (1990). *Muggie Maggie.* New York: Morrow.

Cleary, B. (1993). *Ralph the mouse.* New York: Morrow.

Cleary, B. (2000). *Dear Mr. Henshaw.* New York: HarperCollins.

Cleary, B. P. (2000). *Hairy, scary, ordinary: What is an adjective?* Minneapolis: Carolrhoda.

Cleary, L. M. (1993). Hobbes: "I press rewind through the pictures in my head." In S. Hudson-Ross, L. M. Cleary, & M. Casey (Eds.), *Children's voices: Children talk about literacy* (pp. 136–143). Portsmouth, NH: Heinemann.

Clymer, T. (1996). The utility of phonic generalizations in the primary grades. *The Reading Teacher, 50,* 182–187.

Cobb, R. (2006). *Tongue twisters to tangle your tongue.* London: Marion Boyars.

Cohle, D. M., & Towle, W. (2001). *Connecting reading and writing in the intermediate grades: A workshop approach.* Newark, DE: International Reading Association.

Coiro, J., Knobel, M., Lankshear, C., & Leu, D. (Eds.). (2008). *Handbook of research on new literacies.* New York: Erlbaum.

Cole, H. (1997). *Jack's garden.* New York: Greenwillow.

Cole, J. (1998). *The magic school bus in the rain forest.* New York: Scholastic.

Cole, J. (2001). *The magic school bus explores the senses.* New York: Scholastic.

Cole, J. (2002). *Ms. Frizzle's adventures: Medieval castle.* New York: Scholastic.

Cole, J. (2003). *Ms. Frizzle's adventures: Medieval castle.* New York: Scholastic.

Colfer, E. (2009). *Artemis Fowl.* New York: Hyperion Books.

Colfer, E., & Donkin, A. (2007). *Artemis Fowl: The graphic novel.* New York: Hyperion Books.

Common core state standards initiative. (2010). Retrieved from http://www.corestandards.org

Cooney, B. (1985). *Miss Rumphius.* New York: Puffin Books.

Cooper, J. D., Chard, D. J., & Kiger, N. C. (2006). *The struggling reader: Interventions that work.* New York: Scholastic.

Cordeiro, P., Giacobbe, M. E., & Cazden, C. (1983). Apostrophes, quotation marks, and periods: Learning punctuation in the first grade. *Language Arts, 60,* 323–332.

Courtney, A. M., & Abodeeb, T. L. (2005). Diagnostic-reflective portfolios. In S. J. Barrentine & S. M. Stokes (Eds.), *Reading assessment: Principles and practices for elementary teachers* (2nd ed., pp. 215–222). Newark, DE: International Reading Association.

Cowen, J. E. (2003). *A balanced approach to beginning reading instruction*. Newark, DE: International Reading Association.

Creech, S. (2001). *Love that dog*. New York: HarperCollins.

Creech, S. (2003). *Granny Torrelli makes soup*. New York: HarperCollins.

Crew, G. (1998). *Troy Thompson's excellent peotry [sic] book*. Victoria, Australia: Lothian.

Cronin, D. (2003). *Diary of a worm*. New York: HarperCollins.

Cronin, D. (2005). *Diary of a spider*. New York: HarperCollins.

Cronin, D. (2007). *Diary of a fly*. New York: HarperCollins.

Cronin, D. (2011). *Click, clack, moo: Cows that type*. New York: Simon & Schuster.

Culham, R. (2003). *6 + 1 traits of writing: The complete guide, grades 3 and up*. New York: Scholastic.

Cullinan, B., Scala, M. C., & Schroder, V. C. (1995). *Three voices: An invitation to poetry across the curriculum*. York, ME: Stenhouse.

Cummins, J. (1989). *Empowering minority students*. Sacramento: California Association for Bilingual Education.

Cunningham, A. E., & Stanovich, K. E. (1997). Early reading acquisition and its relation to reading experience and ability 10 years later. *Developmental Psychology, 33*, 934–945.

Cunningham, P. M. (2009). *Phonics they use: Words for reading and writing* (5th ed.). Boston: Pearson.

Cunningham, P. M., & Cunningham, J. W. (1992). Making words: Enhancing the invented spelling-decoding connection. *The Reading Teacher, 46,* 106–115.

Cushman, K. (1996a). *The ballad of Lucy Whipple*. New York: Clarion Books.

Cushman, K. (1996b). *The midwife's apprentice*. New York: HarperCollins.

Cushman, K. (2003). *Rodzina*. New York: Clarion Books.

Cushman, K. (2005). *Catherine, called Birdy*. New York: HarperCollins.

Dahl, R. (1998). *The BFG*. New York: Puffin Books.

Dahl, R. (2011). *Charlie and the chocolate factory*. New York: Puffin Books.

Dakos, K. (1995). *Mrs. Cole on an onion roll and other school poems*. New York: Aladdin Books.

Daniels, H. (2002). *Literature circles: Voice and choice in book clubs and reading groups* (2nd ed.). Portland, ME: Stenhouse.

Danziger, P. (1995). *Amber Brown goes fourth*. New York: Putnam.

Danziger, P. (2006). *Amber Brown is not a crayon*. New York: Puffin Books.

D'Aoust, C. (1992). Portfolios: Process for students and teachers. In K. B. Yancy (Ed.), *Portfolios in the writing classroom* (pp. 39–48). Urbana, IL: National Council of Teachers of English.

Day, J., Spiegel, D. L., McLellan, J., & Brown, V. (2002). *Moving forward with literature circles*. New York: Scholastic.

Dean, D. (2006). *Strategic writing*. Urbana, IL: National Council of Teachers of English.

Deedy, C. A. (2000). *The yellow star: The legend of King Christian X of Denmark*. Atlanta: Peachtree.

Demi. (2002). *King Midas: The golden touch*. New York: McElderry.

Demi. (2007). *The empty pot*. New York: Henry Holt.

Denenberg, B. (2008). *Lincoln shot: A president's life remembered*. New York: Feiwel & Friends.

dePaola, T. (2003). *Things will NEVER be the same*. New York: Putnam.

dePaola, T. (2006). *I'm still scared: A 26 Fairmount Avenue book*. New York: Putnam.

dePaola, T. (2010). *Strega Nona*. New York: Simon & Schuster.

Dias, P. X. (1996). *Reading and responding to poetry: Patterns in the process*. Portsmouth, NH: Boynton/Cook.

DiCamillo, K. (2003). *The tale of Despereaux*. Cambridge, MA: Candlewick Press.

Dickinson, D. K., & Tabors, P. O. (2001). *Beginning literacy with language*. Baltimore: Brookes.

Ditzel, R. J. (2000). *Great beginnings: Creating a literacy-rich kindergarten*. Portsmouth, ME: Stenhouse.

Domeniconi, D. (2002). *G is for golden: A California alphabet*. Chelsea, MI: Sleeping Bear Press.

Domeniconi, D. (2006). *M is for masterpiece: An art alphabet*. Chelsea, MI: Sleeping Bear Press.

Dorn, L. J., & Soffos, C. (2001). *Shaping literate minds: Developing self-regulated learners*. York, ME: Stenhouse.

Dorros, A. (1995). *Isla*. New York: Dutton.

Dorros, A. (1997). *Abuela*. New York: Puffin Books.

Dressel, J. H. (1990). The effects of listening to and discussing different qualities of children's literature on the narrative writing of fifth graders. *Research in the Teaching of English, 24,* 397–414.

Duke, N. K., & Kays, J. (1998). "Can I say 'Once upon a time'?" Kindergarten children's developing knowledge of information book language. *Early Childhood Research Quarterly, 13,* 295–318.

Duke, N. K., & Purcell-Gates, V. (2003). Genres at home and at school: Bridging the known to the new. *The Reading Teacher, 57,* 30–37.

Dunning, S., & Stafford, W. (1992). *Getting the knack: 20 poetry writing exercises.* Urbana, IL: National Council of Teachers of English.

Duthie, C. (1996). *True stories: Nonfiction literacy in the primary classroom.* York, ME: Stenhouse.

Dwyer, J. (Ed.). (1991). *A sea of talk.* Portsmouth, NH: Heinemann.

Dyson, A. H. (1997). *Writing superheroes.* New York: Teachers College Press.

Dyson, A. H. (2003). *The brothers and sisters learn to write.* New York: Teachers College Press.

Edelsky, C. (1989). Putting language variation to work for you. In P. Rigg & V. G. Allen (Eds.), *When they don't all speak English: Integrating the ESL student into the regular classroom* (pp. 96–107). Urbana, IL: National Council of Teachers of English.

Edmiston, B. (2011). Teaching for transformation: Drama and language arts education. In D. Lapp & D. Fisher (Eds.), *Handbook of research on teaching the English language arts* (3rd ed.; pp 224–230). New York: Routledge.

Edmunds, K. M., & Bauserman, K. L. (2006). What teachers can learn about reading motivation through conversations with children. *The Reading Teacher, 59,* 414–424.

Edwards, P. D. (1996). *Some smug slug.* New York: HarperCollins.

Edwards, P. D. (2001). *Slop goes the soup: A noisy warthog word book.* New York: Hyperion Books.

Edwards, P. D. (2003). *The worrywarts.* New York: HarperCollins.

Eeds, M., & Peterson, R. L. (1995). What teachers need to know about the literary craft. In N. L. Roser & M. G. Martinez (Eds.), *Book talk and beyond: Children and teachers respond to literature* (pp. 10–23). Newark, DE: International Reading Association.

Ehlert, L. (2001). *Fish eyes: A book you can count on.* New York: Red Wagon Books.

Ehlert, L. (2006). *Eating the alphabet: Fruits and vegetables from A to Z.* San Diego: Harcourt.

Eisenstein, J., O'Connor, B., Smith, N. A., & Xing, E. P. (2011). A latent variable model for geographic lexical variation. Retrieved from http://people.csail.mit.edu/jacobe/papers/emnlp2010.pdf

Ellis, D. (2000). *The breadwinner.* Toronto, ON: Groundwood Books.

Ellis, D. (2008). *Off to war: Voices of soldiers' children.* Toronto, ON: Groundwood Books.

Elster, C. A., & Hanauer, D. I. (2002). Voicing texts, voices around texts: Reading poems in elementary school classrooms. *Research in the Teaching of English, 37,* 89–134.

Emberley, E. (2006). *Ed Emberley's drawing book of animals.* Boston: Little, Brown.

Eric Carle Museum of Picture Book Art. (2007). *Artist to artist: 23 major illustrators talk to children about their art.* New York: Philomel.

Ernst, L. C. (2003). *Goldilocks returns.* New York: Simon & Schuster.

Evans, D. (2008). *Show and tell: Exploring the fine art of children's book illustration.* New York: Chronicle Books.

Evans, J. (Ed.). (2009). *Talking beyond the page: Reading and responding to picturebooks.* New York: Routledge.

Evans, K. S. (2001). *Literature discussion groups in the intermediate grades: Dilemmas and possibilities.* Newark, DE: International Reading Association.

Evans, M., & Caras, R. A. (2001). *Fish: Pet care guides for kids.* New York: Dorling Kindersley.

Ezell, H. K., & Justice, L. M. (2005). *Shared storybook reading.* Baltimore, MD: Brookes.

Faigley, L., & Witte, S. (1981). Analyzing revision. *College Composition and Communication, 32,* 400–410.

Falconer, I. (2000). *Olivia.* New York: Simon & Schuster.

Fay, K., & Whaley, S. (2004). *Becoming one community: Reading and writing with English language learners.* Portland, ME: Stenhouse.

Finch, M. (2001). *The three billy goats Gruff.* Cambridge, MA: Barefoot Books.

Fisher, B., & Medvic, E. F. (2000). *Perspectives on shared reading: Planning and practice.* Portsmouth, NH: Heinemann.

Fisher, C. J., & Natarella, M. A. (1982). Young children's preferences in poetry: A national survey of first, second, and third graders. *Research in the Teaching of English, 16,* 339–354.

Fisher, D., Flood, J., Lapp, D., & Frey, N. (2004). Interactive read-alouds: Is there a common set of implementation practices? *The Reading Teacher, 58,* 8–17.

Fitzgerald, J. (1989). Enhancing two related thought processes: Revision in writing and critical thinking. *The Reading Teacher, 43,* 42–48.

Fitzhugh, L. (2001). *Harriet the spy.* New York: Yearling.

Flavell, J. H., Miller, P. H., & Miller, S. A. (2001). *Cognitive development* (4th ed.). Upper Saddle River, NJ: Prentice Hall.

Fleischman, P. (1985). *I am phoenix: Poems for two voices.* New York: HarperCollins.

Fleischman, P. (2000). *Big talk: Poems for four voices.* Cambridge, MA: Candlewick Press.

Fleischman, P. (2004a). *Joyful noise: Poems for two voices.* New York: HarperCollins.

Fleischman, P. (2004b). *Seedfolks.* New York: Harper Trophy.

Fleischman, S. (1998). *The abracadabra kid: A writer's life.* New York: HarperCollins.

Fleming, D. (1994). *Barnyard banter.* New York: Henry Holt.

Fleming, D. (1996). *Lunch.* New York: Henry Holt.

Fleming, M., & McGinnis, J. (Eds.). (1985). *Portraits: Biography and autobiography in the secondary school.* Urbana, IL: National Council of Teachers of English.

Fletcher, R. (2002). *Poetry matters: Writing a poem from the inside out.* New York: HarperCollins.

Fletcher, R., & Portalupi, J. (2001). *Writing workshop: The essential guide.* Portsmouth, NH: Heinemann.

Fletcher, R., & Portalupi, J. (2007). *Craft lessons: Teaching writing K–8* (2nd ed.). Portland, ME: Stenhouse.

Flower, L., & Hayes, J. R. (1994). The cognition of discovery: Defining a rhetorical problem. In S. Perl (Ed.), *Landmark essays on writing process* (pp. 63–74). Davis, CA: Heragoras Press.

Fountas, I. C., & Pinnell, G. S. (1996). *Guided reading: Good first teaching for all children.* Portsmouth, NH: Heinemann.

Fountas, I. C, & Pinnell, G. S. (2001). *Guiding readers and writers, grades 3–6.* Portsmouth, NH: Heinemann.

Fox, M. (2001). *Reading magic: Why reading aloud to our children will change their lives forever.* San Diego: Harcourt Brace.

Fradin, D. B. (2008). *Duel! Burr and Hamilton's deadly war of words.* New York: Walker.

Frank, A. (1995). *Anne Frank: The diary of a young girl* (New ed.). New York: Doubleday.

Frank, C. R., Dixon, C. N., & Brandts, L. R. (2001). Bears, trolls, and pagemasters: Learning about learners in book clubs. *The Reading Teacher, 54,* 448–462.

Fraustino, L. R. (2004). *I walk in dread: The diary of Deliverance Trembley, Witness to the Salem witch trials.* New York: Scholastic.

Frazee, M. (2003). *Roller coaster.* Orlando: Harcourt.

Freire, P., & Macedo, D. (1987). *Literacy: Reading the word and the world.* South Hadley, MA: Bergin & Garvey.

Friedman, L. (2009). *Red, white, and true blue Mallory.* Minneapolis, MN: Carolrhoda.

Galdone, P. (1972). *The three bears.* New York: Clarion Books.

Galdone, P. (1974). *Little red riding hood.* New York: McGraw-Hill.

Galdone, P. (2006a). *The little red hen.* New York: Clarion Books.

Galdone, P. (2006b). *The three little pigs.* New York: Clarion Books.

Galdone, P. (2008). *The gingerbread boy.* New York: Sandpiper.

Gantos, J. (2000). *Joey Pigza loses control.* New York: Farrar, Straus & Giroux.

Gardiner, J. R. (2003). *Stone Fox.* New York: Harper Trophy.

Geisert, A. (2008). *Hogwash.* Boston: Houghton Mifflin.

Geller, L. G. (1981). Riddling: A playful way to explore language. *Language Arts, 58,* 669–674.

Geller, L. G. (1985). *Word play and language learning for children.* Urbana, IL: National Council of Teachers of English.

Gentry, J. R. (1997). *My kid can't spell! Understanding and assessing your child's literacy development.* Portsmouth, NH: Heinemann.

Gentry, J. R., & Gillet, J. W. (1993). *Teaching kids to spell.* Portsmouth, NH: Heinemann.

George, J. C. (2004). *My side of the mountain.* New York: Puffin Books.

George, J. C. (2005). *Julie of the wolves.* New York: Harper Trophy.

George, J. C. (2009). *Pocket guide to the outdoors.* New York: Dutton.

George, K. O. (2005). *Fold me a poem.* San Diego: Harcourt.

Gibbons, G. (1997). *The moon book.* New York: Holiday House.

Gibbons, G. (2006). *Owls.* New York: Holiday House.

Gibbons, P. (2002). *Scaffolding language, scaffolding learning: Teaching second language learners in the mainstream classroom.* Portsmouth, NH: Heinemann.

Gill, R. S. (2000). Reading with Amy: Teaching and learning through reading conferences. *The Reading Teacher, 53,* 500–509.

Gilles, C. (2010). Making the most of talk. *Voices From the Middle, 18*(2), 9–15.

Gillet, J. W., & Beverly, L. (2001). *Directing the writing workshop: An elementary teacher's handbook.* New York: Guilford Press.

Gillon, G. T. (2004). *Phonological awareness: From research to practice.* New York: Guilford Press.

Giroux, H. (1997). *Pedagogy and the politics of hope, theory, culture, and schooling.* Boulder, CO: Westview Press.

Giovanni, N. (2005). *Rosa.* New York: Henry Holt.

Glover, M. (2009). *Engaging young writers: Preschool–grade 1.* Portsmouth, NH: Heinemann.

Glover, M. K. (1999). *A garden of poets: Poetry writing in the elementary classroom.* Urbana, IL: National Council of Teachers of English.

Goble, P. (2003). *Mystic horse.* New York: HarperCollins.

Golden, J. M., Meiners, A., & Lewis, S. (1992). The growth of story meaning. *Language Arts, 69,* 22–27.

Gollub, M. (1998). *Cool melons—turn to frogs!* New York: Lee & Low.

Graham, S. (1992). Issues in handwriting instruction. *Focus on Exceptional Children, 25,* 1–14.

Graves, D. H. (1983). *Writing: Teachers and children at work.* Portsmouth, NH: Heinemann.

Graves, D. H. (1992). *Explore poetry.* Portsmouth, NH: Heinemann.

Graves, D. H. (1994). *A fresh look at writing.* Portsmouth, NH: Heinemann.

Graves, D. H., & Hansen, J. (1983). The author's chair. *Language Arts, 60,* 176–183.

Graves, M. F. (2006). *The vocabulary book: Learning and instruction.* New York: Teachers College Press.

Graves, M. F., & Fitzgerald, J. (2006). Effective vocabulary instruction for English language learners. In C. C. Block & J. N. Mangieri (Eds.), *The vocabulary-enriched classroom: Practices for improving the reading performance of all students in grades 3 and up* (pp. 118–137). New York: Scholastic.

Greenberg, J., & Jordan, S. (2010). *Ballet for Martha.* New York: Flash Point.

Gregory, K. (2005). *Catherine: The great journey.* New York: Scholastic.

Grierson, S. T., Anson, A., & Baird, J. (2002). Exploring the past through multigenre writing. *Language Arts, 80,* 51–59.

Griffith, F., & Olson, M. (1992). Phonemic awareness helps beginning readers break the code. *The Reading Teacher, 45,* 516–523.

Guthrie, J. T., & Wigfield, A. (2000). Engagement and motivation in reading. In M. L. Kamil, P. B. Mosenthal, P. D. Pearson, & R. Barr (Eds.), *Handbook of reading research* (Vol. 3, pp. 403–422). New York: Erlbaum.

Gwynne, F. (1988). *The king who rained.* New York: Aladdin Books.

Gwynne, F. (1998). *A little pigeon toad.* New York: Aladdin Books.

Gwynne, F. (2005). *A chocolate moose for dinner.* New York: Aladdin Books.

Hackney, C. (2003). *Handwriting: A way to self-expression.* Columbus, OH: Zaner-Bloser.

Hale, S. (2007). *Princess Academy.* New York: Bloomsbury.

Hall, D. (1983). *Ox-cart man.* New York: Puffin Books.

Halliday, M. A. K. (2006). *Linguistic studies of text and discourse.* New York: Continuum.

Hamilton, V. (2000). *The girl who spun gold.* New York: Scholastic.

Hancock, M. R. (2007). *Language arts: Extending the possibilities.* Upper Saddle River, NJ: Merrill/Prentice Hall.

Hancock, M. R. (2008). *A celebration of literature and response: Children, books, and teachers in K–8 classrooms* (3rd ed.). Upper Saddle River, NJ: Merrill/Prentice Hall.

Hanna, P. R., Hanna, J. S., Hodges, R. E., & Rudorf, E. H. (1966). *Phoneme-grapheme correspondences as cues to spelling improvement.* Washington, DC: U.S. Government Printing Office.

Hannon, J. (1999). Talking back: Kindergarten dialogue journals. *The Reading Teacher, 53,* 200–203.

Harris, T. (2000). *Pattern fish.* Brookfield, CT: Millbrook Press.

Harste, J. C., Short, K. G., & Burke, C. (1988). *Creating classrooms for authors: The reading-writing connection.* Portsmouth, NH: Heinemann.

Harste, J. C., Woodward, V. A., & Burke, C. L. (1984). *Language stories and literacy lessons.* Portsmouth, NH: Heinemann.

Harvey, S. (1998). *Nonfiction matters: Reading, writing, and research in grades 3–8.* York, ME: Stenhouse.

Harvey, S., & Goudvis, A. (2007). *Strategies that work: Teaching comprehension for understanding and engagement* (2nd ed.). Portland, ME: Stenhouse.

Head, M. H., & Readence, J. E. (1992). Anticipation guides: Meaning through prediction. In E. K. Dishner, T. W. Bean, J. E. Readence, & D. W. Moore (Eds.), *Reading in the content areas* (2nd ed., pp. 229–234). Dubuque, IA: Kendall/Hunt.

Heard, G. (1999). *Awakening the heart: Exploring poetry in elementary and middle school.* Portsmouth, NH: Heinemann.

Heard, G. (Ed.) (2009). *Falling down the page.* New York: Roaring Brook Press.

Heath, S. B. (1983a). Research currents: A lot of talk about nothing. *Language Arts, 60,* 999–1007.

Heath, S. B. (1983b). *Ways with words: Language, life, and work in communities and classrooms.* Cambridge: Cambridge University Press.

Heffernan, L. (2004). *Critical literacy and writer's workshop: Bringing purpose and passion to student writing.* Newark, DE: International Reading Association.

Heller, M. F. (2006/2007). Telling stories and talking facts: First graders' engagements in a nonfiction book club. *The Reading Teacher, 60,* 358–369.

Heller, R. (1990). *Merry-go-round: A book about nouns.* New York: Grosset & Dunlap.

Heller, R. (1991). *Up, up and away: A book about adverbs.* New York: Grosset & Dunlap.

Heller, R. (1995). *Behind the mask: A book of prepositions.* New York: Grosset & Dunlap.

Heller, R. (1997). *Mine, all mine: A book about pronouns.* New York: Grosset & Dunlap.

Heller, R. (1998). *A cache of jewels and other collective nouns.* New York: Putnam.

Helman, L., Bear, D. R., Templeton, S., Invernizzi, M., & Johnston, F. (2012). *Words their way with English learners* (2nd ed.). Boston: Pearson.

Henderson, E. H. (1990). *Teaching spelling* (2nd ed.). Boston: Houghton Mifflin.

Henkes, K. (1991). *Chrysanthemum.* New York: Greenwillow.

Henkes, K. (2005). *Kitten's first full moon.* New York: Greenwillow.

Henkin, R. (1995). Insiders and outsiders in first-grade writing workshops: Gender and equity issues. *Language Arts, 72,* 429–434.

Henry, L. A. (2006). SEARCHing for an answer: The critical role of new literacies while reading on the Internet. *The Reading Teacher, 59,* 614–627.

Herrera, J. F. (1998). *Laughing out loud, I fly.* New York: HarperCollins.

Hesse, K. (2005). *Witness.* New York: Scholastic.

Hiaasen, C. (2005). *Flush.* New York: Knopf.

Hildreth, G. (1960). Manuscript writing after sixty years. *Elementary English, 37,* 3–13.

Hill, L. C. (2010). *Dave the potter: Artist, poet, slave.* New York: Little, Brown.

Hillocks, G., Jr., & Smith, M. W. (2003). Grammar and literacy learning. In J. Flood, D. Lapp, J. R. Squire, & J. M. Jensen (Eds.), *Handbook of research on teaching the English language arts* (2nd ed., pp. 721–737). Mahwah, NJ: Erlbaum.

Hines-Stephens, S. (2009). *Show off: How to do absolutely everything: One step at a time.* Cambridge, MA: Candlewick Press.

Hoban, T. (2000). *Cubes, cones, cylinders, and spheres.* New York: Greenwillow.

Hodges, M. (2002). *The boy who drew cats.* New York: Holiday House.

Hofmeyr, D. (2001). *The star-bearer: A creation myth from ancient Egypt.* New York: Farrar, Straus & Giroux.

Holbrook, S. (2005). *Practical poetry: A nonstandard approach to meeting content-area standards.* Portsmouth, NH: Heinemann.

Holdaway, D. (1979). *The foundations of literacy.* Portsmouth, NH: Heinemann.

Hook, J. N. (1975). *History of the English language.* New York: Ronald Press.

Horn, E. (1926). *A basic writing vocabulary.* Iowa City: University of Iowa Press.

Hornby, H. (2010). *DK Eyewitness Books: Soccer.* New York: DK.

Howe, D., & Howe, J. (2006). *Bunnicula: A rabbit-tale of mystery.* New York: Aladdin Books.

Hoyt, L. (1999). *Revisit, reflect, retell: Strategies for improving reading comprehension.* Portsmouth, NH: Heinemann.

Hughes, J., & John, A. (2009). From page to digital stage: Creating digital performances of poetry. *Voices From the Middle, 16*(3), 15–22.

Hughes, M., & Searle, D. (1997). *The violent "e" and other tricky sounds: Learning to spell from kindergarten through grade 6.* York, ME: Stenhouse.

Hughes, M., & Searle, D. (2000). Spelling and "the second 'R.'" *Language Arts, 77,* 203–208.

Hurd, T. (2003). *Moo cow kaboom!* New York: HarperCollins.

Hutchins, P. (2002). *Don't forget the bacon!* New York: Red Fox.

Hutchins, P. (2005). *Rosie's walk.* New York: Aladdin Books.

Hyman, T. S. (2000). *The sleeping beauty.* Boston: Little, Brown.

Hymes, D. (1972). On communicative competence. In J. B. Pride & J. Holmes (Eds.), *Sociolinguistics* (pp. 269–285). Harmondsworth, Middlesex, UK: Penguin.

Ikpeze, C. H., & Boyd, F. B. (2007). Web-based inquiry learning: Facilitating thoughtful literacy with webquests. *The Reading Teacher, 60,* 644–654.

Inches, A. (2006). *The stuffed animals get ready for bed.* San Diego: Harcourt Brace.

Invernizzi, M. (2003). Concepts, sounds, and the ABCs: A diet for a very young reader. In D. M. Barone & L. M. Morrow (Eds.), *Literacy and young children: Research-based practices* (pp. 140–156). New York: Guilford Press.

Irwin, J. W. (2007). *Teaching reading comprehension processes* (3rd ed.). Boston: Allyn & Bacon.

Ivey, G., & Broaddus, K. (2001). "Just plain reading": A survey of what makes students want to read in middle school classrooms. *Reading Research Quarterly, 36,* 350–377.

Jackson, A. D. (1971). *A comparison of speed and legibility of manuscript and cursive handwriting of intermediate grade pupils.* Unpublished doctoral dissertation, University of Arizona. *Dissertation Abstracts, 31,* 4384A.

Janeczko, P. B. (2001). *A poke in the I.* Cambridge, MA: Candlewick Press.

Janeczko, P. B. (2005). *A kick in the head: An everyday guide to poetic forms.* Cambridge, MA: Candlewick Press.

Janssen, S. (2011). *The world almanac for kids.* New York: World Almanac Books.

Jenkins, S. (2009). *Down, down, down: A journey to the bottom of the sea.* Boston: Houghton Mifflin.

Jenkins, S., & Page, R. (2003). *What do you do with a tail like this?* Boston: Houghton Mifflin.

Jiménez, F. (1997). *The circuit.* Albuquerque: University of New Mexico Press.

Jiménez, F. (2001). *Breaking through.* Boston: Houghton Mifflin.

Johns, J. L., Van Leirsburg, P., & Davis, S. J. (1994). *Improving reading: A handbook of strategies.* Dubuque, IA: Kendall/Hunt.

Johnson, T. D., Langford, K. G., & Quorn, K. C. (1981). Characteristics of an effective spelling program. *Language Arts, 58,* 581–588.

Johnson, T. D., & Louis, D. R. (1987). *Literacy through literature.* Portsmouth, NH: Heinemann.

Jorgensen, K. (2001). *The whole story: Crafting fiction in the upper elementary grades.* Portsmouth, NH: Heinemann.

Juel, C. (1991). Beginning reading. In R. Barr, M. L. Kamil, P. Mosenthal, & P. D. Pearson (Eds.), *Handbook of reading research* (Vol. 2, pp. 759–788). New York: Longman.

Kalan, R. (2002). *Jump, frog, jump!* New York: HarperFestival.

Kamma, A. (2002). *...If you lived with the Indians of the northwest coast.* New York: Scholastic.

Kamma, A. (2004). *...If you lived when there was slavery in America.* New York: Scholastic.

Kamma, A. (2008). *...If you lived when women won their rights.* New York: Scholastic.

Karchmer, R. A., Mallette, M. H., Kara-Soteriou, J., & Leu, D. (Eds.). (2005). *Innovative approaches to literacy education: Using the Internet to support new literacies.* Newark, DE: International Reading Association.

Kasza, K. (1996). *The wolf's chicken stew.* New York: Putnam.

Katz, A. (2001). *Take me out of the bathtub and other silly dilly songs.* New York: McElderry.

Kaufman, D. (2000). *Conferences and conversations: Listening to the literate classroom.* Portsmouth, NH: Heinemann.

Kaufman, D. (2001). Organizing and managing the language arts workshop: A matter of motion. *Language Arts, 79,* 114–123.

Kay, A. M., Neher, A., & Lush, L. H. (2010). Writing a relationship: Home–school journals. *Language Arts, 87,* 417–426.

Kelley, J. G., Lesaux, N. K., Kieffer, M. J., & Faller, S. E. (2010). Effective academic vocabulary instruction in the urban middle school. *The Reading Teacher, 64,* 5–14.

Kellogg, S. (1985). *Paul Bunyan.* New York: HarperCollins.

Kellogg, S. (1988). *Johnny Appleseed.* New York: HarperCollins.

Kellogg, S. (1992). *Pecos Bill.* New York: HarperCollins.

Kellogg, S. (1995). *Sally Ann Crockett.* New York: HarperCollins.

Kellogg, S. (1998). *Mike Fink.* New York: Aladdin Books.

Kiefer, B. (1994). *The potential of picturebooks: From visual literacy to aesthetic understanding.* New York: Macmillan.

Kieffer, M. J., & Lesaux. N. K. (2010). Morphing into adolescents: Active word learning for English-language learners and their classmates in middle school. *Journal of Adolescent and Adult Literacy, 54,* 47–56.

Killgallon, D. (1997). *Sentence composing for middle school.* Portsmouth, NH: Heinemann.

Killgallon, D. (1998). Sentence composing: Notes on a new rhetoric. In C. Weaver (Ed.), *Lessons to share: On teaching grammar in context* (pp. 169–183). Portsmouth, NH: Heinemann.

Kimmel, E. A. (2000). *The runaway tortilla.* Delray Beach, FL: Winslow Press.

King, M. L., Jr. (1997). *I have a dream.* New York: Scholastic.

Kinghorn, J. (2002). *My first pocket guide: Seashore life.* Washington, DC: National Geographic.

King-Smith, D. (2002). *Chewing the cud: An extraordinary life remembered by the author of* Babe: The gallant pig. New York: Knopf.

Kist, W. (2010). *The socially networked classroom: Teaching in the new media age.* Thousand Oaks, CA: Corwin.

Klesius, J. P., Griffith, P. L., & Zielonka, P. (1991). A whole language and traditional instruction comparison: Overall effectiveness and development of the alphabetic principle. *Reading Research and Instruction, 30,* 47–61.

Klise, K. (1999). *Regarding the fountain: A tale, in letters, of liars and leaks.* New York: Avon.

Klise, K. (2006). *Regarding the sink: Where, oh where, did Waters go?* Orlando: Harcourt.

Klise, K. (2007). *Regarding the trees: A splintered saga rooted in secrets.* Orlando: Harcourt.

Klise, K. (2008). *Regarding the bathrooms: A privy to the past.* Orlando: Harcourt.

Klise, K. (2009). *Regarding the bees: A lesson, in letters, on honey, dating, and other sticky subjects.* Orlando: Harcourt.

Koch, K. (1990). *Rose, where did you get that red?* New York: Vintage.

Koch, K. (2000). *Wishes, lies, and dreams.* New York: Harper-Perennial.

Koopmans, L. (1990). *The woodcutter's mitten.* New York: Crocodile Books.

Kotwinkle, W. (2010). *Walter the farting dog.* New York: Dutton.

Kraft, B. H. (2003). *Theodore Roosevelt: Champion of the American spirit.* New York: Clarion Books.

Kristo, J. V., & Bamford, R. A. (2004). *Nonfiction in focus.* New York: Scholastic.

Kucer, S. B., Silva, C., & Delgado-Larocco, E. L. (1995). *Curricular conversations: Themes in multilingual and monolingual classrooms.* York, ME: Stenhouse.

Kutiper, K. (1985). *A survey of the poetry preferences of seventh, eighth, and ninth graders.* Unpublished doctoral dissertation, University of Houston.

Labbo, L. D. (2005). Fundamental qualities of effective Internet literacy instruction: An exploration of worthwhile classroom practices. In R. A. Karchmer, M. H. Mallette, J. Kara-Soteriou, & D. L. Leu, Jr. (Eds.), *Innovative approaches to literacy education: Using the Internet to support new literacies* (pp. 165–179). Newark, DE: International Reading Association.

Lane, B. (1993). *After the end: Teaching and learning creative revision.* Portsmouth, NH: Heinemann.

Lane, B. (1999). *The reviser's toolbox.* Shoreham, VT: Discover Writing Press.

Langer, J. A. (1985). Children's sense of genre. *Written Communication, 2,* 157–187.

Langstaff, J. (1991). *Oh, a-hunting we will go.* New York: Aladdin Books.

Larson, L. C. (2009). Reader response meets new literacies: Empowering readers in online communities. *The Reading Teacher, 62,* 638–648.

Lasky, K. (2006). *John Muir: America's first environmentalist.* Cambridge, MA: Candlewick Press.

Lauber, P. (1995). *Who eats what? Food chains and food webs.* New York: HarperCollins.

Lear, E. (1995). *Daffy down dillies: Silly limericks by Edward Lear.* Honesdale, PA: Wordsong.

Lehman, B. (2007). *Rainstorm.* Boston: Houghton Mifflin.

Lehr, S. S. (1991). *The child's developing sense of theme: Responses to literature.* New York: Teachers College Press.

L'Engle, M. (2007). *A wrinkle in time.* New York: Square Fish Books.

Lensmire, T. (1992). *When children write.* New York: Teachers College Press.

Leu, D., Jr., Kinzer, C. K., Coiro, J., & Cammack, D. W. (2004). Toward a theory of new literacies emerging from the Internet and other communication technologies. In R. B. Ruddell & N. J. Unrau (Eds.), *Theoretical models and processes of reading* (5th ed., pp. 1570–1613). Newark, DE: International Reading Association.

Lewis, C. S. (2005). *The lion, the witch and the wardrobe.* New York: HarperCollins.

Lindquist, T., & Selwyn, D. (2000). *Social studies at the center: Integrating kids, content, and literacy.* Portsmouth, NH: Heinemann.

Lionni, L. (2005). *Fish is fish.* New York: Scholastic.

Loban, W. (1976). *Language development: Kindergarten through grade twelve* (Research Report No. 18). Urbana, IL: National Council of Teachers of English.

Lobel, A. (1996). *Alison's zinnia.* New York: Greenwillow.

Logan, C. (2002). *The 5,000-year-old puzzle: Solving a mystery of ancient Egypt.* New York: Farrar, Straus & Giroux.

Long, M. (2003). *How I became a pirate.* San Diego: Harcourt.

Longfellow, H. W. (1996). *Hiawatha.* New York: Puffin Books.

Longfellow, H. W. (2001). *The midnight ride of Paul Revere* (C. Bing, Illus.). New York: Handprint Books.

Lowry, L. (1995). *Anastasia Krupnik.* New York: HarperCollins.

Lowry, L. (2000). *Looking back: A book of memories.* New York: Delacorte.

Lowry, L. (2006a). *Gathering blue.* New York: Delacorte.

Lowry, L. (2006b). *The giver.* New York: Delacorte.

Lowry, L. (2006c). *The messenger.* New York: Delacorte.

Lowry, L. (2011). *Number the stars.* New York: Sandpiper.

Lukens, R. J. (2006). *A critical handbook of children's literature* (8th ed.). New York: Allyn & Bacon.

Lundsteen, S. W. (1979). *Listening: Its impact on reading and the other language arts* (Rev. ed.). Urbana, IL: National Council of Teachers of English.

Luongo-Orlando, K. (2001). *A project approach to language learning: Linking literary genres and themes in elementary classrooms.* Markham, ON: Pembroke.

Lutz, W. (1997). *The new doublespeak: Why no one knows what anyone's saying anymore*. New York: HarperCollins.

Macaulay, D. (1977). *Castle*. Boston: Houghton Mifflin.

Macaulay, D. (1982). *Pyramid*. Boston: Graphia.

Macaulay, D. (1983). *City: A story of Roman planning and construction*. Boston: Graphia.

Macaulay, D. (2005). *Black and white*. New York: Sandpiper.

Macaulay, D. (2008a). *Mosque*. New York: Sandpiper.

Macaulay, D. (2008b). *The way we work: Getting to know the amazing human body*. Boston: Houghton Mifflin.

Macaulay, D. (2010). *Built to last*. Boston: Houghton Mifflin.

MacDonald, R. (2003). *Achoo! Bang! Crash! The noisy alphabet*. New York: Roaring Brook Press.

MacLachlan, P. (2005). *Sarah, plain and tall*. New York: Scholastic.

Macon, J. M., Bewell, D., & Vogt, M. E. (1991). *Responses to literature, grades K–8*. Newark, DE: International Reading Association.

Marcus, L. S. (2008). *A Caldecott celebration: Seven artists and their paths to the Caldecott Medal*. New York: Walker.

Marshall, E. (1994). *Fox and his friends*. New York: Puffin Books.

Marshall, J. (1998). *Goldilocks and the three bears*. New York: Puffin Books.

Martin, B., Jr. (1992). *Polar bear, polar bear, what do you hear?* New York: Holt, Rinehart and Winston.

Martin, B., Jr. (2010). *Brown bear, brown bear, what do you see?* New York: Holt.

Martin, B., Jr., & Archambault, J. (2009). *Chicka chicka boom boom*. New York: Beach Lane Books..

Martinez, M. G., & Roser, N. L. (1995). The books make a difference in story talk. In N. L. Roser & M. G. Martinez (Eds.), *Book talk and beyond: Children and teachers respond to literature* (pp. 32–41). Newark, DE: International Reading Association.

Marzano, R. J. (2004). *Building background knowledge for academic achievement: Research on what works in schools*. Alexandria, VA: Association for Supervision and Curriculum Development.

Mazzoni, S. A., & Gambrell, L. B. (2003). Principles of best practice. In L. M. Morrow, L. B. Gambrell, & M. Pressley (Eds.), *Best practices in literacy instruction* (2nd ed., pp. 9–22). New York: Guilford Press.

McCarrier, A., Pinnell, G. S., & Fountas, I. C. (2000). *Interactive writing: How language and literacy come together, K–2*. Portsmouth, NH: Heinemann.

McCloskey, R. (2004). *Make way for ducklings*. New York: Square Fish Books.

McCully, E. A. (1997). *Mirette on the high wire*. New York: Puffin Books.

McCully, E. A. (2003). *Picnic*. New York: HarperCollins.

McDonald, N. L., & Fisher, D. (2006). *Teaching literacy through the arts*. New York: Guilford Press.

McElligott, M. (2004). *Absolutely not!* New York: Walker.

McGee, L. M., & Richgels, D. J. (2012). *Literacy's beginnings: Supporting young readers and writers* (6th ed.). Boston: Allyn & Bacon.

McGee, L. M., & Tompkins, G. E. (1995). Literature-based reading instruction: What's guiding the instruction? *Language Arts, 72,* 405–414.

McGovern, A. (2001). *. . . . If you lived in the days of the knights*. New York: Scholastic.

McKenna, M., & Stahl, S. (2003). *Assessment for reading instruction*. New York: Guilford Press.

McKeon, C. A. (1999). The nature of children's e-mail in one classroom. *The Reading Teacher, 52,* 698–706.

McKissack, P. (1992). *Flossie and the fox*. New York: Scholastic.

McKissack, P. (1996). *A million fish…more or less*. New York: Dragonfly.

McKissack, P. (1997). *Can you imagine*. Katonah, NY: Richard C. Owen.

McMackin, M. C., & Siegel, B. S. (2002). *Knowing how: Researching and writing nonfiction, 3–8*. Portland, ME: Stenhouse.

McMaster, J. C. (1998). "Doing" literature: Using drama to build literacy. *The Reading Teacher, 51,* 574–584.

McNabb, M. L. (2006). *Literacy learning in networked classrooms: Using the Internet with middle-level students*. Newark, DE: International Reading Association.

McTigue, E. M., & Flowers, A. C. (2011). Science visual literacy: Learners' perceptions and knowledge of diagrams. *The Reading Teacher, 64,* 578–589.

Meddaugh, S. (1995). *Martha speaks*. Boston: Houghton Mifflin.

Mellard, D. F., & Johnson, E. (2008). *RTI: A practitioner's guide to implementing Response to Intervention*. Thousand Oaks, CA: Corwin Press and the National Association of Elementary School Principals.

Merriam-Webster children's dictionary. (2006). New York: Dorling Kindersley.

Meyer, B. J., & Freedle, R. O. (1984). Effects of discourse type on recall. *American Educational Research Journal, 21,* 121–143.

Milich, Z. (2005). *City signs*. Tonawanda, NY: Kids Can Press.

Miller, L. C. (2010). *Make me a story: Teaching writing through digital storytelling*. Portland, ME: Stenhouse.

Milne, A. A. (2001). *The house at Pooh Corner*. New York: Dutton.

Moline, S. (1995). *I see what you mean: Children at work with visual information*. York, ME: Stenhouse.

Montenegro, L. N. (2003). *A bird about to sing*. Boston: Houghton Mifflin.

Moore, C. C. (1998). *The night before Christmas*. New York: Putnam.

Mora, P. (1999). *Confetti: Poems for children*. New York: Lee & Low.

Morgan, D. N. (2010). Writing feature articles with intermediate students. *The Reading Teacher, 64*, 181–189.

Morris, A. (1993). *Bread, bread, bread*. New York: HarperCollins.

Morse, S. (2008). *Magic pickle*. New York: Graphix.

Mortenson, G., & Roth, S. L. (2009). *Listen to the wind: The story of Dr. Greg and three cups of tea*. New York: Dial Books.

Moss, B., & Hendershot, J. (2002). Exploring sixth graders' selection of nonfiction trade books. *The Reading Teacher, 56*, 6–17.

Moss, L. (2005). *Zin! Zin! Zin! A violin*. New York: Aladdin Books.

Moss, M. (2006). *Amelia's notebook*. New York: Simon & Schuster.

Most, B. (1996). *Cock-a-doodle-moo!* San Diego: Harcourt Brace.

Muhammad, R. J. (1993). Mario: "It's mostly after I read a book that I write." In S. Hudson-Ross, L. M. Cleary, & M. Casey (Eds.), *Children's voices: Children talk about literacy* (pp. 92–99). Portsmouth, NH: Heinemann.

Murray, D. H. (1982). *Learning by teaching*. Montclair, NJ: Boynton/Cook.

Nagda, A. W. (2000). *Dear Whiskers*. New York: Holiday House.

Nathenson-Mejia, S. (1989). Writing in a second language: Negotiating meaning through invented spelling. *Language Arts, 66*, 516–526.

National Business Education Association. (1997). *Elementary/middle school keyboarding strategies guide* (2nd ed.). Reston, VA: Author.

National Communication Association. (1998). *Competent communicators: K–12 speaking, listening, and media literacy standards and competencies*. Washington, DC: Author.

National Reading Panel. (2000a). *Report of the National Reading Panel*. Washington, DC: National Institute of Child Health and Human Development Clearinghouse.

National Reading Panel. (2000b). *Teaching children to read: An evidence-based assessment of the scientific research literature on reading and its implications for reading instruction, reports of the subgroups*. Washington, DC: National Institute of Child Health and Human Development.

Naylor, P. R. (1996). *Shiloh season*. New York: Atheneum.

Naylor, P. R. (2000). *Shiloh*. New York: Aladdin Books.

Naylor, P. R. (2006). *Saving Shiloh*. New York: Atheneum.

NCTE Elementary Section Steering Committee. (1996). Exploring language arts standards within a cycle of learning. *Language Arts, 73*, 10–13.

Neeld, E. C. (1990). *Writing* (3rd ed.). Glenview, IL: Scott Foresman.

Nelson, R. (2002). *Pet fish*. Minneapolis: Lerner.

Neruda, P. (2000). *Selected odes of Pablo Neruda*. Berkeley: University of California Press.

Novinger, S., & Compton-Lilly, C. (2005). Telling our stories: Speaking truth to power. *Language Arts, 82*, 195–203.

Numeroff, L. J. (1985). *If you give a mouse a cookie*. New York: HarperCollins.

Numeroff, L. J. (1991). *If you give a moose a muffin*. New York: HarperCollins.

Numeroff, L. J. (1993). *Dogs don't wear sneakers*. New York: Simon & Schuster.

Numeroff, L. J. (1995). *Chimps don't wear glasses*. New York: Simon & Schuster.

Numeroff, L. J. (1998). *If you give a pig a pancake*. New York: HarperCollins.

Numeroff, L. J. (2000). *If you take a mouse to the movies*. New York: HarperCollins.

Numeroff, L. (2002). *If you take a mouse to school*. New York: HarperCollins.

Numeroff, L. (2003). *If you give an author a pencil*. Katonah, NY: Richard C. Owen.

Nye, N. S. (1998). *The tree is older than you are*. New York: Simon & Schuster.

Nystrand, M., Gamoran, A., & Heck, M. J. (1993). Using small groups for response to and thinking about literature. *English Journal, 82*, 14–22.

Obama, B. (2010). *Of thee I sing: A letter to my daughters*. New York: Knopf.

Oldfather, P. (1995). Commentary: What's needed to maintain and extend motivation for literacy in the middle grades? *Journal of Reading, 38*, 420–422.

Olson, T. (2009). *How to get rich on the Oregon Trail*. Washington, DC: National Geographic.

O'Malley, J. M., & Pierce, L. V. (1996). *Authentic assessment for English language learners: Practical approaches for teachers*. Reading, MA: Addison-Wesley.

Opie, I., & Opie, P. (1967). *The lore and language of school children*. Oxford: Oxford University Press.

Opitz, M. F. (2008). *Good-bye round robin: Twenty-five effective oral reading strategies* (Updated ed.). New York: Scholastic.

Opitz, M. F., & Ford, M. P. (2008). *Do-able differentiation: Varying groups, texts, and supports to reach readers*. Portsmouth, NH: Heinemann.

Opitz, M. F., & Zbaracki, M. D. (2004). *Listen hear! 25 effective comprehension strategies*. Portsmouth, NH: Heinemann.

Osborne, M. P. (2009a). *Leonardo da Vinci: A nonfiction companion guide to* Monday with a mad genius. New York: Random House.

Osborne, M. P. (2009b). *Monday with a mad genius*. New York: Random House.

Overmeyer, M. (2005). *When writing workshop isn't working: Answers to ten tough questions, grades 2–5*. York, ME: Stenhouse.

Owocki, G., & Goodman, Y. M. (2002). *Kidwatching: Documenting children's literacy development*. Portsmouth, NH: Heinemann.

Palmer, R. G., & Stewart, R. A. (2003). Nonfiction trade book use in primary grades. *The Reading Teacher, 57*, 38–48.

Papandropoulou, I., & Sinclair, H. (1974). What is a word? Experimental study of children's ideas on grammar. *Human Development, 17*, 241–258.

Pardo, L. W. (2004). What every teacher needs to know about comprehension. *The Reading Teacher, 58, 272–280*.

Paris, S. G., Wasik, B. A., & Turner, J. C. (1991). The development of strategic readers. In R. Barr, M. L. Kamil, P. B. Mosenthal, & P. D. Pearson (Eds.), *Handbook of reading research* (Vol. 2, pp. 609–640). New York: Longman.

Park, L. (2011). *A single shard*. New York: Sandpiper.

Parker, J. K. (2010). *Teaching tech-savvy kids: Bringing digital media into the classroom, grades 5–12*. Thousand Oaks, CA: Corwin.

Paterson, K. (1987). *The great Gilly Hopkins*. New York: Harper & Row.

Paterson, K. (2006). *Bridge to Terabithia*. New York: HarperCollins.

Paulsen, G. (1999). *My life in dog years*. New York: Yearling.

Paulsen, G. (2001). *Guts: The true stories behind* Hatchet *and the Brian books*. New York: Delacorte.

Paulsen, G. (2007). *Hatchet*. New York: Simon & Schuster.

Paye, W., & Lippert, M. H. (2002). *Head, body, legs: A story from Liberia*. New York: Holt.

Pearson, P. D., & Gallagher, M. (1983). The instruction of reading comprehension. *Contemporary Educational Psychology, 8*, 317–344.

Peregoy, S. F., & Boyle, W. F. (2009). *Reading, writing, and learning in ESL: A resource book for K–12 teachers* (5th ed.). Boston: Allyn & Bacon.

Perfitti, C., Beck, I., Bell, L., & Hughes, C. (1987). Phonemic knowledge and learning to read are reciprocal: A longitudinal study of first grade children. *Merrill-Palmer Quarterly, 33*, 283–319.

Perl, S. (1994). Understanding composing. In S. Perl (Ed.), *Landmark essays on writing process* (pp. 99–106). Davis, CA: Heragoras Press.

Perry, N., & Drummond, L. (2002). Helping young students become self-regulated researchers and writers. *The Reading Teacher, 56*, 298–310.

Peterson, C. (2004). *Extra cheese, please: Mozzarella's journey from cow to pizza*. Honesdale, PA: Boyds Mills Press.

Peterson, R., & Eeds, M. (2007). *Grand conversations: Literature groups in action* (Revised). New York: Scholastic.

Pfister, M. (2002). *The rainbow fish*. New York: North-South Books.

Piaget, J., & Inhelder, B. (2000). *The psychology of the child*. New York: Basic Books.

Pinkney, J. (1999). *The ugly duckling*. New York: Morrow.

Pinkney, J. (2000). *Aesop's fables*. New York: North-South.

Pinkney, J. (2006). *The little red hen*. New York: Dial Books.

Pinkney, J. (2007). *Little red riding hood*. Boston: Little, Brown.

Pinkney, J. (2009). *The lion & the mouse*. New York: Little, Brown.

Pittelman, S. D., Heimlich, J. E., Berglund, R. L., & French, M. P. (1991). *Semantic feature analysis: Classroom applications*. Newark, DE: International Reading Association.

Platt, R. (1999). *Castle diary: The journal of Tobias Burgess, page*. Cambridge, MA: Candlewick Press.

Polacco, P. (1994). *Firetalking*. Katonah, NY: Richard C. Owen.

Polacco, P. (2001). *The keeping quilt*. New York: Aladdin Books.

Pooley, R. C. (1974). *The teaching of English usage*. Urbana, IL: National Council of Teachers of English.

Portalupi, J., & Fletcher, R. (2001). *Nonfiction craft lessons: Teaching information writing K–8*. Portland, ME: Stenhouse.

Porter, C., & Cleland, J. (1995). *The portfolio as a learning strategy.* Portsmouth, NH: Heinemann.

Potter, B. (2006). *The tale of Peter Rabbit.* New York: Warne.

Prelutsky, J. (1984). *The new kid on the block.* New York: Greenwillow.

Prelutsky, J. (1996). *A pizza the size of the sun.* New York: Greenwillow.

Prelutsky, J. (Ed.). (2000). *The Random House book of poetry for children.* New York: Random House.

Prelutsky, J. (2004). *If not for the cat: Haiku.* New York: Greenwillow.

Prelutsky, J. (2005). *Read a rhyme, write a rhyme.* New York: Knopf.

Prensky, M. (2006). *Don't bother me, mom—I'm learning.* St. Paul, MN: Paragon House.

Prensky, M. (2010). *Teaching digital natives: Partnering for real learning.* Thousand Oaks, CA: Corwin.

Pressley, M. (1992). Encouraging mindful use of prior knowledge: Attempting to construct explanatory answers facilitates learning. *Educational Psychologist, 27,* 91–109.

Pressley, M. (2002). Comprehension strategies instruction: A turn-of-the-century status report. In C. C. Block & M. Pressley (Eds.), *Comprehension instruction: Research-based practices* (pp. 11–27). New York: Guilford Press.

Pressley, M., Dolezal, S. E., Raphael, L. M., Mohan, L., Roehrig, A. D., & Bogner, K. (2003). *Motivating primary-grade students.* New York: Guilford Press.

Prill, P. (1994/1995). Helping children use the classroom library. *The Reading Teacher, 48,* 363–364.

Provensen, A. (1995). *My fellow Americans: A family album.* San Diego: Browndeer Press.

Pulver, R. (2003). *Punctuation takes a vacation.* New York: Holiday House.

Raphael, T. E., Englert, C. S., & Kirschner, B. W. (1989). Acquisition of expository writing skills. In J. M. Mason (Ed.), *Reading and writing connections* (pp. 261–290). Boston: Allyn & Bacon.

Rappaport, D. (2001). *Martin's big words: The life of Dr. Martin Luther King, Jr.* New York: Hyperion Books.

Rappaport, D. (2009). *Eleanor, quiet no more: The life of Eleanor Roosevelt.* New York: Hyperion Books.

Rasinski, T. V. (2004). Creating fluent readers. *Educational Leadership, 61*(6), 46–51.

Rasinski, T. (2006). Developing vocabulary through word building. In C. C. Block & J. N. Mangieri (Eds.), *The vocabulary-enriched classroom: Practices for improving the reading performance of all students in grades 3 and up* (pp. 36–53). New York: Scholastic.

Rathmann, P. (1995). *Officer Buckle and Gloria.* New York: Putnam.

Ray, K. W., & Laminack, L. L. (2001). *The writing workshop: Working through the hard parts (and they're all hard parts).* Urbana, IL: National Council of Teachers of English.

Read, C. (1975). *Children's categorization of speech sounds in English* (NCTE Research Report No. 17). Urbana, IL: National Council of Teachers of English.

Read, S. (2001). "Kid mice hunt for their selfs": First and second graders writing research. *Language Arts, 78,* 333–342.

Reutzel, D. R., & Fawson, P. C. (1990). Traveling tales: Connecting parents and children in writing. *The Reading Teacher, 44,* 222–227.

Reyes, M. de la Luz. (1991). A process approach to literacy using dialogue journals and literature logs with second language learners. *Research in the Teaching of English, 25,* 291–313.

Rhodes, L. K., & Nathenson-Mejia, S. (1992). Anecdotal records: A powerful tool for ongoing literacy assessment. *The Reading Teacher, 45,* 502–511.

Rico, G. L. (2000). *Writing the natural way.* Los Angeles: Tarcher.

Riddle, J. (2009). *Engaging the eye generation: Visual literacy strategies for the K–5 classroom.* Portland, ME: Stenhouse.

Rief, L. (1999). *Vision and voice: Extending the literacy spectrum.* Portsmouth, NH: Heinemann.

Ringgold, F. (1996). *Tar beach.* New York: Dragonfly.

Robb, L. (2003). *Teaching reading in social studies, science, and math.* New York: Scholastic.

Robb, L. (2004). *Nonfiction writing: From the inside out.* New York: Scholastic.

Robinson, A., Crawford, L., & Hall, N. (1991). *Someday you will no (sic) all about me: Young children's explorations in the world of letters.* Portsmouth, NH: Heinemann.

Rogovin, P. (2001). *The research workshop: Bringing the world into your classroom.* Portsmouth, NH: Heinemann.

Romano, T. (1995). *Writing with passion: Life stories, multiple genres.* Portsmouth, NH: Boynton/Cook.

Romano, T. (2000). *Blending genre, altering style: Writing multi-genre papers.* Portsmouth, NH: Boynton/Cook.

Roop, P. (1995). Keep the reading lights burning. In M. Sorensen & B. Lehman (Eds.), *Teaching with children's books: Paths to literature-based instruction* (pp. 197–202). Urbana, IL: National Council of Teachers of English.

Root, P. (2003). *One stuck duck.* Cambridge, MA: Candlewick Press.

Rosenblatt, L. M. (2005). *Making meaning with texts: Selected essays.* Portsmouth, NH: Heinemann.

Roser, N. L., & Keehn, S. (2002). Fostering thought, talk, and inquiry: Linking literature and social studies. *The Reading Teacher, 55*, 416–426.

Roskos, K. A., Tabors, P. O., & Lenhart, L. A. (2009). *Oral language and early literacy in preschool* (2nd ed.). Newark, DE: International Reading Association.

Rothenberg, C., & Fisher, D. (2007). *Teaching English language learners: A differentiated approach.* Upper Saddle River, NJ: Merrill/Prentice Hall.

Rowling, J. K. (1999). *Harry Potter and the chamber of secrets.* New York: Scholastic.

Rowling, J. K. (2002). *Harry Potter and the goblet of fire.* New York: Scholastic.

Rowling, J. K. (2007). *Harry Potter and the deathly hallows.* New York: Scholastic.

Rumelhart, D. (1975). Notes on a schema for stories. In D. G. Bobrow (Ed.), *Representation and understanding: Studies in cognitive science* (pp. 99–135). New York: Academic Press.

Ryan, P. M. (1999). *Amelia and Eleanor go for a ride: Based on a true story.* New York: Scholastic.

Ryan, P. M. (2000). *Esperanza rising.* New York: Scholastic.

Rymer, R., & Williams, C. (2000). "Wasn't that a spelling word?" Spelling instruction and young children's writing. *Language Arts, 77*, 241–249.

Sachar, L. (2008). *Holes.* New York: Farrar, Straus & Giroux.

Samway, K. D. (2006). *When English learners write: Connecting research to practice, K–8.* Portsmouth, NH: Heinemann.

Samway, K. D., & McKeon, D. (1999). *Myths and realities: Best practices for language minority students.* Portsmouth, NH: Heinemann.

Say, A. (2008). *Grandfather's journey.* New York: Sandpiper.

Scarcella, R. C. (2003). *Accelerating academic English: A focus on the English learner.* Oakland: Regents of the University of California.

Schickedanz, J. A., & Casbergue, R. M. (2004). *Writing in preschool: Learning to orchestrate meaning and marks.* Newark, DE: International Reading Association.

Schneider, J. J., & Jackson, S. A. W. (2000). Process drama: A special space and place for writing. *The Reading Teacher, 54*, 38–51.

Schulze, A. C. (2006). *Helping children become readers through writing: A guide to writing workshop in kindergarten.* Newark, DE: International Reading Association.

Schwartz, A. (1992). *Busy buzzing bumblebees and other tongue twisters.* New York: HarperCollins.

Schwartz, D. M. (1994). *How much is a million?* New York: Morrow.

Schwartz, R. M. (2005). Decisions, decisions: Responding to primary students during guided reading. *The Reading Teacher, 58*, 436–443.

Scieszka, J. (1991). *The frog prince, continued.* New York: Viking.

Scieszka, J. (1999). *The true story of the 3 little pigs!* New York: Viking.

Scott, J. A., & Nagy, W. E. (2004). Developing word consciousness. In J. F. Baumann & E. J. Kame'enui (Eds.), *Vocabulary instruction: Theory to practice* (pp. 210–217). New York: Guilford Press.

Selznick, B. (2007). *The invention of Hugo Cabret.* New York: Scholastic.

Sendak, M. (2003). *Where the wild things are.* New York: HarperCollins.

Serafini, F. (2001). *Creating space for readers.* Portsmouth, NH: Heinemann.

Service, P. (1988). *Stinker from space.* New York: Scribner.

Seuss, Dr. (1960a). *Green eggs and ham.* New York: Random House.

Seuss, Dr. (1960b). *One fish two fish red fish blue fish.* New York: Random House.

Seuss, Dr. (2003). *Hop on pop.* New York: Scholastic.

Seuss, Dr. (2004). *Oh say can you say?* New York: Beginner Books.

Shanahan, T. (1988). The reading-writing relationship: Seven instructional principles. *The Reading Teacher, 41*, 636–647.

Shefelbine, J. (1995). *Learning and using phonics in beginning reading* (Literacy research paper, vol. 10). New York: Scholastic.

Shepard, A. (2001). *Master man: A tall tale of Nigeria.* New York: HarperCollins.

Shiga, J. (2010). *Meanwhile: Pick any path.* New York: Amulet Books.

Siemens, L. (1996). "Walking through the time of kids": Going places with poetry. *Language Arts, 73*, 234–240.

Sierra, J. (2009). *The sleepy little alphabet.* New York: Knopf.

Silverman, R., & Crandell, J. D. (2010). Vocabulary practices in prekindergarten and kindergarten classrooms. *Reading Research Quarterly, 45*, 318–340.

Silverstein, S. (2004). *Where the sidewalk ends.* New York: HarperCollins.

Simon, S. (2000). *From paper airplanes to outer space.* Katonah, NY: Richard C. Owen.

Simon, S. (2003). *Hurricanes.* New York: HarperCollins.

Skillings, M. J., & Ferrell, R. (2000). Student-generated rubrics: Bringing students into the assessment process. *The Reading Teacher, 53*, 452–455.

Slepian, J., & Seidler, A. (2001). *The hungry thing*. New York: Scholastic.

Smith, K. (2005). Enhancing the literature experience through deep discussions of character. In N. L. Roser & M. G. Martinez (Eds.), *What a character! Character study as a guide to literary meaning making in grades K–8* (pp. 124–132). Newark, DE: International Reading Association.

Sniegoski, T. (2010). *Tall tales*. New York: Graphix.

Sobel, J. (2006). *Shiver me letters: A pirate ABC*. San Diego: Harcourt Brace.

Sommers, N. (1994). Revision strategies of student writers and experienced adult writers. In S. Perl (Ed.), *Landmark essays on writing process* (pp. 75–84). Davis, CA: Heragoras Press.

Soto, G. (2005). *Neighborhood odes*. San Diego: Harcourt.

Spandel, V. (2001). *Books, lessons, ideas for teaching the six traits: Writing in the elementary and middle grades*. Wilmington, MA: Great Source Education Group.

Spandel, V. (2005). *Creating writers: Through 6-trait writing assessment and instruction* (4th ed.). Boston: Allyn & Bacon.

Spandel, V. (2008). *Creating young writers: Using the six traits to enrich writing process in primary classrooms* (2nd ed.). Boston: Allyn & Bacon.

Speaker, R. B., Jr., & Speaker, P. R. (1991). Sentence collecting: Authentic literacy events in the classroom. *Journal of Reading, 35,* 92–95.

Speare, E. G. (2003). *The witch of Blackbird Pond*. Boston: Houghton Mifflin.

Speare, E. G. (2005). *The sign of the beaver*. New York: Yearling.

Spinelli, J. (2002). *Maniac Magee*. New York: Scholastic.

Spivey, N. (1997). *The constructivist metaphor: Reading, writing, and the making of meaning*. New York: Academic Press.

Stahl, S. A., & Nagy, W. E. (2005). *Teaching word meanings*. Mahwah; NJ: Erlbaum.

Standards for the English Language Arts. (1996). Urbana, IL: National Council of Teachers of English and the International Reading Association.

Stauffer, R. G. (1970). *The language experience approach to the teaching of reading*. New York: Harper & Row.

Stead, P. C. (2010). *A sick day for Amos McGee*. New York: Roaring Brook Press.

Stead, T. (2002). *Is that a fact? Teaching nonfiction writing K–3*. Portland, ME: Stenhouse.

Stead, T. (2006). *Reality checks: Teaching reading comprehension with nonfiction K–5*. Portland, ME: Stenhouse.

Steer, D. A. (2007). *Mythology*. Somerville, MA: Candlewick Press.

Steer, D. A. (2009). *The mythology handbook*. Somerville, MA: Candlewick Press.

Stevens, J., & Crummel, S. S. (2003). *Jackalope*. San Diego: Harcourt Brace.

Stevens, J., & Crummel, S. S. (2005). *Cook-a-doodle-doo!* New York: Sandpiper.

Steig, J. (2001). *A gift from Zeus: Sixteen favorite myths.* New York: HarperCollins.

Steig, W. (1990). *Doctor De Soto.* New York: Farrar, Straus & Giroux.

Steig, W. (2010). *Sylvester and the magic pebble*. New York: Atheneum.

Stien, D., & Beed, P. L. (2004). Bridging the gap between fiction and nonfiction in the literature circle setting. *The Reading Teacher, 57,* 510–518.

Strassman, B. K., MacDonald, H., & Wanko, L. (2010). Using captioned media as mentor expository texts. *The Reading Teacher, 64,* 197–201.

Strong, W. (1996). *Writer's toolbox: A sentence-combining workshop*. New York: McGraw-Hill.

Sulzby, E. (1985). Kindergartners as readers and writers. In M. Farr (Ed.), *Advances in writing research, vol. 1: Children's early writing development* (pp. 127–199). Norwood, NJ: Ablex.

Sweet, A. P., & Snow, C. E. (2003). Reading for comprehension. In A. P. Sweet & C. E. Snow (Eds.), *Rethinking reading comprehension* (pp. 1–11). New York: Guilford Press.

Taback, S. (1997). *There was an old lady who swallowed a fly.* New York: Viking.

Tan, S. (2007). *The arrival*. New York: Levine Books.

Tanaka, S. (2008). *Amelia Earhart: The legend of the lost aviator*. New York: Abrams.

Tarasiuk, T. (2009). Extreme poetry: Making meaning through words, images, and music. *Voices From the Middle, 16*(3), 50–51.

Taylor, D. (1993). *From the child's point of view*. Portsmouth, NH: Heinemann.

Taylor, D., & Dorsey-Gaines, C. (1987). *Growing up literate: Learning from inner-city families*. Portsmouth, NH: Heinemann.

Taylor, M. D. (2004). *Roll of thunder, hear my cry*. New York: Puffin Books.

Teale, W. H., & Sulzby, E. (1989). Emerging literacy: New perspectives. In D. S. Strickland & L. M. Morrow (Eds.), *Emerging literacy: Young children learn to read and write* (pp. 1–15). Newark, DE: International Reading Association.

Terban, M. (1990). *Punching the clock: Funny action idioms.* New York: Clarion Books.

Terban, M. (2006). *Scholastic dictionary of idioms, phrases, sayings, and expressions.* New York: Scholastic.

Terban, M. (2007). *In a pickle and other funny idioms.* New York: Sandpiper.

Terry, A. (1974). *Children's poetry preferences: A national survey of upper elementary grades* (NCTE Research Report No. 16). Urbana, IL: National Council of Teachers of English.

Thimmesh, C. (2006). *Team moon: How 400,000 people landed Apollo 11 on the moon.* Boston: Houghton Mifflin.

Thompson, T. (2008). *Adventures in graphica: Using comics and graphic novels to teach comprehension, 2–6.* Portland, ME: Stenhouse.

Tiedt, I. (2002). *Tiger lilies, toadstools, and thunderbolts: Engaging K–8 students with poetry.* Newark, DE: International Reading Association.

Tierney, R. J. (2005). Literacy assessment reform: Shifting beliefs, principled possibilities, and emerging practices. In S. J. Barrentine & S. M. Stokes (Eds.), *Reading assessment: Principles and practices for elementary teachers* (2nd ed., pp. 23–40). Newark, DE: International Reading Association.

Tierney. R. J., & Readence, J. E. (2005). *Reading strategies and practices: A compendium* (6th ed.). Boston: Allyn & Bacon.

Tierney, R. J., & Shanahan, T. (1991). Research on the reading-writing relationship: Interactions, transactions, and outcomes. In R. Barr, M. L. Kamil, P. B. Mosenthal, & P. D. Pearson (Eds.), *Handbook of reading research* (Vol. 2, pp. 246–280). Mahwah, NJ: Erlbaum.

Toll, C. A. (2005). *The literacy coach's survival guide: Essential questions and practical answers.* Newark, DE: International Reading Association.

Tomlinson, C. A. (2001). *How to differentiate instruction in mixed-ability classrooms* (2nd ed.). Alexandria, VA: Association for Supervision and Curriculum Development.

Tompkins, G. E., & Collom, S. (Eds.). (2004). *Sharing the pen: Interactive writing with young children.* Upper Saddle River, NJ: Merrill/Prentice Hall.

Tompkins, G. E., & Webeler, M. B. (1983). What will happen next? Using predictable books with young children. *The Reading Teacher, 36,* 498–502.

Tompkins, G. E., & Yaden, D. B., Jr. (1986). *Answering students' questions about words.* Urbana, IL: National Council of Teachers of English.

Tracey, D. H., & Morrow, L. M. (2006). *Lenses on reading.* New York: Guilford Press.

Trachtenburg, R., & Ferruggia, A. (1989). Big books from little voices: Reaching high risk beginning readers. *The Reading Teacher, 42,* 284–289.

Trapani, I. (2000). *Shoo fly!* Watertown, MA: Charlesbridge.

Treiman, R. (1985). Phonemic analysis, spelling, and reading. In T. H. Carr (Ed.), *The development of reading skills* (pp. 5–18). San Francisco: Jossey-Bass.

Trelease, J. (2006). *The read-aloud handbook* (6th ed.). New York: Penguin.

Tresselt, A. (1989) *The mitten.* New York: Harper Trophy.

Tunnell, M. O., & Ammon, R. (Eds.). (1993). *The story of ourselves: Teaching history through children's literature.* Portsmouth, NH: Heinemann.

Turbill, J. (2000). Developing a spelling conscience. *Language Arts, 77,* 209–217.

Turner, A. (1995). *Nettie's trip south.* New York: Aladdin Books.

Turner, P. S. (2009). *The frog scientist.* Boston: Houghton Mifflin.

Underwood, D. (2010). *The quiet book.* Boston: Houghton Mifflin.

Valencia, R. R., & Villarreal, B. J. (2003). Improving students' reading performance via standards-based school reform: A critique. *The Reading Teacher, 56,* 612–621.

Valencia, S. W., Hiebert, E. H., & Afflerbach, P. P. (1994). *Authentic reading assessment: Practices and possibilities.* Newark, DE: International Reading Association.

Van Allsburg, C. (1981). *Jumanji.* Boston: Houghton Mifflin.

Van Allsburg, C. (1991). *The wretched stone.* Boston: Houghton Mifflin.

Van Allsburg, C. (1993). *The sweetest fig.* Boston: Houghton Mifflin.

Van Allsburg, C. (1998). *The Z was zapped.* Boston: Houghton Mifflin.

Van Allsburg, C. (2005). *The polar express.* Boston: Houghton Mifflin.

Vecchione, P. (Ed.). (2002). *Whisper and shout: Poems to memorize.* Chicago: Cricket Books.

Viorst, J. (2009). *Alexander and the terrible, horrible, no good, very bad day.* New York: Atheneum.

Vukelich, C., & Christie, J. (2009). *Building a foundation for preschool literacy* (2nd ed.). Newark, DE: International Reading Association.

Vygotsky, L. S. (1986). *Thought and language* (Rev. ed.). Cambridge, MA: MIT Press.

Vygotsky, L. S. (2006). *Mind in society.* Cambridge, MA: Harvard University Press.

Wagner, B. J. (1999). *Dorothy Heathcote: Drama as a learning medium* (Rev. ed.). Portsmouth, NH: Heinemann.

Wagner, B. J. (2003). Imaginative expression. In J. Flood, D. Lapp, J. R. Squire, & J. M. Jensen (Eds.), *Handbook of research on teaching the English language arts* (2nd ed., pp. 1008–1025). Mahwah, NJ: Erlbaum.

Walker, E., Tabone, C., & Weltsek, G. (2011). When achievement data meet drama and arts integration. *Language Arts, 88,* 365–372.

Watson, K., & Young, B. (2003). Discourse for learning in the classroom. In S. Murphy & C. Dudley-Marling (Eds.), *Literacy through language arts: Teaching and learning in context* (pp. 39–49). Urbana, IL: National Council of Teachers of English.

Weaver, C. (1996). *Teaching grammar in context.* Portsmouth, NH: Heinemann.

Weaver, C., McNally, C., & Moerman, S. (2001). To grammar or not to grammar: That is *not* the question! *Voices From the Middle, 8*(3), 17–33.

Weitzman, D. (2009). *Pharaoh's boat.* Boston: Houghton Mifflin.

Wells, G., & Chang-Wells, G. L. (1992). *Constructing knowledge together: Classrooms as centers of inquiry and literacy.* Portsmouth, NH: Heinemann.

Whatley, A., & Canalis, J. (2002). Creating learning communities through literacy. *Language Arts, 79,* 478–487.

White, E. B. (2006). *Charlotte's web.* New York: HarperCollins.

White, T. G., Sowell, J., & Yanagihara, A. (1989). Teaching elementary students to use word-part clues. *The Reading Teacher, 42,* 302–308.

Whitin, P. E. (1996). Exploring visual response to literature. *Research in the Teaching of English, 30,* 114–140.

Whitin, P. E. (2002). Leading into literature circles through the sketch-to-stretch strategy. *The Reading Teacher, 55,* 444–450.

Wiesner, D. (1995). *June 29, 1999.* New York: Sandpiper.

Wiesner, D. (1997). *Tuesday.* New York: Sandpiper.

Wiesner, D. (2006). *Flotsam.* New York: Clarion Books.

Wilbur, H. L. (2008). *Z is for Zeus: A Greek mythology alphabet.* Farmington Hills, MI: Sleeping Bear Press.

Wilde, S. (1992). *You kan red this! Spelling and punctuation for whole language classrooms, K-6.* Portsmouth, NH: Heinemann.

Wilhelm, J. D. (2002). *Action strategies for deepening comprehension.* New York: Scholastic.

Willems, M. (2003). *Don't let the pigeon drive the bus!* New York: Hyperion Books.

Willems, M. (2004). *Knuffle bunny: A cautionary tale.* New York: Hyperion Books.

Williams, S. (1990). *I went walking.* San Diego: Harcourt Brace.

Williams, T. L. (2007). "Reading" the painting: Exploring visual literacy in the primary grades. *The Reading Teacher, 60,* 636–642.

Wilson, P., Martens, P., & Arya, P. (2005). Accountability for reading and readers: What the numbers don't tell. *The Reading Teacher, 58,* 622–631.

Wink, J. (2010). *Critical pedagogy: Notes from the real world* (4th ed.). Englewood Cliffs, NJ: Prentice Hall.

Wittels, H., & Greisman, J. (2001). *A first thesaurus.* Racine, WI: Golden Books.

Wittrock, M. C., & Alesandrini, K. (1990). Generation of summaries and analogies and analytic and holistic abilities. *American Research Journal, 27,* 489–502.

Wohlwend, K. E. (2010). A is for avatar: Young children in literacy 2.0 worlds and literacy 1.0 schools. *Language Arts, 88,* 144–152.

Wolvin, A. D., & Coakley, C. G. (1996). *Listening* (5th ed.). New York: McGraw-Hill.

Wong, J. S. (2002). *You have to write.* New York: McElderry.

Wong-Fillmore, L., & Snow, C. E. (2002). What teachers need to know about language. In C. T. Adger, C. E. Snow, & D. Christian (Eds.), *What teachers need to know about language* (pp. 7–54). Washington, DC: Center for Applied Linguistics.

Wood, A. (2004). *The napping house.* San Diego: Harcourt Brace.

Wood, J. R. (2006). *Living voices: Multicultural poetry in the middle school classroom.* Urbana, IL: National Council of Teachers of English.

Woodson, J. (2003). *Locomotion.* New York: Putnam.

Worthy, J. (2008). *Readers theater for building fluency.* New York: Scholastic.

Worthy, J., & Prater, K. (2002). "I thought about it all night": Readers theatre for reading fluency and motivation. *The Reading Teacher, 50,* 204–212.

Wylie, R. E., & Durrell, D. D. (1970). Teaching vowels through phonograms. *Elementary English, 47,* 787–791.

Yaden, D. B., Jr. (1988). Understanding stories through repeated read-alouds: How many does it take? *The Reading Teacher, 41,* 556–560.

Yaden, D. B., Jr., & Templeton, S. (Eds.). (1986). *Metalinguistic awareness and beginning literacy: Conceptualizing what it means to read and write.* Portsmouth, NH: Heinemann.

Yep, L. (1977). *Dragonwings.* New York: HarperCollins.

Yolen, J. (1980). *Commander Toad in space.* New York: Coward-McCann.

Yopp, H. K. (1992). Developing phonemic awareness in young children. *The Reading Teacher, 45,* 696–703.

Yopp, H. K. (1995). Read-aloud books for developing phonemic awareness: An annotated bibliography. *The Reading Teacher, 48,* 538–542.

Yopp, H. K., & Yopp, R. H. (2006). *Literature-based reading activities* (4th ed.). Boston: Allyn & Bacon.

Yorinks, A. (1989). *Hey, Al.* New York: Farrar, Straus & Giroux.

Young, E. (1996). *Lon Po Po: A Red-Riding Hood story from China.* New York: PaperStar.

Young, E. (2004). *I, Doko: The tale of a basket.* New York: Philomel.

Zebroski, J. T. (1994). *Thinking through theory: Vygotskian perspectives on the teaching of writing.* Portsmouth, NH: Boynton/Cook.

Zelinsky, P. O. (2002). *Rapunzel.* New York: Puffin Books.

Index